A Note on the Author

Richard van Emden has interviewed over 270 veterans of the Great War and has written fourteen books on the subject, including *Boy Soldiers of the Great War* and *Meeting the Enemy*. He has also worked on more than a dozen television programmes on the First World War, including *Britain's Last Tommies*, *Britain's Boy Soldiers*, the award-winning *Roses of No Man's Land* and *War Horse: The Real Story*. He lives in West London.

OTHER BOOKS BY RICHARD VAN EMDEN

Famous
Britain's Last Tommies
Boy Soldiers of the Great War
All Quiet on the Home Front
Last Man Standing
The Trench
Prisoners of the Kaiser
Tickled to Death to Go
Tommy's Ark
The Quick and the Dead
Meeting the Enemy

THE LAST FIGHTING TOMMY

& THE

SOLDIER'S WAR

Two Eyewitness Tales from the Great War Trenches

Richard van Emden
and
Harry Patch

BLOOMSBURY PUBLISHING
LONDON • OXFORD • NEW YORK • NEW DELHI • SYDNEY

BLOOMSBURY PUBLISHING
Bloomsbury Publishing Plc
50 Bedford Square, London, WC1B 3DP, UK

BLOOMSBURY, BLOOMSBURY PUBLISHING and the Diana logo
are trademarks of Bloomsbury Publishing Plc

The Last Fighting Tommy was first published in Great Britain 2007
The Soldier's War was first published in Great Britain 2008
This edition published 2018

ISBN: 978-1-5266-0479-8

2 4 6 8 10 9 7 5 3 1

Typeset by Hewer Text UK Ltd, Edinburgh
Printed and bound in Great Britain by CPI Group (UK) Ltd, Croydon CR0 4YY

MIX
Paper from
responsible sources
FSC® C020471

To find out more about our authors and books visit
www.bloomsbury.com and sign up for our newsletters

THE LAST
FIGHTING TOMMY

Dedicated to Doris Whitaker,
4 April 1914–19 March 2007,
and
Fred Patch, Lionel Morris, Harold Chivers and
Charlie Wherrett, who died during the Great War,
and George Atkins and Leslie Lush, who survived

It was the men in the trenches who won the war. What they put up with, no one will ever know. I've seen them coming out of the line, poor devils, in a terrible state, plastered with mud. They were like hermit crabs with all their equipment on and they'd plonk down in the middle of the road before somebody helped them up. How did they manage? They were at the end of their tether. They were worn out, absolutely done up. They could hardly put one foot before the other, they were gone, depleted, finished, all they wanted to do was sleep, sleep, sleep.

Air Mechanic Henry William Allingham
No. 8289, No. 12 Squadron Royal Naval Air Service
6 June 1896–18 July 2009

CONTENTS

Harry's father was keen on rabbiting. After he died, his sons found his gun. Nobody knew whether it had ever been licensed, so they threw it down Granny's well.

May Cooper, daughter of George Patch, and Harry's niece, born 1918

I don't think Harry wanted to fight, but he went in any case . . . I never heard him speak about the war, and I somehow doubt he ever spoke about it.

Margaret Ffoulkes, George Atkins' daughter and Harry's god-daughter

When they launched the Somerset Poppy Appeal, they had a great big cannon that shot the poppies out of the muzzle. Of course everybody jumped in shock, but Harry didn't stir a muscle. He just said, 'You haven't heard the guns like I have.'

Pauline Leyton, manager at Harry's residential home

When I first knew Harry he was the champion of local causes. He hates injustice and never hesitated to write to the council or the local newspaper, usually firing on all cylinders when he did so.

David Isaacs, son of Betty Isaacs, Harry's neighbour

I was in the living room with my back to the television. Suddenly, I heard his distinctive voice and it made me feel quite peculiar. I was very still for a moment. I remember thinking, 'Oh my goodness, it's Uncle Hal.'

June Beeching, niece to Harry's first wife Ada, born June 1933

N

*North
Sea*

HOLLAND

o Bruges

Nieuport o

Dunkirk o

Calais o

o Brussels

St Omer o

Ypres o

o Roulers

o Passchendaele

Messines

BELGIUM

o Boulogne

Ploegsteert o

o Lille

Neuve Chapelle o

o Etaples

Loos o

Mons o

o Lens

Vimy

Arras o

Maubeuge

o Cambrai

o Le Cateau

R. Somme

Bapaume
o

Albert o

Peronne

St Quentin

Amiens o

F R A N C E

R.

Rheimes

o Verdun

R. Seine

R.

Paris

The Western Front 1914–18

—··—··— Frontiers

······ Limit of German advance

------ Approximate line of the front from
late 1914 to the beginning of the
battle of the Somme, 1 July 1916

▨ Allied gains in 1916–17, including
ground conceded by the Germans
in early 1917

··········· Limit of German advance in 1918

——— Armistice line, 11 November 1918

0   10   20   30 miles

Battle of Langemarck: advances on 16 August 1917

N

0   1   2 miles

Westroosebeke

Poelcappelle

Langemarck

Boesinghe

Ypres–Staden Railway

7th
DCLI

Steenbeek

Pilckem

St Julien

Passchendaele

Gravenstafel

Yser Canal

Wieltje

Broodseinde

Ypres

Zonnebeke

Ypres–Roulers Railway

Becelaere

Polygon Wood

Hooge

―――― Zero, 31 July – the first day   • • • • • • Advance at Langemarck, 16 August
of the third battle of Ypres

– – – – End, 31 July

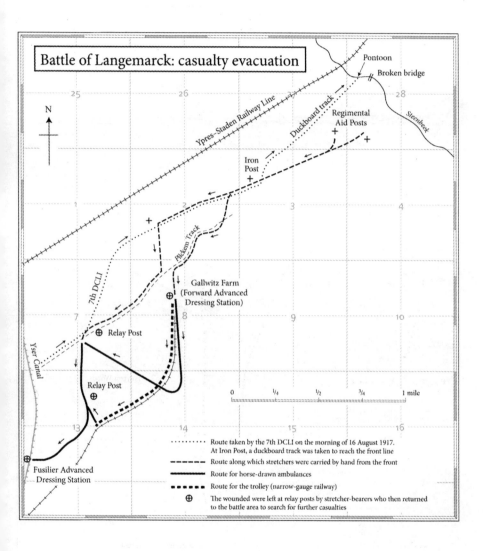

Battle of Langemarck: casualty evacuation

N

Pontoon

Broken bridge

Ypres–Staden Railway Line

Duckboard track

Regimental Aid Posts

Steenbeek

Iron Post

25   26   28

1   2   3   4

Bikem Track

7th DCLI

Gallwitz Farm
(Forward Advanced
Dressing Station)

7   8   9   10

Relay Post

Yser Canal

Relay Post

| 0 | ¼ | ½ | ¾ | 1 mile |

13   14   15   16

Fusilier Advanced
Dressing Station

· · · · · · · · · · Route taken by the 7th DCLI on the morning of 16 August 1917.
At Iron Post, a duckboard track was taken to reach the front line

– – – – – Route along which stretchers were carried by hand from the front

━━━━━ Route for horse-drawn ambulances

■ ■ ■ ■ ■ Route for the trolley (narrow-gauge railway)

⊕   The wounded were left at relay posts by stretcher-bearers who then returned
to the battle area to search for further casualties

DUKE OF CORNWALLS LIGHT INFANTRY.

ROLL OF INDIVIDUALS entitled to the Victory Medal and/or British War Medal

On 11/11/18 or on becoming non-effective		NAME	Unit previously served with. Regtl. No. and Rank in same on entry into theatre of war	Theatres of war in which served					
Regtl. No.	Rank			From	To	From	To	From	To
34934	Pte	PASCOE.WILLIAM JAMES.	1/DCLI.34934.PTE	O	H.S.				
23605	Pte	PASK. WILLIAM.	7/DCLI.23605.PTE 10/DCLI.23605.	O	H.S.				
34677	L/Cpl	PASS. FREDERICK HENRY GEORGE.	6/DCLI.34677.PTE 8/DCLI.34677.HEK 1/DCLI.34677.	O	H.S.				
17441	Pte	PASSEY.HERBERT HENRY.	2/DCLI.17441.PTE 3/DCLI.17441. 2/DCLI.17441.	X					
260089.	Pte	PASSMORE. GEORGE.	2/DEVONS.1755.PTE 7/DCLI.260089. 1/DCLI.260089.		K.S.				
18027	Cpl	PASSMORE. HENRY WALLACE.	8/DCL I.18027.CPL	X					
201476	Pte	PASSMORE. HUGH WILLIAM.	1/4.DCLI.4604.PTE	O	H.S.				
8461	Sgt	PASSMORE. PHILLIP.	2/DCLI.8461.SGT	X					
29295	Pte	PATCH.HENRY JOHN.	7/DCLI.29295.PTE	O	H.S.				
21826	Pte	PATE. HEELYS.	2/DCLI.21826.PTE	X	H.S.				

I certify that according to the Official Records the individuals named in

Place   EXETER.

Date   APRIL 1920.

PREFACE TO THE 2018 EDITION

It is now eight years since Harry Patch died: the last Great War veteran to have seen action in the trenches, the last veteran to be wounded in action. He lives on in the national consciousness, his name still resonant to many of us.

Today, Harry's memorial to his long-gone friends and comrades, erected on the very spot where his battalion crossed the Steenbeck to attack Langemarck in August 1917, is widely visited by pilgrims and tourists to the Battlefields. Harry lived to be 111, and by that strange quirk of great longevity he has become part of the history trail at Ypres. And likewise, in his home city of Wells, a memorial erected to the town's famous son is now sign-posted, alongside directions to the Cathedral and the Bishop's Palace.

Knowing Harry, he would be slightly bemused by such honours; he might even blush with embarrassment, because he did nothing that five-and-a-half million other men and women of his generation didn't do, but served their country in time of war. He was always very conscious of that fact.

Yet, at the same time, it was somehow fitting that the last Great War veteran, the erstwhile Lance Corporal Patch, was fully aware of his surroundings to the end – fully engaged in the world around him, his hearing reasonable with aids, his sight still remarkably strong. It was also a remarkable and a moving coincidence that Harry died aged 111 years, 1 month, 1 week and 1 day, numbers that if divided slightly differently as 11.11.11 are the numbers of the Armistice, signed at 11am at the 11th hour of the 11th month in 1918.

Harry took whatever else he might have said about his life to the grave, but since his death, friends and admirers have been able to fill in one or two gaps in his story. Most notably, the No. 1 on his machine gun team has been identified. Harry said that 'Bob' was uninjured when the rest of the Lewis Gun team was killed and he himself wounded by shrapnel; he also said that 'Bob' came from Henley-on-Thames and that they remained in contact for many years after the war. That man has now been identified: Ernest Charles Hayes served with the 7th Duke of Cornwall's Light Infantry, and his regimental number was 29299 (Harry's was 29295). Ernest's medal index card also shows that he was not wounded.

Ernest Hayes was also underage when he enlisted. This is interesting, because Harry said his comrade was called Bob Haynes. I think I misheard Hayes as Haynes, but, crucially, Ernest's elder brother was called Bob. If Ernest enlisted underage then it seems he used his elder brother's name to disguise the fact and then stuck with it.

This new introduction is to accompany the latest edition of Harry's biography, and is published during the 100th anniversary of the Third Battle of Ypres, also known as the

Battle of Passchendaele. The new edition contains previously unseen images of Harry, his two brothers and his parents. These images were unknown to me; they came to light by pure chance during an off-the-cuff conversation between a battlefield guide and a visitor who remarked in passing that he was distantly related to Harry Patch. I am very grateful to my friend Jeremy Banning for being that guide and to Richard Harris for being that distant relative – a relative who had some remarkable images of this remarkably ordinary man.

Richard van Emden
24 July 2017

PREFACE TO THE
CENTENARY ANNIVERSARY EDITION

It is nearly five years since Harry Patch died, but the memory of this remarkable man continues to live on in the public consciousness. Now, as we reach the hundredth anniversary of the outbreak of the Great War, the nation is remembering once again the sacrifices made by men such as Harry and the generation of like-minded young men and women who served their country in time of war.

In Somerset, where he lived almost all of his life, Harry has been immortalised in plaques, paintings and in carvings too – both in stone and in metal. In Wells, the city in which he died, he is now firmly a part of local history and the tourist trail. Attractive black signs that point to the Cathedral and the Bishop's Palace also direct the tourist to the great stone plinth, two metres tall and almost as wide, positioned next to the Green and dedicated to the city's most famous adopted son. Back in May 2012, hundreds of people turned out for its unveiling, and the warmth and affection felt for Harry was palpable.

The Last Fighting Tommy has sold over a third of a million copies, a figure that has firmly established Harry's book in the category of 'bestseller'. He knew how well it was doing, as he lived for two years after its first publication in 2007. This new, final edition, published to coincide with the hundredth anniversary of the outbreak of the War includes a number of images that were hitherto available only in a special memorial edition that was published shortly after his death.

Harry died on 25 July 2009, just a week after the death of the other surviving veteran of the Western Front, Henry Allingham. For those seven days Harry held the title of Europe's oldest man. Less widely acknowledged, but true nevertheless, was the title he had of the last British male with a nineteenth-century birth date. For far longer, he had carried the mantle of the last man to serve in the trenches: 'The Last Tommy', the accolade with which his name became synonymous.

There was a strange hiatus between the passing of the other remaining veterans of the trenches and Harry's own death. In 2005 there were nine veterans who could claim to have served in the front line: Cecil Withers, Smiler Marshall, Alfred Anderson, Harold Lawton, William Elder, Alfred Finnigan, Charles Lloyd and George Rice. All died that year with the exception of Harry, leaving him alone in the United Kingdom to keep the memory alive of what it was like to fight in the trenches and to go over the top.

It could so easily have been the case that the last veterans were bed-ridden and senile; instead, both Henry and Harry were extraordinarily bright and, in their different ways, eloquent and persuasive. Harry kept his keen eyesight until the end. The final reunion of these two old soldiers was in November 2008 when they met at the Cenotaph with a naval veteran, Bill Stone. Three men each representing one of the armed forces, each man laying a wreath to the dead; Henry, determined to stand, brought proceedings to a halt as he fought to get upright. Finally he had to concede that infirmity would keep him in his chair. It was a poignant reminder that these men who shared 330 years between them were a last, tantalising link with the past. Bill died the following January.

Eight months later and there were two funerals at Wells Cathedral. On 6 August 2009, there was the funeral of Private Harry Patch, no. 29295, former soldier in the Duke of Cornwall's Light Infantry: the last Tommy. And then there was the private man Harry Patch, aged 111, the quiet, self-deprecating Somerset plumber and father of two. The public desire to say farewell to both personae was embodied in an event that balanced the need to recognise his symbolic status as the last Great War veteran of the Western Front with the urge to respect an ordinary man who had worked so hard towards reconciliation between former foes. Harry's coffin, borne aloft by six soldiers of his own regiment, was flanked by six men of former combatant nations: France, Belgium and, perhaps most symbolically, Germany. Harry, as it turned out, had died surrounded by peace.

Later that day, his own wish to be buried with privacy in the little cemetery in the village of Monkton Coombe was respected by the press and public alike. He now lies close to the grave of his parents and behind the headstones of his two brothers, William and George.

For the last decade, Harry had lived a life totally in contrast to all that had happened before. From the age of 100 he had become the focus of more and more public attention, increasingly feted wherever he went. He was honoured by the City of Wells and given an honorary degree by Bristol University; he received honours for his service abroad from the French and Belgian Governments. However, he never lost sight of the fact that any award, any recognition, though channelled through him, was for all those who suffered physically, mentally and spiritually during the Great War, and 'on both sides of the line', as he frequently asserted. He remembered too all those who had suffered at home, all those who lost loved ones and who had to continue to fight – for survival – in the decades afterwards. His last years were spent facing up to the demons of his own war. He came to terms with what he had seen, though he could never forget, and in the end he spoke about the war at length.

Harry returned to the battlefields on half a dozen occasions, the last in September 2008 when he unveiled a memorial on the very spot where he went over the top in August 1917 in front of the Belgian village of Langemarck. It is dedicated to the men of his Division and his Battalion who died that day. That last visit was important to Harry. For the first time he seemed at ease with himself and his surroundings. He visited Toc H, the club run for soldiers, irrespective of rank, during the war, and there he had a cup of tea and signed the visitors' book. He laid a cross at Tyne Cot Cemetery to the British fallen, and then visited Langemarck German cemetery where he paid his respects at the grave of a soldier who had died on the day the village had fallen to Harry's Division. Spying three acorns nestling against the side of the soldier's gravestone, he picked them up and took them back to his residential home where they were planted and where trees now grow. The battlefields no longer held fear for him.

Richard van Emden
December 2013

PREFACE TO THE
PAPERBACK EDITION

Could life get any busier? I don't know, possibly, but since my book came out last July, I seem to have been out and about to the point when I have to be careful what I do. The daily batteries have only so much charge in them!

The paperback of *The Last Fighting Tommy* is now about to come out, and I'm a year older. In fact, I will celebrate my 110th birthday when it is published. I think I'll have a small party to celebrate both the book and my birthday but I'll make that family and friends only; I would prefer it that way.

In the last twelve months, I have been back to Belgium and seen the exact spot where I went over the top. I looked across the Steenbeck towards the village of Langemarck. The ground slopes up from the stream and you can just see the church on the horizon. It was ninety years to the day since I was there. In Ypres I met the mayor of the town, and I gave the oration under the Menin Gate, a very special moment for me. I also went to Langemarck Cemetery to lay a wreath on the grave of a German killed the day we attacked there, 16 August 1917.

With the proceeds from this book I have been able to buy a lifeboat for the Royal National Lifeboat Institution, and I launched it at Poole in Dorset. I would encourage everybody to support the RNLI. Anyway, it is a relief boat, meaning it travels round the United Kingdom and doesn't just stay in one place. It began its service in North Wales and my god-daughter, Margaret, was able to go along and see it. The last I heard it had launched six times and saved seven people.

I have got used to all the publicity, and I am always being photographed.

Recently, I switched on the lights in the Wills Memorial Building in Bristol, a sixty-six metre tower I helped to construct in the 1920s. Then the BBC made a programme about me earlier this year and the Poet Laureate, Andrew Motion, wrote a poem which he read to an audience at the Bishop's Palace in Wells. I very much appreciated the honour.

Lastly, I would like to say that I get requests for autographs from all over the world. I am sure people appreciate that my arthritic hands are too painful to sign now. Can I just say that at almost 110 years old, I have officially retired! Thank you.

Harry Patch, April 2008

PROLOGUE

Harry Patch was 111 years old, and Britain's oldest man when he died. With a good, if not a full, head of hair, and eyes that would recognize a friend at a hundred paces, his looks belied his great age. He was not a man who came across as a potential record-breaker or statistical anomaly, but he was. He was born in 1898, one of only a dozen people (in July 2009) in the United Kingdom who could boast a nineteenth-century birth date.

Currently, there are about eight thousand centenarians, men and women, in Great Britain, compared to 102 in 1911, according to the Office of National Statistics. Nevertheless, fewer than 1 in 200 men reach the grand age of 100, and to survive to Harry's great age is, statistically, rarer than reaching a century in the first place. In June 2008 when he passed 110, he joined the group of so-called 'supercentenarians', of whom there have been just over a thousand authenticated cases worldwide in the history of mankind.

Harry lived to become the last trench fighter of the Great War and, just as significantly, the last man to have gone 'over the top', perhaps the defining experience of that war. Surviving the conflict was fortunate enough but, ninety-two years on, he became the last survivor from amongst 5 million infantrymen who fought between 1914 and 1918; the last of 1.7 million soldiers serving with the British Expeditionary Force on the Western Front in the summer of 1917, the last of both the 759,615 casualties recorded by the BEF that year and of the 77,479 men who were lost, killed and wounded in the bloody salient in front of Ypres that September during the battle of Passchendaele.

Harry was a little bemused that he lived as long as he did. 'Why I'm still here, I can't fathom,' he said, but one had a sneaking suspicion that he was quite intrigued to see just how far he could go while he continued to enjoy life. For a number of years he sat, most days, on a sofa for two, next to his beloved Doris, his companion, some sixteen years his junior. The two were inseparable since she came to the home in 2002.

Doris was no ninety-two-year-old shrinking violet. A feisty Londoner, from Angel Road, Edmonton [a street that, sadly, no longer exists], and the daughter of a gas worker, she learnt as a child to look after herself, and not to let others put her down. 'My mother always told me,' Doris said firmly, 'don't let people shit on you,' and so she never did, but she had a soft side too. Her relationship with Harry was mutually supportive and very caring.

It is clear that Doris was proud of Harry's achievements, but if she thought Harry might be getting too big for his boots she ran her finger up the underside of her nose, to indicate that the man beside her might have been getting just a touch too posh.

Doris died in March 2007 and this was hard for Harry. Loneliness is a recurring problem for anyone who has outlived his generation: everyone Harry ever knew as a child, teenager or young man had died, just one of the difficult aspects of living so long. It seemed strange, more than sixty years since the end of the Second World War, that when Harry said 'after the war', you had to check which war he was talking about, for he served in both.

Henry John, as he was christened in 1898, was an unassuming man, now famous for four months on the Western Front in 1917, when as a young infantryman he served in the trenches in front of Ypres, the town that has come to symbolize some of the worst fighting of the Great War. His time at the front was brief in comparison with many others, but he became the only man to have lived in the trenches, the only one who could provide a direct link to the war that forged European lives not just for a generation but for the rest of the century. He was self-effacing and self-reliant, a man born into a world where self-help and independence were expected. On the tours he made back to Belgium since 2002, he was the object of enormous attention but at the same time he sought not to put anyone out; asked if there was anything anyone could do, he would invariably reply, 'I'm all right, don't mind me,' in his distinctive Somerset accent.

Eleven years ago, few people, if anybody, knew about Harry. His name was just one among approximately 350 British soldiers whose identity was published in the national press when the French Government awarded surviving veterans the Légion d'Honneur for service on the Western Front. Only when the pool of soldiers dried up

and the numbers in the lists were rapidly revised downwards did his name become more prominent. All of a
sudden, people wanted to hear his story.

For eighty years Harry had never spoken about the
war, and when he finally did there was a rawness to his
voice which said as much about his former silence as it
did about his service. Television took an interest. Harry
could tell his story well. By this time there were perhaps
seventy veterans left but how many could actually tell
their story in a way that could translate easily to
television screens? Not many, and most not as well as
Harry. As the pool of veterans became ever smaller, so
the attention grew.

All of a sudden, Harry was in demand, and with fame he
found the corresponding upside and downside to being
public property. He was celebrated by newspapers and
television locally and nationally. He spoke at the Cheltenham Literary Festival in 2001, reading to a packed and
hushed audience segments from his story, and he signed
books by the hundred. He launched poppy appeals, and
opened fêtes and other red-ribbon events. He had his
portrait painted by the artist Jack Russell, the former
Somerset and England wicket-keeper, while in 2004 a
special edition sweet cider was produced in his honour
by a Shepton Mallet cider company. In all, 106 bottles of
'Patch's Pride' were produced to celebrate each year of his
life. Then, in 2005, Harry received an honorary degree from
Bristol University, conferred during a formal congregation
in the Wills Memorial building which he had helped to
construct in the early 1920s.

Then in 2006, as his 108th birthday coincided with the
World Cup, Harry was pictured in an England football

shirt. 'One of Britain's Last Tommies celebrates his 108th birthday on Saturday in the midst of World Cup fever,' trumpeted the *Wells Journal*. 'To find out who Harry Patch and other mid-Somerset personalities rate as their favourite England footballer, see the centre spread.' Harry, as it turned out, was more of a rugby fan.

In the first week after Harry's appearance on BBC1's The *Last Tommy* documentary in November 2005, he received 180 letters, and after that a steady stream brought hundreds more, many speculatively addressed. 'Dear Mr Postman,' wrote one correspondent, 'Harry Patch is a Great War veteran who lives in a residential home in Wells in Somerset. Please could you see that he receives this letter, thank you.' Another letter that arrived was just as vague and was addressed to 'Mr Harry Patch, care of a care home, Wells, Somerset, England,' The postman had no problem finding Harry.

Fame offered Harry opportunities that would otherwise have remained elusive. He was taken to visit the places of his youth, he even returned to the battlefields of France and Flanders and laid a wreath close to the spot where he was wounded and he lost his friends. He spoke about his war at length, and said enough to make him feel more at ease with that time in his life. He met a German veteran, Charles Kuentz, in an act of reconciliation that helped lay many of the private ghosts that had haunted him since the War. More recently, his television appearances alerted long-lost relatives to his continued survival. His *tour de force* on *The Last Tommy* programme was seen by a niece who had not spoken with Harry for more than thirty years. Contact was re-established. Equally, quarrels and arguments that had fractured other family relationships in the past were put to one side, much to Harry's great pleasure.

Fame and great age combined to open many doors, right up to and including Buckingham Palace's. Harry met the Queen, on more than one occasion as he pointed out to her on his last trip up the Mall. He met the late Queen Mother, the Prince of Wales, and the Duke of Edinburgh. He went to No. 10, twice, and met the Prime Minister, too. He undertook a balloon trip, went underground and under-water. He flew by plane and helicopter, and travelled on the footplate of a steam train to Minehead. Space alone re-mained his final frontier.

This book is based upon many interviews conducted with Harry and recorded over the summer and autumn months of 2006. The idea of a biography had been proposed on a number of occasions by publishers and journalists, but it was not until June 2006 that I approached him and asked whether he would be interested in having his memories preserved in a book. I was due to see Harry again a week later, so I asked him to think about it until the next time I saw him. When I went back I deliberately refrained from asking Harry whether he had come to any decision. It was as I was about to leave that he beckoned me over. 'So when are you going to bring your tape recorder then?' He was clearly keen to tell his story.

Owing to my own deep-rooted interest in the Great War, I had frequently asked Harry about his experiences at the front in the summer of 1917, but I rarely strayed beyond that line of questioning. I had fallen into the same groove as so many other visitors, asking Harry about four months at the front while forgetting the other 110 years of his life. However, really to understand

Harry's war and his reaction to it, some context was needed, and it was only with the story of his life that I truly began to understand the effect the conflict had on him.

There were times when Harry became subdued, depressed even. His eyes would take on the thousand-yard stare of a man who has seen much in his life, occasionally too much for his own well-being. I knew that he had lost his friends in the Great War but it was hard to appreciate his level of loss. Death is something everyone comes to terms with; the passing of grandparents and parents is as natural as it is painful, but the loss of children, close relatives and friends, all before their time, is something few of us, mercifully, have to deal with. In a lifetime that has spanned two World Wars, Harry lived with violent death, including the premature demise of so many who were young. This was something that I did not fully appreciate until I spoke to Harry about his life beyond the immediacy of the Great War. I knew he had lost friends at the front, that a cousin had been killed in the First War and a nephew in the Second, but I had not appreciated that so many of the boys from his village had been killed too, lads with whom he had rowed the rivers, explored the quarries, and played rugby. He did not always state that they had been killed, and occasionally I wondered if he knew, but time after time I looked up the names of those he had grown up with, and time and again their names appeared in the records of the Commonwealth War Graves Commission, and many are among the fifty-six names from the Great War on the Combe Down War Memorial.

These are not all of the men and boys from Combe Down, for others with connections to the village are commemorated elsewhere so that, all in all, the community's loss stands closer to sixty-five. They were his friends, his generation, and he outlived them all, and far too many by ninety years or more. He had a right to be depressed at times.

Interviews were divided so that Harry could rest and keep his energy levels up. We held one session in the morning between 10.30 and lunch time, and another in the afternoon between 2.30 and tea, in all perhaps four hours in a day. Conducting interviews was problematic. Driving from West London to Wells, I was never sure how Harry would be that day. In the very hot summer months, it was difficult for both interviewer and interviewee not to wilt in the stuffy weather (he rather took to a hand-held battery- powered fan). On other occasions, the brightness of Harry's eyes and his general alertness indicated that a more purposeful day was ahead. Even so, Harry's voice was less strong than it once was and I was thankful on more than one occasion that the microphone in my recording equipment proved more sensitive than my own ears.

Collating Harry's stories demanded a multi-faceted approach. There are the stories that Harry himself recalled but many had to be triggered by me, and this invariably meant meeting his relatives, talking to local historians, and consulting local newspapers, books and historical documents so that I could go primed with stories that Harry, once prompted, recalled with his usual alacrity.

It took a considerable time to fathom the myriad connections between family, friends and neighbours. Teachers' names, for example, would change, but then, of course, they would, as one incumbent left and a new one arrived. For this reason, every story had to be checked for its context, related to a time and place. As far as possible, I sought to corroborate Harry's stories and to place them in broad chronological order. Finally, when the book was complete, he was given a full copy of the text to read to ensure that he agreed with what had been written and corrected anything that I had misunderstood.

A push-button, fading-to-a-dot black and white television is just a memory but hardly remarkable to anyone aged thirty-five or above, and yet it may one day be worth recalling as an interesting nugget of social history. The problem always is to realise that such detail is fascinating to a new generation. For Harry, much of what we consider so quintessentially a part of the Edwardian age was so mundane to a child of that time that it was hardly worth mentioning. Human history, and not just the devil, is in the detail.

Rural poverty was rife but lack of money did not equate to a lack of fun, and for the children of that generation, such as Harry, adventure, opportunity and excitement were just round the corner, and often no more than a literal stone's throw away. Children lived at a time when danger was accepted and managed, and accidents were an unavoidable fact of life and of growing up.

There is a story that Harry told of a gooseberry bush growing at the end of his parents' walled garden, just beyond the line of potatoes. Harry was not allowed to pick the gooseberries, but, when they were ripe, they hung temptingly, too tempting to be ignored. The only way to reach them was to crawl, stomach hard to the ground, between the heaped lines of potatoes, under the nose of his mother whose kitchen window overlooked the garden. The Boy's Own adventure of the unobserved crawl was just as exciting, and as much the object of the exercise, as eating the fruit.

In the summer, the trees were laden with ripe, sweet fruits and they were the Mars bars of yesteryear; they were treats. But they were also forbidden, in a quasi-biblical as well as literal sense: they hung from the tree and tempted the onlooker or the passer-by. The fruit belonged to the Family Patch, not to any individual, Harry included, and the self-discipline need to resist this ripe temptation was all part of growing up in Edwardian England, when spur-of-the-moment whims went un-requited because life taught you that, for the vast majority of the population, what you wanted in no way equated to what you got.

Ample meals were provided, in Harry's family three times a day, and there was no reason to pick at food in between them. Parents provided for their children as best they could, and if a child routinely supplemented its diet outside mealtimes, it would be seen as a lack of parental care; in a respectable middle class family where the father was the provider, this would border on social disgrace. The fruit trees were symbols of a great divide between our society today and that of a century ago; until he died, Harry Patch was one of the very few who could cross that divide.

Harry grew up in what is now an almost forgotten world. The children who left the textile mills, or played in the narrow alleyways and back streets of northern industrial towns, were Harry's contemporaries. The clothes, the food, the traditions, the attitudes and the sights and sounds remained familiar to him as they are remote to us. We have not quite severed all contact with a time that, for all its perils of industrial disease, child poverty and infant mortality, seems to offer a cosy sanctuary from the new and stark twenty-first-century perils such as global warming and home-grown terrorism. Back then, duty, responsibility, community and church were the pillars that upheld decent society, and paternalism, repression, secrecy, drudgery and narrow-mindedness were its straightjacket, and the ignorance and naivety that were seen as akin to bliss.

The country life into which Harry was born was parochial in the extreme. Decisions of national importance frequently failed to impinge on the rural community, and it is not surprising that events of real magnitude were forgotten or only half-remembered. Even the sinking of the *Titanic* in 1912 made little impression on children, Harry included, who were living in the heart of the countryside where trains rather than ships were the focus of excitement and debate amongst boys.

And what was that wider world into which little Harry Patch was born in 1898? It was just twenty-two years since Custer's Last Stand at the battle of the Little Bighorn, and nineteen years since Rorke's Drift, in time much closer to Harry than the war for the Falklands is to us. The great Prime Minister William Ewart Gladstone died just a month before Harry was born; Queen Victoria still had two and a half years to reign, and Lord Salisbury, the last peer to serve as British Prime Minister, was resident in 10 Downing Street.

In 1899, when Harry was one, the Boer War broke out; he was five in 1903 when Wilbur and Orville Wright undertook the first flight controlled by power. He predates the foundation of the British Labour Party by two years, was nine when Baden-Powell formed the scout movement, and nearly fourteen when the *Titanic* sank. He began work the year suffragette Emily Davidson was filmed throwing herself under the King's horse at the Epsom Derby, the same year that stainless steel was invented in Sheffield and Canberra became the federal capital of Australia.

Harry was seventeen when the cricketer W.G. Grace died, twenty-four when Howard Carter discovered the tomb of Tutankhamum, twenty-six when John Logie Baird transmitted the first television images, and thirty-four when Adolf Hitler became Chancellor of Germany.

During Harry's lifetime, he lived in the reign of six monarchs, he voted in twenty-three elections, and, in 2007, he saw off his twentieth Prime Minister.

And what of the news in 1898? Well, Henry Lindfeld became the first automobile fatality. Hawaii was annexed by the United States, while Horatio Kitchener defeated the Sudanese tribesmen at the Battle of Omdurman. In France, Emile Zola was brought to trial for writing *J' accuse* and Italian football played its first league games.

While 1898 as a date holds no obvious resonance for the British public, those of 1914–1918 certainly do. The Great War has held the nation spellbound for more than ninety years. As it finally passes out of direct human memory, we as a nation must say farewell to a generation of people who, for all their human failings, gave and lost so much in the prosecution of a war the effects of which we still feel today, the results still argued over, the lessons still not learnt.

Since World War II, the West has dealt in small conflicts, where casualties, while individually tragic, have nevertheless been tiny in comparison with the losses of the two world wars and especially those of the 1914–1918 conflict. The horror of the fighting on the Western Front is peculiarly gripping, and continues to attract ever increasing numbers of visitors – around a quarter of a million a year – to the battlefields of the Somme and Ypres.

The soldiers of the Great War were caught in a moment of history. A few years prior to 1914, industrial nations could not have sustained the presence of great, largely immobile armies in the field for any length of time; fifteen years after 1918, entrenched infantrymen could not have thwarted the advance of an enemy utilising strategic bombers, and the increasing mechanisation of fast and armoured vehicles and tanks. The Great War, and the Western Front as we remember it, had to be fought when it was, or it would not have happened at all. No conflict has ever raged for more than four years across such a narrow strip of land, with such devastating consequences.

Harry Patch just happened to be the last to witness this remarkable moment in history, and the last of those infantrymen who held the line in front of Ypres, or 'Wipers' as it was more commonly known by the men who fought there. When he died, the battle and the war joined the long pantheon of other battles and wars that Britain has fought down the centuries and that are now beyond living memory. Yet Harry was hardly warlike: on the contrary, as a reluctant conscript he never wanted to fight anyone but nevertheless he did his duty and remained an unassuming gentleman, in every sense.

VICTORIAN BORN

Harry Patch was born in Combe Down, a small rural community on the edge of the Somerset city of Bath. The name comes from two Anglo-Saxon words: Combe, from 'cume', meaning valley, and Down, from 'dun', meaning hill, which perfectly describe the local geography of steeply rising hills and green valleys where rough stone walls divide fields, and separate one house from another. The village, though its origins date back to Roman times, was hardly a village at all until industralization in the late eighteenth and early nineteenth centuries helped forge its current size and boundaries. For well over one hundred years, the exploitation of the local material, Bath stone, brought about a rapid expansion, as quarry after quarry was opened in the surrounding hills, and workers migrated from Bath to live close to their places of work.

The stone that was removed from Combe Down was a type of limestone. Underground, it was a pale yellow, but once it was exposed to the open air it turned grey and hardened, making it a perfect building block for Bath's Regency buildings.

With the expansion of the quarries came a transport infra-structure, most importantly the Somerset Coal Canal, built in the

1790s. The first great industrial landowner was Ralph Allen, who lived in Prior Park in the 1730s. He dominated quarrying, expanding Combe Down as a settlement, building cottages for his workmen that backed on to the quarries, and finding outlets for the stone not only in Bath but much further afield, in London and abroad. For over a hundred years quarrying boomed and Combe Down as an industrial village grew and grew.

The arrival of the railways heralded the end of quarrying around Combe Down. Isambard Kingdom Brunel's Great Western Railway, opened in 1841, cut a swathe of embankments and tunnels through the Wiltshire countryside revealing new sources of building stone that were easily accessible and transportable by railway. Combe Down could not compete and quarrying declined, so that by the time of Harry's birth only one mine was still in production, leaving tunnels under the village either abandoned or worked by a few independent quarrymen.

What remained was an area rich in geographical and architectural interest, where the surrounding hills were linked by viaducts, aqueducts and tunnels. Natural water resources were harnessed to supply the villages and the mills with water and power. Combe Down was a working village, but for any boy born at the end of the Victorian age it also provided an idyllic and endlessly interesting environment in which to grow up.

Why me? I'm 108 years old, and I'm amazed to be here, quite honestly. No one in my family has lived anything like this long. My eldest brother, who was judged unfit for military service in the Great War, lived to be ninety-six, and my mother lived to ninety-four, but 108! Mother was from a family of six and they all lived to be in their nineties, but no one can expect to live this long. Yet time has passed so quickly. In my mind's eye I can visualize people and places from my childhood and it's hard to realize that these memories are a century old.

I'd like to say I remember the death of Queen Victoria, the Coronation of Edward VII, or the end of the Boer War, but as I was born in June 1898 I was too young, and in any case I don't have the sort of early recall that some children have. My earliest memories are much more mundane, just small episodes around the house or garden that are now pretty much impossible to date exactly. I do recall when I was aged about five or six, there was a big pear tree in the middle of the garden, with very tempting fruit. I remember Dad saying to me, 'I know how many pears are on that tree, so don't you pick 'em.' I didn't, but when he next looked at the fruit, he found that I had taken a bite out of the back of every one I could reach. I remember that distinctly because I was given a good hiding.

My mother's name was Elizabeth and her maiden name was Morris. She was born in 1857 and raised in Monkton Combe. She had gone into service in the 1870s, becoming a cook for a well-to-do doctor in private practice, Dr Henley. He had two spinster daughters, and I used to watch them playing tennis on the lawn. My mother was a Victorian lady, tall, very upright, with a white apron, skirt, bodice and a servant's hat. She was head of the staff, which included a housemaid, kitchen maid, cook and a butler. The doctor's house stood directly opposite Fonthill, the home owned by my father and where I was born. Perhaps that is how my parents met. Otherwise I've no idea how they got together. That said, it's not hard to see how their paths might have crossed, when William, my father, was raised in the neighbouring village of Claverton, just a couple of miles from Monkton Combe.

Dad was about six years younger than Mum, and his family originally came from Wedmore, a village not far from Glastonbury. I believe my great-grandfather had a builder's business there. In fact, building was the family business on Dad's side – they were all involved in one discipline or another. There is a family legend that my great-grandfather, a carpenter by trade, made his own coffin. He hinged the lid and stood it at the top of the stairs, and until it was needed he used it as a wardrobe. I never met him; pity, really, he sounded like a real character.

The family was an extended one and by 1914 there were fourteen different families of Patches in Combe Down alone, including my father's five brothers, Herbert, Alfred, Eli, Walter and Harry.

My father, William, was a master stonemason. If you know Bath at all, there is a big hotel overlooking the weir, the Empire, the founding stone of which was laid in 1901. He was the master mason on that. Uncle Alf and Uncle Eli were also builders; Uncle Herb, who played the banjo, was employed at a nearby earthworks called Tucking Mill. Uncle Walter, and Uncle Harry, after whom I was named, were both professional gardeners, Harry working as a park superintendent in Weston-super-Mare.

On my mother's side, my grandmother (Morris) lived nearby, and had a daughter, Aunt Annie, who was disabled; for some reason she had had her leg amputated. She used to do dressmaking, and I delivered the dresses for her to earn a few pennies pocket money. She was the mother of Fred Patch, my cousin who was killed in the First War. His father was Walter, and he was a gardener.

Who else? Well, there was Minnie, an old aunt on my mother's side of the family, and Uncle John who kept a pub in Bristol. In fact, two of Mother's brothers were publicans; one was in Bristol and the other owned the Brass Knocker on Brass Knocker Hill on the edge of Combe Down.

I was born and brought up in a semi-detached house called Fonthill, with an adjoining property called Beckford Cottage. When the two houses were built, I was told that from the top of the scaffolding it was possible to see Fonthill Abbey, built by William Beckford, at one time the richest man in England, it was said, and a recluse. The Abbey was by all accounts a vast complex, but the central tower, some 300 feet high, kept falling down because of poor foundations and today there is hardly anything left of what was once an amazing but ultimately flawed house.

I had two brothers and we all more or less followed in Father's footsteps in terms of the building trade. My oldest brother, George, was a cabinet-maker, my middle brother a bricklayer, so I was a plumber. Over the years, Father had become something of a cautious entrepreneur. He owned no. 2 Gladstone Place which he rented to Mr Ford, a roadman with a wooden leg; no. 3 he sold to a butcher but in doing so he kept and divided the land and built nos. 4 and 5. No. 4 was my middle brother's house on his marriage, and no. 5 I inherited when I married in 1919. My eldest brother inherited Fonthill as well as another house, no. 2 Laurel Place, which Dad had also bought. The two houses he built cost £400 together, in about 1910.

As well as being a builder, my father was a very keen gardener, and the back garden was thoroughly turned over to provide the family with food all year round. As soon as anyone went through the gate into the garden, they passed by a blue trellis and a laburnum tree to a line of fruit trees. The first was an apricot, the second a pear, the third a peach, then there was a wall and behind that a Victoria plum: delicious. On the other side of the garden were six gooseberry bushes, a Gladstone apple, and then a Beauty of Bath apple, and another apple tree, the name of which I can't remember but a lovely eating apple nevertheless, then another apricot. In the middle of the garden there was a cooking apple, the name of which was Nonesuch As Good. Wonderful names you don't hear much any more.

Of course Father was very keen to protect his produce. Running around the garden was a high wall, at least six foot at a guess. He covered the top of the wall with broken glass, but, as a cunning scrumper could still throw a blanket over it, he built a board out from the wall, so that anyone who climbed up would have to reach right over to get at the fruit, rather than grab it from the branches closest to him. Terry, the family dog, was also around. He ran pretty much wild in the garden and would bark if anyone tried to climb over.

As well as the fruit trees there were two greenhouses. In one were grown orchids and chrysanthemums, and as children we weren't allowed in there. The other greenhouse was more of an outhouse, a lean-to attached to the kitchen. This was heated by a little boiler in the scullery with four-inch pipes passing into and around the lean-to to keep it warm. Here Father grew cyclamens and one or two cacti, but at Christmas time he carried over a mass of chrysanthemums, brought on in the other greenhouse but placed in the lean-to from one end to the other purely for my mother's pleasure. Father was an amateur gardener but, as two of his brothers were professionals, there was a strong tradition of flower growing in the family.

Most of the garden was utilized for food. Dad grew beans,

onions, potatoes, peas, broad beans, sprouts, cauliflower, cabbage, savoys, the lot, and, as if that wasn't enough, he rented the garden next door, no. 1 Oxford Terrace, where he grew more potatoes. It was Mother's job to pick all the vegetables and we would eat them over the winter, with the potatoes kept under the stairs in the dark. Father used to keep his pears until Christmas; they were still all right, but apricots you had to eat as soon as they were ripe.

We were never allowed to take anything from the garden unless we asked our parents first, but the temptation to scrump usually proved too great. I used to crawl on my stomach between the rows of potatoes up to the gooseberry bushes, and heaven help me if Mother spotted me. She had a window that looked straight out on to the back. It was great fun, until I was caught, that is. All the children used to go scrumping anywhere there was a good apple tree, plums, anything that was sweet and juicy. We knew where all the rich pickings were, and it was part of the fun to get away with it.

Alongside the fruit and vegetables were the livestock, including bantam hens, one of which was in the habit of flying at my legs and giving me a nip. We also had about half a dozen chickens, one bantam cock and two hens. Mother dealt with the poultry, that was her job, while Dad looked after the vegetables, and we kids had to weed.

My father used to keep three hives of bees. He had a machine that would separate wax from honey and then Mother would melt the wax down and sell it as floor wax. The honey would be in a bowl and I used to dip my fingers in. Dad would sell the sections of honey, about one pound weight in each section, and some of the fruit, too.

While bees were useful, wasps were simply a nuisance.

There was very little in the way of pest control except what we could buy from the chemist. He was a friendly chap and was a member of the church choir; he knew my family well. He used to sell pretty much anything over the counter: warfarin for rats or sodium chloride powder for weed killer. He couldn't sell cyanide, but he could and did give me a piece as big as a sugar cube to poison the wasps. The only condition was that I had to sign for it. I took the cyanide home and mixed it with potassium in a bucket of water or a watering can. Using a stirrup pump or a syringe, I'd spray the liquid at the nest and kill them all; those that were in the air literally dropped dead in mid-flight. The funny thing was, other than making sure I was down-wind when using the spray, I didn't take any precautions, no face mask or hood at all, but I never got stung and I never suffered any ill effects.

Close to the bees were a couple of pigsties. This worked fine until on one occasion the bees and pigs briefly became rather more than neighbours. Father was taken ill and was in hospital on the day when Spear Brothers, the bacon people in Bath, were due to come and take the pigs away for slaughter. That meant it fell to my eldest brother and me to get the pigs out and into the Spears van; one was OK, but the other took the wrong path and bumped into one of the beehives. He didn't overturn it, but he twisted it round and the damn things came out in swarms. I cleared out. My mother could handle them, but me, I daren't go near them. The pig was running around and was stung all over.

With Dad having a successful interest in so many different activities, it was almost inevitable that we were comfortable as a family, at least by the standards of the day. We had a butler, part of whose job was to wait at table, bringing in the food that was prepared by the cook. Her name was Alma, and she was named after the battle of Alma in the Crimea [1854], although she wasn't old enough to have been born then. My guess is she was about thirty when I knew her at the turn of the century. There was another housemaid, Ella, who helped out, sweeping and preparing the fire grates, and dusting and cleaning the house.

She had to dust a huge glass cabinet in the living room, containing fifty-five different species of local birds caught and stuffed by my father, from the smallest, a wren, to the largest, a peewit. They were all mounted on imitation tree trunks and branches. For many years George and I spent much of our time attempting to match eggs to each of the birds; we never succeeded. Sparrows, woodpeckers, thrushes and blackbirds were easy, but we watched a pair of king-fishers for two years with no luck. We had a pair of field glasses and, when we eventually found the nest, the off-spring had already hatched. They had built their nest right way back in an old water rat's burrow. Otherwise most eggs were up trees; you can guess who did the climbing.

At Fonthill, the staff came daily but as the family income grew we moved to a larger and grander house that has now gone, called Rosemount. This had a nursery, four bedrooms, a drawing room, dining room, kitchen, scullery and con-servatory. This meant that there was a bedroom for the housemaid and one for the cook, who moved in on a permanent basis. Dad was financially secure enough to rent rather than sell Fonthill but in doing so he proved how shrewd he was: in the lease he made sure that he kept the rights to all the fruit in the garden.

Upstairs, my brothers and I shared a bedroom but we had

our own beds. There was an open fire in the room, which you would put out just as you were turning in, then you would have a bed warmer, a pan filled with hot water on a long pole which you used to gently heat the blankets. In the morning the maid would light the fire downstairs in the dining room before we came down. Combe Down is 800 feet up, and in winter there was frost on the inside of the window every morning – you could scrape it off.

In winter, chesty coughs and colds were treated with honey and vinegar, which tasted horrible, as well as goose grease which was smeared on your chest. My mother was also a great believer in a teaspoon of quinine for colds. For anything worse, Dr Morris was the man to see, a wonderful practitioner who would come out at all hours and in all weathers to visit a patient, water dripping off his hat as he knocked on the door on a wet and windy night. He was a man who spoke his mind. Dad was given pills for rheumatism and Dr Morris used to come round and order him to take them. Dad wouldn't, being the difficult man he sometimes was, and the doctor would have no hesitation in letting fly. 'What's the bloody good of me prescribing medicine when you don't take it?' Not many people would speak to Dad like that! The doctor's surgery was his own home. On the occasions I saw him, I used to go into his front room, the waiting room, and he would call you through to the back room that was his surgery. He would always mix you up some sort of jollop or other; heaven knows what it was and whether it did you any good, but you never left empty-handed.

Life at Fonthill and Rosemount was primitive by modern standards. Light and heating in the house were basic and it wasn't until I was an apprentice plumber that I put gas lamps in for my parents. Before that, we had just oil lamps, paraffin lamps and candlesticks. We always went to bed with a tiny paraffin lamp. In the living room, there was a pendant with two weights: you pulled the lamp down, filled it with paraffin, trimmed the wick and pulled it back up. The fire helped light the room. Otherwise you walked around with a little candle in a square brass candleholder that collected the molten wax.

There was no internal plumbing. At Fonthill the toilet was next to the coal shed in the garden, and was reached by a narrow path. It was a small brick building with just a seat with a circular hole in it. Toilet paper was newspaper ripped into square sheets, fastened by a nail into the wall. Behind the toilet was a big pit that would be emptied every so often, when a cart came and took the effluent away. I expect a farmer used it. We would try not to go at night unless we were desperate, because you'd have to get dressed or put a dressing gown on and feel and fumble the way in the darkness. An outside toilet was quite normal in the countryside and that remained the case for a long time. I remember, well after World War I, when I was in Wales, living next door to a builder's merchant who did a round that ended in Shrewsbury. He was going up a place called Horseshoe Pass one night when it was very foggy. He knew there were some farmhouses along the top of the pass, so he decided to stop at one of the houses until the morning. In the night he went down to spend a penny, but as there were no matches on the candlestick he went down in the pitch-black. He told me that he'd crept down very carefully in case the stairs creaked, and felt his way along until he found the latch to what he assumed was the outside toilet, did what he wanted to do, and went back to bed. In the summer, he was doing the same round and came to the farm, and he went to see how they were getting on. Chatting to the farmer, he told him what had happened, and how he had fumbled his way around in the dark. The farmer looked at him for a moment and then went to the bottom of the stairs and shouted to his wife, 'Blodwen, you were right. That's what spoilt the Christmas puddings.' He thought he was in the toilet but had actually gone into an outside pantry.

It wasn't until after the war that my parents had an inside toilet, because they had to wait until Bath Council put the pipework in, connecting Combe Down to the sewers. Just as there were no sewers, so there was no running water. When I was very young, local people shared wells, so there had to be rights of way and access, allowing neighbours to pass along the back of each others' houses. The wells' shafts often passed through quarry workings underground.

At Fonthill our water came from a well in the garden of no. 5 Gladstone Place, at that time rented by the postman. Both neighbouring cottages had a right of way to the well, which was at least sixty feet deep and surrounded by nothing more than a rough stone wall. At the top there was a little structure with a drum and a rope tied to the bucket. You would throw the old oak bucket down until it reached the stream which ran through the bottom of the well. It was quite strenuous to wind it up when the bucket was full, so until we were much older it was Father's job to collect the water. I wasn't allowed to bring a bucket up – it was too heavy – but I was an inquisitive boy and I couldn't help trying. That was all right until one day, when I was winding, I let go of the handle, and it flew round and knocked me out cold.

A couple of full buckets would usually last a day except for when we had baths. The water was used for drinking, cooking, shaving and one face wash. Any used for drinking had to be boiled first, otherwise it tasted pretty foul. I believe there were as many as eight minerals in the water including iron, lead, silver, gold and lime, and drinking it without boiling it was asking for a stomach upset. Taking water from the well ensured that, as a family, we used it sensibly, otherwise Dad would have been making trips back and forth without end. For this reason, most people in the village made an effort to save their rainwater, drawing the water from the lead guttering. It was collected in a tank and used domestically, though not for drinking. I know that the rainwater from the vicarage was collected and discharged to a big tank and was used for washing, while the overflow from that tank went back into a well.

Because water was so limited, we bathed once a week in an old tin bath in front of the fire. There was an Eagle kitchen range: one side was the oven, in the middle the fire, and on the other side was a boiler with a brass tap on the front. The boiler was filled by hand from the well every morning so that we always had hot water. Mother would draw the steaming water from the boiler and pour it into a small tin bath. Then one brother after another got in, using the same water.

Apart from the wells, there were two iron water butts in Combe Down fed from the mains. When a handle was turned on the side of the butt, a chain ran down over a pulley and opened a stopcock at the base, bringing water out of an ornamental lion's mouth. One butt was just outside the church, the other opposite the pub, the Wheelwright Arms. If you didn't have access to a well in the garden, you could draw water from there. Behind both butts was a wooden trough into which water was poured for horses to drink from.

When I was still quite young, the Combe Down Water Company, a private firm, was established and mains water was brought to Combe Down. The wells were then condemned. Dad was upset. He was a cantankerous old sod and would have his own way, but in the end the authorities sealed the wells with two stones across the top, both two foot six in diameter. In the garden, not far from the well, was a cesspit for the sewage. The overflow from that pit was subsequently discharged into the well so it could no longer be used. I later cut a hole in the top of the well and dumped all our rubbish down there too until eventually the sides collapsed and all the rubbish and the sewage ran into one of the old quarries. As for the two butts in the village, they too were disused, but were left as a curiosity. At least one example of these survives in the neighbouring village of Monkton Combe.

From the age of five, I attended Combe Down Church of England School. My eldest brother had his education paid for; my mother used to pay 2d a week. He went to Monkton School, where there was a private schoolmaster. I wasn't worth the expense! I'm glad I didn't go elsewhere for it was at Combe Down School that I met my closest friend, George Atkins. I was about six and he was eight, and we remained great friends for seventy years. He was born in Diss, in Norfolk, but moved when his father took a job as a coachman quite close to Combe Down. For the rest of our time in school we were inseparable.

Our headmaster seemed to us, as young boys of six or seven, to be about 150 years old, although he was probably in his seventies. He sported a long white beard and, given a scythe to hang over his shoulder, you would have Father Time. His name was Henry Henwood, and he had been at the school for thirty years at least, a kindly man and by the standards of the time hardly a disciplinarian. About two hundred children were taught in four large classes of mixed boys and girls, in the same classroom, the girls in one block of desks, the boys in another. As well as learning the three Rs, there was woodwork and clay modelling for the boys while the girls did housewifery, which meant cleaning lessons, cookery and laundry. A local man by the name of Ross was the school inspector and he was responsible for checking on educational standards.

By no means were all lessons class-based. When it suited Henwood, and time allowed, he would march us to his walled garden which he rented from a Major Rawlings, and in the name of science we would turn over and weed his garden for him; we knew all about dande-lions. There we learnt about snails, slugs and caterpillars, too, as well as the many vegetables we planted for him, and the soil we heaped over the potatoes that we had also planted. Our reward was minimal: a few gooseberries and then only when he wasn't looking. Henwood got by far the better deal.

There were other teachers. Lawson was the geometry master, but I was never his best student. I remember that he put two marks on the blackboard, A and B, and he asked what was the shortest distance between them. Of course the answer is a straight line. Then he drew a curve. 'What's the definition of a curve?' I had forgotten that, so I said, 'A straight line caught bending.' I had a rap on the knuckles for that, or rather my hand held out, palm up.

Another teacher, at least informally, was the vicar, the

Reverend Alfred Richardson, who was a noted antiquarian. We used to call him Duck Richards, for reasons lost in the mists of time. On Wednesdays, he would come to the school and ask us bible questions, and, if you got them right, you got a sugared almond.

History and archaeology were by far my favourite lessons. Trafalgar, and Nelson and Hardy. Waterloo and Wellington, the Indian Mutiny and the Black Hole of Calcutta – we knew about them all. Later, just before I left school, we were also taught about the recent valiant death of Scott and Oates, how they fought to reach the South Pole and how Oates left the tent and sacrificed himself for the expedition. We were taught about other great British heroes, too, which meant, more often than not, military commanders. For some boys, this derring-do may have been enthralling but none of it inspired me to be a soldier. I was content with my life.

There were only two places I wanted to go as a boy, Greece or Rome, Rome for preference. I was thrown into Roman history directly I could understand the spoken word. There was the history of their conquests and battles but, because of the influence they had on local life, there were other tales about their everyday lives. There were stories about how they had mined for metals in the area; how they had been unable to remove the silver from the lead taken from the Mendips, and how some of this lead with its high proportion of silver had been found in the Colosseum in Rome. At Charterdown, not far from Wells, it was, and still is, possible to see the old Roman flues where they used to smelt the lead to remove the dross.

This hands-on history fascinated me. Around Bath there

were innumerable Roman excavations, including a Roman villa with coins and pottery and also stone coffins, one with a horse's head inside. Near the vicarage, more stone coffins were discovered, including a skeleton with a coin lodged in its jaw. This was history found while I was at school. Later, as an apprentice plumber, I worked among the Roman remains of Bath, including the famous baths with their lead-lined bottom. When working there, we always took our swimming costumes. So as not to disrupt tourists during the day, all work was undertaken at night by the light of hurricane lamps. Then, when no one was around, we would strip off and swim in the baths, although we weren't supposed to. The pool was eighty feet long and forty feet wide, and it was a great thrill for me to swim where the ancient Romans had been. The water, I have to tell you, tasted disgusting.

In 1910, Mr Henwood retired and a new headmaster was installed and a totally new regime was brought in with him. The new master's name was Henry Collins, and he was a strict disciplinarian, so much so that in two months he lost both Lawson, the geometry master, and a Miss Shepherd, who taught mathematics. They wouldn't stick it, he was that stiff. Bertie, as we all called him – behind his back, of course – would come in each morning and the first thing he did was to tear a sheet out of a magazine, fold it and put it around his cuffs so that they wouldn't get dirty, then he opened the desk and got his cane out and placed it where everyone could see it, then started to teach. We used to get the cane pretty often; you couldn't really avoid it. It was always on the hand, half a dozen strokes, which made the hand a bit numb.

There was one boy, Vernon Bishop, a lad my own age,

who regularly caused trouble. He was always being sent to the Head for punishment, but when Henwood was around all he did was send him home from school for a week, which, of course, was what he wanted. Collins' attitude was different. The first time Bishop played up, he said, 'Now I know Henwood used to send you home, but you won't have anything of that now. If you misbehave, you will be punished.' Vernon didn't like being told and to our complete surprise he kicked Collins square on the ankle. Collins caught hold of him and put him across his knee and gave him the biggest hiding he ever had, then he said, 'Now back to your seat. You come here to learn, not to misbehave. You will never be sent home again.' The next day the boy came to school and his father was with him. 'What did you give him a tanning for?' Collins replied that Vernon had kicked him. 'Would you like me to kick you and see if you like it? That was what he was punished for. And another thing: if you can't tame him at home, leave it to us, he has only got to misbehave a couple more times and there is a remand school at Langport and we'll send him there. The teachers are ex-prison warders, they'll teach him.' This was said in front of the whole class. We were astonished. Many years later, I was to have my own confrontation with Vernon Bishop when his job as a water engineer collided with my own plumbing work, a disagreement that might have led to court action.

Collins had been at the school about six months when he started evening classes. I think he was surprised at the very average level of education, and the idea was to help those who had recently left school to improve their knowledge, but the classes were open to all. He gave lessons, two hours on a Tuesday and two hours on a Wednesday, and I signed up for them with my friend George Atkins. Collins' only condition was that if we started, we had to stick it. The first hour on a Tuesday was English, British English not Somerset! The second hour was Latin. On Wednesday, we had an hour of geometry and an hour of algebra; at thirteen years old, I was sensible enough to see that I needed more education as the time was fast approaching when I would leave school. Indeed, I found a lot of his teaching very useful when, two years later, I sat my exam to become a registered plumber.

Perhaps the most interesting aspect of growing up on Combe Down was the extent of the quarries that honeycombed the ground underneath our feet. I first became aware of them when one of the terraced houses owned by my father shifted slightly. It was built close to an old quarry which had long been abandoned. This was fine until the scullery wall my father was building moved about an inch; it put the wind up him. He found out that the only known entrance to the quarry was in the postman's garden, just the other side of the well we all used for water. He got permission to open it up and he took me down. I was ten years old and it was my first experience of being underground. First we climbed down a short ladder and then, through the second bed of stone, we found a stairway down to the third bed, about fifty feet underground, where the spring ran. I was fascinated. I could see the tool markings in the wall, but much more than that, for there were the workmen's tools, a great saw, teeth an inch long, two stones with a cut between, used to sharpen the saw, and the files stuck in a crevice. It appeared that the workmen had left a shift, never to return.

My father discovered that the walls of the kitchen were

actually resting on two pillars of stone left as supports. The men would cut into the rock about ten feet, and draw a block out, perhaps five or ten tons, and then they would leave a gap, go on and then leave another, resulting in these natural pillars that would hold the ceiling up. There had been a fall in the roof close to one of these supports, and that had caused a crack in the wall of the house above. That was nearly a hundred years ago now and that kitchen wall hasn't moved since.

As the quarries were extended, tunnels led off at all angles and unless you knew where you were going, it was perfectly possible to choose the wrong direction and get disorientated. Once, some boys from Prior Park, a Roman Catholic school, got into one of the caves. They took the outside wall on their way down and they went in thinking that if they kept the wall permanently on their left they could turn round at any time and find their way out, but before long they got lost in these passages. They were three days in there before they were found, and then it was only by a bit of luck. They came across a wall and they tapped on it, and it happened to be the wall of the cellar of the King William pub and the barman heard them tapping. Search parties hadn't found them.

Some people went down to explore the caves unravelling string as they went, but if the string got cut on a rock, you were in serious trouble. To know the way in and out of the quarries, you had to look for markings made by the quarry-men on the pillars. I would find a mark, an arrow pointing in, and after the arrow a number. That was the face the quarryman was working at. Follow it in to get to the face. Under that arrow there is an arrow pointing the other way and that was how he found his way out. Even so, these quarries often broke into each other so you would get confused as to which one you were in.

As kids, if ever a policeman was after us for anything, we used to make a beeline for a cave. Once we were in we'd run just a few feet to one of the stone pillars and hide behind it, knowing the policeman would never risk following us. We might be scrumping apples, or anything else that we'd got up to, and he would chase us. The quarries were our adventure playground and no one really thought much about the danger.

Although the workmen might be gone, the quarries were still full of life and colour. When the weather was bad, wasps would return to where they nested, and very often this was the quarries. Where the stone was a bit rough, the wasps would form a nest, sometimes as big as a football and almost as round. It was like a bees' comb, but a greyish paper-like consistency, full of grubs. Two or three might be suspended from the ceiling by a stalk. This was a tempting target and we used to go along and pelt them with stones, try to stir them up, or even bring the nest down. Of course, if that happened you had to shift and we would tear outside, but even then we frequently got stung on our arms.

All sorts of creatures lived in these caves, including bats, hanging upside down. We'd try to knock them off with a catapult, or if they were low enough we would pull them down with our hands and hold them, like holding a mouse with wings. Later, a rare species of bat was discovered there, and it cost a small fortune to make good the cave entrance so the bats could come in and out.

Outside each quarry there was rubble, stone that was no good for building. These heaps could be quite beautiful, with gooseberry bushes, wild strawberries and even a crab apple tree growing there. Ford, the one-legged roadman who lived at no. 2 Gladstone Place, used to look after the hedges and grass verges of the village. Dad had a habit of giving Ford a couple of pence to buy some seeds, aubrietia and suchlike, and he used to scatter them among the rocks in the quarry. In the autumn, they would flower and look beautiful.

Of course, if we were caught going into the quarries we were shooed off, because some of them were still being worked by independent quarrymen; if they caught us going in, they told us to leave, but in no time we would be back. We used to go in and see if we could find seashells or fossilized fern leaves in the pillars, and we'd try to carve them out. It was very difficult to get one, but that was part of the fun, being careful not to chip it. We never kept them; the entertainment was in getting them out and usually we just threw them away. We were only copying the quarrymen who for generations had cut and saved the fossils, making their own private collections as a hobby.

Bath stone, as it was quarried, had to be laid out to dry, and if it was laid in the wrong direction, it crumbled away. As it was pulled out, each stone was marked on the leading face with a black mark, and that was the way it had to be placed to dry, which might take six months. The men who worked there could tell by the grain what stone it was. My father could look at a block and tell you from which quarry it came, by all the tiny seashells that were in it and the colour. Although we were 800 feet above sea level, the area had at one time been under the sea.

Just as the coal mines used pit ponies, the quarrymen

managed horses underground. They were used to pull the rock from the shaft along a light railway until they came outside, where there was a windlass on a mound. There they coupled a horse on to a long arm and it'd go round and round, winding the rock up the hillside until it got to the flat where there was a shed. These horses spent much of their lives underground for there were stables down there where they slept, and mangers from which they were fed.

Lighting underground was by hurricane lamps or candles. These might be placed in a ledge cut into the wall, or set on anything horizontal; even three nails banged into the stone provided a ledge of sorts. Every now and again a ventilation shaft was dug to the surface; they were called 'light holes'. There were three in Richardson Avenue with just a warning notice board and a small wall to stop unsuspecting walkers from falling in. These holes gave some light in shallower quarries, but after they were closed the shafts were used by people merely to chuck any old household rubbish down. One chap, who owned a garage, used to drop old tyres down the shafts and when he had quite a pile down there, he would chuck in red ash to burn them and black smoke could be seen to rise out of the top.

One of the last men to work in the quarries did so independently although he ought not to have done this alone. One day he went home for dinner and when he came back he found that the roof had collapsed right where he was working. Among his tools was a stone coffin that had fallen through the ceiling and inside was a skeleton and various artefacts. They had an inquest and found he was a Roman soldier. When archaeologists

THE LAST FIGHTING TOMMY

excavated the area, they found yet another Roman villa and attached to it was a private cemetery dating from the same era.

Despite such close shaves, the quarrymen were expert at telling whether a ceiling was secure. An old miner would go in and tap the roof and from the sound alone he could tell whether it was safe or not. Injuries were not infrequent but serious accidents were much rarer. I can recall only one death from a collapse, when, just before the Great War, Fred Davidge was crushed in Vinegar Quarry, a relatively shallow quarry, really, but the ceiling gave way. It closed soon afterwards.

Above ground, the most tangible throwbacks to a once healthy mining industry were the many pubs. Within a quarter of a mile of each other there were the Red Lion, the Mason's Arms, the Hadley Arms and the Horseshoe. Each catered for the workmen from a particular quarry and if a worker from one pub ventured into another, there was a fight. Even when I was a kid, there would be regular free-for-alls.

The man who had been instrumental in the development of the quarries was Ralph Allen, and one of the most interesting places in Combe Down was his estate, Prior Park. In the late eighteenth century this magnate built not just a beautiful home but various follies in the grounds which were wonderful, almost magical, places for children. Sham Castle was one. It was a single wall with turrets, battlements and arrow slits, which he created simply to enhance the view from his house across the valley. The Castle looked enchanting from a distance although there was actually nothing behind it except a farm and ploughed fields. Another construction of his was a folly known as the

Monument. This building was triangular at the base with a circular tower on top. It was derelict even when I was a boy, and was boarded up, but there was no problem gaining access. There used to be a stairway you could climb – in poor condition and probably dangerous – that led up on to an outside platform from which you could look out across the park. On each corner of the triangular base were large decorative pinnacles around which we used to tie a rope, dropping the other end over a stone balustrade to the ground below. We would then climb over and shin down, or run back down the stairs and climb up. Either way it was potentially lethal but incredible fun. Sadly, the Monument fell into such a state of disrepair that it was pulled down in the 1950s.

It was in Prior Park, in 1912, that a string-back plane came to Combe Down to demonstrate the art of flying. It was the first plane anyone had seen, and it drew a big crowd. Its pilot charged a fairly hefty sum to take anyone up for a half-hour's flight. He took off from the grass next door to the Monument, and circled round, and the village turned out to be amazed by the spectacle, little realizing just how dangerous flying was in those days.

About the same time, perhaps a little earlier, I saw my first car. It seemed to me like a block of iron with wheels on. Just down from where we lived was the fellow who owned it. He was a songwriter and poet, Frederick Weatherly [1848–1929]. He must have been in his sixties then, I suppose. I saw him quite a bit around the village, a short, grey-haired old chap, one of the parishioners. He's largely forgotten now but he wrote the lyrics to the song 'Danny Boy', which he set to the tune of the 'Londonderry Air'. He also wrote 'Roses Are Blooming in Picardy', one of the best-known songs of the war. Fred had a friend who wrote the music, while Fred wrote the words. His friend had written the music to 'Friend of Mine', but he died while Fred was writing the words, so instead it became Fred's tribute to his old friend.

2

EDWARDIAN RAISED

Owing to the decline of the quarries, many of the men looked to earning secondary incomes, for instance by helping on farms, particularly during harvesting. Housewives could also help to bring in extra money, by dressmaking, repairing or altering clothes. Other people took in lodgers. That was the legal avenue, and then there was poaching. For many country people it was a valuable and free source of nutrition, hares, rabbits and pheasants being trapped or shot for the pot, and when I was a boy rabbits in particular were almost seen as fair game.

You didn't have to be poor to poach. In fact my old man was a poacher, and a good one too. I don't know if he was ever chased, but I doubt it. Dad had a friend on Combe Down, a police sergeant called Melewish, who liked a bit of rabbiting when off duty. As Dad was partial to rabbit stew, the two of them used to meet and go off together, quite where I don't know.

Sergeant Melewish was with the County Police, the limit of his jurisdiction running through a road called Summer Lane. There was a football club just on the other side of this county boundary, and some of the players used to make fun of him, knowing they were safe. That was until he caught one of them in his county. He took off his tunic and his hat and gave him a damn good hiding. You could get away with those things back then. Much later, when he retired, he took on the Pipers Inn on the way to Bath. Sadly, his son was lost at sea and the news of his death drove his wife blind and in the end Melewish had to give up the pub, a tragic end because he was a real character.

Poaching wasn't risk-free. In the woods, man traps with big iron teeth were still in use. They were hidden in the undergrowth so it was a question of treading carefully. One man who had several was the Reverend Percy Warrington. He owned part of a wooded hill area; well, it was church property really. There were some houses also owned by the church, proper slums, and when Jerry bombed Bath, he settled an argument between the county, who wouldn't buy them, and the vicar, who wouldn't restore them. People were living there, and after the damage he had no choice but to repair their homes.

The Reverend Warrington was not shy of causing controversy. Father helped build the chapel at Monkton Combe Senior School, a school for well-to-do boys, after one row. The chapel was built because the headmaster, the Reverend Hayward, and the Reverend Warrington just could not get on. The story went that before the chapel was built, the schoolboys were given two pews at church. After one service the vicar complained to Hayward that the boys were putting buttons in the collection and Hayward was naturally upset at the accusation. His boys would never do something like that. So the two men fell out and the resolution was the building of the chapel in the school grounds.

As children from an ordinary school, we didn't mix with the boys from Monkton Combe. We occasionally played rugby against them (and gave them a little punch behind the referee's back instead of the flat of the hand). I played at wing three-quarter, so I had to run fast, whereas I have a problem even to walk now! We used to have a fellow come Saturday afternoons to watch us. He'd stand on the touch-line with a double-barrel gun broken under his arm, and we got the reputation among away teams that if we couldn't beat them, we'd shoot them.

The pupils from Monkton Combe weren't local children; they were much posher. Theirs was a preparatory school for Oxford or Cambridge; they were the officers in the army. We didn't mix socially but you would see them walking about, sporting a cap with a white band on it and a blazer. They were smartly dressed and there was a real distinction between them and us. I don't think we were jealous of them, but the class difference was very apparent.

Church in Combe Down was central to community life. Throughout my childhood I sang in the choir, as did many local boys. In the stalls we quietly mucked about. One game was to place a marble on the bench and give it a knock, and the boy at the lowest end had to stop it with his book before knocking it back. I know we missed it once and the marble went off the end of the choirstalls and dropped to the floor, making more noise than seemed possible as it ran on down the aisle. The choirmaster came down at the end of the service to find out what had happened, as did the parson, and marbles became officially off limits.

In church, people rented pews for an undisclosed sum, a label revealing the name of the occupier. These seats were the ones nearer the chancel steps; perhaps the owners felt they were getting a bit closer to God, I don't know. Captain Daubeny rented just such a pew and used to read the lessons in church. He was a wealthy man who had worked abroad in the Government service. I presume he was a soldier of some earlier war, and he would serve again during the Great War, although never abroad. His family owned a large house built above Jackdaw Quarry, The Brow, and in Combe Down church there is a plaque to him. He was to lose his son on the Western Front.

When we were away from church and school, the countryside was our playground. We often walked along the canal side looking for eggs, or around the Midford Brook where the nests were in the long grass or in the bushes. I used to take moorhens' eggs and make a fire and cook them. They were very tasty.

Boys being boys, we made our own weapons: bows and arrows were common, as were catapults, though the trouble was getting the elastic. And woe betide any roaming cats and dogs that passed our way, or pigeons for that matter, indeed pretty much anything that ventured into our path or sat still for long enough. There was no concept of animal rights then and we were a bit cruel at times.

The meandering Midford Brook was a favourite of ours. The steep banks were ten feet across but there was one place where the sides flattened out and we could paddle. The bed then dipped sharply to a depth of fourteen feet, and was known as the 'fourteens'. It was here that we learnt to swim, wading in until it was deep enough, then, well, you sank or swam. We taught ourselves and used anything we could to keep ourselves afloat: two large empty tins, sealed and tied with string around our midriffs, would do. As long as they floated, then, we reasoned, so would we. They were prototypes of the water wings children use today.

One treat was to go to the spa in Bath. For 2d per hour we could bathe in the circular bath or, if we were brave, we could try another pool where the spring came up right in the middle. It was the hottest water of all and was called the two-penny scalder, and was just about bearable. It held about fifteen to twenty people, and you could swim in it. At the end of the hour, they would ring a bell and order you out. There was one other bath we used to call the tepid, that was 3d an hour, and it was all right but less fun. The building that housed these baths is still there but the scalder and the tepid are closed, and are just a curiosity.

There was one place on Hampton Downs, part of Combe Down – it's gone now because Bath University is built there – but there was a field where years and years ago the last duel in Bath was fought with swords. One of the duellists was killed, and someone cut a cross in the turf at the edge of a field in commemoration. As a boy, I used to go and look at it. It was never overgrown, there were no weeds at all, while round it the grass was always well cut. It stayed like that for many years. The land changed hands, and the new owner wanted to discover who attended to it, because no one was ever seen there. He used to watch but never saw anybody day or night, and in the end he set up four cameras, all on tripwires, one in a hedge, one on the footpath, one in a tree and one on the gate to the field, north, south, east and west, all looking towards the cross, while another camera was set up in a tree to cover the whole field. Nothing happened for months, then one night they were all tripped. He developed the film, but there was nothing but a shadow. It was one of the mysteries of Bath and it was never solved.

Not far from Hampton Downs was the old Somerset Coal Canal which ran through Monkton and joined the Kennet and Avon Canal. Before I was born, my grandfather on my mother's side had three barges on the Somerset Canal. They would pull in at Midford to weigh how much coal they had, then come on down through Monkton and when they got to an iron bridge, they'd throw two or three lumps of coal on to the side. My mother and her brother used to run down to collect them and use them on the open fire at home.

The Somerset Canal was closed the year I was born. The water gradually grew wild with weeds and was a wonderful habitat for animals and insects. As children, we spent hours scouring the banks catching newts in fishing nets. We would take them home and put them in an aquarium, but they were forever climbing up the glass and escaping. It was a pity when the canal was finally drained in 1907. They put a railway line next to the towpath and Monkton Combe railway station was built right in the basin of the canal.

That left us with the Kennet and Avon Canal. When we were about fourteen, my friends and I used to go down there to where an aqueduct crossed the canal, and if the lock keeper was asleep we'd pinch his punt. He left a shovel in the punt and we used that to paddle with, and away we would go as far as a swing bridge. It was all a bit of boyish fun, for we used to open the bridge so that the keeper couldn't come across, then we'd tie his punt up on the wrong side of the canal and go up from Claverton and have tea. He had to come down and walk into Claverton before he could get over the canal to walk back to get his punt. Even the Kennet and Avon Canal was very silted up by this time, with lots of weeds, and in time the train superseded the canal as a means of transport. I have a dim memory of seeing a barge come down the canal with timber on it, but that must have been one of the last and as a rule there was very little traffic. In fact there were so few boats that in winter the canal would freeze over and we often took the opportunity to ice skate down there.

As well as the canal, there was a meadow at Midford which was allowed to flood from the neighbouring brook to a depth of about eighteen inches. The water froze, making an ice rink for the children without any danger of anyone falling through the ice to a watery grave below, always a risk with a pond or river. A small charge of a couple of pence was made to skate on the meadow, quite an organized affair as it was possible to rent ice skates out for a small extra fee.

When the snow came, it could easily drift to several feet, and it was perilous even to walk down Ralph Allen's Drive to Bath, never mind drive, when the risk of skidding was extreme. In homes and shops, ice would form on the inside of the windows. Icicles would form anywhere there was a drip of water, such as a tank overflow. Just above the Somerset and Dorset Railway line was a very steep field. In deep snow we'd use it for tobogganing, and if you judged your descent correctly, at the bottom you'd end up on the rails, so we always used to watch the signal to see if anything was coming through the valley. If the signal was down, it meant a train was on its way and, if we had time, we would run up on to the bridge so that the warm, moist steam could billow up all around us. Like every boy, I was fascinated by steam trains and wanted to be an engine driver, but there was no opportunity ever to become one.

THE LAST FIGHTING TOMMY

There's a train tunnel 500 feet under Combe Down. It's not used now, not since the Beeching axe of the 1960s, but it's the longest unventilated tunnel in England. The trains used to get steam up in Bath, enough to go through the tunnel as quickly as possible without opening the furnace door, in order to cut the smoke from the chimney. As a passenger, you'd go with a handkerchief over your mouth, as the air would get very stuffy, almost stifling. It was so filthy, the windows would cloud up, and you couldn't see, while your handkerchief would get smutty. The tunnel was a mile long and took at least a minute or two to pass through. As kids, we tried to walk through it, but it was very difficult to breathe because of the smoke that got trapped in there and more often than not we were forced back out into the fresh air.

The track from Midford to Bath was a single line and before the driver could take it, he had to be in possession of a pouch. The pouch itself wasn't important, it was the ownership that mattered as it gave the driver the right of way, and negated any risk that another train might be on the line. As long as the driver had it, the signals or points could be operated in his favour, otherwise no. Once the train was through the single line, the pouch was handed to the signalman. For the next train passing through, the pouch would be held out on a rod and the driver would grab it without stopping. However, if the train came too fast he could easily miss it or knock it out of the signalman's hand, in which case he would have to stop and retrieve it. At Midford the station was above a bridge, below which was the Hope and Anchor pub. If the pouch fell, the usual place to find it was on the roof of the pub. Retrieval of the pouch was absolutely essential and often took a few more minutes than expected. This was thirsty work, of course!

Despite the precautions, there was one serious crash on this line in 1929. I was very friendly with the signalman at Midford, in fact as a boy I had been quite interested in his daughter, Queenie. Anyway, what happened was that some-where up Radstock way the driver and the fireman of a goods train believed they were about to be involved in a head-on crash with an oncoming train. It didn't happen, but they jumped from the engine, leaving the throttle full open. The train went on down through Midford, through the Combe Down tunnel at full speed, shedding two or three trucks on the way before crashing just before Bath station and killing two people. It was claimed afterwards that the driver and the stoker had fainted in the tunnel, but they weren't even on the train then. The signalman at Midford narrowly escaped with his life, as his signal box was smashed by one of the trucks that separated from the train. I had been working in the station hut the day before; I was often in there mending overflow problems in toilets, and when I returned he told me the full story. Fainted! No, they jumped.

One of the hobbies that I enjoyed in my youth was boating. Along with half a dozen of my friends, I joined the local Forrester Road Boating Club, and learnt to row. When we went there, we changed from our Sunday clothes into a vest and shirt, and a pair of rubber-soled pumps. I was number six in a crew of eight, the one behind stroke, while my friend Lionel Morris rowed at number three. We were quite good and used to compete against other teams such as Monkton Combe College.

At the Club, the boats were lined up on a jetty and were

linked to one another by a chain that ran through a screw eye at the bow. This chain was padlocked at the end in an attempt to stop boats being taken without permission. The rules on borrowing the boats were that we could paddle upriver to the next weir, but we mustn't go down in the direction of Bath. The only person with a key to the padlock was the boatman, called Bowman, who looked after the canoes, and it was to him that I, with Leslie Lush and Charlie Wherrett, used to go to borrow a canoe each, agreeing all the while to obey the Club's rules. So we would go paddling about until the boatman was busy, then, as soon as he was distracted, off we would go downstream. Three of us went in a line in the direction of Bath and the four-foot weir we were intent on shooting.

To reach the weir, we first passed beneath the three-arched Pulteney Bridge. Taking the central arch, where the water was fastest, we got ourselves ready. Then, as we approached the weir, there came urgent calls from tourists above us. They stood on the pier by the Empire Hotel and, believing we were ignorant of the drop, shouted, 'Get into the side, you'll go over the weir!' It was what we wanted to do!

As we reached the weir, paddles were raised in case we turned upside down, and over we went, before paddling down to the North Parade Bridge, where we could pull in on a sandbank. Here we would get out and empty any water from the canoes, carrying them back above the weir before paddling back to the boating station. Whenever we went back, Bowman would say, 'What bloody mischief have you been up to?' I think he knew.

Competitive rowing came on the back of many years of fun on the water when none of us took the sport particularly seriously. We were taught a few basics, such as how to right a canoe, but we would only be given an old tub because they knew we would sink it. If this didn't happen, then there was at least a good chance that one of us might end up in the drink. On one occasion when three of us were in a boat, Lionel informed us he wanted to spend a penny. He should have gone before we left, but seeing that there were families having picnics by the side of the river, we rowed until we reached a spot where there wasn't anybody around, and I pulled in under a large willow tree. Lionel was standing at the front of the boat, one hand holding on to the branch of the willow, while he was spending a penny. The boat must have been rocking slightly, because he said, 'Hold tight!' but I thought he said 'All right' and I put the oars into the water and pulled, leaving Lionel up to his waist in river water.

Looking back at my youth, I can see that it was spent in a community that was in many ways cut off from the outside world. Rural villages and small towns lived their own lives and had little interest in what happened in the wider world; at least that was my experience.

To give you an example, I was fourteen when the *Titanic* sank. We were out at play when the news arrived, and the headmaster called us in and we sang the 23rd Psalm, 'The Lord is my Shepherd': 'Yea, though I walk through the valley of the shadow of death, I will fear no evil . . .', and he gave us an address on the sinking of the *Titanic*, and we sang 'Eternal Father, strong to save . . .' with the prayer 'For those in peril on the sea'. I hardly knew about the ship, but the headmaster told us that on her maiden voyage she had been in collision with an iceberg. We were also told that she was trying to make the fastest trip across the Atlantic. Yet it didn't mean much to us; it was a ship that had sunk but when you grow up in the countryside and perhaps a few of your friends haven't even seen a ship, the significance is rather lost on you. I'm sure there were boys who lived by the coast for whom the *Titanic* meant much more.

I remember, too, the suffragette movement, what was her name? . . . Emmeline Pankhurst, but they were interested in politics and I wasn't. Day-to-day news came from the *Bath and Wells Chronicle*, that was the only paper Dad took. In other words this was Somerset, not London, and as far as I recall my mother never discussed it as an issue. A quarter of a century later, I remember the controversy over Edward and Mrs Simpson and the abdication; we had a radio at that time and we heard the news. But political events made little impression down here. I read about it, and that was it.

Eight months after the *Titanic* sank, my friends and I left school and followed our chosen careers, which usually meant leaving on the Friday and beginning whatever job it was on the Monday. Lionel Morris followed his father into painting and decorating, and Charlie Wherrett left to become a commercial artist, designing posters. I was down for an apprenticeship with Jacob Long and Sons, the firm for whom my father worked as a master mason. The 'Sons' were Charlie and George, the latter also happening to be the Mayor of Bath. With their father, Jacob, they ran one of three big building companies in the city. My father organized the apprenticeship. It would be a five-year legal contract that would be formally signed by the company, myself, my father and his solicitor.

I was allowed the Christmas of 1912 at home, then it was straight to work in the new year. The first job I was

assigned to involved what is now the Spa Hotel outside
Bath. It was being turned into a school, and my first job was
standing at the foot of the ladder while the plumber was at
the top working, and it was a damn cold January morning.
This was the nature of the job. I was expected to watch, to
try and follow what the plumber was doing, and then, in
time, I would be given just a small job, changing a washer
on a tap, perhaps, or adjusting a ballcock in a flush tank.
Simple tasks.

The apprenticeship road had been followed by all us three
brothers: George as a carpenter, William as a bricklayer and
now me as a plumber. For William, bricklaying was not
enough, and early in 1913 he suddenly announced that he
was going to join the army. He had been persuaded to enlist
by his great friend Alfred Logie, a Scot, a carpenter and
joiner who lived in the village, the son of a well-known
shoemaker. Fred was perhaps six or eight months older than
my brother, and had enlisted the year before into the Royal
Engineers. Having completed his initial training, he went
overseas to Gibraltar. Army life suited him and he had
obviously encouraged my brother to enlist and see a bit of
the world, rather than simply pursue a career in the
building trade.

William was keen to join up, and soon after his nineteenth birthday he too enlisted in the Royal Engineers with
the idea of serving together with Fred, although they never
got the chance.

My parents were certainly not at all happy about William
enlisting; Mother in particular had an idea that only scruffs
and villains joined up. I think that was the general
reputation the peace-time army had in those days. However, they didn't try to stop him and so off he went. I don't

recall seeing him again for a long time, in fact I only recall him coming home once. He was in his dress uniform, red tunic, white belt, looking every bit a soldier. In my interest, I put my fingers on his belt and marked it. William whacked me round the head for that as he had to clean it again with Blanco. Then, like Alf, he went abroad, sailing for South Africa and Pretoria, where he remained until August 1914.

3

JOINING UP

History will tell you that when the war broke out everyone went mad, singing and marching about, welcoming the war with Germany. It will also tell you that all the men ran to join up as soon as they could, and that many boys aged sixteen and seventeen enlisted. Well, I was sixteen in August 1914 and I didn't. I didn't welcome the war at all, and never felt the need to get myself into khaki and go out there fighting before it was 'all over by Christmas'. That's what people were saying, that the war wouldn't last long. I am not saying I knew any different, but at my age I was keen to continue my apprenticeship, rather than pick up a gun.

Everyone knew that the war with Germany was only a matter of when, and not if; it was in the papers and in people's talk, but while a lot of local lads went and joined up in the local regiment, the Somerset Light Infantry, I never gave it a second thought as to whether to enlist or not. It is hard with the passage of time really to remember what I thought: I don't recall following news from the front in the newspapers, although I was aware that my middle brother, William, was out there, and I'm sure my parents were concerned, but I don't remember any great fear within the family. I don't suppose people knew what to expect and the long casualty lists were a while away.

On the outbreak of war in August 1914, six divisions of Britain's regular army set sail for France. These troops, numbering just eighty thousand, were all that the nation had readily available to take on the might of the German army which had invaded Belgium and was sweeping south towards Paris.

It was clear to men such as the new Secretary of State for War, Lord Kitchener, that a 'new' army would have to be created, a civilian army, trained and sent overseas, if Britain had any hope of successfully prosecuting, let alone winning, a war in which the German army could call up millions of reservists to fight.

Just days after the war started, Kitchener appealed for the immediate enlistment of 100,000 men, part of what would appropriately be called Kitchener's Army. They would form six new British divisions.

Kitchener's call to arms was answered with a mass rush to enlist from among Britain's young and middle aged. Within weeks, there were enough volunteers to fill every battalion in all six divisions, and on 11 September Kitchener sanctioned the formation of an additional six divisions, to be followed shortly afterwards by a further six.

In Somerset, the men of Combe Down were instinctively drawn to the local regiment. It had two regular battalions, one reserve battalion and two territorial battalions, five in all. In addition to these, a new 6th (Service) Battalion was formed. In the event, this was filled quickly, and in September and again in October two new battalions were formed and were numbered the 7th and 8th (Service) Battalions.

After the initial rush to enlist, the numbers dropped rapidly. It was found that an essentially rural community could not supply the numbers of men required to fill all three Kitchener battalions. Consequently the 'local' composition of each battalion gradually declined, so that while the 6th Battalion was formed with well over 80 per cent Somerset men, this fell to around 70 per cent for the 7th Battalion and to just 25 per cent for the 8th Battalion, which took as many men 'redirected' from the north-east of England as from Somerset. Many of Combe Down's men, Harry's friends, thus found themselves serving alongside men with whom they had very little in common. However, death and injury did not discriminate between backgrounds. At least twenty-four men from Combe Down were killed serving with the Somerset Light Infantry, of whom eighteen were killed serving with the three service battalions, perhaps a dozen of them more or less Harry's contemporaries.

I have only a patchy memory of the outbreak of war. The newspapers were full of it, of course, and as that first week in August was a bank holiday weekend, a few people were being patriotic, walking about Combe Down singing popular songs, among them, as I recall, another Fred Weatherly composition, 'We'll all come up from Somerset, where the cider apples grow . . .'. I think it was a song that was written for the Somerset Light Infantry, more or less as a recruitment song. A number of local lads, some of whom would never come back, were keen to go and see a bit of adventure. Reginald Whittaker was one, although I knew his brother Gus better. They lived a stone's throw from us on Landsdown View and were known to be a bit of a rough family, always fighting, always arguing. Frederick Gerrish was another who joined up, as was Albert Kellaway, a married man and neighbour of the Whittakers. Eric Barrow, from Church Cottages, was one of those who lied about his age to enlist. He was the same age as me and so could not have been older than eighteen when he was killed on the Somme in 1916, serving with the Somerset Light Infantry.

Somerset people are not warlike – it is not something in our make-up – and we are certainly different from people who live in the big cities. We heard rumours, for example, that people in the towns were being given white feathers to embarrass them into joining up, casting aspersions on their manhood if they didn't. I didn't see anyone receive one and no one tried to hand me one either; in fact I never felt any pressure to go, not then and not for the next two years until I was called up.

Soon after war was declared, soldiers began to appear in the village, including a number of men of the Royal Army Medical Corps who were billeted close by in Combe Grove. Perhaps their presence inspired a few to enlist in the RAMC, perhaps it was because we were not anxious to fight that a number of lads enlisted as medical orderlies or stretcher-bearers; I'm not sure, but my close friend George Atkins chose the RAMC as did my mate Leslie Lush and his brother Lewis, both of whom preferred the RAMC to a regiment of the line. In time, almost all the local lads served in one way or another. A few, like my eldest brother, were deemed unfit for the army and worked on the home front in munitions, but most of us were healthy enough and as a consequence the village paid a terrible price for its willingness to serve the country. Lionel Morris, the lad who had spent a penny in the river, he joined up, as did my friend Charlie Wherrett, and both were killed serving with the Somerset Light Infantry, and Lewis Lush, too, was killed sometime towards the end of the war.

I didn't want to join up. I came from a very sheltered family. I didn't want to go and fight anyone, but it was a case of having to. When it came, army life didn't appeal to me at all and when I found out how rough-and-tumble it could be, I liked it even less. I had no inclination to fight anybody. I mean, why should I go out and kill somebody I never knew, and for what reason? I wasn't at all patriotic. I went and did what was asked of me and no more.

I was about eighteen months into my apprenticeship when war broke out. Over the next few months, all the able-bodied plumbers on the firm either joined up or after a couple of years were called up to fight when conscription became law. The firm lost key staff and in the end there were just four men who were over military age and four apprentices. This meant that there was more than enough work to go around for those of us who were left, and inevitably the lads, like me, were sent out to do jobs which normally we wouldn't have been allowed to touch until we had finished our apprentice-ship. We undertook these jobs, working fourteen hours a day, and made a lot of mistakes, being cursed for all eternity by the older men who then had to be sent out to put them right. Nevertheless I gained a lot of experience and with evening classes twice a week to learn the technical details of the job, I was, by the age of seventeen and a half, competent enough to sit for the London Guild of Registered Plumbers exam at the

Merchant Venturer's Hall in Bristol. I passed it, my first examination to become a registered plumber.

Throughout 1914 and 1915, William, my middle brother, was away fighting in France. He had left Pretoria within days of war being declared and had entrained for Cape Town, from where his unit, the 55th Field Company, Royal Engineers, sailed for England, arriving in mid-September. The news from the front was not good: we heard all about the battle of Mons and the famous retreat, and how our small regular army had held the enemy near Paris. Since then the war had bogged down and my brother and his unit were needed at the front. As soon as they were properly kitted out, his unit was turned around and sent straight over to France sometime in early October 1914. I didn't see him before he left and I don't believe my parents did either, and although they heard from him often, it would be the best part of two years before they saw him again.

William's letters home told us something about his time at the front. He had taken part in the first fighting around Ypres, a town that meant nothing to me then. He had been doing all sorts of work: making wire entanglements, repairing the front line, digging communication trenches, mending roads, filling in shell holes, and various other jobs, including making primitive hand grenades for the infantry. He really went through it, by all accounts, although we only heard the full story when he came home wounded, by which time he had taken part in most of the big battles of 1915, including Neuve Chapelle and Loos.

George, my eldest brother, remained at home. He was in his mid-twenties in 1914, had been rejected because of asthma, and began work just outside Bath station. J. Long and Sons had a big builders' yard there and he was charged with making wooden storage cases for 18-pounder shells. Each case had a copper lining which had to be made waterproof. Every screw was soldered at the top, as was every join, so as to stop water seeping in and damaging the shells.

There were just a few casualties from Combe Down in the first year of the war. I don't suppose there were many local men in the regular army other than my brother William and his friend Fred Logie, and in 1914 and 1915 the village wasn't hit hard. I don't think it was until Christmas time 1914 that the village lost its first son, a married man called Bright, a regular: his family still live locally today.

Only in 1916 did the losses become much more serious. The local men who had enlisted in the new battalions of the Somerset Light Infantry were overseas by then, and that summer, when the battle of the Somme began, a lot of casualties began to be reported in the local press, lads that everybody knew. My brother was one of them. He may have come home on leave from the front before he was injured, but if he did I don't remember. Then, in early July, my parents received a letter informing them that William had been wounded, not on the Somme but up at Ypres. He had been hit by shrapnel while revetting trenches and was on his way back to England. He was already in Netley Hospital when my parents went down to see him. He had been wounded in the legs, not too badly because in the long term his wounds did not affect his walking. However, he never went back to France. He had reached the rank of sergeant while abroad and, because of his technical knowledge serving with the Royal Engineers, he was kept back as an instructor.

It would have been August or possibly September when he left hospital and came home on leave. People were beginning to understand what the war was about, and not just because of the long lists of casualties in the papers. At Combe Park, a large war hospital looked after hundreds of injured men, many of whom could be seen, dressed in their hospital blues, walking around Bath city or being pushed in wheelchairs.

William gave me all the details I needed to know about the front line. He used to tell me how lousy and dirty the trenches were, and about the mud and the shrapnel. I knew what I was going into, but being the sort of person I am, I would always have preferred to be told rather than be left in the dark.

There was no getting out of it. In 1915 the Government introduced National Registration when everyone above a certain age, fifteen years, had a legal duty to give the authorities details of their age, occupation and address. Everyone was then issued with a registration card which was to be carried at all times. There was pressure to get more men into the army and this information would be used when conscription came in, to call up the country's manpower, starting with single men. In June 1916, I turned eighteen years of age and from that time onwards I knew that a telegram requiring my service was only months or perhaps weeks away.

Notification came by post and with it a railway warrant from Bath to Taunton, to report by such and such a time the following day. This would have

been around October 1916, and five of us from the
village went down from Bath to Tolland Barracks. Here
we were roughly kitted out and our civilian clothes sent
home. Then, after a few days, it was off to Exmouth
where we did our basic training, squad drill out on the
square, with route marches to build up our strength and
stamina. Quite early on, I was picked out, for reasons
unbeknown to me, and made a lance corporal and given
a stripe. This was the winter of 1916/17, one of the
coldest that I can recall, and we used to go down to the
sand dunes to do physical training and it was perishing.
We did square bashing, left and right turns, about turn,
and were glad of the physical exercise just to keep
warm.

At Exmouth I was put in a billet in Sandwell Road, I
think that was the name. It was a residential house
commandeered by the Government for lodging. This was
not unusual. The size of the army had left the authorities
with a terrible shortage of accommodation and, well before
I joined up, I can remember dozens of soldiers living in
several big houses in Pulteney Street in Bath, all of which
had been taken over by the army.

Our billet was practically empty, no carpets or anything except beds which consisted of three boards on a
trestle and a couple of blankets each. Every room was
full of men of all backgrounds and characters. It was here
that I learnt the first lesson of the army: lock everything
up if you can, or keep a close eye on it if you can't, for it
wasn't very long before someone pinched my boots. I
knew enough to realize that I would not only be in
trouble but indented for a new pair. I made a search and
found out who'd taken them. The thief wouldn't own

up, which meant either I backed off or I fought for them, so I did what I was called up to do – fight. We went outside the house and got stuck in with fists, and after a scrap I got my boots back, plus one rather obvious black eye. It was a silly argument really, but you had to stick up for yourself in the army, or else. Unfortunately for me, the fight was witnessed and I was taken before the officer in charge. The upshot of this was that I lost my lance corporal's stripe over the incident and never regained it.

In early 1917 we went to Sutton Veny near Warminster where I joined the 33rd Training Reserve Battalion. At this point we weren't attached to any regiment, although before we joined the 33rd I wore several different regimental cap badges, the Warwickshire Regiment being one, so I must have been shifted around.

Our training was the usual left, right, turn by numbers. We did quite a bit of route marching around Salisbury Plain with full pack, including an overcoat, water bottle, bayonet, and entrenching tool at the back. We had gas masks issued too, known as box respirators. Nobody liked wearing them. They were a damned nuisance; they misted up and you could neither see nor even breathe properly with them on. I never wore one abroad, but in England we trained in them, going through a chlorine gas-filled hut, putting them on before we went in and then taking the horrible things off once we'd reached the other side.

Bayonet fighting was taught with special vigour by our training sergeants. Go for the shoulders, the two lungs, the heart or groin, though if you had one up the spout, as we called it, which was a live round in the rifle breech, you gave him that instead of the bayonet. If he parried you off with his rifle and bayonet, you went for him with the butt in the crotch or the leg or, if you had a chance to get it up, smash it into his face and knock him out that way. We were always taught that if you got to hand-to-hand fighting it was him or you, and with that in mind you fought with real spirit because anything less was probably fatal. It was him or you: which would it be?

That winter was not just cold but stayed cold for months. The huts we slept in had a Tortoise stove, a round stove in the middle of the room, but unless your bed was close to it, the heat dissipated long before it reached you. Each hut had a coal ration but when our company was on guard over the coal dump, supplies improved significantly! We used to go down; if it was our people, they'd turn their back and we would pinch the coal. The coal dump was behind a gated enclosure on the edge of the camp and this led to an unfortunate incident. An officer came down to check on the guard. He must have been challenged but for some reason he didn't answer and in the dark he was shot in the leg. Of course the sentry faced a court martial, but what happened to him I don't know.

It was at Sutton Veny that we really started training with rifles, firing on the ranges, learning about not only the rifle itself but the slight vagaries that each one had: perhaps yours fired slightly high, or right. At one point, I had a rifle that grouped shots to the left-hand side of the bull at about eleven o'clock, so the only way to get a bull's-eye was to fire down at five o'clock and keep your sights slightly lower.

We were on the ranges on Salisbury Plain, and I wanted

one or two more bulls to get the sought-after Crossed Guns, the badge of a marksman. I needed eight more points but the rifle I was using was firing high, and we were on the 600-yard range. I said to the sergeant in charge, 'Can I lower these sights?' He had a word with the officer. 'Tell him to put it down to five hundred and fifty,' replied the officer. I had five rounds left; my next two shots were bulls, twelve points, four more than I needed, my next shot was an inner, that was another four, and the other two I didn't trouble a damn where they went. It was something to be given the badge to wear on your forearm, but if the truth be told it was the 6d a day extra pay that I was after. Being a marksman meant one of two things: I could be a sniper or I could be sent to a Lewis gun team. I could never have been a sniper – it was far too cold and clinical – so I was sent for training on the machine gun. Here they gave us a badge to go on our sleeve, a wreath of laurels with LG for Lewis gun in the middle. As I was to discover, the badge was known to the machine-gun crews as the 'suicide badge', because if you were taken prisoner by the enemy then more than likely you would be shot.

Throughout my training at Sutton Veny we were given occasional weekend passes out of camp. For those of us who came from Wiltshire or Somerset, it was possible to go home. From the camp, a friend and I walked to Warminster from where, for half-a-crown, we could hire bicycles and ride home for the weekend, just as long as we were back in camp at midnight on Sunday. It was lovely to head back to Combe Down and see our families.

Just as I was about to finish my training, at the start of May 1917, I received the news of the death of one of my cousins. My aunt Lizzie Patch, a widow, who lived a stone's throw from my parents, had heard that her son Fred was missing, believed killed during the fighting at Arras. Fred was just a few months older than me so I knew him well, although we weren't close. He wasn't a sportsman like me, he didn't go boating or play down in the quarries. Instead, he was something of a quiet boy, and a gardener by profession. His body was never found. I was very sad, and his death only brought home the feeling that the war was getting very close.

4

IN THE TRENCHES

A couple of weeks later we were informed that our training was over and we would soon be leaving for the Western Front. After six months' training, yes, I think we did feel prepared to go to France; we were fit and strong but, equally, we were young and some were still keen. Unlike most, I had, of course, been told much by my brother but even so nothing could prepare me for the reality.

As was the custom when soldiers were warned for overseas service, we were given a week's embarkation leave. I went home with Charlie Wherrett and Stanley Pearce to visit our respective families in Combe Down. It was difficult to say goodbye; even today I find it hard to talk about. My mother had seen Bill go overseas and return wounded and now she had to watch me leave. I only understood how difficult that was when, twenty-five years later, I watched my own son leave for war. I can't recall what I did that week. I was no doubt preoccupied with thoughts of going to France; either way, one morning, my leave over, I got up and took the electric tram through Combe Down to Bath station and from there to Taunton. My parents didn't walk me to the tram; instead they saw me leave from the house and after the usual embrace, goodbye and good luck, I went. I know that I met up with Stanley to catch the tram. He had attended the same school as me, but was a few years older and was no more than an acquaintance. In civilian life, he had become a baker's boy, in the family business. Although we had trained together in the 33rd Training Reserve Battalion, we would soon be split up when we arrived in France. He went off to the 8th Somerset Light Infantry and I never saw him again, for he was killed just a few weeks later on the opening day of the third battle of Ypres. Charlie Wherrett accompanied me to France, but we too were parted and never met again.

Yet none of us could have predicted our fates when, in the second week of June, our small group walked up a narrow gangway and was packed together on an old paddle steamer. As the men crowded on board, the group that I was with moved to stand by the port-side paddle. As we pulled out of Folkestone harbour, we watched England and the white cliffs gradually recede into the darkness. I wasn't the only one who wondered whether we would ever set foot on her soil again. Would I come home and, if I did, would I be in one piece? We all knew what we were going to; there were no illusions any more, no excited chatter or joviality. All the lights on board were extinguished and we were forbidden even to smoke, for there was a genuine threat from submarines and an escort of two destroyers would shepherd us across. This was what we were told, but it may have been to make us feel better because in the pitch-dark we saw nothing but the waves breaking around the boat.

I got talking to Jack Fisher, a stoker by trade and a

member of the crew who had previously been in the Mediterranean. He told me that while on the island of Malta he had been ordered to change from one convoy to another. The transport he left then sailed and the next day it was sunk with all hands. He was lucky, and I idly wondered if some of his luck might wipe off on me. That night we slept on deck, if there was room. Lookouts were posted, while the ship zigzagged all the way across the Channel so as not to give any enemy submarines a broadside view.

It was daylight when we arrived in Boulogne, and we disembarked and marched up a steep hill into St Martin's Camp. The sound of guns was just about audible. The sight of soldiers had ceased to arouse any interest among local civilians and we disembarked without fanfare. As we marched away from the dock, I was judged not to be carrying enough, so I was given a fifteen-pound pack of bully beef to carry into camp. We lived in tents, but soon after arrival we were separated and drafted to various regiments. It was at this moment that Charlie and I were parted; there was no choice in the matter. I went into the Duke of Cornwall's Light Infantry, and he was sent to the Somerset Light Infantry and was drafted to a regiment in Egypt, and he died out in India in 1919. My new battalion would be the 7th, a service battalion in the 61st Brigade, 20th (Light) Division, a brigade that, as it turned out, also contained the 7th Somerset Light Infantry and, of course, some of the lads from Combe Down.

When the new draft arrived in France, we were selected for whatever regiment happened to be short of men. That was the fate of conscripts: you couldn't pick your regiment as the volunteers had, otherwise I would have chosen the Somerset Light Infantry. We were lined up and they asked if anyone there knew anything about the Lewis gun. Having had some training, I said 'yes'. The 7th DCLI had a team, and the no. 2 had gone home to England on compassionate leave and so I was sent to join them. On the way over, I had carried a Lee-Enfield rifle but from the moment I was chosen to join the Lewis gun team I was ordered to hand it over and was issued instead with a Webley revolver. As a no. 2 on the team, I would be responsible for carrying the spare parts for the machine gun, enough to build another one if needs be, and so I was not expected to cart around a rifle, too.

A sergeant introduced me to my new friends. At the time, the battalion was out of the line and we were sent to work on the ranges, training, to see how quickly we could do the job. I'd been thoroughly rehearsed on how to take a Lewis gun apart and, if it jammed, what I could do. What I didn't know, Bob Haynes, the no. 1 on the gun, soon taught me. He insisted absolutely, 'You've got to be quick and accurate, our lives and your life depend upon it', and he kept on practising me, when out on rest, changing the magazine and stripping down the gun. I had to know what to do automatically when anything went wrong.

The team was very close-knit and it had a pact. It was this: Bob said we wouldn't kill, not if we could help it. He said, 'We fire short, have them in the legs, or fire over their heads, but not to kill, not unless it's them or us.'

The 7th Duke of Cornwall's Light Infantry had been fighting on the Western Front since late July 1915. Despite the battalion's Cornish connections, many of those who served with the unit were not Cornishmen at all. Just as the Somerset Light Infantry had taken in men from the north-east, so the DCLI incorporated men from almost as far away. Looking at the backgrounds of the first one hundred men killed with the battalion, it is interesting to note that only sixteen were from the Royal Duchy, while as many were from Birmingham, and eleven were from towns such as Leeds, Blackburn and Sunderland. However, by far the largest number were Londoners, some fifty-seven in total. By the time Harry joined the 7th Battalion in June 1917, it was even more diluted, so that his not coming from Cornwall was the norm rather than the exception.

When Harry arrived in France at the end of the first week of June 1917, he joined a battalion resting after an exhausting time in the line. The 7th DCLI was already some three hundred men under strength following its involvement in the battle of Arras in April. Then, in late May, on its last tour in the line, the battalion had suffered a number of casualties from German shelling. C Company in particular had lost a disproportionate number, twenty-six men being killed or wounded, with the other three companies collectively losing just seven. The following month, the Battalion War Diary noted the arrival of three officers and seventeen other ranks, one of whom was almost certainly Harry. Not surprisingly, he, along with a number of other men, was sent to C Company. In July, a further 195 other ranks and one officer were sent out to join the battalion as it prepared for its involvement in the forthcoming third battle of Ypres.

Although the 7th DCLI was out at rest, the word 'rest' itself was something of a misnomer, for the men were not allowed time to recuperate. Rather, they were expected to supply working parties for the trenches. In June, a number of men were required to help the tunnelling companies which were digging deep dugouts in the vicinity of a village called Lagnicourt. On 13 June, the

Harry's parents, William and Elizabeth (née Morris) Patch. Longevity is in the family: Elizabeth lived until she was ninety-four, dying at Fonthill in 1951.

The 1901 Census return, taken in March that year, records that Henry J. Patch, son of William and Elizabeth Patch, was aged just two (*last entry under 'Fonthill'*).

Harry's father outside Fonthill *c.*1905. Harry's bedroom window (*top right*) has an ornate metal guard which his father put in place to stop his young son falling out.

Pulteney Bridge and the weir. Harry, and school friends Leslie Lush and Charlie Wherrett, frequently 'shot' the weir, despite anxious warnings from tourists near by.

Harry Patch aged around fourteen, about the time he began work as a plumber's apprentice.

William Patch in full dress uniform in 1914; his experiences in France were relayed to his brother, ensuring that Harry was left in no doubt as to what he would face on the Western Front.

The spirit typical of Kitchener's Army. The sergeant leading these men over the hedge would later take them to France.

Leaving for the front. Soldiers line the deck to wave an emotional and optimistic goodbye to family and friends.

A Lewis Gun team cleans the machine gun's magazine and the cartridge guide. Such tasks were undertaken daily to ensure that guns did not jam in action. The man nearest the camera has his left hand in the spare-parts bag and may be the No.2, Harry's position on the team. Note the unlit cigarettes, almost certainly handed out by the photographer in exchange for the men's co-operation.

'Ration parties would bring water up in petrol cans which were rarely washed out. There was a standing joke that if you were out there long enough you could tell the difference in taste as to whether the water came in a British Petroleum or a Shell can.'

Unidentified soldiers make their way across the shell-torn ground on Pilckem Ridge. They are heading towards the front line to take part in the fighting around Langemarck, 16 August 1917.

Pioneers laying white tape across the Ypres battlefield. Harry and his comrades lined up along such tape before going into action.

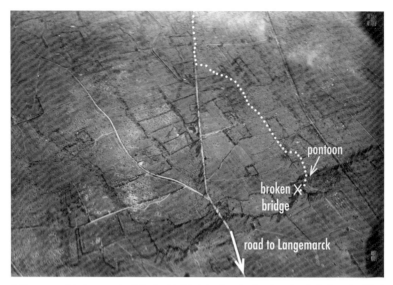

A German aerial photograph of the land behind the Steenbeek, taken shortly before the Allied offensive began. The 7th DCLI crossed these fields prior to the attack on Langemarck. The route up to the front line, the broken bridge and the position of the pontoon over which Harry crossed the Steenbeek are indicated.

A British aerial photograph of the land to the east of the Steenbeek just after the attack on the 16th. The complete devastation of the land, in contrast to the German photograph, suggests the ferocity of the fighting in the first weeks of the third battle of Ypres.

Artillerymen stop to watch the progress of the battle. They would be called into action soon afterwards to bombard the enemy's trenches behind Langemarck.

A shell explodes close to a British forward battery during the attack.

The Steenbeek, pictured shortly after Harry crossed the flooded stream during the attack on 16 August. In the centre is the pontoon constructed by the Royal Engineers and used by Harry and the men of his battalion before their advance on Langemarck.

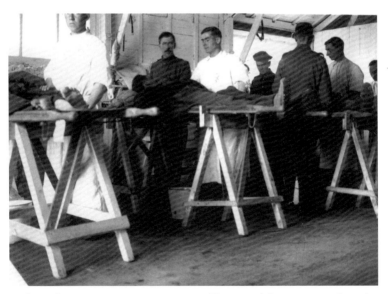

Battle casualties receiving treatment on 18 August. These wounded men are in an advanced dressing station, possibly 'Fusilier ADS' (see map on page x), near the village of Boesinghe. They are directly behind the old front line from where the 7th DCLI attacked, and so may well be soldiers from Harry's battalion.

Summer 1918. Home, wounded and recuperating, Harry, in uniform (*fourth from right*), attends the wedding of his brother George to Lilian Shore. Harry's cousin George Morris (*centre*), also in uniform, survived the war.

Combe Down War Memorial, which Harry attended the unveiling of in 1921. On it are inscribed the names of many of his childhood friends, as well as that of his cousin Fred Patch.

The topping-out parade at the Wills Memorial Building, Bristol, 1926. Harry Patch (*pictured front left, sitting, with a mop of hair*) joins other workers to celebrate the completion of the sixty-six-metre university tower.

Looking up Park Street, Bristol. This picture was taken just after the tower was unveiled by King George V and shows how the building dominates the city's skyline.

The Great Hall where Harry, standing at the back, listened to King George V as he officially opened the new building.

The wooden scaffolding that Harry and his colleagues climbed each day during the construction of the Wills Memorial Tower. In high winds the men could be trapped at the top of the tower.

The countdown to war: Harry (*centre*) joins the Auxiliary Fire Service. Too old to fight again, he chose instead to use his knowledge of plumbing and Bath's water supply to tackle the fires caused by German bombs.

April 1942. After two years of relative peace in Bath, the German bombers attacked. They targeted cities of architectural beauty, in revenge for the RAF's attack on Rostock and Lübeck.

A house in Bath with its walls blown out. Almost 19,000 buildings were damaged and 401 people killed in Bath during several nights of bombing.

Bear Flat, Bath, the morning after a raid. It was here that Harry spent most of the night dousing flames at the National Provincial Bank. One of the pipes he used to tackle the blaze can be seen snaking across the ground. Until daylight, Harry had no idea that his pump was parked across an unexploded bomb.

Harry with Ada, the love of his life. They are pictured in the early 1970s, shortly before Ada died. Their marriage lasted nearly sixty years.

In the caves below Combe Down. In 1990, aged ninety-two, Harry was asked by geologists from Bristol University to help explore the tunnels, using the knowledge he retained from his childhood.

After once vowing never to return to Ypres, Harry agreed to go back in 2004. He returned to Pilckem Ridge and laid a wreath to his fallen comrades in an emotional ceremony.

Harry shares a seat with the late Doris Whitaker, his close companion and soul mate for six years.

Harry holds out his Légion d'Honneur. This highly prestigious medal was awarded by France to all surviving British veterans.

Harry spots the author taking a clandestine picture and raises a salute not typical of former soldiers.

Harry in 2007. Above his medals is the cap badge of the Duke of
Cornwall's Light Infantry.

battalion was relieved once again and retired further back to a place referred to in the War Diary as 'Camp A', close to the village of Vaulx. Here the men underwent further refitting and training, with drill, musketry and lectures followed by instruction in map reading, patrolling and bayonet fighting.

The weather had been very blustery and showery when we were ordered up to the front line before Ypres. I know I passed through the shell-shattered town, and I can clearly remember the Cloth Hall in ruins, smashed to pieces.

It was my first time in the trenches and it just about coincided with my nineteenth birthday. Understandably I was nervous, but I didn't want to reveal any feelings to the others in my team; it wouldn't have helped me, and it would certainly not have helped them, and it was important to show them that I was reliable. They had all seen front line action and they needed to know that I was no danger to them; a windy or nervous soldier was as much danger to the rest as he was to himself. They had lost a member of the team and I was the new boy. It can't have been easy for a Lewis gun team to lose anyone under any circumstances, and I was aware that I had to prove myself before I was accepted.

No. 1 carried the gun and I carried the spare parts. The gun weighed thirty-eight pounds and the spare parts weren't much under, including one spare barrel, so it was quite a weight. Going into the line, nos 3, 4 and 5 carried panniers on straps over their shoulders, two on their chests and two on their backs, fully loaded, which meant they were carrying two hundred rounds.

We moved up with the company, along a muddy communication trench, halting at intervals until we got into the line and the men spread out. We were a little group on our own, five of us, although we were part of C Company, and under the same discipline as everyone else, but we were excused the ordinary duties, such as fatigue parties; that was the job of the infantrymen. As they were being organized by their NCOs, the Lewis gun teams were allowed to find their own spot, more or less, and we set up the gun where Bob directed and patrols were sent out into no-man's-land. The Germans may have been aware that a relief was under way, as it wasn't long before a number of shells landed close to our trenches, followed by some mortars, and enemy aircraft were active overhead. How did I feel? Well, how would anyone feel? It doesn't matter how much training you've had, you can't prepare for the reality, the noise, the filth, the uncertainty and the calls for stretcher-bearers. We took a number of casualties in the company before we were relieved.

At Ypres the land was low lying and the water table very high. It was only possible to dig down a foot or two before hitting water, and as such it reminded me very much of the Somerset Levels. The trenches were hardly below ground at all, and most of the protection was a breastwork built above ground level. The conditions were frequently awful. I quickly got used to sitting on the firing step with my feet up against the trench wall opposite, watching the water flowing underneath the duckboards. Where the floor was particularly bad, we used to get an empty box of ammunition and stand on it until it gradually sank in the mud, when you'd put another on top and stand on that. The ground was absolutely full of boxes lost in the mud.

Because we were Lewis gunners and relieved of the jobs

that the infantry were expected to do, almost our entire occupation was making sure that the machine gun functioned properly. The main problem with the machine gun was an unexpected jam at a vital moment. As a bullet travelled up the barrel, gas was sucked back on to the piston, forcing it back ready for the next round. However, should the gun get too hot, the piston wouldn't come back and compress the recoil spring and it was that recoil spring that was used to fire the next round. As it was my job to sort out any problems, I might have to replace the barrel, no easy job when the metal was hot enough to blister your fingers.

If it was raining, we wore a groundsheet which we could use as a cape, but it was more important to keep the gun dry and we'd cover that first before we covered ourselves. The Lewis gun was our job – lose the gun and we lost the point of our being there – so our main concern was to make sure the gun was clean, oiled, and ready for immediate use: loaded, magazine on.

Ensuring that we remained efficient was the job of the officer who would come down every morning. 'Stand to, right inspection.' The officer would take my Webley revolver out, snap it open and if there was a round missing you had to say who ordered you to fire it, where it had gone and why you fired it. Similarly, if the revolver was in the holster with the safety catch off, I could be on a charge for that because of the danger of shooting myself in the foot, and a self-inflicted wound was always looked on very dimly. Ammunition was hard to bring into the front line so you had to account for almost every round. The rifles belonging to the ammunition carriers were also checked before the Lewis gun was inspected. The officers were very particular that the gun and the spare parts were kept scrupulously clean, otherwise you were put on a charge. If any of the brass cartridges were damaged, then they wouldn't be ejected from the gun, jamming it; likewise a little bit of mud could render the gun unusable, and there was plenty of that around, so they were ensuring that we were ready if the Germans mounted an attack.

I served at Ypres during the summer, June to September; what it was like in the winter I hate to think. But even in the summer it was chilly, too, with occasional storms and frequent squally showers. About three to five in the morning it would get very cold, and you'd do what you could to keep yourself warm, clapping your hands together, moving your feet about, or, if you weren't on watch, moving up and down the trench. The night seemed endless, but then if the sun came out you were all right and as the sun rose, so your spirits rose a little, too.

Each morning at dawn, we stood to, the sergeants and corporals would give the order and the men would climb up on the firestep and look, just to make sure the Germans weren't up to anything, planning a sudden attack or raid. We'd be up there for half an hour, after which you stood down. In the morning, the rum ration would come round. Rum was brought up in a big pottery jar. I don't know what the measure was meant to be exactly because they poured a bit into the lid of your mess tin and you drank out of that. It burnt all the way down, especially if you weren't a drinker, but it warmed you up beautifully. Breakfast followed, then there might be a chance to go to sleep or doze off in the sunshine. If we got peckish we carried something like a square dog biscuit. It was so hard that you had to soak it in water to get your teeth into it.

If we were lucky, the mail might come up. One of the first parcels I ever had contained some of my brother William's wedding cake. It had been packed with an ounce of tobacco, but in transit both had got mixed up together, so it was a case of sitting down and meticulously picking at the cake to separate one from the other if I was to enjoy the cake and smoke the tobacco. I used to write home about once a week, but you got writing paper when you could. To send a private letter required what was known as a green envelope, which you signed saying that you had written nothing untoward, otherwise everything was censored by one of the company officers.

Despite all the rain, there was little fresh water in the front line as everything we needed had to be carried up. Ration parties would bring the water up in petrol cans which were rarely washed out. There was a standing joke that if you were out there long enough you could tell the difference in taste as to whether the water came in a British Petroleum or a Shell can. Washing was almost impossible. Behind the support lines, if you were lucky, you might find an old shell hole where the mud had gradually settled, and, the top of the water being reasonably clear, you would get a wash in that. In the trenches you might get a little lukewarm tea from which you might save a drop to have a shave, but washing in the conventional sense was out of the question. The army did provide baths well behind the lines, but I never got the chance to bathe. Indeed, from the time I landed in France in June until I came away in September, I never had a bath, and I never had any clean clothes.

There was no sanitation at all, and the place used to stink like hell. The latrine was a little recess somewhere in the

trench with a piece of wood across it to sit on. Toilet roll
was a bit of torn-up *Punch* magazine or newspaper.

Boredom was the real problem. We used to sit there and
make up poems about the army, based on the old nursery
rhymes, such as 'Jack and Jill' and 'Mary had a Little Lamb'.
It was one way of whiling the time away. You would be on
lookout for two hours, then off, and someone else took your
place. It was so boring; you have no idea how boring it was.
You'd think about what you were before you joined the
army, and you'd think about the men around you. Up to a
point, you slept. I mean, when they wanted sleep everyone
slept, perhaps on the firestep or in a funkhole scooped out of
the trench wall so you could get out of the way. You might
keep awake for hours on end, but eventually you dropped
off, into a fitful sleep of sorts, perhaps for an hour, two hours
maybe, head in your hands, but the least noise and you
would be awake and wonder for a moment where the hell
you were and what you were doing there.

We took it in turns to keep lookout. You stood on the
firestep and, if you saw anything you thought was a German
working party, you would nudge a friend. 'What do you
think?' Any doubt and we would report what we'd seen, or
thought we'd seen, to the officer and he would have a look
with his field glasses, to see if anyone was showing a white
face or a hand. If he was even a bit doubtful, he would order
a star shell to be sent up. This shell used to break into half a
dozen lights which floated down, shimmering in the night
sky, and they lit up the whole area. When it was sent up, we
were told always to lean forward and keep our faces well
down, with our arms and particularly our hands tucked in
under our bodies so that nothing white could be seen.
Peering out from underneath our helmets, we would try and

count how many lumps we could see in no-man's-land. About five minutes after that light had died, we sent up a Very light, which lit up a much smaller area. Once again we would count; perhaps there would be the same number, well, all right, but perhaps there would be one lump less, or one more. If we knew that none of our men were out there on patrol, then the officer would say, 'Right-ho, give them a burst!' If it was just a bush, then the bush stayed where it was. Bob, as the no. 1, would fire half a magazine at them, then, straightaway, we would move from our position down the trench. It was important not to fire a magazine from the same position because the Germans could see the flash from the Lewis gun and take a bearing on the position. Firing again from that spot was asking for half a dozen whizz-bangs. So we'd always move, perhaps twenty, perhaps thirty, yards either way in the trenches and have another go, and then perhaps, later on, you'd go back to the same part of the line again. While the infantry worked at night, our duty was to carry on watching, watching, watching. Oh yes, the darkness played hell with you, with your eyesight.

After three days, a new battalion came into the line and we would be relieved, making our way out down the communication trench, which was often far from easy. You daren't let anything tinkle, like a cup, or any of your equipment rattle. Not that one person making a slight noise made any difference, but if you have a company moving into position the accumulated rattle would alert the enemy to the fact that a changeover was under way and that was an invitation for a few whizz-bangs. We were being relieved by a Scottish regiment one night, and there was only just about room for two of us to get by one another in the narrow communication trench; what with the machine gun and all the equipment, we damn near had a battle of our own to pass, pushing and shoving and swearing under our collective breath.

Once out of the trenches we took a duckboard track. This was a hazardous journey in itself. We were always told, going up or coming back, that, if a fellow slipped into a shell hole filled with water, to leave him there because it was liquid mud; if you tried to get him out you'd go in yourself and that was it. I thank God it didn't happen, because the thought of leaving anyone stuck in the mud, possibly to drown, would test anyone's resolve. Such orders were not as heartless as they seem; there was a logic to it. A company coming in or out of the line stretches back a long way, and in the dark hold-ups could cause confusion, men could get split up and hopelessly lost. Equally, no one wanted to linger on those tracks longer than they had to, just in case the Germans decided to have a little fun with their guns.

After four days in the line we went back to billets and got ourselves cleaned up. The billets varied, but one I vividly recall was on a farm, close to Poperinge, and still occupied by the owner. You never knew with the Belgian farmers: some were good and some were bad to the Tommies.

The owner of this farm had a pump in the farmyard that was used to draw fresh water from a deep well. Everybody was going to the well to draw water, and this began to grate on the farmer. He complained, and in the finish they put a guard on the well. To resolve the problem, the company was split up into groups of seven, and each one was given a permit to draw one bucket of water a day. From that bucket we could fill our water bottles; the rest was to be used for shaving and washing. Of course it depended on who was on guard – if you knew them, OK, help yourself.

At the start, the farmer left us alone when a guard was put on. However, in the end he was afraid we would pump the well dry, worried enough that he took the handle off so that we couldn't use it. I was a plumber in civilian life, so I got to work. I got a strip of wood, coupled it up to the piston that goes up and down inside the pump barrel, bored a hole and put a pin through. As long as that piston was working, it drew water; when we left, one of our men put a round through the suction pipe. That, of course, destroys the vacuum, and once air got in there was no water. I was sure the farmer would find someone to solder over the holes to make the suction pipe tight again, but for the time being he couldn't use that damn pump. I'm certain he was more than a little annoyed about that. I also made sure I took my handle with me as well, in case we wanted it somewhere else.

Out of the line, the only rest you were getting was a rest from the shells. For most of the men, those few days were spent on fatigues of one form or another, carrying duck-boards up the line, or rations, mending roads; the army never liked you to relax if it could help it. Bored soldiers are restless soldiers and restless soldiers get up to no good, and so a regime was organized to keep us occupied.

You couldn't really relax unless you had the chance to go down to Poperinge into Talbot House, or Toc H as it was known to us. A lot of us used to call it 'the haven' because that's exactly what this place was to the men – a place of peace where you could relax, and that's the only time you could forget the strains of war for a couple of hours.

Poperinge was a busy, medium-sized town, I should say

81

ten miles west of Ypres, and, although it was shelled occasionally by the big German guns, I don't remember that it was badly knocked about, not in comparison with Ypres. Men would come back to 'Pop' if they were going on leave, or they would go there when they were out on rest, and so you always felt comparatively safe there.

Toc H (gunners' signalling code) was named after Lieutenant Gilbert Talbot, the son of the Bishop of Winchester, who was killed during the fighting in front of Ypres at the end of July 1915. His brother, the Reverend Neville Talbot, a senior Church of England chaplain, had been given the task of selecting chaplains to join various battalions, and met the affable Philip 'Tubby' Clayton, whom he attached to the East Kent Regiment and the Bedfordshire Regiment. Clayton arrived in Poperinge in late 1915. With Neville's help and approval, he sought out a house which could be used by all soldiers, irrespective of rank, as a hostel and home from home, 'where friendships could be consecrated, and sad hearts renewed and cheered, a place of light and joy and brotherhood and peace', as Clayton later wrote. The building he chose was an empty mansion rented from a wealthy brewer for 150 francs a month on condition that the house was kept in good order. It had in fact been hit by shellfire in 1915, which had caused serious but not irreparable damage to the building, smashing windows and also badly damaging one corner of a hop loft at the top of the building, which was soon earmarked as a chapel. This room was repaired by the Royal Engineers, and in December 1915 the house was opened as a hostel to any British servicemen going up to or coming back from the front line. In the garden, a carpenter's bench was found and for the rest of the war this bench became a makeshift altar in the chapel and was used throughout the war by Tubby Clayton. It remains *in situ* today.

Discipline in the house was kept not by cast-iron orders or army rules; rather, light-hearted suggestions such as 'IF YOU ARE IN THE HABIT OF SPITTING ON THE CARPET AT HOME, PLEASE SPIT HERE'.

Tubby Clayton was an officer, an army padre, but you wouldn't think he was a clergyman, not at first. He ran the place and was the life and soul of the party. He had a deep, almost bass, voice, and he could sing a good song and tell a good tale. He would sing any old chorus including, I remember, the Ivor Novello song 'Keep the Home Fires Burning'. The only time I heard that song in Belgium was Tubby singing it in Toc H.

The house was as homely as Tubby could make it, with flowers in vases, pictures on the walls, carpets and rugs on the floors, a piano and comfortable chairs to sit in, and open fires. You could have a cup of tea there and a bite to eat if you wanted. There were games going on, and you could join in, or, if you wanted to borrow a book, you could, and the price of a book was your cap, which was returned to you when you brought it back. I believe Toc H at one time was used as a grain store, and all the grain had been stored in the upstairs room. I take it the wheat was in the centre, as the middle was a bit dodgy and Tubby was afraid that the floor would collapse, so everyone used to sit around the edge on benches.

The room at the top was his chapel. Tubby upstairs became a different man from Tubby downstairs. He tried to reassure people in that room, to the best of his ability, that everything was all right. He knew damn well it wasn't. We took communion at the altar made from the carpenter's bench. He knew, as I think most of the people who went into that room knew, that there were people there who were about to go up to the front line and who would not come back. That time in particular was difficult, because we knew we were due to go into battle, and for some that communion would be their last supper. There was a lovely garden in the back, and I can remember going down there and in the middle there was a big shell hole, several feet deep. Today it is a lawn, with flowers. We looked upon Toc H as somewhere we could rest, but it wasn't safe; we were still well within shellfire.

That summer, the number of men visiting Talbot House reached its zenith, and cups of tea by the thousand were sold for a nominal price, and the seventeen staff, the largest number employed at the house, coped with these quantities of men pouring through the front door; these included Harry Patch and his Lewis gun team. In an attempt to assess the numbers using the hostel, a test tally was undertaken by the staff in 1917. The result: 117 men paid a visit in just one ten-minute period. 'And thus we lived through the summer,' wrote Tubby Clayton a year later, 'during which so many of our best friends died, and we came with set teeth to that unforgettable autumn when division after division went forward almost to drown, that those eternal slopes might at last be won, which, had the weather held, might have been ours in the first week of August. With the late autumn there came upon the spirit of the men a darkness hitherto unknown.' That 'unforgettable autumn' was the battle of Passchendaele, and Harry was about to play his part in the struggle.

5

PASSCHENDAELE, 1917

The third battle of Ypres, or the battle of Passchendaele as it is also known, was launched on 31 July 1917. Field Marshal Sir Douglas Haig, the British Expeditionary Force's Commander-in-Chief, was keen to press on with a new offensive in the belief that the German army was near to collapse after the attritional battles of the Somme and Arras. At the same time, British forces would break out of the salient to clear the enemy from the Belgian coast, as German U-boats were using it as a base for successful operations against the British merchant navy. Within senior Government circles, dire warnings had been given that unless the U-boat threat was broken, Britain would be so starved of essential supplies that she would not be able to prosecute the war in 1918.

War Cabinet approval for the summer offensive was given only on 20 July. Just eleven days later, after a ferocious preliminary bombardment, British and Commonwealth troops attacked and made, by the standards of the day, spectacular gains despite the onset of heavy drizzle. This turned to rain in the afternoon. The heavens opened and a battlefield which had proved passable just hours earlier became a veritable quagmire. For the most part, the captured ground was held, but the mud made it impossible for the artillery to move up to support the infantry, who were in places up to three miles east of their morning start line. The rain continued ceaselessly for the following three days, making further advances impossible. The offensive had temporarily ground to a halt.

The weather that August was exceptionally bad. The rain came down in torrents, twice as much as the seasonal average and five times more than in the two previous Augusts. Indeed, for the rest of the month there were only three days when rain did not fall.

For the next two weeks, both sides expended and traded an enormous volume of shellfire as each fought for battlefield supremacy. Vicious localized attacks continued on 10 August, before, on the 16th, the battle of Langemarck was launched in the morning darkness. Eight divisions were assigned the task of renewing the offensive on a wide front. Among the units to be sent into the ensuing mêlée was Harry's 20th Division.

The day before the attack, on 15 August, troops were thrown across a swollen stream known as the Steenbeek, attacking various positions to clear the ground for the forthcoming assault. Close to Langemarck, several pillboxes, including one large concrete fortification known as Au Bon Gîte, had been attacked. A number were knocked out, although Au Bon Gîte held firm, despite at one point being surrounded, British infantry even getting on to the roof of the pillbox. German counterattacks forced the infantry back, but nevertheless a vital foothold had been secured across the Steenbeek, and the next night infantry of the 60th and 61st Brigades would be able to cross and assemble within striking distance of the enemy.

Harry's brigade, the 61st, was given the task of attacking

three objectives known as the Blue, Green and Red lines. These were targets drawn on a map, at roughly 500, 1,000 and 1,500 yards from the jumping-off line. The Blue line would be taken by the first wave of assault troops, two companies of the 7th Somerset Light Infantry and the 7th King's Own Yorkshire Light Infantry. This line was defined as being the road bounding the western edge of the village of Langemarck. The men who reached this line would then pause for twenty minutes while the remaining two companies of each battalion would leapfrog their position and continue the attack to the Green line, clearing the village, on the far side of which they, in turn, would halt and dig in. During these initial attacks, the 12th King's Liverpool Regiment and the 7th Duke of Cornwall's Light Infantry would be expected to make their way forward over the newly won ground, passing through the first waves, ready to continue the assault to the Red line, a complex of German trenches. The direction of the attack would be broadly north-east. A and C Companies of the DCLI would lead the way, A Company would attack on the right of C Company, in all launching two waves of infantry, each approximately two hundred strong. Harry and his Lewis gun team would follow in the second wave to support the infantry by harassing any enemy troops they saw.

Supporting the infantry throughout the advance would be the artillery, firing a creeping barrage across no-man's-land. A creeping barrage consisted of a slowly moving curtain of fire and steel that fell just ahead of the infantry, obscuring their advance and pulverizing any enemy troops who might still be in position. The barrage would lift a hundred yards every five minutes, halting for a period in front of each objective before moving on over the open ground. This curtain of fire would continue until the Red line was taken, whereupon it would drop just 200 yards beyond the objective for an indefinite period, disrupting any possible German counterattacks while the troops dug in.

Throughout July, the 7th DCLI had been out at rest, preparing for the forthcoming offensive.

The third battle of Ypres was under way and we were to play our part in the general advance, that was obvious to see. We undertook intensive training through the early part of August in drizzly weather.

Before we went forward, all the men left their packs to be taken back by our transport into storage. We wouldn't see these again for the next few days. Some of the lads wrote home, and I may have done too; I know I made out my will. We understood what was going to happen in the morning and we had all those hours to sit down and think about it, so we tried to keep ourselves busy.

We were issued with two days' rations and ordered to see that our water bottles were full. Extra kit was issued to the men, shovels and more bombs, that sort of thing, while all the Lewis gun teams were ordered to carry further ammunition. Bob and I had to carry a full Lewis gun pannier in our haversacks, while nos 3, 4 and 5 carried not only one drum of ammunition in their haversacks but also special carriers which looped over the shoulder and in which it was possible to hold another four, all full of ammunition. It was no mean feat carrying all your equipment into action in dry weather, but over boggy, shell-pocked ground it would be hellish.

We were told that we were going over the top and what the objective was and that we were not to go beyond that, we mustn't go any further. Flares were issued to the infantry to signal when they had reached the German positions but in the event I don't recall any being used.

On the night of 15 August, the battalion fell in, single file, along the west bank of the Yser Canal, and at 11 p.m. crossed over, with C Company taking the lead. A gap of a hundred yards between each of the four companies was ordered but as they marched closer to the line, each company split into platoons, so as to minimize the casualties should a shell fall among them. At midnight, the battalion was halted and the men allowed to rest. At 1.45 a.m. the march continued by way of a trench board, and then a mule track constructed a few days before by the Divisional Royal Engineers. Soon after, the battalion crossed the Pilckem–Langemarck road. By keeping the disused Ypres–Staden railway track on their left, C Company arrived at the assembly position just west of the Steenbeek stream. It had been a tiring march, for it wasn't until 4.15 a.m. that the first men were in position.

In the darkness, the mud and occasional German shelling had caused several casualties and, in the confusion, half of A Company and both D and B Companies had become detached and were temporarily lost. One officer with C Company and two men were sent back to find the rest of the battalion and hurry them forward. As C Company waited in position, the Steenbeek was reconnoitred by the Commanding Officer and Adjutant for bridges and crossings.

The leading waves of Somersets and KOYLIs had to assemble on the far side of the Steenbeek in the dark, the men being ordered to advance as quietly as possible. In places, enemy posts were no more than eighty yards beyond the stream, and it was essential that they were not alerted to the forthcoming attack. Despite the 'normal' shelling and machine-gun fire, it became clear that the preparations were successful and that the men had crossed unnoticed.

At zero hour, 4.45 a.m., the advance began. As the KOYLIs and Somersets began to move to the attack, so C Company crossed the Steenbeek and formed up a hundred yards to the east of the river bank. The ground was appalling and in places men waded up to their knees in mud. Even so, progress was going as well as could be expected, for as C Company crossed the stream, the remainder of the battalion arrived just after zero hour, following the leading company over the water. At 5 a.m., the battalion was in position only a few minutes late.

It was now dawn, and soon the first British aeroplanes could be seen flying very low right along the line, observing the general advance. One of the two leading companies, A Company, by moving east of the river, had suffered some seventy casualties owing to machine-gun fire from the right, while C Company on the left was afforded some cover by the fall of the ground towards the disused railway line.

I'm told we attacked on 16 August, but the date doesn't mean much to me. I know it was some six weeks before I was wounded, so I suppose the middle of August is about right. I remember the names – Pilckem Ridge was one and the other was Langemarck – but it is such a long time ago that I can't quite connect them up in my head. How were we to know that a pile of rubble was this village or that, or that a gentle slope was a particular ridge, let alone what was going on across the front? You only knew what was right next to you, and even this was often obscured by smoke and fire. Strategy we left to those higher up. We were only warned to be quiet as we moved up, as this would be a surprise attack and the enemy was not to know that we were there.

A and C Companies were the assault companies so I assume B and D were in support. Ahead of us, two battalions in the division were to undertake the first advance and we would follow on. In the early hours of the morning we prepared to move off. I have a memory of crossing a flooded stream; it wasn't very wide, and I have since been told it was the Steenbeek. There were a number of trees there, like beanstalks, no leaves or branches, they were just smashed to pieces, or toppled into the stream. To my right, about thirty yards away, there was a little bridge that had been blown up, so instead the Royal Engineers had fixed up some canvas-covered pontoons, three or four feet wide. However, one of them broke loose and began floating away and there was a scramble to get it back and anchor it sufficiently so we could cross. We went over in single file, the pontoon rocking from side to side. I can see it now. Beside us, in the dawn light, the artillery was getting a couple of light field guns over, to shell the German support lines, I would guess.

Our guns' opening bombardment had begun with an almighty clap of thunder. You can't describe the noise, you can't, but it was enough to take your breath away; it was ferocious and much of it was dropping not that far ahead of us as the barrage crept forward with the infantry behind. There was an officer going down the line; I say a line: we were effectively in the open. He had his drawn revolver, and I got the distinct impression by the set look on his face that anybody that didn't 'go over' would be shot for cowardice where they stood.

On the far side of the flooded stream, we assembled. There was a look of apprehension in everyone's eyes, and horror in a few. There was white tape laid there so we knew where to stand and in which direction we were expected to go, otherwise we might wander off course, or fall into a shell hole; they were virtually lip to lip. I saw an officer at this time; he came along unravelling and putting down white tape. We saw him for about ten minutes before he moved on. He just laid it on the ground from one shell hole to another, it wasn't pinned down. We now waited for the whistle to blow.

The officer Harry saw was almost certainly Major Percy Norman, MC, of the 84th Field Company Royal Engineers. A mechanical engineer from Taunton, he enlisted in October 1914 and embarked for France when the 20th Division was sent overseas. He was commended in the Divisional War History for completing 'the very hazardous task of laying tapes under severe fire'. Norman and the men under his command laid 600 yards of tape, including 125 yards east of the Steenbeek from where the 7th DCLI commenced their advance. Harry was pleased to hear that Major Norman survived not only the attack but, indeed, the war.

During the initial fighting, German resistance had proved sporadic and confused. This was due, at least in part, to the fact that the exhausted garrison defending Langemarck was in the process of being relieved by fresh troops as the attack was launched. One large pillbox, in the ruins of an abandoned farm, held out for up to half an hour, long enough to threaten the pace of the advance, but this resistance too gave way and very soon streams of prisoners, as many as 150, were seen stumbling towards the waiting men of the DCLI. Fearing that they would disorganize his formation, the Commanding Officer pointed the prisoners in the direction of the railway, the banks of which would give some protection; 'they were only too ready to go and needed no escort,' wrote the CO after the battle.

The first objective was taken at 5.40 a.m., less than an hour after the attack commenced. Five minutes later, at 5.45, and now in broad daylight, the 7th DCLI was ordered forward, passing through the destroyed buildings of Langemarck to a position identified by a single poplar tree on the horizon.

It was just shell holes, and the team made its way forward in a line. It was absolutely sickening to see your own dead and wounded, some calling for stretcher-bearers, others semi-conscious and beyond all help, and the German wounded lying about too, and you couldn't stop to help them. I saw one German – I should think he'd been dead some time – well, a shell had hit him and all his side and his back were ripped up, and his stomach was out on the floor, a horrible sight. Others were just blown to pieces; it wasn't a case of seeing them with a nice bullet hole in their tunic, far from it, and there I was, only nineteen years old. I felt sick.

The ground remained sodden and cloying, with shell holes half full of putrid water. Keeping any formation was impossible and the men were allowed to proceed in any way they could. They crossed the first objective, coming across groups of KOYLIs digging in along the remains of a hedgerow. The KOYLIs' numbers were badly depleted but they had reached and secured the second objective, the Green line. It was now shortly after 6 a.m. and the DCLI halted among their comrades while the British artillery barrage pulverized the ground ahead for well over an hour. At 7.15 the barrage became intense, then, at 7.20, it began once more to creep over the German-held ground ahead. Company officers now ordered the two leading companies to move forward. C and A Companies of the DCLI passed through the KOYLIs, pressing the attack to the Red line in two waves, with another company, B, in support.

I can recall a large pond that we went round. Here and there, dotted around the landscape, there were concrete block houses, which had caused a lot of damage among the first waves but which had, for the most part, now been taken. As we pushed forward, we got mixed up with some Somersets, who had been attacking to our right and were busy mopping up any resistance. Some German prisoners were coming across; they had been pointed in our direction and I remember one was still carrying a Maxim machine gun, which I suppose he had been ordered to take with him, as no one else was armed that I can recall. They looked tired and dishevelled, what you'd expect men to look like after four days in the front. We didn't feel sorry for them. Why should we? They were out of it; we had to carry on.

We came across a lad from A Company. He was ripped open from his shoulder to his waist by shrapnel, and lying in a pool of blood. When we got to him, he looked at us and said, 'Shoot me.' He was beyond all human help, and before we could draw a revolver he was dead. And the final word he uttered was 'Mother!' I was with him in the last seconds of his life. It wasn't a cry of despair, it was a cry of surprise and joy. I think – although I wasn't allowed to see her, I am sure – his mother was in the next world to welcome him and he knew it. I was just allowed to see that much, and no more. Yet I'm positive that when he left this world, wherever he went, his mother was there, and from that day I've always remembered that cry and that death is not the end.

I remember that lad in particular. It is an image that has haunted me all my life, seared into my mind, but you saw plenty of people wounded, crying for help, but of course you daren't stop, for one you didn't have the medical knowledge to help them and for another you didn't have the time; your orders were to press on and support the infantry. Bob, our no. 1, was already forging ahead. I had wanted to go to the lad's tunic and find his identity disc, his name and his number. I would have written to his people, but Bob couldn't wait, and, with me having the spare parts to the Lewis gun, I had no option but to follow on.

The barrage held for a while, then after about half an hour it moved forward. We advanced behind it, hoping that no shell would drop short.

It was up to the DCLI to reach the final objective. Resistance was lighter than expected and as many Germans fell back or ran in confusion, the majority of casualties suffered from machine-gun fire; another eighty prisoners were taken. In little more than half an hour, the attacking waves reached the Red line. By 10.30 a.m., Brigade Headquarters had received reports by pigeon that the DCLI were consolidating the position and were in touch with the battalions on their flanks.

Any barbed wire had been flattened out by the terrific barrage, and by the time we reached the German first line it was clear, as was the second when we got there. We came down into a traverse from which two communication trenches led back to their reserve line where our lads were fighting. It was our job, if anything happened, to cover them with the Lewis gun. The fighting was hand-to-hand, but they were so mixed up that we couldn't use the Lewis gun; you'd have killed as many of your own as you would the Germans.

At one point I knew that Bob was flat on the ground, his hands employed with the Lewis gun. I would lie down on one side of him and, as he finished firing, the finger of my right hand would be on the receptor. As I pressed it in, releasing the empty pannier, I lifted it off just as my left hand pressed a new pannier on. I would then pass the empty pannier back to no. 3 and he would pass it back to no. 4 and no. 5, and they would reload it and pass it up to me, to my left hand. It was a cyclical action between all five of us, and all the time as the machine gun fired it got hotter and hotter to the point when it became difficult to hold.

I'd just changed a magazine on it, and Bob was looking elsewhere in the support line when two or three Germans came out of a trench and one of them spotted the machine gun and came straight for us with rifle and bayonet. Now we were all lying down, under cover – behind a dead German, to tell you the truth – and he must have seen us because he came towards us with a fixed bayonet. He couldn't have had any ammunition in the rifle, otherwise he would have shot us. My right hand was free; I'd just changed a magazine. I drew my revolver and I shot him in the right shoulder. He dropped his rifle but he came stumbling on, no doubt to kick the gun in the mud and us to pieces if he could – it would have taken us half an hour to get it working again if he had.

I had four seconds to make my mind up. I had three rounds in that revolver. I could have killed him with my first; I was a crack shot. What should I do? Four seconds to make my mind up. That Cornishman's 'Mother' was ringing in my ears and I thought, 'No, I can't kill him', and I gave him his life. I shot him above the ankle, and above the knee. I brought him down. He called out something to me in German, I don't suppose it was complimentary, but for him the war was over. He would be picked up by stretcher-bearers, interrogated, passed back to a prisoner-of-war camp, and at the end of the war he would rejoin his family. Perhaps he was married; perhaps he had children.

I've often wondered since if any of those three shots made him lose an arm or a leg. And I've often wondered whether he realized that I gave him his life. He was no more than fifteen yards away when I shot him. I couldn't miss, not with a Webley service revolver, not at that range.

Bob had picked up the gun and we were on our way again. Things had more or less calmed down when we caught up with the front line, getting tangled up in barbed wire as we went. Of course the barrage had blown the wire all over the place and we had to find our way through it. If you came across a piece of barbed wire that was probably obstructing your way forward, you would cut it with a machine gun and push it on one side.

The trench was a mess. There were dozens of German stick grenades lying about, but, though they looked all right, we wouldn't touch them in case they were booby-trapped. In the past I'd seen our own bombers throw a Mills bomb over with the pin still in, and if a German was fool enough to pick it up and pull the pin out, bang, he'd had it. The bomb was already fitted with an instantaneous fuse, and directly that lever flew off, it exploded. It was a trick our bombers did and I had no reason to believe the Germans' own bombers weren't just as crafty. In the same vein, there were any number of little dugouts in the enemy trench we could have gone into, but we daren't in case they were booby-trapped; we had been strictly warned beforehand about this. The bombers used to clear them and they had their own methods. They would go along to a dugout that looked innocent enough, and throw a hand grenade down there. The explosion of the grenade might detonate whatever was in there, or, if there was a German lurking in there, probably kill him too. As a rule, I never touched anything on the battlefield. No souvenirs: you took souvenirs at your peril.

While the bombers cleared the dugouts, we got busy reversing the trench, using our entrenching tools to move the firestep from one side of the trench to the other. As machine gunners, we were usually excused such duties, but not now. We worked as hard as everyone else, moving the sandbags from one side of the German parapet to the other, piling them up with an aperture for the Lewis gun in between, where we could sweep in case there was a counter-attack, because we were certainly expecting one. Where we were, the Germans had found some timber, put it across the trench and covered it with corrugated iron and earth. We set about piling sandbags on top. We hunted round. There were a number of our dead lying about and we took their groundsheets from their haversacks to place on top of our little shelter to make it waterproof. It made a shelter of sorts. We had one man looking out and the rest of us tried to get what rest we could. In front of us there was a pond and what looked like the remains of an orchard and the ruins of a farmhouse, a perfect place for a sniper, but we didn't get any trouble from there.

Some time later a few men were ordered to search the dugouts, looking for anything of interest, documents and letters which could be sent back to headquarters for examination. The battle had been over by mid-morning and so we waited all that afternoon for an attack that never came. We were sitting among a sea of shell holes, you can't imagine how many, craters lip to lip. They were half-full of water and one, just at the back of where we were, well, the stench was terrible, a half-rotting body was in there, no doubt about it. Right across the battlefield, the bodies of the wounded who were dying, or those who had died, would sink out of sight in the morass. They would never be buried. In places we were up to our knees in mud, gluey, sticky mud. The water came oozing through the earth, you couldn't stop it. The trench was boarded up to keep the sides back, otherwise it would have collapsed.

As night approached and the firing subsided, you could hear the moans of the wounded and the cries for help in both languages. We stayed put all through that long night before we were relieved the next day, exhausted but intact. The only casualty was one of our ammunition carriers who found that his overcoat had a bullet hole through the tail, straight through one flap, and out the other, without him being touched. He was lucky.

The wounded were in a bad way. Those who were walking made their own way back as best they could. The battalions' stretcher-bearers were assisted by two hundred infantrymen detailed to help. They had been given just a week's rudimentary training in first aid and the application of field dressings. Their job was to scour the ground and evacuate the wounded as hastily as possible, but there was no such thing as haste in the swamp that engulfed them. One hundred stretchers had been made available, two men to carry each one, but often four men were needed over the most difficult ground.

The wounded had to be carried across the newly won terrain, and back across the Steenbeek. The first rudimentary medical treatment was available at one of two Regimental Aid Posts (see map on page xiii), yet these were over three-quarters of a mile from the swollen stream. From there, the journey continued to Gallwitz Farm, where four steel-and-sandbagged shelters had been constructed on the eve of battle. The farm was a Forward Advanced Dressing Station, another three-quarters of a mile trudge for the stretcher-bearers. It was only here, if the casualty hadn't already died through loss of blood and shock, that he could be removed on either a horse-drawn ambulance or a trolley that ran along a light railway.

Any casualty badly wounded forward of Langemarck on the 16th had to be carried at least two miles across a polluted battlefield before they could be properly evacuated. It might take several hours for two stretcher-bearers to make even one round trip, by which time they would be exhausted.

After the fighting had died down, the battlefield had taken on an eerie silence as both sides needed time to work out and adjust to their new positions. Three or four contact planes of the Royal Flying Corps flew over the lines to clarify the position on the ground. They were engaged by enemy aircraft which brought down one plane, driving the others off. Four more enemy aircraft appeared, flying up and down the newly won ground at a low altitude, as if photographing. These planes intermittently opened up with their machine guns, spattering the ground close to the men who were working hard to dig in. Lewis guns returned fire.

The Germans were unlikely simply to accept the loss of territory and, as Harry surmised, would almost certainly attempt to muster forces to make a counterattack against what they would calculate was a tired and depleted opposition. At about 5 p.m. a force about one battalion strong was seen massing in front of the DCLI, who were ordered to open rapid fire with rifles and Lewis guns. As an extra precaution, a green-coloured SOS rocket was fired in order to bring down accurate artillery fire on the enemy, forcing the Germans to disperse. A second German attack was launched just as the sun set at 7.30 p.m. and got to within 200 yards of the Red line before that too was broken up, and withdrew before darkness fell. Patrols were sent out to reconnoitre no-man's-land, capturing two Germans in the process, but otherwise the night remained quiet.

In the morning rations and water were sent up to the men holding the new line, while periodically the Germans shelled the village of Langemarck. In the evening of the second night, a small attack was launched on a short section of trench that the Germans had reoccupied to the DCLI's right, and this was retaken without much opposition. These would be the last casualties that the 7th DCLI suffered in the operation, for at 1 a.m. on the morning of 18 August they were withdrawn. They arrived back into their bivouac camp at 6 a.m., exhausted.

For the scale of the attack, the 7th DCLI's casualties were relatively light. Two officers and forty-one other ranks were killed or died of wounds, while a further 140 others were wounded. Of the seven battalions closest to the DCLI, the average loss was fifty-four dead, a low casualty return in the context of the Great War.

The 20th Division's attack opposite Langemarck had been a success. The advance had taken the men 1,500 yards east of the Steenbeek, and a large number of casualties had been inflicted on the enemy; twenty officers and four hundred other rank prisoners had been taken. A section of enemy 4.2-inch howitzers and one 77-mm field gun were captured, as well as twenty or thirty machine guns. A number of concrete pillboxes had also been put out of action.

As a result of its success, the division was also awarded two Victoria Crosses. Private Wilfred Edwards of the 7th King's Own Yorkshire Light Infantry won his VC just ahead of Harry's battalion, while Sergeant Edward Cooper of the 12th King's Royal Rifle Corps won his VC to the right of the DCLI. Both medals were awarded for successfully neutralizing German block-houses. Two more Victoria Crosses were won by men of the 29th Division, who attacked just to the left of the DCLI, on the other side of the Ypres–Staden railway line.

Victoria Crosses were predominantly awarded for success and not for failure and overall the day was an almost unmitigated failure. To the south of the DCLI the results of the fighting were nothing short of a disaster and around 15,000 men were lost for little advantage. Among all the other divisions that fought that day only one other Victoria Cross was awarded, and that to a stretcher-bearer. It was symptomatic of the day's effort. The one gain was the village of Langemarck, after which the battle was named, and it was the 20th Division, including Harry's Duke of Cornwall's Light Infantry, that won the plaudits for this.

I am often asked what I thought of our Commander-in-Chief, as if I must have an opinion. All I can say is that sometimes Haig's intelligence was good, other times it was rotten. But we didn't talk about him among ourselves, in the trenches or out at rest. I know people think that we must have spoken about him, but I can't remember ever doing so. We were there to do a job, and we did it. We weren't there to criticize; we knew when they'd gone wrong.

The weather was fine and the men were described as being in 'fine fettle'; while exhausted, they were no doubt elated at having come through such an ordeal. Their battalion's ranks were greatly thinned, and, at no more than 330 strong, their numbers must have seemed shockingly low to the men from the transport who met them at Proven camp. The following day, a voluntary church parade was held, after which the men cleaned their equipment and indents were made out to replace lost items. Twenty recommendations for awards were submitted and two weeks later, on 3 September, the battalion paraded as medal ribbons were presented by the Divisional Commander, and the Divisional Band played. New drafts were sent to the battalion in late August, making good the numbers lost on the 16th, but not the experience.

For the rest of the month, new drafts underwent further instruction and training, and working parties were sent out under the direction of the Royal Engineers. In early September, the Lewis gun teams were sent to the ranges, and battalion sports and football competitions were organized for the men. Photographs were taken of various groups and companies, before the battalion's inevitable return to the front, and to a position close to Langemarck. Here the men were ordered to undertake battlefield salvage, collecting some 250 rifles and two Lewis guns, many lost by their comrades such a short time before.

Only on the evening of 9 September was the battalion deemed fit and ready to return to the trenches, where once again a tour of duty brought its commensurate number of casualties, both killed and wounded.

The period out of the line, after the fighting, is something of a blank for me now. I've been shown pages of the War Diary, but for the most part it's hard to relate to the record. Going over the top, as I did, overshadowed much of the mundane, ordinary life that we lived out of the line. In the Diary, I see we were reviewed on one occasion by a senior officer. I thought it was the King, but I must be wrong. I remember being reviewed only because the officers and NCOs had a hell of a job to get us out to cheer him. We were too damned tired.

*

In billets or in trenches we lived with rats and mice. The rats, in particular, were frequently huge, some say as big as cats; well, I don't know, but getting on that way. They would pinch your rations and gnaw at your leather equipment and they would have a go at your bootlaces if you stood there long enough. When you went to sleep, you would cover your face with a blanket and feel the damn things run over you. They were quite tame and they certainly weren't afraid of you; most rats will scamper away from you, but not those in the salient.

Roaming around the destroyed villages were not just rats but cats, dogs, mice; you name it, we had it. Stray cats would come into the line, and a stray dog occasionally, and, as a rule, they'd be as vicious as hell. After the war, I worked with a builder who had a terrier that had been born in the trenches. How he had got the animal home is anyone's guess. However, if you were in the same room as the dog, the only way you could get out was if you had a saw in your hand and you showed him the teeth. He was fierce. It was the way they had to live. They survived on what was dead, thrown away or abandoned.

There were times when you'd look out into no-man's-land between the firing points, and all you could see were a couple of stray dogs looking for something to eat to keep alive. These ordinary, domestic dogs had lost their homes and their owners were long gone. Having nowhere else to go, they used to come into our trench, and no doubt they visited the Germans, too. I watched them on many occasions and I thought about their struggles to survive. If they found a biscuit to eat – which was probably ripped from a dead man's tunic pocket – they would start to fight over who should have a bite. And I thought, 'Well, what are we doing that's really any different? Two civilized nations, British and German, fighting for our lives, just the same.'

As a Lewis gun team, we took our orders from the officers, but when we were in the trenches we were just that little body alone, and we shared everything. Now, my mother used to deal with a big grocer just outside Bath, and every fortnight he used to send out a parcel to me in a cardboard box, with an ounce of Royal Seal tobacco, two packets of twenty BDV cigarettes, some sweets or chocolate, if the grocer could scrounge them, and a couple of cakes. Number 4 on the Lewis gun and I were pipe smokers, so the ounce of tobacco was cut in half; half was mine and half was his. The forty cigarettes were divided among the other three, thirteen each, and they used to take it in turns who should have the odd one. Cakes, chocolates, anything else, were all divided. If you had a pair of clean socks and a fellow had socks with holes in, he'd have the clean socks and threw the others away. And that was the spirit that was within that team. There was no question of sharing with anyone else; like the bombers, they must look after themselves.

I remember Bob had a good thick sweater came out one time, and whoever was on lookout that night had that sweater to put on.

You talked to your mates in the Lewis gun team. There was always a certain amount of emotional chatter, nerves. Shall we get through tomorrow or shall we get a packet? I am going up the line tonight and am I coming back? It's getting dark, OK, everything may be quiet, but are you going to see the sun come up in the morning? That was why the comradeship was so important.

Anyone who tells you that in the trenches they weren't scared, he's a damned liar: you were scared all the time. We constantly reminded each other, 'Keep your head down, don't look up.' If you didn't duck low enough behind the parapet, or if you were fool enough to look to see where the German lines were, then death could be instant. There's a sniper ready every time, see a tin hat, bang. There was an officer in C Company and out of the line he was very fond of seeing that your buttons were polished and shined. Of course this was the worse thing you could do in the front line as any reflection, any unnecessary glint, would attract attention, so whenever we were going up the line we used to smear them with mud.

There was a routine to staying alive. To calm nerves almost all men smoked, and if they could get enough cigarettes they would chain-smoke. To hide any glow from the pipe I smoked I turned it upside down, placing my thumb over the tobacco so it didn't fall out. During the day I could always get under a groundsheet with a cigarette or pipe so no telltale smoke rose above the parapet.

Front-line service wore the men down. I would get a butterfly in my stomach and my hands would shake, so for a moment or two I would have a job to coordinate my nerves to do anything. You couldn't deal with the fear and apprehension we had about being hit by shrapnel. It was there and it always would be. I know the first time I went to the line we were scared; we were all scared. We lived hour by hour, we never knew the future. You saw the sun rise, hopefully you'd see it set. If you saw it set, you hoped you'd see it rise. Some men would, some wouldn't.

The shelling was ferocious at times; you'd feel the vibration of the ground, you couldn't help but tremble, mild shellshock. There were those, the least noise, anything like a shell bursting, would send them into hysterics practically, and they would be taken down the line because they had nothing but an adverse effect on the other men. They were a danger to everybody, you'd no knowing what they might do; you couldn't trust them. Word would come down, perhaps one of your mates had been wounded or killed, and the news that so and so had had his chips. That always made you think, 'How long is it before I get hit?' Not if, but when.

6

WOUNDED

For Harry, 22 September is the day he remembers as the day he lost his machine-gun team and he was badly wounded by shrapnel. Given the passage of nearly ninety years and the effect of his wound, the actual events are now a little opaque. The battalion was relieved from the line on the 19th and proceeded to a place known as Soult Farm. Owing to heavy fighting at the front line, the battalion stood to at 5.40 a.m. on the 20th, and throughout the day they were ordered to be ready to move at fifteen minutes' notice. On the 21st the battalion remained on alert but once more they were not required. On the 22nd the weather was fine, and enemy Gotha bombers were seen in the neighbourhood of the camp. On two occasions, bombs were dropped near the DCLI and the battalion suffered about twenty casualties. The following day, the 23rd, the bombers returned in the afternoon and more bombs were dropped, with no loss of life. The battalion was ordered to parade, and in the evening, around 7 p.m., they left the camp to return to the line, relieving battalions of the Somerset Light Infantry and the King's Royal Rifle Corps. From 10 p.m., a thick mist fell over the battle area, hindering the relief. However, the mist hid them from enemy observation and the War Diary notes that there was very little shelling. The only casualties were one officer who was slightly gassed and three other ranks killed and four wounded. It is quite possible that Harry's Lewis gun team were among those killed or wounded that evening.

We were returning from the line, going back into reserve. It was a quiet night, with very little shellfire at all, if any, that I can recall. Nevertheless, as a matter of course we walked in single file, about ten feet apart, to lessen the chance of the team being hit. It was always important to stick to communication trenches where you could, but, if there weren't any, then you just went over the top in the open and took a chance. We'd stopped briefly as Bob was attending to the call of nature in a slight traverse, causing us to bunch up a little as we waited.

Heavy shells make a 'whump' sound, but the light shells, the whizz-bangs, they used to come over so quickly with a 'zuppppp, bang, flash', and I guess it was a whizz-bang that got us. The only thing I saw was a flash; I can't recall any noise at all, but I certainly felt the concussion of that shell bursting, because I was taken off my feet and thrown to the ground. For a couple of minutes I couldn't move; the explosion seemed to paralyze the nervous system, and I lay there, conscious but incapable of anything. Two or three minutes later, movement gradually returned. I didn't even know I was hit at first, but a growing pain told me otherwise. I looked down and saw my tunic was torn away, and there was blood oozing out from the area of my stomach. Under the corner of my tunic was a field dressing and I applied it to my wound. After that, I must have passed out. I don't remember how long I lay there – it may have been ten minutes, it may have been half an hour – but stretcher-bearers came along and I was picked up. I was taken by a Red Cross motor van along a bumpy road as the ambulance hit divots or rocked from one side to another. There were four of us in there lying on stretchers, one man above me moaning.

I don't recall anything else until I found myself in a tented encampment, a casualty clearing station where there were nurses and where a doctor cleaned the wound of congealed blood and lice and put a clean white bandage on. The metal fragment in my body had been scorching hot and I guess that is what deadens the feeling, but now that it had cooled an intense pain took hold.

There were a lot of seriously wounded there, so I had to wait for the rest of the night and all through the next day. I just lay on a stretcher with a blanket over me, surrounded by wounded men. You read in the Bible about the Tower of Babel, and you had it there, wounded all over the place, calling for help, in German, French and English.

The next evening, the doctor came. As shrapnel wounds went, mine was serious but not as serious as others'. He could see the shrapnel in my stomach and asked me, 'Shall I take it out? Before you answer yes, we've no anaesthetic in the can, it's all been used on more seriously wounded than you and we've had no more to replace it.' I thought for a moment. The pain from it was terrific, and I felt that perhaps a couple of minutes' more intense pain might be worth it, so I said, 'All right, carry on.' The surgeon called for some help. Four people caught hold of me, one each leg, one each arm, and the doctor got busy. I'd asked him how long he'd be and he'd said. 'Two minutes', and in those two minutes I could have damned well killed him. Sweat poured off me. He cut around and then got hold of the shrapnel with tweezers, and dragged it out. He dressed the wound and put a couple of stitches in and as the pain began to subside he showed me the shrapnel. It was two inches long, about half an inch thick, with a jagged edge. 'Do you want it as a souvenir?' he asked. 'I've had the bloody stuff too long already,' I told him and with that he threw it away. The doctor went over to the table and the fellow in the next bed said to me, 'If he writes anything in the green book at the desk, you're for Blighty', soldiers' slang for home. Sure enough, the doctor took his pen and wrote in the book, and I thought, 'Well, that's it then, I'm going home.' I was lucky, very lucky indeed, for the word Blighty meant everything to a soldier.

I didn't know what had happened to the others in the Lewis gun team at first until Bob wrote and told me when I was back in England. I had lost three good mates. The Lewis gun team was a little band together and the last three, the ammunition carriers, had, I understood, been blown to pieces. My reaction was terrible; it was losing a part of my life. I'd taken an absolute liking to the men in the team, you could say almost love. You could talk to them about anything and everything. I mean, those boys were with you night and day, you shared everything with them and you talked about everything. We each knew where the others came from, and what their lives had been, even where they were educated. You were one of them; we belonged to each other, if you understand. It is a difficult thing to describe, the friendship between us. I never met any of their people or any of their parents but I knew all about them and they knew all about me. There was nothing that cropped up – doesn't matter what it was – that you couldn't discuss with them in one way or another. If you had anything pinched, you could talk to them, and if you scrounged something, you shared it with them. You could confide everything to them. When they got letters from home, any trouble, they would discuss it with you.

I couldn't really believe I was going home until a few hours later when my name and number were called out. Hospital orderlies then came and took me to the railway station, from where I was taken to Rouen with hundreds of other wounded men. Rouen was a massive base camp, but we weren't taken to hospital, rather to a warehouse. Here we were stripped, shirt, trousers, pants, tunic, everything went. Nurses put a waterproof dressing on my injury and gave all of us a hot bath and shampooed our hair. What was in the water, I don't know; we used Harrison's Pomade to kill lice up the line, but the water killed them and when we got out of the bath, you could have shovelled them out. We got into another bath where the water was clean, and then they put us each in a suit of sterilized hospital blue. What they did with our clothing I don't know, but my clothes were ridden with lice and blood so they may well have been burnt. They then made us ready to be taken down to the quayside to embark on hospital ships that would take us back over the Channel.

Once on board, the more serious cases were taken below while those who were stronger, like myself, were placed on the top deck, still lying on a stretcher. We didn't sail that night. There were submarines in the Channel, so we sailed the next night, no lights, and landed at Southampton on a typically foggy autumnal morning. We were laid out on the dockside under blankets to keep us warm. I don't care to admit it, but I was a little tearful, after what I'd been through. The Salvation Army were bringing along hot cups of tea, while members of the YMCA took postcards round, already stamped, on which it was written that we had landed back in England, slightly or badly wounded or sick, whichever it was; all they required was your name and address and they would post them. At the same time, the Red Cross were coming along, saying, 'Where's your nearest military hospital?' Well, the Royal United in Bath was at that time a military hospital so I said, 'Bath', and I thought, 'This is it, I'm not just home, but I'll be among my own people, where my parents can visit me.' For a while I was semi-conscious and half-asleep, and I hardly remember the train journey, but it was interminable, and I thought, 'Well, damn it, this train's a long time reaching Bath.' Eventually we pulled into a station and I could see a glass roof. It obviously wasn't Bath, so I said to the orderly when he unloaded us, 'Where are we?' and he said, 'This is Lime Street station, Liverpool.' So much for Bath!

Outside the station a fleet of ambulances was waiting to take us to hospital, the Hahnemann Hospital in Hope Street, a grand-looking red-brick building, a civilian hospital, part or all of which must have been requisitioned for use by the military. The injury to my stomach was treated on a daily basis with Lysol to clean the wound, and fresh bandages. I was fortunate that no operation was required. As well as the shrapnel injury, I had a badly sprained foot and had torn some ligaments in my chest. When the shell exploded, I was carrying on my left shoulder the machine gun's spare parts in a canvas bag.

I surmised that when I was flung to the ground, I had landed on the parts and they had dug into my side and ripped these ligaments or muscles, which made breathing and laughing difficult. This was unfortunate as in the bed next to me was an Australian I called Digger, although I must once have known his name because right from the start we got on famously. He was a real wag.

Digger and I slept in a big ward, a mixed ward, ladies at one end, then halfway down it went to men. Between the two sexes was a desk where the ward sister sat all the time; there was also a trained nurse about and if you woke up the nurse would attend to you and would report back to the ward sister who would come if it was important. Digger and I were the only two who were out on a veranda. The veranda had at one time been open-air, but perhaps because of war emergencies they had boarded both ends and glassed the front. There were two cast-iron radiators behind our beds to keep us warm and other extra beds which were not in use. I was quite jumpy for a while. The least noise and I wanted to dive for cover – you couldn't help it – but that feeling began to subside.

Because we were on our own, we had plenty of time to talk, which quickly led to fun. I always remember the nurse coming to Digger one day. She was bringing each of us a cup of tea on a tray, tea which was a bit thick, a bit strong. As she handed him the cup of tea, she looked out of the window and said, 'It looks like rain, Digger.' 'Yes,' he replied, looking at the tea, 'looks like rain, got the colour of cocoa, tastes like toffee, but I suppose it is tea.' It took the nurse a moment for the penny to drop, but I was already laughing, difficult though it was.

Digger came from a family of horse breeders down under,

working with his brother, but his brother had lost a leg in the war, and indeed Digger's injuries were caused by shrapnel in his legs. We got on so well that he asked me to go down there and join him after the war, but I told him I'm a plumber, not a horseman.

By November, both of us were up and around, and to speed our recovery we were given permission to go out of the hospital and take light exercise. Down the road from us was a cinema, free to any soldiers in hospital blue; you could just walk in. One afternoon we were watching a serial film there called *The Grey Ghost*, with the latest episodes being shown on Monday and Friday. For dramatic effect, every episode finished just as something exciting was about to happen. One episode ended as the villain was about to shoot the heroine, and as you witnessed the hammer going back on the revolver, 'Continued on Friday' came up on the screen. So on Friday a group of us went to see what would happen; we sat down and the trailer came on, but what we didn't know was that Digger had taken a paper bag with him. He had blown it up and directly the hammer went back, he banged it. I think everybody in the cinema screamed, we got thrown out and we never got to see the resolution of *The Grey Ghost*. It was an interesting film, not least because it was the first time sound was ever put on a silent film.

Sleeping out on the veranda was enjoyable, with one small reservation. Old Digger had a habit of grinding his teeth at night, and it was a horrible noise. Of course he wasn't aware of this and he used to get a bit fed up when the sister came down and gave him a shot of cold water from the end of a syringe, waking him up. He decided to get even, went down town and bought a pound packet of flour. Just for fun, I helped him rig it up on some twigs above the ward door that led out on to the veranda. Digger got into bed and baited the sister by grinding his teeth. Presently we heard her coming down the ward to give Digger a shot, but Digger was not asleep, and unfortunately it wasn't the sister, but the matron. She caught the flour fair and square on the head. There was no argument as to who had done it, and playing such a trick demonstrated that neither of us was that 'ill' any more. Within days, Digger was sent back to Calshot, his regimental depot, and soon after that I was discharged too, to a convalescent camp.

I was sad to see Digger go. We had got on famously and he had done me the world of good with his humour and his mischievous fun. We exchanged addresses and corresponded for a while; I even wrote once after the war when he was back in Australia but we never met again. I never considered for one moment going to Australia. My home was Somerset.

As it was, just about Christmas I was given leave and I returned home before being sent to Birmingham, and then Sutton Coldfield, No. 2 Convalescent Camp. All those who had just left hospital were given a green badge to wear on their khaki epaulettes. This colour would change as health improved, first to yellow and finally red. Red meant that you were A1 and ready to return to your unit for training, but I was still a while away from that.

My time at Sutton Coldfield was unremarkable. I still received minor medical attention, but most of the time the men slept or sat around and played cards, while our overall health improved. I wasn't inclined just to waste the time doing nothing, and while I was recuperating I was allowed to study. Before I left Sutton Coldfield I took and passed the

London Examination to become a sanitary engineer. It was a correspondence course, letters from London, and I had to answer a large number of questions.

The time at Sutton Coldfield was most notable for one thing: I met my future wife, Ada Billington.

I actually met her when I accidentally knocked her down. Three of us were hurrying for a bus to save ourselves a three-mile walk from Erdington to Sutton Park. Once a month, we got a pass out of the camp. It was valid from Friday night to Sunday night, back in by midnight. It wasn't long enough to go to Bath, so we used to book a couple of nights at the YMCA in Birmingham, and get back for Roll Call on Sunday. As we went round the corner, Ada and her friends were coming down the steps from a cinema and I bumped into her. I picked her up, dusted her off, and, as it turned out they were going for the same bus as us, I took her home and the next night we agreed to meet and we went for a walk, and on Sunday we met again.

It was a drizzly February night in 1918, and I was waiting on the street corner for her outside her home. An old chappie came up to the gate, and said in a North Country accent, 'You waiting for the maid, laddie?' 'Yes.' 'Well, don't wait out here. Come inside.' He took me into the house. Ada was staying with her aunt, and the old man was her grandfather. I can't remember the conversation, but you can bet they were quizzing me, finding out what they could about me, who I was and my intentions. 'What are you going to do on a night like this?' her aunt asked, so I said that I thought we would go up town somewhere, find a show. 'Why don't you stay here? Nasty night,' so we stayed there by the fire. Her aunt and uncle found something in the dairy to do   they had a dairy business on the Chester Road – while Ada's sister Maud, who was living there too, made herself scarce and Granddad went to bed early. When Ada's aunt and uncle came back in about ten o'clock, they made a cup of cocoa and asked if I would like to come down and spend the weekend with them, so that's what I did and that's when Ada's and my friendship developed into something deeper. At Sutton Coldfield I'd noticed that there would be lots of girls who would hang round the camp and go out with any soldier, but Ada was different, and it dawned on me that I had found a girl here who didn't chase after everything in uniform.

In time I was introduced to all her family. She was the daughter of a wire drawer who worked for Sankeys, a large Midlands steel business. He had a skilled job in a foundry, rolling steel back and forwards until it came out as thick as your finger. Ada was about three years older than me and was born and raised in Shropshire, in a village near Wellington called Trench Crossings, the fourth of six children. During the war one of her brothers, Tom, had served in munitions and another, Bill, won the Military Medal and was badly wounded serving in the Machine Gun Corps, suffering an experience not dissimilar to mine. His team had all been killed, except for Bill who had been left for dead, next to his machine gun. A stretcher-bearer had seen him twitch and he was picked up and sent home. What the extent of his injuries was I never knew but his face was very badly scarred. While he was in hospital he studied for chartered accountancy in Birmingham, and later emigrated to America to start his own business.

In July 1918 I was given a week's leave. I travelled south with two fellows from Bath with whom I had struck up a friendship while convalescing. Their names were Titch Harding and Bill Taylor, both privates in the 5th Somerset Light Infantry. We had spent a lot of time together, in fact I had been with them both the evening I had met Ada outside the cinema.

Titch Harding was a proper comedian. As we were going on leave together, Bill and I gave Titch our travel warrants to go and pick up the train tickets. Titch got the tickets, and we got on the train at New Street, Birmingham, to Bristol. We had got so far on the way when Titch felt in his pocket and said, 'I've only got two tickets. I wonder where the other one has gone; it must have gone through the lining. What are we going to do?' So he pulled out three matches and struck one and said, 'Whoever draws the burnt match must go under the seat. We'll put our kit bags down and hide him. It'll be all right.' Bill lost. When the ticket collector came in, Titch pulled out and gave the man all three tickets. 'Where's your mate?' the ticket collector asked. 'Gone to the toilet or something?' 'No,' Titch said, 'he's a bit rocky "upstairs",' pointing to his head. 'He suffers from shellshock. When he heard you banging the door, and a loud noise, he dived for cover. He's under the seat!' When we arrived at Bristol, the guard got out and found a Red Cap, a military policeman, and told him about Bill. The policeman led us to his sergeant. 'Hello, what's the matter with these three? Travelling without passes?' the sergeant asked. 'No, passes are all right, but this one's a bit dodgy; he suffers from shellshock.' 'All right, get back on duty,' said the sergeant, whereupon he took over and accompanied us on to the train to Bath, where we were met by our families. A week later, Bill, Titch and I were all travelling together and we got off at Bristol to change trains, and who should be there but the old Red Cap sergeant. 'You again? Have you enjoyed your leave? You going back? Good, now come along with me,' and he took us over and put us on the train to Birmingham. The sergeant called the guard over. 'Give them a packet of sandwiches and a cup of tea and charge it to me. When you get to New Street station there should be a van to take them to Sutton Coldfield. Find a Red Cap there and hand them over.' The guard took us to a first-class coach where he locked the door, allowing us to travel back in style. It was one of the few advantages of being a wounded soldier in wartime.

In early August I left Sutton Coldfield. I returned to the regimental depot at Bodmin and Titch Harding and Bill Taylor returned to their depot at Taunton. From Bodmin, I would be sent away for training, a prospect that filled me with dread. Ada and I were committed to one another and it had been difficult to leave Birmingham, unsure when we would be able to meet again.

It must have been a few days later when I travelled to Perham Downs, near Tidworth, to join up with other men who were returning to training. News from France was increasingly good: the Germans had been turned and were retreating, but we'd heard of retreats before and we didn't think that this might be the beginning of the end. Most of the men at Perham were pretty much back to full fitness, as least as far as the army were concerned. These lads were not fresh recruits by anyone's imagination, and were far less willing to be ordered about by time-served sergeants, or NCOs the men suspected had never seen the front. They would accept orders, of course, but there was a limit. On the notice board one morning was a note that the company would go on parade for bayonet practice. A number of the men objected and said, 'No.' 'We've had the real thing,' they said. 'We are not going to stick our bayonets into a bag of straw.' Some had no doubt been wounded by a bayonet. In truth, they were absolutely fed up with being told to right turn, left turn, about turn, being told to jump through hoops! These men had gone over the top and they'd used the bayonet, damn it, they didn't want bayonet practice! Treating them like raw recruits! I was quite in sympathy with the rest of the crowd but I was about to find out that I wouldn't have to join them.

Directly I put my equipment back on again, I got a pain in my chest precisely where I had landed on the machine gun's spare parts, so I went sick and got a week's excused duty. The following day there was a company officers' parade and, of course, I didn't go on, being excused duty, and they put me on a charge for it. Instead of going in front of the company officer the next day, I went sick again. The doctor said to me, 'I thought I gave you a week's excused duty yesterday?' I said, 'You did, sir,' and told him what had happened. 'When I give you excused duty, that means everything. I'll have a word with your company officer about it. You'll have to go in front of him tomorrow. Who put you on a charge?' 'Sergeant Major Smithers,' I replied. Now, he had served in France but by 1918 he was training the men back home, and nobody liked him. Even the officers didn't like him. He said, 'You can tell Sergeant Major Smithers, from me, he can stick his crime sheet . . .' and he was very explicit as to where he could stick it. Next morning I went before the company officer. Sergeant Major

Smithers was there, too. The doctor had a quiet word with the company officer and the charge was immediately dismissed. It was noted that I had been excused duty by the doctor. Then the officer said, 'Is that *all* the doctor told you?' I said, 'Yes, sir.' He said, 'He didn't give you a message for anybody?' 'Well,' I said, 'he did. He gave me a message for Sergeant Major Smithers but I don't care to repeat it. There are ladies in the office,' I said, pointing towards the WAACs. He said, 'Don't trouble about them, they know all your slang. If you have a message, you'll give it, and that's an order.' Of course the sergeant major was standing there fuming as I told him what the doctor had said – that he could stick his crime sheet up his arse and set fire to it. I added, too, that the doctor had hoped it might burn some sense into his rear end because there was none up top. It was clear that the officers wanted to take Smithers down a couple of notches, he was so overbearing in his manner. I didn't say anything, but that incident was all round the camp in half an hour, and my life wasn't worth living after that. All the dirty jobs were mine, courtesy of Sergeant Major Smithers.

About a fortnight later I went on parade in full kit and I got the pain in my chest again and I just couldn't stick it. I went to the sick bay and an officer examined me, and fetched the senior medical officer and had a probe and asked a few questions. They had a powwow and the senior officer came back and told me to go back to my hut, and pack my kit bag and report to the company office at two o'clock; I was going to hospital. When I went back, the sergeant major came into the hut. 'What have you got now, more excused duty?' I said, 'No, Sergeant Major, I am going to pack my kit, report, and the ambulance will pick me up and take me to Handsworth Hospital.' He seemed surprised. 'Oh,' he said, 'what's the matter with you?' I suggested he went and asked the medical officer. There was nothing he could do now; I was away from that camp, thank goodness. The luck at being sent to Handsworth was almost too good to be true, and as soon as I got to hospital I spoke to one of the nurses. 'Can you ring this number?' It was Dunlops' business number, where Ada was working. 'Whoever answers it, tell them to pass a message on to Ada Billington. Tell them I am in Handsworth Hospital. I don't think we can meet tonight, but tell them what ward I'm in.' Anyway, come six o'clock that night she was there to visit me, and promised to come back every day.

My injury was diagnosed as ligament damage and it was treated three times a day with massage. Ointment was rubbed into my chest, then a small rubber disc was held against me. This disc was attached to something that looked like a drill, from which an electrical cord ran down to a generator which made a low rumbling sound, vibrating the disc which was run up and down my chest.

Ada was working in Aston, as an inspector of gas masks. She worked alternate weeks, one week on night duty, then day duty the next. When she was on night duty, she used to come off at 6 a.m., go home to bed, and then get up about 3 p.m. to make some sandwiches and come over to Handsworth. She would sit with me until 6 p.m. when visiting hours were over, then leave to go off down to the factory, sitting in the canteen until it was time to go on shift.

This had been going on a week or two when one of the nurses asked me one day, 'That lady who comes to visit you, is she a relative?' I told her that she was my girlfriend and she said, 'Oh, we can't have that. She told the ward sister and the ward sister told the commandant, and the next time Ada came in, they took her to one side. 'Don't you bring any sandwiches again, you'll come in here and you'll have dinner with your friend in the tea room and you can stay here until 7 p.m. and then you can go down to the factory.' And that's what happened. When I was able to get out, they gave me a late pass to get back by 8 p.m., the same time as Ada booked on.

I imagine I was at Handsworth no more than a few weeks when the doctors passed me as fit and I was given instructions to report to the Isle of Wight. When the time came for me to leave, the nurse, the ward sister and the commandant all came to see me off and they said, 'You know our address and we know your girl's address. Now keep in touch with us and if we are in England and you come through all right, we'll come to your wedding.' We weren't even engaged at the time but, when we did marry two years later, all three nurses were invited to attend. Sadly, they were serving with the Army of Occupation in Cologne, so none could come, but Ada and I not only stayed in touch with all three, but when they got leave they all visited us and we kept in touch with them by letter until they all died. The nurse came from Handsworth, the commandant from Nuneaton and the ward sister from Aston.

Ada and I corresponded almost every day at this time. Whenever I was off duty I would write her a letter; I remember one was twenty-four pages long. I knew she was the girl for me, and when I was due to return to France once again I asked her if we might get engaged. 'No,' came her reply. So I asked, 'Shall we get married?' 'No.' She wouldn't get engaged and she wouldn't get married. 'I'll wait for you until the war is over, Harry,' she told me. A lot of girls didn't want to marry when their loved ones were returning to France. Perhaps they felt it was bad luck; perhaps the heartbreak would be too much if they were killed. Ada didn't say anything. She would wait until I came home, that was all I knew. It was several years later that I found out why. Just before the war, in 1913, she had been very close to a boy from her own town, Wellington in Shropshire. His name was Harold Thomas, and he was in the Territorial Army. In 1914 he was called up straightaway, but before he left they had got engaged, and he was killed. She never wore the engagement ring after that, and she swore she would never get engaged again until the fighting ended. She didn't want to be a war widow. Harold Thomas' engagement ring sat on our dressing table for years after Ada and I were married. It might have bothered some men, but it never bothered me at all. Much later, Dennis, my elder son, took it and got it resized and he wore it in remembrance of that dead soldier. It was only after the war, over Christmas 1918, that Ada accepted my proposal of marriage and we got engaged.

There was, perhaps, another reason for Ada's hesitation. Ada worked at Dunlops' with her sister Maud. Maud had met and gone out with a sergeant of the Royal Artillery. She got pregnant, but before they could marry he was called up to go to France. The marriage was arranged, but before he could get leave he too was killed. Their shared tragedy must have made them very wary about any other commitments. Maud, however, found herself in a far greater predicament than Ada. She had a son, Reginald, who was brought up by his paternal grandmother, such was the feeling against unmarried mothers back then. Then Maud met a New Zealander from Auckland, Ernie Hurst. She married, settling in New Zealand, where she had a daughter, but even though her marriage to Ernie did not survive, she never returned home.

7

MUTINY

The injury in my chest may well have saved my life. Had I
not had the problem there, and it was a mild injury by any
measure, I would undoubtedly have been back in France by
the late summer of 1918. As it was, in early November I
was in billets at Golden Hill Fort. The Fort was a huge
Victorian building, hexagonal in design, built to defend the
Isle of Wight, and so had superb views over the Solent. In
the centre was a parade ground, and heaven help anyone the
sergeant major caught walking across that hallowed gravel;
you had to double across every time. Hundreds of men were
billeted in barrack rooms inside the Fort, but there were so
many people training there that the overflow was billeted
just outside the Fort's main entrance, in huts.

By this time I was marked down as A1, and had been
placed on the next draft to go back and rejoin the regiment
in Belgium. It was common knowledge that the Germans
were being pushed back all along the line, but we didn't
dare believe that the war might actually end, but end it did.
On the morning of 11 November we were on the firing
range and were told that, if a ceasefire was signed, they'd

send up a rocket. We watched for the rocket and about eleven o'clock we saw it go up and we all cheered. I remember the feelings of joy to think that I would not have to go back and relief that the war was over. We were using a lot of spare ammunition, so the officer said, 'Get rid of it, fire it out to sea, we don't want to carry it back.' The fellow next to me had started blazing away when I noticed that his rifle was pointing across mine and I said, 'What the hell are you firing at?' He said, 'That bloody hut up there.' I said, 'That's where the markers are!' The markers registered our shots on the targets, but at that moment they were inside, taking refuge on the floor as this lad pumped ammunition through their hut. Far from being the last casualties of the war, they were inches away from being the first victims of the peace.

The sergeant got us together and we marched back to camp, and, while still carrying our rifles, we went to church for a service of thanksgiving, after which we were told we would not be allowed out of camp. The men didn't like this, and later that day they chased this same sergeant along the long pier at Yarmouth, and when he got to the end they chucked him into the sea, and that night we had hell's delight, a real party. At the Fort there was Hurst Castle Lighthouse on one side of us and the Needles on the other, and that evening, on the night of the Armistice, the lighthouse sounded its fog horns for the first time in four years in celebration.

Within days of the Armistice being signed, an order came through that anyone who had seen active service wouldn't have to go back to France. There were a large number of men who fitted that description and so they formed an E Company, all light infantry blokes, Duke of Cornwalls,

Somersets and Green Howards. Furthermore, if you could produce a letter from your employer indicating that you had a job to go to, then you were given what was called priority demobilization, but, for all the promises, that simply didn't happen, not in my case, and not in many others either. It had taken three days to get me into uniform but it would be five months before I got out of khaki and out of the army, and this was to cause a lot of resentment.

We were a very mixed bunch in E Company. In barracks, in the bed next to me, was a man by the name of Perkins, an interesting fellow if ever there was one. He was a Londoner from what would be called today the wrong side of the tracks. Nevertheless, you couldn't help liking him. The pair of us were on guard duty one night, and an officer came down from paying the troops. There were so many men coming out of hospital to join E Company that, rather than being about 260 strong, we had grown to well over a thousand, so he must have had a considerable amount of money at one point. Anyhow, whatever he had left over, he brought down to the office where I was on guard and put the money in a safe in the wall and left.

Perkins had only just come back from the canteen with the orderly sergeant, and both had come back a bit merry. Perkins had just come on guard with me when he saw this officer place the money in the safe. Speaking to the orderly sergeant, Perkins offered him a wager that he could open the safe within half an hour, get the money out on the floor and then put it back in the safe and lock it. The sergeant took him on for a small sum, ten shillings I think it was. There were a few people about, so Perkins asked everybody to be quiet and he sat down on the floor next to the safe, twiddling the dial this way and that, in deep concentration. You could hear these clicks, until presently there was a click that must have sounded a little bit different, for he then wrote a number down. In twenty minutes he had done it. He showed the sergeant the money and won the bet. The next day the officer came down, took the money out and back to the bank, and was none the wiser.

Some time after this, one of the filing cabinets in the office went wrong and this sergeant remembered Perkins and said to the officer in charge, 'There's a man here who can open anything. He'll open it for you', and Perkins was sent for. However, he refused to open it, maintaining that if anything was missing he might, for some reason I didn't understand, get the blame. Eventually they persuaded him to open it and Perkins went back on parade, but the officer was interested in him. On the next parade, he spoke to him. 'What are you by trade in civilian life, Perkins, a lock-smith?' 'No, sir.' 'Well, what are you?' No answer. He said, 'What are you in civilian life? I want to know and that is an order.' Perkins said, 'Sir, if you want to know, I'm a London cracksman.' The officer asked if he intended going back to his job after the war and Perkins didn't know. 'It rather depends how many of the gang come through the war, sir.' 'Well,' said the officer, 'if you go back to it, don't pay me a visit.' 'Where do you live, sir?' The officer told him the London district. 'You're OK, sir,' replied Perkins. 'We only go where there is stuff worth pinching.'

Perkins was a character. If we were anything short on kit parade, tell Perkins, and within half an hour I bet you had it; he'd thieve it from somewhere. We never went hungry. The cookhouse door was nothing to him. He was a bright lad as well. He had a set of loaded dice and if he found anybody playing Crown and Anchor, he'd join in. The game consisted of a mat made up of six squares in each of which was one of six symbols: the crown and anchor, and the four suits in a pack of cards, spades, hearts, clubs and diamonds. It was normally a game of chance and no skill. Men placed money on one or more of the squares, and the dice, with the six symbols on the sides, were rolled. The banker paid out on the money placed on the winning symbols shown on the dice, before scooping the rest. The banker rarely came off worst, but they didn't count on Perkins. He used brilliant sleight of hand. You wouldn't see him put his loaded dice down but he did, switching his with the banker's, and when he'd won enough money he'd switch them back. Then he was gone, leaving the banker a little poorer than when he started, which made a nice change.

To stop the men getting bored, the army used to keep us busy with one thing and another, physical training and marching, as well as firing on the ranges. They also had a Lewis gun there, and we went up eighteen men at a time. There were six targets, two sets each at 200, 400 and 600 yards, for us to have a go at. The first time we went up there, a sergeant got us in a circle and said, 'Right, any of you fellows know anything about Lewis guns?' I said, 'Well, yes, I was a number two in a team at Ypres.' So he said, 'Can you show us how it works?' I said, 'Yes, I think so, though it's been twelve months since I handled one.' He told me to take it apart but I asked, before I touched the gun, was the magazine loaded or empty, as we didn't want any accidents. He said it was empty so I put my thumb into it and took the magazine off and straightaway told him the gun was useless. He asked what I meant. 'There is a part missing with two poles on it; one opens the magazine and throws out the round that's been fired, the other drops a live round in, then the piston will come back against the recoil spring, and if you keep the trigger pulled it will fire until you release it. Anyway, that part is missing.' He put his hand in his pocket and said, 'Is this it?' 'That's it.' 'You know your Lewis gun, don't you?' he said.

I don't know what he was trying to do or to prove. Anyway, I told him that if I had had that gun in France, I would have been on a crime sheet. It was filthy, so we cleaned it up and I showed them how it worked.

Before we finished, the sergeant said, 'We've got a live magazine', and asked if I would like to use it. I was to fire at number six target, and see what I could do with it. I lay down, and decided to have a little fun. I fired downwards, then came across once and down once, and put an H on one side of the bull's-eye. I went across the other side and I went up and round to form the letter 'P', and said, 'There you are.' I'd put my initials on the target. Shortly after, I was called into the company office and there was a major there and he said, 'I understand that you are leaving the army?' I replied, 'Yes, sir. I've got a job to go to.' 'That's a pity. I hear you did some fancy firing on the range.' I said that I was told I could use the magazine as I liked. 'Yes, I know,' he acknowledged. At that time the army was offering cash, quite a bit of money, too, to try to persuade men to sign on and stay in the services, but most men weren't interested. Almost all of us in E Company had a job to return to, and why the army was refusing to demob us, I don't know. Only those without a trade were tempted to re-enlist.

This officer was impressed with my shooting, and had been tempted into a little bet with my sergeant. 'I've bet your sergeant a pound at five to one that at six hundred yards you couldn't take the bull's-eye out of the target with one magazine.' That distance was too far, but I said I would do it at four hundred. 'No,' he said, 'six hundred.' We agreed on five hundred.

We went up on the range, six of them round me, and I asked for a practice shot. I was then given the magazine, forty-nine shots, and I went not on the bull's-eye but the inner ring, and I started at the bottom and worked my way around. The sergeant at the target phoned back to the major and said, 'The bugger's done it, sir.' I knew it already, for I could see the grass behind the bull's-eye. I had cut the bull's-eye clean out with three rounds left. The officer repeated that he thought it was a pity I was leaving the army. 'I would have backed you against anybody that would have challenged you, whether with a Lewis gun or a rifle. I've never seen anybody fire like that.' In those days I had good eyesight and a steady hand.

There was a lot of small-time gambling going on to help alleviate the boredom, but in the end there was trouble and it was inevitable. We had an officer, a captain, a peacetime officer risen from the ranks, and he took E Company out for a route march. I was on fatigue duties at the time, peeling spuds in the cookhouse, and it was only later that I heard what happened. This officer was at the head of the men and he started them at the double – well, half the company went at the double – but four Birmingham boys said they weren't going to double for him, and they stayed marching, and the rest of the company behind them followed suit. The officer didn't know what to do. He managed to get the company back to camp, where the men got together and decided that they'd had enough of this officer and wouldn't parade again.

The officer's authority had been well and truly challenged, and he was not the sort of man who was going to put up with it. He ordered the sergeant major to come down to our huts and rouse us. The first door he opened, he shouted, 'On parade, E Company!' He got his answer. Somebody threw a boot at him and he reported it to the officer. So the officer came down. 'On parade, E Company!' 'We are not going,' came the reply. Back to the company office he went.

Things began to get nasty. A group of men went up to the officers' mess and asked for this officer. After they'd spoken their mind, the officer pulled his revolver out and you could hear the click, click, as the hammer went back. Whether it was loaded or not, I don't know. I only heard what the others told me. Nobody said anything; they all dispersed and simply went back to their huts. Some of the men had been on the firing range and so they rounded up what ammunition they could find, sorted it out between them and went back and asked for him again. This time I was with them. He came out, click, click, went the hammer on his revolver, and crash, crash, went back about thirty rifle bolts, mine included, before someone shouted, 'Now, you shoot, you bugger, if you dare.' Had he not backed down, he would have been shot, there's no doubt about it. All those rifles were loaded, one round each. Anyway, down went the revolver and he scarpered back into the mess.

We had mutinied, and so a brigadier with a chestful of medal ribbons was brought from the mainland to sort out the problem. He immediately set about finding what had happened and then he asked for the men and addressed them. He said, 'I've heard the officer's version of events and now I want to know your side, but I don't want to identify you. We'll have a canvas screen put up between the huts, you'll go behind the screen and tell me your grievances.' He interviewed perhaps thirty men from E Company in all, each talking from behind this screen so that they could speak freely without fear of intimidation. One of the lads said what we all felt: 'It's three months since the war ended, we've each got a job to go to, yet we're still in the army. When we joined up, it was for the duration of the war; that was what we were told, so why are we still serving?'

The brigadier listened and gave his verdict. E Company was to undertake fatigues only, no more parades, and the officer was to be taken right away from the Fort, so I suppose we were in a way exonerated. From then on, we picked up the fag ends, scrap paper and litter around the camp, just keeping the place tidy, that's all, until we were demobbed. The army was keen to get shot of us. Most of us were down for immediate demobilization and we had decided ourselves that we were more or less civilians, and that army rules no longer applied to us.

Soon enough we got our orders to leave the Isle of Wight and we were taken to board a ship for Gosport, where we were to stay one night. It was a wintry March evening when we got there, to be greeted by the news that we would have no blankets that night. The boys were not having that: we weren't going to sleep without anything to cover us up, and we started to create about it. The sergeant in charge said, 'Well, where are you from, anyway?' We told him, 'We're the Duke of Cornwall's from the Isle of Wight.' 'All right,' he said, 'we don't want any trouble, we'll get some.' I suppose he must have heard about the incident. So they issued each of us with four pure white blankets from the stores. We noticed straightaway that none had the distinctive Government stamp on them and so, by the time we left the following day, I should think everybody in Gosport had a white blanket; we sold the lot. There were plenty of girls around the camp; well, to put it in plain English, they were prostitutes, so I can't say that all of the blankets were sold for money.

From Gosport we went to Fovant on Salisbury Plain, and that's where I got my demob papers. We were sent to the quartermaster's store and given our civilian clothes, all the same and ill-fitting, or, rather, it would be more accurate to say they fitted where they touched. We were then handed a travel warrant and set free. There was a light railway going from Fovant to Salisbury, from where we took a main line to wherever we were going. I headed for Bath and home.

Harry, 2004

November 2007: the 90th anniversary of Passchendaele was marked at the Royal Albert Hall during the annual Festival of Remembrance. During the evening Harry was greeted with a standing ovation. At the end of the evening he was introduced to the Queen.

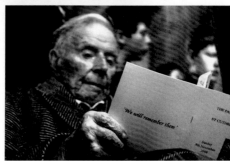

We will remember them: Harry in contemplative mood.

Harry sits with veterans Bill Stone (*right*) and Henry Allingham. Each man laid a wreath at the Cenotaph marking the 80th anniversary of the Armistice. Standing behind Harry is Johnson Beharry who won the Victoria Cross in Iraq.

September 2008: Harry unveils a plaque to the men of the 20th Division on the banks of the Steenbeek, at the point he crossed it in August 1917.

The plaque: *Here, at dawn, on the 16th August 1917, the 7th Battalion Duke of Cornwall's Light Infantry, 20th (Light) Division, crossed the Steenbeek prior to their successful assault of the village of Langemark. This stone is erected to the memory of fallen comrades and to honour the courage, sacrifice and passing of the Great War generation. It is the gift of former private and Lewis gunner, Harry Patch, No 29295, C Company, 7th DCLI, the last surviving veteran to have served in the trenches of the Western Front.*

Harry reads the memorial stone inscription. The spire of Langemark church is on the horizon.

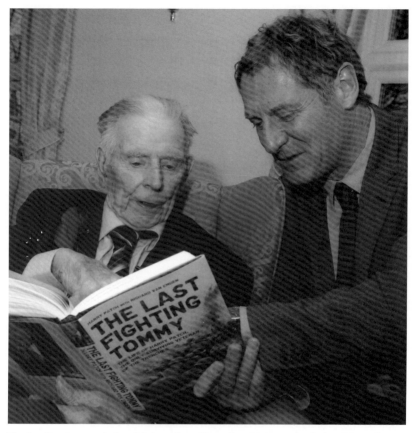

The then Poet Laureate Andrew Motion talks to Harry about his biography. Andrew Motion later wrote *The Five Acts of Harry Patch* as a tribute to Harry.

Harry signs a copy of *The Last Fighting Tommy*. Towards the end of his life he suffered from arthritis in his hand, making signing increasingly difficult.

Harry leaves Tyne Cot Cemetery for the last time in September 2008. Harry always made a point of visiting the cemetery to pay tribute to those friends he lost in the war.

Harry enjoys a break with a cup of tea at his favourite farm a few miles behind Ypres.

Relaxing at a farm in the Ypres Salient where Harry frequently stayed during his visits to Belgium. He thoroughly enjoyed being there and was always overrun by kittens.

The *Doris and Harry* in action just after the official launch at the RNLI Headquarters in Poole.

Launching the *Doris and Harry*, a D Class inflatable lifeboat, in 2007. The boat, purchased by Harry from the sales of his book, has rescued at least a dozen people since its launch.

Harry enjoys a joke with his co-author on the ferry to Belgium, September 2008.

The Great War Society, dressed in Great War uniform, pay a visit to Harry's home in Wells, Somerset.

Harry's funeral at Wells Cathedral, 6 August 2009. Some 1,400 people packed the aisles while outside on the Green and in the streets leading to the Cathedral, another 4,000 people gathered to pay their respects.

A man dressed in Great War uniform holds a copy of the order of service.

Crowds assemble in front of a huge screen which relayed the service inside the cathedral to the Green outside.

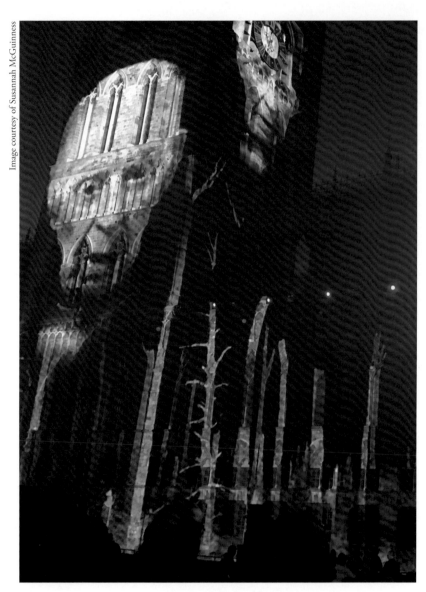

Harry Patch's image projected on to the walls of Ypres' Cloth Hall during the centenary commemorations of the Battle of Passchendaele, 31 July 2017.

8

BACK TO WORK

By the time I was demobbed I was thoroughly disillusioned. I could never understand why my country could call me from a peacetime job and train me to go out to France and try to kill a man I never knew. Why did we fight? I asked myself that, many times. At the end of the war, the peace was settled round a table, so why the hell couldn't they do that at the start, without losing millions of men? I left the army with my faith in the Church of England shattered. When I came home, I joined Combe Down church choir to try to get the faith back, but in the end I went because I enjoyed the music and had friends there, but the belief? It didn't come. Armistice Day parade – no. Cassock and surplice – no. I felt shattered, absolutely, and I didn't discuss the war with anyone from then on, and nobody brought it up if they could help it.

The one thing I could look forward to was my marriage to Ada. With the war over, she left Dunlops' and got a job as a lady's maid in Manchester while I returned to work again in Bath. We soon decided that Manchester and Bath were too far apart and so we set a date for our wedding,

13 September 1919, when we could be married and live as husband and wife in the house that Dad had promised as a wedding present, no. 5 Gladstone Place. Six months later, we married at a little place called Hadley, just the other side of Wellington in Shropshire, with Tom, Ada's brother, acting as best man. It was a very quiet wedding; my parents were getting too old to travel to Shropshire, so only Ada, her sister Wyn and her husband were there. Our honeymoon was in Shropshire, Church Stretton, where the Welsh mountains start, and for a week we walked the countryside and climbed some of the hills and talked about our future.

Marriage came as a welcome break from work. I had sought to return to my job with Jacob Long and Sons in April 1919, but, rather than paying me properly as a fully registered plumber, Mr Amor, the foreman and office manager, insisted that I finish my apprenticeship. That would have taken another two years and pay of just ten shillings a week, and I wasn't having that, not when I was going to be married. I had been an apprentice for three years from the age of fifteen, and you can accept that sort of wage then, but not at twenty-one. I was effectively being penalized for serving my country.

The upshot was that I dug my feet in and refused to go back to work. I told them that, rather than go back at their rate of pay, I would sign on again in the army if need be. It was a bluff. The last thing I wanted to do was go back into the forces, so I returned to Combe Down and over the next few months undertook several odd jobs and some private work to keep myself ticking over while I looked round for alternatives.

Every so often I used to take the train into Bath and called in at J. Long and Sons, ostensibly to see my brother, who worked there as a carpenter. Mr Amor used to see me; he would say, 'We've got nothing to offer you', and I would retort, 'Don't worry, I'm not coming back.' Nevertheless, there was one thing I wanted: I wanted my indentures signed. I asked on several occasions that the firm sign them to signal formally the end of my apprenticeship, and at first they refused.

I pursued the matter again after speaking with my father's solicitor, and what he told me was interesting. In his opinion, not only had the contract been broken when I was called up, but on joining the army I had agreed to serve only for the duration of the war. By March 1919 the war had been over five months and yet I was still in the army. 'Your apprenticeship was a legal contract, stamped and signed by Jacob Long, your father, by me as your solicitor, and finally by you. By failing to release you in 1918, the Government has broken the contract; you are free.' Because I felt that it wasn't me who had broken the contract I wanted the indentures signed, not because I couldn't work without them, but because it was a matter of pride.

The question was what to do in the meantime. I flirted with the idea of joining the Somerset County Police. There were so many demobilized men, and, with unemployment rising, one of the most sought-after careers was with the police force because it was a guaranteed weekly income and for men with families this was important. I applied to join. It was critical to have an exemplary conduct record on your demobilization papers; anything that hinted at second-rate service, convictions for drunkenness or being absent without leave, and they wouldn't look at you. Fortunately mine were fine, and I was invited for a medical at Taunton. There was one problem: my height. I knew I was five feet eight, and that was one inch too short. At the medical I passed everything, and I thought, 'When he checks my height, it'll be all right. I'll stand on my toes, get the inch that way,' but the doctor must have been used to the trick as he told me to lean back and stand on my heels; that did it: no police service for me. To tell you the truth I had no ambition to be a policeman; I thought joining would be a soft option.

For the time being, I worked for next to nothing. I lived with my parents at Rosemount but money was still tight and I did several small private jobs, helping out at home, doing odd bits and pieces such as plumbing in a sink for my mother. The water company was bringing mains water to each house on Combe Down and they asked if I could dig the holes to a terrace of ten houses so that each could have its own separate water supply. There was some haggling over the work. The water company wanted to pay one fixed price for the excavation but I told them I wanted the price of ten excavations, or tappings as they were called, and in the end they agreed to pay.

Yet this was no way to carry on. It was frustrating not seeing Ada, and prospects were not good. Nationally, there wasn't a flat rate in the building trade for plumbing work and the rates in Bath were among the lowest paid anywhere. Ada was keen to move closer to her mum, or at least not to remain in Manchester on her own. I had a think, and decided to find work away from Bath, so I wrote to the plumbers' trade union secretaries at Birmingham, Shrewsbury and Manchester to see if there was any chance of a job. These secretaries would know if there was anything going and, as I was a member of the union, they would help if they could. It was possible in those days to be a freelance plumber without belonging to a union, but you would never get on to the books of a big firm without being a member of the Plumbing and Heating Engineers Union.

Neither Birmingham nor Manchester could give me a job but there was an offer from Shrewsbury for a guaranteed nine months at a housing scheme under development at Gobowen. The rate was half-a-crown an hour and I took it. The following week I went into Long's office in Bath and insisted once again that they signed my indentures. This time I told them about my job offer, whereupon they abruptly decided that they would take me on at the full rate of pay for a plumber. 'You're too late; I've telegraphed to say I am taking the job and I'm going, but I want these indentures signed.' They could see that I wouldn't let the matter rest and reluctantly they signed, just to get me out of their hair.

At Gobowen I lived among a Welsh-speaking community, lodging with another plumber called Parker. Our place was a short walk away in a village called Chirk, where we slept in a miner's cottage. A couple of months after I arrived at Gobowen, Ada and I married. Ada had given up her job in Manchester and moved to live with her brother Tom in Hadley, in Shropshire, and at weekends I used to go over to see her. It wasn't a perfect arrangement by any means but it was far better than we had previously.

I worked for nine months on the housing scheme, just ordinary plumbing jobs, much of it hot-water work, putting in the pipework to the baths and boilers. Ada was pregnant and shortly after the end of my work at Gobowen, in June 1920, our first son, Dennis, was born. He was actually born at my mother-in-law's house at Trench Crossings, just outside Wellington, and I can recall the joy at racing over to see them, getting home in time for his birth.

After I finished at Gobowen, we moved in with Tom and his wife and I took a job with a small firm in Ludlow that specialized in private work. One of the houses I visited was Petton Park, a beautiful mansion house owned by an old lady. The grounds were extensive, with huge flowerbeds, and were occasionally opened to the public.

A considerable amount of work had been undertaken there, with new electrical cables and plumbing installed. On one occasion when I arrived, her ladyship wasn't up, so I wasn't allowed in. I waited until about 11.30 when I said to the butler, 'Look, if I can't get in, I'm going,' as I had a list of other calls to make. A few minutes later I was told her ladyship wanted to see me. I entered a large, imposing room, and there she was, sitting, two dogs either side, looking like Queen Victoria.

'Do you know the water service here?' she asked. I said, 'Yes, I've attended to it on a couple of occasions.' 'Well,' she said, 'I've lost a thousand gallons of water since Thursday. I want you to find the leak.' So I went and found the butler and told him what she'd said. 'Then you will want the keys to the tank room,' he said. The tank was in one of the battlement towers. 'Don't be silly,' I told him. 'If you've lost a thousand gallons of water in the tank room, you won't need me to find it; the place will be flooded.' The house was not on any mains system but had its own private water supply with a pump house called Round Towers, which drew the supply from very deep bore holes. I asked for the keys, went to the house and examined the pumps. They were electric and worked so soundlessly that the only way to tell whether they were working was by looking at the amp meter. I tried both pumps, and they worked all right, so I spent the next two hours hunting round for a leak all over the park, looking for the taps used for watering the flower-beds: nothing doing. I went back and the butler asked what I'd found. When I told him that I'd found nothing, he suggested that I'd better go in and tell her.

Her ladyship was waiting. The only explanation I could come up with was that someone had left a tap running. 'I've had that idea myself, but the staff are as close as devils in hell; I shall never find out.' As the pumps were working perfectly well, I had refilled the tanks for her. With nothing else to do, I prepared to leave when the butler took me to one side. 'I'll tell you the truth now,' he said. The upshot was that the lady's maid was just getting ready to go out. It was her evening off and her boyfriend would be calling in his car. She was running a bath when a message came that her ladyship wanted her. She left the bath with the tap running but now, being short of time, she'd simply changed and forgotten all about the bath. 'That's where your thousand gallons went, down the plughole.' The maid's error, as the butler explained, had compounded another failing, also hidden from her ladyship. It was the gardener's job to switch the pumps on each Monday and Thursday to fill the tanks. However, his wife had been taken ill with a burst appendix, and, in his urgency to go to Oswestry, where she was in hospital, the tanks had not been topped up and so by Thursday the maid had run them dry.

The secret was safe with me but I told the butler that her ladyship would still get a bill for two hours' work, adding, 'But why on earth didn't you tell me this story before I spent two hours looking for a leak?' 'If you hadn't gone round looking for the problem,' replied the butler, 'she would have smelt a rat.' He was protecting the maid and the gardener, while her ladyship was right: the staff did look after their own.

There were several grand houses in the area, owned by long-standing families with influence. Twelve miles from Petton Park was Schotten Park, owned by Lady Mary Cambridge. I went to her house on three or four occasions, taking the train to Whitchurch in Shropshire. On one of these visits, all I was required to do was replace some guttering above and around a dormer window, an easy job, and in a couple of hours I was finished. A coachman and trap usually took me back to the train station, but, as it was such a lovely hot summer's day, I chose to walk. Next to the railway line was a field where I ate some lunch and went to sleep. The next thing I heard was the whistle of my train leaving the platform so I sauntered down to the booking office and asked when the next train to Shrewsbury might arrive. One was due in at 5 p.m. that afternoon so I began to walk away when the stationmaster came tearing after me and told me to come back. An express train was running ten minutes early, so the signal had been put against it. 'You can get in the guard's van and get out at Shrewsbury,' I was told. That train had been halted for me. And why? Because the stationmaster knew I had been working at Lady Mary Cambridge's house, and that still counted for a lot in those days.

In early 1921 we left Ludlow and moved back to Combe Down and into no. 5 Gladstone Place, finally getting a house of our own. Although the house was a wedding present from my father, it had, at the time of our marriage, been occupied by a gardener. He worked for Angels, the millionaire antiques dealers in Combe Down, and, owing to a legal restriction, he could occupy the house until alternative accommodation was found. This was a wartime measure which had remained in force to protect key workers from eviction. Fortunately, in the intervening time between our marriage and my return to Combe Down, Angels had generously built Long Wood, a house on the North Road, and given it to their gardener. It meant that, as he moved out, we were able to move in.

In one sense it was good to have the family together again. It had been nearly ten years since we had all lived in the village, and I'm sure my parents were pleased to see us. I got on well with George, my eldest brother. As well as working at J. Long and Sons as a carpenter, he had made his own furniture out of mahogany, all beautifully inlaid. I recall that he made a fire screen in three sections and each section was made of one thousand individual pieces linked together to create the most intricate honeycomb pattern. The patience that took was incredible and I couldn't help admiring his work. William, my middle brother, had come back to no. 4 Gladstone Place after he was demobbed. He also worked at J. Long and Sons, picking up his trade again as a bricklayer, but later left to take a job as an overseer at the RAF station at Cullern, just outside Bath. In the army he'd risen to the rank of sergeant major and, as the saying goes, 'Once a sergeant major always a sergeant major', and you knew it. After I came back to Combe Down he had a tendency to order me about, silly little jobs really, but he would expect me to do them, and that didn't go down too well with me. No job could ever be done to his expectations, so did we get on? Well, passably!

After the war there were repeated strikes and reports in

the press of riots and a general unease in society. There was still a coalition of the main political parties but it was increasingly in difficulty and under strain. In 1918, there was an election and the number of people who could vote increased dramatically, in part because they could hardly withhold the right to vote from soldiers who had fought for their country.

Up to that point, you could vote if you owned property, so only my father, in our family, had taken part in a poll. With the new law [The Representation of the People Act, 1918], suddenly all men over the age of twenty-one and women over thirty could vote, which included my mother for the first time. Unfortunately for me, the election was held just weeks after the Armistice, which meant that I couldn't vote as I was still six months short of twenty-one.

So it wasn't until November 1922 that I first voted, for a man called Sir John Barlow, a Quaker who had been opposed to conscription in the war. He was a long-standing Liberal MP in Bath – the Frome Division – and I supported him because my parents did. I can't say I took much interest in politics.

The company for which I worked in Ludlow was owned by a man whose brother was managing director of a well-known firm in Bristol called Sculls. This had given me the idea of applying for a job back home. I wrote and had an interview, not with Arthur Scull, the senior partner of the firm, but his son Anthony, who had, I believe, enlisted under age in the Great War. He asked me if I had served in the army, and had I done an apprenticeship? I explained the situation, that the war had interrupted my work but that I was a qualified plumber. He seemed to like me and told me to bring my kit down on Monday morning. 'We will meet you at Temple Meads train station and take you to your job.' As I was leaving the office, I said, 'I've got a letter of recommendation here from your uncle in Shrewsbury.' 'Why on earth didn't you mention it?' he asked me. I told him it was a matter of professional pride. 'I didn't want any influence. I wanted to get the job on merit.' He took the letter and read it, and said, 'Your job's the University Tower.'

The Wills Memorial Tower was a very prestigious development in Bristol. It had been commissioned about the time war broke out and work had been halted in 1916 and was only restarted in 1919. It was situated at the top of Park Street, and when I joined the project it was already well on the way to reaching its full sixty-six-metre height. It was built as a memorial to one of the Wills tobacco empire, and was just part of a huge scheme that included a great hall, library and various other chambers and lecture theatres that would form the core of Bristol University. It was faced with Bath stone and cost over half a million pounds, an enormous sum of money. When I began to work there the following Monday, I little knew that I would work on this site for the next four years, a wonderful project and just the sort of long-term employment that I needed.

I tried to put the war to the back of my mind, although for a long time I remembered the mates that I had lost and used to get very bad dreams about it. The war might have been over but the effects were never far away. Well into the 1920s, those who fought continued to be affected by loud noises. A car backfiring might make a civilian jump but old soldiers were more inclined to duck. I'd see a man duck, and I would know that he'd served in the war; you didn't have to

THE LAST FIGHTING TOMMY

ask. I, too, was affected. A loud noise could bring things back in a flash, and there were more tangible reminders, too. All around the country, every community held ceremonies, unveiling war memorials to their dead. In 1921 a huge congregation turned out in Combe Down to honour those from the village who had not returned. I attended, not least because I sang in the choir; I was a baritone, and the vicar and the choir would naturally lead the commemoration.

Combe Down's memorial was built on the Firs Field, a piece of land given to the residents of Combe Down by two spinster sisters called Stennard, well known to fight each other like cat and dog but very generous to the community. They had owned the field for as long as anyone could remember but nothing had been built there, and the field had remained just rough ground for local children to play on. The sisters instructed their lawyers to draw up the deeds which stated that the land must never be built on, and it remains the community's land to this day.

The unveiling began with a service at the church, after which the choir walked fully robed to the memorial. All those who had served wore their medals. The church, always the focal point for much of the community, had lost so many of its members. The Reverend Richardson's son, Alfred, had been killed serving in Palestine in 1917 with the Somerset Light Infantry. He had at one time served on Gallipoli, I believe. Captain Daubeny, who often read the lessons in church, lost his only son, Charles, who died of wounds in France in the same year. Kendrick Frankling, who stood opposite me in the choir, a bass, he was killed, and the losses didn't end with the Armistice. Eric Grant, a young tenor, died in 1919 while still in uniform, as well as

Victor Wilkinson, a policeman, a member of the congregation and my parents' next-door neighbour.

There was a big crowd there that day, a beautiful late-summer day. Railings surrounded the site which stood in the centre of the field, a large stone cross with brass plaques adorning the plinth, inscribed on which were the names of the fallen. The names of my close friends are on those plaques: Lionel Morris, Stanley Pearce, Charlie Wherrett, Harold Chivers, and my cousin Fred Patch, too, and dozens of others I knew at school, or who were no more than acquaintances around the village, people whose families I spoke to – the butcher, the chimney sweep, a farmer, a carpenter. They had all lost sons in the war, most in their teens or early twenties.

We sang 'O Valiant Hearts', all seven verses; you can imagine how hard it was to sing.

> O valiant hearts who to your glory came
> Through dust of conflict and through battle flame;
> Tranquil you lie, your knightly virtue proved,
> Your memory hallowed in the land you loved.

There was a large Union Jack over the cross, which was pulled down after the appropriate words were spoken. I can't recall who unveiled the memorial – some big noise in uniform, covered in medal ribbons, or scrambled egg as the soldiers liked to call them. Prayers were said, and wreaths laid at the base of the memorial before the service ended and people were left to their own private thoughts.

After I had been working on the tower for six weeks, the foreman came and spoke to me. 'The boss wants to see you tomorrow morning, ten o'clock at the office.' He didn't often see anybody, so the foreman wondered what I had been up to, and I wasn't sure myself. Sculls had a works in Redcliffe Street in Bristol and the next morning I went to see the old man, Arthur Scull. I was called into his office and he told me to sit down in the chair opposite his desk. 'I've been to see my brother in Shrewsbury last week, and I hear you've got the plumbers' certificate and the certificate of the Institute of Sanitary Engineers. Why the devil didn't you tell me?' I said that I didn't think he would be interested. 'You don't intend staying a plumber all your life?' he asked. I told him, 'No.' 'Then what sort of job do you fancy?' I said a building instructor or sanitary engineer. I can remember now, he looked at me over his thick glasses. 'How old are you?' 'Twenty-five, sir.' He shook his head. 'You'll never get a job like that; they'll look at you and say, "Too young, no experience". They'll pass you by. Your qualifications are not good enough. You want the MRSI' [Member of the Royal Sanitary Institute]. I said, 'That's the top exam, I'll never pass it.' 'Have you ever tried? Try. Talk it over with your wife.' I appreciated that he had taken an interest in my career and I took him up on his suggestion, studied for the next three years, took the exam, but failed. The day after I got the result, I went to see him. 'You've failed. Take it again.' 'I can't,' I told him. 'You'll be a fool if you don't,' he replied. By this time I had a wife and two children to support and I couldn't afford the expense. Arthur Scull persisted. 'Take it. I'll pay your expenses, and, if you pass, pay me back out of your wages; if you fail, it's a gamble I've lost.' I studied hard, took the exam again and passed, and in time I paid him back. Arthur Scull was good to me.

On all four sides of the Wills Tower was wooden scaffolding, held together by chains, although none of the scaffolding was actually attached to the building. There were no cranes to haul the materials up to the top, so as well as climbing ladders to the roof level we carried everything else up with us, from the huge tool bags of our trade, full of everything you might need, to the great slabs of lead we used for flashings or for the heavy pipes. We had to carry it all up, which was exhausting, and at the end of the day, at least as far as our plumbing kit was concerned, we had to carry it back down again to be stored away. A plumber's kit cost about £50, several months' wages, so our tool bags were always locked away at night.

Everything on that memorial, all the cornices, was covered in lead that was cast in our workshops, eleven pounds to the square foot. It took some working when the lead was half an inch thick. It was all burnt together by melting the lead to make the joints watertight; it wasn't soldered. The expansion of solder was much greater than that of lead, and the first hot summer it would have split. It was a skilled job, and I was taught the art of lead burning there from a chap called Tommy Smith, fusing the metal together with little drops of lead all the way down. The skill was to get the oxyacetylene flame just right, otherwise the flame would simply melt the lead. It was a very useful and marketable skill.

There was one electric lift that went as high as the belfry, which was used to take bricks up. It was worked externally by one of the men. If the boss came on site to see us or check what we were doing, the man who worked the lift would always take him one floor above us, then let him drop back down fast to where we were, just to shake him up a little; it got him every time. It was also a useful ploy to give any of them who were not working at that moment enough warning to be hard at it when the boss arrived.

The bell for the memorial tower arrived and had to be placed into position. At that time, it was the third largest bell in England, set a half-tone higher but slightly smaller than Big Ben and smaller, too, than Great Tom that hangs in Christ Church, Oxford. Bristol's bell was known as Great George, and it weighed eight tons, heavy enough that when the engineers lifted it a foot off the floor in the Great Hall, the tackle broke. The only solution was to go to Wolverhampton where the bell had been cast, to borrow specialist equipment. They cut a hole in the belfry roof and lifted the bell, placing it in a reinforced-concrete carriage.

The foreman on the job, a Welshman, had a notice printed stating that the bell belonged to Bristol and that nobody must ring it until the tower was officially opened by King George V. It was the worst thing he could have done, because everyone with a hammer, spanner or mallet used to give it a good rap as they passed, and if they didn't have anything to hand, they'd kick it. If he'd said or done nothing and had left the bell alone, nobody would have taken any notice. As it was, the bell was rung all day long.

The work on the tower and the surrounding buildings was impressive and the men worked hard in all weather conditions, keeping the project on track and on budget. Nevertheless, in bad weather work was forced to stop and there was sometimes a risky scramble down the freestanding timber scaffolding. If the wind picked up too much, we could find ourselves trapped up in the tower until it had abated. It was not that the wooden scaffolding was likely to fall, but that the planks were only nailed down, and it was perfectly possible that sudden gusts could rip a plank or two off, injuring anyone still on the scaffolding or indeed down below.

Heavy thunderstorms were also a danger. The top of the tower was shaped like an eight-sided lantern with windows, none of which had glass in them. I was working up there covering the cornices with lead when the sky darkened and a thunderstorm broke. Two of us, myself and the foreman plumber, got under cover out of the rain, and the foreman was standing in one of the windows, a steel knife in his hand. Suddenly there was a terrific bang. Lightning had struck the tower, hitting the bell which had acted as a conductor. Fortunately, the bell was connected to earth by a big copper band. However, the foreman standing in the window had the knife ripped out of his hand. He was thrown to the floor and was incapable of using the arm that had held the knife for three weeks afterwards. The strike must have burnt all the oxygen out of the air, for there was a distinct reek of sulphur, then a second or two later you could feel a gust of air coming back into the tower.

On top of the tower, directly above the bell, was a trap door. One of my jobs was to cover the door with thick sheet lead. The job on the Wills Tower was coming to an end, and so before I placed the lead over the trap door I drilled two holes the depth and width of a penny, and the lad I was working with and I both signed our names in the woodwork underneath and placed two new pennies, each dated 1925, into the bored holes before sealing the door with the lead. I am quite sure the pennies are still there today, although our names would surely have gone by now; must have done.

When the tower was finally finished, we held what was called the topping-out parade, when the last stone was set into position. Very often some money is placed under the stone, just as it is under the foundation stone; it's all for good luck. In our case, a cameraman was there to take a picture, in which I appear clearly identifiable with my thick mop of hair.

All that was left was for King George V and Queen Mary to come and open the building, which they did in June 1925. It was a fine day, crowds of people. I don't remember much. I know the King gave a speech in the Great Hall because we were somewhere near the back, but I can't say I was that interested.

It was at the end of my spell on the Wills Tower that I retook the MRSI exam and passed. Within days of the result being known, Arthur Scull had appointed me manager of his Clifton branch, a significant promotion which acknowledged the efforts I had made. As I lived in Combe Down, I travelled each day to Bristol on a workman's ticket, which cost a shilling return. Each morning I left on the 7 a.m. train to open the shop at eight o'clock, closing at 5 p.m., and then went home. I was very settled at this time, for I had a steady and good income and by this time I also had a second son, Roy, who had been born at the back end of 1924.

Unemployment was rising sharply and the economic outlook was poor. I knew how lucky I was to be with a big plumbing firm, in charge of the branch shop. Sculls employed a number of plumbers and hot water fitters; the boss managed the hot water side of the business, me the plumbing, and we made sure that there was enough work coming in to keep us going. It was all too common to see unemployed men, still in their old army greatcoats, who came in asking for jobs we just didn't have. It kept us all on our toes. With Sculls, to be honest, you had to be a very good plumber to stay there; if you didn't pull your weight, you were out.

When the General Strike hit in 1926, there was no question of missing work and I cycled the twelve miles from Bath to Bristol each day to open the shop. Other than the lack of transport during the strike, we remained fairly unaffected but we certainly felt the effects of the general depression when trade was very bad. There was a lot of gloom and despondency at the time, and business could be quite cut-throat. At the height of the Depression a number of workers who commuted from Bath to Bristol to work were thrown out of their jobs, and Bristol people took their places, while the Bath workers returned home to find a job if they could. It wasn't pleasant.

One big advantage that Sculls had was that the business was related by marriage to another firm in Bristol, which looked after, renovated or sold a lot of property in the area. This relationship was useful, as we received a lot of work through this other company. If they were about to sell a house and they wanted a bathroom put in, then it was my job to undertake the work. Nevertheless, there was a problem. The foreman builder at this other firm was a man by the name of Williams, and I came to discover, quite by chance, that he was pulling a fast one on Sculls.

At the time all orders used to come down from the other company and, because of the volume of work, they had the first call on me. The work was one of two types: contract work, which was subcontracted and charged at a lower level, and day work, which was set at a higher price. Williams would tell me which type of job it was, and more often than not he would add, 'This one's contract, keep your price down', and so I did. My boss at Sculls would only get a certain percentage of the total price, much lower than if it was a day rate. If a client was being charged at the day rate but we understood it was contract work, then there was a considerable excess, and this profit was going to this other firm. I wasn't losing anything; I still got my plumber's rate, but my employers were losing money, and I had a much greater allegiance to Arthur Scull than I ever did to the other firm.

One of the other firm's painters let something slip that roused my suspicions and I followed it up. I knew that all orders were signed and countersigned by a confidential secretary, Phyllis Kay. She was a Sunday school teacher and a friend of mine from church, and I told her what was happening. She agreed to help me out. From then on, if I got an order signed Phyllis Kay, it meant that it was all right and I was to go ahead and do the job, because it was day work. If it was just signed PK, it would mean it was contract. From then on, if Williams tried to pass off something as contract work, I would tell him it was day work and I would undertake the job only if it was paid as such. Williams never found out how I knew the difference. At one point he wouldn't let me go into the office and collect the orders – he'd bring them to me himself – but still I knew and he couldn't fathom how. Sculls never found out that this scam was going on. They were being ripped off, but as there were family connections between the firms there might have been awful ructions if I had said anything.

In the end, the manager of the other firm wanted me moved from Clifton back to be an ordinary plumber at Redcliffe Street. I already had ideas of my own to start a small business. I had ten years' experience so I politely declined, and instead resigned. Whether Anthony Scull

ever asked any questions – because they were very much out
of pocket – I don't know. I already had enough small jobs to
start on my own and I had made good contacts within the
building business, people who trusted me and would put
work my way. One of them was a well-known architect,
Mowbray Green, who got me a lot of business because I
could lead burn.

When I was finally going it alone I decided to splash out
on my first car, an Austin Seven. I had been taught to drive
in the 1920s by a grocer's son, Reg Ings, who was serving in
the cavalry. He used to take me out into Bath to get used to
the traffic, what there was in those days. Back then, I only
needed to apply to the County Council for a driving licence
as there were no actual tests; they didn't come in until the
mid-1930s, I believe. Unfortunately, the Austin Seven was
troublesome. The magneto-ignition, which gave the spark
to start the engine, was always failing, so we swapped it for
a Ford Eight. This car had been owned by two army officers:
one had been drafted abroad and the other didn't want a car
and put it on the market. It was practically a new car and
served two useful purposes: as a family car that took us on
day trips to such places as Weston-super-Mare, and as a
works car that was insured to carry my plumbing tools for
the new business.

Despite my contacts, running my own firm and choosing
my work hardly removed me from the world of sharp
practice. There were too many contractors from whom it
was difficult to get money owed, and that made me wary.
One such man was a chap called Clifford. He had been
working on Midford Castle near Combe Down. The roof
needed considerable work, and in principle I was happy to
take on the job. The Castle had interested me from my

boyhood as it had been built by a man who had once been a society gambler. The Castle was designed in the shape of the ace of clubs, the card he had won a huge pot of money on during one of his games. In all my childhood, I never saw the owner, who was a recluse and married to one of Captain Daubeny's daughters. After he died, the Castle went to the Daubeny family, and it was indirectly for them that I was asked to help put the roof back in perfect order. The place was a time warp: no gas, electricity, just torches and candles. Mowbray Green asked me to work at the Castle but I told him that, as the builder was a hell's delight to get any money from, I couldn't do it. Mowbray reassured me that every time I'd spent £200 in wages and expenses, I was to let him know and he would see that I got it.

During the 1930s, I expanded my company as the effects of the Depression gradually faded and work picked up. Most was very local but I would travel frequently to Radstock and Midsomer Norton, and occasionally further afield to Exeter and Exmouth. The boys were growing up fast, and while Ada was bringing them up I worked very hard to make sure that we had a comfortable life. I gradually took on three other registered plumbers, Jack Bath, who lived next door to us, Leslie Duckett and George Taylor, both of whom I'd known for years. Working locally meant that one of us could be called out at all hours on some emergency or another. A number of houses had large tanks under the roof to collect the rainwater. Water was metered and people were often quite conscious of keeping their bills down to a minimum. The rainwater would be used for domestic purposes, such as washing and the toilets. Drinking water by this time came from the mains. However, with so many tanks in the roofs, there were always small problems, flooding being one of them.

One of my clients was a Miss Davies, a Welsh speaker, and because of my time at Gobowen I could converse a little with her in Welsh. Miss Davies had a recurring anxiety. She had built several houses in Monkton Combe, and in all of them there were problems with the water pressure that made the washers in the taps constantly split, wasting large quantities of water. The water in Combe Down and Monkton Combe was supplied by a private company, the Combe Down Water Company, and the inspector was Vernon Bishop. We had never been friends since school, and the incident when he had kicked the headmaster had always stuck in my mind as being fairly typical of his behaviour. Twenty-five years later, he was in the process of taking over his father's business, which included contract work with the Combe Down Water Company. Owing to the water problems in Monkton Combe, Vernon had been called in and he'd told Miss Davies that she would have to change all the bathroom taps as they were not up to standard.

Now I had changed the washers on these taps on various occasions because the pressure was too high. The taps themselves were fine, indeed, Vernon's father had passed them as being fit. Nevertheless, Vernon's father had written to Miss Davies to tell her I wasn't doing my job properly. He advised Miss Davies to let his son take over from me, blatantly trying to take my business and give it to his son. The problem was that Vernon didn't have either my qualifications or experience.

Miss Davies showed me the letter and I gave it to my solicitor. I said, 'Get Vernon Bishop to come round and you choose any tap in any bathroom you like and he can take it apart.' We had a meeting. Miss Davies' solicitor was present, as well as an independent plumber. I knew damn well that all the taps were stamped JCSWR, a stamp of quality and approval. They chose the tap on the bath, and he dismantled it. The stamp was there and the independent plumber confirmed it was perfectly adequate for the job.

I sat and listened as Vernon claimed that it was critical to keep the pressure in Monkton Combe to force the water up the hill to the village of Windsley, and that he couldn't do anything about it. What he meant was that he didn't want to be seen spending the money to cure a problem that was of the water company's making. However, I had already told Miss Davies that there were solutions. It was possible to build a little reservoir about forty feet up the hill. I said that if Monkton was connected to that, the pressure would automatically be lowered. Alternatively, a pressure-reducing valve could be fitted, a more expensive option that would cost a few hundred pounds. The water pressure hadn't just affected Miss Davies' house but Monkton Combe School's pipes were always bursting too, and a solution had to be found. Once it had been shown that the problem was nothing to do with my work, Miss Davies turned on Vernon. 'You either put that reservoir in, or I will make sure that you are sued for damages.' She was a formidable lady with plenty of money. A reservoir was dug, and Vernon and I remained not the best of friends.

With competition, fair or unfair, there was always pressure to ensure the work came in, but as I could turn my hand to most things, odd jobs were always available if business was quiet. My father had taught me how to lay bricks, so if a wall needed building, I was able to manage.

For anyone working in the plumbing trade, there was exposure to dangerous or noxious substances that would simply not be allowed today. Handling old-fashioned lead piping or lifting any lead flap after a few years would expose the plumber to a white powder underneath, sulphate of lead, which was highly poisonous. You must not breathe it in, otherwise it would cause headaches and nausea. Handling the powder with bare hands would, in time, cause lead poisoning, turning not only the fingernails blue but hands, too. Yet no plumbers wore face masks, and men handled this powder all the time, just as long as they remembered to wash their hands thoroughly.

For many years I mended a lot of guttering using asbestos while lead-burning so as to keep the heat off the woodwork fascia. I mixed up buckets and buckets of asbestos powder with water to coat boilers, smoothing it over to create a good finish. It seems strange, but I don't recall any of us suffering any ill effects.

By the late 1930s, both my boys had left school. Roy followed me into the building trade while Dennis studied for accountancy. In 1939, Dennis was about to take his last accountancy exam and, if war hadn't broken out, he was going to emigrate to America, to Chicago, where Ada's brother Bill now had an accountancy business. Unbeknown to the rest of the family, Ada and I had decided that we would go and start a new life over there too. I never told my parents we were going; of course I would have told them sooner or later, but as the eventuality never arose, they never knew. War had once again intervened to change the passage of my life.

9

WORLD WAR II

It was difficult to watch as Europe slowly slid back into war. Hitler wanted more and more space for a new Germany, a Germany which was re-arming at a frightening rate. I remember watching the newsreel of Chamberlain stepping out of his plane, waving his piece of paper in the air. He had flown back from his visit to Germany, and he told us it was peace in our time, and you hoped it was true, but I was sceptical.

In Britain, Oswald Mosley and his British Union of Fascists were in the news, but this was Quaker country. Clarks, the shoe people, were down here, and they were Quakers; Morlands, the coat company, they were Quakers, and their influence was strong and no one I knew was even interested in his organization, never mind joining it.

In the event of war, I would probably be too old for combat, at least initially, but I felt I needed to do something. About the time of Chamberlain's trip to Munich, the Auxiliary Fire Service (AFS) was set up to equip and train civilian firefighters should the deteriorating European situation lead to war. It made sense to join. To start with, I knew about water, and I knew where all the hydrants were on Combe Down. There were two water mains in the village: one was just ordinary pressure, about ten pounds per square inch, and the other was high pressure, and I knew one from the other, so I, along with one or two local ex-Great War men, joined the AFS Combe Down in one of three teams.

Preparing for war was difficult. For those of us who had been through the 1914–18 war, the idea that we were going to go through it all again was difficult to accept, let alone contemplate, not least because my own sons were teenagers and just about the same age as I had been in 1914.

I was forty-one in September 1939 when Hitler invaded Poland and war was declared. I was indeed just outside military age [18–40] to be called up for national service. Dennis, however, was nineteen and studying for chartered accountancy; he only had his final exam to pass. Dennis didn't want to join the army so he went to Portsmouth, took a test, and joined the navy as a writer, which meant he dealt with the captain's administration, mail and correspondence. He signed on not just for the duration of the war but for twelve years.

For the first few months nothing much happened. It was known as the phoney war. In 1914, Germany had invaded France almost from day one, but in the second war we dispatched an expeditionary force for the Continent, but it would be the best part of nine months before Germany invaded France and all that meant for the troops and their retreat to Dunkirk.

In Bath, preparations were made, with air-raid shelters being built, wardens given rattles and whistles, and sirens erected, but I don't think we heard a siren for real for the best part of a year. In Combe Down, a lot of iron railings and four gates from around the church were taken away to be melted down for the war effort. They took some railings from in front of our house, but there was no point in protesting; you couldn't argue with government directives. Besides, how unpatriotic would you look if the railings from your neighbours' homes were taken away and yours remained intact? No, we were all in the war together, as a community, and you were willing to do your bit. I believe that most of the railings were of such poor quality that they were fit for nothing, and the idea of collecting the iron was as much to do with keeping up local morale as anything else.

With the threat of invasion very real, a system consisting of three lines of defence was established to protect Britain. The first line of defence was still the navy, the second line was troops under training, including, I believe, the Dad's Army which would occupy, among other things, the concrete pillboxes you can still see today. At the end of the war I saw a map which showed every pillbox from the Wash to South Wales, and there were hundreds of them. As a member of the AFS, I was to be part of the third line of defence along with those who manned searchlight batteries. Because I had served on a Lewis gun, I was given particular training on the belt-fed Vickers machine gun, a much better piece of equipment than the Lewis gun.

While there were searchlights round about Bath, there was little or no protection, no anti-aircraft guns, and right up until 1942, when we were bombed, Bath was an undefended city; I don't think anyone imagined we would be a target. We all had blackout curtains in our houses, and some people taped up the windows against the risk of a blast shattering the glass, but we didn't bother. We also made some curtains for Combe Down church. You had to watch it: the first glimmer of light and you were in trouble. At one point, a policeman threatened to report me because he said the curtains showed light through them. I told him to carry on. I also told him the material had been officially supplied by Somerset County Council. I heard no more about it.

Everyone could do something. Dad, although he was nearly eighty, took a job as a firewatcher, while others in the village, such as my great friend George Atkins, were air-raid wardens. As part of the AFS, our crew was regularly training. We used to go out on a Sunday morning, the whole crew, having a practice, sometimes with Bath Fire Brigade, sometimes on our own. We were very competent but we also had a lot of fun. We went out one morning to a very tall building on Combe Down. We ran the hose out, started the pump, put the ladder up, and the no. 1 on the crew, called Williams, went up. The idea was to rescue a dummy from a notionally burning house and bring the dummy back down the ladder. As it happened, Williams couldn't get the window open. Chief Officer Gibbs, who was watching him fumbling around, called out, 'Go on, Williams, make it realistic', so Williams pulled his axe out and smashed the window to pieces. When he got the dummy and brought it down, Gibbs was unimpressed. 'You bloody fool, that window was already unlatched.'

We often used to practise with the professional crews of Bath Fire Brigade, but on Sunday mornings we were usually on our own and we would operate in front of crowds of local people. We would compete with the other AFS crews: no. 1 crew would run so many lengths of hose out in such and such time, and our crew, no. 2 crew, had to see if we could beat it. Sometimes we would actually use the pump. The hosepipe was rolled in a coil and was coupled to the pump, while the suction pipe was placed in water, in the canal, a canvas reservoir or perhaps the Midford Brook. We had to be very careful. The pump turned the water into high pressure, and if the hosepipe was folded or twisted and they turned the water on, it would throw you down, you couldn't hold it.

Most public displays weren't designed simply for entertainment. They were essentially instructive, showing what civilians could do in the event of a raid, or how to handle small incidents. The vicar of Claverton proposed to give a public demonstration of how best to tackle an incendiary bomb. It was to be held at the vicarage, and he thought it would be interesting to see how long it would take us, from an initial call, to drive from Combe Down to Claverton. It was supposed to be a dry practice. We would arrive, smartly jump into action, and run a hosepipe out, but with no water. The call was taken and we raced to Claverton, two miles in four minutes, only to find the vicar's demonstration had gone totally wrong. Somehow, during his efforts, he had managed to set fire to a lot of undergrowth in a wood, and so the dry run became a wet one.

The field was very steep, and we left the car at the top end and pushed the petrol-driven pump down to the fire. The nearest water was the canal, so we uncoupled the suction and delivery hoses and put the fire out. By this time the ground had got a bit slippery, so we asked if a few of the civilians would help push the pump back up the hill to the car. There were five of us on the team, two on one side, two on the other, and me at the back. A number of civilians helped us, but, as we started, we got too close to the canal edge. One of the team slipped on the canal side and, grabbing at his pal, took him with him into the water.

At Combe Down we had three crews; no. 1 crew would go to the fire, no. 2, which might be ours, would stand by, and the third crew would be resting. In a proper raid, all three were called out. We kept our Bewick fire engine in an old stable attached to the vicarage; we had the stable downstairs for the car and the pump, while upstairs was a hayloft. One of the firemen built a fireplace in there, and we had four beds and a telephone. We were told by telephone which fire we should go to. The Chief Officer, Gibbs, lived a short distance from us. He would take a call, then he would come to our front door. If it was night, he pressed a button which activated a buzzer under my pillow; it was like an electric front-door bell without the bell, and was just enough to wake me up. It was my idea, actually, to help wake me up, and I would depress a button to let him know I'd received it. I'd then get up and dressed and run down to the stable while he'd go round four more houses and shake them up. Ten minutes, and we had a crew out.

We had to know the roads well. The rule governing illumination included vehicles as well as houses, and we drove with masked headlights and just a thin strip of light showing. In the dark, you never knew what you might come across.

In 1940, the first heavy raids on Bristol took place, which meant that the professional Bath fire crews went to give help and the AFS were left to tackle any emergencies. One concerned the train station at Monkton Combe. The railway ran through the old disused coal canal and the station was actually built in the bed of the canal. Right opposite, there was a factory belonging to a family called Freeman. They used to tear up rags, making them into flock for stuffing furniture and mattresses. Anything metallic was meant to have been removed, but evidently a button or something similar had gone through the machines in the rag mill and caused a spark. For a time the material must have smouldered. The rags had been bundled up and loaded on a railway truck which burst into flames. We were called, and as the material was thrown out of the wagon it was our job to damp it down. The suction was from a nearby brook so we had plenty of water. As we damped down the flames, I climbed into the carriage. It was dark, and with the truck doors open on each side, I pointed the hose outside until I was alerted by somebody running along the station plat-form shouting and waving his arms furiously. 'What the hell are you doing?' I didn't know, but in the gloom it seems that the power of the water had smashed the window of the ladies waiting room and completely flooded it.

The raids on Bath in 1942 came as a direct response to the Allied attacks on German cities of culture, notably Rostock and Lübeck. There had been unbridled anger at the Allied raids, and it was quickly concluded that Germany would retaliate by working its way through the Baedeker tourist guide, bombing historic towns in Britain. Thumbing through the guide, they decided to hit those picturesque towns given three stars or more, notably Exeter, Bath, Norwich, York and Canterbury, all of which were hit between late April and early May.

The raids came just as German attacks on Britain's major cities had begun to wane. By 1942, Germany was heavily engaged in fighting in Russia, and was committing vast forces to new spring offensives after the initial invasion the previous year. Britain's key industrial cities and ports were better prepared and defended, so that softer targets such as Bath were, in reality, the only available option.

Although air-raid sirens sounded in Bath on average one in three days throughout the war, the vast majority of alarms were purely precautionary, as German bombers, picking up the Avon, had followed the river to Bristol, or swung round in a wide arc to attack towns and cities in the Midlands, dropping their bombs as they continued onwards for home. This time would be different. On the nights of 25 and 26 April, eighty Junkers and Dornier bombers took off in eight waves from airfields in northern France and headed for sleepy Somerset. Such was the dire shortage of men and machines that the Luftwaffe was forced to scrape together every airworthy aircraft.

Using both crews in training and their instructors to pilot the planes, the Junkers and Dorniers set off for Bath, crossing the cliffs of Dorset before picking up the river that would take them directly over Combe Down.

I was at home when we were called out. I remember it as a clear, moonlit evening and as we left the house the first German aircraft began to circle around the city. Aircraft engines droned above us as numerous flares were dropped, lighting the whole area up. My wife commented how beautiful it looked. I couldn't see the beauty myself, and told her to get inside quick. We didn't have an Anderson or a Morrison shelter as we had never expected Bath to be raided; it was an open city, no guns, nothing at all, just a few searchlights. The only thing Ada could do was to go next door and get under the stairs with my sister-in-law, as I went on duty. My brother, William, like my father, was a firewatcher and he was already out that evening.

We got news that the Germans had dropped a large number of bombs on Wellsway, a steep hill that led indirectly from Combe Down on to what was known as the Bear Flat, before descending into Bath proper. The National Provincial Bank on the corner of Wellsway and Shakespeare Avenue was reportedly on fire, and our engine was directed to go and put it out. We raced to take the pump down, parked it along the road and tried to deal with the fire, which was already very extensive. My job was to couple the sections of hosepipe on to the pump and put the suction hose wherever we had water, but by this time many of the water mains were fractured and the water flooded uselessly away. Bath had prepared for such eventualities and had erected static canvas tanks around the city, and it was on a corner where two roads met on Wellsway that we drew our water to tackle the blaze. Although these tanks held thousands of gallons of water, the pump's water pressure damn soon sucked up every last drop. The bank was ruined and all we could do was damp it down and save what papers were left in the cellar.

All the time we could hear aircraft overhead. We could tell by the sound of the engines which was a British plane and which was German. Anyway, at about 11 p.m. one of their damn bombers went out, turned round and came back up, dropping flares as he went. He was no more than fifty feet – in fact he was so low he seemed to skim the roof tops – and as he came back down the Wells Road, over the Devonshire Arms pub, he opened up, machine guns blazing. In the darkness he must have seen us clearly illuminated by the firelight. I dived under the pump as bullets spattered all down the road, ping, ping, ping.

We dealt with fires all night as best we could, until about 9 a.m. We were just damping down smouldering houses when a warden came along and said that we'd parked our pump across an unexploded bomb. We had no idea. When we bent down, we could see the bomb lying on the road; in the dark we'd almost driven right over the top of it. We tentatively shifted the pump, but it was a close shave.

For all the crashes and reverberations that each bomb made, the Germans had pretty much failed to hit their targets. The railway had been missed altogether and famous sites such as the Royal Crescent and Circus were hardly touched at all. Even so, the damage to the town was extensive and lots of roads were closed off to everyone but the emergency services. One place that was destroyed was my old firm, J. Long and Sons. Their offices were close to the railway, and, in missing the station, the German bombers had a direct hit on my old plumbing and building firm, and all the machinery was destroyed. Another site to take a hammering was the gas-works in the Lower Bristol Road. This was hit by several bombs. A huge gas-fuelled flame shot skywards and the gas-holders quickly deflated, cutting all supplies to the town for the next three days. Williams, a Combe Down member of the AFS, was already there. His father, George, had been in the fire service before the Great War and was on HMS *Hampshire* when it was sunk in 1916 with Lord Kitchener aboard. His son had always been a very keen member of the AFS, and when little happened in the first years of the war, he'd moan about how he wished he could get some action. Well, he got his action at the gas-works that night, and he got it in the neck from us too. 'So what about it now, Williams? Keen for more action?' He'd been bloody scared out of his wits, and didn't fancy action after that, although we never quite let him forget it: 'Keen for more action yet, Williams?'

The second night, the German bombers came back again and we were called once more to the Bear Flat. Part of our immediate problem was that the Germans were targeting the railway station and the track, both of which lay in the dip just below the steep ridge on top of which sat the Bear Flat and Wellsway. The enemy aircraft chose to attack over the top of Combe Down and the Flat because all other routes into Bath were protected by a tremendous number of anti-aircraft positions, not protecting the town itself, but strategic sites of importance further away such as the Cullern fighter/bomber base, and to the north and to the west, those guns defending Bristol and the docks. The one undefended route into Bath was from the south, over the Bear Flat. In failing to hit the station, they were bound to hit the buildings where we were working.

On both nights the Germans dropped sticks of incendiaries as well as bombs, and once again houses burnt across the city, and roofs and walls gave way, filling the streets with debris. After nearly seventy years, it's hard now to distinguish much between the raids; all I can recall is putting out a fire in a residential house. The flames had been extinguished but, as we turned the pump off, a chair in the dining room suddenly burst into flames. We were in the process of leaving the house when we sent the message to turn the water on again, not noticing that we had twisted the hosepipe. Two of us were holding the pipe but we lost it. The nozzle flew off, hit the wall and bounced back, the water pressure driving it across the room, where it flew off again in a different direction. By the time we had chased it all round and caught it, both of us were wet through.

In the morning the full extent of the damage was evident. Those houses not badly damaged had all their glass smashed and front doors blown off their hinges. Elsewhere, homes had been reduced to near-dereliction, and, among the debris, our hosepipes snaked through the halls and living rooms of homes opened up to the world. It was like looking into a large doll's house, with pictures or mirrors still hanging on the wallpaper-covered walls, fireplaces intact even if the floor had gone. The risk of collapse was severe, and roof tiles frequently slipped, causing a small avalanche into the street below. Many streets were closed off, and a chequered flag marked the spot where an unexploded bomb lay awaiting the bomb disposal squad.

A German propaganda picture came to light after the war, marked 'a badly bombed area'. It showed Bath, but it was actually that part of the city that had undergone slum clearance and was waiting to be rebuilt; they thought it was bomb damage, but it wasn't.

The clear-up operation was immense. Teams of men began digging in the rubble, removing bodies, while families made homeless sifted through what was left of their houses to see what they could salvage, pulling out personal possessions and looking for any useful timber. Neighbouring towns such as Bristol sent down vans to serve mugs of Oxo and tea to civilians and those in the services, and mobile kitchens dispensed vegetable soup. Meals were served in municipal buildings that had escaped damage. There were some houses along Clevedon Road, all of which suffered at least some damage, but Jerry had dropped a bomb and blown one of these homes out. I knew this street well because the houses had been built after the First War by the family of my friend Titch Harding. He had got in with Bath City Council, and, as his people also ran a decorating business, they had built these houses from start to finish. In all honesty, they weren't built to the highest specification, and as I walked by I couldn't help but smile. Some wag in the know had stuck a notice out on the rubble in the morning: 'Jerry built and Jerry bombed.'

After the raid was over, all the small firms went together to put things right. As a plumber, I had been issued with a builder's licence which meant I could get access to plumbing supplies at cost price from a place called Memories in Bath. I went back to Shakespeare Avenue and met an electrician there who was going from house to house trying to get the electricity working again, while I went in to trace the plumbing and the gas. In one house I told the lady that the electrician who was following me was a bit deaf and that she should shout at him to make herself heard. I then popped out and spoke to the electrician, and mentioned that the owner was a bit deaf and that he needed to shout. Anyway, we watched as the two of them shouted at each other, until they rumbled that we were pulling their leg.

The raids on Bath were the worst I was called to deal with. The damage on the Bear Flat was truly awful. Off Wellsway there are a number of streets all named after poets, Shakespeare Avenue, Wordsworth Avenue, Milton Avenue, Chaucer Avenue, and so on. They all suffered damage, but Wordsworth Avenue got the worst of it – it was destroyed. Combe Down was relatively untouched. Clevedale Road had a hit, and the road to Purbeck College had a crater, but there were no casualties. After the raids on Bath, most people used the caves for shelter when the sirens sounded, and there you were guaranteed to be safe. As for the three teams in the Combe Down AFS, no casualties were suffered either night, although I understood that two lady messengers were killed.

In all, I went through four raids, one in Bath, two in Bristol and one in Weston-super-Mare, but nothing was as bad as those two nights. Did the bombs remind me of Ypres? Of course they did; I was going through it again, and it was tough. One thought did flash across my mind, though. When that German plane machine-gunned our team, I couldn't help thinking that if I'd had my Lewis gun I could have downed him easily, he was that low.

The Baedeker Raids, as these attacks became known, were highly destructive. In all, 401 people were killed in Bath and 875 people wounded, 360 of them seriously. The final death toll was the highest among the towns hit during the Baedeker Raids and reputedly higher than any single raid on Coventry. Nor was the attack on Harry's AFS crew an isolated incident. As the raid was designed as a reprisal, firemen, policemen and ambulance crews were targeted.

Despite the precautions taken since the outbreak of war, including the construction of forty-three municipal air-raid shelters, no one expected any raids. The best-laid plans went quickly awry as buildings which had been set aside for casualties were hit and put out of action, and people fled into the surrounding countryside.

In all, some 19,000 buildings were damaged, including the famous Assembly Rooms. They had just been refurbished at great expense and were completely burnt out. However, Bath was not quite the benign city of culture and tourism it appeared to be. Elements of the British Admiralty had relocated from London to Bath, while an engineering works in the city was designing torpedoes for the navy, and at Kingswood School the famous

Mulberry Harbour was being planned. Sporadic, largely opportunistic, raids continued for the next two years; indeed, it was not until three months after D-Day, in September 1944, that the Government gave the all-clear to the West Country.

Because I had my own business in Bath, I found myself in the same position in the Second World War as the company to which I had been apprenticed in the First, namely that all the people I had working for me – and I had three plumbers – were called up. I struggled on, trying to cope, but I couldn't do four men's work, it was impossible; so towards the end of 1942 I sold the business to a fellow in Holloway in Bath and looked around for a new opportunity.

In one of the trade papers, I noticed that the Ministry of Works was advertising for a civilian garrison engineer to come to Wells to look after the plumbing and sanitation at a number of military camps at Glastonbury and Street. The applicant had to be over military age; well, I was forty-four by then, so that was all right. I had the qualifications and I sent them through to the Colonel-in-Chief at Houndstan who interviewed me and offered me the job as a sanitary engineer. I was glad to go and soon after we moved to a pretty little village outside Yeovil called Compton Dundon, where I would live for the next ten years.

The job itself was money for old rope, really. I had to sign the Official Secrets Act because by the nature of my work I would see all the troop movements. If a regiment was coming in, I knew where it was coming from, and if a regiment was going out, I knew where it was going to, because of sending barrack-room damages after them.

From 1942 the Americans had begun to arrive in increasing numbers and all the camps gradually filled

until they were absolutely bursting at the seams, with bell
tents erected between the huts. One thing I noticed
straightaway was that none of the black and white GIs
shared a tent. Nor would they walk down the street
together. It was very marked that the whites couldn't
stand the blacks. I didn't know why. I was surprised at the
antagonism; in fact, I got on very well with the black
troops, not least because I found them better behaved. I
couldn't get on with the white GIs. The black soldiers'
accommodation was just as good as that of the whites, but
the segregation was seemingly accepted. At one camp, the
black GIs were billeted in what was the old Glastonbury
railway station. They had their own cookhouse there, and
as part of my job I went to see that everything was all right,
repairing the brick ranges where they made their food. The
black GIs had a way of cooking that was different from the
English. Instead of cooking Brussels sprouts and cabbage
and such like, they used to stew up prunes and raisins and
sultanas, and it made quite a decent variation on what I was
used to. I made a point of visiting them quite a lot during
meal times, because I would be invited to sit down and
have lunch with them.

There were several incidents between white and black
GIs that caused quite a bit of ongoing friction. One
incident occurred at a wedding reception in Glastonbury.
It was being held at a pub, the First and the Last – today it
is the Pike and Musket. Anyway, the marriage was between
two local people, but invited to the reception were several
black GIs and some of the whites didn't like it, so they went
down with the intention of disrupting the party. In
Glastonbury, there was a policeman known as 'Ginger'
Rogers, an amateur boxer, and when he heard about the

disruption he went down and restored order by laying six of the white GIs out.

As well as dealing with the fresh water and sanitary arrangements in the camps, I was given a similar role for a group of four searchlights that were permanently manned just outside Yeovil. One of the group was far more powerful than the rest and was known as the Master Light. This shone an incredibly powerful beam into the night sky, and, if it picked up an enemy aircraft, then one of the other three searchlights would join the fray, holding the plane in the glare of the crossbeam. This helped in calculating, by triangulation, the height of the plane so that the anti-aircraft fire could be aimed more accurately.

The men working the Master Light lived in an underground bunker. I was never allowed beyond this bunker or to approach the Master Light too closely for reasons of security. Nevertheless, I did watch the crews light up the bulb which was powered from a large generator. It worked when two carbons in the centre of the light were brought together, creating a spark that lit the beam. The heat was intense, and for twenty feet in front of the searchlight the grass would be scorched.

During a raid, these beams would search the sky trying to pick out an enemy plane which, when caught in the searchlight, often tried to dive down the beam in order to fire at the crew and knock out the light. At the same time, night-fighter Spitfires would scramble from nearby Yeovilton, flying above the enemy aircraft. Directly a Spitfire was about to attack, the beam was switched off. The sudden darkness blinded the enemy pilot who, until this point, had been swathed in brilliant light. As it took a few seconds for his eyes to adjust, he was momentarily vulnerable as he couldn't see what he was doing. On a number of occasions, we saw German bombers caught in the beam and brought down under heavy fire, while we looked out for the crash and telltale flames on the ground. One German bomber came down just outside Street, and, after the war, five crosses could be seen, marking the place where the crew of a Dornier or Junkers was buried. Only after D-Day, when there was no further threat from German air raids, were these searchlights no longer manned.

Throughout 1943 enormous preparations were being made by the Allies for an invasion of France. American forces were continuing to pour into Somerset, and everywhere there were secret dumps of ammunition in the woods, while along the roads long convoys of lorries were often seen. Heaven help you if you got caught behind one because it was impossible to get past.

One of the best kept secrets during this period was the Allied decision to build a secure oil pipeline across southern England that would, in time, stretch across the Channel to Europe and would help resupply the vehicles and tanks of any landing force there. The pipeline was called PLUTO [Pipe-Lines Under The Ocean] and during my work around Yeovil I had come to hear of its existence. The Germans could bomb as many army lorries as they liked, but they wouldn't be able to break the supply of fuel unless they knew where PLUTO was, and this was secret. Sometime in late 1943 or early 1944 I happened to stumble across it.

I was in Combe Down on my way to a cottage in Monkton Combe when I saw three men in khaki on private land belonging to the Reverend Warrington, and as far as I knew they had no business to be there. I wandered across and asked them what they were up to and they told me they were laying a three-inch gas pipeline. 'Who are you kidding?' I laughed. 'I'm a plumber and I know a gas main is identified by a continuous red mark painted along its side.' Marking identified every type of pipe. If the red line was dotted, it was domestic hot water. A blue line meant mains drinking water, a dotted blue line meant water fed to domestic tanks for sinks and lavatories, and not to be drunk. The pipe they were laying was a natural colour with no markings. That is the pipeline under the ocean, 'Pluto'. The pipeline began in South Wales and ended at Fawley Oil Refinery, and at various points this fuel could be tapped for use in military lorries. They also had one line that went to the RAF station at Yeovilton to refuel the aircraft there. After that I don't know where it went. The men told me that I would have to sign the Official Secrets Act, but I already had. In fact they were not laying the line at all but were checking it for obstructions. One of the men was walking along the route of the pipeline with a little instrument. As long as the instrument was ticking the line was all right. If it stopped ticking, it meant there was an obstruction and they dug down to the pipe to see what the problem was and that was what I had seen.

In the weeks before D-Day, the camps became utterly choked with American soldiers. As I've said, I knew the time and date of all movements in and out of every camp in this area, except for one, and that was D-Day. We knew that a major assault on Europe was planned, for there was an extraordinary number of men and huge quantities of ammunition, trucks and tanks, too many for there to be any other explanation. I knew all about the ammunition dumps in the woods around Street; these woods were army property, and sentries were always around, warning off kids. I can only be thankful that the town was never bombed! But that day, 6 June 1944, was kept secret by everyone. I went away one night, everything was normal, camps full of Americans, everything as it should be. Came back in the morning, and not a soldier was to be seen, they were gone. It was quite eerie. Fires in the camps' ranges were still burning. There were urns of cocoa, coffee, tea, all hot. Cheese, butter, bacon, it was all there, in the dining room, with half-consumed meals on the tables. It came as a complete surprise to me to hear that D-Day had happened.

After the troops had gone, a number of men, including me, were given the job of dismantling some of the camps and giving them back to the owners. There was a prisoner-of-war camp at the foot of Bristol Hill, Sobury Park, and the clerk of works would obtain permission to borrow prisoners to help dismantle the various sites around Street. We were never particularly friendly with these prisoners, but we treated them as we would expect to be treated, and they responded likewise. I understood that these prisoners were well looked after, almost too well, for as far as I know none ever tried to escape. They were all clearly identifiable and wore clothes with large bluish cloth patches on their backs. All these men seemed content to see out the war in relative safety. Who could blame them?

We were instructed that, once a hut was dismantled, the POWs would load all the corrugated iron on to a lorry which would go to a returns depot at Shepton Mallet. However, the very first time we did this the lorry returned fully loaded, with a message, 'We don't want this. This is American.' We then tried a depot at Taunton but the same thing happened. They wouldn't accept anything. In no time, we had a hut full of corrugated iron sheets that no one wanted, so in the end we sold them to the farmers at two shillings a sheet. And not just corrugated iron. All sorts of things littered the camps, and we packed up and sold spirit levels, saws, carpenters' tools, gardening tools to anyone happy to buy. We gave some of the proceeds to police funds, always a wise thing to do, and the rest? Well, don't ask!

One of the camps we cleared is where St Dunstan's car park in Glastonbury is today, right in the main street. At this camp there were four petrol pumps. All of them had been more or less wilfully damaged by the GIs before they left, ensuring they couldn't deliver petrol. Any fuel was more or less liquid gold during the war, so I said to the clerk of works, 'I wonder if the whites have left any petrol in the tanks?' He didn't know, but we soon found out, borrowing a dipstick from a garage. The first tank we found to be empty, but to our great surprise two of the four underground tanks were full and the third about half full. We had with us what was known as a semi-rotary pump, and we pumped the petrol out into anything that would hold fuel. Given my profession, I could get hold of a number of hot-water cylinders which I plugged to seal them. Each took about fifty gallons of petrol and I filled to the brim just as many as I could get hold of. We then drove the cylinders to Street, where the clerk of works had some Nissen huts on a site which, ironically, was being used as part of a camp for petty criminals. The clerk had sole access to some of these huts, so we stored the cylinders there under lock and key. There would be no shortage of petrol for us, and for the rest of the war I was able to travel around, often visiting my parents in Combe Down. Indeed, there was too much fuel for just the clerk and myself, so we sold petrol to anyone who wanted it, or rather to those who were 'in the know' and could be trusted. Do you know who our biggest client was? It was the chief superintendent of Glastonbury police, who had his own car. In the end, we cleared the lot. The pumps were repaired and then handed back to the owner, a firm based in Shepton Mallet.

The job of repairing damage, as well as clearing the camps, took many months. The American troops had certainly left their fair share of problems, having been accommodated in buildings right across Somerset. A large number of soldiers were housed in Prior Park, which had been standing empty for about eleven years. It had been a Roman Catholic school before the Americans arrived. Despite all the talk of how much they got paid, some at least obviously felt that this was not enough. They stripped all the lead from the huge porch in front of the main entrance and sold it to some scrap-metal merchants at the bottom of the hill. These merchants had a business under one of the viaduct arches and were happy to buy whatever the soldiers could get hold of. After the war the site went back to being a Roman Catholic school and I was given the job of re-covering that porch with lead.

Another site I dealt with was a big house in Glastonbury called The Populars, which had housed a number of GIs. In their spare time, these men started to build a brick swimming pool at the back but, for whatever reason, it was never filled. Instead, they built a cookhouse in the bottom. I went to inspect the site prior to pulling it down. I took a team of men to the cookhouse and we looked around. I had one lad with me, very inquisitive, and he opened the door on the range and looked inside. Sitting in the middle of the range

were two boxes of Mills bombs, all live, with their deto-
nators in. What possessed them to put them in the oven,
I've no idea. We had no option but to call the bomb squad
in and they destroyed them.

With so many camps empty, a lot of squatters began to
move in. Some were young people with children who just
wanted a home; some were people who got married and
wanted a house; others were much older people. Few, if any,
had money to buy coal, so wardrobes or any other furniture
that was left behind was gradually broken up for firewood.
On the Somerton Road, just by Millfield School, there had
been a large tank camp, No. 1 Camp, and squatters had
moved in almost straightaway and established themselves
to the degree that they set up their own committees, and
held residents' meetings which I would attend in my
official capacity as Garrison Camp Engineer. There were
always disputes about who would pay for the electricity,
and a man from the electric light people would be there and
try to sort out the issues. The problem was that the
electricity was communal; it wasn't metered for individual
huts. On one occasion, he told the squatters that unless an
electricity bill was paid they would be cut off. I remember
one old lady moaning that some other lady in the next-door
hut was using an electric machine to make gloves and was
therefore consuming far more than she was, but the man
held firm. 'Unless it's paid, I shall cut you all off.' It all got
rather heated. 'All the switches and fuses are in my hut. I
shan't let you in,' she said firmly. 'Don't worry about that,'
he said. 'I shall climb the bloody pole and cut you off.' On
another occasion, I was given the order to turn the water
hydrant off to stop them from having water but at the last
moment that was rescinded, so these squatters had a

sympathetic ear somewhere on the council. I must say that most of the squatters were very nice, with the exception of one or two, and in the end the council allowed them to stay for years.

War or not, Somerset always had its fair share of people on the move. Many were itinerant workers looking for casual employment. Gypsy caravans were a frequent sight around Glastonbury and Yeovil, while roaming the country were a large number of vagrants and tramps who lived off the land and did odd jobs to stay alive. I remember, as a child, that there was once an old workhouse near Bath, what is now St Martin's Hospital, at the top of Wellsway. There was a rough dry-stone wall surrounding the building. The nearest workhouse to Bath was Frome and tramps used to walk to Bath, have a night there and then be on their way again. Some of them had a regular round. They daren't enter the workhouse with any money, so if they had any coins on them they used to find a suitable fissure and press their money in to hide it in the wall. Of course they would be looking around to see that no one was watching. We knew that money was hidden in the wall and so we used to go along and search, looking carefully into every gap, and pinch what we could find. Of course, there were times when we would see the tramps looking along the wall, trying to recall where they had left their money. It seems heartless, looking back, but as kids you didn't always think.

During the war, and for many years afterwards, there used to be an old white-haired tramp who was different from most. He used to come through Wincanton, work his way round through Castle Carey, come through Compton into Street working his way round Street and back to Wincanton again. He had an old bike, and he used to cuss like a trooper if he got a puncture. I often used to walk up Compton Hill with him and, if I saw him anywhere round Castle Carey, I'd go and say hello. He was often down a little side road, making his tea for breakfast, and I would go and have a cup and a chat. He was always neat and tidy, clean-shaven; you would hardly think he was a tramp. One day a policeman from Castle Carey asked, 'You don't know who he is?' I said, 'No, but I often meet him.' He said, 'I won't tell you his name, but we always know where to find him. In the winter he sleeps under the racecourse grand-stand at Wincanton and, wherever he goes, the local police always tell us. During the First World War he was an admiral of the fleet, and he lost his only son, and since then he's just gone as a tramp.' This man never spoke about the war, he just talked about ordinary things, where he'd been and the people he'd met, but you could tell he was well educated. Local people would keep a friendly eye on him.

When I moved down to Compton Dundon, I remained in the Auxiliary Fire Service but nothing was happening, and in effect I was responsible for fires that were small enough for me to deal with almost on my own. There had been no more alarms for a long time, no sirens that put us on guard in case of a raid, and when I realized Hitler was no longer a threat I left the AFS for good and returned to civilian work.

Victory in Europe Day (VE Day) soon followed, and at Compton Dundon there were enthusiastic celebrations on Street Hill. I went along and watched as fires were lit at the top of the hill, at a place called Marshall's Elm. People sang and danced, but as I'd never learnt to dance I watched and had a drink. It was impossible to get excited. My oldest brother, George, and his wife, Lilian, had two children, May and Bob. At the outbreak of war, Bob had come back from

Canada where he had gained his 'wings', and met a man called Reginald Hughes, the son of a chemist. Hughes had come back to Britain from training in South Africa and they teamed up as bomber pilots but were transferred and flew as test pilots on the new jet engine. In November 1943, Bob had a flying accident and was killed. He was just twenty-three, the same age as my own elder son. Bob was buried at Haycombe Cemetery, Bath. He lies close to Reginald Hughes, who had been killed back in June 1943 in another flying accident, while testing the same engine. The saddest part of the story was that Hughes was engaged to my niece, May. They were real soul mates. So May lost her fiancé and her younger brother, and my brother and sister-in-law lost their only son. The shock of his death caused Lilian to have a heart attack; she could only watch Bob being taken through the house for the funeral, and she died soon after. May did not marry until she was fifty-eight, and has no children. Yet again, war had cost my family dear.

10

GROWING OLDER

Harry turned forty-seven the month after the war in Europe finally came to an end in May 1945. With the cessation of fighting, the Government no longer needed Harry's services and he returned to purely civilian work, joining E. R. Carter's as a plumber, and staying with them until he retired. In due course, he moved once more, leaving the village of Compton Dundon where he had lived since 1943, and going to Yeovil. Here he remained until well after retirement.

After the war, Harry's two sons returned from fighting overseas. Dennis eventually chose to sign on for further service, remaining with the navy for the next seventeen years, finishing with the Admiralty in Bath. Roy left the Royal Army Service Corps, taking a job with Morlands, a sheepskin factory in Street. In 1946, he married a local girl he met through work; she had settled with her family in Somerset after leaving the East End of London as an evacuee during the Blitz.

By 1945 Harry was sick of war and its terrible consequences.

I felt then, as I feel now, that the politicians who took us to war should have been given the guns and told to settle their differences themselves, instead of organizing nothing better than legalized mass murder. I had no interest in what happened to the Nazi war criminals. Another war was over, and once again both I and my family had paid a price that was always too high. Fortunately for me, both my sons had come back; Dennis was on HMS *Sheffield*, a light cruiser. This was the ship that took part in the sinking of the *Bismarck* and later the *Scharnhorst*, but I didn't discover that from Dennis. He never spoke about his war, and I never wanted to ask.

Just after Christmas 1945, Harry's father, William, died at the age of eighty-two. He and his wife, Elizabeth, had returned in the late 1930s to their former home, Fonthill, selling Rosemount, which had become too big for them. For the next six years, Elizabeth continued to live at the family home, looked after by various members of the family including May Patch, eldest daughter of Harry's brother, George, who frequently popped in to see how Elizabeth was, right up until her grandmother's death in May 1951 at the age of ninety-four.

Throughout the late 1940s and early 1950s, Harry remained with Ada at Compton Dundon, living in an idyllic thatched cottage. In many ways, these were some of his happiest times. Like his father, he had a large vegetable plot, and also reared pigs and chickens. In the extensive gardens, there was an orchard with valuable cider apples, more valuable than Harry realized. For a while, he grew and sold the apples, ignorant of their true worth as a rare variety of cider apple, a mistake he soon corrected! As his father had done, he cultivated as much land as he could, while continuing to hold down his full-time job. Harry even found time, and space, to build his own caravan. 'It was made out of hardboard. It had two single beds, a table, no washing facilities but a two-ring cooker that was heated by oil. The tyres were the front wheels off a Morris car and it was towed behind one of the company vehicles that I was occasionally permitted to borrow.' Throughout the 1950s, Harry holidayed frequently on the south coast in the caravan, meeting up with relations as well as with his best friend, George Atkins. George's wife had moved to Chickerell, close to Weymouth, during the war, but as chief air-raid warden in Combe Down, George remained behind, only joining his wife after VE Day, when he took a job at the Portland Dockyard, taking supplies to naval vessels in the harbour. After the war, Harry and Ada spent much of their free time in Weymouth.

Increasingly, Harry looked towards a time when he could enjoy life. His love of history had already drawn him into public speaking about Bath and its Roman history, a subject about which he had enormous hands-on experience from his work at the Roman baths, as well as his knowledge of the local countryside. However, it was his love of one book in particular that drew him into a ten-year-hobby-cum-quest, to find the truth behind a story he had read as a boy.

That book was *Moonfleet*, written by the popular writer J. Meade Falkner. Falkner had written two other adventure stories for boys, but *Moonfleet*, his classic yarn of smuggling and murder, in the same tradition as *Treasure Island* or *Kidnapped*, won popular acclaim among Edwardian boys brought up on the *Boy's Own* comics and books that extolled heroism and daring adventures. George's move to Chickerell was significant because it was less than half a mile from the tiny hamlet of Moonfleet, so small, indeed, that it does not even appear on motoring atlases.

As children, both Harry and George had read *Moonfleet*. It tells the story of a fifteen-year-old boy, John, who by chance discovers a secret passage under the church at Moonfleet. The tunnel is being used by smugglers with whom John becomes entangled. Inevitably in stories of its time the villains die and John returns to a peaceful life. However, rumours that the tunnel actually existed led Harry and George to set about their own part-time search.

Falkner's story was based, at least in part, on truth. Smugglers had used a secret passageway to the church's crypt, where they had stored kegs of rum. The church, located just behind Chesil Beach, was a useful staging post for the illicit smuggling ring. One evening, as the congregation was singing, a violent storm blew up during which the sea broke through the beach and into the crypt. The sound of strange, unearthly noises emanating from beneath their feet terrified the worshippers. They fled, unaware that, rather than the knocking of the dead, the noise was in fact the floating kegs bumping against the crypt ceiling.

The smugglers' tunnel was believed to have been dug close to a gravestone, and any search required permission from the Bishop of Salisbury. We went to Moonfleet and read as much as we could about the history of the church. The hamlet was originally called Moenfleet, Moen meaning west, and this was gradually changed to Moonfleet.

In the second chapter of the book, there is a storm, that is true, but there was supposed to be an underground passage going from the church down to Fleet Water, but we could never make out how this was possible. According to George's compass – he had a non-magnetic compass – it was going into Chesil Beach but we couldn't find anything for a long time.

George was in the habit of having a walk around, and he climbed the hill opposite the church. It was a hot summer and that night he wrote me a letter. 'Come down for the weekend.' He'd noticed a difference in the grass behind a tombstone. He said, 'I've got some pegs; I'll get on the hill and tell you which way to move and drive a peg in.' We had a spade and took the turf off, and underneath we found two big stones. We lifted them, and there was the passage. George wanted to go down, but I insisted on testing the air first, and we put a candle down. It was all right, and we went in. The tunnel was two feet four inches wide and less than four feet high. It was the right one but it was not a smugglers' tunnel. Now George, before he died, met a fellow from Charleston, well over ninety, and as a boy he had seen the crypt opened in the 1870s, and he told us what it was like. There were six coffins inside. The kegs bumping about under the chancel floor had smashed all the coffins to pieces. The parson gathered up the bones and the brass plates and put them in a space in the vault and it was sealed again. We'd noticed that the tunnel we found led towards the vault but that it ended in solid masonry. The book tells you there's an entrance; well, there isn't.

In 1963, I retired at the age of sixty-five. The owner of the firm said to me, 'You've got your health and strength, Harry, why don't you carry on?' But I told him, 'I've got my health and strength, and that's the time to enjoy life. I've had fifty years in the building trade and that's enough for me.' The boss had four daughters but no son to carry on the business, so in time the company itself closed.

For the next decade, Harry and Ada lived quietly in Yeovil. Then, in 1976, Ada had a stroke which incapacitated her.

It was a massive stroke after a period of ill health. She was in hospital in Wells but in the end they felt she was well enough to be discharged home again. One afternoon, Dennis took us for a drive round Wedmore and back; she seemed all right then. That evening we were sitting upstairs and I said to Dennis, 'She's not with us.' We called the doctor and she was taken to hospital straightaway. Dennis and I stayed with her until late evening when we came home. When we went back up next morning she was dead.

Harry was devastated. Ada was eighty-one years old, and their marriage had lasted over half a century. She was cremated and her ashes interred at Haycombe Cemetery in Bath. The following year, George Atkins also died, and a close friendship that had lasted seventy-four years was also broken.

The late 1970s were difficult years for Harry. Dennis had been very close to his mother and her death hit him particularly hard. Within a year, he had turned to drink, financed by a generous naval pension and supplemented not only by further income from his subsequent civilian career as an accountant for Clarks Shoes, but also by a state pension. By this time Harry had left Yeovil and moved back to live with Dennis in Wells, but life in his new home became increasingly intolerable. 'Dennis would come home, have the tea which I prepared for him, shower, change, and go to the pub with his friends. He soon turned alcoholic, whisky and brandy, never beer, and that destroyed him.' Dennis grew progressively difficult to live with. He began to sell off family heirlooms, including Harry's own Great War medals. 'Eventually he sold everything that he could lay his hands on, all the silver, so he could drink whisky with his friends.'

In 1980, Harry met a widow called Jean and soon afterwards they were married, moving to Valley Close in Wells. Harry married partly, as he himself admits, to escape life at home. 'To be honest, I married to get out of my son's way; you couldn't live with him.' Jean was about Harry's age, and had moved from rather poor accommodation in Wells to sheltered housing, close to where Harry had been living.

It was shortly after Harry and Jean married that a chance conversation with a friend took Harry abroad for the first time since the Great War. He returned to France, not to the battlefields of his youth but to those of World War II.

A friend of mine in Street, who was part-owner of a coach company, phoned me one night and said, 'We've had a cancellation for two people who were going to Normandy to see the beaches. Would you like to take it up?' After much thought I said that we would, and my wife and I went to France. I didn't really give it enough thought and what I saw made me regret going. The experience was more than enough for me, and I was shocked at my reaction. The tour took us to see the beaches where the men had landed, and the Mulberry Harbour which had been built to supply the troops. We saw the German dugouts and the gun emplacements, some of which had been blown to pieces by our fleet out at sea, but it was the cemeteries that I found too much to bear.

We went to one American cemetery, above Omaha Beach. I met an attendant looking after the graves and he told me there were 9,500 Americans buried there. I surveyed the scene and I thought how I must have known some of them. I stood in the pathway, gravestones on each side of me, but I could not bring myself to walk down among the graves. I stood and I cried, and some people helped me up the steps to a pavilion with more names, those of the missing, all round. Those GIs that I had known, none of them by name of course, but their names were all round me, no doubt about it, and I sat there as the people from the coach trip went off, walking through the cemetery. I looked at those tombstones; they didn't die a normal death, they were shot, bayoneted or torn to pieces with shrapnel. Many must have died a terrible death, and those tombstones took on an entirely different light to me. At that moment I felt there could not be a god, and I became an agnostic. Those 9,500 men must have prayed that they would go home safe, and their families prayed as well, but it was decided that they should not live. I thought, too, of the differences between the blacks and the whites in Somerset, and the problems between them, but they must have been as one when they landed in France to fight, and they were certainly as one in this cemetery; no distinctions here.

It was doubly hard to see such wasted life. My own son at home had served in the navy throughout the war and had been fortunate enough to come through when others hadn't, but he was drinking his life away. I was glad to get out and go back home, and I swore that I would never go abroad again.

Shortly afterwards, back in Wells, Dennis came round to our house. He was in a bad way. He pulled his trousers up, and I could see his legs were very badly swollen. We picked up the phone and got the doctor to see him. I was approached by one of Dennis' boozing friends and he told me Dennis had sclerosis of the liver. My son had never told me anything. We spoke to a doctor and decided to get him to London to see a specialist. I asked what would happen if they couldn't do anything for him; then what? The doctor said, 'I'll give him a fortnight to live.' He went to King's Cross Hospital and he lived eight days. He was sixty-one.

After Dennis died, I told my solicitor I didn't want any money from my son's estate and it was passed to Roy, including the house Dennis had bought. The car went to one of his boozing friends.

The death of Harry's elder son was compounded soon after by the death of his second wife. His marriage lasted just four years before Jean died of cancer. The distress over Dennis had led to a confrontation between Harry and his other son, Roy. A rift developed between them that was never healed, and for the last twenty years of Roy's life they never spoke. Roy died of cancer in 2002.

By the mid-1980s, Harry was on his own once again, though he continued to be supported by long-term as well as new friends. His neighbours in Wells, Fred and Betty Isaacs, were particularly close, and they helped Harry through many of the dark days. When Fred eventually died in 1988, Harry returned the kindness he had been shown and cared for Betty. 'They had two bedrooms in their house and if Betty was ever ill I used to go and stay in their spare bedroom. Fred had asked me before he died, if anything happened to him, to look after Betty. I promised I would. I said, "For what you've done for me since my wife died, yes, I will", never expecting to live as long as I have.'

By the mid-1980s, interest in the Great War had begun to grow, as people became aware that the number of veterans was diminishing rapidly. The seventieth anniversaries of the battles of the Somme and of Passchendaele were commemorated widely in the press and on television, but Harry was not interested.

I didn't meet any old comrades from the regiment after the war and I made a point not to watch war films. Anything to do with war on television, and I turned it off straightaway.

Even when I finally appeared on television talking about the war in 1998, well, to be honest, I slept through most of it. I didn't even like the old wartime songs, because they brought back too many memories, and Passchendaele was about as deeply buried at the back of my mind as I could possibly make it.

While Harry's war experiences remained dormant in his mind, his vast knowledge of Somerset and particularly the now-closed quarries was increasingly in demand. In 1990, aged ninety-two, he helped geologists from Bath University explore the ground under Combe Down. Council interest in the quarries and their potential danger to the village was growing. In the Firs Field, where the war memorial stands and where local children played, a light hole or ventilation shaft was exposed by the fall of a beech tree during a storm. It revealed the floor of a quarry just twenty feet below the surface. Immediate action was needed. Harry, wearing hard hat and dungarees, was taken underground. It was the first time he had been down there in seventy years, and he was featured in the local press for the first time. 'Henry (aged 92) shows the way' the local paper trumpeted, and reported that Harry not only helped check the underground workings for Bath City Council, but showed them a quarry that no one else knew even existed. The trip revealed several roof falls, including one that Harry judged to be below the important road junction of Richardson Avenue and The Avenue. Urgent repairs were undertaken, including a concrete cap to seal the light hole in the Firs Field, and Harry's opinion was frequently sought. It was the first time that Harry's age was significant, for few people still alive had such a thorough knowledge of the quarries, most of which had been sealed to prevent access for more than sixty years.

Despite much private sadness, Harry remained resolutely positive, and with Betty he began once more to travel around the United Kingdom and Ireland. They travelled by coach tours organized by a company in Shepton Mallet.

Locally, we went to Ilfracombe, Bodmin, Westward Ho! We also went to places as different as London and Llandudno. Later, we travelled to Cork, then all round the Ring of Kerry, while another trip took us as far as Fort William in Scotland. Eventually, Betty became too frail to tour and in time the doctor told her that she should give up her independence. She must go where somebody would look after her around the clock, and that's why we came here to the residential home, over ten years ago now, and here I am today.

LIFE BEGINS AT 100

They say life begins at forty, don't they? Well, for me it began again at 100. On that day, back in 1998, the home had a big party for my birthday, and it was after that, that I suddenly started being contacted by newspapers and television, and it hasn't really stopped since.

People talk to me about that war. I find it easier to talk about it now, having talked since 1998, but until that birthday I wouldn't mention it. I didn't mention the war even to my first wife and we were together for fifty-seven years. I don't think she had any idea about my service, and never brought it up. Now it is usually all people want to talk about, and I'm tired of talking about it. I appreciate the fact that people want to write to me about that time, but it's too much: photographs, autographs, letters asking for an interview, you get fed up. I'm not available!

I've been told that I'm the last survivor of the trenches, the last fighting Tommy; I like that title. Henry Allingham, who is a couple of years older than me, was air force, so I think I am the only one left who actually lived and served in the trenches. My entire generation fought that war and

I've turned out to be the last, and it does make you wonder. I read that one woman who died recently was 116. I shan't make that, but 109 – fingers crossed.

Going back to France was nothing I ever thought I would do, and certainly not at 105 years old. I was asked on many occasions whether I would consider going back and I said, 'Never', but in the end, I don't know why, I decided to go and I'm pleased that I did. Seeing Ypres again and the battlefields was very emotional. I've been back by coach with Genesta, a battlefield group, and when I first went back I travelled with two other veterans, Jack Davis and Arthur Halestrap. Jack was Duke of Cornwall's Light Infantry as well, and we formed a bond. We visited the cemeteries, and the places where the effects of war can still be seen, and I have returned to Pilckem Ridge. The first time I went back there, we drove to my Divisional Memorial, the 20th Division. I was on a coach and we parked opposite, and the idea was that I would lay a wreath to the memory of my dead friends, but I couldn't. I looked from the window and the memories flooded back and I wept, and the wreath was laid on my behalf.

I've also been to Toc H in Poperinge, visiting the chapel at the top of the building where Tubby Clayton held his services. I don't know if either Jack or Arthur ever went there during the war. Now they are both gone, and I've had no desire to go back again, and it's harder to go, physically, in any case.

I'm aware that it's the ninetieth anniversary of Passchendaele in 2007 and I don't know whether I will be able or willing to go, although no doubt someone will suggest a trip. I never thought I would return to the Ypres salient in the first place, and each time I have returned I have said and accepted that it would be my last visit. I don't feel the need to go. I know that Arthur Halestrap always felt it was his duty to go until the end, but I don't know, we shall have to see. Each visit has been that much more exhausting and, coming towards 109 years of age, perhaps it will be just too much.

My last visit was in late 2004. The BBC were making their series about the last Tommies and I was asked if I would meet a German veteran, Charles Kuentz. My first reaction was 'no' but I came round to the idea. Charles was conscripted just like myself and fought for the Kaiser as I had fought for the King, relations, of course, cousins, so it was a family affair. It shows you how stupid war is.

I shall never forget the German cemetery at Langemarck and the British cemetery at Tyne Cot. I went with Charles and I put a wreath of poppies on one of the German graves. He couldn't speak English; his father was born French but he lived in Alsace, and Charles was conscripted into the German army, and he fought against me. We had an interpreter, and we exchanged presents: I gave him a bottle of Somerset cider and he gave me a tin of Alsatian biscuits. I was glad I met him before he died, a few months later.

War is organized murder and nothing else. Charles told me that he was ordered to fire his artillery gun; it was nothing personal, he said. He couldn't see what he was firing at, and it was just done by coordinates. I told him that we fired at the legs and didn't aim to kill, and that was the truth. I enjoyed the meeting; we had lunch together on Kemmel Hill where he had served at one time, and toasted each other and shook hands. I was very happy to shake his hand. Later that evening, we went together and sat under the Menin Gate in Ypres, side by side, during the 8 p.m.

ceremony there. I never felt sorry for the Germans during the war, but I did for Charles. I felt sorry for what he had to go through; no one deserved to go through that war.

Each evening under the Menin Gate they play the Last Post, and when I was there they asked me to say the oration, 'They shall grow not old, as we that are left grow old . . .' But that is not what Tubby Clayton taught us. He used to say, 'With proud thanksgiving let us remember our brethren who fell', and then he would say, 'They shall grow not old . . .' They always miss that line out and I don't know why. That was the prayer we always used to finish those meetings with at Toc H, and they always leave out that little bit under the Gate, and I think that is wrong, so I've made a point of saying it.

It always amazes me how much interest there is in the Great War. You only have to see all those people standing under the Gate when they sound the Last Post to see what I mean. I also know there are issues that still stir up much controversy. Was Field Marshal Haig any good? I've given my view on that subject. One thing I will say is that I'm glad to see they are pardoning those men who were shot at dawn, but that's just a personal opinion. There was a veterans' day held at No. 10 Downing Street recently and I spoke to the Prime Minister. I said the people who were shot at dawn as cowards, they were no cowards. I said you get a shell and the concussion robs you of all powers of movement for two or three minutes. Since then I've read in the papers that the sentences had been repealed because of a court ruling over one family's father. They should never have been shot. What about the relatives left behind? We say on Remembrance Day, 'They shall grow not old, age shall not weary them . . .' All right, remember the dead, but I also remember the people left behind, mourning.

For me, 11 November is just show business. Take the Armistice Day celebrations that night on television; it is nothing but a show of military force, that's all. I don't think there is any actual remembrance except for those who have lost someone they really cared for in either war. That day, the day I lost my pals, 22 September 1917 – that is my Remembrance Day, not Armistice Day. I'm always very, very quiet on that day and I don't want anybody talking to me, really.

From 1918 until he died in the 1970s, I kept in touch with the no. 1 on our Lewis gun, Bob Haynes. On the Somme, in the last months of the war, he had been injured in the shoulder and had come back to England. After the war he worked on industrial electrical engines, settling down in Henley-on-Thames before eventually moving to London. We never met again but we occasionally wrote. We both kept faith with our understanding that we would never write and tell the families of those who died in our team exactly what had happened. I mean, there was nothing left, nothing left to bury, and I don't think they would have wanted to know that.

When I received the Légion d'Honneur, in 1999, I received it not for my own good. I received it in memory of the three friends I lost, and that's why I wear it. My friends earned it more than me. We had a little ceremony here at the home, and Major Watson from the British Legion came and pinned on the decoration. It is a very prestigious honour, I know. I was also told by someone that when I wear it I am entitled to free public transport in France, and one or two other things besides, but I don't know if that's true or not.

I don't know what they intend to do in France, but there
is an idea about giving a state funeral to the last veteran in
Britain. The newspapers came and asked me what I
thought, telling me it would be something like Churchill's,
but then he was a great Prime Minister. I said that the
honour must be given to a veteran who had seen action on
the Western Front, not to anyone who happened to be in
uniform when the war ended. Overall, the idea was all right,
I suppose, wanting to honour the generation who fought,
but I wasn't interested. I don't know what Henry Allingham thinks. He wants his body left to medical science, does
he? Well, there you are then. It's not for me. I want to be
buried in Monkton Combe alongside my family in the
churchyard. I've been back there recently. As you walk
along the path, you pass on the left the grave of William
John and Elizabeth Patch, my parents, who were also
married in the church. A little further along, there is
George, my eldest brother, and his wife Lilian, and also
my middle brother, William Thomas Patch, and Hilda
Ann, his wife. So why would I want to be anywhere else?

I am very fortunate to have such good friends who take
me out. I know the area so well that I show them little cuts
through, and back lanes that most people do not know. I
usually give a running commentary. History, geology and
archaeology have been my fascination all my life, and I can
give a guided tour to whoever happens to be taking me
round. There are Roman remains everywhere, there are rock
formations that are two million years old, and further away
in the Mendip Hills there is an extinct volcano, Emborough
Pool, and the other extinct volcano is Bath itself, hence the
famous springs. Going back to my home village of Combe
Down is lovely. Nick Fear has taken me back on a couple of

occasions to the house I was born in, and I can look up to my childhood bedroom and to the little ornate Victorian grill my father placed on the concrete sill outside to stop his toddler son from falling out. Last time I was in Combe Down I saw that the war memorial is in the middle of a construction site. They are not building; rather, they are filling the empty quarries below with concrete. The council is pouring concrete – and tens of thousands of pounds – into the old workings to shore them up, and at the same time thirty-ton lorries pass over these quarries and shake the roof to pieces. Best of luck, is all I can say. According to one man I met, it would take a ten-ton lorry every ten minutes for eleven years to fill it up. There are sixty-two acres of quarries underneath Combe Down, and that's only one part of the entire system which stretches for thousands of yards in every direction.

I am fortunate to have kept my eyesight so I can enjoy all these things. Otherwise, you'll have to ask the doctor how I am physically. All I can say is that I feel all right. I've currently got an infection on my arm which I went to see the doctor about. Whatever I had, it was itching like mad, and in scratching my arm I've managed to infect the skin, so he tells me, but a bit of cream in the morning is clearing that up. Otherwise, I'm in pretty good shape.

When I was wounded, well, it must have been as I fell down, this ankle here, I don't know whether I sprained it or fractured it; either way it has never been right since. It has always been swollen, and if I used to walk on it too long, it was a bit painful. I also have a small scar where the shrapnel was taken out. When I told a doctor recently and showed him where it was, he told me that a quarter of an inch deeper and I would have bled to death. Even now I occasionally get pain from it. Sometimes if I stretch, I can feel there is something there, an ache, that's all, nothing regular about it. It comes and goes when it wants to.

And that's about it. The memories remain, of course. In the home right opposite my room upstairs there's a linen cupboard and the girls who are on night duty often go to store away folded sheets and, until recently, when I was lying in bed at night and the nurse switched the light on outside my room, if I was half asleep and half awake, I was back on that battlefield; there was the flash. Now the staff have blacked out that top window, so I don't have that problem any more.

I don't take any tablets, except one for iron; they say I'm short of iron. I see other residents here swallowing handfuls of tablets, and they are thirty years younger than I am. I have hearing aids in both ears, and I have reading glasses, but I don't use them now, not since my cataracts were done. I went into hospital for that small operation and I was quite tense about it as it was the first time I'd had an operation since 1917; otherwise I have never been in hospital, not as a patient, anyway. I have lived in the countryside all my life; fresh air, perhaps that's the secret. I've hardly ever seen a doctor either, no broken bones as a child.

I don't drink alcohol any more; I saw what it did to my boys. I smoked a pipe until I was sixty, Royal Seal tobacco, but I gave it up after I was taken ill at work and had to go home. My wife called a doctor; it wasn't my own doctor, he was a Czech. Anyway, he gave my wife a tablet, and said, 'Give him this and on no account wake him. Let him wake naturally.' She gave me that tablet Thursday night, and I woke Saturday morning as right as rain. What I had, I don't know.

What is the secret of a long life? No idea. I wish I could tell you. I'm happy and that is all that concerns me today. I don't have any ambitions now. I achieved what I wanted when I became a Member of the Royal Sanitary Institute, when I wanted to be either a building inspector or a sanitary engineer. I am glad to see my family and friends, and I'm glad that I have had the chance to be reunited with relatives with whom I had lost contact. Otherwise, it's a day at a time.

They will have written their pieces in the papers for when I finally go; the last trench fighter has to be newsworthy. I've seen obituaries of other veterans and there is now only Henry Allingham and myself in this country who served on the Western Front, and one British man in Australia, so you tell me. Can you imagine how it feels to be one of the last ones? Always hearing that another has just died, then another and another, waiting to hear who's gone and always wondering if you're next. Well, if they've written the obituary, all I can say is that I hope to live long enough that they will have to update it, and more than once! Then I can fade away. Isn't that what old soldiers are meant to do?

EPILOGUE

HARRY: HIS FAMILY AND FRIENDS

The author talked to Harry's friends, family and, in one case, a work colleague. Each had a different perspective on Harry's life and personality; together they represent over three hundred years of personal and affectionate contact. Their insights help to complete the picture of Harry and the influence he has had on a wide range of people throughout his long life.

May Cooper, daughter of George Patch, and Harry's niece, born 1918

I got a letter recently from Uncle Henry. I've not seen him since he was about 103, as my health is not good and it's difficult for me to get out. I'll be eighty-nine next birthday myself. He signed the letter 'Uncle Henry' which pleased me, because I notice everyone refers to him as Harry now on television, or Hal. Well, he was always Uncle Henry as far as I was concerned.

The Patch family was what I would call a proper nature family because they all loved and understood the natural environment. This stemmed directly from Granddad. From my earliest childhood, I can remember a big glass case in the sitting room of my grandparents' house and inside was every kind of stuffed bird you could think of, perhaps forty or fifty that he had collected over the years: jays, robins, blackbirds and goldfinches, and another case had a squirrel inside. As a child I used to look intently at all these creatures and learn about the wildlife.

Granddad was a wonderful gardener. He grew fruit, even grapes, and vegetables, and the two greenhouses were always full of flowers, geraniums and orchids. As well as the bees he kept and the animals he reared, I know that Granddad was keen on rabbiting. It was only after he died, when his sons were sorting out his affairs, that they found his gun. No one was sure whether it had ever been licensed, so they threw it down Granny's well.

This love of the countryside was transmitted to all three boys. Father and I walked for miles around Combe Down and Midford, and I don't suppose there's a walk around here that we didn't cover. He would talk to me about the flowers and the wildlife, show me the different leaves, and the mushrooms you could eat safely and those that were deadly. We'd walk down the valley to Tucking Mill and the canal. It wasn't as overgrown as it is today, and we'd pick sloes and make sloe gin.

Granny was a lovely person, too. After Granddad died, I used to pop round two or three times a day and would often find her sitting contentedly in her arbour near the back door, a shaded place surrounded by sweet-smelling jasmine. I always went in very gingerly so as not to frighten her, as she was stone deaf. She lived on her own until she died aged ninety-four, and managed to look after herself very well. Uncle Bill could get to Granny's house by a little path that ran directly to her back door, and he would often walk over and help put her to bed. Only when she was nearing the end of her life was her bed brought downstairs into the sitting room, and then everything else was moved out to make space, including that glass case with the birds in. I think it was eventually given to the Scouts.

We all used to visit Granny to make sure she was all right. She lived on a pension of just five shillings a week, so if she needed a new pinafore I would go to Bath and buy one, knocking a bit off the price as she would have been horrified had she known what they cost.

I'm making it sound like village life was idyllic, which it wasn't. It was wonderful in many senses, but just ordinary, too, nothing special. The world has changed so much even since the 1950s when all the family looked after one another, and it was all part and parcel of village life. When I was a child, there were thirty shops in Combe Down, including a butcher, baker, tailor, a dairy, but they've slowly disappeared and now there are just two, the Co-op and a newsagent. There were once five pubs; there are just a couple now and the Post Office closed two years ago. The only shop that has opened up since then is an estate agent's; it's a sign of the times.

The quarries and the work they gave were once the lifeblood of the village, but even when I was a child they had practically all gone as a viable industry. Now, those same quarries are threatening the village and the council is spending millions to shore them up. There's a quarry underneath my sitting room, and I get letters all the time from engineers wanting to inspect my house for subsidence. It's always been a threat. Granddad had a problem with some building work years before I was even born. He went to check under the house and found a large amount of cut stone down there, abandoned, so he used it in the building of nos 4 and 5 Gladstone Place; he clearly wasn't overly concerned about the quarries back then and he was a master mason.

His sons followed him into the building business, all with different skills. My father was a wonderful joiner. Like Uncle Henry, he served an apprenticeship at J. Long and Sons and he made some beautiful furniture. I have a wonderful fireguard here with me now, and he also made me a doll's house with all the individual pieces, chairs and tables, in minute detail. I often thought that perhaps the three boys could have gone into partnership together, but they never did.

Margaret Ffoulkes, George Atkins' daughter and Harry's god-daughter

Harry, or Henry, as I know him, has always called me 'my little girl' from as far back as I can remember, and he refers to me in the same way today, and I'll be eighty-five later this year. Last year, on Henry's 108th birthday, he had a party at a restaurant and he gave his 'little girl' a bowl of flowers, roses and carnations. I cried for several minutes and he cried too, I don't know why, but it meant such a lot. I placed the flowers in the memorial window in our local church in North Wales, and I was delighted to see that they lasted for several weeks.

Uncle Henry was lifelong friends with my father, George Atkins, right from school days, and was best man at my parents' wedding in 1921, and so a natural choice as my godfather. He held me, so he has told me, when I was just half an hour old, and we have remained close ever since. He is a very, very loyal and honest friend and a counsellor to me even now, and very witty as well. To me he was always Uncle Henry, and his wife, Aunt Ada, indeed our families were so close that it wasn't until I was about twelve that I discovered they weren't blood-related at all.

I was a very naughty child, pulling the heads off four rows of leeks in a neighbour's garden, or letting mother's canary fly free from the cage; I had a thing about cages and so did the canary, because it never came back. I would get a good wallop, of course, and Mother would tell me, 'Your sister wouldn't do it.' My sister was terribly spoilt, and I frequently fought with her and when things got too much I would say that I was going to run away, but I would go no further than down the lane to Uncle Henry's house. Aunt Ada was always sympathetic. 'Oh, she's a little cat,' she would always say of my sister, in her strong Birmingham accent. Of course, my parents always knew where I was going and in due course Dad would come and get me.

Each year we went to Uncle Henry's for Boxing Day, and in the summer we would all holiday together at Boleaze's Cove, near Weymouth. At the end of his garden, Henry had built himself a little caravan which he hitched on to the back of his Austin Seven, with Terry, the white-and-brown spotted wire-haired terrier, in the back. We thought Henry was very posh, camping in a caravan. My father followed in a Morgan. My sister and I were sent by trailer as our seats in the car were used to carry the large ex-army bell tent and its gear that my family slept in. It was a blissful childhood, walking and cycling for miles, every year, all of us together. In fact, when war broke out in September 1939, that was the first year that the Patch family was not with us. During the war, my father was an air-raid warden manning the telephone in the church hall, while Uncle Henry was in the fire service with its headquarters at the vicarage stables.

My father spoke very little about the First War unless asked. He joined the Somerset Yeomanry but transferred to the Royal Army Medical Corps because he wanted to be a non-combatant. I don't think Henry wanted to fight either, but he went in any case. Henry was a quiet man, in fact I never saw him get annoyed – I don't know if he could get angry, because he would always want to reason – but I would see him often having very long and meaningful conversations with my father. What about, I don't know, but I never heard Henry speak about the war either, and I somehow doubt they ever spoke about it. We were to forget about the war, and although I remember seeing Dad wearing his medals on Armistice Day, the day of remembrance itself was something for the men; children were not involved that I can recall.

Derek Andrews, apprentice plumber under Harry Patch

School broke up at the end of July, and two weeks later, on 14 August 1943, my fourteenth birthday, I started work for E.R. Carter's, then the biggest plumbing and heating firm around. When I started, the boss had only three or four men actually at work, because all the rest had been called up in the forces. There wasn't too much heating to do, more plumbing jobs, because there weren't new buildings or installations going up because of the war. While the scope of jobs was reduced, there was, nevertheless, so much demand that you were forever running from one job to another; because there weren't enough plumbers around for you to take your time, you had to rush into everything.

I was what was known as a boy mate. The boss gave evening classes to the young lads to show them the As and Bs of the business, but he never signed on apprentices, not officially, because that way he could get rid of you if you were no good. That's how he looked at it. As a consequence, my wages were very little indeed, not much more than one shilling and two pence a day, so I was on an apprentice's wages without ever being called an apprentice.

There were always half a dozen of us boy mates to go with one of the experienced heating engineers or plumbers. As the war ended, more plumbers became available to be taken on and I was sent with Harry Patch who had recently joined the firm. My job was to watch what Harry was doing, and eventually I would go and practise it myself. It wasn't his job actually to show you as such, because you could see what he was doing. Nevertheless, you had to have confidence to do plumbing, especially when you are dealing with water in private houses! So you've got to be really confident in what you are doing before you start.

Harry never had any transport, not that I can remember. He always came in on the bus from Compton Dundon, where he lived, and whenever possible he preferred to walk everywhere, and was a quiet man. We had a pick-up driver. He drove the van and would take all the materials to the next job, and would take you too if he had room. Otherwise, I can remember carrying Harry's tool bag all round Yeovil; you couldn't get any lower than that, walking round Yeovil with a tool bag.

A plumber's tool bag was pretty weighty back then. There were wrenches for the steel pipes: you could get them in different sizes, 8-inch, 10-inch, 12-inch, 14-inch, right up to 24-inch, and you carried three or four of these as well as pliers, hammers and wood chisels, and a blowlamp for the lead joints, because it was all lead or steel then, no copper piping; even the waste pipes underneath sinks were lead, not plastic like today. Yeovil is quite a big town and our business place was right down one end, in Henford. If you had to climb an incline like Mudford Road, you had half a mile uphill carrying this bag, and by the time you got halfway up, you were looking to Harry to take the bag out of your hands.

The boss's mate was the Somerset County Engineer, a chap he went to college with, so we had all the educational buildings in this area to maintain because his mate gave them to him. I would be assigned to the plumbers according to what jobs were available on the day. I could be with Harry for weeks, until such time as someone else needed two mates on another job. Harry would be given a job card, and we would tackle one job after the other, I suppose six or seven in a day. If Harry was working underneath a sink, he would want this tool and that, and I would hand him the tools, and similarly if he was up a ladder or a pair of steps; wherever the plumber went, you went. That was the life back then of a boy mate.

If you see Harry, remember me to him and tell him my arm still bloody aches from carrying his tool bag.

David Isaacs, son of Betty Isaacs, Harry's neighbour
Harry was great friends with both Mum and Dad, and, when Dad died, Harry more or less took over the care of

Mum. He'd known them both for many years, through the church and clubs, and I know that the day Dad died, Harry brought Mum up to see him.

They were all neighbours in a sheltered housing scheme in Wells. Harry was ninety-three at the time of Dad's death, and he took it upon himself to mow not only his own lawn, front and back, but Mum's too. In fact, as Mum became less and less able, he did everything for her, washing, ironing, shopping. He looked after Mum for many years and he was devastated when she died in 2001. His second wife had died many years before. She had been bed-ridden with cancer for a long time and Harry looked after her with total devotion. I think that is Harry through and through. He needs someone to look after, someone he can concentrate on, and this is when the gentleman in him comes out best. I was so pleased when Doris arrived at the home later that year, after Mum died. I think that saved him.

There is a natural fighter in Harry. His experiences in the war made him want to fight for justice, and I think they changed his attitude to life. But his instinct to fight is not something entirely derived from the war; I think it comes from his nature when, as a child, he learnt to stand on his own two feet.

When I first knew Harry, in the early 1980s, he was the champion of local causes. He hates injustice and because of that he never hesitated to write letters to the council or the local newspaper, usually firing on all cylinders when he did so. On the ring road, the council proposed to put in traffic lights which Harry felt would only hamper and not relieve congestion, causing more problems for local people. Harry and Mum did their shopping down the high street and frequently struggled to get across the road. So he fought the proposal. In the end, he lost. Nevertheless, a pedestrian crossing was put in. There was another time when permission was sought by local people to erect a communal hut on some open ground. The council refused the proposal and Harry took up the cause but lost that, too. You'll have to ask him which campaigns he won! He was a one-man band, and that helped him remain active.

One day, Harry and Mum went on an outing. As they came through the front door, Mum tripped and fell, damaging her hip very badly. Harry redoubled his efforts to look after her, but he was probably ninety-eight by this time and I was frequently called to go up and help. Then one day he said, 'David, I want you to make arrangements for us to go into the residential home, we've decided that it's time.' As it happened, a double room was available and Harry and Betty moved in. Both homes had to be cleared quickly. I called in a house-clearing company and they came round and took all the furniture from both houses. It was heartbreaking; a lifetime's possessions gone. The men were breaking the furniture up as it was being taken from the house. They offered £100 for the lot, but Harry wanted to get rid of everything; as he said, he couldn't use it any more; but I don't know what he thought of the money, I really don't.

June Beeching, niece of Harry's first wife, Ada, born June 1933

My mother, Winifred, was the youngest of six children, one of whom was Ada, my aunt, who married Harry in 1919. When I was a child we often went to visit my aunt, but over time, as Ada died and then my mother died, we somehow lost touch with Uncle Hal, as we called him. I don't quite know how it happened. I suppose people move house; I know we moved to Devon, and after a while you just assume that all that generation has gone.

When the BBC1 programme *The Last Tommy* came on, I'd actually seen the name Harry Patch on the screen, but as he had always been Uncle Hal to us the penny did not drop that it could actually be him. I was in the living room with my back to the television, as I had turned to get something out of the bureau. Suddenly, I heard his distinctive voice and it made me feel quite peculiar; it was quite a shock, and I was very still for a moment. I remember thinking, 'Oh my goodness, it's Uncle Hal, but then it can't be.' Hal had quite a few relations in Somerset and I wondered if it could be one of them. So I picked up the phone and rang my daughter, and Daniel, my grandson, answered. I said, 'Get your mother to put the TV on to BBC1 straightaway and I'll ring a bit later.' I didn't say anything else because I didn't want her view to be coloured by anything I said. I went back and watched again, and the more I watched, the more I thought, it is him, it is, but at the same time I thought it can't be, because of his age. We thought he had died a long time ago. My daughter rang back. 'Do you think Uncle Hal is still alive?' I asked. She said, 'Surely not', and my husband doubted it was Hal, too, but I was convinced it was him. It wasn't what he looked like, it was his voice that convinced me; that hadn't changed at all since we'd last met in the late 1970s. In the *Western Morning News* there was an article about Hal. Other newspapers ran stories and we took a look at everything. One newspaper said Hal had lost touch with all his relatives and that his two boys had died. I had no idea of any of this; it was very sad. Another went on to mention his friend Nick Fear. I went to the local library and explained the situation and they gave me two telephone numbers, neither of which was correct, and after that the trail went cold for a while. Then, when it was Uncle Hal's birthday, he appeared again and I went back to the library, explained the situation once more and asked if there was a local British Legion which could help. They gave me the number of the Bridgwater branch, and one of the members, as it turned out, visited Harry. I explained I wanted to send a birthday card and he promised to see that he got it. I wrote and put one or two things in about the past, just to prove it was me. I mentioned the thatched cottage near Somerton where we'd all been as a family, and where I used to cook up baby potatoes in a large copper for Uncle Hal's pigs. I thought, 'It will tell him that I am who I say I am.' Shortly afterwards, I got a letter which said how pleased he was to hear from me.

A visit was arranged, and we went to his residential home. He was sitting on a sofa and I just walked straight up to him and said, 'Hello, Uncle Hal, you look very well . . .' And we went from there. It was marvellous to see him looking so fit and well. Nick brought Hal down to see us, and we've been each month since then and hope to go again before Christmas. He seems to have perked up even more since we got in touch; I don't know, perhaps it's my imagination, but it feels like that.

Jeremy Banning, close friend

Harry was always adamant that he wouldn't meet a German veteran, so it was a surprise when he changed his mind. He doesn't make an instant decision, he needs space to think.

So he mulled over the idea and by the time he agreed to meet Charles Kuentz, he wasn't nervous at the prospect, he was looking forward to it. By 2004, he'd been back to Belgium twice, and he knew that the whole trip would be tailor-made to be as easy as possible for him.

The meeting was filmed for a BBC1 documentary, *The Last Tommy*, and the production company provided three of us with a people carrier as it was easy for Harry to get in and out. We kept an eye on him through the rear-view mirror, and when he fell asleep we were glad that he was at ease with his surroundings and with us.

When he's out of context, Harry doesn't necessarily stand out and isn't recognized, but when he's at the Menin Gate memorial in Ypres, he's mobbed, people standing six deep wanting to shake his hand and say how proud they are to meet him; one or two want to tell him about their own relatives who fought. It can get overwhelming, although Harry never seems to find it too much. On several occasions, I've been handed money by people, total strangers, who say, 'Make sure Harry has a drink on me.' But he doesn't drink, so he gives it to the British Legion. I always joke with him, that he's the most photographed man in Belgium, and he just smiles and says, 'yeah', as only he can.

The first time I looked after Harry was in 2002 when he went back to Pilckem Ridge. That day he was too distressed to leave the bus and lay a wreath. When I helped him to bed, he said, 'I was a bit wobbly today.' So we sat on the edge of the bed and talked about it for an hour, one to one, away from the hotel bar and the general hullabaloo downstairs. It's the time veterans are most likely to give you their thoughts, and that talk with Harry is a very precious memory.

In September 2004, we reached Belgium and stayed overnight in a small farmhouse in Elverdinghe. Of course Harry, being a countryman, was in his element; given a pregnant cat or a duck with one leg, he's just wonderful. I have a mental image of Harry surrounded by cats, and because his fingers are not as flexible as they once were, the cats pushed against his hand instead of being patted. One or two would get quite playful and Harry would hold up his index finger as if to say, 'Now, that's enough.'

If Harry has a big day ahead of him, such as meeting Charles Kuentz, he'll choose to go to bed at 7 p.m. He's very much in tune with his body and with himself. He knows what pills he needs to take and that he likes to eat little but often. He is also used to a routine, so it's good to keep to that as far as possible.

The following morning, Harry had a big breakfast and was raring to go. The film crew came to see what his thoughts were at meeting a German veteran, but Harry just said, 'I'm all right, looking forward to it.' I think they were hoping he would say much more, but that isn't his way. After the event, he'll give a measured response. I think the meeting with Charles Kuentz helped Harry enormously. It wasn't a momentous occasion, just two very old men meeting, shaking hands and smiling broadly. Charles was very deaf and everything had to be written down and then translated. Perhaps the symbolism of the meeting was more important than what they actually said. At one point Harry was asked if he would still have met Charles Kuentz if Charles had been the one who fired the shell that killed his friends, and without hesitation he said 'Yes.'

Later that day, we drove to Tyne Cot, the largest British cemetery on the Western Front. Harry was much more depressed there, sitting with his hands together under his chin, as if in silent prayer. As he looked around, he could see nearly 12,000 graves, all of them of men who will always remain his peers. Behind, there are panels with the names of another 35,000 men, who simply disappeared in battle. Harry sat there, hunched over, looking almost haunted, deep in thought. It was clear to see in his eyes that he was back in time. It's hard. You don't want to break into his thoughts but you have responsibilities as a carer and you can't leave him there for too long in the cold. It took quite a while for him to perk up.

There are three places at Ypres that Harry is always going to struggle with: Tyne Cot, the Menin Gate and Pilckem Ridge. We always tell Harry, 'We're going to Pilckem Ridge now, OK?' It's only fair to give him warning. To me, it feels as if it is something he has to do. I don't think he gains comfort or pleasure by being there, by seeing that it has been rebuilt or that kids are playing nearby; rather it is simply that he feels he must go. In 2004 there was a grey, leaden sky, and just as he laid the wreath and sat there in contemplation, a shaft of sunlight came out from behind the clouds, and touched Harry's head and the wreath.

Pauline Leyton, manager at Harry's residential home
Harry the soldier, the war veteran, was someone everybody wanted to talk to, but only about the war. They wanted to hear what his experiences had been, and I thought there was nobody who was really just interested in Harry as the whole person. There's an awful lot of Harry as the husband and the father, and as a resident in an elderly persons' home, so I organized with Age Concern that someone would come

down, what they call a befriender, and talk to Harry, to support him.

I often sit down with Harry and we talk and put the world to rights. Equally, if he has a problem, he always comes to the top, to the manager. A few years ago, he said that he was having bad dreams, and that it was all coming back to the fore, memories which he had suppressed or put to the back of his mind. I think it was after his 100th birthday, when people began to come and talk to him, and there was all the interest in the press and the media.

One of the most moving things for me was when he paid his first visit to the Wills Memorial Building in Bristol, the building he had helped construct in the 1920s, and for the first time I really had a realization of what he'd gone through, because he was talking to the television crew, and I saw that so much of his war was inside him, and had never come to the top. It upset me to hear it.

I knew Harry as the man who had come in with his friend Betty back in October 1996. He had made a pact with her husband, before he died, that he would look after Betty. They came in for a trial, for day care, and that didn't quite work, as they were coming in and going home, and it was a lot for them. So we invited them to come in and live here for a while, and that was when I first met him, but of course I had no idea of what he had been through.

I took him twice to launch the Somerset Poppy Appeal at Weston-super-Mare. They always have a different way of launching the appeal and on one visit they had a great big cannon that shot, or rather exploded, the poppies out of the muzzle. Harry had to press the button and of course everybody jumped in shock and Harry didn't stir a muscle. He just said, 'You haven't heard the guns like I have.'

One of the best feelings in life is when you actually achieve something, and in Harry's case it was receiving his honorary degree from Bristol University; at that moment he was right at the top of the pinnacle. When it was offered to him, seeing him there, I'll never forget that as long as I live, his eyes sparkling, looking down on the assembled congregation. The recognition meant so much to him.

Another example was meeting the German soldier, Charles Kuentz. We applied for a passport for Harry, and when it arrived he not only got the passport but an enclosed note from someone at the office saying, 'Dear Harry, I hope you have a wonderful time.' It was funny, no one queried the application to check we'd got his birth date right. It was lovely. I think the trip abroad helped him come to terms with his past.

Nick Fear, close friend
Harry is such a capable and caring man that he likes to answer as many of his letters as he can. In the week after *The Last Tommy* was shown in 2005, he had something like 180 letters from the public. A lot of them were fan mail of the sort that says 'We loved you on the programme, thank you for what you did for us in World War I', but quite a few were asking for answers that Harry couldn't possibly know. Some people were asking, 'My grandfather was in the Great War, did you know him?' Some were in Harry's regiment, the DCLI, but in another battalion; sometimes they were in a completely different regiment, fighting in a different battle on a different continent! But fair enough; some people didn't realize that Harry didn't fight on Gallipoli, or that he didn't know East Africa.

There is a side to Harry that likes the attention, but it

can get too much. Harry was concerned to answer his letters and he just needed a bit of help. I now visit him every couple of weeks and come away with mail that needs answering. He had his double cataract operation on the NHS two years ago, and his eyesight is remarkable. I know that we moan about the NHS, but I am rather proud of that investment in a gentleman of advanced years because it has improved his quality of life tenfold.

Nevertheless, he gets asked the strangest things, such as, 'What cigarettes did you smoke in the trenches?' Recently a gentleman sent a cassette tape and wondered if we could ask Harry about World War I. A few years ago he was happy to talk about it, but now he's fed up, because there was a lot more to his life than just the Great War. The man asked if we could interview Harry on his behalf because he thought it might be therapeutic. It was very kind, but that was the last thing he wanted. We sent the tape back and said we were very sorry but we couldn't help him. Harry has had a request recently from abroad asking for his autograph, or, more accurately, asking for fifteen copies of his autograph, on photographs or bookplates; the writer even included a special pen that signs pictures, but Harry has a problem with arthritis in his writing hand and it pains him to write, so he will nowadays dictate the letter to me and then I'll send it off. Requests for autographs have come so often in the last two years that he's saying no, because he just can't do any more. Inevitably, we have had one or two strange letters, not in a harmful way, but ones where you couldn't quite understand what the writer is talking about. The upside to all the letters is that Harry cuts off the stamps for the Royal National Lifeboat Institution, and of course foreign stamps are the most useful.

FUNERAL ADDRESS BY JIM ROSS

Patch, Harry Patch, that's a good name,
Shakespearean, it might be one of Hal's men
at Agincourt or not far off, although in fact
it starts life and belongs in Combe Down.

These are some of the words Sir Andrew Motion penned
when writing his poem for Harry. And to me they seem to
sum up the wonderful thing about Harry, for he was both a
national icon and, at the same time, an ordinary man – a
retired plumber from Combe Down.

When I first met Harry he took me into a little room in
Fletcher House and told me of his war. It was not a discussion.
Harry told me what he wanted to say and that was it. That was
eleven years ago and we didn't talk of the war again.

There were better things to talk about and some fun to be
had.

I would sit there with Lesley, and Harry would tell us his
stories. There was the one about the train journey to Bristol
Temple Meads. One of his mates was trying to dodge the
fare. A pretty ordinary story you may think, but then you
remember that the train journey was in 1918 and the way of

skipping the fare was by feigning shell shock. The ordinary had become extraordinary.

As Harry grew from being very old to being very very old, his spirit was undaunted. He could charm the ladies. I remember once being with him and his fellow veteran Bill Stone in the Town Hall here some years ago. There were a good number of ladies there. All attractive and all gathered round Harry and Bill. Yes, you know who you are. The ladies knew who the real characters were. Characters formed in Edwardian England. Not fifty-year-old whippersnappers like the rest of us. He was an ordinary man with extraordinary charm.

As Harry's fame increased with his age and the declining number of Great War veterans, so too did the demands on his time and energy. On one occasion he was launching the Somerset Poppy Appeal at Weston. The Royal British Legion had arranged for their poppies to be puffed from a small cannon, but unfortunately had employed a pyrotechnics expert who was a bit over enthusiastic. This poppy launch was becoming exciting. The poppies had become soaked in the rain and were now forming a glutinous and potentially dangerous mass in the cannon from which they would be expelled. The cannon was duly fired with a bang which rattled the windows in Swansea. The gathered crowd collectively jumped out of their shoes. Including Pauline, who had taken Harry to the event. 'Ooo,' she said to Harry, 'Didn't that just scare you something terrible?' Harry looked at her. He pointed that index finder he used so much to help make his point. 'You haven't heard guns, Pauline. Not like I've heard them.' Harry was an ordinary man with extraordinary experiences.

Some years later, Harry was to appear at the Cenotaph with Bill Stone and Henry Allingham to commemorate the ninetieth anniversary of the armistice. Harry didn't want to go up to London the night before. Better by far to sleep in his own bed and make an early start. My instructions having been given I then commenced detailed discussions with my friends in the Ministry of Defence who organise such ceremonies. At all costs, Harry had to be there on time. And the only way to get him through central London was with a police motorcycle escort. At this point may I ask the Chief of the General Staff to allow his attention to wander. The MOD pulled strings which really shouldn't have been pulled and the motorbikes appeared and whisked our limo through central London in a blur of red lights and startled motorists. As we sped past Harrods at 60 mph on the wrong side of the road my wife asked Harry if he was aware of just how many laws we were breaking. 'Oh yes,' he said turning round with a smile which stretched from one ear to the other. 'I know exactly what we're doing!' That was Harry, the ordinary man. One hour later he was representing his generation. Creating images which are seared on our minds. The last Tommy clutching the wreath for his mates. For his Regiment. For his Army. And for the Army that was on the other side. All of their lives were precious to him. They were all victims. He was Harry, the extraordinary man.

I mentioned earlier that Harry had that certain Edwardian character which appealed to the ladies. He could summon the care staff at Fletcher House by looking them in the eye and – using that index finger again – beckon them to him. Gentlemen do not try that at home. Harry could do that for two reasons. First, he was Harry. And second, he was dealing with the staff at Fletcher House. To work there, only angels need apply. For they didn't just care for him. They loved and they cherished him.

And when he grumped, for Harry was an ordinary man,

they put up with him. Harry would have wanted me to say this and to use my finger to emphasise the point. 'Thank you'.

He brought out the best in people. When you are 109 years of age you can't wait several months for new hearing aids. No. You go to a complete stranger, an expert in audiology, and he moves heaven and earth to get you the best there is. Free.

When you are so old that you have decided that its time to go. You bring the best out of people as they spend hour after hour sitting beside you, holding your hand as you sleep.

Harry was honoured by the King of the Belgians, the President of France and the people of Britain. He accepted these honours with great humility, for he knew that they were his only by reason of his great age. He knew he was just an ordinary man.

When Harry had reached 100 he had faced a choice. Put yourself in his position. You have spent eighty years imprisoning the horror of the trenches in the furthest recesses of your mind. But you know that some nights they escape and torture you. You have a choice. Keep it under as much control as you can or let it out. Keep it under control or tell the world what it was really like. Keep it under control or think again of the lad from 'A' Company. Harry let the demons out. And they did their work, emerging in his dreams to torture and torment and terrify him. He didn't 'go public' to become our oldest author or to meet fine people in fancy places and palaces, for Harry was an ordinary man. Harry let it out so that we could hear his message. His message of peace and reconciliation.

I wouldn't have had the courage to make the decision Harry made. Would any of you? No. We are the ordinary ones. Harry was the extraordinary man. The plumber from Combe Down who showed us true heroism. Now, at long long last Harry, you can rest in peace.

ACKNOWLEDGEMENTS

I would like to thank everyone at Bloomsbury, particularly Bill Swainson, the senior commissioning editor, for his belief in the project and his unstinting encouragement, and Emily Sweet for her expert editorial advice and support. I am also grateful to Nick Humphrey, Colin Midson, David Mann, Jessica Yarrow, Lisa Fiske and Polly Napper, all of whom have worked hard to produce and market this book.

I would also like to thank Jason Williams for the rear cover photograph, as well as my good friends Jeremy Banning, Peter Barton and Taff Gillingham for their help and expert knowledge on the Great War. Thanks also to Jim Ross for providing his funeral address to Harry that is a fitting conclusion to the book.

I would particularly like to thank my agent, Jane Turnbull, for all her enthusiasm and constant support throughout this project.

Thank you, too, to the large circle of friends of Harry Patch, many lifelong, including his niece May Patch, the daughter of Harry's eldest brother George; his god-daughter, Margaret Ffoulkes, who has 'known' Harry since she was half-an-hour old; David Isaacs, the son of Harry's beloved neighbour Betty Isaacs; Nick Fear and Lindsay Vasey, his close friends; Jim and Lesley Ross, his frequent visitors; and June and Richard Beeching, who, owing to Harry's numerous television appearances, have been reunited with a relative they both assumed had died a long time ago.

I am grateful to Pauline Leyton, the senior manager of Harry's residential home in Somerset. She has been unfailingly considerate and, with her excellent staff, has been enormously helpful in facilitating my visits and supplying me with numerous cups of coffee and tea.

A big thank you is due to the late Doris Whitaker, Harry's feisty confidant and soulmate, who has been kind enough to let me interview Harry on innumerable occasions. She would have had no need to read this book, as she must have heard every story five times over.

As always, I must thank my wife, Anna, for all her unstinting enthusiasm and her understanding as I disappeared to my study to write. A special thank you to my indomitable mother, Joan van Emden, whose superb knowledge of the English language has helped get rid of errors, daft and otherwise, which crept in.

Lastly, I am grateful to Harry himself. He has been a willing participant in this project from the first day, but could not have expected the regular and extended grilling he underwent as we revisited his 108-year life in detail. 'It's a long time ago,' he would sometimes say, when tiredness stopped him from remembering an event that had taken place perhaps one hundred years earlier. This did not stop him thinking about it, and on my next visit he would often have the answer. Thank you, Harry. It has been a great pleasure to help write your story, or rather, your story so far.

PICTURE CREDITS

I would like to thank the *Bath Chronicle* for their kind permission to use three images taken during the Bath Blitz of 1942, as well as the Imperial War Museum for permission to use the following images: Q2751, C.O.2253, Q5865, Q17654, Q2708, Q2706 and Q8460. Thank you to the Hauptstaatsarchiv, Stuttgart, for permission to use the German aerial image of the Steenbeek taken on 22 July 1917, and to Bristol University for permission to reproduce the image of the topping-out parade at the Wills Memorial Building in 1925. I am grateful to The National Archives for permission to reproduce the aerial image of the battlefield close to Langemarck, August 1917; the image from the 1901 Census return; and a page from the Medal Roll for the Duke of Cornwall's Light Infantry. I should also like to thank Jason Williams for his pictures of Harry Patch and Doris Whitaker, and Harry holding his Légion d'Honneur. Many thanks to Jason Bryant for the picture of Harry around the time of his 110th birthday, Harry reading the order of service at St Paul's and Harry with the Great War Society, and to Rob Wicks for the picture of Harry and myself on the ferry to Belgium. I am very grateful to Jim Ross, Johan Vandewalle and Peter Barton for pictures of Harry in the final years of his life. The pictures of Harry's funeral are courtesy of Getty Images. Thanks to the RNLI for the pictures of Harry's lifeboat, and to Pen & Sword and Roderick Field for the final picture in the plate section. All other images are courtesy of friends and close relatives of the Patch family or from the author's personal collection.

INDEX

THE
SOLDIER'S WAR

Dedicated to my wife Anna and to our wonderful son Benjamin

CONTENTS

ABBREVIATIONS

The following abbreviations are used throughout the text:

Ranks	Units
Brigadier – Brig.	Battalion – Bttn
Captain – Capt.	Battery – Batt.
Company Sergeant Major – CSM	Company – Coy
Corporal – Cpl	Division – Div.
Gunner – Gnr	Machine Gun Corps – MGC
Lance Corporal – L/Cpl	Regiment – Rgt
Lieutenant – Lt	Royal Army Medical Corps –
Lieutenant Colonel – Lt Col	RAMC
Major – Maj.	Royal Engineers – RE
Private – Pte	Royal Field Artillery – RFA
Quarter Master Sergeant – QMS	Royal Garrison Artillery – RGA
Reverend – Rev.	Royal Horse Artillery – RHA
Second Lieutenant – 2/Lt	Yeomanry – Yeo.
Sergeant – Sgt	
Sergeant Major – Sgt Maj.	
Trooper – Trp.	

INTRODUCTION

During the later stages of the Battle of the Somme, Major A. G. P. Hardwick surveyed the morass in front of him. He was standing outside a large dugout which, he was informed, had previously been an enemy bakery. It was situated in a communication trench leading to the front line, a captured German trench. 'The dugout is a huge place,' he recalled, 'and many direct hits have made no effect on it. Its entrances are three, leading in from the trench, and it is below ground level about twenty-five feet.' He admired the technical skill required in its construction, lined as it was with twelve-inch-square timber, both roof and walls; the floor, too, was made of wood. Until they were relieved, it was the temporary home for the 76th Field Ambulance, and in the preceding days Hardwick and his comrades had brought many a casualty in for treatment. The issue had never been the quality of the accommodation, but rather, how, once they had left the dugout and the trench, they might find it again in a largely featureless terrain, blasted into utter submission by shellfire.

'Our landmarks to this place are very few and a compass is going to be indispensable here – our chief marks are in order. (1) Trench-board over a wide trench, (2) Then made due N for a smashed up harrow, (3) A smashed Boche limber cart in a shell hole, (4) Then two dead Huns lying in a shell hole.'

His description reflects the common perception of the Western Front, a place of desolation and destruction, but it is a vision that ignores and excludes all other reality.

Some eighteen months earlier, in 1915, Denis Barnett, a young lieutenant in the 2nd Leinster Regiment, was faced with a similar problem to Hardwick's. In his case, he was leading a working party forward to undertake a job near the firing line at Ypres. In the dark, he had only a few pointers to guide his way, but he had carefully noted them so as to avoid going astray: 'It is a very difficult journey from here to where we are digging, and the "sailing" directions are like this: "across field to haystack; bear half left to dead pig; cross stream 25 yards below dead horse; up hedge to shell hole, and then follow the smell of three dead cows across a field, and you'll arrive at exactly the right place"!'

Both Hardwick and Barnett had, it appeared, an equal chance of getting lost, but there was one stark difference: the terrain in which they were working. The once picturesque Somme had, by November 1916, taken on the mantle of the best moonscape ever fashioned by man. On the other hand, in 1915 the Ypres Salient still maintained its distinctive agricultural feel.

Nearly twenty years ago, I was fortunate enough to travel back to France and Belgium with a friend, Benjamin Clouting, a former trooper in the 4th (Royal Irish) Dragoon Guards. He had served on the Western Front for the duration of the war, and was wounded twice. As we travelled away from the Belgian town of Ypres into the infamous Salient beyond, we stopped to look at the ground where he was wounded in May 1915. Ben peered from the coach window towards the railway cutting where, seventy-five years earlier, he had taken shelter from German shellfire. I remember looking in the same direction. I saw the cutting and in my mind's eye I pictured Ben sitting there, shrapnel in his ankle, surrounded by a marshland, a place of lip-to-lip shell holes and uninterrupted mud. I was not, as I realise now, picturing 1915, but 1917, the world of the Battle of Passchendaele – a landscape I had been educated to expect, from school lessons and Great War poetry. The history of that war was not taught in the context of 1915 but firmly that of 1916 and 1917. Understandably, the 1914–18 war was pictured as horrific, endlessly brutal and at times beyond human endurance. It would have been hard to inspire such a vision had the teacher mentioned the luscious fields of wild flowers – a bee's paradise – or the grass growing wild in uncultivated fields, to be nightly scythed by soldiers. It would not have helped if he had told of agricultural implements lying redundant near unkempt haystacks, of partially intact farm buildings, or intrepid farmers who still sought to harvest a least a little of their crop within sight of the trenches.

The annals of any war, it is said, are told in the history of its great battles, its decisive turning points, primarily military but also political. The rights and wrongs of decisions to launch offensives are still hotly debated, the tactical success or failure of new instruments of war are reviewed and reviewed again. Those key moments in an offensive which were exploited or missed are still argued over, and ideas are developed as to what might have been. And then the history of the battles themselves is told from the point of view of the High Command, and then told again through the voices of those who took part in the fighting at Mons, Gallipoli, Loos, the Somme, Arras, Ypres, Cambrai et al.: they have all had books written about them.

Bombardments, hand-to-hand combat, casualties, mud, blood and guts: they are essential elements in understanding our history and often they are superbly told. But inevitably the momentum behind these tales has been the fighting, sometimes to the exclusion of almost everything else. Yet the extraordinary story of the Great War is as much about the lives the soldiers led when *not* in battle as it is about their time in combat.

It is often said that the British Tommy was 80 per cent bored stiff, 19 per cent frozen stiff and only 1 per cent scared stiff. In assessments made by former soldiers who were there, direct contacts with the Germans in terms of 'battle' days were few and far between, and most of the time they were involved in trench maintenance and observation of a rarely seen enemy.

The Soldier's War is a broadly chronological examination of the Great War, but with a difference. Instead of concentrating primarily on battles, I have looked at the men's everyday lives, drawing out aspects that are rarely mentioned; indeed, they are largely forgotten. These seem to fall into two categories, one of which is intrinsically linked to overseas service itself, such as the problems and the drama of going on leave, or the unrelieved boredom of sitting in the front line waiting for something to happen. The other aspect is scarcely noticed in the books that concentrate on major events: the moments of 'normal' life that the soldier experienced, such as the beauty of a sunset, or the delights of fishing in a river; the adoption of stray farm animals such as a puppy as a pet, or a goat as an unofficial unit mascot. And then there are the more obscure but equally authentic stories that never find a mention elsewhere, such as the finding of prehistoric, Celtic or Roman archaeological souvenirs when thousands of miles of trenches were dug, or where sites of historical interest were uprooted by shellfire.

It is, of course, important to remain balanced. The horror of war is not expunged from this book; far from it. I have chosen a number of the best accounts that I have read to illustrate the brutality of fighting, as well as the terrible nature of the wounds and the remarkable attempts to render assistance to the wounded and to save life. Equally, the purpose of this book is not to challenge any established orthodoxy or set views of the war: there is no thesis to prove here or argument to substantiate. Rather, it is to offer a range of thoughts, perspectives and ideas (which are sometimes contradictory) but which were recorded by the soldiers themselves – that myriad collective of men from all walks of civilian life.

The book teases out their attitudes towards the world around them, their feelings towards the enemy and each other. It highlights the moments of humour and pity, the occasions when the natural world surrounding them refused to depart even from the most desolate of environments, and it features examples of the weird and wonderful, the unlikely, and the seemingly implausible, that inevitably occur when millions of men stand opposite each other across a small strip of no-man's-land. But equally importantly it includes deeply personal insights into their own lives, their hopes, their challenges and predicaments. How they dealt with those challenges in the context of a conflict is what has always fascinated me about the Great War.

On a glorious summer evening in mid-August 1916, Major H. M. Dillon wrote to a friend, with unquestionable glee. He had put off writing until something really exciting happened and at this point, during the Battle of the Somme, he felt that he had reached his moment.

'Guns, guns, guns of every sort and size hammer and pound the Boche line and we continually work forward, killing the devils as we go. This battle is being run on the right lines, I am sure, i.e. for every man we lose, we "out" more than one German . . . There is a suppressed excitement among the men I have never noticed before, an absolute craving to get at the swine. I think they know that the whole nation and Empire are in it now and they feel that the German will is bending.'

A month later, one of Major Dillon's letters struck a slightly different, more reflective tone. He talks of the thousands of tiny lights he can see in the darkness behind the lines, of braziers flaming in the cool evening air; he talks of the colonel's seeming fearlessness in action and of the noise of the distant guns, searching for enemy ammunition dumps and crossroads, and then he adds:

'I watched it [the barrage] for a long time last night, absolutely fascinated, with the watery old moon looking down and saying what d——d fools you men are! Well, there it is, and two thousand years after Christ came on earth, we can't do better than try to kill each other . . .'

It is impossible to say whether this reflects a temporary change of mood or a permanent change of attitude. Nevertheless, a soldier's story can be heavily influenced by mood swings, affected by multifarious battlefield influences, and not just which side of the bed he happened to get out of. Make assumptions about the Great War and the men who fought in it and those assumptions have a habit of coming back to bite you. It is always tempting to claim that soldiers did things 'this way', or that they 'felt like that', when inevitably such a statement courts a reply from someone with plenty of evidence to the contrary. This is hardly surprising. In excess of two million men lived on the Western Front from 1916 onwards, reflecting every hue of society, and so it is difficult to be definitive about anything except to say this was how it was done at that moment in time – probably – and that this was how many men felt – but by no means all.

Because this book is chronological, each year is inevitably given shape by the famous battles, but, while they provide a framework, they are of secondary importance to the individual lives of the characters portrayed. Set-piece battles in the Napoleonic tradition, lasting one or two days, quickly gave way in the Great War to attacks lasting a week or two, then rolling offensives of many months' duration. There would be little point in attempting a blow-by-blow account of the battles of the Somme, Arras or Passchendaele; there would be neither room nor, I suspect, enough readers' patience to justify reproducing endless gory accounts of vicious fighting, well-written though they might be. It is perfectly possible for readers to suffer their own form of battle fatigue.

As the book is organised in this way, then it should follow perhaps that stories should appear roughly in their date order. On the whole this is the case. However, there are occasions where I have sought to develop a theme or idea and have grouped stories together, in such a way that they complement each other and, in the philosophy of this book, to give a balanced perspective on a particular subject. For example, the British fear over enemy spies in and around the trenches is examined and three or four examples given. There would be little point in breaking them up simply because two anecdotes fall in November 1915 and two in January 1916. This said, I have moved stories out of their contextual 'year' only on few occasions and where it makes little or no difference to historical veracity; I would not, for example, place the description of an Allied barrage from 1918 into the chapter on 1915, as the change in the technicalities and the weight of such barrages altered so enormously in those three years.

The Soldier's War overwhelmingly draws its stories and anecdotes from unpublished material: diaries, letters and memoirs. They come from many sources: the established archives such as the Imperial War Museum and the Liddle Collection in Leeds, but also from dozens of regimental archives whose resources are too rarely mined. Private sources have also proved fruitful, and I am grateful to have been given access to a number of diaries and memoirs that have never previously come to light. Occasionally, I have quoted from letters reproduced in books privately published during or shortly after the war. These were of very limited print runs and were primarily put together for the benefit of close family and friends, not for wider circulation. Sadly, the majority of these books were produced by parents in memory of deceased sons, using the letters to create a fitting tribute and a lasting memorial to their service. Only on very exceptional occasions have I used published material, where I have wished to make a very specific point but have failed to locate material evidence from unpublished sources.

In using the soldiers' own words, I have had to make a few small changes. Inevitably, when men wrote diaries or letters under front line conditions, punctuation and grammar were the last things on their minds. In order to make their records easier to read, I have tidied up these aspects from time to time, and changed a word if its repetition seemed cumbersome to the modern reader, or when it referred to other unquoted material and so would not make sense in this context. I have also occasionally modernised the expression: for example, men spelt 'dug out' as two words, or with a hyphen, or, in the more usual way from our point of view, as one word, and we have settled on the modern usage. I have tried in all cases to keep something of the character of the writer and the sense of stress under which many soldiers wrote.

The soldier's life on the Western Front is illustrated with a selection of images taken by the soldiers themselves. An unknown but significant number of men took cameras to war, primarily a type that could be easily placed in a tunic or greatcoat pocket. The most common was known as a VPK, or Vest Pocket Kodak. Manufactured between 1912 and 1926, it was actually marketed during the war by Kodak as 'the Soldier's Camera' because of its durable all-metal construction. It used roll film (producing 4.5x6cm negatives) and, with a retractable bellows lens, it folded into a steel surround about the size of two cigarette packets. Its popularity was not only due to its price but its solidity, and it was responsible for bringing photography to the mass market. In 1914 and 1915, the VPK was used to capture some of the most evocative images of the Great War, including the very few pictures of men in action, as well as the remarkable photographs taken at the Christmas Truce of 1914.

The extraordinary images may lack the pin-sharp clarity of official photographs, but they tell a different story – the story that those who actually fought wished to tell. Of course, a great many are the typical images any young man abroad would wish to take, images of friends and comrades, normally not posed but taken spontaneously. However, many others were taken by men with an interest in this newly popularised medium, and present a remark-able record of a world descending into carnage.

The British Government, fearful that the enemy could glean useful information from these pictures if they fell into their hands, banned the use of cameras on the battlefield. In a War Office Instruction dated 19 April 1915, it was stated that 'the Field Marshal Commanding in Chief, the British Army in the Field, prohibits the taking of photographs and the sending of drawings and photographs to the press, and by an Order issued on the 16th

March, 1915, photographic cameras are not allowed to be in possession of officers, warrant officers, NCOs or men while serving with the British Army in the Field. Instructions should be issued by General Officers Commanding in Chief to all serving under their command that on no account are cameras to be taken when any unit or reinforcing draft proceeds overseas.' The order was quickly disseminated through the military hierarchy. While serving in France, Denis Barnett wrote in a letter home dated 20 April, 'Isn't it sickening about the camera? He's got to go, though I don't want to lose him.'

Interestingly it was an order repeated by the British First Army, which saw reason to issue an order banning cameras again on 9 September 1915. The warning was given that 'Any officer or soldier or other person subject to Military Law who disobeys this order will be placed in arrest and the case reported to the Headquarters of the Army or Lines of Communication Area.'

Although there was no direct threat of court martial, such a sanction was used on a number of occasions, while records survive of one officer in the Royal Garrison Artillery who was cashiered from the army after being caught taking pictures. For this reason, the vast majority of cameras were packed away in valises or kitbags to be returned later to England, so that while VPK images are common before mid-1915, they become increasingly rare after this date, although nothing like as rare as the authorities would have liked to believe.

Any photography after this date was unofficially sanctioned by the attitude of a battalion Commanding Officer. If he saw no reason to act, then, on the whole, neither did the officers under his command, and it is clear from the very 'public' nature of some pictures taken later on the Somme, at Arras and at Ypres that a blind eye was frequently turned to the use of the VPK, especially behind the lines. Despite the fact that anyone of whatever rank, excepting the most senior officers, had an equal chance of being captured, it may well have been the case that officers were trusted more than other ranks to use their discretion when taking images, and most surviving images were taken by commissioned ranks, who, of course, were also more likely to be able to afford the expense. However, other ranks' images survive. Lance Corporal William Smallcombe, whose pictures appear in this book, not only took photographs throughout his time on the Western Front from 1915 to 1918, but was happy to mention the fact in letters home, something the censor saw fit to overlook.

The images that appear in the plate section have been taken from my own personal collection, those of friends, or from archives across the United Kingdom. They tell the story of the Great War inasmuch as they cover every year of the conflict, including shots taken of the battlefields in 1919, and reflect the changing nature of the war from the lush open countryside of 1914 to the desolation of 1917. They have been chosen not only to give an overall impression of the war itself, but also as a link to some of the aspects of daily life covered by stories in *The Soldier's War*. Images taken in action are extremely rare, for obvious reasons. Of the very few known, two were taken by a private in the 1/10th King's (Liverpool Scottish). His name was Frederick Alexander Fyfe, aged twenty-six, and before the war he had been a press photographer. His images, taken in June 1915, show an attack by his battalion at Bellewaarde Farm, just hours before he was shot and wounded in the leg. His civilian profession and his deep interest in photography are probably the only reasons why, as men were being killed and wounded around him, he would even think to take pictures.

All too frequently, books are published with a selection of images taken by the official war photographers, and all too often they are the same images that we have seen over and over again. To my knowledge no books have been published, certainly in recent years, that have attempted to use the remarkable collection of VPK images; they have, until now, been largely ignored or forgotten.

It is ninety years since the end of the Great War. This is a significant date as 2008 has proved the effective watershed between the Great War as a living record and the Great War as history. On 1 January, the last German veteran, Erich Kästner, who served on the Western Front in 1918, died aged 107, the last of Kaiser Wilhelm's Imperial Army. He was followed in the next two months by the final three French veterans. Yakup Satar, taken prisoner of war by the British in 1917, was 110 years old at his death, and acknowledged to be the final Turkish veteran. There are no known surviving Canadians, Australians, South Africans, Russians, Indians or Americans who saw action.

Of the three British servicemen still alive, two, Henry Allingham and Harry Patch, served on the Western Front. Henry is the oldest of the surviving veterans at 112 years. He is also the oldest British ex-serviceman ever recorded. Harry Patch, the last fighting Tommy, is, however, the only British serviceman who can now recall what it was like to serve in a trench. The public's interest in the Great War appears undiminished: Harry Patch is fêted for being the last Great War veteran of the trenches. He enjoys the benefits of his status, and why not? He never asked to be famous, or to become the focus of public attention.

I well recall, in the mid-1980s, a London regional television programme carrying the story of a Great War veteran living several floors up in a tower block in London. He was paying a couple of pounds an hour to a man living below to come and listen to him talk, not necessarily about the War, just about anything. I was hardly interested in the Great War myself at the time, but I recall the pathos of the story and I realise now that only in recent years have we, as a nation, become aware of these men and their histories.

Someone out there, a Second World War veteran, will take on Harry's mantle in thirty years' time. He may or may not have spoken about his war, he may well not have said much about what he did sixty-five years ago, but he too will become fêted, not for what he is so much as for what he symbolises. When the Royal

Family and the entire Royal Albert Hall audience stood to applaud
Harry Patch at the Field of Remembrance Festival last November,
it was in appreciation of what his generation undertook, what they
faced and suffered, as well as a sign of respect for Harry's own
service. He has become the face of a generation and the repre-
sentative of an era that has profoundly influenced our lives.

In almost inverse proportion to the declining number of
surviving veterans has been the growth in popular tourism to
the former battlefields of the Western Front. It is a huge and
growing business. In the last twenty years the desire of millions of
Britons to visit the sites where their forebears fought and where so
many died has been extraordinary. For some, one visit is enough;
for many more, it is the start of a regular pilgrimage, and for a few
it is a place of endless fascination to be tramped over from one
corner to another, working out enemy dispositions, trench lines
and lines of attack. Yet, for all the appeals such scenery makes to
the imagination, it is impossible really to take in what happened.
Once we could sit enthralled as the veterans themselves talked;
now we are left only with the stories, but what stories they are!

1914

The War in 1914

Great Britain went to war outnumbered and outgunned, not a good starting scenario for any war, but it had two undeniable aces – the British Tommy, the best-trained soldier in Europe, if not the world, and the rifle he carried, the superbly manufactured Lee Enfield .303. That combination, man and rifle, was a formidable force for any opposing army, however large. Nevertheless, many historians now believe that if Germany had any chance of winning the war it had to do so by mid-1915, when its superiority in numbers and, in particular, artillery could be made to tell, otherwise it was on the slippery and unavoidable slope to defeat. The fact that Germany did *not* win said as much about the fighting spirit of the British soldier as it did about the German generals' own catastrophic battlefield miscalculations.

There was something wonderfully British about the way the country went to war in August 1914. When Germany invaded Belgium on 3 August, in a pre-ordained plan to sweep down from the north and take Paris, the French were not even certain that Britain would come to their aid.

The system of alliances and hidden agreements between the great powers of Europe had precipitated the war. The fatal gunshots in Sarajevo in June, when a Serbian nationalist, Gavrilo Princip, assassinated the Archduke Franz Ferdinand, presumptive heir to the Austro/Hungarian Empire, triggered the initial international crisis. Austria had subsequently claimed Princip worked for the Serbian Government, an unsubstantiated assertion. Threats and demands by Austria were rejected by Serbia, safe in the knowledge that secret agreements of support from its ally Russia would mean that it would not be left alone. An Austrian ultimatum caused a relatively minor crisis in the Balkans to spin out of control. Countries went to war, sure in the knowledge that their alliances would guarantee them support. Austria could, in the last resort, depend on its ally Germany for military assistance; Serbia, in turn, could rely on its long-standing ally Russia to remain firm against the Austro-Hungarian threats. Russia, in turn, knew that if it were attacked it could rely on France, an ally since 1892, to come to its aid. The chips were down. When Germany launched a five-pronged invasion in an attempt to knock France out of the war, France turned to England for support, but help was not instantaneous. Britain had entered into an entente cordiale with France in 1904. Subsequent to this informal agreement, discussions had been held on the basis that the most likely scenario for a European war was one against Germany and, in the light of this, that a small force of six divisions would be sent to fight on the left flank of the French army. But despite the French expectation that Britain would automatically feel obliged to come to their rescue and send an army, Britain did not feel equally indebted. It would need to consider its position.

Despite a well-known naval arms race with Germany for many years, there were still close family ties between the British and German royal families. The Kaiser was Queen Victoria's great-nephew and therefore a cousin to King George V. The Kaiser was a recent visitor to Britain and there had been close military ties between British and German regiments for many years. If none of this was particularly significant in British politics, it certainly was in Germany. There was genuine surprise and consternation in the Fatherland when Britain chose to declare war on Germany.

Britain went to war with the largest navy in the world but one of the smallest standing armies. Ever since the South African War had exposed serious problems with the army, a series of root-and-branch reforms had significantly transformed its capabilities. Not that the army had grown as a result of these reforms, and relatively small numbers of British troops had been entrusted with the maintenance of imperial power across the globe, effectively policing the Empire with the tacit or reluctant agreement of the local people. Even so, if truth be told, Britain's standing was already on the wane. For home defence, the Royal Navy could be expected to hold sway against an attack by an enemy fleet. However, fear of invasion was such that at first only four infantry divisions and one cavalry were sent to France. Although two divisions followed within days, the size of the British army was, on paper at least, still rather paltry.

The force had yet to engage the Germans when, in an 'Order of the Day' issued by Kaiser Wilhelm II at his headquarters in Aix-la-Chapelle, he decreed, 'It is my Royal and Imperial Command that you concentrate your energies, for the immediate present upon one single purpose, and that is that you address all your skill and all the valour of my soldiers to exterminate first the treacherous English; walk over General French's contemptible little Army.'

The word 'treacherous' gave some indication of the feeling against Britain for entering the war; 'contemptible little Army' was a sign of what the enemy thought of four divisions of infantry. News of the order was filtered down and read to the ranks of British infantry within two weeks of its issue. For those who survived, a new name would soon be adopted to describe them: the 'Old Contemptibles'.

The men who stood their ground at Mons were certainly aware that they were the recipients of the concentrated energies of large numbers of enemy troops. Outnumbered six to one, they at least held the south side of the Mons-Condé Canal and, until the Germans forged a crossing late that first day, they were able to give the enemy a bloody nose that they were unlikely to forget. Their rapid fifteen rounds a minute, combined with deft accuracy,

ensured that the Germans who pressed on were cut down in
swathes before their numerical supremacy began to tell. Along the
canal, the Germans began to forge crossings and the British troops,
much to their consternation, were withdrawn from the town.
Unbeknown to them, the British Expeditionary Force (BEF) had
become separated from their neighbouring French forces and a
retirement was required to buy time to re-establish contact. That
withdrawal, however, would become a headlong two-hundred-
mile retreat that would not stop for two weeks, until the British
were south-east of Paris.

The retreat from Mons has gone down in the annals of British
military history as one of its greatest endeavours, but, for all its
heroism, it could hardly hide the reality of the situation. The
British Army was, if not on the run, then on the march, and then
quickly on the hobble, as the hard-paved roads took their toll of
the BEF's collective feet.

In Britain the popular enthusiasm for war had translated into
large numbers of recruits to the army. Lord Kitchener, the new
Secretary of State for War, had initiated his recruitment drive,
calling for 100,000 volunteers to form a New Army. He knew, if
no one else did, that the war would last not for months but years,
and that if it was to be won it would require a civilian army,
Kitchener's Army. The call to arms had been excellent, but the
news of the British Army's desperate straits brought about a
spectacular rise in enlistment, overwhelming recruiting offices.
These soldiers would not be ready for the front for the best part of a
year; they could not be the saviours of the Regular Army. It would
have to depend on the territorials. However, their deployment to
the front was still weeks away, and in the meantime the regulars
would have to take the strain.

The BEF retreated out of Belgium and into France. A confrontation was effected at Le Cateau on 26 August, a daring and
successful attempt to halt the pursuing Germans in their tracks,
allowing the bulk of the exhausted troops to gain a bit of time

before the enemy rejoined the chase. Elsewhere, the cavalry acted as a screen to the retreating men, coming in and out of action to buy a moment's respite for the infantry.

As the British and French fell back, the Germans themselves became exhausted in their relentless chase. Their own lines of provision were becoming strained and overextended. The desire to 'walk over' the BEF was intense, and a fatal error was made when the German High Command, instead of encircling Paris as their own detailed invasion plans had intended, redirected their efforts to annihilating the BEF once and for all. As the German forces swung south-east, away from the capital, the French rapidly organised a fresh Sixth Army in the city and advanced towards the flank of the German army pursuing the BEF. The Germans were oblivious to the French Sixth Army's existence until they were attacked. Almost overnight, the tables were turned. The British Army, which had crossed the Aisne and Marne rivers, turned and suddenly found themselves in pursuit of the German army, which was retreating in confusion and in risk of being cut off and surrounded. The Germans fell back on the Aisne and the first defendable high ground, known as the Chemin des Dames, and it was here that both sides came to a standstill. It was the middle of September, and they dug in. The first trenches were constructed that would one day form an unbroken chain of defence from the Belgian coast to the Swiss Alps.

For the army commanders there was a brief deadlock. The Germans had no intention of coming down from their command- ing heights, and the British and French troops were in no state to push them off. The only way was for one side to outflank the other, and so began what became known as the 'race for the sea' as, by instalments, German and British troops sought to outflank each other while all the time heading in one direction: north-west. It was a race that would finish for the British close to the pretty Belgian town of Ypres, with its outstanding medieval Cloth Hall in the centre. It was here, in the fields and villages just outside the eastern side of the town, that the Regular Army, supported later that year by large numbers of territorials, would stand their ground as the Germans once again used their numerical supremacy and their superiority in artillery and ammunition to force a decision. In massed attacks, the Germans launched wave after wave of assaults against a rapidly thinning British line, which heroically stood its ground. On many occasions, unbeknown to the enemy, they had all but breached the line, as nothing but a handful of men held the British position. The situation was extremely serious, but mutually assured exhaustion had held the enemy back at critical moments. 'If they had but known' was the feeling amongst many of the British soldiers who held out as the first flurries of winter snow began to settle on the battlefield and icy winds blew across a rapidly established no-man's-land. Slowly, the British troops consolidated their position, tripwire hung with tin cans was replaced by stakes and barbed-wire entanglements, and holes in the ground began to be linked into shallow trenches with sandbag breastworks and floors of wooden planks. The Great War, as defined in popular imagination, had begun.

Comrades

One evening, in a coveted hour's rest, stretcher-bearer Private Vero Garratt wrote a letter home. It was dark, but with the aid of candlelight shielded by an old battered tin can, he spoke about what he could see around him.

'When I look up, my eyes meet a mass of darkness that is studded here and there by lights similar to my own, and near which weary boys are turning their thoughts to homeland with a very expressive look on their faces. They are good boys. Rough and ready as many of them are, yet the joy and happiness their comradeship has brought to me is beyond telling. You would be surprised how easy it is out here to sink one's differences and personal prejudices that may have weighed with one under different circumstances. And it is difficult not to make certain limited concessions to the other fellows' use of Anglo-Saxon, etc, and conduct, which would have occasioned no end of rebukes under less trying conditions.'

It was that comradeship perhaps more than anything else that veterans spoke of with equal pleasure and pain when remembering the Great War. In its context, few veterans shied away from using words such as love, when it came to those with whom they had served, shared terrible privations, and from whom they were too frequently parted through death or injury.

In one sense, the close bonds of friendships between men serving at the front were no different from those established at home; some people they naturally got on with and liked, others they did not. But friendship and comradeship, while inextricably linked, were not one and the same thing. In times of war, comradeship transcended all 'normal' friendships. It was hardly surprising that few men ever replicated those extraordinarily close ties, characteristic of lives lived on the edge. Many regretted their eventual loss, and bemoaned the absence of such links in civilian life when they came home; others were grateful for the love they felt and the bonds they developed. Sidney Rogerson, an officer in the West Yorkshire Regiment, wrote that the war years stood out for him and for others as 'the happiest period of their lives', for the very reason that 'in spite of all the differences in rank, we were comrades, brothers dwelling together in unity'. When old soldiers met after the war, some of that comradeship could be rekindled, but it was impossible to feel again what they had known in the trenches.

Trench warfare was a great leveller. In France, far away from home, it no longer mattered what job a man had done previously, how much he earned, or even what sort of life he would return to, should he survive. Instead, there was a tacit acknowledgement that everyone was in the same boat and everyone's chances of survival were about equal. This was collective comradeship, drawing its strength from various sources. It was love of the regiment that bound men together, establishing an *esprit de corps* that maintained unit cohesion under the most difficult circumstances. In the cold light of day, men might reply when questioned that they were fighting for freedom; to halt the march of German Prussianism, but in reality, on a day-to-day basis, men fought for each other, for the name of the regiment, and sometimes the division, not for highbrow notions of patriotism or democracy.

Comradeship in this sense had a united objective; men were all notionally fighting for a common aim that those at home could not understand or fathom. And the greater the estrangement from home, the more soldiers were bound together psychologically, their common experience the cement which kept them together.

Those feelings cut right across boundaries of rank and status. Lieutenant Walter Ewbank noted its potency in a letter to his parents in 1916. The unit he had trained with and the platoon he had led had gone into action and had suffered heavy casualties. He described the action in terms of a 'terrible and glorious end' to the 'flower' of the British Army. His pride is tangible.

'They were men of magnificent physique and astounding courage, and went to the attack in the face of terrible odds, like a pack of hounds. Never have men presented such a fine spectacle . . . What happened I cannot tell you. Not a man flinched nor hesitated. On they went, and tears are in my eyes now when I think of them and how it was I did not go under with them . . . Never did I believe such a feeling could be aroused in one's breast nowadays.'

The feeling was reciprocated, NCOs and other ranks willing to do anything or go anywhere with an officer they respected and trusted. Sergeant Ryan of the Royal Irish Fusiliers thought highly of his Medical Officer and, when that officer was killed, Ryan carried his body back to a dressing station where he laid it out on a stretcher. 'Ryan was very much put out, and mourned as if he had lost a dear relation. He cleaned the dead officer's face, combed his hair, and arranged his tie,' recalled John Lucy, an old regular who had recently been commissioned.

The stress of action, whether under fire in the trenches or going over the top, threw emotions into tumult. 'A few hours under bombardment, with the knowledge that one may at any moment be blown to pieces, gives one a wonderful insight into the character of one's comrades,' wrote Signaller Charles Birnstingl to his family back in England, 'and living under these conditions you take either a violent – and often inexplicable – antipathy or feel a real love for your fellow sufferers.'

In great danger, soldiers who were often strangers to one another frequently overrode their own feelings of self-interest and preservation to help each other. Nineteen-year-old Private

George Fleet, of The Queen's (Royal West Surrey Regiment), had been endlessly terrified in action until he jumped into a shell hole to find a boy of similar age.

'One glance at the boy's face told me all the guts the poor devil ever possessed had vanished . . . The tears rolled down his cheeks. There, in the midst of carnage, he made a pitiable spectacle. I think I persuaded him to join me and we linked up with the others. I never met him again. Whether a member of The Queen's or not, I cannot now say. He may have been killed, he may yet be alive, but his weakness gave me courage. God knows I was scared, but seeing this fellow with practically every vestige of control gone, I felt strong again.'

Comradeship between friends or within small groups of friends was the strongest bond of all. In Kitchener's Army, it might be amongst those who had enlisted together, mates from work, from sports teams or social clubs. But friends were often parted in training and new groups would be formed around an infantry section, a machine-gun section or amongst the bombers and signallers; even the teetotallers got together, as did those who liked a drink.

Harry Patch, the 110-year-old veteran who is the last man to have seen front line service on the Western Front, has recalled evocatively what comradeship meant to him. In his Lewis gun section it meant sharing everything, dividing up parcels from home with one another, right down to the last piece of chocolate and the final cigarette. Nothing was kept for oneself that was not offered to another whose needs were greater. Any trouble at home was a problem for all in the section, and sharing concerns was part and parcel of their continued survival.

That did not mean there were no grumbles. 'Men would swear at one another, swear about each other, but the true fact was there was always that other bond of friendship; we were still friends. Your pals are almost family,' asserted one old soldier. Frederick Manning perhaps summed up the relationship best of all:

'These apparently rude and brutal natures comforted, encouraged and reconciled each other to fate, with a tenderness and tact which was more moving than anything in life. They had nothing; not even their own bodies, which had become mere implements of warfare . . . They had been brought to the last extremity of hope, and yet they put their hands on each other's shoulders and said with a passionate conviction that it would be all right, though they had faith in nothing but in themselves and in each other.'

To lose a friend or to lose a comrade during the fighting was not quite the same thing. Many men who lost close friends were entirely bereft by the loss, and sometimes cared little about what would happen to them. Unwilling to contemplate losing anyone close to them again, such men refused to bond entirely with anyone else around them, preferring looser associations of comradeship. Losing a comrade was always sad, but not the same as losing a close friend.

Men naturally became hardened to death. Often, although they would do all they possibly could to help another wounded soldier, once he was killed, though he was not forgotten, he was gone and they did not dwell on the fact. Death was an accepted state of affairs, and there were those who looked upon the dead as the fortunate ones: 'he can't be worse off the other side of death than we are here . . .', wrote one soldier about his dead colleague.

Lieutenant John Capron, of The Queen's Own Cameron Highlanders, recalled one incident that made him wonder at his own indifference.

'We soon saw a target, a body of some 100 Huns, and gave them five rounds rapid. They seemed to be walking towards us in quite the ordinary way. None of the glory of a charge, or bugles, or singing. In fact the whole battle seemed extraordinarily silent. I fired twice and the range was such that I couldn't miss. Moreover I was absolutely steady in my aim and know it was good. Then they stopped walking forward and my men started curling up on the ground wounded, or rolling on their backs, kicking up their legs, again quite the natural thing to do. Had anyone spoken to me I should have told him "Oh yes, they're casualties, that's all." It all seemed so natural and commonplace.'

Private Herbert Chase, a stretcher-bearer, bore witness to how suffering and death could be met with cool indifference. 'Blood, mud, filth, frightful smells, shattered men – one sees but passes them by almost without a shudder. One eats one's food beside dead men without a thought, where, before the war, the very thought would have turned one sick. One sees one's own comrades killed and lying in pools of water, face downwards – it is all terrible but, fortunately perhaps, one does not feel it extremely.'

Apparent indifference did not entirely suppress emotions. When Sergeant Ryan left the Medical Officer to venture back outside to help the wounded and was almost instantly killed by shrapnel, Lucy saw his body, laid next to the Medical Officer's, and the tragedy was too apparent.

'I went in slowly again to visit the dead Ryan and his officer. I prayed for them both. These devoted men had died directly to save their fellows . . . The red compassionate lips of Ryan were white-grey. His discoloured teeth showed between them. I patted his cheek in farewell. Then I stood up, and I could not move away. The world turned over. My manhood seeped from me. Ryan's death had hammered the congealed nail of grief deeper into my heart, and a long suppressed tide of sorrow rose and flowed about me. I heard strange sobs coming from my lips, and felt my spirit fainting. In the little dressing station I missed all my dead friends again.'

Soldiers' Memories

Maj. George Walker, 59th Coy, RE
We were all sitting at tea and it was a lovely evening, when two of
the subalterns poked their heads in the drawing-room window and
announced that 'it' had come, 'it' being the telegraph order to
mobilise for war. Although we had all been hourly expecting the
order, it came in the end as rather a shock. Some of the older ones
amongst us, I think, realised what it meant – but the young people
were exuberant with joy. I remember going into the Mess a few
days before, and finding two of my subalterns reading the morning
paper, and, on asking what was the news, one of them replied
rather disconsolately: 'I believe the blighters will wriggle out of it
after all.' That was their only fear. Well, the blow had fallen at last
and the comparative peace of an annual course of musketry was
turned into the turmoil of preparations for war. Fortunately the
whole thing had been worked out very carefully in detail during
the previous winter. Everyone knew what he had to do and when
he had to do it.

Trp. Alfred Tilney, 4th (Royal Irish) Dragoon Guards
On mobilisation, the quiet cut and dried routine of the regiment
at once changed, and everything became one long bustle from
morning until night. Every train brought in loads of reservists
from all parts of the United Kingdom and the usually quiet station
of Tidworth became very much alive. The reservists were a cheery
lot (until their first dose of inoculation) and of course they told us

youngsters all about active service. The spirit of everyone was most optimistic, some, who thought so much of our own army and so little of the Germans, going so far as to think they would all be home for Christmas; some were, but not in the condition they had expected.

Sgt Bradlaugh Sanderson (Reservist), 2nd King's Royal Rifle Corps

5 August: The scene remarkable. Meet chums of early soldiering days. Within two hours was equipped and ready, 4,000 King's Royal Rifles, 4,000 Rifle Brigade to be dealt with. My old colour sergeant wants me to stay and go with the 6th Battalion, but I wish to go with the 2nd so I'm shoved into the first draft of 300 proceeding to Blackdown. It's quite a remarkable system at the Mobilisation Stores. You give in a ticket, and at once you are taken to a pigeonhole where your name and number are pasted above. There is a brand-new outfit, to size in every detail, no trouble whatsoever. Feels nice to be in regimentals once more.

6 August to 11 August: Time occupied in training and route marching. Colonel says he has never seen such a well-set-up battalion. General Hutton and the King inspected us today. We were told that we had no reputation to make, but one to keep. Issued out with ball ammunition, this means business. We are off tomorrow.

12 August: Battalion parade at 3 p.m. All the married soldiers' wives see us off. A little weeping naturally, but no gnashing of teeth this journey. The men are happy and look forward to active service. Arrive Southampton, same secrecy. Gates closed after entering the docks. Embark transport *Gateka*. Nobody knows where we are going. The captain gets a letter from a torpedo boat, and then we're off. Some say Havre, others Boulogne or Dieppe.

Maj. George Walker, 59th Coy RE

We left the Curragh by train for Dublin and on the Sunday we were all embarked and we sailed that night. After an uneventful voyage we arrived at Le Havre, our only excitement was being held up and boarded by a French destroyer off the Channel Islands. It was rather an amusing scene. We were all asleep about midnight. I was in pyjamas in the skipper's bunk when the alarm sounded. I dashed on some clothes and found the destroyer's searchlights fixed on us. The Officer Commanding and his adjutant were, when I got to them, trying to make up their minds which of the many secret papers should be burnt. The question was settled by myself and the adjutant dashing down to the galley; we burnt the lot.

The French naval officer came on board. Such was the relief of the skipper and our Officer Commanding that they got angry and refused to show him anything unless he produced his credentials, which seemed to me, at least, to be sufficiently substantiated by the destroyer, its searchlight and its guns. However, all was well in the end and our naval friend was consoled with a drink and so to bed again.

Trp. Alfred Tilney, 4th (Royal Irish) Dragoon Guards

What a time we had crossing the Channel. Usually the trip can be done in a couple of hours, but it had taken us eighteen. The explanation was that we had been dodging submarines during the night. One had to laugh later, on recollecting how we all scrambled on deck to see the lights off the coast of France, and our surprise when we were informed by a member of the crew that they were still the lights off Hastings; we must have been round the Isle of Wight a few times.

Anything more lacking in life or more unlike war would be difficult to imagine than the sight which met our eyes on steaming into the harbour of Boulogne. Bells were ringing for mass, but the only person to be seen was a gendarme with his blue coat, red baggy trousers, carrying a long rifle with a longer bayonet, quietly patrolling the quay as if it was an everyday occurrence for British cavalry regiments to land in France.

Sgt Bradlaugh Sanderson, 2nd King's Royal Rifle Corps

13 August: Arrive at Havre. Strange sounds in the shape of 'Vive Les Anglais'. Seem quite pleased to see us. We were the first infantry to land, and they march us right through the town, and at such a pace, and on cobbles, too. Anyhow, we stick it manfully. The people are everywhere, even on roofs, and such a clapping. A halt, and people press us with beer and cider. The NCOs keep them back, because there's no beer this trip, however tempting it seems. People, I am sure, can't understand it, but we accept other things such as flowers, etc. Eventually we arrive at the top plain, and go into camp. Thousands of people gather round. We introduce ourselves, and pretend we can understand them.

15 August: All this day we are travelling, and the people at each station simply throw groceries, cigarettes and cider to the troops. We stop at Amiens. There's more fun. People clamber for souvenirs, and my cap badge disappears with an amazing speed. Get back into the carriage before they pinch my clothes. Anyhow, we are well off in cigarettes (French), which aren't like English, they haven't the bite. I heard one fellow say, 'It's worth being shot to get such a spread.' We get to Arras, where there is such a splendid welcome. I've seen gay gatherings in India, but the scene at Arras beggars description. Feels nice to be an Englishman.

Back in England the public support for conflict, while not universal, was extremely robust. Across the country, people poured on to the streets in their hundreds of thousands galvanised by the news of war with Germany. Some were worried, a few cautious, but fears were rarely voiced amid the popular clamour for action.

Recruiting sergeants were soon besieged by willing recruits. The army, which normally recruited 35,000 men a year, found that they were getting these numbers in a week and simply could not cope. Far from

donning khaki, many volunteers wore their own clothes for months; were
trained by septuagenarian officers, and even police officers, and hardly
saw the breech end of a rifle, let alone a live bullet.

2/Lt John Bellerby, 1/8th West Yorkshire Rgt (Leeds Rifles)

The war came to me as a surprise. For people of my age – I was eighteen in 1914 – substantially the whole of life since we had become effectively 'aware' had been passed in conditions in which there was neither war nor rumour of war. I remember in the summer of 1913 listening to a tub-thumper, who was haranguing a small party of citizens in a farmyard in the village of Helmsley and attempting to arouse in them a readiness to share his foreboding that war would shortly break upon us. I thought he was crazy, as most certainly did all his other listeners.

Cpl Harold Jones, 1/1st Montgomeryshire Yeo.

August Bank Holiday 1914! We are all at home with Mother in her country cottage, quite out of touch with the newspaper world. Full of the holiday spirit, we set out for a picnic in the mountains and have a very happy, carefree time. Passing a wayside railway station on our homeward journey, the signalman very excitedly calls us and shows us a newspaper special edition. Right across the front page, in big letters was the word WAR. We are at once subdued and finish our return journey trying to imagine what is in store for us. Next day in town all are full of martial ardour, little guessing that it would soon be tested.

Pte John McCauley, 2nd Border Rgt

The World War was a fortnight old when my employer came up to me in the workshop and said, 'Well, John, England is at war, you know; she badly needs young men like you today.' He knew that I had served in the Special Reserve before the outbreak of war. Perhaps that knowledge gave him the courage to ask me to go, for, after all, it needs a little courage to ask a young man to go out and face death, even for his country's sake. My only reflections then were: 'How romantic it will be, what can war be like? I might just be in time to see the end if I join up at once.' My imagination was running away with me. I could see the soldiers of the different countries dumped into three or four fields to fight it out. If I didn't join up quickly, the war would be over and I would miss this wonderful spectacle.

I told my employer I was willing to go. How pleased he was! Perhaps he thought he had done his bit. My decision seemed to give pleasure to my workmates, too; why it was so, I never could tell, but they shook me by the hand, clapped me on the back, and wished me good luck and a safe return.

It was not because I was bloodthirsty and eager to slay my fellow creatures that I volunteered to go to war. I had no craving to kill or maim either German or Turk, or any man of another country. Youthful folly and impetuosity were the main reasons for my presence in the uniform of a British soldier: an overwhelming curiosity to see the war and experience new sensations; to taste war for myself.

2/Lt John Bellerby, 1/8th West Yorkshire Rgt (Leeds Rifles)

My mother was a pacifist and had instilled in her children the belief, at least in principle, that war was wrong; and in August 1914 I was not prepared to make a decision one way or the other. One thing was definite in my mind – that I would certainly not be a party to having the country overrun by Germans. If they came, I should wish to know how to fire a gun. Training in this was necessary, even though I was not then disposed to go abroad. It was made possible by joining the Leeds University's Officers' Training Corps, which I did within ten days of the declaration of war – saying, when questioned by the Commanding Officer, that I was not a candidate for a commission.

Cpl Harold Jones, 1/1st Montgomeryshire Yeo.

A town meeting was called after a few days and patriotic speeches made, ending up with appeals to the young men present to signify their willingness to defend their country by signing a roll in the Mayor's parlour. With several colleagues, I signed. A squad of businessmen in the town was formed, which I joined, but after one evening of squad drill and sloping arms I chucked it and decided to become a pukka soldier. Hearing that the Montgomery Yeomanry were a few men under strength, I wired them to ask if they would take me! Sounds funny now, but they were mighty particular the first few weeks of the war. The reply came to proceed to Llandrindod Wells and report at the depot there. Two other recruits and myself were very cordially received, and having passed the medical examination were sent on to Welshpool, the regimental depot.

Fully expecting to be housed in barracks, imagine our pleasant surprise to find that we were to be billeted in a hotel. Here we had a very easy and happy-go-lucky time. There were only three instructors for over a hundred raw recruits and, although we were supposed to be trained as horsemen, there were only six horses between the lot of us. However, none complained. We were well housed, amply fed and had a few parades.

After a fortnight of this, volunteers were called for to join the first line of the regiment now stationed on the east coast. Not being satisfied with the easy life we were leading, a number of us stepped out and in a few days were sent off on our cross-country journey to Aylsham, near Cromer. The town band played us to the station and at last I felt the real 'goods'.

Pte John McCauley, 2nd Border Rgt

The barracks were spacious and comfortable, and things began to look bright for us. We had been the first group of infantry to arrive, but further contingents began to flow in and we then experienced discomfort and congestion. We were a strangely clad army. Some wore khaki trousers, civilian jackets and boaters and bowlers. Others had khaki tunics and civilian trousers. Finally, the authorities commandeered the entire stocks of boots, shoes and clothing from the local shops. Then the real burlesque commenced. Wagons loaded with all kinds of men's coats, trousers, boots and shoes drove into the middle of the barrack square and shot their contents on to the ground. Hundreds of men assembled round the pile, and the colonel and quartermaster stood in the middle of the ring. 'Who takes size nine?' the colonel would shout, holding high a pair of boots. A great roar of voices would be the answer, the boots would be tossed over and a scramble for possession ensued. After the distribution, we looked funnier than ever. One chap, whose feet were so big that no ordinary-sized boot would fit him, walked round for nearly a month with the toes cut from one pair of boots tied with string to the heels of another pair. The town was searched in vain for a pair big enough to fit him and eventually they had to be specially made for him.

Pte Ernest Aldridge, 2nd Welsh Rgt

I was a boy of seventeen years old. The uniform I was given was made for someone of about 28 stone. I didn't know whether I was inside or outside it. If the neck of the coat had been a little larger I'm afraid I would have slipped right through! When we were making a turn, I would be halfway round before my uniform would start to move – which always worried my drill instructor because I would never be in line with the other fellows.

2/Lt John Bellerby, 1/8th West Yorkshire Rgt (Leeds Rifles)

Immediately on getting my uniform, I was sent for training to the first line battalion at Strensall. This, the 8th West Yorkshire Regiment, was a territorial battalion with only one regular officer, the adjutant, Captain Dundas. The training was almost entirely on Boer War principles, so it mattered little who was in command, or

what had been their training. Apart from musketry, nothing that
we learned was of the least value for later trench warfare, but it was
all deeply exciting, and made us a coherent unit. We learned how
to move about the country as a battalion, how to give and take
orders, how to march and bivouac and take meals in the open, and
find our way around the country by night. Everyone was keen, in
the usual nonchalant sixth-form way.

In the early months there was a tension and a zest in life
imparted entirely by anticipation of what was to follow. It is
impossible to continue for months, training with one specific aim
in view to which all have implicitly committed their whole being,
without becoming seized with eagerness to put the training to the
final test.

It was probably this sort of feeling which led me to say 'Yes' when,
after three weeks of training with the first battalion at Strensall, the
adjutant asked me if I would fill a vacancy in it. I think I rationalised
my decision by saying to myself that if I was prepared to shoot
Germans in the event of their landing in the UK, it was obviously
more sensible to meet them on the other side.

Cpl Harold Jones, 1/1st Montgomeryshire Yeo.
We reached our destination and soon realised we had to prepare to
rough it. The meal awaiting us was soup served up in 'dixies' and
every man had to dip in for himself. The dining place was a
leaking marquee and the floor was a quagmire. We found – in the
dark – that the camp was based on a small farm. The officers were
billeted in the house and all other ranks in the buildings. The only
corner four of us could find was in the entrance to the big barn.
We slept there until, after being buried under drifting snow a few
times, we decided to force our company on others better placed.
We succeeded in squeezing into a horse stall with eight other men.
We found it as hot there as it was cold in the doorway. Fortunately
the horses were stabled outside.

Every man now had a horse and the first thing the raw recruit had to do was to satisfy the sergeant major that he could ride. I satisfied him the first morning that I could not. Personally I thought I could, but he had other views and expressed them rather forcibly. It seemed that riding a horse without falling off was not enough. He did his utmost to make me tumble but to his great annoyance failed. One man was so sick and disheartened by this tyrant that he decided to 'work his ticket'. This wily one made it appear that he found it very difficult to keep his seat when the horse was only walking and as soon as the order 'Trot!' was given he immediately fell to the ground, not troubling to wait for 'Canter!' He was soon sent home as being unlikely to make a good and efficient soldier.

Pte James Racine, 1/5th Seaforth Highlanders

Bayonet fighting was a daily occupation and together with Swedish drill [physical exercise], we were put through it severely. A squad was formed into a ring, facing inwards, with the men about two paces apart with their hands behind their backs. A man was detailed to run round on the outside with a strap in his hand, which he dropped into the hands of one of the men in the ring who, in turn, immediately gave chase and endeavoured to catch the other man before he could complete the circle, and occupy the vacated place. If he was successful in catching the running man, he hit him with the strap; the prospect of such punishment naturally provided an incentive for fleetness of foot.

Pte Charles Heare, 1/2nd Monmouthshire Rgt

This life is grand, marching and singing. I have a fairly loud voice and let it go. How fond we all are of marching and singing! 'Tipperary' is sung, as is 'A Soldier Man' and 'Who's Your Lady Friend?' and a host of others.

All who had volunteered for foreign service are given a silver brooch with 'Imperial Service' on it with a crown on top; our first medal. How we show it off! Mr and Mrs Wyman, our landlord and landlady, say the war is serious. We all laugh and say we won't see a clothes line in France never mind the front line, and if we go and the Germans knew the 2nd Mons were coming out, they would give it [the war] up as a bad job.

A new lot joined my company on a Saturday route march of twenty miles. I am behind a bandy-legged man. I can't take my eyes off his legs and I'm always out of step. We all sing on the marches. What a great holiday, all the boys say. It's the best war we've ever been in.

Pte Reginald Wilkes, 16th Royal Warwickshire Rgt (3rd Birmingham Pals)

One certainly lives in an atmosphere which tends to broaden the mind and vision. The familiarity amongst fellows living in a hut gives one an idea of what other folks, in different circumstances, think and do. Small faults in fellows, which were often much exaggerated by our narrow-minded society and social convention, are now more easily condoned and lost sight of, in the face of new qualities, many of which have before been dormant. One of the most notable of these is the general desire to help a fellow in trouble, whatever its nature and origin. I have seen fellows give up their leave, to let some fellow with trouble at home go, and then make a collection and pay his railway fare. Many a lie is told when another fellow can be helped by it, and can one really consider them as black when there is no desire for personal gain behind them?

2/Lt John Bellerby, 1/8th West Yorkshire Rgt (Leeds Rifles)

The responsibility for discipline and for minor punishments fell upon the youngest officers, with the consequence that there was much inequality in the penalties for similar 'crimes'. My own principle was never to give any punishment whatever except for something really heinous, for which I should have proposed to give the maximum. I fell-in the platoon and told them my principle, and said that I should do my utmost to cause the ejection from the army of any member of the platoon who might be caught taking the property of another. I did not realise how empty such a threat was at the time, but it worked. The only subsequent offender was Busby, the cook, who had the misfortune not to be present when my remarks were made. Some weeks later I discovered, by a piece of detection simplified by Busby's largeness of foot, that he had stolen the slippers of another member of the platoon similarly distinguished, and I induced the colonel to give him a stiff dose of detention. For some odd reason, this raised me in his estimation. One hears stories of irate other ranks threatening to shoot dastardly officers in the back once they had them in no-man's-land. I doubt whether much of that ever existed in the British Voluntary Army. At all events Busby, released from detention, was the first to volunteer when I asked for aid in a somewhat sticky task during our first days in the trenches, and I felt no apprehension as to his motive.

Gnr Stanley Collins, 137th Heavy Batt., RGA
One day we were going up Deptford High Street, people cheering us as they went by. In those days a soldier felt proud of himself; every man in the colours was a hero. The 60-pounder guns were drawn by six heavy draught horses, and at the rear of each gun there were two wheels that put the brakes on if you were going downhill. I was the brakesman on the off-side. One particular day, we were going on a route march and came out of Deptford High Street into Deptford Broadway just as a tram came along, a number 40. Our sergeant, Glossop, a big six-foot man who thought a lot of himself, a real bastard he was, he started shouting out, 'Keep to your left, keep to your left', passing it down the line. When this tram came by, I looked up and it was my dad. Proud little bugger I was, bandolier on, all highly polished, 'Wotcha, Dad,' I said. Dad slowed up, 'Hello, my son, where do you reckon you're off to?' 'Plumstead Common,' I said, and no sooner had I

got the words out of my mouth than Sergeant Glossop put me under arrest.

We went and did our route march, and directly after we got back, after we'd put our gun away, they slung me in the Guard Room, took my money away, took my fags, everything. I was really offended, I didn't know what it was all about. When the sergeant had said, 'I'm putting you under arrest', I thought he was going to give me a rest or something. Evening time came and I was still in the Guard Room. Not many yards away was a coffee stall, and I asked if I could go up there, but the NCO guard told me I wasn't going out of there tonight because I was a prisoner. That made me sweat.

Next morning, Sergeant Glossop and two men, a prisoner's escort, hauled me up in front of Captain Moore. They took my cap off and in I marched and stood there anyhow. 'Stand to attention,' said Sergeant Glossop. Attention! I didn't know what attention was, we hadn't done any infantry training. Then Sergeant Glossop gave his evidence . . . Captain Moore said he'd deal with it and he dismissed the sergeant and the escort. Then he asked me whether what the sergeant said was true, so I told him it was. I was never one for telling a lot of lies. Then Captain Moore explained that we were at war with a very powerful enemy, and that when you were on a march you should never divulge to anybody where you were going, because the enemy had spies everywhere. He laid it down rotten to me. Then he asked me where I lived, so I told him, and he said that I'd better go home for the weekend, and he wrote me out a weekend pass.

Pte James Racine, 1/5th Seaforth Highlanders
Our duties consisted of maintaining order in the town and arresting any men who were drunk and disorderly, or who were in the town without permission. We had one particularly difficult man to deal with, for he reeled along the High Street and sang at the top of his voice. Twice he was advised to return to his billet but

the third time he swung round and hit one of the pickets in the face. We carried him kicking and swearing through the main street, accompanied by the usual interested band of spectators, into the presence of the police inspector at the civilian police station. Here he was released and dropped on the ground but immediately got up and struck the inspector in the eye. He was thrown to the ground, searched, and finally deposited in a cell after his boots had been forcibly removed; we left him singing, swearing and making as much disturbance as he possibly could.

Pte Charles Heare, 1/2nd Monmouthshire Rgt

The battalion are to dig trenches on the east coast. We are all down to sleep that night when a telegram arrives. Our sergeant opens it: 'Congratulations, your battalion is accepted for active service. Orders following.' On Friday 5 November we leave Northampton, women crying, some fainting. A real parting this time. All Northampton turns out to see us off.

———

Once the British Government had made the decision for war, the Regular Army had mobilised and travelled to France with the greatest efficiency. The troops, to be known as the British Expeditionary Force (BEF), had quickly moved up by train from the Channel ports in a north-easterly direction towards Belgium and the town of Mons. No one yet knew exactly where the enemy was, but the news was clear: they were in great numbers and sweeping south.

Capt. Hubert Rees, 2nd Welsh Rgt

First night in Belgium. My company went to Peissant and we arrived there in pitch darkness, bumping into some French cavalry in the street. It was rather a near thing, for a few moments, whether we began the war by shooting the French. Until one had actually seen Germans, French and Belgians, it was not very easy to decide at a little distance whether they were friend or foe.

The Belgian inhabitants were sure that we were the Germans and shut themselves up. After some time we managed to induce a woman to come out on to her doorstep to parley with us. She had a lantern in one hand and a child of about five was holding the other. We put our best French scholar in the front row and they began. It would have gone all right if a subaltern, who was more excited than I had any idea of, hadn't been holding a loaded revolver and fired a shot into the ground at our feet. The woman screamed loudly, bolted inside and locked the door, leaving us with the lantern and a screaming infant. I went round the house to find the back door and fell into the local river. However, after some time we did manage to get the men billeted. They were extremely tired and it was very necessary to try and give as many as possible a good night's rest. There was only one practicable road into the village at our end and I was lucky enough to find a brand-new harrow in a neighbouring farmyard. I put the harrow, spikes uppermost, in the road, told a section under a sergeant to watch it and the rest of us went to sleep. It appeared to me fairly certain that anyone who tripped over that harrow would create enough noise to wake most of us. I had been asleep for perhaps half an hour when I was awakened by the sergeant in charge of the harrow. He had a Belgian peasant with him. 'Beg pardon, sir,' said the sergeant, 'but this gentleman want 'is 'arrow back.'

Trp. Alfred Tilney, 4th (Royal Irish) Dragoon Guards
On the evening of 21 August, the regiment was to the left rear of the town of Mons. B Squadron had gone out on a job and C Squadron, being next on duty, received orders to set off as contact squadron.

We crossed the Mons-Condé Canal and reached some woods and a village. I was in 4th Troop, so we found a picket and were given orders to fire on anyone coming down the road. It was agreed that Corporal Thomas should shout, 'Halt! Who goes there?' and we were to fire.

In the morning we moved up on to a side road. Some of the lads were having coffee and bread and butter, which was being given out by an Englishman who came from Windsor. I had a job as orderly to Captain Hornby. He gave me two eggs, which I ate raw, and we were just going out to see what was delaying the war when Trooper Vincent came round the corner. He was awfully excited, and said to Major Bridges, 'They're coming! They're coming!' The major said, 'What's the matter?' This seemed to pull Vincent up. He stood to attention and said, 'Enemy advancing down the road, sir.'

The major had a look and turned to Captain Hornby. 'You have a go at them with two troops, and I will give you covering fire.'

'Mount the first two troops, draw swords, right wheel!' and we were off. I followed the captain as he went down the right-hand side of the road. He took a German on the point of his sword, just as I saw the lads do at Shorncliffe with the dummies. I couldn't have a hand in the fun, so I crossed over to the other side of the road and took on a chap with a lance, whom I captured.

We set off back to Headquarters. I led the way with the German lance well out in front, we arrived at the canal and found a troop of the Bays holding the bridge. I recognised a chum, and he asked me where we had been. I pulled his leg, said we had been out to fetch a sample, and if they saw any chaps like these they were to shoot them, as they were Germans.

When we reached the regimental headquarters, Colonel Mullens asked, 'Who caught this one?' I stuck out my chest and said, 'I did, sir.' He told me I was a damned fool. The order was that prisoners should be searched, stripped and turned away some distance from our troops. This was to save dealing with them and hampering the advanced troops.

This was the first action of the BEF on continental Europe since the Battle of Waterloo ninety-nine years earlier. In 1939, just days before the outbreak of the Second World War, a memorial was unveiled to commemorate the incident. Both Tilney and Hornby attended the ceremony.

Capt. Hubert Rees, 2nd Welch Rgt

We were ordered to rejoin our battalion at Fauroulx. When we got there, we had a view of the Battle of Mons. It was dark when we arrived but the flashes of the guns and flames from the burning houses made a very impressive sight. It also brought home to us that there really was a war on, a fact which up to then many of us had had some difficulty in visualising. After many years of complete peace, one's mental outlook required a considerable amount of readjusting which accounted for a brother officer asking me a few days later whether I felt savage.

'Savage?' I asked. 'What about?'

'Savage with the Germans,' he explained, with a serious and rather puzzled look. 'What I mean is – Do you want to kill them?'

'Not especially.'

'Nor do I. I expect we ought to eat raw meat or something.'

Lt Rowland Towell, 41st Batt., RFA

Suddenly a mob of horses came dashing along the road from the east with inhabitants and others with them. Alarming reports were spread by interpreters: Germans within a mile and in force. It was a depressing entry into the war. Apparently a troop of 15th Hussars had dismounted, leaving a minimum guard over the horses: two whizzbangs [German shells] burst close to them, and off the lot went. This was the simple unvarnished explanation. At 4 p.m. the batteries were ordered up to a position that had been reconnoitred and prepared. 29 Battery led, then 41, and lastly 45. As 29 Battery disappeared over the crest of the hill, three bangs were heard. I remarked to the Battery Sergeant Major that they had opened fire very smartly. The explanation followed immediately: three crashes on the ridge, German shelling. It looked nasty and more shells arrived just in front on the road. I was ordered to wheel to the left across the field behind the hill. However, the lead driver of the leading gun went on obstinately up the road. The Battery Sergeant Major galloped after him, cursed him for not following my order and asked him why he had not done so, when the man unexpectedly and in astonishment said, 'What, across that wheat?' The fruits of our careful peacetime training!

After heavy fighting, the Germans forced the British infantry to retire from the town of Mons. A great retreat had begun that would take the BEF to the gates of Paris and beyond. As the infantry fell back, there was every danger they might be enveloped and captured. The cavalry were used as a moving screen to protect the infantry and, when necessary, to come into action and charge the enemy.

Lt Alexander Gallaher, 4th (Royal Irish) Dragoon Guards
We were dismounted in the village street, watering our horses from buckets, when we received the order to mount and charge. We jumped into our saddles and tore off down a narrow lane without in the least knowing where we were going or what was up. The dust was thick, so thick one could hardly see the man in front. We went off in a rush and rode down that choking lane with no other thought than keeping going. We had no order to draw sabres, and just galloped in a bunch. Before we reached the end of the lane, men began to fall. I remember seeing our colonel shouting, 'Not there, not there!' but it conveyed no meaning to me. We dashed on after the leading squadron round the corner and into a very inferno of shell and small arms fire. No time to wonder what was happening. Shrapnel was bursting right in amongst us, and men falling every inch of the way. Not far beyond the corner, I saw a flash which seemed right in front of my eyes, and my horse went down.

When I came round, I was lying on my side, with one leg under my dead horse. My head was bad. Alongside me was a French officer who had been attached to us, a count, someone said. He was dead. A bullet had hit him right in the centre of the forehead. All seemed quiet for a moment, and everything seemed strangely still. Down the lane I saw Major Tom Bridges ride out into view. He stopped, shaded his eyes with one hand, and gazed about oddly. The Germans saw him and opened fire, the bullets singing by him as he turned and galloped away.

I struggled out from under my horse and tried to run towards the point where Bridges had disappeared, but my leg was sore and numbed and I fell. Another attempt resulted in another fall, so I crawled on my hands and knees to the nearest shelter, a cowshed by the lane. Creeping inside, I found a wounded French interpreter and two wounded troopers. The shellfire began again, and rifle bullets whizzed all about. One of the cows in the shed was hit in the back by a bullet and, with a startled effort, broke the chain by which she was tied and rushed out.

A moment later a German officer and two German soldiers with bayonets came through the doorway. In the officer's hand was a tiny pop-gun of a pistol, which he kept pointed at each of the four of us as he went from one to the other. Reaching my corner, he stopped and relieved me of my revolver and my map-case, the latter containing a notebook in which were an entry or two that I knew would hold his big, round blue eyes.

Running through my pockets, he came to a sovereign purse with seven sovereigns in it. This he tucked back in the pocket of my tunic, then stepped out of the door to examine my notebook in the fading light. The moment his attention was well engaged, one of the German soldiers lost no time in extracting the sovereign case and its contents from my pocket in a manner that left no suspicion in my mind that he intended replacing it.

2/Lt Eric Anderson, 108 Batt., RFA

The infantry must have had a terrible time. We suffered more than they did from sleeplessness, as care of the horses made large inroads into the time available, but the infantry suffered from sheer exhaustion. It is a pitiful sight to see a man who is really footsore trying to get along. Some cut chunks out of their boots at the heel or round a toe that has rubbed, others tried carpet slippers given them by the inhabitants. Many just gave up, not caring whether the Germans got them or not.

Sgt Bradlaugh Sanderson, 2nd King's Royal Rifle Corps

We have lost a few taken prisoner, the army sergeant and some stragglers who were footsore. I keep my feet in condition by putting Vaseline around my socks, but ain't they sore all the same! Nine o'clock we are still marching. I didn't believe one could sleep and march. A few are falling out, it's not nice marching and fighting. We have filled our stomachs with apples which grow by the roadside. This night we only have two hours sleep.

Trp. Alfred Tilney, 4th (Royal Irish) Dragoon Guards

Retreat!!! . . . hateful enough to soldiers at any time, but when we were ordered to retire time after time, no wonder we could not understand it. What seemed to hurt our fellows most was the sight of the refugees; the roads were full of them, all with their few belongings, and carrying babies in many cases, hopelessly hurrying out of the invader's path. The fate of many of those who were too late needs no repeating. Only a few hours before, these same people had been cheering us on to victory, and now we were retiring, it seemed as if we had let them down; they didn't understand. Could we blame them? We did not understand ourselves.

Maj. George Walker, 59th Field Coy, RE

We laid out a [trench] line and got to work and stuck at it all day. Meanwhile the battle in front went on. It was the finest pyrotechnic display I have ever seen. The German shells were bursting all about. They came from all directions, except the rear, and the bursts were of all colours, white, black and white, black and pink and yellow. We could see but little of the infantry but could see the yellow bursts of our Lyddite shells in the enemy's lines. It was a lovely day, brilliant sun and no wind, and a German plane sailed placidly to and fro over our heads, directing the fire.

At about noon, some of the 19th Brigade made a counterattack. I, in my enthusiasm and ignorance, thought we were going to win. Very soon they reappeared over the ridge and came dribbling back, many wounded and all shaken, very few officers.

I met one huge Highlander of the Argylls who said to me, 'They call this war, I call it bloody murder.'

We spent our time collecting straggling infantry and putting them into our trenches, the sappers being evicted and made to lie in the open. It was a trying job as the infantry were shaken and we officers knew nothing. However, we were determined not to go back and we gradually steadied the men. One incident at this time struck me very much. I saw a company of infantry led by an officer deliberately rise from their trench and begin to retire. I dashed over to him and asked why. I was told by the captain that he had had the order. On asking from whom, he replied, 'From that officer there,' pointing out an individual who promptly replied, 'You are a bloody liar.' I mention this as an instance of how such things may happen. I am pretty certain that someone who wanted to be off passed the word down to the officer, who, thinking it bona fide, acted on it.

2/Lt Eric Anderson, 108 Batt., RFA

It was dark by now and raining steadily. There seemed to be a never-ending stream of troops, ambulances, and every sort of vehicle. I dodged over to a staff officer standing at a crossroads and tried to get some sort of information. My men, meanwhile, who I imagined had heard me tell them to wait, wandered on. I soon gave up looking for them as hopeless. At a crossroads I met an officer who was directing the 5th Division straight on and the 3rd Division to Beaurevoir where the infantry were being sorted out. Officers stood in the road and collared their men as they went by.

I went on to a collection of houses about 1 mile to the north-east, where I was told the artillery was. They were in a narrow lane and it was no fun trying to get along. It was a continual obstacle race, round horses, stepping over or on to sleeping men, team after team in never-ending line. At last I struck my own people. It was now 11 p.m. and we heard we were to have two hours' rest. We managed with much difficulty, and in pitch dark, to clear the road and with still greater difficulty to get the horses fed. The men were simply foolish from fatigue and lack of sleep and just dropped off to sleep in the middle of whatever they were doing. Going round in inky darkness to feel whether horses have their feeds on or not is no jest, before all the men had to be kicked up again to take the nosebags off.

We were to move off at 1 a.m., so about twenty minutes before, in pitch black and drizzling rain, I got the sergeants up and the manhunt began. A man might be five yards away and still completely lost. No amount of shouting could rouse them and as they could not be seen, we had to sort of sweep for them. The drivers were made to mount and so were the gunners and then we looked for the absent ones. At last all were collected, safely sleeping, on the horses and carriages and we moved off.

L/Cpl Arthur Cook, 1st Somerset Light Infantry

Most of the men have discarded all their equipment; this would have meant severe disciplinary action in normal conditions, but nobody seemed to mind as long as they retained their rifle and a bandolier or two of ammunition. I stuck to the whole of my equipment in spite of being advised by the men to get rid of it. I was tempted on many occasions as the days were terrifically hot and I envied others with their lighter load, but the nights were very cold and I was glad of my overcoat to keep me warm, whereas the others were shivering, so I humped that greatcoat on my back mile after mile in the blazing sunshine to have the benefit of it at night, to the envy of my comrades.

After three hours' rest, we were off again and continued up to 10.30 p.m. (6 hours). God only knows, our throats were parched with heat and dust, and every few minutes' halt was spent in a sleep of exhaustion. We are too far gone to look or converse with anyone, we move as in a dream; every now and again one drops down, we help him up and try to urge him on. Others fall out at the side of the road, too exhausted to go another step, nobody takes any notice, perhaps he will die of exhaustion, perhaps he will be picked up, but more often he is taken prisoner. Our feet are red raw and full of blisters, our limbs are numbed for the want of rest, all life and interest in things are gone, but we keep going, how, we do not know.

Sgt Bradlaugh Sanderson, 2nd King's Royal Rifle Corps
Well, we awoke at daybreak, hardly able to realise that we weren't marching. I went scouting, and got two eggs and some milk from a house nearby. After breakfast I tinkered up my feet, and finished up this attempt at a diary. Then one of my chaps gets some vegetables, and we have a dinner in fine *table d'hôte* style. Our happiness is short-lived. Cannon sound again. We are ordered to parade at 6 p.m. We march on far into the night. I hear the French have let them through and all sorts of rumours . . . we're fed up. Why can't they let us scrap them, and chance it?

———————

The heroism displayed by officers and other ranks was remarkable. The casualties amongst the officers were particularly heavy. In one action that was to become legendary, L Battery, Royal Horse Artillery, fired their guns at the Germans just a few hundred yards away. Assailed by counter-battery fire, the gun crews were knocked out one by one, until a single gun remained in action, the officers taking their turn to load and fire. Three Victoria Crosses were awarded amongst the few surviving gun crews.

Maj. Walter Sclater-Booth, L Batt., RHA

I got into a root-field on the opposite side of the road to that in which the battery was situated. I saw at least one gun of L Battery firing and could see some flashes of German guns stabbing the mist from the near heights. There was a heavy shellfire and just as I realised I could hardly hope to reach the battery, a shell burst close in front of me and knocked me over, wounding me severely. For five hours I lay unconscious and unseen among the high roots and was only finally found when I had partially come to and was staggering around like a wounded animal. Being temporarily blinded, I was placed on a horse and handed over to Captain Burnyeat of I Battery, who led me away.

Capt. Hugh Burnyeat, I Batt., RHA

After sending L Battery's guns away, we got on to our horses and were going back to the battery when I caught up with Captain Stone of the Bays who had just found Major Sclater-Booth, who commanded L Battery. A shell had burst close to his head and had stunned him without, I think, actually cutting the skin anywhere, but his cheek looked as if someone had caught him a hell of a smack with a many pronged fork, it was deeply ridged and furrowed, and his eyes were all swollen.

Stone put him on to one of his own troop horses and asked me to take charge of him, which I did. He was not a pleasant companion, for at times he went into peals of the most demonical laughter and was quite off his head. He recognised my voice, although he could not see me and I managed to quieten him down and get along. He was in a very poor way when I got back to my battery and, seeing some motor cars at a crossroads close by, I led him across and asked one of the staff officers to take him along with them. This he refused to do, and I was told to tie him on to one of my limbers. In the meantime, Major Sclater-Booth fainted and fell off his horse. I tried another motor car, but with no better result. At last I had a brainwave and told the staff officers that the officer was the Hon. Walter Sclater-Booth, brother of Lord Bassing; this piece of information quickly changed the whole picture and a big limousine car that had nothing but some signalling equipment inside was made available. I was so furious that anyone could have behaved in such an abominable way. It would have killed him to have tied him on to a limber in his state.

L/Cpl Arthur Cook, 1st Somerset Light Infantry
We are feeling the effects of all this marching, but our platoon officer, Lieutenant Pretyman, is smiling. He found a stray horse and he goes along in front of us stretched out on the horse's back, fast asleep. We expect to see him fall off any moment but he doesn't. Today's march was roughly twenty-five miles. We look like a lot of millers, our clothes, faces and hands are covered with a thick coating of dust. None of our relations would recognise us now; everybody has a beard and with no washing facilities we look a sight of horror. Our numbers are gradually declining, with men falling out every day. Being so near to Paris, we expected to see some kind of defence line set up, but it looks as if the French are going to surrender the capital without a fight.

The retreat was about to end. The Germans, having overextended their own exhausted forces, were attacked in the flank by the French Sixth Army driven by taxis to the front line from the streets of Paris. The enemy was forced to pull back and dig in on a ridge, the Chemin des Dames. Trench warfare was about to begin.

Sgt Bradlaugh Sanderson, 2nd King's Royal Rifle Corps
6 September: What a glorious day! Instead of going to Paris, we are to take the offensive, and we are going back. There wasn't half

a cheer. Perhaps they heard it in Paris. Someone started the Tipperary song and 'Rule, Britannia!'. To use a Tommies' term, 'we did give it socks'. Off we went, and it was at once apparent that the boys meant business. That night our advanced cavalry got in touch with the enemy. It was reported that we had them in a tidy knot. So this was the plan. We began to take an interest in our surroundings. Once more we heard 'Vive Les Anglais', accompanied by a significant gesture of the hand across the throat, and 'Allemandes', which is French for Germans.

Our transport, mechanical, is quite up to date. They come in the night, a long convoy of them, dump rations down where the respective quartermasters are, pick up the casualties, and off they go. We haven't many footsore ones now. I've got corns under my feet I could have a horseshoe on. My section holds a record. No one has fallen out yet, but there's one chap who has real grit. Ever since that long march to Mons he has had such awful bad feet, we have left him behind scores of times. Sometimes he would catch us up at halts, then behind again, but he always came marching into bivouac to take his place next morning. He comes from Keighley, quite elderly. His knees gave way once on a march, but he won't go sick.

Today we had read out to us the Kaiser's statement about us being a 'contemptible little Army', and it made us mad. Just let us get a chance at them. Today we cross a river, the Germans are on the other side. Our cavalry had captured a lot of transport and prisoners. Now we began to see where the Germans had been. Bottles – empty, of course – everywhere, and beds and tables pulled out of houses, and windows smashed.

As British troops re-advanced, they passed amongst desperate civilians who had been, it was claimed, brutalised and even tortured by the enemy. Allegations of rape, murder and theft against civilians were soon

stoked up by the press in Britain, and inevitably, while many of the
more lurid cases were without foundation, a number were certainly true.

Sgt William Peacock, 1st South Wales Borderers

We went further down the village to buy a drink of coffee off a
poor French woman. She told us a pitiable tale of what the
Uhlans, that was the German cavalry, had done to her little boy.
She said they held him up by the arms and cut off one of his legs
with their sword and she showed us the heel of his boot he was
wearing at the time, that they had cut clean off as they missed his
leg the first blow. Afterwards we went and saw where he was
buried in the churchyard along with others who were killed in
the village. They have also molested every girl and violated them
as well.

Sgt Bradlaugh Sanderson, 2nd King's Royal Rifle Corps

14 September: This day will ever remain in my memory. It was a
rainy morning, simply pouring. We went gingerly through a
village, Troyon, and up the slope of a big spur in front. We got to
the top, re-formed, and were going through a cutting in the
hillside when a terrible rain of bullets came amongst us.

Our officer, Captain Cathcart, was hit, and shouted, 'Extend
over the ridge right and left.' I went with my platoon officer, Mr
Davidson. We extended about three paces up to the edge of a
mangold patch. Day was just breaking when we got into position.
We had two killed in a few seconds. Then the Germans turned two
machine guns on us from a haystack not ten yards to our front. My
officer seized hold of a man's rifle, stood up and deliberately fired. I
shouted 'Get down, sir!' He was shot through the eye immediately, and died a few minutes after. Before he did die, however, he
said, 'Hold on to this position, as it is on the flank, don't retire
until you get orders.'

Bullets were clipping the leaves off the mangolds in front of us.
One went through my cap, another hit the safety catch of my rifle,

which made me mad. Every time the Maxim stopped, I bobbed up and took aim, at the same time ordering the men to concentrate their fire on the left side of the haystack. Word was passed on to watch the flank as well. All officers were out of action, so still having that infernal Maxim in mind, I crept to the left front, and got a beautiful view of him as he was sitting manipulating his gun. I avenged Mr Davidson, and felt pleased.

After about thirty minutes, another platoon arrived. Then the [2nd] Sussex came up on my left. I heard a lot of shouting, and everybody was standing up. The Germans had put up a white flag, and were coming in by hundreds to surrender. I noticed a battery of twelve guns away on our right front. The gunners were coming in, and I had a sneaking fancy all wasn't right. They were coming in with rifles, so I ordered my men back. When the Germans got to our front line, they realised what a small number we were. Then they deliberately opened fire at short range. Our chaps gave them rapid [fire], with the result that about 300 made for our lines as prisoners. The others ran back . . . We dispatched the prisoners to the rear, and settled down to work again.

The actual sequence of events was disputed by both sides. Everyone agreed that a white flag had been flown. However, the Germans asserted that the British had opened fire without provocation, a fact that would have serious ramifications for some British prisoners of war captured the next day.

Pte John Cooper, 1st Coldstream Guards

We were taken to headquarters to an officer who was, I think, a general. He was very angry about some incident having to do with the use of a white flag. He spoke very good English. We knew nothing about the incident, but apparently it had something to do with the Sussex Regiment. This general talked about shooting the men and hanging the officers. Finally he gave an order, and two or three battalions of Germans, armed, lined both sides of the road, and we were made to run between them for a distance of about 400 yards, and they set about us with their rifles and big sticks. Captain Robins had an eye knocked out. We were all knocked about, and two men of a kilted regiment were knocked down and killed.

Capt. Lancelot Robins, 2nd Welsh Rgt

I was marched under a blazing sun to Laon. I was without a cap, this having been lost when I was first captured and struck. The sun and blow affected my head. I was suffering from concussion, and the whole facts of the journey are not clear to me. The men with me told me I fainted twice and the whole party was badly treated along the road. I can recollect being assaulted when walking in front of several prisoners. The man struck me on the chest, and I know I hit him in the face. I was knocked down either by a German or by the rush of the other men behind me all of whom I heard afterwards were hit or kicked. On getting up, I picked up my water bottle which had fallen over my head, and seeing a German running at me with his rifle held up in both hands, I swung my water bottle, which was full, clean into his face. I was then knocked down and struck over the face, and this blow I believe destroyed my eye. I know from the men that we were brutally treated because we were accused of having fired on the white flag.

Accusations and counter-accusations were made of barbaric treatment. The regulation British jackknife, used for opening tins of food, was an object for a German obsession that it was used for gouging out the eyes of their wounded; the German saw bayonet, with its serrated edge, used by German pioneers for cutting wood, was seen as a deliberately fiendish implement for killing British Tommies.

Lt R. H. Johnston, 1st Lincolnshire Rgt

The glades became resonant with loud, raucous German commands and occasional cries from wounded men. After about an

hour and a half, I suppose, a German with a red beard, with the
sun shining on his helmet and bayonet, came up looking like an
angel of death. He walked round from behind, and put his serrated
bayonet on the empty stretcher by me, so close that it all but
touched me. The stretcher broke and his bayonet poked me. I
enquired in broken but polite German what he proposed to do
next; after reading the English papers and seeing the way he was
handling his bayonet, it seemed to me that there was going to be
another atrocity. He was extraordinarily kind and polite. He put
something under my head, offered me wine, water and cigarettes.
He said: 'Wir sind kamaraden' [we are comrades]. Another soldier
came up and said, 'Why didn't you stay in England – you who
made war upon the Boers?' I said: 'We obeyed orders, just as you
do; as for the Boers, they were our enemies and are now our friends,
and it's not your business to insult wounded men.' My first friend
cursed him heartily, and he moved on.

---

*One of the most heinous crimes attributed to both sides was the use of so-
called dum-dum bullets, bullets which were round or deeply grooved so as
to split on impact and cause devastating internal injuries. Anyone
caught with such ammunition was liable to be shot almost out of hand.
During the first few days of fighting, an order had been passed around
British officers that flat-nosed revolver bullets should be thrown away.
It was not clear whether these bullets contravened internationally agreed
rules of war laid down by The Hague Rules in the 1890s. Lieutenant
Aubrey Herbert first considered their disposal only after being wounded.*

Lt Aubrey Herbert, 1st Irish Guards
As I lay on the stretcher, a jarring thought came over me. I had in
my pocket the flat-nosed bullets which the War Office had served
out to us as revolver ammunition. They were not dum-dum
bullets, but they would naturally not make as pleasant a wound

as the sharp-nosed ones, and it occurred to me that those having them would be shot. I searched my pockets and flung mine away. I did not discover one which remained and was buried later on, but neither did the Germans. It was first hearing German voices close by that jogged my memory about these bullets, and the Germans were then so close that I felt some difficulty in throwing the bullets away. The same idea must have occurred to others, for later I heard the Germans speaking very angrily about the flat-nosed bullets they had picked up in the wood, and saying how they would deal with anyone in whose possession they were found.

Sgt Bradlaugh Sanderson, 2nd King's Royal Rifle Corps
That night we had a roll call, and found that all officers except three had been killed and wounded, and about 500 of other ranks. The Northants and North Lancs, and Sussex, lost their colonels. One of our sergeants who had been killed left a wife and ten children. This is war with a vengeance. One prisoner this morning put his arms around my neck, but I told him I wasn't in courting humour. I saw several cases of wounded men giving Germans water. One of my men, Hunt from Derby, got shot through both lungs. He came back with me. I helped him down to the rear. He wanted a fag before he died. He said 'It's wonderful how soothing a fag is.'

All sorts of rumours are going round. Some say a Peace Conference is on. I fancy we will be in pieces before that happens. It's marvellous how ignorant we are here. We don't know what is going on except on our own immediate front. We got some English papers and we see that our army saved France. That's some consolation, anyhow, but we didn't know what we were doing.

Sapper Perks, 1st Signal Coy, RE
19 September: During the day we move back about half a mile to some houses just outside Bourg, where we are much more comfortable than before, as we have a loft to sleep in. The house

is still inhabited by two old ladies, one being over ninety, while her daughter is well over sixty.

They are not very pleased to see us, although they get a good meal of food out of us and make a great row when we dig up some of her potatoes. On telling her that if we weren't here the Germans would be, and would take all her food without asking, she replies that she had the Germans in her home in 1870 and wouldn't mind if they came again.

Sgt Bradlaugh Sanderson, 2nd King's Royal Rifle Corps
20 September: Got blown out of our trenches yesterday, but now we have strengthened them by digging under, and making independent traverses. The enemy seems to have plenty of ammunition to waste. If the Kaiser could only see the number that hadn't burst, or gone in the valley, he'd have a fit. All the same, it isn't nice dodging them. One dropped right in my dugout whilst I was absent. Think I was born under a lucky star.

The general in front of us is called von Kluck; we call him 'One o'clock' because he starts shelling about that time.

Capt. Hubert Rees, 2nd Welsh Rgt
The evening of 24 September remains in my mind as one of the most beautiful I ever remember. There was not a cloud in the sky and the landscape stood out clean cut in a pearly pink light which seemed to accentuate the peace and warmth of a perfect day. Not the faintest suspicion of any movement of the air stirred the leaves and the quiet beauty of the evening seemed to have communicated itself to the opposing armies on the Aisne so that even the sporadic shelling ceased and no sounds of war marred the tranquillity of this peaceful interlude. I lay on top of the bank above a sunken lane, basking in the rays of the setting sun, and looked up the valley, the upper part of which was heavily wooded, woods which we had defended recently for an anxious eight days until brought back to the present position. Above and beyond the woods ran the

great bare limestone ridge of the Chemin des Dames stretching away for miles to right and left. Not a living thing moved on the wide stretch of country within view. With the sun behind me every tree, bush, hollow and rock stood out with intense clearness right to the skyline and with this clear-cut immobility went a stillness which nobody appeared wishful to break.

Suddenly from the German lines came a tremendous roar of cheering which swept along the Chemin des Dames in a great wave of sound. 'Antwerp has fallen,' I thought. [This was not the case. However, a U-boat, U9, had sunk three British cruisers on 22 September.] We had been expecting it for some days. The sound was awe-inspiring in its volume, if merely as an indication of the thousands of men who were immediately opposed to us. I looked down into the sunken lane to see what effect this had on the troops, if any. There were only two men in the fifty yards visible. The nearest was sitting on the bank trying to open a tin of bully beef with his clasp knife, having apparently lost the key. He was looking up and listening. I turned back. The Germans, having finished shouting, sang with great patriotic fervour 'Deutschland, Deutschland, Über Alles', followed by the Austrian national anthem. It was really magnificent, and very impressive, and when they had finished there was for a few minutes a great silence. Then the retort came from the British lines in the shape of a cockney voice which cut the stillness like a knife, singing, 'Come, come, come and have tea with me, down at the Old Bull and Bush.' The many English-speaking Germans must have been furious at this careless reduction of the sublime to the ridiculous at a stroke. As for me, I laughed till my ribs ached and incidentally decided that there was no possible chance of the Germans winning the war.

Sgt Bradlaugh Sanderson, 2nd King's Royal Rifle Corps
24 September: Still in billets. Sir J. French came in when we were cooking, without any instruction, and started talking to us, and saying how pleased he was with us all, that he was proud, and that

England was proud, too. He went round all the billets in the same manner. So once more we were pleased, and everyone came to the conclusion that Sir John French is a trump. Everybody simply adores him. Regiments have added new glories to their records, and whatever the outcome of this campaign may be, it won't obscure them. Sir John said we were only there for a short rest, as he couldn't spare seasoned troops, which is quite natural.

The British troops would soon be on the move. In what was known as the race for the sea, each side sought to outflank the other, and in doing so eventually extended the thin line of trenches all the way to Nieuport on the Belgian coast. The British troops would now congregate around a new place, so far undamaged by war: Ypres. The following extracts are taken from a diary written by a trooper as he advanced north with British forces. They cover the last week of the march and give an impression of the distance covered.

Trp. Henry Dyer, 4th (Royal Irish) Dragoon Guards
Moved off again at 12.30 p.m. Had a long march of thirty-eight miles. Saw a man of the Royal Field Artillery lashed on a limber – sentenced for being drunk. Am writing this by the light of a fire whilst on guard. The time is now 1 a.m. We are in an orchard. Am just going to be relieved; can hear the sentry coming . . . Moved off 9 a.m. Marching all day. Thirty years old today. Shall I see thirty-one? Am very doubtful . . . Nothing doing. Moved on again. Marched thirty-two miles, passing through Amiens . . . Horse very lame, too lame to keep up. Waited by the roadside for an hour and a half then started off to find troops on my own, tracing them by their footprints, hoof marks, dung, bully beef tins and occasionally a cigarette packet . . . Rejoined the regiment after marching all day through pouring rain; wet through to the skin . . . Moved off at 4 a.m. on a horse pinched from the 9th Lancers. Crossed the Franco-Belgian frontier again. Nothing doing; had a singsong around a campfire. Each man sitting round

the fire has a loaded rifle in his hand ready for an emergency . . .
Near Ypres. Had Catholic souvenirs served out by Sisters of Mercy
in the trenches. The people were very kind to the British, giving
us all kinds of useful articles such as gloves, scarves and jerseys.
Lieutenant Water shot in the neck.

---

*In early October a 7th Division arrived to join the BEF. Landing at
Zeebrugge, they had originally been charged with helping to save the
fortified Belgian town of Antwerp, but, as this had fallen on 9 October,
they were sent south. By the 14th, they too were at the beautiful Flemish
town of Ypres.*

Cpl Charlie Parke, 2nd Gordon Highlanders, 7th Div.
On 14 October the 7th Division, halfway to being convinced that
the war would be over before they had participated, came to Ypres;
we had marched 103 miles of which the last forty miles had been
covered in a little under forty hours.

To the weary British, Ypres seemed as peaceful and welcoming as
Lyndhurst after a long route march through the New Forest. The
quaint old-fashioned Flemish town, lying sleepily by the side of a
serene, tree-shaded canal, seemed very remote from war. At every
cottage door there were rosy-cheeked women with tempting jugs of
wine since there were very few T-totallers in the British contingent.

Sgt Bradlaugh Sanderson, 2nd King's Royal Rifle Corps
Ypres is a lovely town. One wouldn't think, to see the people
talking and walking about, the shops lit up, etc, that fighting was
going on five miles away. The Germans haven't been right in. Our
chaps got here just in time. We are ordered to wash and shave, to
make the spies think we are fresh from home. I got a Belgian
refugee to do the needful. He charged 2d; if ever a fellow earned it,
he did.

Cpl Charlie Parke, 2nd Gordon Highlanders

My first responsibility was to see the men under my command had somewhere to sleep at night; most people offered their homes immediately and those that didn't were told they would house soldiers, this being an absolute necessity. Men slept on floors and in outhouses with officers having conventional beds in the most affluent houses in the town; the class gulf between officer and men was still as wide as it had ever been. The hell they were all about to enter was to virtually destroy that differential; when men are at their Maker's door and flying shrapnel can open that door at any minute of the day, every day, there was to be a bond built up between the two.

L/Cpl Arthur Cook, 1st Somerset Light Infantry

The Germans have set fire to many houses and ricks in the vicinity by shellfire. Most of the houses have been hit, places that had been vacated only a few hours previously by peaceful inhabitants. Birds were singing in their cages as if nothing unusual was going on; pigs were grunting for food in their sties; horses were neighing for fodder; remains of a hasty meal were left on the table and hot embers were still burning in the grate. The furniture was still orderly except where a hostile shell has penetrated the room and disturbed it. The houses have the appearance of being hastily abandoned with the hope of returning again in a few hours. God only knows if they will ever see their homes, or what is left of them, again.

During our stay in Plugstreet [Ploegsteert] or, rather, during the early part, we sometimes billeted in the village houses in the daytime during our occupation of the support lines, and occupied the lines only at night. A number of civilians were still there. They seemed reluctant to give up their homes, although two or three were killed during most weeks. I remember one day, eleven of us were in one bedroom. Shells were dropping all round us – some short, some just over – so we decided to quit. Next day, on passing, I noticed a shell had struck the bedroom windowsill and had crashed through the floor. Had we not moved, these notes would not have been written. After leaving the houses, we were lodged in Plugstreet Wood in canvas bell-tents – some protection against shellfire! The tents were originally white, but we spent one hot afternoon colouring them with cow manure and ochre. We used long poles with lumps of rag tied at the ends. The task was tedious and malodorous. Until then, I had no idea so many flies existed! But the result was good, and the tents were much less easily seen afterwards.

Sgt Bradlaugh Sanderson, 2nd King's Royal Rifle Corps

Marched out of Ypres at 9 a.m. We looked clean, and a sergeant with the Army Service Corps insulted me, and asked if we were Kitchener's Army. The answer is unprintable. That night we're in the thick of it again, and making acquaintance with the old Jack Johnsons [5.9-inch German shells]. Had a charge. One old fat German at the last trench put up his hands, and said something like 'merci', I thought that he meant thanks in French, but I was surprised when he pulled out his watch, a safety razor, money, and laid down his arms. Whilst I was picking them up, he scooted, but didn't get far. Evidently he meant the English mercy, and was bribing me.

Cpl Charlie Parke, 2nd Gordon Highlanders

My first experience of strafing set me stiff with raw fear, especially when the German artilleryman started searching for his length; at the outset there was an interval of about eight minutes between consecutive shots, eight minutes of apprehensive waiting to discover whether the gunner's search for length would bring death, an early wound ticket out of the mess, or a miss with more attendant waiting tension. The German firepower was tremendous, the British artillery being exceedingly minimal in comparison.

We could see some movement in the trees some 1,000 yards away. Time was meaningless in those pre-battle nervous moments but it would be about eight o'clock in the morning when the enemy came from out of the trees, packed shoulder to shoulder. The Germans wore grey uniforms which, when massed, gave a suggestion of a blue hue. They started advancing at a fast march pace, firing their rifles into the air, an exercise that killed nobody but was just another of the Hun's frightening tactics. At 800 yards we started intermittent firing, approximately six rounds per minute. At 400 yards the enemy increased the speed of charge to a slow double, but at the same time we switched to rapid fire. It was bloody murder, the grey masses fell like ninepins, the man behind climbing over his dead comrade and continuing the advance. It was as though those brave men had been told by their ruthless, ambitious Kaiser that they could walk through bullets.

After rapid fire for approximately fifteen minutes, the wooden casing over the barrel of our rifles became too hot to hold, so the men would either use the webbing sling to protect their left hand or scoop soil and grass from the top of the parapet as a heat shield.

That first day the Hun made seven charges, always literally shoulder to shoulder in four rows and always with the same result, the wholesale slaughter of the cream of German manhood. That first day drew to its close the same way it had started, with constant strafing of the British lines; mounds of dead, wax-moustached Germans littered no-man's-land. Through the nocturnal hours, we could hear the enemy removing their wounded but we never fired at an enemy we couldn't see and to waste bullets was sacrilege.

Lt Col C. K. Burnett, Commanding Officer, 18th (Queen Mary's Own) Hussars
One of the most thrilling sights I have ever looked on was the battle line by night round Ypres, when fighting was at its most furious pitch. Once, a violent thunderstorm accompanied the

combat, while the continuous display of rockets of all colours round the semi-circle of the salient, the constant bursting of shells and flashes of the guns, so visible at night, aided by the vivid storm of many-coloured sheet lightning and abetted by the roll of the thunder and the noise of the guns, all this with the flames of many villages burning in the distance and the mass of smoke and fire rising from the town of Ypres, as a centre setting to the picture, produced a scene which few will ever forget.

Trp. Henry Dyer, 4th (Royal Irish) Dragoon Guards
We are taking cover behind a wall, but if a shell hits it we will be taking cover *underneath* the wall! One shell has just burst about ten yards away, but I am untouched. I am writing this while the firing is going on. Just ordered into the wood for better cover, but it's nearer the German guns. Winslade, Skates and I spent about an hour in trying to catch a partridge. The King's Own, who are in the trenches, cannot advance or retire owing to the close position of the enemy. Our own artillery is dropping shells short into our trenches; one just burst amongst the Lancashires. At last a shell has found us out and burst among us. There are many horses killed and also two men, one, Private Skates, blown to pieces. I was near him and found I had got a bit of shell in my leg. There are some terrible sights; one horse had his head from his eyes down blown off and also one foreleg.

L/Cpl Arthur Cook, 1st Somerset Light Infantry
Another day of Hell under the continual hail of shells and bullets. Have lost a considerable number of men today. Oh, why have we no artillery to retaliate? Why have we to live in such a Hell? The ground is vibrating all day long with the concussion and the continual thud, thud, thud of shells. Men are being buried alive and blown to pieces all around me; perhaps death is preferable to this infernal life. The Germans have made tremendous efforts to push us back but have failed up to now. We were relieved in the

evening by the Lancashire Fusiliers and went back to a wood on the other side of the chateau and had a good sleep, the best for days.

Lt Col C. K. Burnett, Commanding Officer, 18th (Queen Mary's Own) Hussars

We noticed at this period how weary the infantry was with its incessant fighting, the men seemed to have that faraway look on their faces which betokened general inability to realise the horrors which were surrounding them. Their almost continuous and superhuman exertions for week after week, practically since the war began, had left them now with just a fixed determination to go on until they dropped, without notice of other events beyond what occurred in just their immediate front; one could too plainly see that the limit of human endurance had almost been reached.

Cpl Charlie Parke, 2nd Gordon Highlanders

There was an overwhelming stench of death. The almost sweet but acrid smell of decaying flesh could not be compared to any other, but suffice it to say that even someone new to this horror would know its source instinctively and immediately. In hot weather, corpses of horses and men would explode in about three days. The whole body would swell up, although different parts to different extents. Fingers inflated only slightly, whereas stomachs swelled the most and, in fact, it was at this point that explosion would normally be expected to occur; in military bodies, however, the extremely strong webbing belt held the stomach in, so bursting occurred in two places, just above the belt and just below, near the crotch.

In that hellhole, one creature came out on top whatever the result of the skirmish; that creature was the rat. These vermin performed so well in stripping flesh from corpses that they were a protected species, the standing order being that none were to be shot.

I watched at first hand one of these monster rodents start ripping at the freshly felled German uniform, almost at the edge of the British parapet, fiercely searching for the prime Hanoverian flesh beneath. Rats were an extremely efficient demolition unit, usually starting at the peripheries, either head or toes; where there was an abundant supply of human flesh, which was usually the case, they would leave the stomach, the container of waste products, and start on a fresh corpse. Although they were an obnoxious sight, they performed a necessary duty in baring skeletons and I, from my own experience, found they never troubled live humans, not even when the men slept.

Sgt Bradlaugh Sanderson, 2nd King's Royal Rifle Corps

I have to see about the issue of rations to the section, and if anyone wants to try a Chinese puzzle, let them try to issue 2 loaves of bread, about 11 small tins of bully, 23 biscuits, 3 tins of jam, cheese, and a lump of bacon with a bone in it, in a wood where no lights are allowed, to fifteen men, each to have an equal share, otherwise there's ructions. Always about 9 p.m. Sometimes there is one tin of Vaseline, a piece of soap, a pipe, chocolate, a pair of bootlaces, so we raffle them. One consolation, we get plenty of food, and Tommy has always some to spare for the kids. All one can hear in towns we have passed through, is 'souvenir, biscuit, Anglais'.

Cpl Charlie Parke, 2nd Gordon Highlanders

At night those tired, ravenous men eagerly looked forward to their nightly visit from their regimental comrades from the support positions, anticipating rations. Once again the ammunition came, but there again the ammunition always came, taking priority over food. They did, however, get tea brought in a cooking can with a lid, so stewed you could stand a spoon up in it. The men used this lukewarm tea to soften the rock-hard emergency biscuit ration in order to protect their teeth.

L/Cpl Arthur Cook, 1st Somerset Light Infantry

We found a pig wandering about and decided to kill it, but no one seemed game to do the deed. At last it was suggested we put him in a sack and shot him. We burned him off and sliced and divided him up. In the meantime, some fowls and rabbits and a goat were found and all went into the pot together. My word, it took a lot of cooking, as Jerry kept on shelling and we had to run for cover, leaving the pot to carry on stewing. The best of it was when Fritz just missed putting one shell right into the pot, which threw up a lot of dirt that settled in our stew. But we didn't mind a bit of dirt – we were not going to lose that stew, and it turned out to be excellent! I had two or three helpings. We also nearly had a calf. It was wandering along the road behind us, and one fellow said, 'Here, bring me a rifle, I'll have a pot at him.' It was about fifty yards off so he had his pot but with no fatal result, it just swished its tail, looked round as much as to say 'Who did that?' and wandered off again, this time into German lines. I think it must have been a spy!

Had a lovely hot bath and change of clothing this morning. On arrival at the brewery where we were going to have our bath, we undressed in a room, taking off everything except our shirts and boots. Our khaki coats, trousers and caps, less the chinstraps, were tied in a bundle and placed in the fumigator, and our vests, pants and socks were carted off (lice and all) for boiling. We then had to go out in the open and proceed along the canal towpath for about fifty yards, in full view of the ladies on the canal bank. Remember, we only had shirts on and it was bitterly cold, so we did not loiter for the benefit of the Mademoiselles much, but high winds did not help conceal our modesty! We were glad to get inside the bathroom which was nice and warm. Our bathtub consisted of large beer vats. Ten men were allotted to each vat, so on discarding shirts and boots we clambered up into the vats like a lot of excited kids. Every now and again we peeped over the side to see if our boots were OK, for we had been told to keep our eye on them as they were likely to be pinched.

By this time we were a very lousy crowd, the lack of washing facilities had bred louse by the thousand, and the surface of our bath water had a thick scum of these vermin. But we didn't care, we helped scratch each other's backs (which already looked as if a lot of cats had been scratching them) to ease the itching. We were, of course, given a piece of soap and towel, and after ten minutes we were ordered out and dried ourselves and were given a clean shirt. We then had to retrace our steps along the towpath to the dressing room where the girls were still waiting. It must have been cold for them but I suppose they thought it worth their while! We were then issued with clean vests, pants and socks, then out came our clothes, all steaming hot, which we put on. My! What a sight we looked with everything creased and our hats all shapes. Anyway, we felt nice and clean for a while, but it would not be long before our warm bodies became alive again with nits which had not been destroyed in the washing process, making themselves active in our vests and pants.

Cpl Charlie Parke, 2nd Gordon Highlanders
The thin khaki line at Ypres had stood its ground. The contemptible little army had repelled the Kaiser's crack divisions. I believed then, and I still believe, that the Germans lost the war at Ypres in 1914. If the Hun couldn't pass a thin line of troops, then how were they going to stop hundreds of thousands of British reinforcements?

Those reinforcements had been pouring into France at an ever-increasing rate since the first territorial regiments arrived in mid-September. In late October and early November, dozens of new and eager battalions were setting sail to do their 'bit' and win the war, despite the scepticism of the regular soldiers they would meet, who often doubted their part-time comrades' abilities and training.

Pte Charles Heare, 1/2nd Monmouthshire Rgt

The boat – *Manchester Importer* – and off we go. The sea is like a table, calm. One of the draft, Byron Thorne, a friend of mine, said, 'I have broken my gun.' 'It's a rifle,' says Fisher. 'Well, my gun is broke,' says Byron. 'Let's see it,' says Fisher. The rifle was half cocked, Byron was trying to load it. 'How many rounds have you fired?' asks Fisher. 'None,' says Byron. 'Never had a gun until I had this one two days ago and most of the draft are the same.' 'Good job we got a navy,' says Fisher. 'Our army is slightly bent.'

We arrive at Le Havre and had to wait until evening to get off. How excited we all are. Let's hope it doesn't finish before we get off the boat. If we only step off the boat, we can get a medal [for service overseas] . . . At last we get off. Great is the excitement. I get tangled up on the gangway with my bicycle. The boys behind me say, 'Move the old iron out of the way, Charley, you are stopping good soldiers going to war.'

A soldier of the Lancashire Fusiliers asks me what lousy mob this is. I tell him this is a regiment not a mob. 'We are the 2nd Mons.' 'Never heard of 'em. English, or what are you? And what are you here for?' 'We are territorials and the London Scottish have just done well at La Bassée, and we are going to do better,' I say. He smiles and says, 'When the Germans know your mob are here, they will take out their knives and forks and come over and have you for dinner.' He damps my spirit a bit.

CSM Cornelius Love, 1/2nd Monmouthshire Rgt

We met some Field Artillery coming down for a rest or to be made up to strength. We were lucky to get replies to our questions, for they were all practically asleep as they jogged along. One good chap (whose leg we pulled by asking him 'what time the teams were kicking off') promised us we would get all the information we required when we got on the field and that there would be no entrance fee. He said all this without a smile and this was for a very

good reason. He had been there and was returning with a very
small percentage of his battery.

Pte Charles Heare, 1/2nd Monmouthshire Rgt

I fancied my French was good. Listening to these old soldiers saying,
'Malon the batt' (speak the language), 'Honey' (for water), 'Chub-er-
now' (for shut up), 'Kidner budgy' (what's the time?). Now I find I
haven't got French at all but India talk, Hindustanee. I am learning.
I learn 'Merci' for 'thank you' and I try it on a Frenchman who says in
good English, 'It's justice you want, not mercy.'

---

*The winter had settled in with a vengeance, and both sides hunkered
down in waterlogged trenches. For all the combatants, Christmas was
approaching and while goodwill would not necessarily be extended to all
men, the hope amongst those in the line was that a temporary peace might
reign for at least a day. No one could have predicted the events that
followed.*

Cpl Arthur Cook, 1st Somerset Light Infantry

Very sharp frost last night. Received plenty of gifts of puddings
and cakes. Was also presented with Princess Mary's Gift, containing tobacco, cigarettes and pipe; these I gave away, but the case is
still in my possession. Had a walk around Ploegsteert; the roads are
lovely and hard with the frost. It is obvious the Germans made
sinister use of their short time in this small place, for all the young
maidens from eleven onwards appear to have been raped, and are
now showing signs of motherhood. The troops in the front line are
having a quiet time today.

Maj. R. T. Fellowes, 1st Rifle Brigade

A most interesting day. We all went to church at 9 a.m. in
Fleurbaix. I then went with the general to attend a conference to

decide what was to be done about getting rid of the water that is getting to be a serious menace to our trenches. We have got to clear out a lot of the ditches behind us and cut a lot of extra drains, and thus try and divert the flow of water. After this, we went down to the trenches to see how things were getting on – in the left section things were very much as usual – everyone at work, digging and clearing away fallen-in trenches, etc. The usual sniping was in progress, and the general and I got shot at when we made a dash across the open for a few yards to escape a lot of water that was lying in the trench.

When we got to the right section, a very different state of affairs was in progress – an armistice was on and the whole of the neutral ground between our trenches and the Germans was covered with men – they were mostly over the ground where the night attack took place a week ago, and they were busy collecting the dead bodies that had been left out there all that time. It was a weird sight, English and Germans all hobnobbing together perfectly friendly. Our fellows were digging three enormous graves, and the Germans were collecting the bodies and bringing them along. It was a beastly sight seeing all those poor frozen bodies lying about in every kind of attitude, just where they had fallen.

CSM Cornelius Love, 1/2nd Monmouthshire Rgt

The enemy and our men commenced shouting to one another across no-man's-land (the distance between the trenches was about 150 yards). It came to offering cigarettes and bully beef to one another as souvenirs. The heads began to bob up over the parapet. A couple of the bolder spirits went out and met the enemy and exchanged small gifts. There were several dead lying about in no-man's-land, and we took this kind of armistice as an opportunity to clear away the dead and give them a decent burial. Sufficient time was arranged for this, but it was not carried out: instead of helping to bury the dead, the enemy proceeded to collect rifles and bayonets and carry them to their front line. Of course, it was some time before our officers realised what was happening, and then the order was given for all NCOs to stand-to in the front line. There was a feeling that a big surrender was coming from the other side, but it was not to be.

Cpl Arthur Cook, 1st Somerset Light Infantry

A few days ago, we were trying our hardest to slaughter each other, and here today are our men and the enemy walking about together in no-man's-land, laughing and joking with each other and shaking hands as if they were old friends meeting after a prolonged absence. You had to see it to believe your own eyes. After exchanging cigarettes for cigars, they would stroll along arm in arm. Not to be done out of this little armistice, I too went out and had a chat with several of the Germans, most of whom spoke very good English. They all looked extremely well and assured us that they would not shoot as long as we didn't, so I don't know who will start the ball rolling here again. Anyway, we are making the most of this fantastic situation while it lasts. This truce had its advantages, for it enabled us to collect our dead which had been lying about here since 19 December, and give them a proper burial in the cemetery near Somerset House (battalion HQ) in Ploegsteert Wood. The Germans themselves handed over the body of Captain C. C. Maud, and told us he was a very brave man.

Maj. R. T. Fellowes, 1st Rifle Brigade

There were several German officers about and they told us that they knew perfectly well what was happening behind our lines. They knew that we had received reinforcements the other day, and they knew the numbers of both officers and men. They knew that up to a short time ago we were doing three days in the trenches and three out, but that we changed a short time ago, and that the longest time a battalion had been in was seven days; all this was perfectly correct, and it makes one marvel at their system of intelligence. Whether they have got spies behind our lines with underground telephones, or what it is, I really don't know, but the fact remains that they know infinitely more about us and our doings than we do about them.

It was weird walking about overland and seeing our trenches from the top, after having lived in them and walked in them for six weeks underground, and when the only view we got from them was from ground level. Everything seemed so different and the distances so short when one was not threading one's way amongst a labyrinth of zigzag trenches, going round traverses and up and down endless communicating trenches. It was quite an experience, and the whole thing made it difficult to realise that we were at war.

Capt. Sir Edward Hulse, 2nd Scots Guards

We talked [with the Germans] about the ghastly wounds made by rifle bullets, and we both agreed that neither of us used dum-dum bullets, and that the wounds are solely inflicted by the high-velocity bullet with the sharp nose, at short range. We both agreed that it would be far better if we used the old South African round-nosed bullet, which makes a clean hole . . . They think that our press is to blame in working up feeling against them by publishing false 'atrocity reports'. I told them of various sweet little cases which I had seen for myself, and they told me of English prisoners whom they have seen with soft-nosed bullets, and lead bullets with notches cut in the nose; we had a heated, and at the same time good-natured argument, and ended by each hinting to the other that the other was lying.

Maj. R. T. Fellowes, 1st Rifle Brigade

When one sees and hears of these things, it rather makes one realise what a stupid, senseless thing war is; the Germans, I expect, are just as good fellows as we are, and don't really hate us with that ferocious hatred that we are told they do — and yet tomorrow we shall be plugging away at each other and doing our best to kill each other again. I suppose it is only a small proportion really of the Germans that deserve the epithets of 'Huns', 'Murderers', 'Pillagers', etc, that the English press hurl at the German nation as a whole!

Pte Charles Heare, 1/2nd Monmouthshire Rgt

All our papers are crying out at the Germans for using dum-dum bullets [. . .]; the papers say it is not war. A King's Own orderly asks Black [a friend] and me to go up and see their sniping post in a house. We go. A rifle is fixed on a tripod. 'What a large rifle,' says Black. 'Yes,' says the sniper. 'We use soft-nose bullets here. They are three times as large as ordinary bullets.' A wet sack is spread across the window, in front of the rifle. 'That stops the flame being seen,' says the sniper. 'Look through this pair of glasses and see what this rifle can do.' I look. A German is on the barbed wire with only half his head. 'We caught him at daybreak,' says the sniper. 'See what this rifle can do.'

Cpl Charlie Parke, 2nd Gordon Highlanders

I never saw, and never found out, how that truce started but it soon spread through the trenches like wildfire. As an NCO, I stayed in the trench, it was only the privates who mixed with the enemy; the officers from both sides paced along the top of their own parapet refusing to acknowledge each other, pouting and clearly disapproving of the events. The men played good-natured football games with empty Maconochie tins and exchanged their ration of rum or cigarettes for generous-sized German cigars. Close to dusk, the two sides were ordered back to the trenches; the ceasefire had been scrupulously adhered to by both parties.

CSM Cornelius Love, 1/2nd Monmouthshire Rgt

After a few more greetings, there was a kind of 'wind-up' on both sides, as no one seemed to know the meaning of this miniature armistice. One of our company sergeants [Frank Collins] was spotted in no-man's-land and was fired at from the enemy's reserve trench and hit in the breast. I honestly think it was the act of a maniac. I could see he was badly hit. He staggered to where I was standing and just managed to reach our wire. I helped him in and commenced to bandage and treat the wound where the bullet had entered, but when I turned him over I could see that he was a hopeless case. The bullet had entered his lung. We did the best for him. He was sent on a stretcher to the Medical Officer but he did not live long.

While open fraternisation did not last for very long, the truce itself lasted for many days, with neither side wishing to be the one to break the peace. In many places, where orders were received to open fire once more, a message was sent to the enemy warning them that hostilities would recommence so that anyone still out in the open could regain their lines. The Christmas Truce was over. The struggle was about to begin again in earnest.

Cpl Charlie Parke, 2nd Gordon Highlanders

Christmas was the time by which many had expected to be home but now, as I peered across the 300 yards of no-man's-land that morning, I knew it was going to be a long, long haul.

1915

The War in 1915

The present was well-intentioned and no doubt heartfelt, too. It was a gift of a small brass box containing tobacco and cigarettes for smokers (acid tablets for non-smokers), and it came from Princess Mary, daughter of the King, as a Christmas present to those serving abroad that first winter of the war. It was accepted by soldiers and sailors alike with obvious pleasure and gratitude. The boxes had in fact been paid for by public subscription, and were a visible sign that people back home were thinking of them. Inside, there was a small card wishing the soldiers 'A Happy Christmas and a Victorious New Year'.

The second sentiment was patriotically bullish but, all things considered, somewhat optimistic. In 1914 the BEF had held on, but only just. The winter had given the Commander-in-Chief, Sir John French, and his senior commanders, including General Douglas Haig, time to think. Approximately 400,000 men had so far made it to the Western Front, a number greatly increased by the arrival of the territorials from September 1914 onwards. Of that gross figure, around a quarter had been killed, wounded or were missing, the vast majority of them regular soldiers whose replacement, like for like, would be well-nigh impossible. The remainder of those under arms were taking their turn in and out of the line, adapting slowly to the bitter winter conditions and the frequently appalling nature of the ground in which they managed to exist. The British Army was hopelessly unprepared for winter life, a lesson learnt quickly but at the expense of large numbers of men, who, succumbing to trench foot and hypothermia, were removed from the line. The British troops had also tended to hold positions close to the Germans' but geologically disadvantageous, and in time small strategic withdrawals to firmer ground were made.

Historically, armies do not launch offensives during winter, and all sides on the Western Front did not diverge from this norm. It would be the Allies who would open the fighting season with a joint offensive in early March, but the French attack was postponed while the British went ahead with a plan to capture the village of Neuve Chapelle and the high ground of Aubers Ridge, threatening the enemy's possession of the city of Lille. The attack was also designed to demonstrate to the French that the BEF was a fighting force to be reckoned with. The four-division assault was initially successful but a lack of coordination, and supply problems, quickly brought the offensive to a halt. The Germans counter-attacked, retaking much of the ground lost. Losses on each side amounted to around 13,000.

The stalled offensive in France came at a time when a political split between so-called 'westerners' and 'easterners' grew ever deeper. It was a division between those who supported the continued campaign on the Western Front as the essential crucible of fighting, and those others (the 'easterners', including the First Lord of the Admiralty, Winston Churchill) who preferred an alternative pre-emptive strike elsewhere, to alter the course of the war. The decision to launch a campaign in the Dardanelles against Germany's ally Turkey was supported by the failure at Neuve Chapelle, but it was a risky strategy. Two divisions, including the 29th, a regular division made up of battalions brought back from the far corners of the Empire, would be entrusted with a landing alongside French and Australian forces on the beaches of the Gallipoli peninsula, with the long-term aim of capturing Constantinople and knocking Turkey out of the war. However, tight restrictions on the expenditure of ammunition in France and

Belgium, and the still-weakened effectiveness of the BEF, opened up a potential danger much closer to home. The 1st Canadian Division had arrived in February to relieve at least some of the burden, and there had been an Indian Division in France since October 1914. Nevertheless, there appeared no immediate prospect of getting one of Kitchener's New Army divisions to the front line. If the Germans launched an offensive here, disaster might be difficult to avert. The British were committed to the Gallipoli campaign when, just three days before the landings on the peninsula, the Germans launched an offensive near Ypres on 22 April, using a new weapon: poison gas.

Fortunately for the Allies, the German High Command intended to concentrate its efforts in 1915 on offensives in the east against Russia, limiting operations in the west to short offensives with limited objectives. The decision to attack in the Ypres Salient was made for strategic reasons; there was no intention to launch a decisive blow. However, the hard-pressed troops in the line were not to know this, and the fighting was intense as the British and Empire troops were pressed back into a smaller and smaller defensive ring in front of Ypres.

In May, the postponed French offensive in the Artois was launched with a supporting attack made by British troops on 9 May, at the Battle of Aubers Ridge. The offensive achieved nothing other than to draw off enemy reserves from in and around Ypres. By late May the fighting around Ypres had largely abated, just five weeks after it had begun. Had the Germans known, they might have broken the British line decisively. They had the manpower and the artillery to do so, but had chosen to stay their hand. It was their last major offensive against the British until March 1918, and the last opportunity to win outright.

The short-lived British offensive at Aubers Ridge would have passed into history largely unnoticed, but for the fact that its apparent failure brought about one dramatic change which, in the long term, would have a huge influence on the outcome of the war.

A *Times* newspaper correspondent, with the support of Sir John French, placed the failure of the offensive on a lack of artillery ammunition. The revelation brought forth a storm of protest both public and in the House of Commons and had the effect of waking up the British Government from its indolent slumber. Ever since August 1914, when they had proclaimed 'Business as Usual' just as they also declared war, there had been an excited recruitment drive which had robbed industry, in particular vital industries such as coal mining, of valuable workers, but elsewhere there had been little effort to turn the island's economy on to a war footing. British immersion in the fighting, in comparison with other nations, had been gradual. 'Business as Usual' might easily have been translated as 'complacency and inevitability'. It had taken an offensive and nine months of war to make the Government realise the seriousness of the situation. Ammunition could not be made by the established munitions factories alone. For any successful prosecution of the war, a huge expansion of the armaments industry would be required. To undertake the task, David Lloyd George was made Minister of Munitions, and he set about a radical reform with his usual energy. It was an appointment that would pay huge dividends.

The British Army took the summer to recuperate from its exertions. Their losses hastened the arrival of the first of Kitchener's Divisions, the 9th, which arrived in mid-May, to be followed over the next few months by several more. At Gallipoli, the campaign had ground to a halt close to the beaches where the men had landed in April, so in August a second landing was made, but to little avail. The failure at Gallipoli turned the attention back to the Western Front and a second joint Anglo-French offensive. The British would attack in the mining district of Loos while the French would attack near Arras. For the first time, Kitchener's New Army would be tested in action. The offensive began after a heavy bombardment of the enemy lines, and met with rapid success. However, a problem that was to dog so many operations until 1918, with communication and supply, halted progress, while German reserves were brought up to counter-attack. On the second day, Kitchener's men were sent into action and suffered heavily. The offensive was temporarily halted, to be renewed in mid-October but with further heavy loss for little ostensible gain. The failure was to cost Sir John French his job, and he was removed in December. General Haig, who had never believed in the offensive at Loos, replaced him.

The year's activity was brought to a close, and the men settled down for another winter, at least much better equipped than they had been in the previous year. At Gallipoli, the campaign was stopped and the process of evacuation began. In one of the most extraordinary operations of its kind, the entire garrison on the peninsula was safely withdrawn at night under the nose of the Turks, by a combination of subterfuge, downright trickery and no little skill.

Attitudes to the Germans

From any distance other than at close range it would be impossible to determine whose khaki-clad body lay on the German wire. However, one telltale piece of evidence attached to the prostrate form left no room for doubt. Before attacking that morning, Second Lieutenant Laurence Forrest had pulled on a black armband in memory of his sister-in-law. It was two years since she had drowned when the *Lusitania* was sunk by a German U-boat, with the loss of 1,198 civilians. The press had called the sinking deliberate mass murder of innocents, among them many women and almost a hundred children. Second Lieutenant Forrest, for one, had certainly not forgotten.

Reported atrocities are the easiest way to foment hatred between two nations at war, and in 1914 both Britain and Germany required a certain baiting. In Britain, newspapers ran lurid stories of soldiers' (mis)behaviour. Some of it was fanciful but much of it true, not least because war is a natural theatre for excess. On the battlefield there were claims that British soldiers had shot at men surrendering under the white flag; that British and German soldiers had used flat-nosed dum-dum bullets. The Germans were rightly accused of crimes against civilians, and of wanton destruction. They in turn countered that Britain had used prisoners as labourers within range of artillery fire and that many had been killed, thereby breaking one of the articles of war prohibiting their employment in an area of danger: the list was endless.

After a brief war of mobility both sides had dug in and, with the proliferation of trenches, there developed a largely static conflict in which the enemy, other than the dead, was rarely seen. Brief conversations, or more often jibes, were exchanged across no-man's-land, but there were moments, too, when something said would make men think. 'We're Saxons and you are Anglo-Saxons' was one German call which highlighted the similarities rather than the differences between men in opposing trenches. The great revelation was the Christmas Truce of 1914, when both sides swapped carols and greetings rather than bullets, and then met in no-man's-land to exchange gifts and to talk. Yet, for all the short-lived fraternity of the occasion (and many men refused to join in), Britain was at war with Germany and, though there was no individual quarrel between opposing soldiers, there was a recognition that the war would continue; as one private in the Rifle Brigade noted in a letter home, 'One fellow (a German) said to us, "today peace, tomorrow you fight for your country, and I fight for mine."' These soldiers saw no contradiction between enjoying the novelty of the occasion and then returning to war, even though, as the same private wrote, 'Several of them came from London, and one asked us to write to his wife, and gave her name and address.'

War had been expected. *Der Tag*, an apparently inoffensive German phrase meaning 'The Day', held a resonance with the British public in the years leading up to 1914 that is all but lost to our collective consciousness today. The words were broadly interpreted to mean 'the day' when Germany set out on a pre-determined course of war and conquest. Who had said them, and when, was not altogether known, but the words had been digested in Britain without question and their implication accepted as gospel.

Historically and culturally the nations had much in common. Germans were the second largest immigrant population in Britain pre-1914, setting up bakeries and butchers' shops across the country, and working in many of London's best hotels and restaurants. They were well integrated into British society. Similarly, it was common for British boys of well-to-do families to travel to Germany to finish their education, studying at many of the great universities, or to develop their business acumen and language skills by working in German industry.

Familiarity, rather than reducing the risks of war, had only managed to enhance them. Neither side was in any doubt as to the interests and ambitions of the other. Nevertheless, there was no history of bitterness between the two nations, no hurtful disputes on which to fall back as a pretext for war. There was just a growing sense that, as ruler of a third of the globe, Britain was about to be challenged for its place at the head of the international table. On the eve of the Battle of Mons, when Captain Hubert Rees was asked whether he felt 'savage' towards the Germans, he spoke not only for himself but for the majority of others when he said 'No'. But he was a professional soldier and he would fight whoever he was told to fight, to the best of his ability.

Throughout the war, the nicknames given to the enemy by British soldiers reflected the attitude and feelings of men towards their counterparts at any particular time. Hun, kraut, Boche, squarehead were the more abusive; Allyman, Jerry, Fritz, Johnny, even (surprisingly) Dutchmen, were less abrasive, while sometimes the names seemed to combine respect with abuse, such as 'Brother Boche'. According to one tank officer, Frank Mitchell MC, the names changed as the war progressed. The talk of German 'frightfulness' was at its most vociferous in 1914 and 1915 and as a consequence 'when feeling against them was very strong, they were called the Hun, or simply Huns'. During the Somme offensives of 1916, Fritz came into use, probably from a growing respect for the enemy's fighting qualities. Mitchell believed that the name 'Jerry' came into common usage later in the war, also as a sign of respect.

With the war's growing industrialisation, many infantrymen felt themselves to be victims of firefights over which they had little or no control; they were merely left to sit it out and to suffer the consequences. Shellfire was by far the biggest killer of the Great War, whereas bayonet wounds were responsible for only a tiny proportion of all injuries. It was not untypical that enemies, trapped in the trenches, felt more in common with men suffering equal discomfort a hundred yards away than with their own 'comrades' manning guns two miles behind the lines. Bombardments of the German lines might be greeted with relief, by men who were thankful that the enemy's fighting capacity was being whittled away, but that did not necessarily negate a certain sympathy for the enemy, knowing for themselves what it was like to go through such a terrifying ordeal. As he stood on sentry duty one night, Norman Cliff, a private in the Grenadier Guards, contemplated his enemy across no-man's-land.

'In solitary silence I mused. Behind the opposite parapet was a German sentry standing in mud, as I was; feeling cold as I did; perhaps scanning the bright company of stars, as I was; thinking what folly war was, as I thought; his mind hovering over the family at home, as mine did.'

There were naturally those who gave little thought or consideration to the enemy; those who were out to settle old scores, or to avenge the loss of a friend or brother. A mindset was easily reached in which 'the only good Boche was a dead Boche', and there were plenty of men who were not interested in taking prisoners, in the belief that every prisoner had to be fed and housed at a time when supplies were running short at home.

Equally, units varied greatly in their attitude to the enemy. Just as Bavarian and Saxon soldiers were noted for their 'friendliness' and Prussians for their aggression, so British units were markedly different, depending on whether they were recruited from more sedate rural areas such as Somerset and Devon or from tougher cities in the industrial heartlands of the North and North East.

During combat, most humanitarian thoughts were set to one side. Kill or be killed was the rationale, and few soldiers would think twice about dropping bombs down an enemy dugout rather than call out for those inside to surrender. As troops crossed no-man's-land, they were frequently either cut down or forced to take shelter in shell holes, advancing by short rushes. However, if soldiers managed to gain the enemy's parapet quickly enough, they often found either that the enemy was in the process of running away or that hands were already in the air in surrender. Few men, in reality, will fight to the death, and a general fear of cold steel ensured the bayonet's use was limited.

In the frantic, confused nature of battle, surrender and the chances of its acceptance were always problematic. There were occasions where no quarter was given and enemy soldiers killed out of hand; equally, occasions of great compassion were shown. To increase the chances of a surrender being accepted, a German might remove his helmet, speak what little English he knew, and hold out images of family members, of children, or offer souvenirs. Most were keen to carry stretchers, to be seen as useful to the enemy when removing wounded, augmenting their own chances of survival. It was then, away from the white heat of battle, that the attitude to the enemy rapidly softened. Arthur Wrench saw a kilted Scotsman 'walking arm in arm with a wounded German and passing the coffee stall there. One man ran out with a cup of coffee which he handed to the Argyll. He in turn handed it to his stricken companion . . . Enemies an hour ago, but friends in their common troubles.'

Similarly, in September 1917 the Reverend Bere, serving at a Casualty Clearing Station (CCS), noted that 'On Saturday a British Tommy stuck a knife into the shoulder of a Fritz during a hand-to-hand fight. The Tommy was wounded, too. They came here together in the same ambulance and smoked each other's cigarettes on the way.' Duty done, honour satisfied, there was no reason for continued animosity.

Soldiers' Memories

Pte John McCauley, 2nd Border Rgt
The floor of the barn was covered in straw, and it was up to each man to claim some unoccupied spot for his bed. I threw down my pack and equipment and sank beside it. I gazed at the men who had been through the fighting with feelings of respect almost approaching awe. They were quiet, determined-looking men who seemed to have some great secret locked in their heart. They had seen. What could they tell us? Their uniforms were dirty and torn, and solid chunks of mud hung about their boots, puttees and equipment. While trying to rid themselves of some of this mud, they calmly surveyed the new arrivals as though trying to figure out what sort of fighting material we would make. We, for our part, felt rather subdued in the presence of these men who had already faced the dangers and horrors of war. Our jaunty air and cheerful spirits were rather quelled by their quiet demeanour, and, for the first time, perhaps, we began to appreciate the serious nature of this war business.

The winter of 1914–15 was extremely cold, though no more so than normal. Nevertheless, the British Army found itself ill-equipped to supply thousands of men living for extended periods in appalling conditions. As a consequence, the men were struck down with ailments ranging from trench foot to lumbago. Nor were the conditions conducive to maintaining morale: Christopher Fowler had been less than a month near the firing line.

Pte Christopher Fowler, 1/1st Honourable Artillery Company (Infantry)

Oh, how I loathe those trenches. Going up last time, I fell in a ditch three feet deep in water and by the time I was pulled out I was drenched right through to the skin. Then it rained nearly all the time (as usual), and to crown the lot we had the greatest misfortune to lose our junior captain and three men. We are now without an officer in our company, a captain being on leave. There are now under 100 men left in our company out of 180.

Capt. Herbert Flemming, 9th London Rgt (Queen Victoria Rifles)

Some days I get most terribly down, and feel I could fly from the horror and misery of this war – I hate the darkness so – and loathe taking my men out, feeling their way very slowly along the muddy, slushy fields and not being able to see more than a few yards ahead. The nearer you get to the trenches, the more frequent the bullets and the responsibility of knowing that a false step, a wrong turn, might lead to disaster. It takes a long time to get your men into the trenches and I always heave a sigh of relief when they are all safely in, and again when we are relieved and they are all safely away from danger. You have to creep about noiselessly and perhaps suddenly up goes a flare from the German lines, which lights up the whole country. You lie flat and wait until the light is finished and then creep on a bit further.

2/Lt Leslie Sanders, 2nd Prince of Wales' Leinster Rgt

I estimate my chance of getting wounded at one in four; of getting killed or totally disabled at one in ten. These are pretty heavy averages, and I would be foolish not to be prepared for the worst. In a sense, therefore, I count myself already dead . . . The only thing I fear at all is the loss of both limbs or total blindness. Both of these are improbable contingencies. If a bullet gets anywhere near your eyes it usually goes into your brain. Still it does happen sometimes; there have been so far twenty-two cases of men blinded in the British Expeditionary Force . . .

Pte John McCauley, 2nd Border Rgt
On my first morning in the trenches, just as dawn was breaking, I was foolhardy enough to risk my head above the parapet of the trench at a spot where I thought I was safe. I could not resist the urge to have one quick glimpse of no-man's-land. As I peered out across the waste of desolate ground, my senses reeled. I could see the mangled and partly decomposed bodies of cattle and horses and the remains of boys and men who had 'gone west'. The remains were clothed in German, French and British uniforms, and God alone knows how long they had lain there, to be further mangled and torn in death by the screaming shells which exploded in that dreary waste. My nostrils were breathing in the foul air of rotting flesh, and the stench of stagnant water in shell holes, and I dropped back into the trench with a horrible feeling of fear and nausea. That sense of fear clung to me from that day forward and stayed with me to the end of the war.

There was an absolute requirement to keep warm that precluded any sensitivities when it came to ripping up the wooden floors of outlying farms or houses in Ypres. Throughout that winter, abandoned homes were systematically stripped of wood for duckboards to line the trench floor and for firewood.

Lt Denis Barnett, 2nd Prince of Wales' Leinster Rgt
My fellows went out one night to get firewood, and came in with a beam about 30x3ft, which they put on a fire. About five minutes

later, the house fell down, and the Germans cheered, and we joined in. In daylight, the place was seen to be flat. It is better like that, as it won't draw fire so much . . . There are several smaller cottages about, all rather depressed, some with only one wall, others with none at all, but only heaps of bricks. A lot of the work of destruction is due to our men pulling down beams for firewood after the walls have been partially knocked away by shells.

Pte William Brown, 1/4th Oxford and Buckinghamshire Light Infantry
'German House', an isolated stronghold in our front line, was unapproachable except by night, and it was therefore necessary for the garrison to obtain sufficient supplies of firewood during the hours of darkness for the following day. One day I had no wood with which to cook our breakfasts, so I prowled about for some odds and ends. I noticed a broken wheelbarrow lying in no-man's-land, some twenty yards in front of our position. It was a risky proceeding to fetch it in during daylight, but we sadly needed a hot drink, and therefore I crawled cautiously out and procured the prize. It was a foolhardy thing to do, however, as we were not more than about eighty yards from the Germans. I got back safely, but had been seen – no doubt just as I was on the point of disappearing behind cover. Immediately I reached safety, a terrific burst of machine-gun bullets streamed across our parapet, tearing the top layer of sandbags to threads and scattering the earth in all directions. We lay prone, and spent some fifteen minutes on our stomachs, not daring to move. However, all's well that ends well, and we much enjoyed our breakfasts. It is surprising, when calmly reviewed later, what stupid risks one is sometimes willing to take so needlessly.

2/Lt Cyril Winterbotham 1/5th Gloucestershire Rgt
It is a strange sight, this firing line. Imagine two untidy lines of sandbags looking more like rubbish heaps in the distance and between them straggling lines of wire on rough poles at all sorts of

angles with a dead cow here and there and odd articles scattered about. Then dotted about are ruined houses with tileless roofs and broken walls standing in the remains of their gardens. Over all, absolutely no sign of life or movement.

I sat and looked round on Sunday morning. An aeroplane was being shelled up above and the sky was dotted with little white puffs of smoke. I couldn't help trying to reconstruct the scene in peace and imagine all the roofs on and all the mess cleaned up . . . Waller and I remarked simultaneously that the whole thing is preposterous nonsense and that men ought to leave each other in peace to enjoy the weather and, I added, go fishing. After which we went off to try and spot a sniper and if possible put a bullet in him.

Pte Vero Garratt, 2/5th (London) Field Ambulance, RAMC
Yes, the trenches are a veritable wonderland. From a road swept by shellfire, and showing the desolation it might have done the day after the Flood, you enter the communication trenches and commence the most remarkable tour it is possible to imagine. Winding in and out, twisting and turning like round the edges of a jigsaw puzzle, you walk on and on through trench after trench, and seem to be going miles and miles ahead, when in reality you may have advanced only a few hundred yards. The dugouts you pass generally have some inscription, over them which signify the purpose of their existence – the more flowery names, as 'Paradise Alley', etc, more often than not indicating that the cynic has been at work.

Lt John Bellerby, 1/8th West Yorkshire Rgt (Leeds Rifles)
The essential point in maintaining fitness was food, the supply of which was invariably abundant, while the cooking – at least for the officers – was astonishingly good, even within 100 yards of the enemy. There were times when life was comparatively quiet and time even hung heavily on our hands. This had its rewards for any

whose aesthetic sense was well developed, for the scenery had its special beauty even though carved into a queer kind of tracery by the twisting trench tops. Anyone who cared to weight his luggage with a book could find opportunity during the sunny days for indulging his reading appetite. I personally read very little, though just for a whim I took a book with me in bright moonlight to see whether I could read it in a shell hole in no-man's-land.

Pte William McNeil, 1/5th South Staffordshire Rgt

I was with a party filling sandbags which we usually kept in readiness for repairing our trenches and parapets during the night. Suddenly, one of our field batteries behind us opened fire, and a shell came straight through our Royal Engineer officer's legs, taking away his two kneecaps, through the body of a machine-gunner who was lying asleep in the dugout, through the parapet and burst in no-man's-land. I'll never forget that officer as he lay on the stretcher, just asking for a cigarette. What a fine example to put in front of the men!

Maj. George Stevens, 1/8th Durham Light Infantry

One of the many duties of an officer was the censoring of the letters of his section. Most of my section had no clue on the subject of letter writing, and the average letter read: 'Dear Mother, I am glad to say I am all right, and the grub is good. Your loving son, George.' These, by their brevity, needed only a glance.

My section had a number of casualties, including an Irishman named Fitzgerald, a bricklayer by trade, but a poet at heart. Fitzgerald's letters to his wife May covered many pages, closely written in a good hand, and like it or not, I had to read them. They were a joy to read, full of tenderness and love, poetically expressed, and after his death must have been a great consolation to poor May. The only good thing I know about King Charles I is that he wrote letters to his Queen almost as good as Fitzgerald's. We buried him beside a hedge in a field on the bank of the Zonnebeke. Some weeks later, I received a letter from his widow, in which she thanked me for my description of his resting place, but said she was in a state of bewilderment because she had received a letter from the Roman Catholic padre giving her another location for his grave, many miles away, and she was wondering if he was really dead. I sought out the padre, and gave him a good ticking off for the distress he had caused her, and wrote again telling her that there was unfortunately no doubt about his death and that he really was buried where I said, as I had myself selected the spot, and assisted in the burial.

Sgt Charlie Parke, 2nd Gordon Highlanders

In practice, the Company Sergeant Major would read all letters in order not to bother the Company Commander; in that position I would later read dozens of letters and always initialled the outside of the envelope over the seal in order to guarantee their passage to the old country. Pen and paper were available to the men when in reserve to facilitate writing letters but most of them, including myself, preferred to use the more convenient 'lazy card'; approximately eight inches long, it contained numerous phrases, a man striking them all out save the one he wanted to send. Mrs Parke, struggling to bring up the rest of the family in Aberdeen, always received the same message from her eldest child: 'I'm keeping quite well, hope you are the same, your son Charlie'.

Capt. Herbert Flemming, 9th London Rgt (Queen Victoria Rifles)

It is curious to have the whole brigade in barracks again [in Ypres] and the men have thoroughly enjoyed it. They have had plenty of room and plenty of food. The stone floors were rather hard to sleep on, but it is wonderful how one gets used to a thing. I offered a bed to my faithful batman, Stanley Derby, but he told me he preferred the floor now! He is a real good boy and I am awfully lucky. He is only twenty-two and very, very deeply in love. He told me all about it, one night in my dugout. He used to write the most

pathetic letters to his lady love, who lives in Kilburn – I expect he
does now – for he writes almost daily, but I never read them. I just
sign and let them go.

Pte Reginald Wilkes, 16th Royal Warwickshire Rgt (3rd Birmingham Pals)

I have just received your parcel and papers. The cake was a bit
squashed, due probably to the parcel being on the way a day or two
longer than usual. It would be better in future to send them in
those light chocolate boxes, or to put plenty of corrugated cardboard round the packages.

The cheese came all right and went down well. We happened to
be in the firing line when it came, so it added a little to our rations.
Any time you send something, can you put in a slice of raw ham or
a rasher of bacon? We can always cook such things and the very
fact that they came from Blighty adds extra flavour to them. Do
not worry to send cheese. The issue we get is generally fairly good
stuff and we get plenty of it. Also do not put in carbolic soap as it
is apt to taint the other contents, and we can always get plenty of
good soap such as Pears etc. Tinned fruits (pears, peaches and
apricots) we can get very easily, and we eat a lot of them. In fact, in
almost all the small villages about five miles or so behind the line,
you find a canteen run by soldiers and stocking most tinned meats
and fruits, sauces, biscuits, etc. It is when one gets a bit further
back to villages which are not used permanently as billets for
battalions temporarily out of the trenches, that one finds trouble in
getting these things, together with cigarettes.

You will think that this letter is all on one subject but I know
that both of you are often at a loss what to send. The cream
crackers Ernie sends go down well with the cheese . . .

Pte John McCauley, 2nd Border Rgt

Shortly before the hour of an attack, the mail was delivered to us,
and I found myself the recipient of a parcel and letters. I was in

doubt what to do, whether to burden myself with my mail or leave it in the trench and probably never see it again. Others who had received parcels were frantically rummaging through them, and selecting what they wanted most and throwing the remainder away. At any minute the order to go over might be given, so I got a comrade to tie my parcel on the equipment on my back, as I did not feel like leaving it after its long journey. He had scarcely finished putting a secure knot on the string when the order came ringing down the trench 'Over, boys!'.

Lt Denis Barnett, 2nd Prince of Wales' Leinster Rgt
The post corporal has just staggered in with something wrapped up in a newspaper. It appears to be a large mess as big as an ordinary cranium, which, on examination, proves to be the remains of a large tin of honey, which has leaked all over the country. There must be a sticky trail from here to Boulogne. There is half a pint left, which will be very welcome indeed. I am writing to Eling Farm to thank them.

Enclosed is a rather comic souvenir. When the post corporal was giving me a parcel, a half-spent bullet hit plop in the middle of it. The said bullet proved on examination to have splintered the bullseye, gone through the chocolates, and finally stuck in a bit of Turkish Delight which I send you *exactly* as I took it out of the packet. It's one of the funniest freak bullets I've ever seen or heard of.

PS The post corporal has just discovered that the bullet hit him in the breast pocket, tore across his paybook, and the front of his tunic and his sleeve, before it plopped into my parcel, so it is what you would call *some* bullet!

Pte Cyril Chitty, 2/4th Field Ambulance, RAMC
One night when I was on duty in the ward, a patient came towards me holding a bloodstained handkerchief to his ear. 'Whatever have you been up to?' I said. 'Well,' he replied, 'I reckon it was my gal's

fault. Last Thursday was my birthday and my young woman – meanin' kindly of course – sent me a bottle of sweet-smellin' 'air oil. Of course it ain't no good to us out here, let alone addin' to the weight of yer pack, but I didn't like to chuck the stuff away, seein' as 'ow she'd sent it, so I give my 'air and 'ead a tidy dose of it last night and woke up to find a rat a-sittin on me shoulder and a-lickin' of it orf, and when I moved me 'ead why 'e bit me through the ear.'

Lt Alan May, 49th Machine Gun Coy, MGC

I will never forget my first night in the trenches. The dugout which has been turned over to me was certainly not much but I felt quite safe. The shells that came over, the Boche MG fire, and an occasional sniper shot did not seem very alarming. But the huge rats scared me, great beasts that refused to be intimidated. Two or three kept coming up on the foot of my 'bed' and throwing things at them did not faze them. If I shot one of them I thought they might disappear. Having heard about the chap who shot his foot off when aiming at a rat on his bed, I was careful. Then a large piebald rat came to the foot of the bed and I shot it. At first I thought the whole dugout was collapsing and I was almost deafened by the explosion in that confined space. Dirt fell from the roof and filtered through the walls, making the air too thick to breathe. So that was that, no more rat- shooting in a dugout.

Cpl Arthur Cook, 1st Somerset Light Infantry

Where we are is the worst we have struck for rats, there are thousands of 'em. We have to suspend our food in sandbags from the roofs of our dugouts, and wake up in the night to find them having a swing on the bags, cheeky rascals. We have to cover our faces at night as several men have been bitten, and we only have our greatcoats for cover, we keep our boots and puttees on to protect our legs. They crawl over you at night, and we give the thing a biff from under the coat and send him squealing in the air, there is a short silence, then a thump as he reaches the ground, a scuffle, and he is gone.

At a cursory glance, much of the battlefield in 1915 resembled an unspoilt landscape. Houses close to but not in the line were often only semi-derelict and one of the sights to which many soldiers referred in their diaries and letters was that of animal life left to run wild, both abandoned farm livestock and domestic pets. Many farm animals ended up as food for the soldiers' pot; dogs and cats were often adopted and lived in the trenches.

Lt Denis Barnett, 2nd Prince of Wales' Leinster Rgt
When I was doing my rounds, I saw a hare sitting on the road in the moonlight, so I seized a rifle and rolled him over, and my platoon made the most of him! There was not much left when they'd done. One of my lads once went out of the trench (without permission) to a farm between the lines to steal chickens. While so engaged, he ran into a German who was doing the same. As neither had a rifle, they nodded and passed on.

Capt. William Croft, Adjutant, 1/5th The Cameronians Scottish Rifles
A weasel with a litter of six cubs crossed the road just in the rear of our trenches, in broad daylight. She seemed rather surprised. She then hopped up the parapet to reconnoitre and finally came back and carried her cubs over one by one, taking no notice of the men standing about.

Lt Denis Barnett, 2nd Prince of Wales' Leinster Rgt
There is a little grave about 2ft by 3ft in the middle of a bust-up farm, and on the cross there is this: 'Here lies Tim, a little brown

dog, killed by a shell during the bombardment of this house by
the Germans on April 23, 1915. R.I.P.' That was the end of our
mascot. He went out of the trench into the farm to see why the
bricks kept jumping about. He did his bit all right. The Rifle
Brigade had a kitten, but she was shot by a sniper while walking
on the parapet with her tail straight up in the air . . . Please send a
bullet-proof tortoise.

Maj. F. W. Johnson, 88th Field Ambulance, RAMC

In a disused dugout, I found a litter of pups; next day, the mother
deserted them. I suppose the noise was too much for her; so I took
a pup and I am, with the aid of my servant, trying to rear it. At
least I suppose I should say my servant is bringing it up with my
assistance, because he does all the work and I look on. He was
probably about ten days old when I got him and caused us no end
of amusement in the trenches; he was not too steady on his legs at
first as you would conclude and when he wandered round the floor
and anything tickled his ears he would shake his head, promptly
overbalance and roll on his back. He is growing fast and is much
more steady now and knows where to look for his breakfast. I am
sorry to say that his manners in all respects are very unsatisfactory,
but with a little judicious application of the hand, I have no doubt
that this can in time be remedied.

Some of the men took two of the others, but a sad fate befell the
three remaining: one was trodden on and two days after a big
'stunt' we had a particularly severe thunderstorm which flooded
the dugouts and the two leftovers were drowned. We had 'banked'
up the door of my domicile when it started to rain, but the barrier
carried away and in came the water very fast. Fortunately the pup
was in a bucket hanging on the wall. I managed to rescue him, an
electric torch and a pair of boots. When I went in again to see what
could be done, the water was up to my neck and all things that
would float were practising naval manoeuvres with my torch for a
searchlight.

Lt Denis Barnett, 2nd Prince of Wales' Leinster Rgt

I've lately made the acquaintance of a great character, the machine-gunner's goat. She's a most extraordinary beast, and has taken to machine-gun tactics in a wonderful way. She will fall in with the gun teams; you can pull her away by main force, but she comes back at the double. She gets awfully excited at the command 'Action!' and helps the gunners by running between their legs, and standing where they want to mount the gun; she's never more than a yard out at most. When the guns are up, she stands in front and licks their noses lovingly. We're all very fond of her, and the gunners have adopted her entirely; and she now bears the mystic sign MG on the side of her, in emerald-green paint.

The winter had been tough, but as spring arrived the mornings were lighter and spirits rose commensurately. In the trenches, day and night were effectively inverted. The darkness was used to carry out work, the day to catch up on sleep. The first defensive holes dug in 1914 had gradually been deepened and revetted, while the front line had been extended, with communication trenches leading back to safer ground. Even so, by early spring the trench system was not yet one continuous line and it was easy for relief parties to walk through the front line and find themselves on the enemy wire. Any work carried out at night had not only to be done quietly, but the location of the work itself found with a minimum of fuss.

Pte Henry Clarke, 1st Suffolk Rgt

An officer explained that we had to go and lay wire in front of a trench occupied by the Welch Regiment. None of us knowing the exact route turned it into rather a chance game on account of trenches not being all connected up. We proceeded by compass walking 100 yards to the top of a wood then taking a direct turn to our left where we found an old communication trench not far ahead. We thought it best to get well under cover as we were now completely in the open. One man ventured in first and found himself submerged to the waist in mud and water and did not stay long, so we followed this trench instead for about 250 yards when we were halted rather abruptly by someone shouting 'Get down, you bloody fools!'; we were down, wire and all, before he had finished his decent and expressive sentence, then we were greeted with, 'You are bloody lucky', but at least we had found our destination.

Lt Denis Barnett, 2nd Prince of Wales' Leinster Rgt

It is a very difficult journey from here to where we are digging, and the 'sailing' directions are like this: '. . . across field to haystack; bear half left to dead pig; cross stream 25 yards below dead horse; up hedge to shell hole, and then follow the smell of three dead cows across a field, and you'll arrive at exactly the right place'! The best of these landmarks is that you can use them on the darkest night. I brought my lads back on a short cut I devised for myself, including a couple of dead dogs and a certain amount of one German. It is a much better way, and I got the bearing so well that I walked right into the last cow without even smelling her, so strong was the wind blowing the other way.

Pte John McCauley, 2nd Border Rgt

We arrived at the point where the work had to be done – within seventy yards of the Germans' front line! It was a very dark night and I fancied I was surrounded by silent, ghostly figures from another world. All orders were conveyed by signs, and in a short time we were filling sandbags and laying them in position to strengthen the trenches. Never a word was uttered, and the only sound was the panting of men, and the occasional scrape of a shovel. The Germans had evidently located us and were suspicious, for all through the night there were occasional bursts of shooting in our direction. Some of the bullets found targets. Even the task of making trenches in the dead of night cost valuable lives, and the groaning of mortally wounded men reached my ears during those first few hours. It was all so eerie and strange, I didn't know what to think about it. I had imagined a terrific din and wild excitement everywhere. Yet, in the midst of the darkness and stillness in which we were shrouded, death was quietly stalking among those phantom figures. The thought that a bullet might strike me down at any moment caused me to tremble.

Cpl Arthur Cook, 1st Somerset Light Infantry

My platoon had orders to dig a communication trench from a captured line to our front line. I spaced the men out – a ticklish job in a very exposed position – and to keep the men on the task I had continually to walk up and down the line. Captain Marshall, our Company Commander, came along and inspected the work. The following incident then took place. The captain asked me where the platoon sergeant was and I had to admit I had not seen him. He took me with him to find the sergeant, whom we eventually found crouched in a dugout on the canal bank. The captain took out his revolver and, pointing it at him, said, 'Come out before I shoot you, and take charge of your platoon.' He came out and we started back towards the front line, when to our surprise we ran into my platoon, who had run away from their task. I loaded my rifle, fixed my bayonet and drove them all, including the sergeant, back to their task. I had to continue walking up and down the line to encourage the men, as the cowardly behaviour of the sergeant was demoralising them.

Sgt Charlie Parke, 2nd Gordon Highlanders

The old soldier was a wily character and, if there was something he wanted to miss, he would use his head. He'd pull the bullet out of a cartridge and take a small length of cordite, a cottony type of thread, placing it under the tongue. It would make him physically sick and then, of course, he'd spit it out. The doctors took a while to catch on, but eventually numerous men having the same symptoms the day before going into action suggested something more than coincidence. That set of symptoms later constituted a charge and the practice died out by the end of 1915.

Occasionally soldiers endeavoured to take fate into their own hands by lying in a trench with their feet up, to see if they could get wounded and hopefully 'buy a Blighty'. Another ingenious trick was to fire a bullet into a fleshy part of the leg through a tin of bully beef, no less, in order to avoid telltale powder marks.

Pte John McCauley, 2nd Border Rgt

We were nearing the eve of the fight for Neuve Chapelle, one of the grimmest fights in the history of warfare, and crowded with deeds of immortal heroism, when a new terror fell upon me. The sergeant of my platoon visited our billet, and without any preliminary warning, he solemnly said:

'A private of . . . Company has been sentenced to death. The sentence will be carried out at sunrise tomorrow, and the following men will parade with rifles to form the execution squad.'

The sergeant proceeded to read out fifteen names, twelve members of the firing party and three reserves. A sickening shudder went through me when I heard him read out 'Private . . .' That was my name.

I pictured the condemned man, wherever he might be on his last night on earth, and thought of the awful suspense he must be enduring and the poignancy of his sufferings. Who could fail to feel the deepest sympathy for the miserable wretch? There was the wider issue of the safety and security of the British Army as a whole. It might well be imperilled, we had been told, by the abolition of the death penalty for desertion.

As the first glimmering of dawn appeared, there was a melancholy air of activity among the troops. Every member of the firing party had spent a restless and unhappy night, and the nearer approach of the hour of execution increased our misery. Shortly before the order to parade was passed round, my own fears and sorrows were partly allayed by a visit from the sergeant. The final selection of the execution squad had been made, and I was not to be one of the twelve executioners after all. My duty was to parade as one of the three reserves. I inwardly offered a prayer of thankfulness to God for my deliverance from the terrible task.

Every man in the battalion was on parade on that unforgettable morning. It was a public execution so far as the battalion was concerned. We were compelled to witness this cold-blooded murder of a comrade. We marched for about a mile along the main road, and then turned off through the entrance to a farm. Passing by the farm buildings, we entered a field at the rear of the farmhouse and were then ordered to halt.

A small party of men move slowly across the field and halt in front of the stake. It is the firing squad. They ground arms, about turn, and march several paces away. Their rifles are still lying on the ground, and they stand stiffly to attention with their backs to the rifles. The manoeuvre puzzles me for a moment, until I see three military police approach the rifles. They pick them up one by one, and slip a cartridge in the breach of each rifle. A live round in this one, a blank round in that one, and finally every rifle is loaded.

Suspense deepens and pale faces on all sides are grimly set as the next act in the awful drama is awaited. We have not long to wait. A slight movement in the direction of the farm buildings attracts our attention. A small group is making its way to the centre of the field. The doomed man is being escorted to his execution. He is hatless and unbound – a limp, quivering creature, stumbling forward with bowed head as though perfectly resigned to his terrible fate. His legs seem to be heavy, as if something is weighing him down, and he only drags them along with difficulty. My own eyes are transfixed; the sight of that pathetic figure casts a spell upon us all. He is nearly abreast of me when he slowly lifts his head and takes a glance at the parade. I obtain a clear view of his haggard-looking face.

The shock of what was revealed to me in that brief glimpse sent me dizzy with horror. I had to fight hard to resist the impulse to scream aloud. The man who stood there on the brink of eternity was known to me, and I wanted to run out to him and snatch him back from the cruel death that awaited him.

It was Private Briggs. My thoughts flashed back to England – to Shoeburyness. The words of the colonel as he uttered his solemn warning to Private Briggs: 'Young man, if you don't alter your ways when you get to France you will finish up in front of a firing party of British soldiers.' How full of tragic prophecy was that grave warning.

I watched as if in a trance, and saw his escort guide him to the stake. He was in a stupor now – paralysed with fright. They pinioned his arms and legs, then bound his poor, trembling body to the stake. A blue and white bandage which had been carried by one of the escort was placed over his eyes and firmly fastened at the back of his head. I could see his lips moving, but could hear no sound. Maybe he was murmuring a farewell to this world. No, that could not be the meaning of that strange twisting and contortions of the mouth. A moisture filled my eyes, and drew a curtain of mist across my vision. Then came a tear. I feel no shame in making this confession. There were many tear-filled eyes on that parade.

There was no one near the poor wretch at the stake now, and the order rang out sharp and crisp through the early morning air: 'Present arms.'

The front rank of the firing party were on their knees, and the rifles of the twelve executioners were levelled at the shoulder. As they took aim, they visibly trembled, and not a single rifle was held steady. I could imagine their thoughts: should they shoot to kill or merely wound? What a damnable duty to thrust upon brave British soldiers.

'Fire.'

A momentary pause, then the crack of the rifles rang out. It was not a clear volley. The shots were spasmodic; some of the firing party had hesitated longer than others. The result was ghastly. A terrifying moan, and the thing that had been a man sagged at the stake, doubled up on its toes and hung there in a huddled position, until the escort went to it and cut it down from the stake.

While the battalion was being formed up in marching order, the body was placed on a stretcher and covered with a Union Jack. The small group surrounding it suddenly moved towards a corner of the field, headed by the padre. In the corner of that beautiful green field, the body of the deserter was laid to rest. Private Briggs there found the peace which passeth all understanding.

Lt John Capron, 56th Divisional Ammunition Column, RFA
Most of the night there would be minor flashes and flickering up and down no-man's-land – rifle or machine-gun – or sometimes the faint report from a trench mortar, followed by the heavy detonation as its bomb burst. Now and again the night would be pierced by a soaring Very light, fired by a nervous outpost hearing noises in the undergrowth and fearing the sudden rush of a raiding party. The light would hang for a minute, throwing its cold white radiance over all the broken landscape, before falling and fluttering earthwards – to leave the blackness blacker still. It was eerie watching through the night and around 2 a.m. a dreadful drowsiness would steal over you – it became an effort to keep staring into night . . . Now was the value of your companion, the telephonist – over a mug of strong and tinny tea, brewed over methylated, sleep could be held at bay.

And gradually there came a thinning of the gloom – faint signs of coming dawn – black turned to grey, and at last a pale streak of light showed low over the eastern dark horizon – the tide of life ceased to ebb, and slowly flowed again. A thistle head suddenly visible in the pallid light confirmed another day was born. Daylight brought greater activity as the early mists lifted the red tiles and broken brickwork, the jagged rafters of a German-held village appeared – and then the woods and copses and the countryside beyond. Then a wisp of blue smoke escaping from a broken cottage roof would catch your eye. A shame to spoil someone's early cup of tea – but you order your signaller to pass the word 'Battery – ACTION!'

When they respond 'Battery ready', you decide that one gun will do – 'No. 1 gun, 3,500 (range) 5 minutes (elevation), 1 degree 25 minutes left of zero, Corrector 150, one round – FIRE!' This should ensure an airburst over the target – the point being that by bursting in the air observation is easier than if the shell landed and burst in the confused rubble of the village. If the burst is well and truly over the cup of tea (unlikely first shot) you can go on at once to sending over a salvo to burst on percussion. You hear your guns fire a faint crack away behind you, and the shells whistle overhead. Your eyes are glued on that wisp of smoke and the red tiles round it crack-whistle crack-whistle crack-whistle, over they go – then, oh joy, three plumes and jets of ruddy brick dust and tiles fly up gloriously close, it seems, to the little blue twist – you MUST have upset the teapot!

Pte Cyril Chitty, 2/4th Field Ambulance, RAMC
The far-off blue horizon melted into a misty golden sky, while the ruined tower of Saint Eloi, solitary and grand, crowned a near slope. All the foreground and the fields, as far as the eye could reach, were beautiful with flowering plants, poppies, marguerites, the yellow tansy . . . After the drumming gunfire of the night before, the sense of peace, the grandeur of desolation, and the beauty of triumphant nature sank into my inmost being, exalting it in praise and prayer.

All too soon, alas, I was bought back cruelly to earth for, glancing at the ground beneath, I saw to my horror that my foot was resting on a dead man's knee protruding from the soil, and as I hastily jumped aside, the kneecap and the fibula fell clattering into the trench.

Pte William Brown, 1/4th Oxfordshire and Buckinghamshire Light Infantry

While in the Plugstreet [Ploegsteert] district, we built a fine new trench on Hill 63 just in front of Messines. Many exciting nights were spent on this task. It was very open country, and we were frequently swept with machine-gun fire. However, our casualties were few, and we had the pleasure of completing the trenches and holding them for a few days afterwards. The grass in front of these trenches was very tall, and the enemy could easily have crawled to within bombing distance without being seen. We therefore spent some nights out in front cutting the grass with sickles. Every time we hit an empty tin - and the ground was literally covered with them - we drew rifle fire, but we lost no one on these occasions.

Pte James Racine, 1/5th Seaforth Highlanders

We obtained water for washing and shaving purposes from shell holes which the rain had filled. I daily adjourned to one to carry out my toilet and it was situated behind the parados of the trench; the water, on which a green scum floated, was rank but had to serve its purpose for ablution requirements. The water receded, as the days passed, until one morning I discerned the body of a man at the bottom when I knelt down to wash; it occurred to me that the time had arrived when I should seek a more savoury position.

Pte Harry Emans, C Coy, Heavy Branch MGC

Our two 'sanitary wallahs' as we called them, responsible for keeping the latrines clean, were also characters. They were classed as C3, not fit for active service, and were known to all as Spit & Cough. They were both from Tyneside and true Geordies, about 5 foot 2 inches in height, one thin and the other much stouter built and cross-eyed. Both were sentimental and sometimes at night when we were having a singsong in the billet they would sing almost with tears in their eyes 'Come speak to me, Thora'.

Lt Denis Barnett, 2nd Prince of Wales' Leinster Rgt
I am in a sort of house, having a nice cushy time . . . We've got a
shell sticking in the wall (about halfway through) which has not
burst yet, and we're trying to think of a way of getting it out. At
present we've had no volunteers for the job. The gunners won't
have anything to do with it, and I think it is safer where it is . . .
There is a framed and illuminated document on the wall of this
room which certifies that the family Delacque was made associate
of the Society of Christian Families in August 1899, signed by
Jules Duval, parish priest. I wonder where they are now . . . It's
funny how a house that's been absolutely censored with shellfire
and long deserted, leaves you entirely unmoved till you find
something to stimulate your imagination, like a boot scraper or
any little thing inside. In most of these places there are enlarged
photographs of Monsieur and Madame and the children; in one, I
found Madame's accounts of the housekeeping. There is nearly
always something left to make you think a bit.

This morning there was a thick mist, so we could carry on with
our work on the parapet. Young and I went out and looted a farm
in front. We got a framed picture for the dugout, some glasses, a
decanter, a ladder, and some coat-hangers! We came back to the
trench à la Kronprinz with our arms full of things of human
interest.

*Many civilians clung on to their homes, desperate not to leave until
absolutely necessary. Before the advent of overwhelming and devastating
shelling in 1916 and 1917, civilians were a common sight near the
trenches.*

**Lt Col John Longley, Commanding Officer, 1st East Surrey
Rgt**
Neuve Eglise. German aeroplane over, get under cover, about half
an hour later over come six shells. Two dropped on left of church,
next two drop on a house next door to General Maude's head-

quarters, completely wrecking it. I bunk a fat old man and a woman over the wall at the back away from the debris. Later we find a couple of women buried in the cellar under dust and bricks and we dig them out. They are smothered in dust and apparently suffering slightly from shock but are more concerned about some money they have located somewhere and can't find. We try and find it for them but cannot.

Lt J. A. C. Pennycuick, 59th Field Coy, RE
A Belgian blew himself up near our stores with a dud shell. It had landed in his garden and he tried to unscrew the nose with a hammer and chisel! He was holding the shell between his knees and it went off and blew his legs off and blew him through the wall of the house. When he was dug out from under the bricks, he was still alive and conscious but died about three hours later.

Lt Denis Barnett, 2nd Prince of Wales' Leinster Rgt
I found a couple of small kids wandering about yesterday, not worrying a bit about odd bullets. I had to go out, though I was in a blue funk, and get them into the ditch, and make them crawl back out of the way. They loved it, but I didn't a bit! Of course what civilians there are left lie pretty doggo day and night, and don't need much coercion to keep them away from the lines. Those kids had come out to look for souvenirs and were very lucky not to get them. (I may tell you the word is regularly used in this euphemistic sense.)

I had a conversation with a German the other morning. I began just at dawn: 'Guten Morgen, Allyman', and we soon got going. I told him about the Kaiser, and he said we were all sorts of things I didn't know the English for, and also one thing which is a favourite appellative among the lower orders of English society, which he was awfully pleased with.

Sgt John Grahl, 1st Highland Light Infantry
A German had been heard to shout over our trenches 'Hang on until October and you can have the damned war.' This is the third time it appears that the same remark has been shouted on this front. Wonder if there is anything in it; I expect it's more of their bluff.

There was a great exchange of greetings between our fellows and the Germans opposite. The complimentary remarks passed were something like the following:
Our men: 'We are the bulldogs!'
Germans: 'Bulldogs, yah, yah!'
Our men: 'Come over, Fritz, you ___ ___.'
Our men: 'Gott strafe the Kaiser!'
Germans: 'Gott strafe the King!'
This went on until each side got exasperated and then bullets were exchanged for words.

———————————

Everywhere, both in and out of the line, spy fever gripped British forces. Greatcoats and uniforms removed from British prisoners were assumed to have been used by spies, while the more daring went for a complete change of clothes. A chaplain riding a brown – then later a white– horse with a distinctive spot on its forehead was one individual sought amongst many. The British High Command was always fearful that the enemy could steal an advantage at a time when the Germans already held the upper hand militarily.

Pte Henry Clarke, 1st Suffolk Rgt
We had a good view of Neuve Eglise. The Germans were continually shelling that place, and the church turned out a very handy spot for the Germans who used its clock for semaphore until someone passing noticed an alarming difference in the hour. The place was searched and a spy was found. Needless to say what

became of him! Apparently through his handiwork a company of East Surreys were badly shaken up whilst lying in billets.

Lt J. A. C. Pennycuick, 59th Field Coy, RE
There is a report of the capture of two damned spies, a man and a woman. They apparently spread washing out in squares and triangles to indicate to aeroplanes that troops were in certain districts. The aeroplane passed on the information to the guns who consequently shelled the desired areas.

War Diary, 9th East Surrey Rgt
Instruction received of two civilians driving around in car endeavouring to obtain information from troops:– car shabby and old. Roi de Belge open touring [car] probably Darracq but with Darracq badge removed from radiator. Colour dark. Radiator brass, car noisy. Individual I. Oldish, going white, scrubby beard, appearance French, speaks French, last seen wearing brown cap and dark suit. Individual II. Well-built 5 foot 10 inches, forty years, pasty face, fairly heavy, black moustache. Both seen driving. Units warned to instruct guards on roads to stop and arrest individuals (whether they have passes or not). Separate them and send to division HQ under officer's escort. If car seen and challenge disregarded, guards to fire at tyres. Duties detailed to regimental police. Doubled at night. Magazines charged. Guards warned that if these individuals are spies they will not hesitate to shoot.

Pte John McCauley, 2nd Border Rgt
We were fighting against heavy odds all along the line. The Germans were a vastly superior force numerically, and they possessed enormous supplies of guns and ammunition. Our shortage of these things placed us at a perilous disadvantage. In order to deceive the Germans as to the strength of our armaments, we had to resort to various ruses. We had to run up and down the whole

length of our section of the line and fire off a few rounds from different points, thus leading them to believe that at least a dozen machine guns were posted along our piece of front.

Pte Charles Heare, 1/2nd Monmouthshire Rgt
The guns behind us never fire more than a dozen shells a week. 'No ammunition' say the gunners. It seems strange to us. We are all looking forward to going to Berlin this summer . . . Our signal officer sends for all orderlies to come to the signal office. We are now in a room of a house on the borders of France and Belgium. You can lie with your head in Belgium and your feet in France.

Capt. Hubert Rees, 2nd Welsh Rgt
Not for one moment do I wish to imply that the war was anything but a horrible business, but a sense of humour was almost a necessity to prevent the combatants from going mad. There is no doubt that the men who took the war too seriously, and were able to see no humour in it, could not stand the strain . . . I say 'combatants' advisedly, because a sense of humour was not confined to the British. Therefore, one or two notorious war books, dealing with the horrors of the war in which is depicted a state of affairs in which it would be impossible to remain sane, cannot be accepted as a true reflection.

Pte Henry Clarke, 1st Suffolk Rgt
Men belonging to the East Surrey Regiment intermixed with a few Middlesex passed us on our way up to the line. They were all in an awful state and shouting 'We are all that is left of our respective regiments', telling us what *hell* it was. One hearty fellow even asked for our names and addresses so as to be able to let our people know that we were gone under [dead]. They had indeed had a rough time so they could easily be excused.

Pte Charles Heare, 1/2nd Monmouthshire Rgt

Black and I are taking periscopes up the line on our bicycles when a shell drops clean through a house and on to the other side of the road, where it spun round and started to roll. It didn't explode but we fell off our bicycles and lay flat, expecting it to go off. Talk of waiting for death, we are both trembling from head to foot. After a while we get up. 'If that had gone off we should have lost interest in this war,' says Black.

In April the Germans launched an offensive at Ypres, attacking the thinly held trenches opposite them. In their attempt to press the Allied troops back, they used a new weapon of war: chlorine gas.

Cpl Arthur Cook, 1st Somerset Light Infantry

The German trenches in front of my platoon are about 800 yards away, but there is a hedge which runs from the enemy lines straight towards us and finishes up about 300 yards away. Early in the afternoon, I was gazing over the top of the trench when I saw a German walking along behind his trenches, and on his back was a large, flat container. Suddenly I noticed he was leaving a trail of smoke behind him, which later turned into a dense green mass that commenced to roll along the ground gradually towards us. The wind was no more than a breeze. With horror, I realised that this must be the gas we had heard so much about. I hurriedly went around and warned all the men what was happening.

Only a few of us had been issued with some sort of protection, that consisted of a flat piece of cotton wool about three inches square with tapes attached, the pad being kept in position by placing it over the mouth and securing it with the tapes at the back of the neck. I ordered those who had these to put them on at once, and those without them to scoop a hole in the ground, which would immediately fill with water, soak their handkerchiefs in it and ram them in their mouths. As this was being done, I got everybody to line the trench, and, when the enemy appeared, to open up rapid fire.

Lt J. A. C. Pennycuick, 59th Field Coy, RE

The men got into a trench but very suddenly found that they were all unable to breathe and were coughing. I got them out of the trench in spite of the shelling, which was still very close, and got to some dugouts. Here they lay down for a couple of hours, very sick and completely exhausted. Then they made their way back to billets. When I got down both officers and men looked exceedingly ill and were lying down coughing and gasping for breath. They had put their handkerchiefs into their mouths and tried to breathe through them, but apparently only Corporal Maclean and a couple of sappers had been at all successful at this and they were not so bad as the rest. The smell on one of the handkerchiefs appeared to be a faint smell of chlorine or bromine.

Sgt Charlie Parke, 2nd Gordon Highlanders

A gas death was a cruel one indeed. Evidence could be seen everywhere, in ditches and at first aid posts. An initial whiff gave one the impression somebody had a tight hold on one's throat, but further exposure produced hideous scenes. Men would claw at their throats in a futile attempt at relief, while their brass buttons were chemically converted to green by the action of the chloride. Their bodies swelled as they writhed on the ground in agony, their tongues hanging out; a bullet at this stage, whether of German or British origin, would constitute a merciful escape.

CSM Cornelius Love, 1/2nd Monmouthshire Rgt

During the battle I had no platoon officer. This added to my responsibilities, as I had to find my company officer to get direct orders. I had the luck to meet him crawling along for a bit of cover. Captain Bowen wanted to see me to issue an order which I shall ever remember. It was:– 'The present line must be held at all costs, even to the last man.'

He was cut about the head and face, and he was covered with blood and dirt, of which he was not aware. He was badly wounded in the back. He was holding his shirt away from the skin, as it was sticking and causing added pain. I really thought he was 'going on' [dying]. I suggested to him that it would be better to get his wounds dressed, as he was bleeding badly, but he had no intention of leaving the line because we were so short of officers. He was sick and becoming weaker, and the Commanding Officer gave him instructions to go that evening.

I felt a bit lonely without Captain Bowen, who was one of the best of officers, and always with his men when the dirty work was on. He had no mercy on the shirker. He was christened 'Worker' because he was always doing something to protect his men, and we felt fairly safe whenever Jerry felt like doing a goose-step towards our front line.

Pte Charles Heare, 1/2nd Monmouthshire Rgt

The snipers are active here. Ration parties get caught and many killed. The shelling has got quiet but the Jack Johnsons – three at a time – start to come over, then a gas attack. Our bit of flannelette is useless. The gas burns the eyes, throat and is terrible on the chest. We are all coughing and swearing. Black has made a drink of tea. Very sweet – we gulp it down and both of us vomit all green. No doubt it saves us.

Cpl Arthur Cook, 1st Somerset Light Infantry

It was not long before the Germans emerged from their trenches, keeping at a safe distance from the gas cloud in front of them. Our line was very thinly held, but we had the satisfaction of inflicting many casualties on those advancing Germans, so much so that, after about 200 yards, they scuttled back to the shelter of their trenches, probably surprised at the resistance they had met; they left many dead and wounded. I'm afraid we had no sympathy for them, for as soon as an attempt was made to get them back to the lines, we picked them off. Such methods of warfare got no sympathy from us. I had the satisfaction of getting several bulls that afternoon.

Although we stopped the attack, that deadly gas was still rolling towards us. Owing to our concentration on stopping the enemy's advance, we had overlooked the fact that the German with the canister continued his walk alongside the hedge towards us, ejecting his gas. This was a risky business for him, for had a high wind got up the gas would have overtaken him. I don't think we would have lost much sleep over that! The trouble was that the gas coming from the hedge was much denser than that coming from the front line. As gas is much heavier than air, I begged the men to keep their heads above the trench, as anyone sitting in it would be affected when the gas rolled over us. Unfortunately, some of the men did not take my advice and became gas casualties, whilst those of us who kept our heads up escaped with no ill effects.

Pte Henry Clarke, 1st Suffolk Rgt
Shells were raining all over the shop, especially around us so as to prevent our supports getting up. I was in the dugout with the CO and adjutant working the telephone when the neighbouring dugout was struck by a shell, badly wounding one man in the head, and burying all the rifles and causing those inside to scatter for the exit. Our dugout lasted about another ten minutes or so until a shell exploded just in the rear, knocking out the telephone and wounding the adjutant who was directly behind me. I hardly knew what was happening for a few minutes or how we had got off so lucky. All had disappeared with a hole staring at us a few yards in circumference. We withdrew to an emergency trench which had been dug in the rear of a ditch and which turned out to be far worse, being up to our waists in

water. I had just time to get properly soaked and shaking with cold when a shell dropped just on the edge of the trench, burying me and Lance Corporal Game who was horribly wounded, having two large holes in his back, one on either side of his backbone. Not one of us knew what was happening in front but more or less knew what to expect.

Men could be seen retiring to our right. A few minutes afterwards the Germans appeared, forcing us out of our trench or we would have been enfiladed. We went back or rather struggled back on our chests to a shell hole, nine of us in a helpless condition and not a weapon amongst us. The colonel made the best of things by handing round cigars, but we had only just managed to get steam up when a German appeared on the edge of the shell hole shouting 'end-der-off' ['*Hände hoch*'] which apparently meant 'hands up'.

Lt J. A. C. Pennycuick, 59th Field Coy, RE

The doctor, a very good chap, came round at once to look after the men. He made them lie down wrapped up warmly in blankets and had their chests rubbed with turpentine. He also gave them various medicines of glycerine and aspirin, I think to ease those that had headaches and coughs. In the major's room we got a kettle going on a primus stove so as to get the steam into the room. Eleven of the men were sent off to hospital in an ambulance. I did not believe in this poisonous gas business before today, but there is evidently no doubt about it now.

The Germans had been held, but the enemy's first use of poison gas caused a sensation in the British press, which was able to seize upon its introduction on the battlefield as yet another example of Teutonic frightfulness. Nevertheless, once one side had used it, the other was bound to follow, and the Allies retaliated five months later at the Battle of Loos.

Pte Henry Clarke, 1st Suffolk Rgt

The Germans were all of the same opinion, that they were simply making a walk of it to Ypres then to Calais, finally reaching London. They undoubtedly thought that we were all that was left of the Contemptible Little Army. We started back. I cannot estimate the strength of the Germans but villages were simply crammed with them; our artillery seemed lost.

There was any amount of sarcastic and cowardly remarks passed, swines, etc, one idiot calling us 'Cousins from over the Channel', telling us also that we were prisoners (hardly knew that, I suppose), finishing up with a sneer and also spitting upon us.

We were questioned by a number of officers, trying to pump us for information. If they had not asked so many questions they would not have had so many untruths. They thought we were all Kitchener's men, we told them they were still in England and didn't they look shocked. They had the impudence to tell us our Regular Army was absolutely wiped out during the latter part of 1914; they were more surprised than ever when they were shown some of our paybooks proving we were regulars, we told them there were also lots more to come from India.

Pte Charles Heare, 1/2nd Monmouthshire Rgt

What I cannot make out is what is keeping the Germans back. You can walk or crawl along a mile of trench and find about one man in a dozen yards of trench. Our colonel very often fires a few rounds here and there and tells us orderlies to do the same. A battery of French 75s [rapid-firing light artillery] go to La Brique. It is interesting to watch them fire. Our artillery is small in number. An argument arises over what day it is. Six of us bet and we are all wrong. I thought it was Wednesday. It was Monday.

Cpl Arthur Cook, 1st Somerset Light Infantry

When darkness set in . . . some Germans came forward and started digging a trench 200 yards away, while others came within 50 yards of us and dug snipers' pits, and we had to stand up and watch them do it. I was itching to align my sights on a few more Jerries, but for some unaccountable reason we were told by our officer that we had to keep perfectly quiet and do nothing. And there we stood all night, with our finger on the trigger watching Jerry dig right in front of our eyes; it was in my opinion a fantastic and ludicrous position to be in. If only the enemy knew our strength, he could walk over and take the line, which may have been the cause for holding our fire.

Pte Charles Heare, 1/2nd Monmouthshire Rgt

Going up to the battalion I saw the worst sight of the war: a man of our regiment was crying 'Shoot me!' When I looked, he had his two legs and right hand blown off. He said, 'Shoot me out of it, shoot, you coward!' My God, I ran from him to the battalion. Going back the same way, the man was still alive, and when I got near, he said, 'I know what I got, shoot me out of the way.' At last I get behind him but my courage fails me, but when I look again at him, he is dead. I drop my rifle and ran to Irish Farm. Sergeant Shaw is there. 'Hello, Taff, seen a ghost?' I tell him of it; I am trembling and sweating.

CSM Cornelius Love, 1/2nd Monmouthshire Rgt

After being in the front line for several days, we were well-nigh beaten from hunger and thirst and with being 'shook to pieces'. I crawled across with the idea of finding an officer, but, to my surprise, I discovered that the remnants of our battalion had left at daybreak. The Irish officer to whom I spoke told me he had only a few men – relics of his company who had held the line a few days previously. It was impossible to relieve me. I was covering nearly 100 yards of front line with twenty-six men. The Irish officer and his men were quite twenty yards apart, and every man was standing to. When I returned, I had all I could do to cheer up our lads. I thought it best to tell them a lie, which was to the effect that the relief had lost their way. The language that followed this information is not fit for publication.

Cpl Arthur Cook, 1st Somerset Light Infantry

During this period, I ran dangerously short of small arms ammunition and reported back to the CSM. He ordered me to send an NCO and two men back to battalion HQ for two boxes, and this I did. About an hour later, the NCO struggled back to our trench covered from head to foot with blood and human flesh. He could not speak, he was the worst 'shock' case I had seen. I got him to sit down and started to remove the ghastly reminders of his recent experience, and after a while he calmed down a bit, but his speech was still incoherent. After a while I was able to gather that he had started off with the ammunition, and then his mind was a complete blank. I reported the matter to the CSM and asked permission to take two men to collect the ammunition. About twenty minutes later, I found the two boxes lying in the middle of the road and the remains of the two men completely dismembered – a 'whizzbang' had caught them and torn all their limbs asunder. The amazing part of this incident is almost incredible: it appears the NCO was in the centre holding a cord of the two boxes in each hand and the two men were on the outside each holding one cord, yet the NCO escaped and the men on either side of him were blown to smithereens. The ammunition, too, was intact, which we carried up to the trenches as fast as our load would allow us, for all around were signs of death and destruction. It was a mystery to me how the NCO found his way back to our lines after his ghastly experience.

It might be expected that those who had fought such a determined rearguard action at Ypres would feel rightly proud of their collective effort. Yet regiments, though they were all fighting on the same side, could be mutually antagonistic. In late 1914, regular soldiers had been contemptuous of the arrival of the territorials and, in turn, both were at times disdainful of Kitchener men. Even within regiments there were rivalries, and not always pleasant ones. In late May, days after the end of the Ypres battle, three Monmouthshire battalions were amalgamated. At around the same time, the first of Kitchener's Divisions, the 9th (Scottish), reached France, to be followed soon after by the 14th (Light) Division.

Pte Charles Heare, 1/2nd Monmouthshire Rgt
Our battalion joined the first and third Monmouths. Our battalion is about 200 men, and altogether with the other two battalions we are about 500 strong. Our first [battalion] have been at Hill 60. They have suffered, and so has the Third [Battalion] who have been at Zillebeke and Zonnebeke. Colonel Bridges of the Third is in charge. We march off to a nice quiet country place called Herzelle. Glorious weather – it is so peaceful it seems we can all feel ourselves getting normal again. It's like a tonic but what a mistake to put us together! The three battalions quarrel amongst themselves all the time. The First would say, 'You Seconds came out by mistake in 1914. And when you did, you were only resting out here. You lot haven't seen a war yet.' Then the Seconds would say, 'You First are the Kaiser's bodyguard. Some of your Battalion have gone to their country and the Army put us with you to stop the rest of you going (as the First lost a number of prisoners on Hill 60).' Then the Thirds would chime in. 'You lousy lot – the two of your battalions should have been at Zonnebeke or Zillebeke to know there was a war on. None of you have woken up yet.'

Pte James Racine, 1/5th Seaforth Highlanders
All the troops were eagerly awaiting the arrival in France of the New Army, recruited by Lord Kitchener, for it was anticipated that their appearance would mean a longer rest from the trenches and shorter spells on the line. We had heard so much about the

formation of this New Army and had waited so long for it to appear, that the men were becoming sceptical of its existence, for they thought that it was another rumour circulated to keep up the morale of the troops already fighting. The following conversation could be heard shouted, as one battalion passed another on the march: 'Seen any of Kitchener's Army?' Reply: 'Oh, shut up, you know darn well it is only a yarn and that there is no such thing.' This army was to have been ready in May and even the enemy had shouted across – 'Vere is dot Kitchener Army?'

Pte William Brown, 1/4th Oxfordshire and Buckingham-shire Light Infantry
Our occupation of the trenches was of short duration. We then gave them over to a battalion of Kitchener's Army. There was considerable ill feeling between the territorials and Kitchener's men in France in the early days, and the different battalions frequently hooted and hissed each other when passing on the march. However, this soon died away, and no distinction was made or thought of. After all, we were doing the same job, in the same way, against the same enemy.

Lt J. A. C. Pennycuick, 59th Field Coy, RE
The working party for tonight consisted of the 7th King's Royal Rifle Corps, Kitchener's Army, 14th Division. They marched past here about 8.15 p.m. looking a little footsore. They were rather amusing and wanted to do everything by drill such as picking up of shovels, etc. It is something to actually have 'K''s army out here at last.

No one could accuse Kitchener's Army of lacking enthusiasm. They had trained for at least nine months, were very fit and highly motivated. The same could not be said of those men who had been wounded and were

being drafted once more to France, men like Private John McCauley. He
had been wounded at the Battle of Neuve Chapelle in March 1915. His
three months in France had been enough to last him a lifetime. That
attitude was reflected in another group of men: coal miners. These
civilians in khaki were required to transfer their skills to the Western
Front to take part in an underground war. This would require
professional tunnellers to join in a dangerous job of mining and
counter-mining opposing trenches. These tough men had little interest
in military authority.

Pte John McCauley, 2nd Border Rgt

I was determined to avoid any possible chance of ever being
ordered to an overseas draft again. The same thoughts occupied the
minds of all the wounded men in barracks. They made no secret of
it, but openly vowed that nothing on earth would induce them to
return to the battlefield if it could be avoided. How different a
mood had crept over us all in a few short months! In 1914, we
were overjoyed at the prospect of going to France and marching
into battle; and, now, nothing but absolute compulsion would
ever send us back there.

For all their determination, there was no challenging 'absolute compul-
sion' and they were ordered to return.

The day of departure, or rather the night, for we were due to march
out of barracks at midnight, arrived. The draft contained a number
of men who had been through the early fighting in France, and
they were preparing for the second journey overseas very unwil-
lingly. There was a wild orgy of drinking in the barracks that
night, and discipline was thrown to the winds. At half past eleven
pandemonium prevailed, and almost every man in barracks
appeared to be drunk. They were in an ugly mood, and ripe
for any kind of mischief. Windows and barracks room property
were wilfully smashed, and they roamed about the building bent

on destruction of any kind. I could sense some serious trouble
ahead, for any attempt to suppress the wild behaviour would have
stirred up mutiny in an instant. The colonel handled the situation
with tact. It was obvious that he would be deeply relieved to get
the drunken draft off his hands, and he displayed unusual patience
while the troops were being rounded up on the barracks square
just before midnight.

Lt John Godfrey, 103 Field Coy, RE
Never shall I forget that march down: I went before another officer
named George; in the midst were the miners, playing upon the
beer tanks – or obviously at some previous period they had done
so. They rolled and lurched disgracefully: they fell out in their
tens, and in their hundreds: it *was* a hair-raising trial. But we put
into them the fear of God by taking some of them down under
escort, and I pride myself immensely on the fact that George and I,
without the help of my efficient NCOs, got the full 105 men,
drunk or sober, into the boat that night.

What a tightening of the heart-strings there is when you see the
boat that is to take you away, rolling and hissing gently like an
implacable monster! Of course it took hours to get the men on
board, and the crush there was terrific.

Pte John McCauley, 2nd Border Rgt
The troops looked more like a mob of rebels as they bunched
together, and angry cries and the singing, laughing and swearing
of drunken men drowned the colonel's speech. He might just as
well have saved himself the trouble of trying to pour out any
patriotic platitudes to men who were deaf to such talk, for nobody
paid the slightest attention to him. He soon realised the futility of
speech-making for he suddenly broke off, and gave the signal for
the draft to be marched away. The troops maintained their
defiance of authority by refusing to march in proper military
formation. They spread all over the streets and on to the pave-

ments, and many were actually reeling and staggering about from the effects of the liquor they had taken. In this confused state, we pressed into the railway station where free fights and much struggling and scrambling took place for the best seats on the train.

Lt John Godfrey, 103 Field Coy, RE

It was rather misty weather, and the English coast came and went as we approached or receded from it. George and I went down below for a bit, and when we came up again after having arranged our kits on the floor of the saloon, all we could see was cold, grey water, a white wake, and a destroyer and a couple of other boats going over with us. That was the only time I felt down in the dumps at all – that first moment that I realised we were out of sight of England.

The voyage was fair: the weather was pretty rough, and discovered the weaknesses of numerous Tommies, who were so crowded as literally to be lying on top of each other on deck and below: half of them were sick, and with that and the lack of ventilation and a lot of uneaten food scattered about, things were pretty awful. The officers were bang in the storm centre of the whole stench, and I didn't sleep very well.

For those new to the Western Front, going up the line for the first time absorbed the imagination. This was what they had been training for. But they little knew what to expect, and excitement mixed freely with apprehension as the night sky lit up with distant flashes and they could hear the rumble of gunfire.

Pte Ernest Aldridge, 2nd Welsh Rgt

We marched many miles, really about ten, but the weight of the fighting outfit made it so much worse. We broke off the road and crossed some fields. All talking now dropped to a mere whisper. The order came for all cigarettes to be put out, and that we should, as much as possible, prevent the rattle of the brasswork of our equipment. I could see flashing lights rising in an arc, lighting the place up with a brilliant white light. All was quiet and still, the silence being broken only by a whispered command or someone stumbling. The darkness, the moving men, the silence and, more than anything else, the expectation of something unknown gripped the whole mind.

Pte Sydney Fuller, 8th Suffolk Rgt

We were warned during the day that we were to go 'into the line' that night. Many of the men who were fond of booze indulged in what they no doubt thought might be their last 'bust-up', and when the time drew near that we were to parade, several were well 'oiled'. One man in our section was quite maudlin, and wandered round the billet repeating, at short intervals, 'Might as well die 'appy if [I] gotter die', and shedding bitter (or beery) tears. He paraded with the rest of us at 5.30 p.m., as if he were a martyr going to execution. We marched off at 6 p.m., full of natural curiosity and wonderment as to what we were to experience in the line.

Pte Ernest Aldridge, 2nd Welsh Rgt

We met a guide at the appointed place. It was a dark night and it was usual to warn the man behind of any obstruction such as a shell hole or telephone wire. After a time, we came to a sentry who called out the usual challenge, 'Who goes there?' The guide replied in a whisper, 'Welsh.' Then, when warning of some obstruction, he would whisper, so the officer in charge thought that we were nearing the enemy, so proceeded with caution. But after going for about a mile and seeing no sign of our near approach to the enemy, the officer requested of the guide how far we were from them. The guide replied about a mile. 'Then why the dickens have you been whispering all the time, making us think that we were very close?' 'I've got a bad throat, sir,' replied the guide.

Cpl George Foley, 6th Somerset Light Infantry

We seemed, as we moved up the road, to have left behind us the last link of the chain which had connected us with civilisation. From now onward we were in a world apart, where men moved openly only by night, where the scream and bursting of shells, and the rifle fire, fitful and desultory, were the only interruptions to an unearthly silence – a desolate, scarred world, the playground of Death itself . . . I remember at one point that a whizzbang, bursting close above us, appeared to blow a man's hat off just behind me; no one was hurt, however, and we were rather encouraged, taking it to be an example of the actual harmlessness of shellfire.

Capt. Eric Whitworth, 12th South Wales Borderers (3rd Gwent)

A company was entirely in the hands of its guides; a mistake on the part of a guide one night delayed the relief two hours, and such a mistake might have much more serious consequences. The front trench was not continuous, in fact only a very small proportion was held, and there were large gaps of 150 to 200 yards. A guide who lost his way might easily find himself in the middle of no-man's-land; where the German lines were only fifty yards away, the error might not be discovered in time to prevent the party wandering into the enemy's lines.

Cpl George Foley, 6th Somerset Light Infantry

Preparations for our first trip to the line were now actively carried out, and we were introduced, as a company, to the 6th North Staffords, who were to be our guides and comforters during the great event. At dusk, having mixed our sections with their platoons so that the old hands predominated about four to one, we marched the long three miles first by road, then by communication trench, until, almost before we expected it, we were in the front line.

There was no one between us and the enemy. It was a great moment for every one of us, and my diary announces with pride that on this night I 'fired my first shot at them'. It was merely a blind shot in the direction of the Hun trenches, some 300 yards away.

Sgt William Peacock, 1st South Wales Borderers
I was on duty patrol in the trench and we had just received a draft from England the day before, so of course they were anxious to look over the top to see if they could see the Germans. One man said to me, 'Sergeant, shall I have a look over, just a minute?' and I said, 'No, it is not safe to look over in daylight as they will snipe you the minute you put your head over the top.' We had boards up along the trench saying 'Beware of the sniper'. I had only just turned my back when he put his head up to have a look and a bullet came over and knocked him clean through his temple and killed him dead on the spot. That man had only been in the trench twenty-four hours altogether and only a week in the country. It was no trouble to get killed out there, you did not need to ask them to do it, perhaps your turn would come plenty soon enough. Yes, many a life was thrown away out there through carelessness and for want of judgement.

Pte Martyn Evans, 1/6th Gloucestershire Rgt
During our first stay at Ploegsteert we made our acquaintance with a first-class German sniper, periscopes were smashed time after time. Cook and Dyer were killed outright during the morning and several men were wounded because they would not stop looking over the top. Strict orders were given that during the day, except in case of attack no one was to use anything but the periscope for observing the enemy.

Pte Sydney Fuller, 8th Suffolk Rgt
We could see the German lines plainly. They were between 400 and 500 yards from ours, and were in chalky soil, whereas ours were in sandy clay. No-man's-land was just ordinary farmland, grown wild since the trenches were dug. There was a field of mangels, which had run to seed, and so made good 'cover' for patrols. In one place was a four-cylinder 'flat' roller, not far from our trenches. This was often fired on, as it was thought possible that a German sniper might have concealed himself behind it overnight. In another place was a cultivator, standing just as it had been left by the farmer when the Germans came. It was queer, seeing all those miles of trenches in front of us, showing not a sign of life, and yet swarming with the enemy.

Pte Martyn Evans, 1/6th Gloucestershire Rgt
My platoon was attached to the 2nd Rifle Brigade and immediately on entering the trenches we were told off to be placed with the sentries to see what was going on. I found myself standing on the firing platform near by a lance corporal who told me to remove my pack and fix my sword. The last part of the order rather scared me, but I suddenly remembered there was no such thing as a bayonet in a Rifle Regiment. I stood on the firing platform and rested my rifle on the parapet, an occasional bullet whined past, but otherwise I could see nothing. My instructor told me to take his place for a few minutes while he fetched a very light pistol. He discharged a star shell from it, and I could make out the line of white sandbags forming the German line. I was told to fire at the sandbags, which I did, thus discharging my first round on active service.

Pte Sydney Fuller, 8th Suffolk Rgt
Came off duty at 'stand down' – 4.45 a.m. During the afternoon I saw my first German. He was working in their trenches to the left

of us, apparently building up or repairing the trench with sandbags. I had a good look at him through a telescope. He was a tall, thin man, wearing a dark grey or green uniform and it was noticeable that he sported 'sideboards'. We judged the distance to be about 1400 yards, and set our rifle sights for that distance. Our shots had no effect beyond making him stop work and glance up every time a shot was fired. Later on, the machine-gunners used their rangefinder, and the distance was found to be only 800 yards. A Lewis gun was used shortly afterwards, at this range, when three or more Germans were visible at the spot. This, one of the machine-gunners told me, made them move very quickly. A 'miss' was signalled by one of them, with a piece of board, as soon as they were under cover.

Capt. Alexander Shaw, 1st King's Own Scottish Borderers
I had some shots at long range at two Boches who were engaged in digging. The first shot they took no notice of, so I lowered my sights 200 yards and fired. They stopped work and pointed over to the right and talked. The third shot I lowered fifty and aimed left and the effect was instantaneous. They fell flat into the trench and crawled out of sight on all fours: we laughed heartily. At night the Germans had a concert in their front-line trench. Good bass voices. They sang 'Bluebell'. I got my piper to give them a tune.

Lt John Bellerby, 1/8th West Yorkshire Rgt (Leeds Rifles)
Our targets were the periscopes of varying sizes held up by sentries along the line. The nearest ones were visible to the naked eye and these we demolished by degrees till ultimately only one remained and that was at a distance of about 400 yards. In firing at it, we discovered a phenomenon never before experienced, namely that if a rifle were fired with a telescope within a couple of feet of it, and if the sun was shining brightly, the telescope would pick up the trajectory of the shining bullet and then follow the bullet right up

to the target. Thus, while I could not see the periscope, its upper mirror being only about two or three inches square, Sergeant Webb was able to tell me whether I was firing high or low, or too much to the left and right. The German holding the periscope was obliging enough to wave us the wash-out sign after every miss, and then replace the periscope to give us another shot. It took me eighty-five rounds to get it. The German then turned it wrong end up, in the hope that we would waste more ammunition. However, Sergeant Webb was insistent that the final shot was truly a bullseye.

Brig. P. Mortimer, 3rd Meerut Divisional Train

After having a glass of beer in a dugout mess I had a look through the machine-gun officer's telescope at the German trenches and actually saw, as clear as daylight, the reflection in the top mirror of his periscope, of a German officer's head as he searched our trenches through his periscope, a most uncanny sight – the grey peaked cap and face as he looked down into the bottom mirror could be clearly seen. It was decided to 'strafe' the periscope with a Maxim which, after being trained on it carefully, was let off to the tune of fifteen rounds. The periscope immediately disappeared. A 'miss' was signalled from the German trenches by waving a spade backwards and forwards.

———————

The controversy over the illegal use of dum-dum bullets that had caused such consternation in the autumn of 1914 never faded away. Then, the Germans had accused the British of using flat-nosed revolver bullets, and the British returned the accusation with interest. On numerous occasions, soldiers reported finding German bullets reversed in their cartridges, creating a snub-nosed end. Sometimes boxes full of such ammunition were found, as if it were deliberately manufactured. No alternative reason for its production was ever discovered and the question

*remained: would not the reversing of a bullet in its cartridge utterly
undermine its aerodynamics?*

Maj. Henry Hance, 179 Tunnelling Coy, RE

I obtained a clip of cartridges taken from the body of a German
sniper whose bandolier contained about ten such clips. In every
case the bullets in the clips had been reversed, exposing the lead
base, making them in effect into explosive bullets. I saw the effect
of one fired at close range, which hit the man next to me in the face
and blew the back of his head off. I have often tried to see if a
British bullet could be reversed in the field, i.e. by means of wire
cutters, scissors, etc, or gripping it in the jamb of a door, but never
succeeded, whilst it was easy to reverse a German bullet.

Capt. Henry Kaye, 43rd Field Ambulance, RAMC

There was quite a large proportion of rifle bullet wounds and some
of the usual talk about 'explosive bullets'. This is mostly rubbish –
for one thing, a bullet cannot 'explode' and I have yet to see any
surgical evidence of an expanding bullet, such as one is accustomed to with a sporting bullet in a stag. A solid bullet will and
does blow a bone and soft parts to smithereens, but I have never
seen a mushroomed nickel casing or the effects of it out here. I
should like to have a rifle expert's view of the effect on the
shooting of reversing a solid bullet in the case (which I believe *has*
been done by the Germans) for one would imagine it would then
fly anywhere between third man and square leg – before believing
that it can be a paying policy.

Hewitt [another doctor] brought down one of the German clips
containing bullets reversed, of which there are many thousands in
Sanctuary Wood. The odd thing is that all that have been opened
contain no powder. Of this there seem to be three possible
explanations. (1) That the Huns find that for short ranges the
explosion of the [percussion] cap is sufficient (this could easily be
tested). (2) That our Tommies who occupied these trenches for

months amused themselves by reversing all the bullets and removing the powder. (3) That they are a bad lot, issued in error.

The miners brought to France by Lieutenant Godfrey were among the hundreds employed by tunnelling companies given the specific job of burrowing beneath no-man's-land and laying charges under enemy positions. At the same time, the enemy were actively digging in the opposite direction, and a deadly underground war took place, in which each side endeavoured to set off explosive charges before the other. Great attention was given to listening for the noise of the enemy working, and the telltale noise of picks and shovels, and the sliding sound of sacks of soil being removed. Then there was a chance to blow what were known as camouflets, small localised charges designed to kill the enemy rather than wreck a tunnel system.

Lt Alan May, 49th Machine Gun Coy, MGC

The miners were a group of men one hears little about. I don't think enough credit was given to these men for their laborious work. These miners worked in shifts, much the same as if they had been mining coal at home. While at work they know the Boche are mining, too, and that they could go up in smoke at any moment. Not exactly ideal conditions for working underground. Often we would see them trudging back to their billets, tired out and covered with clay and dirt. As well as miners they, of course, have to be soldiers, too, though they certainly don't look it but they carry rifles with them all the time.

One day a Boche raid happened to reach the mine entrance just as the chaps were coming out. Although carrying rifles, they preferred to fight with shovels and picks. They put up a fine fight and held the Boche off till assistance arrived, even capturing five of the enemy.

Lt J. A. C. Pennycuick, 59th Field Coy, RE

28 June: Went up to 15th Brigade in the morning and on to 38 trench. Went round the mines and spent a long time listening near the shaft out of the end of 38 trench. The corporal reported sounds of German mining but I could hear nothing at all. 38 trench was knocked in by a shell just to the right of the communication trench. Report also that there were noises behind 41 trench in a saphead. We put down bore holes and listened but could hear nothing

30 June: I went on up to 15th Brigade Headquarters on my motorbike and went up to 38 trench to the mines. We heard the Boche distinctly under the end of 38 trench in our mine working below us and also began preparations to camouflet them.

1 July: There were noises of Boches in part of the mine gallery and I went all round including the wet mines. Came back about teatime and at 6.30 I got a wire saying that they had just let off a camouflet in one of our galleries. I went off on my motorbike and went up to 38 trench again. However, they were quiet and not worried and so I came straight back.

2 July: Went down to 15th Brigade and went up to Hill 60 by the valley. I found they had let off another camouflet this morning as they had again heard Germans. One of our 4.7-inch shells, high-explosive, burst short of the bridge on the opposite side of the railway to us and nearly did for us at our mine shaft. I crawled all round the mines at about 1.30 (about 2 hours after the last explosion). We went very cautiously and I had a rope round me in case of gas but it was quite all right. Some fallen earth at the last camouflet scared us and a good deal of our gallery was wrecked. Apparently the Boches also let off a camouflet close to our second one this afternoon.

3 July: We found another charge ready to fire as the Germans could be heard at the end of our first gallery. We got it tamped up but were going to wait until we could distinctly hear the Germans at work before firing it. After tea I got a message saying that the

Boches had fired a camouflet and killed one of our men. The man at the head of our gallery was clearing it and was killed by the shock of the explosion and buried. Two other men with him were nearly blinded but they were all right. They got the dead man out and were going on with the work. I crawled all round to see that everything was all right.

4 July: Everyone was jumpy. Our camouflet had been blown up successfully. Noises of Germans were reported all over the place and in one gallery I found two men posted with rifles ready to shoot anyone who appeared. As they were not very clear who they were to shoot, I turned them out. I crawled all round the mines and spent most of my time cursing the various workers as they were most of them too frightened and doing nothing.

In September 1915 the British launched the final offensive of the year close to the village of Loos. It would be the first time that Kitchener's Army was used in such operations, and in the event they acquitted themselves well, although they suffered heavy losses.

The following anonymous account, though not written about the battle itself, gives one of the best evocations of the lead-up to an attack that I have read, giving some indication of what it was like to wait for zero hour. Unusually, the time for the attack was set for early afternoon as opposed to early morning, when attackers usually looked to take advantage of the half-light.

Anonymous account given by an officer

The infantry will advance to the attack at 1.30 p.m.

8 a.m. We are only four officers, with the two companies who are going to lead the attack, for we are going in (under strength). While we breakfast, my Company Commander and I pore over our maps spread out on the parapet of the trench. For the hundredth time, we discuss the plans we have made for keeping our direction

as we advance to each successive objective. We disagree violently as to whether we turn half left, on leaving the trench, as he maintains, or a quarter left, which is my opinion.

8.30. We still breakfast. The subaltern of the other company, pointing at the landscape with a piece of bread and butter, says, 'Doesn't their wire look beastly?'

8.45. The sun comes out and floods the scene with light, even tinting the shell bursts with gold. You catch yourself looking at your watch. 'Only a quarter to nine' is what you say. What you are thinking is that in five hours, any hour, this rotten waiting will be over, one way or another.

9.30 a.m. The other Company Commander retires to his Christian Martyrs tomb [dugout] and reads *The Field* [magazine]. His subaltern is still eating bread and jam. My Company Sergeant Major writes a note to the Company Commander. I watch two grey-coated Huns plodding stolidly among the shell bursts, carrying a plank. They disappear.

10 a.m. Three aeroplanes come out from over our lines. Rather more noise in consequence, 'Archies', [anti-aircraft] and machine-gun fire.

10.30 a.m. German high-explosive shrapnel, very black, very smelly, very noisy, very erratic. The other Company Commander leaves his hole and demands to know why the blazes we are kept loafing about like this all the morning. People always attack at dawn, why make a matinée of it?

11 a.m. Frantic demands down the trench for Sergeant Bradall. Pass the word down for Sergeant Bradall. One of the servants vouchsafes the information that the sergeant was killed last night. 'On the water fatigue, sir,' he said. 'I saw him dead myself.'

More aeroplanes, more noise, more German shrapnel, most objectionable, but wide.

11.30 a.m. Two hours more! My Company Commander and I agree we will stay where we are until one o'clock, then go along the trench to the right where the company is, see that the men can all get out of the trench easily, and pick a good jumping off place for ourselves.

Noon. The servants produce a bottle of port. It betrays considerable signs of the agitation of the night. We partake of port wine and a biscuit, in approved style. Wine does not taste well out of a chipped enamel mug, especially port, after it has been under shellfire.

12.15 p.m. We lunch off tongue, bread and sand. The port is by this time so thick that it fortunately veils the interesting mineral deposits in the bottom of the mug. I retire to the Christian Martyrs tomb and read several pages of *The Field* without understanding them.

12.30 p.m. One hour more. Great map and compass work by everybody. Much discussion about the final objective, somewhere beyond the smoke wreaths round the village. My Company Commander produces a two-franc piece. 'We'll toss up who goes over with the leading platoon,' he says. Winner goes second. I win.

12.45 p.m. My servant, wearing the chastened yet hopeful air of a second in a prize-ring, divests me of my raincoat and cap, then girds about my waist my belt with all the complicated paraphernalia of modern war – revolver, compass, field glasses, gas helmet. The other officers are similarly occupied. Conversation languishes.

12.55 p.m. Our orderlies appear mysteriously, unbidden, at our sides, as is the way of orderlies. We four officers compare watches. My Company Commander and I set off along the trench.

1 p.m. The British soldier is as full of angles as he is in a Nevinson war picture. [C. R. W. Nevinson, a war artist of the Vorticist school, known for his angular style of painting.] He and his equipment stick out all over the trench. We are squeezed, battered and bruised as we force our way along the trench foot by foot. The men are singularly quiet, the old ones phlegmatic, the young ones thoughtful.

1.10 p.m. The din is awe-inspiring. The very air seems to tremble with noise. This must be the intensive bombardment. It makes the nerves tingle with excitement. The men are waking up. You look at your watch and wonder how much longer you can bear the strain of waiting, not for what may happen but to fight, to get at them.

1.20 p.m. We find a good spot to get out of, right in the centre of the company. The men of the platoon that is to lead are standing in the niches they have cut, ready to leave the trench at the sound of the whistle.

1.25 p.m. 'Three minutes more, I make it,' bawls my Company Commander in my ears. I nod without lifting my eyes from my wrist.

1.28 p.m. A man beside me points excitedly to the left. 'They're off!' he yells. I see a stream of fellows moving forward, ever so slowly, on the extreme left. It is a false start but they keep on.

1.29 p.m. We are still waiting. My Company Commander has one foot on the parapet. He turns round and grins at me.

1.30 p.m. A whistle just above me sounds all along the line; men are scrambling, stumbling on every side. The first platoons are off. Lord – What a row!

1.31 p.m. How leisurely everyone seems to be moving forwards. My platoon is tumbling out of the trench. I presume I blew my whistle. Smoke and noise and figures swarming through the haze. My Company Commander waits for me as I come up and roars in my ear. 'Half left. You see I was right.' A man beside you exclaims 'Oh!' in pained astonishment, as it seems, and you see him at your feet with the blood gushing out of his head. It is then you realise you are over the top and never knew it.

———————————

In attacks, wounded men were not helped at all by their immediate comrades who were under orders to maintain the momentum of the advance. Instead, recovery was undertaken by stretcher-bearers belonging to the battalion. However, if casualties were heavy, the wounded man would often attempt to make his own way back, crawling in and out of shell holes, often meeting others in a similar predicament. When John McCauley was shot in the knee, he effected his own salvation but in doing so felt oddly ill at ease.

Pte John McCauley, 2nd Border Rgt

Strangely enough, as I lay wounded on the battlefield, no further use for fighting in my condition, and free to make my escape from the hell we were enduring, I felt genuine regret at the thought of parting from my chums. Fine, loyal comrades they had been, tested and tried by the most severe ordeal ever faced by human creature, and proved steadfast and true to one another. I began to appreciate what the splendid spirit of comradeship, born out of the horrors and hardships we had faced together, meant to me. I had a feeling that I was imposing on these splendid fellows, leaving them just when my help was most needed. Two dead and one wounded in our little group meant that extra burdens would be thrown on my pals, and I thought that I would like to stay with them, wounded though I was, to prove that I was as loyal as they had been to me. Those kinds of thoughts flit through the mind, especially in action.

L/Cpl Roland Mountfort, 10th Royal Fusiliers

After being wounded I can remember now what a curious feeling it gave me to be leaving my equipment behind, even at that time and place. There was my rifle, on which for more than twelve months I have spent hours and hours of labour to keep clean, looked after better than myself often, fixed bayonet, one cartridge in the chamber, cocked and safety catch on. My equipment I have greased and polished many a hundred times, my ammunition, all laboriously cleaned a few days before, iron rations, until then clung to like life itself; groundsheet, haversack with razor from Hadden's, and brush from Leytonstone years ago, and all my portable property that I had carried until it seemed almost part of me – chucked into a shell hole and left there to rot.

Pte C. Young, 2/4th Field Ambulance, RAMC

Except for a grunt when one of us is relieved of the stretcher, our journey is continued in silence. We are too wet and miserable for speech; we are automatons wound up and propelled by one fixed idea, the necessity of struggling forward. The form on the stretcher makes not a sound; the wet, the jolts, the shaking, seem to have no effect on him. An injection of morphine has drawn the veil. Well for him!

There is no house – merely a heap of ruins to mark what once had been the site of a brewery or wine establishment – but beneath the ruins are commodious vaults, once containing vats, but now housing a dozen or so stretcher-bearers who will take over our 'case' and complete the journey to the dressing station.

In a few minutes our patient is off again with a silent 'goodbye' from each of us, and a slight feeling of envy at the thought that in a few days he will probably be in Blighty. He passed from us; we knew not his name, his face was hidden – to us a stretcher-case; but, in so far as we, sweating and cursing, had carried him nearly a mile, despite and because of this, his going was like that of an old friend. Some day in these post-war years, we may pass one another in the street, unconscious of our intimate acquaintanceship.

Capt. T. I. Dun, 36th Field Ambulance, RAMC

Our Tommies, what tender hearts they have got! I heard one of them speaking to a badly wounded pal just before he was put on the ambulance car. I did not hear all that was said, but I felt strangely touched at the depth of expression in his voice as I heard him say simply, 'Goodbye, old chum.' It looks bald in writing, but look at that stretcher with its burden of blood and pain in it, see the anxious way the Tommy's old friend bends over him, hear those few words, as the machine gun goes 'pit-pit-pit' to the time of the rifle and the white trench rocket lights up the scene, and it is there that one sees the depth of Tommy below his smirking devil-may-care, I-don't-care attitude.

Capt. Henry Kaye, 43rd Field Ambulance, RAMC

At 1 p.m., Taylor, Edwards and I fell upon a poor man in a dreadful state – brain protruding from an evil hole between his eyes, right eye destroyed, wound in the neck, lacerated right hand, right foot almost torn off and a terrible sloughy hole in it; tibia and fibula fractured just above the ankle – both legs riddled with holes of all shapes and sizes, and the whole of him of course in a state of mixed blood and dirt, which is indescribable.

Well, this meant a two-hour job, and we got him all nicely fixed up, free from pain and off to the CCS later on. Curiously enough, we had another man in almost the same state during dinner, but farther gone, and he died peacefully in the dressing room, being too bad to touch.

In the summer of 1915 British troops moved south to the pleasant, rolling countryside of the Somme. The Germans had arrived here in November 1914 during the 'race to the sea', and had spent much of the next year digging in, building highly elaborate defences, choosing the high ground to establish themselves. Their enemy then had been the French and, on the whole, there had been a policy of live and let live, the Germans happy to entrench, the French happy to look elsewhere to attack. Just behind the Allied lines was the town of Albert.

Lt J. A. C. Pennycuick, 59th Field Coy, RE

Rode into Albert in the afternoon on a bicycle. It had several shops open but had been a good deal knocked about, and looked like Ypres at the beginning of April. The church tower had been a good deal hit and one shell had knocked over a golden statue of the Madonna at the top of the tower. It was hanging over at rather more than a right angle and the figure looked exactly as if it was doing a high dive from the top.

Pte James Racine, 1/5th Seaforth Highlanders

We came to rest in the village of Autuille which is situated at the foot of a hill just behind the line. We were the first division of British troops to relieve the French on the Somme. The sector was extraordinarily quiet, and, although the village was in such close proximity to the front line trench, it had been very slightly damaged. Several estaminets still dispensed their refreshments.

Here we found large dugouts, and the French troops had evidently believed in comfort, for they had constructed beds, made from struts and covered with wire netting, which were very comfortable. They had also constructed rustic tables and chairs. In an old house, I found a very much out of tune piano and accompanied a mixture of French and British troops in a singsong. The French troops gave us a hearty welcome and informed us that the sector was extremely quiet and that only eight light shells a day were fired into the village. These were sent over in pairs at the following times: 11 a.m., 2 p.m., 4 p.m. and 8 p.m., and the French artillery replied similarly.

At the times stated, the troops had gone into the dugouts whilst the shells burst, and then returned to the estaminets at the conclusion of the comic bombardment. We thought this to be an extraordinary way of carrying on a war, but were prepared to enjoy our improved surroundings. We were also informed that, previous to our arrival, the enemy shouted across to the French that they were being relieved by Scottish troops and the French had ridiculed the idea. The secret intelligence of the enemy was extraordinary and he seemed to know, in detail, the movements of our troops.

Lt J. A. C. Pennycuick, 59th Field Coy, RE

Lovely sunny day. In the morning I went to Vaux Wood and visited the observation stations. One, a new one, close by the French heavy battery, one in a tree, and one in a boiler near Vaux

Ecole, which looked like the conning tower of a submarine. Through a telescope I could see a Boche sentry in front of a house in Curlu. He was rather a sloppy individual and lounged about and talked to a lady friend. I also saw the Herr Colonel's cook in white overalls and apron and two other Boches and some children and cows; it was quite an amusing half-hour.

Maj. George Stevens 1/8th Durham Light Infantry
The other evening one of our fellows got hit in the shoulder by a bullet, his best pal rushed up to give him help, tore off his coat and shirt and had a good look at the wound. He then caught the patient a ringing slap on the back and said, 'Ee man, it's champion.' The wretched victim didn't seem to mind, but simply said, 'Howay, Geordie, gan awa and shake hands with the German for me for bein' sae canny.'

Pte James Racine, 1/5th Seaforth Highlanders
At dawn on the first day, we found on our barbed wire entanglements a piece of paper on which was a written request that two or three of our men would, at a given time, proceed halfway across no-man's-land and meet a similar number of Germans in order to exchange periodicals and souvenirs, as the French had been accustomed to do. After a consultation, our interpreter and two men agreed and, at noon, met the enemy halfway; the heads of the troops on each side were above the parapets and no firing took place. Later, when we left the trenches, we were paraded before the Commanding Officer and severely reprimanded. He stated that 'it was impossible to fight a man with one hand and give him chocolates with the other'. We were given to understand that any similar action in the future would be severely dealt with.

Capt. John Laurie, Adjutant, 2nd Seaforth Highlanders
The battalion came down from the Ypres Salient in the summer of 1915, having been brought up to strength after the heavy

casualties of the first and second gas attacks in April and May respectively. We were glad to take over a quiet section of the Somme front from the French, east of Mailly-Mailly, in a very different scene to the Ypres Salient. The French were no believers in disturbing a quiet sector by raids or shelling and I believe that the story of an incident in one sector of the 4th Division front is true, that the German officers (ignorant of the relief) came over for their evening game of bridge with their adversaries and were very disgruntled by their reception!

Pte James Racine, 1/5th Seaforth Highlanders
The brigadier made a tour of inspection of the front line. This particular sector was quiet, which would no doubt account for the appearance of the general and his staff, for they generally kept well to the rear when any activity was evidenced. The general passed along the trench, halted, and having enquired as to whether it was safe to look over, he gingerly hoisted himself on to the firing step, looked over the top and took a hurried glance at the enemy trench opposite. He stepped down, not having been fired upon during the moment he had looked over the top, informed the captain of my company that, as it was so quiet, it was possible that the Germans were not occupying their front trench and that, as a test, a tunic and cap were to be placed on a rifle and held just above the top of the trench, whilst he continued his inspection of the sector. Upon his return, we would examine the tunic and, if it was found to be riddled, it could be safely assumed that the enemy had not forgotten the war and gone home.

We knew quite well that the enemy occupied his trench in an exceedingly efficient manner, by reason of the rapid fire to which we had been subjected. However, as soon as the general had passed on and the tunic and cap had been exposed as ordered, the captain whispered hurried instructions to several of the men to open fire on the tunic with their rifles; when the staff returned, ample evidence was afforded of the activity of the enemy. The captain knew perfectly well that, had the clothing by some unforeseen chance not been bullet-ridden, parties would have been detailed to go over to the enemy trench after dark and investigate. None of us were exactly excited at the prospect.

The second Christmas of the war, and British soldiers were far better prepared than they had been a year before. The infrastructure of the front line was far more advanced than twelve months earlier with well-constructed dugouts, raised duckboards on the trench floor, and much better drainage with the use of mechanical and manual trench pumps.

Something else had changed, too. The military authorities were determined that there would be no repeat of the Christmas Truce. Strict orders were issued that there was to be no contact with the enemy. It was an order that was broadly obeyed, although there were still isolated cases of fraternisation. William Gordon, a lance corporal in the Scots Guards, took part in one large-scale meeting and recalled the serious repercussions.

L/Cpl William Gordon, 1st Scots Guards
Towards daybreak voices could be heard from the German side shouting 'Tommy, Tommy, Good Christmas'. Some of the boys from our side took up the call shouting 'Good old Fritz, Merry Christmas'. The Germans were also beckoning to the British to come over and meet . . . and it was then an easy matter for the first steps to be taken by both sides to meet halfway between the trenches.

Within minutes I had reached the main crowd in no-man's-land. The Germans dancing to their harmonicas which they had brought with them. I got talking to a few Germans, some of whom could speak a little English. One especially, I liked, was a fairly tall young man who some years before the war had been a waiter in the Savoy Hotel, London. I exchanged a few of my tunic buttons for a few German regimental badges and learnt thereby that the units facing us were the 13th and 15th Bavarian Regiments. So far as my memory serves me there must have been over two hundred soldiers, German and British, between the trenches in groups of between ten and twenty . . .

Time was getting on and sometime between 10 and 11 a.m. news was received that the division on our right of the trenches had orders to commence at twelve noon artillery fire on the ground where the unofficial ceasefire was taking place . . . Exactly on the hour the field gunners commenced firing. It only lasted for a few minutes but it succeeded in its object by chasing stragglers back to the trenches.

News had clearly filtered back about the informal truce. When the Scots Guardsmen were relieved two days later, the incoming battalion was ordered to fire fifteen rounds rapid over the parapet to leave no one in any doubt that the truce was over.

On reaching our farmhouse billets, we were instructed to remain where we were and in no case allowed outside. Immediate action was taken re letter writing and men warned not to mention any of the Xmas Day happenings. All letters were subject to censorship by company officers, that being the usual rule, but in addition the men were informed that the issue of green envelopes was to cease at once. Green envelopes were not subject to local company censorship but were subject to examination at army base before going on to the UK.

A big enquiry followed our return to billets, the outcome being that several officers lost seniority in rank . . . Our sergeants were reduced in rank to private soldiers, corporals were also down-graded; but I, being of low rank, suffered no punishment. Leave to the UK for soldiers serving in France used to take place once in every eight months or so; but, as a further punishment and to block news of the event, all leave was cancelled for six months. In my case I was in France from early September 1915 to late January 1917 before I had my first ten days' leave to the UK, so in a way I did pay for getting friendly with the Bavarians.

The archetypal studio portrait: Captain Richard Heumann, 2nd London Regiment (Royal Fusiliers), photographed while on leave.* He was killed in action on the Somme, September 1916, and buried where he fell, with two other men from the battalion. Their isolated grave remains in a field close to Falfemont Farm.

*This studio photograph is the only image in the book not taken on a VPK or similar camera.

August 1914: the 11th Hussars arrive at the port of Le Havre. The men crowd the decks for their first view of France.

Moving up to the front line: regular British soldiers receive an effusive welcome from French soldiers and civilians.

Unknown British cavalry photographed shortly after the epic retreat from Mons, 10 September 1914.

Royal Engineers, wearing blue and white armbands, stand beside their horse as it runs out telephone cable from a frame on its back.

Men of the London Rifle Brigade, 1914: three were killed and four wounded. An eighth, the photographer, was also wounded.

Heating up water for washing in winter billets, 1914. This privately taken photograph was made into a postcard and sent home.

Relaxing in an estaminet. The man reading, Douglas Belcher (London Rifle Brigade), went on to win the Victoria Cross in May 1915.

Ploegsteert Wood: men of an unknown regiment use their jack knives to open a tin of food.

A Maxim machine gun manned by two soldiers of the South Staffordshire Regiment, early 1915.

Men of the 3rd Rifle Brigade in a primitive trench: surprisingly few men are wearing their kit. On the parapet are their groundsheets, hanging out to dry.

Playing cards while at rest. Trench routine meant that men relaxed and slept during the day and used the cover of darkness to work at night. They are wearing 'Gor blimey' trench caps, issued in the winter of 1914/15 and discontinued soon afterwards.

Putting out and
securing barbed
wire, early 1915:
the jumbled mess
is in contrast to
the neat designs
described in
military manuals.

Filling sandbags: literally
millions of sandbags were used
to line the trench parapets,
constantly being replaced as
they were destroyed.

An officer looks through an early trench periscope, which uses
mirrors to reflect an image of no-man's-land. His walking stick
rests on the fire-step.

Spotting for a sniper: an army
issue telescope is used to look
into no-man's-land,
May 1915.

An 18lb gun team with ammunition and ammunition limber to the right.

A remarkable image of a shell burst caught on camera: the size of the explosion suggests a 5.9-inch German shell.

Hit by enemy shells and on fire: Morteltje estaminet at Wieltje, Ypres Salient, is slowly reduced to rubble.

The effect of a shell burst on a soldier's uniform: the shrapnel has completely shredded his clothes.

Over the parapet, looking towards the German lines at Ypres: this was a risky image to take when snipers were around.

The 'Strand Palace Hotel': an unidentified unit holds the front line near Armentières, early 1915.

Cooking in the support trenches: note the rum jars, bottom right. Labelled 'S.R.D.' (Supply Reserve Depot), fragments of these jars still litter the battlefields.

Action panorama (two VPK photographs): men of the 1/10th King's Liverpool Regiment fighting in the Ypres Salient, June 1915. Very few images of actual fighting were ever taken.

A Lewis gun team of the 12th Gloucestershire Regiment (Bristol's Own).

After the first German chlorine gas attacks of April 1915, British soldiers were issued with gauze pads soaked in hypo-sulphate, as well as goggles to protect their eyes from tear gas.

Men of the South Staffordshire Regiment pose with carrier pigeons used to fly messages back to headquarters.

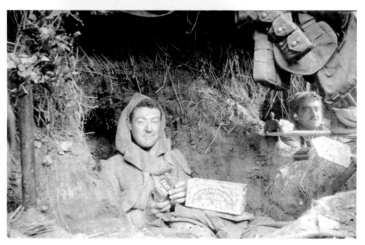

'Biscuits and Bully': Huntley and Palmer's 'Superior' biscuits and 'bully' (corned) beef fed millions of British soldiers throughout the war.

An officer of the 1/5th York and Lancaster Regiment resting in an early dugout. This wooden construction offered little or no protection from a direct hit.

Snipers at work: the men are wearing sack cloths over their heads to ensure no light can be seen behind them.

A dummy is held above the trench parapet in order to draw sniper fire. By firing, a sniper might reveal his position, so enabling retaliatory action.

Men of the 1/2nd Monmouthshire Regiment: they are holding a portrait of a soldier. Like the dummy, it would be used to draw sniper fire.

Exhausted: an officer catches up on his sleep after a night's work. His Mark V Webley revolver hangs from a lanyard on the wall.

Table and chairs 'borrowed' from a nearby house for trench use. The officers are wearing other ranks' webbing to help conceal their rank from the enemy.

Arras: a soldier of the 12th Gloucesters strips to the waist during a hunt for lice living in the seams of his shirt. The search was known as 'chatting'.

Men of the South Staffordshire Regiment take a much-needed bath: the farm cart has been lined with a tarpaulin and filled with water.

While in billets, soldiers mixed freely with civilians on farms behind the lines.

A quick hair wash: not all civilians were happy with soldiers using their wells and pumps, for fear that they would run dry.

These men are preparing food in a billet and may well be officers' batmen. The man on the right wears South African War campaign ribbons.

Ypres, 1915: in the
distance are the
famous, and badly
damaged, Cloth Hall
and Cathedral.

Loos, 1915: British
infantry advance
towards the enemy
lines.

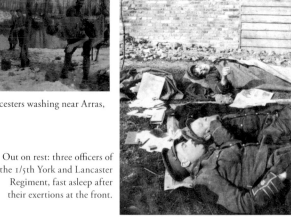

Men of the 12th Gloucesters washing near Arras,
winter 1915/16.

Out on rest: three officers of
the 1/5th York and Lancaster
Regiment, fast asleep after
their exertions at the front.

British dead await final interment. Chloride of lime was normally sprinkled on the dead to aid decomposition.

CSM William Gamlin, 6th Somerset Light Infantry, lies critically ill. A veteran of the South African campaign, he died soon after this picture was taken, in August 1915.

L/Cpl William Smallcombe holding a Lewis gun in the trenches at Arras. He is wearing a Lewis gunner's qualification badge on his left sleeve.

1916

The War in 1916

Very slowly, imperceptibly, the tables were turning against Germany, only this time, in January, there were fewer voices in Britain predicting a victorious year ahead. Militarily, the war was not going particularly well for anyone.

However, there were definite signs of improvement as far as Britain was concerned. The shell shortage which had plagued each offensive in 1915 had been partially alleviated in the early autumn at Loos, but the guns were still not fed as well as the gunners would have liked. However, under Lloyd George's boundless energy, things were changing and, in a war that would be largely won or lost by the resort to overwhelming firepower, the balance on the battlefield was turning one way and one way only. The results of improvements in the quality and supply of munitions would be witnessed on the Somme later that summer.

January also saw another change for the better. An enlistment crisis which had become evident from mid-1915 onwards had been solved at a stroke. Conscription was introduced, and with it a guaranteed source of manpower to the army. Of all the belligerents, Britain was the only one that had relied on volunteers to fill the ranks. The Government had long felt unsure that the British public would be willing to accept compulsion, and had tiptoed towards conscription in August 1915 when all civilians between the ages of fifteen and sixty-five were required to register, giving details of both their occupation and their address. This survey was undertaken to help ease manpower shortages to industry, allowing the Government to manage labour, but it was clear that such an authoritative list would be just as useful to the authorities when it came to conscription. In a last gesture towards volunteer recruitment, the Derby Scheme was introduced in September 1915. Men could enlist, but would be allowed to return to their civilian employment and would not be called until required. Its success in bringing forward fresh recruits was decidedly limited, and the more cynical perhaps felt that the scheme had been used as a ruse to convince the British public that compulsion was the only way, now that voluntary enlistment had so obviously foundered. The Government need not have worried. The public broadly supported enforced enlistment into the services, even if those already serving were dubious about the quality and morale of men forced to wear khaki and fight.

The two great issues, ammunition and enlistment, were being properly addressed, but nothing ever goes smoothly in war, and in the first months of 1916 the British public were once again to find themselves disappointed and shocked in almost equal measure. With the arrival of Kitchener's division in France, an agreement was made with the French, who had taken on the greater part of the workload of the war to this point, for the BEF to take over the trenches in a relatively sleepy backwater of the line, so showing their commitment and freeing up French forces for action elsewhere. The backwater was the Somme.

It was of no great strategic value, and for that reason little serious fighting had happened here. Indeed, a policy of live and let live had developed between the French and German soldiers, and no one more senior had seemed to mind. This would change. All previous joint offensives had seen the French attack at one location, the British at another. Here, on the Somme, it would be possible for the Allies to launch one massive assault on the enemy, hand in hand, so to speak. Plans for the offensive were begun at the end of 1915.

The problem was the Germans. They may have been happy to leave the Somme well alone, but their attention had been turned to the Western Front, and a decision was taken to make an enormous effort against the French forces at Verdun. Here, they felt, they could fight the French army to a standstill, bleeding them white in the process. The offensive, which began on 21 February, was colossal in its prodigious expenditure of men and materials. The shock to the collective French psyche was immense. Verdun had to be held at all costs and later, in their Commanding Officer, General Henri-Philippe Pétain, they had a man with the resilience to see the fight to the finish. The problem was that the proposed Somme offensive would now have to be scaled back. France could not commit anything like the men once envisaged; it would have to be a largely British affair. There was a further twist to the new arrangement: Britain would have to attack much sooner than expected in order to draw off German forces from Verdun. It was a demand reluctantly agreed to by Field Marshal Haig. Throughout the early spring of 1916 the process of planning was relentless.

Elsewhere, the reports were depressing. News reached the press that a British force numbering some 13,000 men had been forced to surrender in Mesopotamia to the Turkish army and was marching into captivity. Hot on the heels of this piece of bad news came the Easter Rising in Dublin, a rebellion that shocked the public and required a number of troops, who might otherwise have been gainfully employed in France, going to Ireland to quell the uprising. Then, in late May, news reached home of the inconclusive Battle of Jutland. Britain's great pride, the navy, had not even beaten the German fleet in an engagement on the open sea; indeed, the initial news had been even worse, that a tactical defeat had been sustained. It was only as newspaper editors were finally digesting this that the press announced a further tragedy. Lord Kitchener had been drowned when the ship he was travelling on, the *Hampshire*, was sunk by a mine in the North Sea while on its way to Russia. Most of the ship's hands had gone down with the vessel.

Little wonder that the public set so much store by the forthcoming offensive on the Somme. The Big Push, as it was popularly known, was in the offing and, it was hoped, would break the stalemate once and for all. The responsibility of the offensive had been left in large part to the men of Kitchener's New Army. Division after division had arrived in late 1915 and early 1916 straight from England or from training camps in Egypt. They were well trained and highly motivated.

To soften up the enemy, a five-day bombardment of the German trenches took place, later extended to seven days when bad weather put a temporary delay to the infantry assault. The expenditure of ammunition was prodigious. The British fired four times as many shells in one week as had been used at Loos in three. The problem was that the display of firepower was let down by its relative ineffectiveness. Most Germans were in dugouts thirty feet below ground, and, while many were driven mad by the noise, the vast majority were uninjured as the British shells thundered down, making a mess of the trenches and wire above, but not affecting those deep underground. When the British infantry attacked on the morning of 1 July, the Germans were able to race up their stairs and meet the oncoming infantry with withering fire. The ratio of British to German losses that day was somewhere in the region of 10 to 1.

That first day may be considered as the worst in British military history, but no Commanding Officer was going to call a halt to an offensive after one day; it would have been militarily disastrous for morale, and politically impossible. This was the first truly great battle of attrition that the British had fought, and in a process of two steps forward, one step back, the British and Empire troops slowly but surely drove the Germans back across the battlefield. Every wood, every lane, every field, every ridge was contested, as British troops and their commanders entered a steep learning curve that would ensure, at least for the most part, that some early mistakes were not endlessly repeated. There was an awful truism that no one would openly acknowledge but many knew: in manpower the Germans could not afford like-for-like losses. The Somme battlefield had little strategic value, but, in an effort to grind the enemy into the dust, it was as good a place as any to turn a war in one's own favour. It was also the place where the British Army learnt to fight a modern war.

In September the British introduced a new dimension to the battlefield: the tank. Heralded in the British press as a new wonder weapon after its initial success in taking the village of Flers, it had, in truth, been useful but, as with all new technology, there had been faults and problems. Most of the tanks had broken down or became stuck. Nevertheless, it was a sign of the increasing sophistication and industrialisation of the battlefield and the shape of things to come. The other signs were the unmistakable predominance of Allied firepower, and a temporary Allied advantage in the air war as the latest British aircraft dominated the skies. However, no breakthrough occurred and the Somme battle petered out in the winter mud. The Germans were only too glad to see the end of a battle they had psychologically lost. For nearly five months their men had been on the defensive. Small tactical counter-attacks may have won back ground temporarily, but they had never taken the fight to the Allies and their losses had been roughly comparable.

The end of the Somme battle also signalled the end of what had been a great political career. The British Prime Minister Herbert Asquith, who had lost a son, Raymond, in the fighting in September, was increasingly seen as a beleaguered and ineffectual wartime leader. In December, his tenure was brought to an end when the Liberal David Lloyd George, in cooperation with the Conservative Party and the press, brought down the Cabinet. A Coalition Government was formed and at its head was a new Prime Minister, Lloyd George, the man who as Minister of Munitions had radically altered Britain's armaments manufacture; the man who had become the Minister for War after the death of Lord Kitchener, was the obvious natural successor. There was one problem. Lloyd George was a meddler. Deeply suspicious of Haig after his campaign on the Somme, he could not and would not trust his Commander-in-Chief to run the war on the Western Front. His increasingly exasperated relations with his army commanders, Haig in particular, were to hamper rather than support the offensives of 1917 and seriously jeopardised the entire campaign on the Western Front in 1918.

On Leave

The contrast was as stark as it could be, whether going on leave or returning to France. All soldiers took time to make the adjustment from the mud-sodden trenches of the Western Front to the bustling streets of London and the provincial cities. Some men loathed the difference, reeling at the normality of street life, and the seemingly frivolous pursuits of civilians going about their daily business when, almost within earshot (for those in London, at least), the guns maimed and claimed more lives.

Yet other soldiers rejoiced at the spectacle, delighted to be amongst normal people, doing normal things. The chance to take in a West End show, go to the cinema, dine in a restaurant with white linen tablecloths, or simply to walk in the open without the need to duck, was a powerful stimulant; the only problem was that people would always ask about the trenches. Wherever a soldier went, he was an object of wonderment. Until mid-1916 the service dress cap – worn in France with the wire stiffening removed on active service – was a good indication that this was a man home on leave, but there was more to it than that, as Private Christopher Massie knew.

'Someone will approach you, or a barmaid will drop flirting and ask quietly across the bar:

"Young man, do you come from the front?"

"Yes, why?"

"Oh, I thought you did. There is something different about the men who come back. What is it like out there? Terrible, I suppose."

You wander up and down your mind to find out really what it is like. Good times you have, and damned bad ones; but you can't recollect anything useful, so you say: "Well, my dear! I don't know what it's like out there, but it's just heaven here."

"Fancy that!" she comments, "Everything seems so quiet and slow to us." '

Massie did not mind the questions, although he evaded a telling answer. Others, such as Driver Percival Glock, who served in the Royal Field Artillery, could not abide them.

'For the benefit of anyone who has not experienced leave, I will try and explain or rather describe it. The first question I was asked was, "When are you going back?" Just think of it, one comes home with the idea of forgetting the war and the first question reminds one of it and so it happens, every person one meets asks the same question, which is invariably followed with "Have you seen any Germans?" "Do you want to go back?" "Have you seen any fighting?" "What's it like out there?" "Have you had many narrow squeaks?" "When's the war going to finish?" and so on, but of course you can't blame them, it is only natural.'

The soldier's desire for leave was intense and the expectation that it was about to be given made men exceptionally jumpy and unwilling to take risks. In October 1917, Albert Martin recorded in his diary how he was 'sweating on leave very violently' and the following day he wrote how 'Leave fever has reduced me to a frightful state of fidgets. Can't keep still for two minutes together.'

Waiting for leave was especially difficult for those who were married with children. Their leave was no greater or less than all 'other ranks' and was rarely granted until a man had served at least a year abroad. There was a very practical logic to this, and it was in no way a desire on the part of the military authorities to keep men unnecessarily from their loved ones. By the end of 1916 there were, on average, two million men serving on the Western Front; even one week's leave per year, per man, involved the authorities in a huge administrative undertaking, processing in theory more than 38,500 men every seven days, transporting them down to the base and shipping them back home. Allowing for casualties in deaths and wounded, even half this number was a serious drain on resources.

In the early part of the war, leave was not distributed evenly and this caused friction. Some lucky men received as many as three leaves in two years, others none. An incident was recorded in which an Army Service Corps sergeant, with just three months under his belt in France, who had never seen a shell burst, receiving leave, news of which nearly caused a riot amongst the infantrymen. Later on in the war, a proper rota was enforced, logs of names were kept and a man could anticipate the rise of his name on the 'leave list' as others in his platoon were given their passes. Nevertheless, at any moment leave could be cancelled owing to an emergency at the front. The anticipated enemy offensive in March 1918 robbed thousands of men of their leave, just days before the assault began.

The authority's determination to keep to a strict rota removed the opportunity for men to return home on compassionate leave, an allowance that had been granted on occasions earlier in the war. There was also no added allowance for those who would have to travel further to see their families. A Scotsman from the far north was given just the same time in Britain as a man living in Kent.

When a man's leave was granted it usually came with little more than a day's notice. He would swiftly gather up his belongings and make his way down as quickly as possible, always conscious that he could still be robbed of his leave by a stray shell. Lieutenant John Godfrey recalled one such incident close to the damaged ramparts that surrounded the town of Ypres. As he looked around, a shell burst close by, splinters hitting a despatch rider who was 'brought in to be patched up only to die within a few minutes, bewailing the fact that he had just started to go on leave'.

Once on his way, a man was taken on a long, laborious train journey down to the coast, the speed of which was not 'out of place for a funeral', according to one soldier. These trains were specifically reserved for men going on leave, and were frequently in poor condition, although no one heading towards the coast, except perhaps in deepest winter, minded too much. Once at the coast, a certificate was required, stating that they were vermin-free. Then, once passes had been thoroughly checked and rechecked, the men boarded a ship bound for a Channel port and another train that would trundle north from the coast to Victoria Station.

How men spent their usually ten-day leave was up to them, as long as they returned on time to Folkestone. Some, utterly exhausted by their experiences, slept for a greater part of their time in Britain, while others did little more than remain at home with their families, not wishing to see anyone else. Christopher Massie chose to go to the cinema. Far from shying away from the war, he was interested to see how his Somme battle was reflected in the official films. He was not impressed.

'Does that monstrous insult, *The Battle of the Ancre* film, deceive many people as to the real facts of our experiences on the Somme? It is not like that, ladies and gentlemen. I saw it when I was at home and very merry. It was a good joke. With me were two Australians, a South African, a fellow in the Rifle Brigade, and a bottle of whisky. The whisky was for after the performance, but things turned out so badly during the showing of the film that the cork had to be drawn. We noticed an old lady weeping in a seat close to us, and the Rifle Brigade man bent over to her and said in a voice all sympathy, "Cheer up, bless yer 'eart, it ain't so bad as that!"

'I saw other film pictures and other shows before I returned to France, but they only impressed me by their cheapness and vulgarity. London was the great show. London's people and my comrades "on leave". One is not exactly happy. Perhaps beneath it all some of us are hurt. They say we look well. But all these days of fighting leave a mysterious malady for which we have not yet got a name. Something has happened.'

It was easy for soldiers to feel totally dislocated from their surroundings, unable to make the psychological transition from trench to civilian life. Many bitterly resented those who appeared to prosper from the war effort, earning many multiples of the soldier's shilling a day by working in munitions factories. As for war profiteers, the men could hardly stomach the thought of the sums they earned at the price of their comrades' suffering. The sight of fit men who had managed to duck conscription owing to 'important' war work also made them angry. Robert Cude, a private with the Royal West Kent Regiment, was furious.

'The "necessary" man will tell you, even as several have told me, that the army relies upon his efforts; what a man! Yet wherever one goes, one can see such specimens knocking around. Money is all that their patriotism is worth. To shoulder a pack and rifle, well, that is the job of fools. Heaven, if I do come out of this safe and sound, I will never serve such a disgusting country again. Moreover, men who have not served will get short shrift from me.'

Frank Richards, serving in the 2nd Battalion Royal Welsh Fusiliers, had waited eighteen months for his second leave of the war. He escaped for a while to tramp the hills, but he also attended a ceremony in which he was given a gold watch inscribed with his name, for winning the Distinguished Conduct Medal. Richards was realistic. People at home 'were wonderfully patriotic at smoking concerts given in honour of soldiers returning from the Front, but their patriotism never extended beyond that'. He noticed how every man of military age had come up to him to shake his hand before asking for advice. They wanted to evade military service. How, they asked him, should they go about it? If they failed and were forced to go, what advice could he give them as to which corps was the best one to join so as to stay away from the trenches?

And then all too soon it was time to return. A small number of men overstayed their leave and accepted the punitive consequences on their return. The vast majority, such as Hal Kerridge, serving with the London Scottish, parted company with family and friends and arrived on time.

'My father came with me to the station. He said, "Cheerio, son, look after yourself, I'll be glad to see you back again", and that was that. My father was a great scout. He was a gentleman, yet he'd got nerves of steel. He'd never show his emotions, it would upset me, so at the station we shook hands . . . I said goodbye to my mother at home, she could not bear to come. Many mothers were crying, in floods of tears, hanging on to their husbands' arms. It was usual at any station, some signs of hysteria. You saw it every time you got a crowd going back to the Front.'

Soldiers' Memories

2/Lt John Godfrey, 103 Field Coy, RE

Life is really divided into two parts: (a) the ordinary day-life in billets, which is a fair approach to peacetime conditions (b) night-life in one's work, which is simply an entry into Dante's Inferno – it is all an eerie abomination of desolation, full of unpleasant sights, sounds and smells which simply cannot be pictured by anyone who has never been there – it is so utterly unlike anything that one has met before. For the first month or so, the novelty of it is highly interesting: but after that has worn off, the life becomes intensely wearisome – the jobs are always the same, and the brain-work required for them is nil . . .

If the war and every job in it were not so protracted, it would be high-class excitement; the long strain, though, merely makes it sickening. On the job, one's only amusement is watching other people hop for it when a shell pitches near.

L/Cpl R. J. Smith, 19th King's Liverpool Rgt (3rd City)

Armed with a dozen Mills bombs, my mate Walter Stirrup and I crept out to the shell hole which constituted a listening post, and there relieved the two Wiltshires in more senses than one. After whispered advice from these two mud-covered figures who were constantly consigning the mud, the Germans and the British War Office to 'HELL – B – HELL' and various coloured 'HELLS', we sank into the mud beds their bodies had made, and commenced to listen.

According to a report, Jerry had a similar listening sap about forty yards away.

Except for an occasional whine of shells travelling both ways, and the spasmodic stammers of distant machine guns, our own line was fairly quiet. Suddenly an enemy machine gun opposite to us opened up. Perhaps the two Jerries in the sap were nervous, for without warning a bomb exploded on the near lip of our shell hole, to be shortly followed by several more not quite so near. To that there was only one reply, and raising myself up the crater I pulled the pin from a Mills and lobbed it into the sap. The sudden crash was followed by a shuddering moan and then silence. As I slid back to Walter's side in the mud, his eyes reproached me in the dim light.

Silence reigned for several minutes and then an inferno was let loose from the German front line in the form of rifle and machine-gun fire, and, still more deadly to us, the whine of rifle bombs. Two dropped close to our left and, warning Walter to keep down, we sank into the mud. A third whine grew closer, to be followed by a vivid flash and hard metallic crash of exploding bomb. If Walter cried out, I did not hear him in the din, but I felt his body relax and a sigh gurgled into the mud into which his face was buried.

The bomb had burst at his side, as was evidenced by a curl of smoke from a new indenture in the side of our crater. Kneeling in the mud, I softly called him and, receiving no answer, I turned him face up. His right shoulder was blown away and blood oozed from his neck and head.

With bloody hands and sobbing breath, for what seemed like hours I dragged him by the feet through the sap to the trench. Here he was taken over by the CSM and stretcher-bearers and laid in a dugout. A relief was posted up the sap and I was free to take a place at his side. An hour dragged by without movement, and squatting on my heels with my back against the earth wall, I commenced to doze.

'Bob, Bob.' Walter's lips barely muttered the words as he grasped my outstretched hand. He attempted further speech but fell back, dead. I leant over and touched his face with my cheek. I heard my own voice say, 'He's gone', and remember stumbling out into the trench. Walter was the first casualty in the brigade and before many hours passed several more joined him. The following night we blew the Jerry sap and forty yards of his front line to hell with Mills bombs and felt some relief.

How often in the next three years I envied Walter his brief war life and quick and painless end.

At night, no-man's-land was anything but vacant of men and dominating this ground was a keenly contested occupation. The British High Command in particular felt that by enacting an aggressive form of ownership, British spirits and confidence would rise as German morale fell. Apart from listening posts that would give warning of enemy activity or possible attacks, other men ventured into no-man's-land on working parties sent out to secure, repair and extend the front line barbed wire. On another night, fighting patrols might be sent to make contact with the enemy. Alternatively, a raiding party was deployed to enter the enemy trenches and seize a prisoner for interrogation, or simply to wreak mayhem, instilling fear into the enemy, wearying those who never felt off guard.

2/Lt John Godfrey, 103 Field Coy, RE

The line hardly moved at all: our front line trenches were often no more than fifty yards from the Germans' line: within close rifle fire. All repair work was only possible at night, and our days became a routine – marching the section up as soon as dark fell, at first over weed-grown tracks and paths or remnants of grass-grown roads, and then, within German machine-gun fire, diving down into a communication trench deep enough to hide your head, and so finally up to the support and front line trenches. Then you allotted your men to the various jobs, which you had reconnoitred by day or were merely continuing from the previous night – renewing a parapet here with sandbags or revetting, repairing barbed wire gaps there, or putting in duckboards where the water at the bottom of the trench really got beyond a joke – say two feet.

Cpl Arthur Cook, 1st Somerset Light Infantry

There is wiring to be done in front of our trenches; this is always an unpleasant task and invariably it's a pitch-dark night and raining. But the darkness, of course, has its advantages. Sometimes we have to go and fetch the wire from a dump in rear which is usually a camouflaged shell hole, our only equipment being a rifle, gas mask, and a bandolier of ammunition. Each man would carry a roll of barbed wire and two stakes, one would be pushed through the centre and the roll heaved on to the shoulder. Anyone who has not had the experience of carrying wire in the trenches on a dark wet night, with shells and MG fire whizzing over the top will find it difficult to conceive what such a journey is like. First you bump into the man in front who, on a dark night and in the bottom of a trench, is very difficult to see; and if you don't scratch yourself from his roll of wire you are lucky. A false step will land you in the bottom of the trench more often than not full of water, with your chums behind falling on top of you; rolls of barbed wire, soldiers, rifles, and iron stakes are all mixed up in one cursing heap.

Every few yards the stake or wire drags against the trench or a signaller's telephone line. The rifle does not help, as it invariably falls off the shoulder or else the muzzle gets tangled up with wires. Altogether it is a business that would shatter the temper of a parson, let alone a Tommy. The climax is reached when we are asked to leave the trenches and continue the journey in the open by going over the top to fill in the gaps made in the wire during the day by enemy shellfire. The men clamber cautiously out of the trench with the barbed wire balanced on their shoulders, and, after a few fearful glances at the front, set about their task in feverish haste, stakes are hurriedly erected and the wire interlaced, making a formidable obstacle. Clothes, hands and face are continually being rent and scratched. When a light goes up from the enemy lines, one has to stand perfectly still and hope we shall be mistaken for a post or a broken tree stump, a move by anyone and all are doomed.

2/Lt John Godfrey, 103 Field Coy, RE

It was just your luck whether the enemy decided to shell that area tonight or not: if he did, you just had to lump it until the strafe was over. Then, unless there was a severe strafe on, at the last of the dark, you would begin packing up for the return journey: tools had to be checked and materials for further work put in some shell hole. Any wounded were removed by stretcher-bearers if they couldn't walk, as soon as possible after they were hit; the dead, even if killed in the day, were usually left in some side trench for removal by night: it was pointless to get more people killed merely burying corpses.

Then the section began its tramp back to its billets, if any, or more usually trench shelters, about a mile or two. This was a memory that will always live with me. You assumed that you had had the worst of the night's work over, and began taking more notice of the general surroundings. The dawn was gradually driving away the mists in the valleys over the miles of weeds and poppies, and the day seemed to bring out the peculiar smells of weedy vegetation – a smell like camomile seemed to predominate.

About halfway back, when just out of range of machine-gun fire, the communication trenches ended, and you rose on to the tracks and paths again. You had to take care not to get strangled on the network of field telephone wires which ran promiscuously all over the place. In the gun position area you were occasionally startled by one of our own guns firing off almost, it seemed, in your face. Field guns you got used to, but the occasional 60-pounder really shook you. If you were riding, which was still sometimes possible in the battery areas at this stage, I am sure the gunners let off one or two just for the fun of seeing you and your horse jump.

Capt. Eric Whitworth, 12th South Wales Borderers (3rd Gwent)

Trench raids fulfil a policy to give the enemy no rest, to weaken his morale and above all to obtain constant and certain identification of the troops in front of us. It is often hard, in the hideous and pitiful circumstances which surround many raids, for the regimental officer to bear in mind this larger point of view, and foolish criticism of a staff officer, who orders raids, is sometimes heard. Yet only those who have taken part know that a trench raid is the sternest test of morale and leadership which any officer or man is called upon to face.

Except for the bravest, the anticipation of a raid, as compared to an attack at dawn, is as a nightmare to a dream! For in a raid the nervous strain is infinitely greater and at times the casualties in terms of those missing are relatively heavier than when a battalion is engaged in a formal attack. Instead of enjoying the confidence acquired in acting as a unit or a regiment, the raiders are a handful of men separated from their comrades, and the very isolated nature of the task forces them often to anticipate and enlarge the danger of the work in hand.

L/Cpl R. J. Smith, 19th King's Liverpool Rgt (3rd City)

My new job was first thrower to the bombing squad, which entailed creeping out through the wire, supported in the rear by four or five riflemen and, when chance permitted, getting close enough to a German machine gun to drop two or four Mills grenades in quick succession and get away again. Out of twenty-five to thirty attempts, not without loss to the rest of the squad, myself and Tommy Corwen managed two successful stunts, wiping out a German gun crew the first occasion, and the relief crew the second time. For this we were magnificently rewarded with a strong tot of whiskey, and naturally deduced that the intrinsic value of sixteen German machine-gunners and three first-class guns was worth two francs of whiskey to the British Headquarters.

Shelling was heavy and so were the casualties. Night patrols and bombing patrols became a regular nightly affair, and it was not therefore with any great surprise that I was called to the CO's dugout one afternoon.

The CO and the adjutant were closely studying a trench map when I entered. My heart sank in my boots. 'Hello, Smith,' called the CO. 'We are just studying some of the ground you and Corwen have been joyriding around lately.' 'Yes, sir,' I managed to get out. 'Now we want you and Corwen along with five or six others to bring in a German prisoner, dead or alive, but alive if possible. Headquarters want to know who occupies the line opposite us.'

For half an hour the details were discussed and it was arranged that on our left a bombardment should serve to kid Jerry that he was being attacked there, whilst we slipped over and attacked one of his trench posts. 'Then,' continued the CO, 'all you have to do is snaffle one of his sentries and shoot back to our trench.'

How damn simple!

I returned to the front line, and having found Corwen I casually remarked, 'Tommy, we are pleasantly requested to slip over to our friends across the way tonight and borrow or steal one of their hale and hearty sentries as the brigadier would like to send his little boy at home a complete German uniform, and he begs us to bear in mind that a blood-stained tunic would make his little boy sick. So keep the gentleman clean.'

'What does he think we are, bloody magicians?' snorted Corwen.

For several minutes we described the origination of this insanity in lurid terms and, after discussing the plan thoroughly, we felt sure that our names would be on the next ROLL OF HONOUR issued by the War Office, probably as missing.

Night crept on, and my stomach felt as though it was liquefying rapidly as we loaded up with Mills grenades, a bombing club each, and swallowed a small tot of rum thoughtfully provided by our captain.

With Corwen and I in front, and three riflemen strung out on either flank in the rear, we crept through the wire. Occasionally a burst of machine-gun fire swept the ground, but we luckily managed to flatten ourselves in time and miss the deadly hail. At last we reached his wire and after waiting for several minutes to locate the exact position of the machine gun after a burst of fire we separated, as arranged: Corwen moved along the wire to the left and myself to the right, followed by our three men each. After worming our way for about thirty yards, we turned inwards and I commenced to cut the bottom strands of the wire and crawl under.

Throughout, the machine gun was spasmodically firing. I had reached the parapet, my three men followed and slid into the trench, where all three waited, two to creep towards the machine gun and one to face the other way to guard against anyone coming along the trench. Corwen and his men were in the same position on the far side of the post, and were to await the signal, which was a Very light fired straight at the Germans manning the gun . . . Minutes passed as I edged to seven or eight yards from the gun. I was covered with mud, face included, through flattening myself in it so often. I could just see the outline of two heads by the machine gun. They appeared to be peering well ahead, and would hardly have thought of looking for movement so near at hand. My heart was pounding until I thought they would hear its beat. I suddenly felt horribly afraid that the muzzle of the gun was being turned in my direction and then, realising that any second would see it spout death, I let fly with the Very light and sprang for the heads. Corwen and I crashed on to the gun at the same time as the two men from the rear flung themselves forward. Crash went the Mills bombs down the dugout, and within thirty seconds we were dragging the two German gunners through the wire.

Immediately out of the trench, I flung a bomb on to the post to blow up the gun, and this we had arranged to be the signal to the two men along the trench to beat it. It also prevented the machine gun being used against us while we got through the wire. One German commenced to be awkward; him I tapped on the head pretty hard with the club. The first hands to grab us and pull us to safety were the colonel's. Crouching in the trench, he flashed a torch on the Jerry I had stunned. 'What the hell is up with this fellow?' he whispered.

'Oh, I had to biff him to keep him quiet,' I chimed in. 'Biff him? You've cracked his skull like an egg!' chuckled the CO.

That night Corwen and I staggered out of the CO's dugout feeling at peace with the world. We had been treated to a jolly good feed on tinned fish and best part of a bottle of whiskey between us.

The last words I remember from the CO were, 'Smith, you're damnably funny when you're drunk, and I am going to make you a corporal when you are sober.'

There had always been a certain amount of fraternisation between enemies. Often it was no more than a 'Good morning, Fritz' shouted across no-man's-land, with a similar or rude reply. Sometimes the communication went further, and taunted the enemy.

8th Royal Munster Fusiliers War Diary, 10 May 1916
Little enemy activity . . . Lieutenant Biggane went out to enemy's sap at H25 d49. It was unoccupied. He brought back two notice boards put up by the Germans with the following announcements.

(1) 'Irishmen! Heavy uproar in Ireland; English guns are firing at your wifes and children! 1st May 1916.'

(2) 'Interesting war-news of April 29th 1916. Kut el Amara has been taken by the Turks, and whole English army therein – 13,000 men – maken prisoners.'

The German intelligence was clearly good, and was aware that an Irish Regiment was opposite them. Shortly afterwards, the War Diary of the 9th Munster Fusiliers noted:

An effigy labelled 'SIR ROGER CASEMENT' which had been suspended by the neck from a tree by one of our patrols yesterday was brought in. It appeared to annoy the enemy and was found to be riddled with bullets.

Sir Roger Casement was a former British consul turned Irish Republican. In 1914 and 1915 he visited Germany to raise a brigade from amongst Irish prisoners of war who would be willing to fight against Britain. He failed, returning to Ireland just prior to the Easter Uprising, when he was captured. He was subsequently tried and executed for treason.

The messages continued. A few weeks later, the first that any British soldiers knew of the death of Lord Kitchener, the Secretary of State for War, was another message from the Germans opposite.

46th Infantry Brigade War Diary. Left Subsection 11/6/16
The sentry posted in the sap opposite Boyeau 46 noticed an envelope on a stick outside our wire with the following written on the inside:

'The English Ministre of war and the general Kommandre Lord Kitchener is on the trip to Russia with all his generals officers trowened in the east see by a german submerin. Nobody is sowed.'

Lt Col John Longley, Commanding Officer, 1st East Surrey Rgt
In the trench on our left, whilst a party of RE sappers and miners were at work, a note was thrown over from the Germans in the

opposite trench. The note, which was stuck in a cartridge case and thrown right into the sap, contained the following: 'Good morning. I see you have started sapping', signed 'Ernest'. This was written in English and goes to show how hard it is to catch these Germans 'asleep'.

War Diary, 1/5th Leicestershire Rgt

The enemy patrols were active during the night but, although they were heard, our patrols were not able to get in close contact with them. In front of B Company, they were heard near our wire. Our sentries at once opened fire, when a voice exclaimed in most idiomatic English, 'I'll put my xxxxxxx fist in your face in a minute', and 'You're a nice xxxx to lead us.' Our men ceased fire, naturally thinking it was one of our own patrols that had wandered off its course; however it turned out to be yet another Hun ruse.

Pte James Racine, 1/5th Seaforth Highlanders

At dawn on one occasion, we saw a flag on our barbed wire entanglements in front of the trench. Apparently during the night some enterprising German had crawled across and fixed it. The previous day, a draft of new officers had arrived and one young fellow, who looked about nineteen years of age, was most interested in the flag and annoyed at the temerity of the enemy in placing it there – it could only be looked upon as an insult to the British Army. He stated his determination to go out after dark and bring it in. The old campaigners viewed the whole business with distrust and strongly advised the officer to be very careful. Acting upon advice, he set off after dark with a sergeant and one man armed with a ball of string, with the intention of tying the string to the flag, returning to the trench whilst unwinding the ball, and then hauling in the offending object. When he reached his objective, however, he unfortunately appeared to lose his head and instead of carrying out the arrangement, took hold of the flag and dragged it out of the wire. An enemy bomb had been attached and it exploded and killed the officer and wounded the sergeant and man. An enemy machine gun, which had been trained on the spot, also opened fire.

2/Lt Dennis Neilson-Terry, 7th Queen's (Royal West Surrey Rgt)

You've no idea how ridiculous this war is, you sit in a trench and wait and fire and send bombs over and shell and wait again, and bury a few men and wait and fire and sleep possibly and wake and wait and shell and that's all; why, it should never have been allowed to reach this pitch, it isn't warfare, it's civilised savagery and barbaric civilisation, to use an impossible expression, and there seems no end unless we spend our money . . . I must think out some novel idea for 'Hating Huns'. Oh, they're a foul lot, but I bear them no grudge now, at least they're patriotic, aren't they? I sent them over a large lemon by means of a catapult the other day, do you think they understood?

Lt William Vince, 14th Royal Warwickshire Rgt (1st Birmingham Pals)

I wonder if you are as full up of rumours as we are here. We live on them and they come tumbling in with perfectly alarming frequency. The Roman poet Virgil has a passage regarding Rumour which makes her out to be a pretty meretricious creature. But even the language is too mild for Rumour as she stalks about the trenches. I will tabulate the chief rumours that have come through the last forty-eight hours:

1. Lord Kitchener drowned in North Sea battle.
2. Lord Kitchener saved.
3. Memorial service to Lord Kitchener, attended by the King.
4. Eighteen German ships sunk in second naval battle.
5. Russia (she is always good at rumour) advances on a 400-mile front.
6. Russia takes 40,000 prisoners.
7. Russia takes 30,000 prisoners.

8. Russia takes 13,000 prisoners.

9. Russia captures an army corps.

10. Russia captures four army corps.

11. A German army corps surrenders at Verdun.

I suppose this is the result of no newspapers turning up. The last one I saw was Monday.

But what is one to believe? Probably the truth is that Austria is giving Italy the trouncing that she deserves; meanwhile I mark time and believe nothing.

12. A big push is coming.

13. Peace is coming. But this within a few weeks or (more exactly) on 26 June or 7 July.

14. Lieutenant William Vince is suffering from mental giddiness and prostration.

Men were rarely left with nothing to do on active service, as the army always took care to fill their time, to avoid disciplinary problems. However, that did not stop boredom, or a dull resignation, taking a grip on minds. Many men were desperate for home leave, although other ranks could expect a year's service before the opportunity arose. If home leave was not forthcoming, then a spell of rest behind the lines was always welcome.

Lt Arthur Terry, 23rd Northumberland Fusiliers (4th Tyneside Scottish)

Do you know how leave is managed out here? So far as I can judge, someone in the army says to his superior, 'What about some leave?' The superior says, 'Oh, ah, um – yes, I'll see about it.' The army form QX5846 is filled in and sent to GHQ. GHQ officials look at it and, 'God bless my soul, have these people been out three months? Just fix a date for leave to start.' So the date is fixed and leave lists prepared. Everybody is happy and leave trains are arranged for months ahead. Then GHQ rests from its labours.

A week before the date on which leave starts, a confidential report is sent to GHQ to say that a German has been seen opposite the point held by the 5685th Brigade (map reference G10 a 9.5 sheet 989a). GHQ immediately says – 'What! Amassing German troops there, are they? Stop all leave at once – move every man you can spare to the threatened spot.' Troops are then moved to any distance within 100 miles! About a week after all the troops have settled down in the new area, someone at GHQ discovers that the confidential report said 'A German' not 'a German Army' and they then say, 'As there is no danger now, we'll start leave again. Fix a date.' And so it goes on, ad lib!

Lt William Vince, 14th Royal Warwickshire Rgt (1st Birmingham Pals)

Well, the tale of this letter will be the tale of my effort to get to you. I was on tenterhooks on Wednesday morning, until my warrant came through, which eventually it did all right. We were due to take over the front line on Wednesday night, so Bryson and I, who were going together, started out from our reserve trench about midday, got lunch at the battered town behind our lines, and then marched back to the village where our spare kit was stored. The way was enlivened by a high shrieking wind and pretty heavy driving rain, but all the same I enjoyed the walk immensely. It is something to do a walk, instead of a battalion march in columns of fours: besides, was I not going on leave? Getting wet didn't matter, for we were able to get a complete change when we picked up our valises. We rushed the transport officer (who lives in state behind the lines) for a room to change in and an excellent tea. A motor lorry arrived to take us to the railhead, which was just as well, as said railhead was some fifteen miles away. We arrived here about 7.30 p.m., in time to get some dinner at a hotel, where we should have eaten more, only we got entangled in conversation with some kindly, but pardon me if I call them 'bourgeois', French people who were dining there too and we fled before we got too far out of our depth.

The train being a military one, you will not be surprised to hear that, though it was made up and in the station by 9 p.m., it was not allowed to start until 12.35 a.m. Nevertheless, we took possession of two corner seats and read and slept. Daybreak woke us up, and we played bridge for an hour or two, and so eventually we arrived at the sea port about 9.30 a.m., having taken nine hours to do a journey which in ordinary times you would do in about one hour. But then we beat a sort of circular tour (average rate eight to ten miles per hour) round most of France and Belgium. No boat until evening, so we spent today eating and wandering around the town, then on to the quay to find that leave was stopped and no boat was there.

L/Cpl William Smallcombe, 12th Gloucestershire Rgt (Bristol's Own)

Arras was once a lovely large town, but now it is a shameful sight. Thousands of houses are knocked to atoms and almost every one bears some trace of shellfire. A few civilians still live in cellars but the majority of the people have disappeared. Oil paintings, lovely furniture and valuables of all kinds are strewn all over the place. Near this home (we are in a cellar) is a room used for a museum and there are hundreds of fine Egyptian pottery pieces in splendid condition. Two jars in particular I noticed stand three feet high. A lot of them are covered with writing in Egyptian. There is also a lovely carved oak chest there being knocked about. Some of the pottery has been used as commodes for soldiers who were here before. It is heartbreaking to see the inside of the church. Magnificent silver candlesticks and valuables are everywhere, but it will only make you sad for me to try to describe it.

Pte Reginald Wilkes, 16th Royal Warwickshire Rgt (3rd Birmingham Pals)

I am writing this in the shadow of the ruins of one of France's cathedrals. This is the second one I have been over since I arrived out here, but whereas the other was a place of beauty, this is the house of desolation. Occasionally a German shell still hits and further demolishes it, but the greater part of the damage was done long ago.

The interior is a debris heap, composed of pieces blown in from the walls, the brickwork of the roof, mosaics and the carved woodwork of the pews and shattered pieces of stained glass from the windows. Here and there a statue still stands, minus perhaps a head or a limb. By some stroke of luck, two of what I should think were amongst the finest of these statues are left with only a few shrapnel marks on them. Both are figures of old prelates of the place, now dead. They are kneeling as in prayer, facing the altar and are in full robes. The carving of the lacework of these robes is amongst the finest I have seen, while the expression on the jaws is fine.

Gnr Stanley Collins, 137th Heavy Batt., RGA

We were up on the bank of the River Somme, filling sandbags and digging holes and I don't know what we weren't doing. They phoned up from Hemmingcourt Wood where our horse lines were, and said there was some ammunition to come up but they were a driver short. Sergeant Glossop came up to me. 'Gunner Collins, get down to Hemmingcourt and take over a pair of horses.' Now I hated horses at any time, but I had to go back there. We had to harness up and the sergeant down there asked me what I could ride, could I lead, centre-lead or wheel? I told him I couldn't ride, and I couldn't, I'd never been on a horse, but I said I'd try with the long reins. Going up the line in the dark with a load of ammunition on the GS wagon, I thought, 'This is nice, sitting on the old horse and just walking along taking it easy.' We got up to our gun position, unloaded the ammunition and started on our way back.

There was a fellow I used to know, Darky Norris, he was the lead driver. There were three pairs of horses and I was on the middle pair. Just as we were coming down through Albert –

Albert itself was all in ruins – old Jerry started strafing in no uncertain measure. So Darky Norris didn't worry about anybody else, he said, 'Right, break into a gallop.' I nearly shit myself, I did, I'm cuddling the bloody horse's neck to save myself falling off, never mind about the reins. Anyway, we got back to the horse lines, and I didn't half have a sore arse. Being a gunner, I only had slacks on and the others had riding breeches. I had a bloody great boil with the skin off, only through sitting in the saddle going up the line and back. I went sick and saw the doctor, but any time after that if there was any ammunition to go up, I used to sit up on the GS wagon and do the long reins, not that I could drive, but I thought that wherever the front four horses went the back pair would go as well.

Capt. J. C. Procter, 13th Gloucestershire Rgt (Forest of Dean)
The other night when I was cycling up to the trenches just at dusk I passed one of the numerous roadside cemeteries, with its neat row of graves and wooden crosses. On the roadside outside were numerous stretchers and carrying parties, and on the stretchers lay the mummy-like figures of some of these poor little fellows, tightly and neatly stitched up in blankets, waiting till it was dark enough for the parson to come and do his job. The sight was sufficiently depressing . . . I hurried on. I'd not wish to see the last act, the hasty words of the burial service, the one sordid Union Jack snatched hastily from a body 'finished with' and flung over the next, while the bearers smoked in the road outside. I think it was the littleness of the bodies that worried me.

The build-up to the Great Push was well under way. However, in the months and weeks preceding the offensive there was relatively little fighting. Men were able to enjoy the sun in the trenches while others,

whose jobs took them away from the front line or those who were
withdrawn on rest, enjoyed the spring weather and beautiful country-
side.

Lt Arthur Terry, 23rd Northumberland Fusiliers (4th Tyneside Scottish)

It is grilling weather out here just now and the roads lie white and
dusty like ribbons through the fields. Being out in the open is a
perfect delight – one hears the hum of insect life, the song of birds,
and one sees the swallows darting past nearly under your horse's
nose and butterflies of all colours and sizes, and now and again a
flying beetle comes smack against one's face as it sails along
without any steerage way.

These beetles look very funny as they drift along perpendicu-
larly and industriously fluttering their wings as much as to say
'Don't you dare to imagine I'm not as good as any bird at flying for
I am' – and all the time they haven't the faintest idea where they
are going and blunder on until somebody's face or something else
brings them up with a sound turn! This afternoon I had a swim in
a very muddy stream, but it was very cool water with a beautiful
sting in it and I enjoyed it immensely. I hadn't intended to do so
and had no towel with me, so sat in the sun 'in puris naturalibus' (I
think that's right) till I was dry! . . .

Signaller Cyril Newman, 1/9 London Rgt (Queen Victoria Rifles)

'Tis a beautiful morning and the air is full of the restless buzzing of
aeroplanes. Not only has the sunshine brought out aeroplanes, but
also the small inhabitants of the lower world – ants, huge beetles,
things with 'umptun' legs and other creepy-crawly insects found
in freshly dug earth. I have just been watching a large greenish
beetle trying to scale the walls of the trench. On his hind legs he
has a pair of spurs – like climbing irons, which he digs into the soil
to get a hold. However, either he hasn't learnt how to use them

properly or has lived too well and grown fat, for four attempts have failed. He would doubtless have made many more had I not had compassion, spread one of *your* envelopes before him, enticed him on it and thrown him overboard. Now, was not that kind? The ants are too industrious; not content with the trench, they must needs crawl over me – as if I had notions to spare them! There is a nasty, black, jumping tribe of spiders – I kill any who come near me. I don't like them.

Capt. Alexander Shaw, 1st King's Own Scottish Borderers
On fatigues from 8 a.m. to 2 p.m. digging sumps at side of big communication trench. These roads are six feet deep and six feet wide at top, three feet wide at the bottom, with a small drain. At intervals are small sumps, four feet deep, bridged by a sort of plank ladder. Big sumps are dug at longer intervals out to one side and are ten feet deep. Hundreds of mice, field voles, moles and small deer fall into these trenches and finally get to the sumps where, in spite of some clever galleries dug up the face to within eighteen inches of the turf, the soil, alas, is too wet and slippery so engineering operations fail. They have no discipline and the galleries get crowded; the tail of the queue push forward and the workers at the head get forced over and fall six or seven feet to the bottom. If one gets injured in this fall, his fellows immediately set on him and tear him to pieces and fight over the cannibalistic feast in a dreadful orgy of hunger and despair. The moles do better, and where there is a mole he digs a tunnel whereby all escape and are saved. I found a bewildered mole lying at the bottom of a sump in hard chalk. Here all his ingenuity and perseverance failed. I carried him to a bit full of mice and he set to work at once and soon disappeared, followed by all the mice. This mole had wonderful black velvety skin. Mice do not understand the law of gravitation; they dig galleries mostly vertically where an incline would save them.

Acting Bombardier Alfred Richardson, 116th Siege Batt., RGA

I had a lovely day in the city of Amiens last Wednesday. Captain Walker gave me a pass along with one of our sergeants and we both made the journey of 25km on bicycles, it being a simply delightful morning. The road is superb, the last ten kilometres being absolutely straight. We left here at 9.30 a.m. and arrived there at 11 a.m. I did a little shopping for Mr Walker and then I took my sergeant to a nice restaurant, where we had a good dinner (the French menu is peculiar, quite different to our style, but I might say that we did *not* eat any snails or frogs!!)

In the afternoon, we went and looked round the cathedral (this being my third visit; I would go and see it every day if I could – it is wonderful). Inside, there is a small piece of St John the Baptist's bone . . . The altar and choir stalls are a wonderful piece of work, but the whole structure is marvellous throughout. I had a look in the Gare du Nord (Railway Station) and I happened to be there when the French 'Leave' train arrived. Scenes such as I witnessed at Victoria last Xmas took place. What an excitement and rush there was when fathers, mothers, sons, daughters, brothers and sisters met! I stared and stared at the sight and recalled my arrival in London.

We set off at six o'clock and had a stiff ride back, the wind having risen and being full in our faces. We kept going until we arrived at a large village seven miles from 'our' camp and in the pitch darkness, we happened to take the wrong turning and went miles out of our way . . . We arrived home at 9 p.m.; so we did not do so bad after all.

Pte Reginald Wilkes, 16th Royal Warwickshire Rgt (3rd Birmingham Pals)

Although only a matter of 1200 yards or so from the Hun lines, we are living in a basement room of a cottage. Of course it is hidden from view by a fold in the ground and well screened by trees. The roof has been blown away, but the ceiling of the ground floor still remains intact. At the back many of our English garden flowers are blooming amidst weeds and grass as high as themselves. I have a bunch of flowers by me as I write. The young fruit has set on the tree, apple and cherry trees at the back, while the gooseberry and the currant bushes are laden with fruit in the green stage. In the hedges, a garden rose is a mass of lovely white bloom, while sprigs of lilac show up, laburnums hang gracefully in yellow profusion.

At the far end of the garden runs a river for us to bathe in and catch fish. Major Deakin took a photo of half a dozen of us fishing with sticks, cotton and worms for 'tiddlers', which were pulled out by the dozen. We were just a crowd of happy boys for the time, deaf to the sound of the guns. If the weather keeps like this, we shall all be as brown as berries soon.

2/Lt John Godfrey, 103 Field Coy, RE

I passed an epoch-making event in my history yesterday – to wit, I had my first meal of frogs! I have a large pool not five paces from my tent, and during a thunderstorm dozens of them hopped out. So under the directions of the interpreter who was attached to me as I do most of the acquisition of stuff from the local people, we captured them in empty tins and slew about twenty of them and the cook fried them, also under the interpreter's supervision. And they were excellent! Like very tender chicken. I may say that only the hind legs are eaten, skinned and fried – the green skin is taken off, of course. They rather remind one of eating wishbones. The next thing he's going to teach me to eat is snails! Soon I shall be quite the complete Frenchman!

Acting Bombardier Alfred Richardson, 116th Siege Batt., RGA

Captain Walker sent for me, and asked me to take a horse, and Stead as orderly, and go for a long ride up the river to the source, and then come down slowly and notice all the good places for fly and minnow fishing.

The source of the river was quite a peculiar spot – a small lake with about half a dozen deep holes round the sides through which the water issued out of the ground. In the centre of the pond, I saw at least forty or fifty fine trout lying in the bottom. I made about a dozen sketches of the whole length of the river in sections, marking all the nice trout 'streams', weirs, gravel and stony bottoms, etc, and all the essentials appertaining to fly-fishing. We arrived back at 3 p.m. after a grand day. Captain Walker was delighted with the sketches and greatly complimented me on them.

This morning I got up at 5 a.m. and went in the trap with Mr Walker up the stream and we spent a lovely three hours' fishing with the minnow on a stretch of three miles. We had two good 'runs' just below a small sluice; Captain Walker has up to now caught forty-seven fine trout – oh! and we are on 'active service!!'

Capt. Walter Ewbank, 1st Border Rgt
Things are getting lively now, and before this reaches you I shall be fixed up one way or the other. However, whatever happens I am looking forward to it with heart and soul. I have a sort of craving for another scrap. I have many debts to wipe out, and I have spent all my spare time in training my company that way, with the result that, when B Company goes over, they will take very few prisoners. It is either 'kill or be killed', I tell them, and God help the loser. Each man knows every vital point on the Boche's body and where to make for, I think. I have now a perfect fighting unit of 240 men, who will go to hell with me if necessary. Perhaps you consider this rather like a threepenny novel touch. I assure you, if you do, you were never more mistaken. I mean it. I have secretly lived for this time, this moment when debts, which can only be atoned by death, can be wiped out. I shall take care of myself, never fear, as much as possible . . .

Well, if the next thing you hear or have heard of me is a short message on a cable, don't worry about me. I shall have enjoyed myself and will have had a good run for my money.

Pte Charles Heare, 1/2nd Monmouthshire Rgt
The 109th Brigade are all suspicious of everyone. They are told
that if they catch a spy they will get ten pounds and a leave to
Ireland. It is agony to go out at night, 'Halt, halt!' everywhere you
go. Coming back from White City one night, a sentry stopped me
and said, 'I'm off to Belfast.' 'What, sick?' I said. He says, 'No, I've
got a spy, a minute ago.' 'Let's have a look.' I did and nearly had a
fit. It was our Colonel Bowen. By this time we all wore sandbags
on our helmets and the officers wore other ranks' tunics with their
rank on their epaulettes. Our colonel always wore puttees, with a
broken sandbag on his hat and he walked with his head down. The
Irishman in the dark rushed him. Our colonel said he liked his
keenness.

---

*On 24 June the bombardment of the German line began. It was
anticipated to last five days.*

2/Lt Dudley Lissenburg, 97th Batt., 147 Brigade, RFA
I can well remember the first moments of this preliminary
bombardment. It was early morning, I recall, and a miserably
wet day. The lavatory was situated at the end of a long communication trench, running parallel to and twenty yards or so below
the line of guns and terminating in a square recess six foot by six
foot with a roof of sandbags supported by spars of timber beneath
which was the usual 'squatting pole' over a deep and narrow
trench.
    I, of course, knew the barrage was to commence that day, but
with other personal matters on my mind, I sat on the pole in a
contemplative mood – alone. The silence was, indeed, eerie.
Suddenly, as if struck by an earthquake, the earth shook and
the roof began to collapse, as hundreds of guns – field and heavy –
opened fire simultaneously – wonderful synchronisation. I rushed

out and was just in time to escape the collapse of not only the roof, but the whole recess.

Lt George Mallory, 40th Siege Batt., RGA

We were busy with Fritz's trenches pretty continuously from last Sunday week onwards – mostly with a slow rate of fire, but sometimes taking part in a furious bombardment of particular places – villages, etc. Our guns have been firing well and as most of this shooting was observed we can say with certainty that they did a lot of damage – for instance, for one shoot when I was at the guns and Glen observing, of around sixty rounds or so, $^1/_4$ exploded right in the trenches, another $^1/_4$ on the parapets (one round certainly blowing up a dugout) and of the rest only about eight rounds altogether which didn't fall into the barbed wire. Such results make a real difference to my peace of mind. I want to feel we're some use; and I can feel certain we are.

Pte Frank Williams, 88th Field Ambulance, RAMC

25 June 1916

Attended two services and enjoyed good sermons. Our light gunfire continues unabated. 6.45: Whilst in church some of our largest guns opened out – up to six-inchers. The ground has begun to tremble now and the bombardment seems ever-increasing in intensity. Though our heavy batteries have not fired a shell, the crashing roar of some of the reports made me pray for the Germans.

Night. The whole heaven is lighted up by the glare of the gun flashes, one orderly was called out to fetch a wounded from Mesnil; he had a confused impression of a sort of hell let loose. The night sky was a mass of lurid light from the star shells and the incessant flash of the guns, while the scream of aerial torpedoes and tear gas shells and the general booming artillery was punctuated by the explosion of mighty monsters of destruction, the whole combined coming to us behind with an ominous rumble, like the sea on a cavernous coast.

The date for the attack was set for 29 June but, owing to heavy rain, it was delayed by two days. It was difficult to wait. However, for many men it was a chance to write 'last letters home' to be sent to their families in the event of their death.

Pte Edward Higson, 16th Manchester Rgt (1st City)

The delay was to our fellows like a red cloth to a bull. Everybody was eager to be 'over the top', our first big stunt. One felt proud to be with such fine fellows, men who, two years ago, were ignorant of the dangers of war. Now their only thought was to get at this nation that had set out to ruin all freedom and to endanger their homes, or to die a glorious death in the attempt. There were no white faces, no trembling limbs. In their hearts they were hoping to come through safely, not for their own sake but for the sake of those at home, but on the other hand they were quite prepared to die for the glorious cause of freedom and love.

Pte John Scollen, 27th Northumberland Fusiliers (4th Tyneside Irish)

My Dear Wife and Children
It is with regret I write these last words of farewell to you. We are about to make a charge against these awful Germans. If it is God's Holy will that I should fall, I will have done my duty to my King and country and I hope justly in the sight of God. It is hard to part from you but keep a good heart, dear Tina, and do not grieve for me, for God and His Blessed Mother will watch over you and my bonny little children and I have not the least doubt but that my country will help you. For the sake of one of its soldiers that has done his duty. Well, Dear Wife Tina, you have been a good wife and mother and looked after my canny bairns and I am sure they will be a credit to both of us . . .

My Joe, Jack, Tina and Aggie not forgetting my bonny twins
Nora and Hugh and my last flower baby whom I have only had the
great pleasure of seeing once since he came into the world, God
bless them. I will try and get to do my duty whilst on this perilous
undertaking and if I fall, then you will know that I died in God's
Holy Grace. Tell all of my friends and yours also that I bid them
farewell now. My Dear Wife and children, I have not anything
more to say, only I wish you all God's Holy Grace and blessing so
GOODBYE GOODBYE and think of me in your prayers. I know
these are hard words to receive but God's will be done.

From your faithful soldier
Husband and father
John Scollen. B Coy. 27th. S.B.N.F.
Goodbye, my loved ones, DON'T CRY

Pte Charles Heare, 1/2nd Monmouthshire Rgt
Our orderly room sergeant says, 'Charley, we are up to our eyes in
this advance. It will cost some men but we will have to go on. Our
Headquarters will be Beaumont Hamel Cemetery after the breakthrough.' We are all excited and full of fear. Our Adjutant Ibbs
says, 'Heare, you know where to find us tomorrow?' 'Yes, sir, in
the corner of Beaumont Hamel Cemetery.' 'It may be,' he said,
smiling. Perhaps he is the only one who has doubts of us
advancing.

Pte Sydney Fuller, 8th Suffolk Rgt
The CO had us on parade in the afternoon, when he gave us a
short, serious address, the main thing he impressed on us being,
'Kill all you can, and *don't* take any prisoners.' He also said that
'the only *good* Germans were *dead* ones'. We were issued with three
days' rations and two empty sandbags per man. Our orders were to
march off at 7.30 p.m., but this was amended to 9.45 p.m. We
were visited by a French soldier (who could speak English very
well), in the evening. He had, he said, been at Verdun, and he

described to us some of the things he had seen there. At 9.45 p.m. we marched off, loaded with our rations and various necessary instruments.

Cpl Arthur Cook, 1st Somerset Light Infantry

Bombardment continues all through the night and day. The attack starts at 7.30 a.m. tomorrow. All private correspondence, cap badges, numerals and spare kit has to be left behind. We are fully charged with ammunition, grenades, water, emergency rations and all the paraphernalia needed for modern warfare. The men were in excellent spirits and full of hope for the morrow: it was going to be a welcome change from lying in a trench and taking everything without the opportunity of hitting back. Paraded at 9.45 p.m. and marched to the assembly trenches, and then told to get a couple of hours' sleep. We certainly rested our weary limbs, but sleep was out of the question.

L/Cpl Harold Bisgood, 1/2nd London Rgt (Royal Fusiliers)

1 July 1916: At last the long-looked-for day and hour has arrived; broad daylight, the rain has ceased and the day is quite bright. The din now is beyond all imagination, every gun in France seems to be turned on the Hun on our front. Surely none can live in this hail of shells and still the German guns remain quiet. Meanwhile all our front line men had been engaged in lighting smoke candles and firing huge smoke bombs. Now arises a dense cloud of smoke all along our line and the time has arrived when we must show our hands and advance. The Germans, as soon as they saw the smoke, knew what was to follow and rapid fire was opened at once. Nothing daunted, the London boys climbed up the parapet ready for the fray.

Cpl Arthur Cook, 1st Somerset Light Infantry

The brigade was attacking on a three-company frontage, with the 1st East Lancs on the left, 1st Rifle Brigade in the centre and the 8th Royal Warwicks on the right, my company being in support to the Rifle Brigade. At 7.20 a.m. a huge mine exploded under Hawthorn Redoubt on our right front, the force of the explosion rocking our trenches.

Punctually at 7.30 a.m. the attack was launched. It was an amazing sight, for as far as the eye could see, to the right and left, lines of men were advancing across no-man's-land in perfect skirmishing order as laid down in the drill book; everything was going smoothly and not an angry shot barred their progress. But just before the forward troops reached the German trenches, the enemy opened up a murderous fire with machine guns. We were supposed to follow the Rifle Brigade at 7.40 a.m., but everybody was eager to get into the fray and was following up the Rifle Brigade in a few minutes. So with a prayer on my lips we went over the top, and had not gone far when the enemy guns opened fire, and we were caught in the middle of no-man's-land. Men started to fall like ninepins, but we had to push on. Soon my platoon officer was hit (2/Lt Tilley), then my platoon Sergeant (Will Mott) was killed, and I was left in charge of the platoon within five minutes of our advance.

Pte Henry Russell, 1/5th London Rgt (London Rifle Brigade)

During our advance, I saw many of my colleagues drop down, but this somehow or other did not seem to worry me, and I continued to go forward until I suddenly became aware that there were few of us in this first line of attack capable of going on. At this stage I found myself in the company of an officer, Lieutenant Wallace. We dived into a flat, shallow hole made by our guns, apparently both wanting to decide what we should now do. He asked me whether I thought we should attempt to go on or remain there for the time being and, thinking the position over very rapidly, I came to the conclusion and told him that going on would, in my opinion, be suicidal, and that the best thing we could do would be to stay there and attempt to pick off any Germans who might expose them- selves. We were not very clear as to how we were situated, but had a fairly shrewd idea that we were, in fact, surrounded. Lying on the ground, it was quite impossible to get any idea of our position. Lieutenant Wallace said, however, that we had been ordered to go on at all costs and that we must comply with this order. At this, he stood up and within a few seconds dropped down, riddled with bullets. This left me with the same problem and, having observed his action, I felt that I must do the same. I, therefore, stood up and was immediately hit by two bullets.

Cpl Arthur Cook, 1st Somerset Light Infantry

It is extraordinary how some men die. I happened to slip into a shell hole and on clambering out saw a man sitting up on the top of the hole doing his puttee up. I entered into conversation with him and was annoyed at getting no reply; he was dead. Another man was leaning against a trench parapet, a natural thing to do if you feel a bit weary. I asked him to follow me, he failed to do so and going back to give him a piece of my mind, I discovered he too was dead and had no interest in earthly things.

By now the Germans were trying to force us out of their trenches. Those of us that were left then got together and started to collect bombs from the dead and wounded, and then commenced a grenade battle in real earnest; but after two or three hours our supply of bombs ran out, and there were no more to be got. The Germans then gradually drove us back, inch by inch, through their communication trenches, with their superior supply of bombs.

Pte Sydney Fuller, 8th Suffolk Rgt

We did not move further forward, as evidently the redoubt had been captured. In the early afternoon the enemy's shelling gradually died down. Later, we moved to the left, taking up a position behind our own (53rd) Brigade's front. We passed along one of the 'Assembly' trenches. It had been heavily shelled by the enemy, apparently during the morning. Several of our men were lying dead in it, killed by the enemy's shells. In one place a man was kneeling, as if in prayer, his hands covering his face. Lying in the trench behind him was another man, face downwards, half buried in the earth thrown into the trench by the shells. A little farther along the trench I slipped on something, and looking down I saw a piece of a man's backbone, and pieces of flesh strewn about the trench. Hanging down from the parapet, in the corner of the traverse, was a mass of entrails, already swarming with flies.

Cpl Arthur Cook, 1st Somerset Light Infantry

A second lieutenant of the Warwicks and myself had a little pow-wow on the situation and decided to split the men we had equally between us, and barricade the trench left and right, leaving the open space between us to look after itself. He took his party to the right and I took mine to the left, until we gained contact with the enemy, then we made our barricade.

I then got a few men to collect all the bombs, German ones and all. Whilst they were doing so, a German approached us – I killed him; but many others were following with bombs and there now started another grenade contest, and the only bombs we had were German stick bombs. We could see each other as the bombs were thrown and we were actually throwing back the ones they threw before they burst.

My numbers were becoming rapidly reduced but we were holding our own until the enemy worked round to our right rear and began bombing us from this quarter. This was getting pretty hot, but my orders were to hang on until midnight when we would be relieved, but we seemed to be the only British troops here and my party now numbered nine.

Pte Henry Russell, 1/5th London Rgt (London Rifle Brigade)

Observing the wounds later, I realised that one had been made from behind and one from in front. I must say that this action had a profound effect on me in later years. I had thought that a man who could stand up and knowingly face practically certain death in these circumstances must be very brave. I found out that bravery hardly came into it. Once the decision was made to stand up I had no further fear. I was not bothered at all even though I believed that I would be dead within seconds and would be rotting on the ground, food for the rats next day. I did not even feel appreciably the bullets going through and this was to me something extraordinary. I am now convinced that when it comes to the last crunch nobody has any fear at all; it is not a question of bravery. In some extraordinary manner, the chemistry of the body anaesthetises it in such a way that, even when fully conscious, fear does not enter into the matter.

I had crawled into another shell hole some distance away, into which another colleague of mine had also crawled. He told me that he had been shot through the middle of the back and that the bullet had emerged through his left ear. We were lying in this shell hole together, he wondering whether we would finish up in the same hospital. In this, I could not help feeling that he was being rather optimistic. I did not expect that we could survive the day and, a little later, after the failure of our attack, a heavy barrage of shellfire fell upon us . . . We had not long to wait before a shell burst on the edge of our hole; it killed my colleague and injured me in such a way that I was virtually emasculated. [Now] even if a miracle happened and I did, in fact, get away, I would not be fit for anything in this world.

I, therefore, decided to kill myself. To this end, I was under the impression that I had three choices. The first was to explode a Mills bomb which I was carrying in my pocket and kill myself in this way. This seemed to be a silly procedure because it would only be doing what the Germans were already attempting to do. The second was to take a very large dose of morphine tablets which I believed to be in my pocket. The third course was one which came to my mind as a result of a talk given to us by the Medical Officer before going into action. He said that, if wounded and bleeding, we should never take intoxicants, as the result would almost certainly be fatal. I therefore managed to get hold of the bottle of rum which I had put in my haversack and I drank the lot, hoping that it would result in my death. In fact, it did me no harm at all. It probably made me slightly merry and bright and rather stupefied. It also probably caused me to drop off to sleep, though I am not aware of this. However, I came to the conclusion, when I had recovered my senses that, in spite of my condition (my left arm being torn and the bone shattered, my left thigh damaged, my right leg wounded and strips of flesh hanging down from my abdomen) it was still worth while making a serious effort to save myself.

L/Cpl Harold Bisgood, 1/2nd London Rgt (Royal Fusiliers)
Suddenly at about 7.30 p.m. the firing died down to a minimum, and looking out, I noticed a man had boldly climbed out of the German trench and was holding up a large white board with a brilliant red cross painted on it. This man advanced well into the centre of no-man's-land and beckoned to us, whereupon one of our stretcher-bearers jumped over the parapet and went to meet him. The man with the board was a German doctor who spoke quite good English; he offered an armistice of one hour and this after much ado was accepted by our people. The Hun doctor then signalled with his hand and immediately a party of about fifty German stretcher-bearers doubled out and started attending to the wounded. This was good enough for us and over we went again.

Lt. R. H. F. Allen, 13th London Rgt (Kensington)
That armistice was a very fine act on the part of the Germans and should be remembered in their favour. Another act of chivalry was also performed by the Germans of the 2nd Guards Division. A few days later they dropped from an aeroplane a complete list of the men taken prisoner by them, thus relieving the anxiety of their

next of kin, who only knew that their sons or brothers were 'missing'. I am glad to say we did the same and those few acts help to show that even in war, humanity does not deteriorate except temporarily.

Pte Henry Russell, 1/5th London Rgt (London Rifle Brigade)

It was an extremely hot and lovely day, and I had to wait probably till about eleven o'clock that night before I dared to make any move to get away. When I did, I met a serious difficulty. I found that lying on the ground, it was quite impossible to decide in which direction to crawl and, in the end, decided on my direction solely because I could see a fire on a hill, and as I knew that we had come down a slope during our attack, I crawled in that direction. It turned out that this was the right way to go and I continued to crawl. After a long time, to my relief I was challenged in English. I crawled into an advanced post as well as I could and the occupants said they would do their best to get a stretcher to carry me away as, by that time, I was nearing exhaustion. I must have become unconscious at this stage because I remembered no more until dawn was breaking.

Cpl Arthur Cook, 1st Somerset Light Infantry

We were relieved at 11 p.m. and ordered to go back. At the end of a German sap I ran into our signalling sergeant (Sergeant Imber), the first Somerset I'd seen for hours. I said, 'Come on, Sam, we are relieved.' He had about six German helmets hung on him – I would have liked one of these as a souvenir, but I couldn't be bothered with it just then. How I escaped I do not know. I tripped over dead bodies, fell headlong into shell holes full of dead, my clothes were torn to ribbons by the barbed wire. I lost all sense of direction and eventually fell sprawling, dead beat to the world.

Pte Henry Russell, 1/5th London Rgt (London Rifle Brigade)

I was put into this train, no doubt by this time being in a very distressed condition. I do not remember much about the train except for one thing. I looked up in a sort of half coma to see a Red Cross nurse looking down at me. I was never to forget this, because I have always thought of it as the most beautiful sight I have ever seen in my life. I never saw this girl again, and I only know that her name was Miss Jones, which does not leave me much chance of ever identifying her.

I have been asked what is the most beautiful thing I have ever seen, and I have always given the same answer. A woman. I have seen the sun rise on the Jungfrau; sunset at Corbière; the midnight sun in northern Norway; evening light on the Taj Mahal; the Mediterranean blue; England and Paris in the spring; the Eternal City; the glory that was Greece; and sunrise in aircraft several miles above the Alps and many other things. I can, therefore, claim to have seen a lot of wonderful sights, but I still give the same answer to this question.

For many more days, men continued to crawl into the front line. One of those who had come out of the battle unscathed was Charles Moss; although unwounded, he would never be the same again.

L/Cpl Charles Moss, 18th Durham Light Infantry (Durham Pals)

Roll call wasn't until late in the afternoon, and as I sat waiting for it while I scraped the cement-like mud off my uniform and equipment, I was filled with a grand feeling of satisfaction at having weathered my part in the battle so well. But the feeling went deeper than that. I had passed into a new and fuller understanding of life. I became more fully conscious of being alive than I had ever been before I had seen such awful killings and suffering – mental as well as physical.

In such battalions as ours, the suffering was often more mental than physical. Our feelings had not been brutalised by our civil life occupations, we were not time-serving professional soldiers, most of us had left soft jobs. We had in the ranks many with college and university educations, who had 'volunteered' for the duration of the war only – there was no conscription in 1914 when our battalion was formed – we had not been psychologically hardened for the hardship and mentality of the rank and file of the PBI, the 'Poor Bloody Infantry'. Yet, as a contrast, we had a few miners in our company, and they took to soldiering as they thought it was a great game. Their intrepid and sporting spirit never deserted them in or out of the trenches. Death seemed to be nothing to them. When they spoke about any of their pals being killed, they said 'He's gone west' as though he'd gone to a football match.

The casualties had been terrible. From the time the whistles blew to go over the top that morning until midnight that night, there was a British casualty for every one of the 59,400 seconds that had elapsed. The dead included Private John Scollen, who had written so movingly to his wife and children. That day was, and remains, the worst in British military history. The dead lay in great swathes, quickly turning black in the summer heat. For those fatalities, and for the ones that followed, it was difficult to feel compassion, and most men became largely indifferent to bodies, though not necessarily to the horror.

Lt George Mallory, 40th Siege Batt., RGA

I don't object to corpses so long as they are fresh – I soon found that I could reason thus with them. 'Between you and me is all the difference between life and death. But this is an accepted fact that men are killed and I have no more to learn about that from you, and the difference is no greater than that because your jaw hangs

and your flesh changes colour or blood oozes from your wounds.'
With the wounded it is different. It always distresses me to see
them.

Cpl Arthur Cook, 1st Somerset Light Infantry

During the night [12 July] I went into no-man's-land, taking
another man with me, searching for dead bodies. I found four but
their condition was too bad to move, so I collected their paybooks
which I handed into the orderly room for identification purposes,
making sure their identity discs were left on the body. The stench
of these bodies when I turned them over was horrible, and the
gasses inside gave forth a belching noise. A bullet had passed
through one man's paybook and entered his heart. They took
particulars of the dead men in the orderly room, and then calmly
sent for me and ordered me to return the books to the bodies! I told
the adjutant this was not necessary as the men still had their
identity disks, but it was no good.

Well! Night is setting in [13 July] and I have to get those
paybooks on to the dead men in front. I got hold of the man who
got hold of me last night and told him what I had to do. He said,
'I'm not going out there again, I was scared stiff when those bodies
started to belch.' I did not press him, as I had done an un-
authorised thing and must put it right myself. So I got out of the
trench and wandered about no-man's-land looking for the bodies.
I found them eventually and put the books back in their pockets;
it took an hour to find them. I vowed from then on I would not go
out on a similar stunt, and I kept that vow.

Pte Daniel Sweeney, 1st Lincolnshire Rgt

It was on the evening of 18 or 20 July (not sure of date) that I found
the body of Private Salway. I was sent with thirty men out of the
firing line which was then in Mametz Wood. We were on what was
known as the Sunken Road, just at the corner of the trench, when
we saw two men lying, one on one side of the road, the other on the

other side. The moon was very bright and we could see plainly both men were wounded terribly. Now something seemed to tell me to look into the pockets of the man on the right side of the road; he was the first dead man I have ever touched but I did and I found a few photos of himself and his wife and children, a pipe and tobacco and one franc and a half. We got a light and looked at his letters to see who he was and when I saw the address at the top of his letter (his home address) I knew it very well and I believe I knew the man, too. The letter was the last one from his wife and I kept it until after the battle and we got relieved. I left his paybook and also his identification disc on him so as the burying party would know who he was, then we went on our journey . . . After we were relieved we went by train to a place called Arras. I then sent that letter which I had found on Private Salway to his wife and she wrote back and thanked me and asked me if I happened to find out where he was buried if I would let her know. When we left Arras to go to that 'Hell' again, I had a look at a good many graves around the spot where I found Private Salway but I could not find him there. I know where he must be buried now. It is one of the big grave grounds. I passed it on the march; there are about 800 buried there, the graves are well looked after but some of the poor chaps are buried where they fell and a bit of wood made into a cross to show that some poor lad is buried there; some have no names, others bear on them 'An Unknown English Soldier'.

Gnr Victor Archard, C Coy, Heavy Branch MGC

Since we could do no work, we decided in a momentary calm to make for a dugout, so we ran, one at a time, to the trench. Here we found a German dugout, number 34A. It was entered by between twenty-five and thirty stairs, boarded above and on the sides. The stairs gave place to a landing, and then a sharp turn and an ascent of about nine steps. The first room entered contained a table, chairs, lamp, shelves and a large clock, while an exit led from the opposite wall. The room was papered and evidently well kept.

From the middle of either side a passage led to a kitchen and store respectively, while the passages were of sufficient width to allow bunks with spring mattresses to be erected. These were stationary affairs and looked comfortable. On these beds were numerous expensive valises and new uniforms, also ammunition, tins of dubbin, boot polish, etc. One bunk contained a dead German who had probably been killed there, or had crawled there to die. In the stores were several cases of lager beer and mineral waters, and a fair quantity of tinned meat of superior quality. There were also supplies of matches, some cigars and various articles of kit. We sat down and made a good dinner from the articles of diet kindly supplied by Fritz. This completed, we regained the trench and made our way back to the nearest road.

Lt Carrol Whiteside, 7th Border Rgt
On relief, we went back to deep and very fuggy saps in Fricourt Wood – deep dugouts made by the Hun. When the battle was to all intents and purposes over, we had a look through the German brigadier's apartment down below. The place was sixty feet beneath the surface, down a steep flight of steps all boarded on the walls and roof and moreover distempered white. There were about eight fair-sized rooms, including an orderly room and servants' rooms. The whole place had been left in a terrible hurry and the only live things left were a cat and a puppy which positively quivered with terror and started looking round apprehensively on each shell burst or gunfire. The puppy finally followed us out to billets and went the unknown way of all other dogs.

Maj. A. G. P. Hardwick, 59th Field Ambulance, RAMC
Heavy rain again this morning. Six dead Boches have become exposed in the parapet about our dugout – through falls of earth caused by rain. They were probably only buried by a shell there, as they had not been 'souvenired', as the men say, i.e. one still had his wristwatch on. He was promptly 'souvenired'.

Taking weapons home as souvenirs was forbidden, and could result in the immediate cancellation of leave. Nevertheless, many soldiers smuggled weapons home, many still live and dangerous. Major Edward Wellesley MC, a descendant of the Duke of Wellington, served with 178 Tunnelling Company REs. He died at home in October 1916 while on leave from France, when a bomb he was dismantling partially detonated.

2/Lt John Godfrey, 103 Field Coy, RE

I am enclosing the epaulette from the greatcoat of a Royal West Kent man who was killed in a very famous stand here. I took it off him as a memento before he was buried by the trench. I am trying to send home certain Boche souvenirs – with which this country is littered. I enclose here the epaulette from the shoulder of some defunct German, with the number of his regiment on it. I am trying to send the bolt of a German rifle, a German soft forage cap and the outer case of a German bomb: I hope they reach you. I have collected one or two good souvenirs: two bits of nose-cap that I found sticking in the parados of the trench over my head, two days after that first strafe; a French bullet found in these trenches; and a bit of shell that fell from the skies, off an 'Archie' – one of ours. I am going to make a valiant attempt to send home some Boche souvenirs: bombs, cartridges, mess tin and the autograph of a Boche soldier who I hope is now extinct: one Tas. Kraus. The bombs are in pieces, after explosion, therefore perfectly safe.

L/Cpl Roland Mountfort, 10th Royal Fusiliers

More pleasant to behold is the stuff left by the Germans. In their old trenches you can get any mortal thing you fancy as a souvenir, from a sniper's rifle in a grey blanket to a Prussian helmet or a clip of dum-dum cartridges. If you like, you can have the battery that supplied the electric light for a dugout: or the notice board from the one with all the bottles outside marked 'Lager Vorwalker', or the special cardboard case used for carrying explosive bullets. Or you may prefer to collect postcards to 'mein lieber, lieber Hans' from 'Deine Elise'. Personally I took nothing at all. After I had seen dead bodies lying on all sides in the weird attitudes of sudden death, souvenirs seemed a bit paltry.

Maj. M. J. F. Fitzgerald, 39th Batt., RFA

I had an interesting experience with a poor wounded German whom I found in an artillery dugout in Mametz Wood. His leg was smashed and he had been without food or water for two to three days, so he said. But the thing that interested me was his terror when I discovered him. The dugout out was pitch dark and I had no torch, so I felt my way down with revolver in one hand. When I came to the shelf where the man lay, he shrieked 'kamerad' in terror. I had to strike matches at intervals and light paper. My orderly officer was with me, but neither of us could speak German. I understood that the man had been told that the British shot their prisoners, hence his terror. We gave him some biscuits and chocolate, but had no water bottles on us.

Pte Sydney Fuller, 8th Suffolk Rgt

One badly wounded German lay writhing in agony on the ground near where we stopped. He was evidently past help. One of the signallers who had managed to get a little more than his share of rum issue was desirous of shooting the dying German. 'Bastard,' he called him, but we put a stop to that business. I saw two bullets strike the wounded German immediately afterwards and he ceased to move, so evidently someone had no scruples about it. Possibly (but not probably) someone shot him to 'put him out of his misery'. However, there were many men who shot down any of the enemy, regardless of circumstances – wounded or prisoners, it made no difference – and it was noticeable that the men who did that sort of thing were loudest in condemning the German 'atrocities'. Two wrongs evidently made a right with them.

Maj. A. G. P. Hardwick, 59th Field Ambulance, RAMC
A young Hun about twenty-one was brought in this evening, who
had been lying out for six days in a shell hole with multiple bomb
wounds (slight). He was in an awful condition and smelt like a
badger. He had had to eat a few stray biscuits and to drink his own
urine. Wounds not deep but maggotty. He said that 'they were all
dead sick of the war and that people in Germany had no idea of
real state of affairs out here' – but neither have ours!

Capt. Walter Ewbank, 1st Border Rgt
A general feeling of optimism pervades the whole army now, and I
hope that it will not be necessary for us to spend another winter
out here; though who knows? When I think things over, I find
that life at present is full of enjoyment. These occasional amusing
episodes help to keep me going, and it is always pleasant to get
one's own back on the Boche. I killed one the other day. He was a
sniper up a tree in no-man's-land, and just by luck I spotted him. I
turned a machine gun on him, and down he came. Splendid, what!
The greatest joys I can get out of life at present are:
    1st, to kill a Boche.
    2nd, to get a parcel from home.
    3rd, to get letters.

Lt George Mallory, 40th Siege Batt., RGA
I wonder how much the German shortage of ammunition amounts to.
Certainly he can't use it as extravagantly as we do in these parts – and
less just lately. They molest our communications very little compared
to all the firing of our own batteries on crossroads, etc. There are days
nearer the front when he seems to have plenty – but again there is no
comparison when one thinks of what we give his front line.

Lt Col Henry Dillon, 1st West Yorkshire Rgt
There is a suppressed excitement among the men I have never
noticed before, an absolute craving to get at the swine. I think they

know that the whole nation and Empire are in it now and they feel that the German will is bending. This I suppose, from a military point of view, one would describe as superiority in morale. But there is a certain indefinable, telepathic communication in the minds of a crowd, and an army is, after all is said and done, only a disciplined crowd. They feel they are on top and want to finish it, and I think more than that, they want to feel that England has struck the deciding blow.

Maj. Francis Gull, 13th Rifle Brigade

One has to merely pray to God to spare one as I do firmly believe he will in my case and put one's entire faith in him. Only one thing do I dread, that is disfigurement – real disfigurement, it would be too awful for my girl. To be deaf, blind or dumb or lose arms or legs I do not care twopence for, but to be an eyesore would be too much. Gladly would I give my life for my home and country.

I go into this battle with an entirely clear conscience and pray to my God and my girl to give me strength to do my best and my duty and keep my nerve strong. To do anything cowardly or base would be the worst thing that could happen. How easy it is to put all before God and so to speak to go naked and with a clear mind before him. If he wills (as I believe he does) that I shall come through, it will be done. If not, then I will not and nothing I can do will alter that. I have thought it all out and cleared all the muddle from my brain and to God I give myself with the surest Faith of his bringing me back to my girl.

L/Cpl William Smallcombe, 12th Gloucestershire Rgt (Bristol's Own)

Murder! Murder! Everywhere! Gracious God! How can it be allowed? My comrades lay around – on the parapet – just in front – dead – discoloured – and oh God! *So* lonely.

Some dear son of a weeping mother. How she must long to

know where he is – but to see him laying cold and dead, would break the heart of any parent. Death is raining every few seconds – taking its horrible toll. We dodge and duck to escape that death-dealing shrapnel – but it claims its victims. We struggle on a few yards. One poor lad tries to rise, but utters a cry of pain as the shrapnel bites into his back. We drop again and find ourselves lying by another poor lad who was killed five minutes ago. Into the trenches – those of us left. Word comes along. 'Two men are crawling in.' They come in.

Pte Daniel Sweeney, 1st Lincolnshire Rgt

Devil's Wood is another sight I could tell you something about, but it is too horrible to mention and I shall not forget it to my last day. It is impossible for me to try and describe to you what these woods look like after a battle; there are hundreds of things I could tell you which nine people out of ten would say were all lies, it is only those who have seen them who can believe them, but ask anyone who was in the battle of Mametz Wood or Delville Wood and see what they will tell you. Murder is not the word for it. These are places where hundreds of men have said their prayers who have never said them before. This war is teaching people a lot of things that they never gave a thought to before. I will just tell you one little thing that happened to me on the Somme in the early hours of 14 Sept, just a few words only – I was wet to the skin, no overcoat, no water sheet, I had about three inches of clay clinging to my clothes and it was cold. I was in an open dugout and do you know what I did – I sat down in the mud and cried. I do not think I have cried like this since I was a child, I pity the poor lads who are up there now.

Lt T. G. Taylor, 1/10th London Rgt

One day, after going along the trench in part of the intermediate line, west of High Wood, and having the usual hair-breadth escapes, I met the brigadier commanding our brigade. He said,

'Taylor, have you just come along that trench?' I said, 'Yes, only just!' He said, 'Then down on your knees and thank God you're alive after doing it. I always do!' Good for him, wasn't it? I don't think he was far wrong!

Lt Col Henry Dillon, 1st West Yorkshire Rgt

Absolute desolation everywhere, shell holes and huge dumps of shells and barbed wire and ammunition and thousands of men covered in chalk and dust. Every trench has its name and as one goes along, in and out, round the traverses and winding along, you see a board up on every trench that leads off:– Piccadilly and Bond Street. – This way Wounded – RE Dump. Every dugout also has its board, so if you came along Buckingham Palace Avenue, a 10-foot-deep ditch, you would see a hole and two boards above it, one 2nd in Command and the other adjutant, if you then descended a winding staircase in the dark you would find myself and the adjutant. We each have a bed and boxes for tables and some shelves, boards on the floor and iron girders with sandbags for roof and sacking in a wooden frame for walls. Of course this is a good deal better than most and really comfortable, and down here the guns are not uncomfortably loud.

Maj. A. G. P. Hardwick, 59th Field Ambulance, RAMC

The dugout is a huge place and many direct hits have made no effect on it. Its entrances are *three*, leading in from the trench, and it is below ground level about twenty-five feet . . . Our landmarks to this place are very few and a compass is going to be indispensable here – our chief marks are in order. (1) Trench-board over a wide trench, (2) Then make due N for a smashed up harrow, (3) A smashed Boche limber cart in a shell hole, (4) Then two dead Huns lying in a shell hole, and then fifty yards in front we drop into the trench leading to Stuff Redoubt: except for these points there is nothing to distinguish one [place] from another.

Lt George Mallory, 40th Siege Batt., RGA
For the first part of yesterday Glen was my companion. A dumpy
little man rather fat and jolly to look at but not coarsely so; his
forehead bulges slightly and he has small sparkling eyes; his hair is
close cropped. His mouth is one of the most expressive I have ever
seen – consciously so in large measure and particularly for
enjoyment and horror. Human and humorous he is really, and
a great blessing. I feel quite an affection for him. His age is three or
four years short of mine but he must look at least ten years older. I
find that he is rather easily depressed and put out. I suppose the
trouble is that he has been out too long without leave – oh I don't
wonder fellows get bored out here – after a year or so!

Pte Charles Heare, 1/2nd Monmouthshire Rgt
An orderly called Dutton arrives in the division. He calls outside
our dugout, 'I say old chappie, where are the 29th Division
Headquarters? Can you show me, old boy?' What a voice, like a
girl. Then the boys lead off, 'Oh George kiss me', 'nurse the child',
'come to mama' and all that nonsense. We make room for him. He
has just come out and an orderly was wanted from the 1st Essex. It
appears he is sent out of the way. He proves to be the worst orderly
I have ever known all right. He has a book on *Astronomy for
Amateurs*. I read it and get interested in the sky and we chum up
together. One night he comes to the dugout and shouts out,
excited, 'Come and see Cassiopeia, she looks fine.' 'Oh hell,' say the
boys, 'he's got a tart out there.' There is a rush outside. When the
boys saw it was only a star, I thought they were going to dump
him. We all laughed afterwards. The nearest civilian was twelve
miles away.

Pte Vero Garratt, 2/5th (London) Field Ambulance, RAMC
When I look up, my eyes meet a mass of darkness that is studded
here and there by lights similar to my own, and near which weary
boys are turning their thoughts to homeland with a very expressive

look on their faces. They are good boys. Rough and ready as many
of them are, yet the joy and happiness their comradeship has
brought to me is beyond telling. You would be surprised how easy
it is out here to sink one's differences and personal prejudices that
may have weighed with one under different circumstances. And it
is difficult not to make certain limited concessions to the other
fellows' use of Anglo-Saxon language, etc, and conduct, which
would have occasioned no end of rebukes under less trying
conditions.

Pte Charles Heare, 1/2nd Monmouthshire Rgt
Dutton is sent out later on. One of the orderlies came in and said,
'Taffy, you had better go and look for your Queenie. He is up in a
shell hole just off the Longueval Road, crying out. I couldn't get
him to move.' I find Dutton. He is saying, 'I can't go up', and
yelling out as a shell drops. It is hot with shelling. A Scotch
orderly joins us and we get him out at last. It gets warm again and
he lies down again in a shell hole. 'It's too awful, I can't go on.'
'Hold your arm up,' says Scottie, 'and Taffe will put a round
through that fleshy part, then you will get out of it.' 'You're
murderers!' he yells and moves on just as a piece of shrapnel caught
him, breaking his arm and gashing his leg. We left him at an
advance dressing station, glad for our sake as he gave us all nerves,
and glad for his sake.

Cpl Harold Bisgood, 1/2nd London Rgt (Royal Fusiliers)
I am rather at a loss to know where to begin. This last awful month
has driven us all as near mad as possible, nothing but mud and
blood and terrible loss of friends on all sides. Success to our arms,
yes, plenty, but at what cost!
    Passing on from Happy Valley, I found myself in the small
village of Carnoy. Leaving Carnoy, I came across the most
extraordinary sight; as far as the eye could reach, the ground
was torn up into a series of holes, and it was impossible to find a

level square yard; here were the most famous Trones, Bernafay and Delville Woods, almost touching one another, now represented only by holes and sticks of shattered and torn trees; the dead lay almost everywhere, and the smell was beyond one's imagination. Guns there were by the hundred of all sorts and sizes, regardless of any cover, blazing away for all they were worth. Now one was able to see and realise what the artillery were doing for the cause, it made one pleased they were on the British side; at the same time I knew it was hell up in front where I had to go.

I learned to my disgust that the battalion had just moved into the line at Angle Wood, to the rear of Combles, and that I should have to follow at once. I set out for Angle Wood some twenty miles off, passing on my way through that awful 'Happy Valley' so well known to the lads out here. As I neared the edge of the valley, I came across some twenty weird animals, nestling together. I learned these were of the now famous Mr Tank tribe. Mr Tank is a most extraordinary person to describe. He is composed of steel plates, rivets and caterpillar bands. He is able to travel on his head, back, base, or front, can climb any hill, shell hole or trench, can push over any ordinary house or tree, and is a perfect devil for machine-gun emplacements. These latter, he simply rolls on and squashes; his weight is only thirty tons.

It was getting dusk when I reached Angle Wood, and owing to the lack of trees it was hard to find. However, having found it, I reported to Captain Heumann, and was greeted with the remark, 'Oh! I'm glad to see you've come, you're just in time for the stunt tomorrow.' I knew what that meant, and wished I'd lost my way.

That night amid preparations for the show in the morning, I managed to snatch a few winks in a friendly shell hole (not too muddy). The rumbling of the tanks awoke me at 3.30 a.m. Fritz was searching the sky with searchlights, imagining the noise was aeroplanes. At four, we had to move up to Falfont Farm trenches, our bombardment was intense, the enemy also were replying with not a few, and at 6 a.m., just before daylight, we moved up to the assembly trench. We had not been long in these trenches when the captain called a meeting of his officers, during which the Germans shelled the trenches heavily, and all the officers and a sergeant major of both A and B Companies were killed or wounded except one, a young subaltern, and he was suffering more or less from shell shock. Here it was that we lost Captain Heumann, or 'Dickie' as he was better known to all ranks. His loss put a damper on everything, as he was the life of the battalion, he was killed by concussion only. I left him seated on the fire platform as though he were asleep. Now came the order to advance to another trench, and I was compelled to leave the captain and the major in the hands of the King's Own Scottish Borderers who promised to dispose of the bodies.

2/Lt George Foley, 7th Somerset Light Infantry

I was looking out across the battered ground in front of us, wondering how long it would be before we took our place in that dense cumulus of smoke that marked the battle line, when out of the mist there suddenly loomed an apparition, the sight of which fairly took my breath away. Slowly it rolled and swayed towards us; its motion was not that of a snake, nor of an elephant, but an indescribable blend of the two. It had all the easy sinuosity of the former as it slid over the tumbled ground, coupled with the clumsy attempt at dignity which one associates with the latter. From its gaping jaws issued steam and smoke, and from its belly came forth a mighty rumbling. For a few tense moments we gazed in dumb and awe-stricken amazement; and then it flashed upon us that here before our eyes was one of the new land ships.

Gnr Alfred Reiffer, Tank D17, D Coy, Heavy Branch MGC

Our tank was filled up with stores of all kinds: drums of engine oil, iron rations, gas masks, equipment, overalls, revolvers, anti-'bump your head against the roof of the tank' leather helmets, carrier pigeons in a basket, semaphore signals (flaming red in colour) on the outside of the tank on either side of the exhaust pipes.

There was a terrific amount of noise in the tank made up by the engine, the tracks and the tumbling about of the drums of oil and various paraphernalia that we had to carry. Our own barrage was going on outside and the German barrage, but really we couldn't hear a lot of this because of our own noise.

We were fired on by German machine guns. First of all they were firing on the starboard side and the impact of their bullets was making the inside of the armour plate white hot. And the white-hot flakes were coming off and if you happened to be near enough you could have been blinded by them.

Sgt Harold Bisgood, 1/2nd London Rgt (Royal Fusiliers)

The Germans seemed at first awestruck at the tanks, but they soon pulled round and offered a most stubborn resistance, so much so that we did not quite get all we wanted to, though we were very successful; we took NO prisoners. I found it terribly hard to keep my end up, we broke into the German line and biffed Fritz here properly. I then sent a party down trench B and took a party along trench A and bombed as we went. We reached points A and B and cleared the whole of the loop trench, but we were unable to get any further as we lost many of our best bombers, and also the Germans had strong barricades erected at these points, on which were mounted machine guns. We then withdrew a few yards round the corner, erected barricades in a similar manner, placing Lewis guns in gaps between sandbags. For several hours after this, we tried to bomb each other out. We were lucky enough to get hold of some rabbit wire and make a cover for our trench, which spoilt Fritz's chance, as bombs alighting on the wire would invariably bounce off and explode on one side or the other of the trench . . . Mr Tank settled down, having met with an accident, a Hun shell hit one of the caterpillar bands. You may well imagine how we felt, perched in already smashed up trenches receiving the awful shelling which the tank brought forth. However, our friend held his own, firing from his Maxims every shot he had, and using up all his shells in the Hotchkiss gun. The mechanics then set the petrol tanks alight and retired into our trenches.

During an attack when the battlefront became fluid, there was an immediate difficulty for the artillery of both sides to register correctly on to targets. Often artillery fire slackened as both sides endeavoured to work out where the respective positions lay.

Sgt Harold Bisgood, 1/2nd London Rgt (Royal Fusiliers)
After several hours of this hide and seek game, we managed to get up our two-inch trench mortar battery, and my word didn't the enemy shift, two shots and they were off, leaving about twenty casualties. We rushed the barricade only to be faced with another; and then our troubles began, as OUR artillery, not knowing exactly how far we had advanced, began dropping shells in our new line; one wiped out the whole of one of my bombing sections. I was simply frantic as shells were coming all ways. I sent runner after runner back to HQ but evidently many of these became casualties; at last, however, one got through and the range increased, but not before I lost two of my best sergeants and several men.

Lt George Mallory, 40th Siege Batt., RGA
I was back at another point which we have been using as an observation post, and there I carried out what appeared to be a successful registration. I was back at 8.30 p.m. and went to bed very tired after food. Before I went to sleep, I heard distinctly from the murmur of voices in the tent some mention of our troops being shelled out of a trench by our own guns. [It was] my suspicion that this battery was accused of the mistake. I can't tell you what a

miserable time I had after that. You see, if my registration had been untrue, it was my fault. The conditions for observation had been very difficult – a lot of smoke had been blowing across at intervals and other shells were bursting near the point on which I was ranging. I went over and over again in my mind all the circumstantial evidence that it was really our shells I had seen bursting, and had horrid doubts and fears.

Lt Edward Allfree, 111th Siege Batt., RGA

Mistakes of this sort were not often made, but, of course, at times the human element was bound to come in. Even the best of gunners were, at times, liable to make mistakes. I can remember Hartley making a curious bloomer – and not only a bloomer, but a bloomer on a bloomer. It may seem unfair to record other people's mistakes, but I don't mind recording this one of Hartley's because Hartley was, of all people, the most precise, careful and accurate, and it therefore goes to show that *if* Hartley could make such a mistake, anyone might. The major was at the observation post and Hartley was acting as battery commander, and was doing the shoot.

The first three rounds were fired in succession, and each one was 'unobserved' by the major. He at once suspects some bloomer, and rings up Hartley. At the same time it flashes across Hartley that he has forgotten to put on the necessary right switch from zero line. He hears the major on the phone and at once tries to pacify him, before he begins asking questions, with 'All right, sir. All right, I know why you did not see those rounds, – just a slight mistake – look again, you'll see it all right this time.' He tries again – 'Unobserved. Repeat.' Next round – 'Unobserved.' The major rings up again – 'My dear Hartley, what on earth are you doing? Have you got the right target?' Yes, the target is right. 'Then, for goodness' sake, check your figures again.' He does so. The blood rushes to his head. – 'Good Lord!' After the first mistake in not putting on any switch, he put on a left switch instead of a right switch, and made things ten times worse. He explained what he had done to the major, who forgave him, feeling, I believe, rather glad to think that even Hartley could make mistakes such as that.

Lt George Mallory, 40th Siege Batt., RGA

Yesterday afternoon was very unpleasant; I had to attend an enquiry held by some senior artillery officers with the object of discovering which of several batteries was firing into our own trenches some days ago. A hateful business – hateful that the infantry should have that cause of complaint, hateful to feel the uncertainty and doubt which must be felt in the best conducted battery under the circumstances, hateful because everyone was really there to save his own skin – or, to put it just a little higher, to save the credit of his battery – and hateful finally because it was such cold work waiting three hours before our evidence was taken. I was only concerned with one morning as FOO (forward observation officer) and was quite happy about that as far as our own guns were concerned because I had been able to give a very good registration.

Capt. J. C. Procter, 13th Gloucestershire Rgt (Forest of Dean)

I saw the most thrilling of air fights the other day. I was lying in my tent when I heard faint machine-gunning up in the sky. I went out but couldn't see anything at first, as it was a cloudless day and very sunny, under which conditions aeroplanes become transparent and almost invisible. Finally I detected six machines in close combat, at about 10,000 feet. In a short time, two of them broke out of the fight and went off towards the Germans. I found out afterwards that these were one of ours chasing one of theirs. The other four came lower and lower, till it was possible to see that it was one machine being driven down and down by the other three. The rattle of machine guns was continuous. Finally they got so low that every detail of the fight was obvious, and the hapless victim had a cross on his wings. Every moment I expected to see the machines collide. At times they appeared to actually touch each other. As soon as the Boche tried to go straight, one of ours would get in line behind him and when this happens the machine gun of the aeroplane behind has it all its own way. The Boche of course had the initiative in the course he set, but our chaps followed his wild twistings in a marvellous way, and there was always one ready to follow his most fantastic turn. His flying was almost unbelievable.

Pte Sydney Fuller, 8th Suffolk Rgt

In the afternoon there was a bigger scrap in the air, over Longueval – about half a dozen planes of either side. The most peculiar thing about this scrap was that it stopped all shelling for a time. When it began, the guns on both sides were at it hammer and tongs, but no sooner did the planes get really busy with one another, than the men serving the batteries round us ceased their work and stood watching the fight. In about half a minute the German shells ceased coming over and everything seemed to be strangely quiet, the only sounds being the rattle of the plane's machine guns and the roar of the engines overhead, and the excited comments of the men, spectators on the ground. When the scrap finished, away went the guns again, – 'the mixture as before'.

Capt. J. C. Procter, 13th Gloucestershire Rgt (Forest of Dean)

It looked like a fight between birds. The sudden dartings and swoops and savage sideways jabs were utterly surprising. This fellow thought nothing of looping the loop and at the same time spinning his machine on its long axis *and* firing his gun all the time. I never knew aeroplanes could spin like that before. This went on for twenty minutes, and at the end of that time the whole four of them weren't more than 500 feet up, and immediately above our camp. I momentarily expected to be shot, as often they were fighting on the vertical descent of a loop, as well as upside down. A hundred times I expected to see the machines crash to earth. At the end, when they were too near the ground for further gyrations, Boche tacitly gave up, and made a straight long slant for earth. Even then I believe he hoped to trick our chaps into thinking he'd given in and then make a dash for it. Anyway they stopped firing and followed him in his slant. He never made a dash, for he must have been dying as he planed down, and his wonderful skill deserted him. He caught the top of a willow and his machine crumpled into a mass of wreckage in a pond. He was fished out, but was full of water and bullet holes, and died. It was a wonderful show. One minute these brand-new glittering machines doing such wonderful things, and the next a mass of twisted scrap in a dirty pond and a dead man with a blue face and his uniform covered with black slime, and a cheering crowd scrambling to be first on the scene.

Acting Bombardier Alfred Richardson, 116th Siege Batt., RGA

A large enemy aircraft attacked one of our kite balloons. Although attacked by some six or seven of ours, and although a terrific barrage was put up by 'Archie' round the balloon, the enemy aircraft succeeded in peppering it but nothing happened, to his disgust, except that the two observers came down in their parachutes. Again he attacked it with his MG but still the thing did not catch fire – six separate times did he try and failed. All this time he was surrounded by our chasers but, by skilful pilotage, he evaded them.

Now the excitement came. The enemy aircraft decided to make for home, evidently thinking the balloon was fire-proof or bullet-proof! He flew on until almost over our position, when he suddenly turned back and met his opponents – four in number – face to face. Again he evaded them by looping, turning, and finally doing a spinning nosedive until he almost touched the ground. All the time machine guns were simply ripping away: it was marvellous how no plane came down.

The enemy aircraft was now only some fifty feet from the ground and directly overhead; one of our chasers stuck to him. Sergeant Walden and I decided to bury ourselves in a shell hole, as bullets were whizzing past our heads. I could see both the pilot and observer as easily as if they had been on the ground. Never before have I seen a Boche plane so frightfully low down and still fighting. By a skilful movement and turn and then a zigzag course, he finally succeeded in evading our machine and was last seen flying very low down, with our chaser still in pursuit and still potting at him. I would have given pounds not to miss it. It was so exciting: really you cannot possibly imagine how fine it was.

2/Lt John Godfrey, 103 Field Coy, RE

4 a.m.: Cold, wet and filled with a foreboding of evil – my state can better be imagined than described. Well, we got to work by 7 a.m. in a filthy wet trench in the worst possible position as far as vulnerability went – bang by the side of the main road to Flers. At about 8 a.m., as a matter of course, the shells began coming over. Amid the various noises I suddenly noticed an unfamiliar kind of burst – so trained does one's ear become to the noise of each particular shell – and I looked around. More and more of these came over till they were falling literally in hundreds. By that time I had twigged that it was something nasty: a chemical, and told the men to put on their gas helmets. I went over to a little group of my best chaps and told them they were absolutely safe if they wore their gas helmets properly – a Tommy can't stand gas – and by that time the Germans had the range too jolly well for pleasantness. I left that group and walked along to another one to chase them up. Poor fellows, they were cowering like paralysed rabbits.

Just as I had left group 'a' – I heard the horrid double thud that means a couple of shells in the trench. I was knocked into the mud, but when I got up heard a howl of agony. I fairly tore up to see what they'd done, and it was beyond the worst pessimist's expectations. Everything was black: the trench, the men, their clothes and skins, looked as if they had been burnt. I couldn't see well enough with the gas helmet on and had to take it off – and promptly nearly died of a kind of general choking. Eyes streaming and my whole face red hot with irritation. However, poor old Arthurs had to be got out, so I yelled for a man to go and get a stretcher. Dead silence (they had all bunked), except for the senseless hiss of shells coming over. So I held my breath and took a puttee off Lawrence, who was dead, and with a rifle made up a pretty fair bandage and splint. I never realised a man could lose so much flesh and live. His leg bone was broken and most of his calf shot away. At last Shepherd crept up – I damned him for a cur and told him to get a stretcher. Arthurs, meanwhile, was howling to me like a babe. I shall never forget that as long as I live: I was crouching on the naked dead bodies of five of my men, coughing like a consumptive, holding up old Arthurs' head and pouring water down his throat. It is curious how one thinks at such times. While I was waiting for the stretcher, I was reminded irresistibly of Pig and Pepper: Arthurs being the howling baby, and me the sneezing and coughing Duchess.

Poor old Dell was grinning madly at me with no jaw and his eyes like a fish's – and he was such a nice handsome chap. I could see his heart and bones where the shell had torn bits off him. I wonder I didn't go mad. At last Shepherd arrived with a stretcher and an infantryman to help. They two got him (howling still) into the dressing station and I lumbered back with another wounded chap clinging on to my neck.

Pte Frederick Aylett, 133rd Field Ambulance, RAMC
It must have been about midnight when we filed out, carrying a stretcher between two. We made our way across an open space of about 200 yards, and then dropped into a communication trench. All the way up, we were heavily shelled and it was a wonder that nobody was hit. The earth that was flung up came down like rain upon our helmets. [We] came to a dugout where one or two

wounded had been brought in. Four of us offered to carry a man down. He was a big fellow and we had no end of a job before we reached the aid post. The trench was a good one as far as protection went, but a bad one for carrying laden stretchers. Occasionally our hands scraped the sides of the trench and sometimes sharp turns and square bays made it exceedingly difficult to get a stretcher round.

At last, however, we reached the aid post and deposited our man safely. We were in a bath of perspiration and thoroughly fagged out. The wretched sergeant in charge got his lists muddled up, and I had not been in five minutes before I had my name called to take the man we had just carried from the line down to the relay post. There were men there who had not carried a case down that night, who had hidden in funk holes and come back when the coast was clear. However, it was no use expostulating or endeavouring to explain things to a wooden-headed NCO so we just went out and grabbed our man. I had cooled down, but my clothes were still wet with my former exertion, and the night air struck chilly as we emerged from the stuffy dugout. We were soon warm again, going over the rough ground, stumbling occasionally as our weary legs almost gave way from time to time. We reached the post on the roadway and returned. We were thoroughly weary and used up and could hardly drag our legs forward. By the time we reached the dugout, we were ready to drop from sheer fatigue. The brain felt curiously numb, and one felt a hundred years old.

Pte William Brown, 1/4th Oxford and Buckinghamshire Light Infantry

Rations for a battalion had to be indented for several days in advance, so that during our stay in Bouzincourt we were drawing for a full-strength battalion, but were considerably below strength. Therefore we were surfeited and a great deal was wasted. As I was the senior private, I had temporary charge of the platoon, and for two days I drew two loaves per man per day, and other

food, in like proportion. In addition to this, we had several days'
post, and this included many parcels. Letters and articles of value
belonging to those who had left the battalion were returned, but
food and perishables were divided amongst those who remained. I
was obliged to take a great heap of cakes to the cooks to be burnt!
Such waste was unavoidable.

Cpl Arthur Cook, 1st Somerset Light Infantry

The next few days were a succession of daily trips forward and
backward with the rations . . . I soon discovered what a thankless
task it was getting those rations up to the front line. It is a route
march every day, and sometimes a very unpleasant one. The time
of our return and going up again gave us a narrow margin of about
two hours' rest when the quartermaster got us up to draw the
company's rations. This did not take long, but then we had to
share it out into seventeen equal portions, plus a bit for the CQMS.
The seventeen portions would then be placed in sandbags. We
based our distribution according to the strength of the section
when it went to the trenches, and if there had been any casualties,
the remaining men were lucky, for they had a large share. The
preparation of the bags was a long business; a portion of tea was
placed in the empty bag, then shaken into one corner and tied,
sugar was then put in and tied in the opposite corner. If there was
any tinned stuff, this went in next, then bacon, sometimes raw,
sometimes cooked, bread and cooked meat (this was always a
messy job cutting it up), parcels and mail (if any). The bag would
then be tied up with the number of its section or company
headquarters. When this was completed, it was time to start
our journey. In the majority of cases these bags reached their
destination in good condition, but occasionally the sugar was
mixed up with the tea but no one worried much as the majority
liked their tea sweet. They did not, however, appreciate it being
scattered all over the meat and bacon. There were occasions when
the bags arrived soaking wet – the carrying party having fallen

into shell holes or trenches full of water, but this soggy mess was never wasted.

Pte Frederick Aylett, 133rd Field Ambulance, RAMC

For breakfast we had bread, bacon and tea. For dinner about half a pint of stew made usually with corned beef, and for tea, which was our last meal, we had a couple of hard biscuits with jam and grease and not quite a pint of tea. We had nothing between four in the afternoon and eight the next morning. This scanty food with bad water told on our health. Before we went down, there was hardly a man who was not suffering from acute diarrhoea and passing blood. It was no use to report sick because there was nowhere to rest and so there was nothing to do but just to keep going as well as one could. Once or twice I came over so queer I could hardly stand, and the food we had revolted me, so that for a day or two I subsisted chiefly on tea.

Pte William Brown, 1/4th Oxford and Buckinghamshire Light Infantry

Our sector was an abomination, consisting of nothing but ditches – sometimes very shallow – partly filled with slime and water. There was no shelter of any description, and our only possible occupation was to endeavour to scrape away some of the mud. An idea of the state of the country may be imagined when I say that on one occasion, when we were wearing rubber waders, several men arrived up the line barefooted, having had their waders sucked off in the mud. I have seen strong men lying down in partial hysterics, crying like children through sheer exhaustion. To add to our miseries, the shelling was practically incessant; but we soon became so indifferent to everything that we cared little whether we were hit or not – in fact, we often said we would willingly lose a limb to get out of it all.

Pte Frank Harris, 6th King's Own Yorkshire Light Infantry

Bert thinks he stands a chance of leave later in the year, what is known as the back end. Relinquishing a promising career as a foreign correspondent, would it not be nice if we both scrounged leave simultaneously? It certainly would, Bert lad, but a few days following these brotherly thoughts, Bert himself is dead, and, whilst not wishing to sound harsh, in some ways death out here seems such a small part of our lives that we accept it as an ever-present risk, that whatever you can stand has to be endured. Yes, death is wholesale, I am afraid – live in its midst by day – sleep in its midst by night – we are cognisant with it in its most atrocious forms – you grow hardened – submit without demur twenty-four hours a day – yet I wonder, before all these killings, how many of us had gazed on death as a result of a natural cause?

There was one category of soldier who could leave the front, and without the need first to lose life or limb. They were the boy soldiers. Lying about their ages, they were enlisted in their hundreds of thousands in 1914 and 1915, and willingly went to France. Few knew what to expect, least of all the parents who then saw longer and longer casualty lists in the newspapers. Under pressure, the Government allowed boys under the age of eighteen to be recalled to Britain.

Gnr Stanley Collins, 137th Heavy Batt., RGA

We went through the Battle of the Somme, which I believe lasted until November time, when one day the sergeant major called for Gunner Collins to see Captain Moore. Captain Moore was down in a dugout. He asked me how old I was, and I had to do a bit of quick thinking. Nineteen when I joined up and I've been here almost a year.

'Nearly twenty, sir,' I said.

'I don't want any bloody lies, Gunner, how old are you?'

So then I told him, near enough seventeen. Then he showed me a letter from the War Office that my mother had sent to have me returned home, and he said I'd have to go but I would probably be put in prison for false attestation. That didn't worry me. So an NCO escorted me from there back to where the horse lines were, and I had to go down to the railhead, Boulogne or Calais, I forget which, and I was handed over to the Railway Transport Officer. The next morning I was put on the boat, full of wounded, people groaning, hollering and screaming, and we landed at Folkestone.

You couldn't go wrong there, anyone came off a boat and they'd give you a handful of fruit or cakes or something like that. Then we got on the train and I landed up at Woolwich, all on me Jack Jones I was. I got there about eight or nine o'clock at night and I went to the Shrapnel Barracks where the Royal Artillery were, to report to the Guard Room. The NCO of the Guard asked me who I was and where I'd come from, they didn't know anything about me. 'We've got no beds here,' he said, 'there's an old bed over in one of the rooms but we haven't got any mattresses.' I dumped my kitbag on this old empty bed and then I thought, 'Sod this, I'm going home.' I knocked at the door, and when my mum saw me, she swooned. She soon came round and then got the old frying pan on the go. I had a wash and brush up and a good old scoff [meal].

Maj. A. G. P. Hardwick, 59th Field Ambulance, RAMC
A day of days. We were up at 6 a.m. and were greatly surprised to find the ground covered with snow – it has been very cold during the nights, but snow in November is not common here.

Zero hour was 6.10 a.m., and to the second our artillery started – it was even noisier than that of Monday last, as this time we were amongst the lighter guns whose noise is even worse than that of the 'heavies' – it was a wonderful sight, dawn just beginning to break through: the ground, trenches, shell holes all dead white, a low white mist above the ground and with this the flashes and noise of the guns and in the distance the Boche star signals of red and white. It was the weirdest, most awe-inspiring sight that I have ever seen – words fail. The gun flashes were wonderful and of every hue – dull red, yellow, green-yellow, purple and white according to the nature of the explosive. Overhead was the dull swish and clanking of our heavy shells which had been fired off at Ovillers, etc, and immediately above us was that infernal 60-pounder battery that seemed to never stop. No Hun shells came over in reply . . . The bombardment lasted twenty minutes only – but it was a terrific one.

Pte John McCauley, 2nd Border Rgt

German prisoners began to arrive: poor miserable wretches. Fear and anguish was writ plain on their faces, and perspiration poured from them as they hurried past our position murmuring almost mechanically, 'Kamerad, Kamerad.'

Orders were given to stand guard over the mouth of the dugouts and we could hear the frightened Germans shouting 'Kamerad, Kamerad.' They would not emerge into the open, however, and we were ordered to go down into the dugouts and turn them out. I and a comrade cautiously entered the dugout over which we had been standing guard and descended very slowly, keeping a keen lookout for any signs of treachery on the part of the men who were now virtually our prisoners. I was hesitant and nervous, afraid of a bullet coming out of the darkness, and the only consolation I could give myself was that if such a thing did happen, my comrades would avenge my death by blowing up every man in the dugout. Step by step, with my finger on the trigger of my rifle, I went down into the dark, until I nearly stumbled over a young German on the bottom step.

He seemed to be in great pain and clutched at his stomach where I observed blood gushing from a wound. I was astonished at his youthfulness. He was only a young boy, hardly more than a schoolboy, and the youngest German I had seen in the line up to that time. He gave me a most appealing look, and kept crying out 'Lazarett [hospital], Kamerad, Lazarett.' Fear and anguish were clearly reflected in his face, and a bitter revolt against the horror of war flooded my very soul. I offered him water, cigarettes, and attempted to bandage his wound, but it seemed that I was only increasing his agony for he only gripped me, and cried 'No, Kamerad.' If only he could understand a few words of English or I speak a few words of German, I thought. I wanted to comfort him, to assure him that my heart held no hatred against him. All that was in my heart at that moment was a great ache for the poor wounded boy, who should have been at home on some happy playing field instead of wallowing in this filthy hole with death lurking so near. It made me feel ashamed of my manhood. I badly wanted to stay by the side of the young German who had stirred up such a well of pity within me. I wanted to see him safely behind the lines. He seemed to understand my feelings towards him, and when I rose to carry on with my grim work, he clutched at my tunic as though he did not want me to go . . .

As I passed him at the foot of the steps leading from the dugout, he held both his hands out to me in appealing fashion, sobbing and murmuring some words in German. Heaven knew what he was saying, but his anguished tones stabbed into my very heart. I shall never be able to erase from my mind the terrible scenes in that dugout. Years after the war, I still sit by the fireside and see in the flickering flames that poor German boy with his hands outstretched in tearful appeal, and I fancy I hear his pleading voice, 'Lazarett, Kamerad, Lazarett.'

As I passed him, I gripped both his hands, gave him an affectionate touch on the shoulder and stumbled up the steps with tears dimming my eyes. I prayed earnestly for many a day afterwards that that little German boy would find his way back home to safety and happiness.

Pte Frederick Aylett, 133rd Field Ambulance, RAMC
While we were round Thiepval, we carried a good many wounded Germans down. Most of us had no feeling of hatred for them, and we always carried them as gently and with as good a heart as we

did our own men. They were only fighting for their masters just as
we were, and were to be pitied rather than reproved. I always used
to think of the man's wife or mother or little ones at home, and I
used to wonder how much longer the men of Europe would
continue to be exploited in the interests of a select circle of
professional soldiers, diplomats and armament shareholders. That
grey-clad figure broken in war was nearer to me, was more my
brother, than Lord Northcliffe in England, raking in thousands
and gaining influence by the sale of his papers. He was more my
brother than loud-voiced Bottomley [proprietor of the patriotic
journal *John Bull*], gulling the people of England and making
inane prophesies about the end of the war. To me the German was
not an enemy, but a comrade in misfortune, and I always hoped he
would recover and get an easy job in England.

Pte John McCauley, 2nd Border Rgt
My old wounds were troubling me now that the cold weather had
arrived, and I was suffering badly from frost-bitten feet. My hands
were swollen to twice their normal size, and frequently my arms
were completely numb up to the elbows. For nearly a month I had
not had my boots off, and most of my companions were in the
same miserable state as myself, owing to the intense cold. Putting
the backs of my swollen hands to the barrel of my rifle, I could feel
nothing, and I could lift it up only by holding it between my
elbows. God help us if we had been called upon to defend
ourselves. Fifty yards away, the Germans were, no doubt, thinking
the same thing.

Frostbite was a terrible enemy. How terrible only those who
lived in the trenches for weeks on end know. Men were actually
being frozen to death and others were fighting against sleep and
the cold until they could fight no longer. Some we had to pick up
and massage vigorously until the stiff cold limbs could be brought
into use again, and those who had the use of their hands and arms
would put cigarettes in the mouths of their helpless comrades and

light them for them. Faces were covered up as much as possible with woollen scarves, and the wool would be covered with small icicles formed from the breath.

Col John Bateson, 24th Siege Batt., RGA

The conditions in front were beyond words to convey. The trenches were filled up with an earthy gruel through which you moved along as best you could, now and again stumbling over a submerged corpse. I have a vivid mental picture, to this day, of two young soldiers in an alcove scooped out of the side of their sludge-filled trench, their table was the back of a dead soldier, lying on his face and half buried in the mud; their light, for the alcove was inclined to be dark, under the gloomy skies, was a fag end of candle, standing in a blob of its own grease on their 'table'; and they were playing cards: decent lads from civilised homes, it was well they could take such evil conditions so.

Rev. Roger Bulstrode, Hon. Chaplain to the Forces (2nd Class)

A trifling incident of this time has remained in my mind. When the Germans had been driven back some miles, I was walking up beyond Le Transloy into the captured territory. Some distance beyond the old German front line, I met a man returning. 'If you go on a bit further, sir, you'll see some grass by the road!' That was his great bit of news.

Capt. QM Ernest Laman, 2nd South Wales Borderers

I am reminded of a Somme yarn during a damp spell.

Officer passing (or wading) along the road sees a tin helmet move. Reaching out with his stick he tips it over and finds a head underneath.

'Hello, who are you?'

'No. 45678 Mechanical Transport, Driver Thomas Sticklebottom, sir.'

'Where's your lorry, then?'
'Standing on it, sir!'

Pte Sydney Fuller, 8th Suffolk Rgt

Quiet with more snow. A robin perched on our dugout chimney and allowed us to touch him – he did not appear to be at all afraid of human beings. Perhaps he had shell shock, or it may have been that he was loath to leave the warmth of our chimney.

Lt Leslie Sanders, RGA attd Field Survey Coy, RE

I haven't anything to write about, at least anything that I'm allowed to write about. For the annoying thing is that all the things which happen and are of any interest are also forbidden subjects. I'm afraid I've rather strained the regulations in what I've said before. I'm supposed to maintain a deathly silence as to the conditions on this side; I'm not supposed, for instance, to describe the dugout I write this in, nor the state of the roads, nor the features of the landscape, nor anything except perhaps the weather – which is cold and rainy.

Pte John McCauley, 2nd Border Rgt

There came a day when the bitter cold and the pain of my wounds rendered me useless for fighting, and I was sent down the line. I was attached to a company of about 150 men, and our task was to search for dead bodies and bury them. Two issues of raw rum were served out to us daily, to kill the dangerous germs which we might inhale. It was a ghastly job, and more than ever I learnt what war meant. We commenced our grim work in the early morning, and set out in skirmishing order to search the ground. For the first week or two, I could scarcely endure the experiences we met with, but gradually became hardened, and for three months I continued the job. We worked in pairs, and our most important duty was to find the identity discs. After our morning's work was over, a pile of rifles and barbed wire stakes would mark the place where we had buried our gruesome discoveries. There they lay, English, German, Australians, South Africans, Canadians, all mingled together in the last great sleep.

Often have I picked up the remains of a fine brave man on a shovel. Just a little heap of bones and maggots to be carried to the common burial place. Numerous bodies were found lying sub-merged in the water in shell holes and mine craters; bodies that seemed quite whole, but which became like huge masses of white, slimy chalk, when we handled them. The job had to be done; the identity disc had to be found. I shuddered as my hands, covered in soft flesh and slime, moved about in search of the disc, and I have had to pull bodies to pieces in order that they should not be buried unknown. And yet, what a large number did pass through my hands unknown. Not a clue of any kind to reveal the name by which the awful remains were known in life. It was painful to have to bury them, be they British or German. Very often my chum or I would collect small stones and pebbles, and work out some epitaph above the grave, as a last worldly tribute to men who would probably be living today if the world had really striven for peace in the opening years of this century. In those three months, I assisted in the burial of over ten thousand dead – known and unknown. The womenfolk of those thousands who may be yet mourning their loss in British and German homes can rest assured that we carried out our work with reverence and care for friend and foe.

Lt Leslie Sanders, RGA attd Field Survey Coy, RE
A little while ago, I stood at the entrance to my dugout. A slender moon was setting in the west, and a faint glow lingered there – tender, delicate colouring. Elsewhere, the sky was limpid with the colourlessness of twilight ere the stars began to peep. The grey veil of nightfall mercifully hid the desolation of the landscape. The great expanse of brown and naked mud, the overlapping shell holes, the loathly pools, the spindly, shattered stumps of trees, the

indescribable medley of rusting wire, broken tools, unexploded shells, rotting sandbags, and rubbish of every sort – the kindly cloak hid all these. The lurid green flashes of the guns which later would stab the darkness like lightning were not yet so apparent as to catch the eye. No battery near me was firing, and only a distant rumbling and occasionally the cheerless sound of a shell passing overhead could be heard. The traffic on the road nearby was still.

Two men were talking quietly. The murmur of their voices came to my ears; somewhere a fire began to twinkle . . . One's eyes went to the peaceful west. The darkest day was past; already it seemed lighter at this hour than it had been, and there floated the slim crescent of the New Moon: the New Moon with the old Moon in its arms . . . The darkness deepened; far away the first star shell of the evening flared up and lit the battlefield . . . Somewhere a man died.

1917

The War in 1917

It was not unlike the final evacuation of Gallipoli, only this time it was the Germans who disappeared from right under the noses of the British. Throughout the autumn and winter months of 1916–17, the Germans had been busily engaged in constructing a new defensive system forty miles to the east of the Somme, a seemingly impregnable line which, above all else, would shorten the front that they had to hold, thereby releasing manpower. In mid-March they were ready, retreating almost overnight, leaving the Somme battlefield to the Allies, who were suddenly able to walk the ground that had been fought over so aggressively without risk of death or injury. Ahead were open fields that had proved so tempting through field glasses and telescopes, but which had always seemed beyond reach. In following up the Germans, the Allies discovered that their enemy had not been so accommodating. Trees had been cut down across all major highways, so hindering the Allied advance. Crossroads and buildings had been destroyed for the same purpose, and anything that would benefit the enemy – fruit trees, crops or water supplies – had been cut down, uprooted or poisoned. It was not quite a scorched-earth policy, but it was wanton destruction that angered many British soldiers. Furthermore, an elaborate system of booby traps had been left attached to tempting souvenirs, bottles of wine, even beds, making progress hazardous.

The retreat to the Hindenburg Line had disrupted but not halted the Allied proposal to attack the enemy that spring. In

December 1916, the French had turned to a new dynamic Commander-in-Chief, General Robert Nivelle. He had been the architect of a series of successful counter-attacks in the autumn and winter of 1916 and his stock was riding high, not only with the French military establishment but, crucially, with the French public, too. The demand in France, after all the previous losses, was for a decisive breakthrough, and Nivelle promised that he could hand them such a success on a plate, victory, in effect, 'within forty-eight hours'. All available resources for the attack were mobilised, while the British promised a secondary attack near Arras where the Germans had not withdrawn. The huge public expectation of victory was therefore mirrored by their abject horror when the April French offensive failed miserably. Continuing with the offensive in the face of huge tactical disadvantages only cost more lives and brought the French army to the brink of outright mutiny. To the north, the British campaign had opened a week earlier and with some success, including the Canadian Corps' seizure of the strategically important position of Vimy Ridge, but casualties had been enormous and, although the battle continued for the next month, there was little further tactical success and a daily cost in lives that was proportionately greater than that on the Somme.

Nivelle was sacked and the French army never again took the offensive lead, handing the baton to the British. The remarkable fact was that for all the German intelligence that had predicted Nivelle's offensive, there was no knowledge of the mutiny which might have galvanised the Germans to an all-out fight to the finish.

Once more both sides took stock, but this time for only a brief period. The British had been devising an audacious attack on another important ridge, this time south of Ypres. The Messines Ridge had been held by the Germans since 1914 and had commanding views to the north and south. For over a year the British had been tunnelling underneath it, digging five miles of tunnels in order to lay twenty-one enormous mines literally to blow the enemy off the position. Significantly, the attack was a limited operation. There was no intention to break through, merely to take the Messines Ridge and hold it. On 7 June 1917, 600 tons of explosive utterly destroyed any German resistance there could have been. The noise of the explosions was heard in London, and completely broke the enemy morale, killing thousands of troops almost simultaneously. Under a creeping barrage, British troops took the Ridge for remarkably few casualties; indeed, for the first time on the Western Front, defensive casualties had exceeded attacking ones, a significant milestone in the war and a pointer to future campaigns.

Within eight weeks the British were on the offensive again, this time at Ypres. The campaign signalled a move away, in effect, from the joint Allied offensives of the Somme and Arras, for the French troops could no longer be relied upon to take the lead as they had done for so much of the war.

Field Marshal Haig's objective was to sweep out of the Salient, attacking the German submarine pens on the Belgian coast. German U-boats were causing havoc in the Atlantic, sinking huge numbers of the British Merchant Navy that was transporting food and ammunition across the Atlantic. The Allies had their own blockade against the Germans which was proving massively damaging to their war economy; the Germans in turn had waged a similar war and the threat of starvation appeared in Britain as the number of U-boat attacks could not be significantly diminished. However, Haig was also convinced that the German army was close to breaking point and that another appreciable shove in that direction might just prove decisive.

The weight of British bombardments of the Western Front had continued to grow almost exponentially, and the ten-day bombardment to soften up the enemy prior to the infantry attack on 31 July was to prove no exception. Some 3,000 guns were ranged against the enemy and over four and a quarter million shells were expended before the infantry attacked on a twelve-mile front. Once more, the initial success was halted but while a stout defence had proved difficult to overcome, it had been the weather which had proved impossible to defeat. The great bombardment had proved a double-edged sword. On that first day, drizzly rain had turned into a downpour, and the battlefield, with drainage ditches destroyed by shellfire, became a veritable quagmire. Bringing up supplies and moving the guns was an exhausting process, as was casualty evacuation. Nor did the rain stop; it went on mercilessly for much of the next two weeks, halting the offensive until it could be renewed on 16 August. Once again there were gains, but in what was to prove one of the wettest summers in living memory the campaign floundered. This inspired a debate that has raged for ninety years, as to whether Haig should have halted the entire campaign.

For the rest of August, September, October and the beginning of November, the Allied troops ground their way forward, halting on 10 November, four days after the seizure of the village of Passchendaele, by which name the offensive has become known. Both sides were exhausted and with comparable casualties. It was to prove the last great attritional battle of the Great War, and showed once again the remarkable resilience of the British and Empire troops: some sixty-one VCs were awarded, more than one every other day. It also proved that the Germans were not quite at breaking point.

The fighting of that winter had not quite finished. A final offensive to be launched on 20 November near Cambrai was set into motion, with, on this occasion, the first attempted use of tanks en masse. No preliminary bombardment was used, in an endeavour to take the Germans completely by surprise. It was an idea achieved with a remarkable degree of success. Within hours, the British had punched a hole four miles deep into enemy territory, smashing through the seemingly impregnable Hindenburg Line with astonishing ease. Church bells pealed for the first time since a wartime ban had silenced them, and the euphoria in Britain, after the desperate fighting at Ypres, was tangible. Once again, initial high expectations would be rapidly dampened. Ten days later, the Germans committed twenty divisions to a counter-attack, using a new tactic of rapid infiltration, which they had successfully tried on the Eastern Front in September. This tactic was to use storm troopers who, attacking under a hurricane bombardment, bypassed opposing strongpoints so as to get in behind the enemy, attacking artillery positions and throwing the defenders into a state of confusion. Forward positions would be effectively cut off and mopped up by a large force following on. By this technique, most of the ground lost was recaptured and within a week the fighting simmered down.

The campaigns of 1917 were over, but the balance of power was now radically changing. In October, the beginning of what would become the Russian Revolution had effectively signalled the end of Russia's participation in the war, formally ended by the treaty of Brest-Litovsk signed in early March 1918. But the demise of one great nation on the Allied side had been replaced by another. The United States of America had joined the war in April 1917, and although her active involvement in it would take time – the first American troops would not be ready to take offensive action for a year – it signalled to Germany that the war had to be won, and won quickly, before the USA committed enough troops to turn the tide.

Pressure on Officers

Alan Thomas' Commanding Officer was a well known fire-eater, a man seemingly imperturbable and fearless in action. His name was Lieutenant Colonel William Dawson, DSO and three bars. Wounded in action nine times and mentioned in dispatches on four occasions he was, at the age of twenty-five, young to be a battalion commander, even by the standards of the Great War. Once, while in action, Lieutenant Thomas recalled him strolling around, smoking a pipe, encouraging the men, even cracking a joke; on another occasion when they were walking together in a very dangerous place, Dawson strode on ahead, pipe in his mouth. 'Had I been alone,' recalled Thomas, 'I could scarcely have dared to creep along even on all fours.' With Dawson, 'you felt safe.'

Dawson inspired respect and devotion amongst the men under him. 'Did he know what fear was, I often wondered,' wrote Thomas. 'Then, one day in 1917, I came across him alone. Our lines were being heavily bombarded and I was going along my sector to see if the men were all right. Turning into one of the bays, I ran into Dawson. He was standing in an odd position: instead of leaning with his back to the side of the trench, he was standing facing it, gripping the mud wall with crooked fingers. His expression was drawn, as though he were in pain . . .

'Are you hit, sir?' I asked.

'Hit?' He repeated the word as though he did not know what I meant. Then he went on: 'I suppose it's never occurred to you that

I could be frightened . . . when I'm with other people I don't show the fear I feel, that's all.'

'Other people' did not just mean NCOs and other ranks, but officers as well. The pressure on these men to appear unflappable and imperturbable was immense. Accusations of 'being windy' (fearful) were always hotly denied, and officers would frequently rather risk death than to be seen to baulk or break. Sergeant John Lucy, serving with the 2nd Royal Irish Rifles, recalled an incident when he was sitting with two officers in a house that was being peppered by German shells. At any moment he judged one would hit the building but still these officers continued to talk. 'I swore to myself at their pride and folly, and quaked. I could not show cowardice.' Months later, after Lucy had been commissioned, he spoke to one of the officers, a captain. 'We were waiting for you to get up and out of it first,' the officer admitted, 'but as you were a sergeant, we had to kind of hold ourselves in.'

There are two statistics that are very revealing about the officer class during the Great War. They are not found in the number of Victoria Crosses won, or the percentage of junior officers who went on to high command. Rather, they are to be found amongst the courts martial records. The first is that of more than 3,500 officers sent for General and Field General Courts Martial charged with a crime against military law, just twenty-one, or 6 per cent, were convicted of desertion while serving overseas. However, of all those thousands charged with offences, over 37 per cent were convicted of drunkenness.

The pressures on officers during the Great War were intense: to conduct themselves properly at all times; to show leadership and fearlessness; to hold and exercise responsibility correctly – these were all expectations placed on the shoulders of men holding the rank of second lieutenant or above. All these qualities were encapsulated in one over-arching word: duty.

'Doing one's duty' was the minimum requirement for an officer on whose frequently youthful shoulders the lives of many men under his command rested. Indeed, one of the anachronisms of the conflict was the age at which officers, as opposed to other ranks, could be enlisted in the first place. On the outbreak of war, recruitment of other ranks was set at eighteen, but it was stipulated that for service overseas a recruit had to be nineteen or above. For officers, the age was lower. They were invited to enlist at seventeen with the expectation that they would not be sent overseas until eighteen. Why there was this difference in age is not clear. It may have been felt that public school boys were naturally more mature. However, officers with six months' training were sent overseas aged as young as seventeen (and very occasionally younger still) to take command of a platoon of nominally sixty men, many old enough to be their father and perhaps even their grandfather.

The reason they were sent was the disproportionately heavy losses amongst the officer corps. The nominal strength of a British infantry battalion in the Great War was around 1,000 men of all ranks with roughly 1 to 40 the proportion of officers to men. However, approximately 1 in 19 of all deaths were officers, a figure that grew to 1 in 17 for those serving on the Western Front: the ratio for wounded was commensurately bad. Officers might survive many months when the battalion was not directly in combat, but, once over the top, they took their role in leading the men forward, and in directing operations to their immediate front. This made them extremely visible to snipers and machine-gunners, and they suffered accordingly.

The losses amongst officers during the great battles of attrition in 1916 and 1917 were heinous. A wounded officer returning to his unit often found few, if any, of the personnel he knew prior to his injury. The expectation amongst officers was not if, but when, death or injury would strike, and for junior officers that reality was the starkest of all.

The pressure on an officer to set an example in front of the men he commanded was simply accepted. Until later in the war, when commissions were granted to men from the ranks, a regular officer, especially a Commanding Officer, was almost invariably the product of the rigid class system of the time. He had gone to a public school before moving into the army and one of the military academies, or perhaps to university and the Officer Training Corps.

The correct characteristics for leadership were indoctrinated at school, where young men were taught to play up and play the game, implicitly learning that the interests of the individual were relegated or suppressed for the general good of the whole. In effect, by the time they were sent for officer training, it was taken for granted that the building blocks to becoming a subaltern were already in place. Such a man would not need to be taken and rebuilt in the mould of an army officer: the mould already existed; it simply needed to be filled with the correct particulars of military drill and tactics.

Once on the Western Front, the officer's own expectations of himself, combined with the traditions of the regiment, would ensure he stuck to his task when in action, as Second Lieutenant Dennis Neilson-Terry, of The Queen's (Royal West Surrey Regiment), knew: 'The only thing I ever fear really is not coming up to scratch when the moment arrives; unless you have perfect control over yourself out here you're not too much use, that's the one thing I hope for, a clear vision when the moment comes. It's no use wanting success, as I've wanted it all my life, and then to fail at the last moment through one's own fault.'

Such high expectations could lead to tragedy. During the first tank attack in September 1916, the nervous strain, coupled with the intense weight of expectation for the new weapon of assault, made several officers break down. In one company alone, an officer went mad and fired his pistol at the engine in order to make it go faster, and two others had nervous breakdowns. A fourth, a twenty-year-old officer named George Macpherson, took his own life. It was his first time in action and he ended the day convinced that he had failed. He shot himself, leaving a note that simply said, 'My God, I have been a coward.'

For those officers who continued to serve for any length of time, telltale signs of strain became all too apparent. Complaints of severe headaches and stomach problems were common, as well as stammering and trembling hands. Norman Collins, a twenty-year-old subaltern serving at Arras in 1917, found his teeth chattering when under bombardment. 'The sergeant was making me a cup of tea . . . I apologised to him and said, "It's cold, isn't it?" Actually, I knew perfectly well that my teeth were chattering because I didn't like the shells dropping closer and closer, and he said, "Yes, it is cold, sir", and passed it off. And then it stopped and you pulled yourself together.'

In recognition of the pressures placed upon them, officers were granted substantially more leave than other ranks. Mental break-down was also treated with greater sympathy, officers being relieved of their duties or command and sent down the line for rest and recuperation; incompetent officers were more likely to be removed quietly and without ceremony out of the line to serve out their time at the base or regimental depot in Britain. In all, 173 officers were cashiered from France and another 670 dismissed, a remarkably small proportion of the number of men given com-missions.

Many officers with impeccable service records could not take the strain of front line service for ever. Lieutenant Colonel George Stevens, commanding the 2nd Royal Fusiliers, broke under stress during the Battle of Arras. He had served over two years in France and had been awarded the Distinguished Service Order in 1916. In a letter home to his father, he wrote candidly, 'I am deeply sorry to say I have had a nervous breakdown and am now in the VI Corps Rest Station (officers). I never, never thought this would happen to me, but I cracked up all of a sudden and now I suppose all my prospects in the army are gone.' Stevens complained bitterly that he had not been given time to recuperate when others in the division had been offered a month's leave. 'They have been damnably unfair to me just because I wasn't always grousing.' By the end of the month, he was evacuated to England. 'The doctor says it will be three or four months before I shall be fit for France again. I feel so sick over the whole thing; if only I had been given leave for a short time to get right away from all the horrors here, I should have been all right now.' Stevens later recovered and took up his old command, though his intense hatred of the fighting only deepened as time went on.

Soldiers' Memories

Capt. Eric Whitworth, 12th South Wales Borderers

I discovered him on a wiring party in no-man's-land. A subaltern
and a few men were repairing the outside edge of our wire and, as
Company Commander, I went out to visit them. I found the
covering party lying in shell holes in front, and then turned to
make my way back to the trench. There was a thick mist and in a
few moments I had lost myself. I returned to the wirers and the
subaltern told Private Knight to show me the way back. I noticed
how unerringly he led me to the small gap in our wire through
which I had come, and soon afterwards I made him my orderly and
kept him at company headquarters.

Knight was only a boy of eighteen, but he proved a most
capable and devoted orderly. At night, he had a wonderful sense of
direction and instinct for choosing the best path: darkness was
perhaps less strange to him, as previously he had worked in the
mines in South Wales.

A great deal of work fell to him, owing to his skill as a guide:
he was, of course, constantly taking messages, and on nights
when we were to be relieved, he always went back to bring in
the leading platoon of the new company, but his chief work was
coming with me on the ordinary rounds of trench duty every
night. Indeed, he became also a companion, though quite
unconsciously, for we rarely, if ever, spoke of anything to break
down the barrier of our official relationship. Nor did he expect
or receive any reward, other than an occasional hot drink from

the sergeant major and some extra socks which had been sent out from my home for him.

Knight is now dead, officially missing. He was last with me in an attack. After I was wounded, but able to walk, he acted as my orderly for the last time and helped me back to the aid post. As he left me, I felt instinctively the contrast of all the attention and comfort before me, and the dangers and hardship of the next few days in front of him. There was nothing to be said, but I was able to fill up his water bottle from mine and give him some rations as he turned back to join the company. Four days later, the battalion attacked again, and the officer who had taken over the company was killed by a shell. Knight was never seen again, but was known to have been with him. During my convalescence, I wrote many letters to the homes of those that were killed or missing, but none with the same sense of loss and gratitude as to Knight's mother. One morning there arrived in a cardboard box some lilies of the valley from his garden, 'sent from his Mother in memory of Arthur Knight, a faithful orderly'.

The bonds that grew between officers and servants/orderlies were often incredibly close. The orderly might prepare food for his officer, although a man specifically detailed for the job usually cooked for the company's officers. Despite the best television efforts of Baldrick, an officer's servant in the television series Blackadder, *these meals could be surprisingly good, with dinners supplemented by luxuries sent from officers' families back home or from hampers sent directly from some of the leading stores, such as Fortnum & Mason.*

2/Lt Dudley Lissenburg, 97th Batt., RFA

Gunner Waterhouse is the officers' mess cook; a grand lad, who, though a habitual imbiber when given the opportunity, and an uncontrollable 'foul mouth', never let me down. He was a most loveable lad and an expert cook, who could produce a meal, 'à la Savoy', at a moment's notice, and though at times I had to almost drag him out of an estaminet, half an hour before officers' dinner, in a state of semi-intoxication, the meal was dead on time.

Lt George Mallory, 40th Siege Batt., RGA

By far the worst of our discomfort has been caused by our cook – quite a character this man; in spite of his sloppy overgrown appearance, with sloping shoulders and puffy cheeks, he retains a distinct boyishness – the boyishness of the 'regular pickle'; if there's a mess, one feels, he's sure to be in it. I don't whether it's worse to see him peeling his greasy potatoes and fingering raw meat with his filthy hands than to sit down before the dirty dishes he sends to our table.

Capt. Eric Whitworth, 12th South Wales Borderers

I am writing this quite comfortably on a bench and table with a cloth of sandbags, and there is a wooden seat to sleep on. Unfortunately, there is no place for the servants, who have to live and cook on our brazier on the steep stairs! However, they are used to this. I have just got a new company cook; he is a great improvement on the last, who got slack. However, a week in the ranks will probably cure him as, though an officer's servant or cook has less leisure time and is more constantly at work, still he is assured of good shelter, plenty of food and is more certain of seeing the war through! He also has the art of making a decent stew; very often, in fact most days, the meat ration only admits of stewing, unless one is dining out at Headquarters, where one is sure to find a recognisable joint and even a sirloin and undercut with curious regularity! But here in the front line, the less one eats the better; one is living for many hours a day in a stuffy dugout, the only outlet of fresh air being the short staircase which is always filled with servants who, besides cooking for us there, feed and sleep themselves.

Pte Daniel Sweeney, 1st Lincolnshire Rgt

You will be surprised to hear that I have stopped cooking for the officers. I have six new officers and one of them I did not like at all;

they wanted me to do impossible things. I told them that I had satisfied other officers for two years and as I could not satisfy them they had better find someone else to do the cooking. Perhaps I have done a silly thing by leaving the job but I will chance it. I know everything will be a lot harder for me and I shall have to do sentry and all other horrible things. We are expecting to go back for a rest soon so if all goes well I may get another staff job.

Capt. Eric Whitworth, 12th South Wales Borderers
My servant is irreplaceable. He has studied my likes and dislikes and my fads and always attended to them; he never allowed me to go out, whether for a ride or for the trenches, without my having all I needed; and with every move of the battalion, when I have many other things to think of, I could leave my personal effects to him entirely; he knew my possessions out here in every detail, and at any moment could tell me where my smallest possession was, and I don't know how I shall keep my things without him, and no longer shall I find myself the only officer having toast for breakfast when apparently nothing but a smoky fire is available! Often I had said of him that he was unsurpassed as a servant, but a bad soldier.

In March, the German army began its prepared retreat from the Somme to the newly constructed Hindenburg Line. The Germans had shortened their lines and at the same time taken up residence behind what they believed would be a near-impregnable position constructed with deep belts of barbed wire, heavily fortified machine-gun posts and concrete pillboxes. The countryside between the Somme and the Hindenburg Line was surrendered to the Allies.

2/Lt George Foley, 7th Somerset Light Infantry
The next few weeks were for all of us a time of pure and unalloyed delight. I should think that a man unexpectedly freed from an

unjust imprisonment could hardly feel more elated than we did at this new turn of events. To appreciate this, it must be clearly remembered what a complete deadlock trench warfare really was. Belts of well-sited barbed wire, strongly manned trenches and a thick concentration of artillery made the country behind the enemy lines a goal in our eyes well-nigh inaccessible. It became a sort of promised land, to which, after a long and bitter struggle, we might one day carve a way for those who survived us.

And in a single night, the enemy had vanished. We were free to roam for miles over ground which, but a few hours before, had seemed inviolable . . . Rich, the bombing officer, and I had a race for the honour of being the first Somerset officer to enter Le Transloy, which I believe I won by a neck.

The main road ran north and south through the village, and almost seemed a dividing line between the old battered world we were leaving and the comparative virgin soil that stretched before us. Beyond the road, the shell holes were few and far between. Although we were soon to find that the evacuated villages had been left in ruins by the Boche, they were at any rate surrounded by pleasant, smiling uplands and wooded knolls. Try as he might, the Hun could not set his seal of desolation on everything.

We soon began to hear alarming stories of booby traps cunningly set by the enemy before his retreat; of dugouts which blew up when an overzealous explorer reached the third step down, of 'souvenirs', to move which was to fire electrically an explosive charge, and of still more subtle slow-action mines, actuated after many days by clockwork, or by the action of acid gradually eating through the holding wires.

Sgt William Peacock, 1st South Wales Borderers

They were such a crafty, cunning lot, up to all manner of devices to kill or wound you. One man got into a bed which blew up and killed him, another went to play a piano in a house and it blew his hands off. Another man went to pull a clock down from a wall and it blew his two fingers off. You might go down into a cellar and when you trod on one of the steps, up you will go. Houses have been blown up by delayed mines a week after the German have left the place. A party of men were sleeping in the kitchen of one of the houses in Cambrai when it went up and killed eighteen of them. Yes, they were a crafty lot, the Germans, we learnt a lot off them, I can tell you.

Pte Joseph Baynes, 8th Gloucestershire Rgt

In a room was an old bed with a dirty mattress on it. The first two chaps in the room jumped on it and claimed it for the night. We others had to sleep on the floor. When the chaps were out, my pal and I found the innards of an old clock, no face, but the springs were all right and it ticked. We got a piece of wire and hung it under the bed. Well, the two chaps got on the bed and we all kipped down. After a while all was quiet and one of the chaps on the bed heard the ticking and no doubt thought of booby traps. He gave an almighty yell and in seconds flat the room was empty, including my pal and I. Now in these events you will always find a brave one and he lay down on his belly and crawled back to the farmhouse. He discovered the old clock and came running out. Of course, no one would own up and, if we had confessed, I don't think I would be telling the tale.

Sgt Harold Bisgood, 1/2nd London Rgt (Royal Fusiliers)

I paid a visit to the battlefield of Gommecourt where exactly nine months ago we lost practically all our battalion. I went right over the field where we started on 1 July and carried right through Gomme-court, now a mass of mangled ruins. One of the largest and most dense woods in France now represented by only a few shattered tree trunks and myriads of holes. Passing over the ground between the old lines, we even now found bones, bits of cloth and gas helmets belonging to our boys killed and never buried. The civilians had buried quite a number of our men and named the graves.

2/Lt George Foley, 7th Somerset Light Infantry

The camp next to ours was built on the site of the old front line of 30 June 1916. On the evening of 15 March, we were whiling away an idle hour after tea, when we were startled by a terrific concussion. We rushed out, and, seeing a cloud of smoke over the other camp, thought that a big shell must have fallen there. On going over to see the damage, however, we found the whole place a complete wreck, and in the midst of it all was an immense crater. A mine, laid before the first offensive, had, for some inexplicable reason, waited until this moment before exploding, and the result was the chaos we saw before us. The King's Liverpools were occupying the camp, but by a great stroke of luck practically the whole battalion was attending a performance of the Very Lights [the divisional concert party], so that casualties were comparatively light.

War Diary, 12th King's Liverpool Rgt

At 5.50 p.m. an old mine situated between the officers' huts and the main camp exploded, completely wrecking the whole camp. Assistance was hurriedly obtained, and occupants of damaged huts released. Three officers and nine other ranks were killed and fifty-two wounded. One man last seen crossing where the crater appeared could not be accounted for.

Sgt Harold Bisgood, 1/2nd London Rgt (Royal Fusiliers)

I have to go to Poperinge on business so shall visit our old pal Charlie Chaplin at the cinema (6th Divisional Cinema).

I visited the cinema at Poperinge and saw Charlie Chaplin in a six-part piece, almost forgot the war, but not quite as a shell screamed through the canvas roof of the cinema at 9.20 p.m.

2/Lt George Foley, 7th Somerset Light Infantry

A large wooden theatre was built for the Very Lights and christened 'The Coliseum'. Here during our short spells of rest we were able to forget for a few hours the dangers and discomforts of the trenches. The shows were extremely good, and I can testify how thoroughly we appreciated them, and what a splendid asset such a place of amusement was to us. No performers could have wished for a less critical audience. The least thing was enough to amuse us. One song, or at least part of it, sticks in my mind. It was sung to a catchy tune and will show what simple stuff sufficed us:

> Up on the duckboards it's lovely to go
> Specially when there is fog, rain or snow,
> I met a Sapper, a terrible swell,
> He said, 'You're looking as muddy as hell.'
> He said, 'We're building deep dugouts for you.'
> I said, 'That's splendid, if only it's true.'
> Down came a shell, and we gave a great lurch –
> Lone Tree to Saillisel Church.

> *Chorus*
> Lone Tree to Saillisel Church
> All on a winter's day;
> We stepped on to the duckboards,
> And started right away;
> When we got to the end of the boards
> He asked me to stop for a drink;
> But I said, 'They're shelling the Chateau,
> So – I don't think.

Capt. QM Ernest Kirkland Laman, 2nd South Wales Borderers

We have had the 'Ginks' concert party over from the 87th Field Ambulance and another from the 89th FA – both good shows, especially the former, topping 'girls' they both have. The divisional band also came over once, and the brigade sports were a great event. The battalion didn't shine particularly. The great event of the day outside the obstacle race was the Gallipoli Race, with a yard start (in 100) for every year's service over seven. The only competitors being those at the Landing. Various tin cups had been turned out by a silversmith of the RE for prizes, and there were two for the Gallipoli Race.

About thirty starters lined up including Gen. Lucas, Col. Ellis – Border Rgt, Lt Col. Taylor – 87th FA, Capt. Dent – RI Fus., Capt. Graham – 87th FA, Capt. Blake – our MO, Capt. Fraser – 87th FA, Capt. & QM Simpson – KOSB who had twenty-six-yard start and won easily. Managed to get 2nd place myself with a yard start in front of Capt. Fraser Raine who was third. Clearly shows that a yard start for each year of service even above seven is too much. My prize was a jam tin bomb on a wooden pedestal. An exact copy of the tin bombs we made out of jam tins on the Peninsula in the early days, filled with horseshoe nails, shrapnel bullets and any old iron and 'ammonal' as the explosive, with a bit of fuse sticking out. On the outside of the tin is a brass plate with the inscription 'Gallipoli Race 2nd Prize' and another on the base explaining what the article is – absolutely the best prize of the lot.

Sgt Walter Sweet, 1/2nd Monmouthshire Rgt
In the evening a corporal and a man from 'A' Company came looking for me. They had dug up a strange rifle and wanted me to identify it as no one knew what it was. I had no difficulty in naming it as soon as it was in my hand. I knew it was a Canadian Ross Rifle and I proved it by scraping the mud off where I knew the name was engraved – just in front of the breech. They had evidently been digging in the old 1915 battlefield where the Canadians caught the first lot of gas.

Lt Francis Buckley, 1/7th Northumberland Fusiliers
The German ammunition was mostly stored in large wooden boxes, and we had to get rid of it. This was done by emptying the boxes into the nearest shell holes, so that the ground outside was littered with ammunition. In one of these shell holes, amongst a lot of rubbish of this kind, I found four old pewter dishes and two

pewter spoons. They had been heaved out of the dugout along with the rest of its contents. One of the plates was dated 1733, and all were marked with a foreign maker's stamp. They afforded, when cleaned, a rather unusual decoration for the walls of the mess room. This little collection was disposed of 'under Divisional and Brigade arrangements' but I managed to secure the spoons.

The Germans had often stripped homes of furniture and crockery to make their own accommodation more comfortable, with beds, chairs, pictures, even grandfather clocks taken down underground. However, digging trenches, scavenging round old dugouts or churned-up ground, soldiers often found not just contemporary souvenirs but ancient ones, too. One of the most extraordinary stories of the Great War was the archaeological finds discovered on the Western Front. The French alone were reputed to have dug over 6,000 miles of trenches, frequently cutting through areas of historical interest. Bronze Age axe heads were found, as were Roman jewellery, pottery and knives. Some artefacts were more recent, including Napoleonic rifles and cannonballs.

Lt Francis Buckley, 1/7th Northumberland Fusiliers
Lieutenant Colonel G. R. B. Spain of the 6th Northumberland Fusiliers came to command the brigade during the absence of Brigadier General Riddell on leave. He was a man of remarkable erudition and a collector of prints and other things. And I soon found that we had many things in common and many interesting talks I had with him on a variety of subjects.

We discovered together several early flint implements and arrowheads about Serques, and he told me a lot about the early Stone Age which interested me greatly and set me looking for these interesting relics wherever we happened to be quartered. At Coigneux I found a series of early implements in which the British Museum took considerable interest.

Pte Will Bird, 42nd Bttn (Royal Highlanders)
About one o'clock we heard one of the Hun's 'freight trains' arriving, the huge 'coal box' type that went deep before exploding. An anxious five minutes ensued, but there was not another. After a time I told Tommy I was going to crawl over and see how big a crater the shell had made . . . it would be something to kill time, so off I went. Ten yards of crawling put me where I could stand up, and soon I was over to where the huge crater had been made. It would accommodate a bungalow and was shaped like a vast bowl. Bits of metal glinted in the sun. Then, at the very centre, at least ten feet below earth level, I saw a glitter different from the others. Curiosity got the better of me. I edged over the crater lip and carefully felt my way down, watching for any hot metal. It was slow going, as the chalky soil was powdery, and I did much sliding. At last I was at the spot and used a boot toe to knock away earth from the metal thing. In a moment I became excited. The shell burst had revealed the very tip of a sword blade, buried perpendicular in the earth. I had to crawl from the crater and explore until I found a sharp stick like a tent peg. I used it to excavate and after a long session I had the sword loosened and pulled it forth. It was a Roman sword, with an embossed pattern on the hilt.

It would never do to let the lads see it. Some others might go over and dig. There would be tales of all kinds, leading to investigation. Finally I tried to fix it under my tunic, but it would not stay there. And what could I do with it going into action? I stood and debated a dozen ideas and in the end went over to where a post of some sort had been broken off close to the ground. After a long effort I managed to sink the sword beside the post, covering over all sight of the hilt with tramped-down earth, and then I went back to my platoon.

Will Bird returned in November 1918 while absent without leave. He found the sword and eventually managed to take it back home to Canada.
In 1998, I discovered a coin right on the German front line at Ovillers, on the Somme. Accepting that it was probably German, I went

*home and cleaned it up. It turned out to date from 1754, the reign of
Louis XV. Dropped by a farmer 250 years ago, it had survived the
Somme battle intact.*

---

*Most soldiers paid little heed to matters of history or culture when they
were out of the line. They were interested in spending what little money
they had, and, in the case of Charles Heare and his small group of
friends, writing to those back home who might send a small parcel of
gifts that they could share between them. In Britain, there was no
shortage of people willing to help a soldier in need, a small detail well
known to the recipients.*

Pte Charles Heare, 1/2nd Monmouthshire Rgt
At Poperinge we all had our photographs taken and exchanged
them with one another as well as addresses of girls. All the boys
then send letters and photographs telling these girls of lonely
soldiers short of smokes. I had no end of letters and cigarettes. The
letters said how sorry they were to hear I was short of cigarettes,
but as I didn't smoke I had my suspicions as my friend Black used
to say 'more fags for me'. One girl in Cheltenham wrote to me
thanking me for my photo, sending me cigarettes and saying how
sorry she felt that I had lost all my brothers. I caught Black this
time and so his cigarettes ended. 'But you ought to have your
photograph taken regularly,' says Black.

Capt. Eric Whitworth, 12th South Wales Borderers
We had a wonderful present some time back: six aluminium baths
from the Empress Club, London. This must be the Ladies Club, I
think. These have enabled the whole battalion to get a bath at
times when it would otherwise be absolutely impossible. Today,
for example, all my company have had a hot bath and clean socks,

shirts and pants; the bath is just put in a hut and water heated in a field kitchen; and one bath reserved for officers. It is a great thing; for a few hours at least they will be free from lice. This problem has become terrible. Not even the cleanest men can keep free from them. The doctor lectured to officers and NCOs on it the other day, and I handed it on to my company today, and not one could hold up his hand as being free from them. Some have almost sleepless nights from lice, and the irritation leads to boils. The various powders are of no real effect, and it is a problem one feels it is hopeless to grapple with, though I never realised till today how serious it was.

Pte Frederick Aylett, 133rd Field Ambulance, RAMC

The dugout had formerly been used by the French. It was an extremely long, narrow place running lengthwise under the bank of a valley. The men were packed in so closely that once you had lain down for the night it was next to impossible to get out. It was so narrow that men lying crossways found their feet in the small of another man's back who might be lying opposite. Then the lice!! They abounded everywhere. They dropped like the gentle dew of heaven from the roof, and crawled in the cracks and upon the floor. They were small red fellows and black spotted ones; there were great fat grey beggars, too gross and well fed to be able to move. Twice daily we examined our shirts, sitting on top of the dugout, stripped to the waist and going down the seams, cracking the lice with our thumbnails. Occasionally a juicy one would spurt in one's face. We had a good scratch of about half an hour's duration before returning to rest each evening, and for many a day we had marks and spots all over our bodies.

Pte Charles Heare, 1/2nd Monmouthshire Rgt

Although the mud is bad and the rain we get as lousy as ever. One fellow suggests we all take our shirts and trousers off, rub fat salt bacon on them, put them by some water and when the chats go off our clothes for a drink, run away with our clothes. That's one way of getting rid of them but we don't try it.

Lt Leslie Sanders, RGA attd Field Survey Coy, RE

The campaign that is opening now, it seems to me, will be the bloodiest in history. For nearly three years, both sides have been straining every nerve to perfect and accumulate the means of destruction. They will be expended now with the most lavish prodigality. All the horrors in history will pale into insignificance beside the hell that will rage over Europe during the days of the coming struggle.

I dread beyond most things a peace bought about by any other cause than military victory. The Boche knows as well as we that our ultimate victory is certain. If he staves it off, in whatever way – even by granting our terms – it is a victory for him . . . I shall be sorry if he is starved into submission. That would give him a leg to stand on: 'It wasn't our army's fault: it was our cursed populace, that didn't know how to take up a hole in their belts.' And so our sons get the job to do again, and the blood of those who have perished up to now is betrayed. 'The War that will end War?' Perhaps. And maybe not.

Capt. William Ferrie, 196th Machine Gun Coy, MGC

The scene of desolation is undoubtedly depressing. To live among ruins, to see on each day's tour of inspection – even if you walk for miles – nothing else but ruins – begins to weigh on the spirit, and, in short, it induces the 'blues'. Of course you may be in the blues anywhere and it is always the result of not being usefully and energetically employed, and the remedy here is the same as anywhere else; namely, to put your nose to your work and give up moralising.

So this is what I do. I am now properly interested in my work. I am quite anxious to win the war for Britain, France, Russia, Italy, America, China, Serbia, Montenegro, Japan and Portugal. If Cuba and Guatemala come in too they will find in me their obedient servant. We are on trial. The side that endures the most, and suffers the best, and most of all works the hardest, will win the victory. I, having made the quarrel mine long before Brazil thought of it, and being notoriously 'dour', am disposed to show myself the better man of the two with the people over the way.

Cpl Arthur Henry Cook, 1st Somerset Light Infantry
The following gives some idea of what each man carries into action. Pack containing cardigan, cap comforter, ground sheet, mess tin, iron rations, unconsumed portion of the day's rations, knife, fork and spoon, rifle bayonet, 170 rounds SAA [small arms ammunition], two No. 5 grenades, two P bombs, two aeroplane flares, three sandbags, box respirator at the alert, entrenching tool and handle and a full water bottle. Other articles to be carried in the company would be two Very light pistols, a number of illuminating and SOS cartridges, wire cutters, etc. That is a picture of a soldier in the Great War as he plodded his miserable way through seas of viscous mud, weighted down with all the above equipment, stumbling, slipping, ever expecting death; of the constant expectation of attack and the tremendous nerve strain and tension when moving against a concealed enemy.

Anonymous letter by 'Tom', a stretcher-bearer, Arras
April 1917
Now let me tell you a bit about the largest battle in the world's history. You would gather from my letters that I was about to 'move' again, or in other words, go over the top. It did not come off as soon as we expected, so that was why I managed to drop you a line on Easter Saturday or was it Good Friday? No matter. On Saturday we moved to a deep dugout in 'battle' order, that is, without our spare kit. Never shall I forget the roar of the guns, hundreds of them. On Easter Sunday we had nothing to do except load up with bombs, ammunition, rifle grenades, Very lights and other weapons of war. We stretcher-bearers packed our bags full of

bandages and shell dressings. That done, we smoked and sang and *thought*. I was wondering what you were all doing, and I kept looking at my watch and guessing so and so was happening at the various times, six, seven and eight. I thought of the Holy Communion services being held, and of the prayers that were being offered on our behalf. At eleven, I fancied the choir singing 'Jesus Christ is risen today' and all the beautiful Easter hymns. Again at six, I wondered how many bells were being rung, and wished I could have made another. No use wishing, though. Night came, and I noticed more men saying their prayers than usual, and it was rumoured that the chaplain was coming round to hold a short service, but he did not turn up. I was very sorry, for the fellows would have responded. However, we sang hymns and sometimes broke off into some old songs.

Midnight came, and the order ran down the dugout, 'Get your equipment on.' That done, we filed out and had a march over the ground we recently took, into some assembly trenches. Everything was done as quietly as possible, so that the enemy would not know we were there. We deepened the trench, and then we sat down, and talked about cold and rain! I was frozen to the marrow, and we could not stir because no movement was to be made. So the time rolled slowly by, and all the time our guns were pounding away, and it was very few who had not got a severe headache. I can vouch for mine being 'rocky'. 2, 3, 4, 5 and 6.30 a.m. came and went, and then we saw four tanks lumbering over the shell-swept ground. Then the fun began. Fritz began to shell us and up went our temperatures a few degrees. (Shelling always makes one warm.) Down came the metal, mingling with the rain and sleet. No casualties so far. Then there was such a crash, and I tried to look but it was dark. Am I blinded? I thought. No, only buried. Next I felt a shovel striking my arm, and I tried to move but couldn't. A few more digs from the shovel, and another heave and out come my 'nut'. 'Are you hurt?' everyone near me was saying, but thank God I was right as rain, only for a shaking. My pal was in a like plight, but we both got 'normal' again after a while. We moved away from there, and bless me if the same thing did not occur again. I began to think Fritz had got us two 'taped'.

Ah well, nothing else happened, and the order came ringing down, 'Over the top, boys', and up we jumped, every man as one. A finer sight I never saw. Wave after wave in perfect order marching into the jaws of death. Down went many a good husband and son, but on went the remainder without a flinch. We stretcher-bearers were soon busy putting dressings on the poor fellows who had been hit, and ever and anon the cries went up. Oh, it was awful. Our platoon officer and his servant got a leg blown off and I put a tourniquet on each and left them for the RAMC to carry back, but both of them were hit again and killed. Our orders were to carry on until we reached our objective, and bandage all, and then start to carry. Some of the poor fellows prayed for us to take them back, but we could not.

My pal was mortally wounded only a yard from me. I showed him his wife's photo, and read her last letter to him, and part of St John 17 and so passed away a real Christian soldier, and I could not but think of the Easter message as I saw the smile on his face as he died. 'Oh Death, where is thy sting?' It was with a heavy heart and wet eyes that I left him with the snow falling on his body. All around lay dead and wounded, and I did what I could for the latter, giving water to those wounded in the legs and arms, but flinging the water bottle away from those wounded in the stomach. You will gather how we suffered when I tell you that out of forty-two in our platoon who mounted the parapet, only eleven are left and I am one of them . . .

Your soldier boy, Tom

The fighting around Arras produced one of the heaviest daily casualty rates of the entire war, with over 4,000 killed, wounded or missing each

*day between 9 April and 17 May, when the battle ended. This rate is a
third higher than that of the Somme, and almost twice as heavy as that
suffered at Passchendaele three months later. The battle also confirmed
what many knew, and reaffirmed to others, that while the Germans
were not beaten, they were suffering greater and greater privations.*

Pte Herbert Chase, 2/1st (London) Field Ambulance, RAMC

This time my squad occupied a German dugout near a place
known as Pine Trench. The Germans had only been driven out the
preceding day and had evidently left in a hurry. They left behind
several souvenirs including three German loaves, a mouth organ,
two refills of solidified methylated spirit, a haversack, a newspaper
dated 7th and one or two letters from Germany not even opened.
One of these letters we found to be from a mother to her son and it
said she regretted she could not send him an Easter cake but the
shortage of flour prevented it.

Lt John Godfrey, 103 Field Coy, RE

Our fellows 'went over the top' as the saying is, raided successfully,
secured much booty, and returned. When the booty was examined
later, among a host of helmets, rifles, packs, etc, was found a small
parcel addressed to Herr Fritz (private, Schlinkenslopcher Rifle
Regiment) and labelled 'from your loving wife'. Inside the parcel
was found a small – a very small – rasher of bacon!

---

*Those who fought and survived the Battle of Arras, like every other battle
of the Great War, marvelled at how they come through barrages of both
artillery and machine-gun fire when so many fell around them. Some men
became superstitious, others fatalistic, believing that if their name or
number was on a bullet, then there was nothing they could do to avoid it.
Some men fought for months and years confident they would come through*

and then suddenly appeared to become prescient about their immediate future, predicting death. Survival depended on luck, and there were plenty of men whose luck simply ran out. There were men who died from non-war-related injuries, not just illness or disease, or even undiagnosed physical ailments, but who died unusual deaths such as in storms and lightning strikes — hardly surprising when millions of men stood in front line trenches, holding their lightning-conducting rifles and bayonets.

Gnr Ernest Drane, 197th Siege Batt., RGA

A squad of enemy planes came over, bombing us. Poor Bombardier Dobson killed and Tirrell and Parsons wounded. Only yesterday we saw some crosses on a lorry and Dobson said, 'I wonder if one of those crosses is for me.' I wonder who will tell his girl; he was single and I went with him to help select a gold brooch before we left England — his last present to her.

Lt John Godfrey, 103 Field Coy, RE

A new subaltern joined up, called Dixon: a nice man, but very quiet, not to say depressed. He told me that he felt that he was not going to last long, and I actually noted this down in my diary on the day he said it:

'Dixon arrived to take Green's place. A pleasant Irishman, evidently a bit of a pessimist. He says he has a presentiment he is not going to survive this war! I am glad I am not cursed with such gloomy forebodings.'

An infernal shame: Dixon was killed last night by a shell, and his orderly with him . . . They brought him in this morning, and I had to arrange his burial. We managed to knock up a bit of a coffin. He was in a horrid mess, but when he was finally laid out in the coffin he looked quite peaceful, very pale, of course. Then I had a hunt for a padre: this meant a lot of painful walking over Kemmel. However, the funeral went off all right. Poor old lad, he was only in the company a week.

Pte Sydney Fuller, 8th Suffolk Rgt

One of our men was wounded beside me in a rather unusual manner. He suddenly complained that something had 'stung' him on the left shoulder, and on removing his tunic, etc, found that a bullet had entered at the top of the shoulder, and had passed down in the front of his chest, under the skin, coming out near the centre of his chest. He was standing upright when he received the wound. I also saw one 'C' Coy man who had been wounded in the hand and had had a hole drilled through the side of his tin hat by one bullet. He said that his tin hat was blown almost off his head by the explosion of the shell, and as he put up his hand to pull the hat straight again, the bullet smashed his fingers and passed through the tin hat without, however, injuring his head.

Maj. Bertram Brewin, 16th Royal Scots (Lothian Rgt)

Richard Lodge, a son of an Edinburgh professor, was a captain, an awfully good lad, some 6 foot 5, and he was hopeless in the line owing to his height. He told me that he had given up trying to take cover as the pain he suffered from so much stooping was far worse than being hit, so he used to stalk around at his full height, showing nearly to his waist above the parapet. I really think the Boche took him for a dummy – the gifted R. Academicians had sculpted and painted busts of men stuck on poles, and one used to carry them round the line to encourage the Boche to snipe at them (they really were most natural), and as the Boche was pretty cunning he refused to be drawn. Anyway Lodge got a free and unsurpassed view of no-man's-land and the Boche lines, and was in great request by Stephenson on any question concerning them. The irony of fate was that he was killed in a dugout above Roisel, near Peronne, by a direct hit from a shell on the dugout entrance. He was a very fine lad.

Sapper Albert Martin, 41st Signal Coy, RE

I was given up for lost. I was crouched down in the trench with my back to 'Jerry' when a small shell landed on the parapet, a matter of only inches from my head. The trench came in on top of me, and but for the fact that it was strongly revetted, I should have been completely buried. When the smoke and dirt had cleared away, the other fellows were surprised to see me pick myself up unhurt. Aitken said, 'That one had got your name on it, Joe.' 'Yes,' I replied, 'but it was the wrong number.'

Pte Sydney Fuller, 8th Suffolk Rgt
I helped to lay a telephone line from Battalion Headquarters to 'A' Coy. The company was in a redoubt which lay on a hill behind the Albert–Peronne road. While engaged in this work, I picked up a shell fuse on which was the number 14598 – my regimental number. Someone remarked that I was quite safe from shellfire now, as the shell made for me had already been fired.

Lt Gerald Brunskill, 1/5th Royal Sussex Rgt (Cinque Ports)
Some days ago when there was a heavy wind blowing, during the night a tree crashed on a tent in the transport lines and crushed under it RQMS Abraham and Sergeant Hunt. The former died in a Casualty Clearing Station the day after the accident and the latter succumbed to his injuries today. This was a terrible accident and the victims are all the more of a loss to the battalion as they had both been out with us since the beginning.

Lt Edward Allfree, 111th Siege Batt., RGA
We had one casualty. Bombardier Stevenson was unfortunately hit by a falling pavé stone, which was blown high in the air from a shell burst in the road, and fell on him about 300 yards away. He died the next day. I saw him fall, but could not understand the cause, as it seemed so many seconds after the last shell burst. The stone must have gone an enormous height before it struck him. Everyone in the battery was most awfully sorry to lose Stevenson. I remember he was one of the very few men who

stayed to receive Holy Communion after Church Parade on the
Sunday previous.

Lt R. Macgregor, 5th Queen's Own Cameron Highlanders

The more I think of it, the more determined I am that God alone
protected me. Seventeen times during four days I was hit by
shrapnel. One piece about four inches long lodged in my haversack, which saved my spine. Another time I was hit by a branch of
tree that laid me flat. My steel helmet saved me injury. It is strange
that I should be spared, when so many better men went down.
Still, it is fate, the Will of God. Thank Him for it.

Lt John Bellerby, 1/8th West Yorkshire Rgt (Leeds Rifles)

I was cured of any belief that it was admissible to appeal to the
Almighty for any aid, personal, or general, in fighting . . . To me
it was manifestly senseless to link a God of love in any way with
the kind of calculated murder I had been engaged in. How could
one invite any member of the Trinity, for example, to pay heed and
cooperate as one was coolly preparing to shatter the lovely red scalp
of a German officer? Admittedly, it was love of country that was
the chief originating motive but the method was that of an
executioner. The crime of those who were to be dispatched was
only that they also loved their country. After this introduction to
trench life, I found prayer impossible and absurd. I never again
prayed in the context of battle – not because I was shocked,
perturbed or conscience-stricken, for I was not emotionally
affected in any significant degree after having once accepted
the role of executioner – I just could not see any logic in expecting
a God of love to be interested in this role.

Pte Sydney Fuller, 8th Suffolk Rgt

The German prayer book found in the pillbox at Poelcappelle – on
the cover, 'Mit Jesus in der Feld', and inside a coloured picture of
Christ looking with pity on a dead German soldier. The same

picture as in our own Field Prayer Book, 'With Jesus in the Field'. The only appreciable difference was in the uniform of the dead soldier – German in one, khaki in the other – and the feeling experienced on seeing that picture compared with one of our own, that the whole war was a horrible mistake.

Capt. Eric Whitworth, 12th South Wales Borderers
It is curious how Sunday inevitably completely disappeared; days out of the trenches are rest days; days in are days of work; that is one's frame of mind unless, of course, in billets as here, when we have no work on Sunday and a church parade. As a matter of fact, there was a voluntary service on Sunday morning and thirty-four of my company went; but very few altogether. This is very curious as the men's letters – almost in every case – are full of expressions of trust in the Almighty both re themselves and their relatives at home.

Signaller Charles Birnstingl, 1/9th The London Rgt (Queen Victoria Rifles)
If the journey up to the line is tedious and slow, the return is rapid enough, every man pushes himself along as quickly as he possibly can, and it is only when he has left shells behind that the pace slackens, and he realises just how weary he is. Firstly they wearily drag themselves into camp, in the early hours of the morning, to be welcomed by those who did not go up to the lines . . . then comes porridge or soup, tea, and if one isn't too tired – a wash – then roll up in a blanket and sleep the clock around.

Cpl Arthur Cook, 1st Somerset Light Infantry
The battalion move to Arras and are accommodated in a shed; it is hoped no shells or bombs will be dropped on this place, for not only does it accommodate the whole of the battalion, but thousands of shells as well, also thousands stacked around the building outside. One high explosive on this place and up goes the 1st

Somerset Light Infantry for ever! Why on earth they put a complete battalion in such danger completely beats me, you expect to be blown to kingdom come in the trenches, but when you are out for a rest period, you expect some kind of security.

Sapper Albert Martin, 41st Signal Coy, RE
Now that I am so far from the line, in a spot where the heavy guns can only be heard when the wind is in the right direction, where there is no sign of war, and where the rural occupations of peacetime plod along as if totally unconscious of the awful horrors that are taking place only a few leagues away, I feel my old love for the countryside reviving. I was half afraid it was dead, killed by spending so many months in about the most monotonous and soul destroying region imaginable.

Signaller Charles Birnstingl, 1/9th The London Rgt
(Queen Victoria Rifles)
I went to bed this morning to the sound of cocks crowing, but for some time could not sleep, lying awake enjoying the sounds of lowing cows, the bells on the horses being harnessed in the farmyard, and a fine-toned bell with a deep, sonorous note, ringing for Mass.

The country as we marched from the station last night looked so fresh in the moonlight and smelt so clean that one forgot the horror of the past week, and I am sure the one feeling uppermost in all our minds, as we marched along singing 'The Pilgrims' Chorus', was one of thankfulness at being alive. I awoke today from a comfortable bed and found the sun shining brightly on a whitewashed farmhouse and its garden gay with dahlias. I'm sitting now in the orchard revelling in the glorious sunshine. Every house in the village looks clean and the people seem unusually pleasant; one could easily imagine oneself in an English village; all the gardens are neat and bounded by trimmed hedges.

Pte Charles Heare, 1/2nd Monmouthshire Rgt

It is the end of our day marching, getting near the line we are to move by night now, our new RSM is at Arras when the companies are crawling in, word is passed back to get the men in anyhow as they have tonight and tomorrow to rest before moving again. They are coming into Arras in some shape. Twos, threes, some fours, sore feet, chaffed legs, sore shoulders. The RSM stopped the boys and started to put them in fours, 'What the hell is the game, the shape these men are marching, it's a disgrace to the British Army.' 'Go away,' says Sergeant Major George who has no fear, 'these boys have been out here since '14, you humbug. Slogging it for you to be preserved in England.'

One of the best soldiers in France is George, always smiling. If you are feeling rough on the march he will take your rifle. 'Try and stretch it now lads,' he will say. He is six foot and fourteen stone. Like a horse. A good athlete.

Lt Carrol Whiteside, 7th Border Rgt

One heartily, and forcibly, agrees with one of our most apt Tommies, who remarked apropos of this continued route marching: 'It's not the fucking marchin'' I object to, it's the fucking fucking about!'

Pte Edward Wanless, 1/5th Border Rgt

Well, this is the flaming limit. After marching for five days – from the Somme district – you can imagine what the poor fellows' feet and legs are like. Well, to pile the bloody agony on, they give one hour's pack drill to the men who couldn't stick the marches. That means to say anybody dropping out on a route march has to do this bloody thing as if he has committed a crime.

Sgt Harold Bisgood, 1/2nd London Rgt (Royal Fusiliers)

Started on march for Poperinge with all our possessions on our backs. Joke: Little Boy: 'Oh, Daddy, what are soldiers for?' Daddy: 'To hang things on, my dear.'

A day or two later, the CO and I had a long ride together and he acknowledged for the first time that, after all his work and efforts, his subalterns missed something he could never give them; and this small incident shows clearly what it is.

The popular view of senior First World War officers is that they were singularly lacking in intelligence and were disliked by those serving beneath them. This was far from the case. Many senior officers, including Army, Corps and Divisional Commanders, were highly respected, even adored by junior officers and the ranks alike. However, as with all professions, there were exceptions to the rule.

Capt. Eric Whitworth, 12th South Wales Borderers

Such was our divisional general [Ruggles-Brise], a man of justice, a soldier who inspired in all ranks a feeling of confidence and loyalty, and not merely a picturesque figurehead, unknown and misunderstood. A man whose personality breathed kindness but never weakness, and lastly a soldier who, while he showed us that he understood our difficulties, made us feel that they were there to be overcome at all costs.

His successor was a man whose equal for charm of personality I have rarely, if ever, met in any sphere of life. He was older than most brigadiers appointed to the New Army, but a man of great activity. He had been wounded while in command of his regiment in France and decorated with the CB and DSO. To many, he has two great characteristics as a general: his study of the men, their capabilities and necessities, was incessant, and like all great soldiers, the idea of the impossible was abhorrent to him. During our last musketry course in England, he was on the range morning and afternoon. A few men, owing to shortness in the arm, had been allowed to keep the left hand under the magazine instead of in front of it. His keen eye saw this at once, and he insisted on the correct position, showing himself how it could be attained by a slight adjustment of position.

On the line of march, he was not content merely to remain on his horse and watch the battalion go by. He would dismount, walking along with the men, studying their physique and condition at the end of the march, the fitting of the equipment, and here and there in the hot weather showing men how to open their tunics to breathe more easily.

The new GOC (Brigadier F. P. Crozier, DSO) was different in every respect from his predecessors. He lacked the presence, charm and the dignity of them both. He was essentially a hustler, who probably overestimated the results obtained by energy alone, and his authority was not strengthened by the issue of impossible orders, which could not be carried out owing to conditions he never saw. No doubt he had hustled his own battalion with great success, but his reputed boast on arrival, that he had never obtained discipline in his own battalion until a man had been shot, was indicative of his own characteristics rather than of strength or greatness as a commander of men. Not that the efficiency of the brigade suffered much under his command; in many details it was more efficient than it had ever been before, but this was from fear rather than as a response to any real leadership.

2/Lt Harold Jones, 12th South Wales Borderers

Early one morning, soon after we had our trenches in fair order again, I was looking out over no-man's-land with my eyes glued to my glasses, when I heard a voice alongside: 'What are you doing, sir?' Thinking it was my sergeant or corporal I did not trouble to turn but mumbled something about watching Jerry. Again the voice and again the same answer. Then the voice: 'Are you asleep, sir?' I replied rather shirtily, 'Damned near it.' Then the voice, now like thunder: 'Come here, sir!' I turned and to my horror found myself facing General Crozier and his staff in all their glory. Phew! How he ticked me off, threatened to place me under arrest, and made me follow on his heels for a considerable distance, finally dismissing me with more awful threats. A general in the front line was a very rare event and one I had never expected. Notwithstanding all the brave deeds which in his book he says he performed, this was the only occasion I saw him in the front line.

Crozier wrote two books, A Brass Hat in No Man's Land *and* The Men I Killed. *Both Jones and Whitworth claimed Crozier was rarely seen in the front line, never mind in no-man's-land. His surviving service records hint at this man's apparently flawed character, both before and after the war.*

Pte Herbert Chase, 2/1st (London) Field Ambulance, RAMC

After two days, instead of going down to Agny to rest, we went further up, this time right through the newly taken village of Neuville Vitasse. On the way we passed Sir Douglas Haig on horseback and with a troop of lancers in attendance. It was quite inspiring to see the Commander-in-Chief, he looked smaller in features and considerably older than we imagined him to be from his pictures – but of course very grim and soldierly and bedecked with ribbons.

Sapper Albert Martin, 41st Signal Coy, RE

Sir Hubert Plumer, the Second Army Commander, arrived by motor car. He marched on to the ground in true military fashion making right and left turns and going round two sides of a triangle instead of taking a short cut across the diagonal. He was radiant in two rows of ribbons and a monocle which was very refractory. He inspected each man in the brigade and spoke to all those who had ribbons up, asking for particulars of how they had won their decorations.

Capt. Eric Whitworth, 12th South Wales Borderers

I halted for lunch on the road on Rich Mixed and Dates and while so doing saw a general with pennant approaching. I stood up and saluted and he drew up and asked me where I was going, my regiment, etc. He then asked me if I had heard the good news of our push further north and he told me the figures. I was so attracted by the charm of his personality and presence that I stopped his last mounted orderly and he told me it was Sir Henry Rawlinson, Commanding Fourth Army.

Preparations for a summer offensive at Ypres were under way when Major Sidney Greenfield was instructed to proceed to a base camp at Etaples. He was to work as an instructor in the disciplines of trench life to new recruits out in France for the first time. What he saw did not impress him.

Maj. Sidney Greenfield, MC, 1/6th Northumberland Fusiliers

My notes indicate that the weather was excellent and I was not a bit overworked and probably thoroughly enjoyed the rest. I spent time shopping and visiting Paris Plage and neighbouring places, meeting officers bringing out drafts, getting up to date with letters and replenishing my kit. One thing stands out in my mind about this period, which does not appear in my notes: the looks of despair on the faces of the men as they passed through my hands. Each draft had to undergo fresh training for a few days before rejoining their units or joining them for the first time.

It seemed to me that we had mainly the dregs of the army to deal with. Each draft was probably mixed. Some would be youngsters of eighteen coming out for the first time whilst others would be men who had been wounded and were now returning. Many of them had more experience of trench warfare than I. They knew the dangers and there was a hopelessness in their faces which almost made one weep. My job was to instill enthusiasm and efficiency and I felt it was extremely difficult. To put men through the elements of trench warfare and trench behaviour and discipline when they had already experienced many months of it and knew as much of it as I did was no easy task and I spent much time in explaining that it had to be done for the sake of those who had not experienced it. To instill smartness and efficiency in these fellows seemed almost impossible and so they passed through my hands with the dread of the trenches before them.

Cpl Arthur Cook, 1st Somerset Light Infantry

Arrived at a camp near Proven at 4 a.m. Here training for the impending attack took place in real earnest; battles were won, trenches were captured and consolidated day after day. We have had this before many a time, but there always seems to be a fly in the ointment somewhere on the actual day. All hard and fast training manuals, parade ground instructions, etc, all go by the board in action, and each individual is left to work out his own salvation by common sense and initiative.

Pte Sydney Fuller, 8th Suffolk Rgt

Usual parades. The Archbishop of York gave the 53rd Brigade an address, or sermon, his text being a part of the 20th verse of the 6th Chapter, 1st Epistle to Timothy – 'Keep that which is committed to your trust.' He said, 'You must all do your best in the coming operations, which may, if successful, bring about the end of the war in a short time.' His address was given from an old wagon, the brigade forming three sides of a hollow square in front of him.

Pte Thomas Bickerton, 2nd Essex Rgt

Just before the attack was to take place, we had a brigade muster, and General Carton de Wiart addressed us. He told us that one dead German was worth two live ones. He hated the Germans and of course had seen a great deal of the war and the suffering in Belgium, so it was possible to understand his outlook. We were

addressed afterwards by our padre, and I felt rather sorry for him –
he'd got to tell us to be merciful, and I think we all began to
wonder whether Christianity came into warfare.

Sapper Albert Martin, 41st Signal Coy, RE
The weather is bad and we wonder whenever the attack is to be
made. Each day we expect to receive the order but it doesn't come,
and nobody cares for this suspense. We know we have come to
make the attack and we would prefer to get it over quickly, for we
know that the sooner it is over the sooner we shall get back out of
this hell of mud and shells and gas. We know that there will be a
lot of casualties, but hope springs eternal, and each man reckons
that *he* will get back safely.

Gnr George Hollett, 217th Siege Batt., RGA
It was pitch dark and fairly quiet, but exactly on the hour, there
was a tremendous roar as all the guns spoke at once, and a
zigzagging, flickering belt of flame covered the countryside as
far as we could see. The ground shook and quivered and we had to
shout in one another's ears to make ourselves heard, above the
inferno of crashing guns and shrieking, whining shells of all sizes.
It was hell let loose with a vengeance! Fritz sent up his SOS signals
from the trenches, and then his guns and shells helped swell that
infernal chorus.

Pte Frederick Aylett, 133rd Field Ambulance, RAMC
On 31 July the attack was made. For the first day things went
pretty well; but on the second day came the rain and washed away
our hopes and our chances of success. I was helping in one of the
dugouts washing down, ripping off muddy clothing, handing
dressings and splints to the Medical Officer besides taking the
names of the men who came through. We worked with hardly a
break for three days, and then we managed to work in twelve-hour
shifts. A good many of the cases had been lying out for five or six

days, and in some cases gangrene had already set in. We could not get the smell of it out of the place, and all the blankets reeked of it. A good sprinkling of Germans came in wounded. One I remember must have had remarkable powers of endurance, as he had an arm severed, and he had himself placed two tourniquets very tightly upon the stump. He had been lying out for some days, but he was still a long way from being physically exhausted. He asked for drink and I gave him some water. He seemed very grateful and murmured his thanks in French.

Lt Alan May, 49th Machine Gun Coy, MGC

The big concrete strongpoints and dugouts we saw had been blown to bits. From the remains of one of these I saw a miserable little Boche run out. Here was my chance to shoot a Boche personally but he raised his hands when he saw me so of course I could not. I judged him to be about fifteen years old, weak and about half my size. He looked at me like a dog that knows he has done something wrong and croaked 'Kamerad'. By shouting and gesticulating I made him understand that if he wished to live he was to carry some of my load. The agility with which he picked up two boxes of ammunition was astounding considering his physical condition.

Sapper Albert Martin, 41st Signal Coy, RE

Every night when the weather has been favourable Fritz has treated us to a heavy dose of gas shells and each time the gas guard has had to wake us and we have been compelled to wear our masks for a couple of hours at a stretch. We also use fans (pieces of thin wood on handles) to fan the gas out of the tunnels. Owing to the gas curtains being kept down at night and the ventilation shafts being shut, the air in the tunnels becomes most fetid. Seventy or eighty men crowded in one of these galleries, many with wet clothes, and all in a filthy dirty condition, breathing the same air over and over again, their bodies stewing in the close

Captain Birrie, MC, an Australian medical officer attached to the
8th East Surrey Regiment.

Sgt Harold Bisgood standing in the doorway
of his billet. Note the German stick grenades
on his webbing. This and the other images
on these two pages are taken from Bisgood's
personal album.

Short back and sides: an RAMC orderly gives
a friend a haircut.

Trying to have a wash: trench life, 1916.

Grave markers ready for use. Five men
were killed by a shell exploding on the
parapet, 4 June 1916; they are buried in
Hebuterne Military Cemetery.

Royal Flying Corps wireless operators.

On a route march: the normal routine was to walk for fifty minutes then rest for ten.

Souveniring: a Tommy of the 2nd London Regiment with a German *Pickelhaube* and pioneer's sawback bayonet, pictured on the Somme, 1916.

German prisoners of war mingle with British soldiers in the trenches near Combles, on the Somme, September 1916.

Sgt Harold Bisgood returns to the Somme battlefields, March 1917. Behind the two men is Gommecourt Wood, where British troops suffered terrible casualties on 1 July 1916.

A British tank knocked out during the fighting around Tilloy on the Somme.

'A lonely grave on the Somme', as photographed by Sgt Bisgood.

The gas attack prior to the infantry advance at Gommecourt on the Somme, 1 July 1916.

British prisoners of war captured just prior to the Somme offensive. All the images on this and the following three pages (with the exception of the 'gas attack') were taken by German soldiers.

A German lieutenant wears a British greatcoat and steel helmet while standing in a captured communication trench, 1916.

A shell explodes on the edge of Delville Wood during the Battle of the Somme, as seen from the German trenches, August 1916.

German stretcher-bearers carry away a wounded comrade.

German machine-gunners (Maxim MG08) man a post overlooking no-man's-land. Note the telephone wires with their insulators.

German wounded being removed from an aid post based in a barn. The rickety nature of the transport often exacerbated injuries.

An unexploded 24 cm British shell is examined in a trench. The German is holding his gas mask container with his name on its base.

German tunnellers working underground, possibly on a large dugout.

A German pumps water from a sodden trench in the Ypres Salient, 1917.

A small-calibre British shell sticks out of a tree, Ypres Salient.

British prisoners of war on a working party: prisoners on both sides frequently worked close to the trench lines, against international law.

An acrobat turned soldier demonstrates his high-wire act to his German comrades.

A German soldier examines his shirt before killing the lice between his thumbnails or by running a candle up the seams.

Bathtime: German soldiers enjoy a dip in tubs. Men were rarely allowed to bathe for long before they were ordered out.

August 1916: German soldiers enjoy themselves behind the lines at Mennen, in what appears to be a reservoir.

A Lewis gun team at Ypres: the section commander, a
sergeant, carries a pistol rather than a rifle.

A shell explodes in the ruins of an unnamed village in the Ypres Salient.

A wounded German soldier is found three days after the launch of the British offensive at Ypres, 31 July 1917.

A party of men halt for a short rest by the side of a road. The man nearest the camera is wearing non-regulation shorts.

A dead German lies in a trench taken by the British during the Passchendaele offensive.

The shell-pocked landscape of the Ypres Salient.

A German soldier ducks for cover close to a broken light railway line.

D Company Headquarters, 8th East Surrey Regiment, August 1917: soldiers smoke outside a dugout in Jeffery Trench, Ypres.

A damaged trench: note the corrugated iron (known as 'elephant iron'), used to construct the roof of a dugout.

A Drumhead service carried out by a padre. Many different denominations were represented on the Western Front.

Mail arrives and the men gather round the post corporal. Regular contact with home was vital for morale.

Pay parade: a soldier signs for his money and the amount is entered into his paybook.

Boys of the Royal West Surrey Regiment enjoy a swim behind the lines.

A litter of puppies: animals such as cats and dogs were frequently adopted by soldiers in and out of the line.

Out on rest: a man takes a short nap on a plough.

Fishing in a pond: incredibly, these men are barely half a mile from the front line at Hill 60, Ypres.

German soldiers walk past a captured British Expeditionary Force canteen, March 1918.

March 1918: the German offensive swept over the old Somme battlefield and with it the cemeteries built for British war dead.

Two years after: a poignant image of British and Australian dead killed at Fromelles in July 1916.

The summer of 1918: the town of Albert is recaptured from the Germans. In the distance the famous Basilica is in ruins.

1919: the Cloth Hall at Ypres under reconstruction. Work to restore the medieval building was not finished until the 1960s.

The village church at Herlies in ruins. A German mural adorns one of the walls.

A British tank on display in a French town square proves a magnet for British tourists.

Civilians revisit the battlefields during the 1930s. These men, some former soldiers, are happy to pose while holding rusting rifles.

A tour party stands over battlefield debris including trench pumps, rifles, barbed-wire pickets and entrenching tools.

Two women visit a trench during a battlefield tour. The wooden duckboards still line the floor.

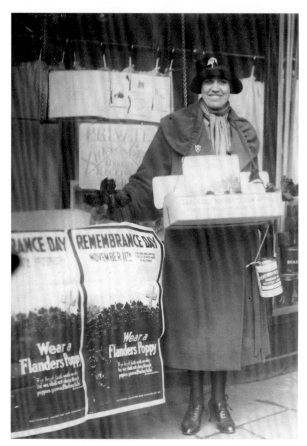

'Wear a Flanders Poppy'. On Remembrance Day, 11 November 1925, a
poppy-seller stands on an unknown British street.

damp atmosphere and exuding all manner of noxious odours – this alone is sufficient to make us ill. It is positively choking to enter the tunnels in the early morning, before the curtains have been raised and a draught created. You choke and splutter and gasp for breath, but if you have slept in it you do not notice the aroma; you only realise that you have got a rotten headache and feel beastly sick. But foul air is better than poison gas, and dugouts are to be preferred to shell holes.

Pte Frank Harris, 6th King's Own Yorkshire Light Infantry

It is a case of 'Gas masks, Out! and on!' and 'Lively, me lads, lively' – whether they give you the torture of the devil or not. The next hour or so is purgatory indeed, as lungs are near to bursting point, we flounder on and on. Masks off a few seconds for lightning test – gas still coming over, whip 'em back on. Due to faulty valves or taking a damned silly chance, several blokes get caught – start retching, coughing and spluttering like a lot of old men. We curse our way along – so to the shambles on ahead – could you hear our comments and language, you would think my patriotic peroration a short time back was poppycock indeed . . .

Fritz has been mainly using tear gas up to now, or we would not be risking this 'mask off' lark so much. Your blood, nonetheless, pounds, likewise eardrums, old boy, and when your eye pieces have blurred you are what is known as 'quids in'. Be grateful it is tear gas and hope Jerry doesn't switch to a lung full or two of the other, you choke or bleed to death. Who knows, we may get a dose of this ourselves.

We eventually reach the end of the boards – proves fortunate again – shelling not too bad and as far as flesh and blood will permit we try to pick up speed. We pass now a solitary Boche, swollen, too, floating in a miniature pool, if a crater it was certainly some shell. How the hell did he get there but he is some poor mother's son and met a violent end – you can tell that by his eyes – apart from a belly full of gas. Death is supposed to compose but it does not compose here. Fritz bobs to the edge of the pool as we go by. Some other poor mother's son belts him in the jaw with his boot – starts him bobbing from side to side like a waterlogged tree stump.

Word travels round we're nearing zero – watching shells burst just ahead, we rise and gird our loins. The shell bursts creep on up the slope until the earth erupts in fountains all along the crest. Whistles blast and we are away. However, progress is slow, dead slow in fact. Apart from the slope we cannot get along for shell-scarred stumps of trees, plus the wreckage of old concrete strongholds.

Fritz starts shelling and machine-gunning, too. No alternative but to swiftly hit the grit and try short, spasmodic rushes, and when sufficiently near try some of our precious bombs. Spot any Fritz, then a bit of sniping, too – even so we are apparently losing time and a sergeant yells, 'You lot there, get a move on.' 'And you,' we say, but we eventually reach the crest to find that Fritz has decamped leaving, as at Arras, their dead and wounded behind. Maybe they were 'Suicide Club Wallahs', in any case what cover they had is pulverised by our shells and it is a case of 'Dig, dig!' so it could be a case of Fritz falling back for a time to give his artillery more scope.

The air is now filled with German shells sighing for our blood. It is incredible to us that some of them do not collide before they reach the ground. As I have said before, curse the lot, 'Dig, dig deep' or we will soon be cold meat. No such luck as any shells colliding in mid-air, and as if exalted all pour down, pounding our eardrums until they feel as though they will burst. Yes, old chap, shrapnel keeps us low and a lot of Yorkshire Light Infantry must think that their own time has come at last. Perhaps Harris is one, but blokes seek comfort in the fallacy common out here that you do not go west until the particular piece of shrapnel – that particular bullet bearing your particular name.

The blokes are shouting for stretcher-bearers and they will be fortunate indeed, for there is even worse than this to come. Who are my nearest fellow beings? Sergeant Thorpe and Corporal Blake – two of our ancient sports – Thorpe and gay cavalier Blake! with whom I sniped at the opening day of Arras. Blake, the mimic and the wit – all three of us cursing in a lurid monotone as we shovel like hell. My own pick falls clear for a second, something is transfixed on the point – not another skull, I hope – I have already encountered enough of those. This is something extra special – a German water bottle half full of rum seeping cruelly through the gash. Thorpe sniffs and looks, then sniffs again, by Jove! whilst his eyes take on the appearance of ping-pong balls. Blake sniffs and looks, all three take a damned good swipe just as Fritz drops two or three beauties a yard or so away and we scatter like scalded cats to find Blake partially buried. We return, dig him out and the old so-and-so can breathe again; he spits out a pound or so of rich, good German soil, deeply inhales a little more, has another swipe of rum and then lets fly the choicest of his profanity. Music to our ears – all things considered he is not in bad shape at all.

Soon, I am roughly shook, awakened by a panic-stricken gunner intent on clearing out. I ask him what is amiss and almost incoherently he shouts, 'Fritz using flame', then he is off and away in a flash. There is meagre half-light by now and, although I hear heavy rifle- and machine-gun fire, I see no sign of liquid flame. We have already seen old discarded gear – dum-dum bullets, too, another refinement coughed up by Fritz, saw-edged bayonets another, none of which we are supposed to use ourselves. We are not supposed to drop bombs down the pants of captured Boche but I am afraid that at times we do.

Over fly a few Boche planes, mad devils, too – the old Death or Glory boys. Flying so low one could almost touch them and see the smirks behind the goggles. In a blind fury a bloke feels so futile and impotent when machine-gunned from the air, as he does when being bombed. You feel futile, of course, under shellfire, but somehow or other in a different kind of way – aerial gunning and bombing really gets under your skin and debases you more than ever.

Three or four of us, disregarding shells, spring erect, and let loose several magazines of concentrated fire but without wishing to boast, expert marksmen though we are, we do not allow for air speed, and inflict no damage at all with our well-intentioned volleys whistling aimlessly into space. This is just a gesture I suppose but always the odd chance . . .

Apart from the other wounded, three of our best Lewis-gun team are hit. Halliday in the shoulder, pipe-loving Barnes in the rump and Hudson, a bullet clean through the jaw and so on.

Fritz has this ground taped to an inch, and has held it for years. In fury and confusion we jump down whence we came, dragging behind the nearest wounded men. The three gunners manage unaided, and whilst we can manage without 'windy Hudson', Halliday and Barnes, two of the best Lewis-gunners in the business, will be sorely missed I am afraid. Halliday grits his teeth, spits out 'By God, it stings'. Halliday sheds his pack and is away. Barnes, whose evil-smelling pipe fumes must have been detectable for miles, due to the nature of where he got his particular packet, is not quite as rapid as Halliday, actually grins and also is away. Hudson, likewise, is not grinning; however, the wound is spouting blood like a whale and he is windy looking now and personally could not care less.

During an unexpected lull I make a swift dash and succeed in recovering a gun which by a miracle, although caked in mud, still works. I then spot Moxon, now a stretcher-bearer, working like a Trojan tending mutilated flesh. His work is set out with one poor devil who has already got a wound in his back in which one could sink a man's clenched fist, but Moxon, true to form, nonetheless bawls at him, 'Lie still, you bloody fool, lie still.' All whilst another chap, a youngster, the same age as myself, waits for dressing without a single word until a razor-sharp sliver of shrapnel gives him a second packet, slicing off the fingers of one hand. There is little wonder that he goes berserk. The bloke with a hole in his back, I am afraid, has no chance at all, as he is losing too much blood, but is cursing back at Moxon all the time.

We endeavour to peg out for the night, unaware what to expect next in a pretty parlous plight. What is in store comes at early light with a mass attack by Fritz using flame-throwers pumping jets some thirty yards in length.

No living creature in the path of these has any chance at all. The nearest jet being twenty or so yards distant – it appears that we have had it when a slight breeze causes it to veer and takes it from our immediate front. We breathe again, but the outposts on our flanks, poor devils, a hellish spectacle and fate, are barbecued almost to crisps. My division, though not of late, has faced flammerwerfen attacks before. It is my first taste and, by George, familiarity, old boy, will never give way to nor breed contempt. We imagine we know what will follow, the flame which is exhausted, flickers and subsides.

Deutschland über Alles – the massed Boche I mentioned intent on pushing off any survivors of ours, and winning back their ridge and here the bastards come. There are, however, many Yorkshire Light Infantry, also Durham Light Infantry, who have managed to survive, and, whilst we are famished, parched, unbelievably fatigued, plastered with muck and filth in our eyes and teeth. Whilst we are more or less resigned, light a Woodbine if you have one, we accept this bloody challenge, pull our belts in, deploy, spit on our hands, and wait, for Fritz to come a little nearer.

By a miracle we have two Lewis guns that still function, and we put up concentrated rapid fire. Fritz wavers, re-forms and keeps coming nonetheless. Lights are improved by now; not so much wasted fire, and the Squareheads go down like ninepins. What are left are crumpling and endeavouring to retreat. This lot though, pal, sure hate our guts as we hate theirs. Maybe the equivalent of our Guards, certainly tall and burly enough. They have also, like us, been taught to kill, the creed of war of course.

I was a bloody fool I suppose when I fell on top of a Boche who had just sunk his bayonet into one of my best pals a foot or so away. I lunged myself, missed, parried, then got the 'Squarehead' in the breast, but then, not content with that, followed him to ground, thumbs gouging at his throat until a bloke dragged me away. 'You can only kill the bastards once,' he observed. I shot a quick glance at my pal, with a penetrated artery, undoubtedly no chance, gave the Boche some boot, and resumed the mêlée, and what a ghastly bloody business it was.

Pte Sydney Fuller, 8th Suffolk Rgt

Saw a few prisoners come back – most of them young men . . . One of them lay on a stretcher beside us all day, there being too many of our wounded, who were attended to first. The RAMC chaps bound up his wound and left him until later. His wound was in the leg and must have been very painful for he often signed to us to cut his throat for him. At intervals he begged for 'coffee or vasser', and drank quite a lot of my water. J. C. ate sandwiches in front of him, evidently with the idea of tantalising him, but he was too far gone to worry about grub.

Lt Edward Allfree, 111th Siege Batt., RGA

In the afternoon I made my way to the forward position, where I was to spend the night in the mud. When crossing the canal, I met a party of Hun prisoners being brought back. As they reached the bridge, they one and all with a smile, and a sigh of relief, heaved their steel helmets over into the water, and produced and donned soft, round caps. The war was over for them, and they would have no occasion to wear their heavy helmets again, and they seemed heartily glad.

Pte Daniel Sweeney, 1st Lincolnshire Rgt

There is every sign of this war ending soon but I do not think it will be over before April but Haig says himself Xmas will finish it and he knows more than I do. The boys are not blind, they know very well that Fritz is beaten; even his own men say that Germany cannot last out much longer.

Lt Edward Allfree, 111th Siege Batt., RGA

To give some idea of the mud, I need only mention that I saw a horse, harnessed to a French wagon, with its hind legs so deeply sunk in the mud that it could not move. Its hind legs were buried right up to its haunches, so that its stomach was level with, and lying on the ground, with its front legs stretched straight out in front of it along the ground. It had to be dug out.

Just the other side of the sandbags, about two yards from the entrance to the pillbox, was a dead Boche, lying with his face in a shell hole; a few yards down the trench behind us was another, and just in front of us was a dead British Tommy. They never got buried – it was not worth exposing oneself to the enemy to perform the task. Each time I went to the observation post I saw them rotting away – getting thinner and thinner – till at last they were actually skeletons in discoloured uniforms. In the meantime great green-bodied bluebottles swarmed over them, and it was only with difficulty that one kept them off one's bully beef or sandwiches, when partaking of lunch. I suppose they rather fancied a change of diet. At night, I think they went to roost in our pillbox.

Pte Christopher Massie, 76 Brigade, 25th Div., RAMC

The horse will stand his ground against shellfire but shies at a piece of fluttering paper, trembles at a traction engine and shudders at the sight of one of his dead fellows. The mule is not so mysteriously wounded as the horse. When he is wounded he walks away from the battlefield in the direction of the field hospital. The humour of this situation is crowded out by its simple pathos. Men and mules, broken in battle, dragging themselves back down the awful road to Ypres. Often the mules are bandaged with the men's first field dressings. There is the same 'fed up' expression in their sad eyes, the same selfless humility – a humility which gives one the impression that men and mules are rather ashamed of their wounds.

The horse will stand wounded at his post. I remember coming down from Messines one misty dawn finding a horse standing by the body of his dead mate. He stood quite motionless as I patted his strong neck. 'All right, old chap?' I asked. He looked at me with those mysterious eyes of sorrow. Like a mother's, and turned his head away. I looked over him and found a long gaping wound in his stomach. And then, when I had found it, he ventured to glance at me once more, as if he would say quite simply, 'You see, my friend, it is all over.'

Driver Percival Glock, 281 Brigade, 56th Div., RFA

Six big strong horses could not pull an empty ammunition wagon weighing about five cwt through the mud and if a horse fell down, five times out of ten it had to be shot as it was a terrible job to get it on its feet again. We have tried for as much as twelve hours to get one horse up. Can you imagine being pinned under a horse in thick, sticky mud; of course you can't even imagine the mud. I had one of my legs pinned down by a horse and a few shells dropping round about to make it more pleasant. The other fellows tied a rope round me and another round the horse's neck and legs; previously they shot the horse so that it should not kick. There were between thirty and forty men pulling on the ropes and it took them over two hours to get me out of it. On another time a fellow was pinned more securely than me. We tried every way to get him out. We even tried about twenty horses hooked together to pull the horse away but that couldn't budge it an inch; they even broke the harness on the job. The poor fellow underneath was giving instructions how to act. Several times he told us to leave him until it was daylight, but of course we couldn't do that. We eventually freed him by digging away all round him and propping the horse as we dug. After all this and a good stiff dose of rum he was all right again.

Lt Godfrey Skelton, 205 Field Coy, RE

I think at this time I was becoming 'nervy'. The strain, the constant fear of death or wounding, the responsibility for the work and for the sappers and the large working parties of infantry began to take their toll. When I reported to the company or battalion headquarters, on going out and on returning I would probably have a drink of whisky to help me on my way. One put off the moment when one had to leave with the runner and face the machine-gun bullets, the shells falling around and standing still when the enemy flares went up.

Capt. George McMurtie, 7th Somerset Light Infantry

I went to the brigade HQ dugout so as to be near at hand; I saw what a strain was put on the staff in an occasion like this. The brigadier was absolutely worn out and the staff major had his hands full. Reports were coming in by runners and telephone from all four battalion commanders, describing how the fight was progressing. Messages were being sent off for more ammunition and bombs. Orders were being sent to the artillery, infantry, Machine Gun Corps and occasionally the telephone wires were broken by shellfire and the telephone operators had to go out and repair them at once.

Maj. Sidney Greenfield, 1/6th Northumberland Fusiliers

I have always maintained that I went three days and three nights without sleep. It ended by the CO telling me that he wanted me to take a letter to Geordie Bell (captain) who was in charge of the reserve company. When I found the reserve company I handed Geordie the letter which he read and then said I think you had better get to bed and get some sleep. This I did and slept through twenty-four hours or thereabouts. It was here I met a new Baptist padre who was to be attached to our battalion. Some said that although he had not even seen the front line he took one look at me and the next they heard was that he had applied to be sent back to the base.

It was some months afterwards when talking to a fellow officer about these events he suddenly said to me. 'Do you know what was in that letter you took to Geordie Bell?' To this I naturally replied that I had no idea and frankly I was not particularly interested at that time. To this he said, well I'll tell you. It simply said 'Greenfield is done in put him to bed'.

Capt. George McMurtie, 7th Somerset Light Infantry

The adjutant kept on ringing all the Company Commanders on the telephone when there was no need for it at all. It's the most annoying thing, being woken up in the few moments of sleep one can snatch in the line, having to wade through mud and water, in a desperate hurry, revolver, tin hat, compass, papers falling in all directions, grasping the telephone and thinking there is some important message to come through and then hear a voice from the other end, 'The adjutant has gone now, do you mind waiting, sir?' Having waited several minutes, you hear the adjutant, 'I say, old man, have you got those things yet?' 'Those things' being duckboards or wire which you received ages ago. He woke me on one night on a fool's errand and so I told him what I thought of him. Funnily enough, he had done the same thing to all the other company commanders and so there we were, all four Company Commanders shouting down our different telephones and cursing him at the same time for the same offence!

2/Lt George Foley, 7th Somerset Light Infantry

A little book called the BAB Code was issued to Company Commanders. It contained all the words and phrases likely to be wanted in trench warfare or an attack; opposite each word and phrase was a number, so that we were now able to speak or send messages through the telephone in code. This was a measure to prevent the enemy acquiring information by means of listening sets, and it was now forbidden to communicate anything over the phone in plain English within a considerable distance of the front line . . . Sometimes the use of the code was a little irksome. I remember on one occasion, when shells and trench mortars were falling and everyone was feeling rather strung up, a message was handed to me, in code. With the help of the little book I struggled through it, but mathematics under any circumstances were never my strong point, and under fire they were positive torture. However, the message, coming at such a time, must be important and I ploughed on. Imagine my disgust when, having finally decoded it, I read 'Report at once number of Canadian Military Policemen in your company.'

Lt Edward Allfree, 111th Siege Batt., RGA

My dear old friend Marshall left us at this time, much to my regret. He was sent back with a nervous breakdown and neurasthenia, and got to Blighty with it. He had been clearly getting worse for some time, and I think the experience he had one evening 'put the lid on it'. I forget exactly where he had been, but the major had sent him somewhere, and on his way back he had to meet a lorry load of our men. On coming through Woesten by himself, the place was being heavily shelled and there, near the crossroads, he found a lorry which had just had a direct hit. It was in the charge of two drivers, both of whom had been wounded, and one of them severely, and would undoubtedly bleed to death unless he received immediate attention, which the other appeared quite helpless to give.

Now Marshall was one of those highly strung, sensitive, imaginative people, with a horror of blood and a dread of shelling (most of us had the latter to a greater or lesser degree), and, as I have said, with his nerves already in a very bad state. He possessed, however, a stronger characteristic, and that was a keen sense of what he considered his duty and of what was right and wrong, and he never let his sense of fear prevent him from doing what he felt he ought to do. Marshall was therefore, to my mind, a truly brave man. A brave man is surely not one who knows no fear, but rather one who, though fearful, and with a lively sense of danger, yet acts nobly.

So with the shells still bursting near on the crossroads, with that horrid shattering roar, he gave directions to the other man, and together they bandaged the wounded, and got him on a passing lorry. He then took him to a Belgian dressing station, which, though some way off, was the nearest one, and after some persuasion, succeeded in getting them to take them in. He could speak French well, and was therefore able to make strong representations to those in charge.

He then went back to the battery, arriving in a badly shaken condition, and almost in a state of nervous collapse, and reported to the major what had happened, and that he was quite unable to take the men in the lorry to the billets. So Hartley was sent.

I am afraid his evening's performance was not properly appreciated by the major, who was inclined to adopt rather the attitude that would cause him to give expression to such words as, 'What the Devil does he go tinkering about with wounded lorry drivers for, instead of doing the job I sent him to do?' Marshall himself said he felt a worm for allowing someone else to do his job.

That night it was Marshall's turn for duty in the map room, so I stayed with him. He was not at all in a fit state to be left on duty all night alone. We did in fact have a target come through on the phone that night; which I worked out, and got the guns in action. The next day, Marshall was sent off to the CCS, feeling, as he said, that he was a rotter, and 'swinging the lead'. But there is no doubt that he really was in a very bad state.

Pte Robert Cude, 7th The Buffs (East Kent Rgt)

It is perfectly beastly to see the poor devils coming out, for standing for days on end, waist-deep in water and mud, has left its mark on them, and a considerable number of them have trench feet, some of them are so bad that they are on improvised crutches (a pair of rifles), and others cannot put their feet to the ground at all. What a war this is to be sure for everyone out here (in the line of course) is heartily sick of it all, and wishes it was over. Personally, I do not think that anyone troubles as to which side will ultimately win; all we ask is to go back quietly and live a life according to our own tastes.

Pte Ernest Douglas, RAMC

I've seen some very nasty sights, and carried some nasty cases down, all under shellfire; they talk about a soldier going out and fetching a comrade in under shellfire – and he gets the Military Medal or Distinguished Conduct Medal. We are always under shellfire, and can't dump our stretcher and run for it to a safe spot; we have to plod on, up past the knees in mud – balancing on the edge of shell craters, slipping and sliding; shells bursting above and in the earth quite all around us. It's God's mercy that we get through, but we have the patient to think of and quickness probably means his life.

What annoys me most is when we get a chap 'serious' and makes a dash and he dies at the door of the dressing place – love's labour lost. But I suppose God wills it, and He is 'Boss'.

Rev. Roger Bulstrode, Hon. Chaplain to the Forces (2nd Class)

In some ways, work on a battlefield was the most characteristic part of a chaplain's life. In going from one wounded man to another, he would have endless opportunities of ministration. He could often relieve the torment of thirst, perhaps by a drink from the man's own water bottle which he was unable to reach. He could take down a message from dying lips. I recall one lad in the Shropshires, lying in a shell hole, whose one thought was 'I don't know what my mother will do'. I could at least write to that mother and tell her how her boy had forgotten his pain in his thought for her. And one could speak, often in dying ears, the Saviour's precious Name, and the Blood that cleanses from all sin. The simple lines

Jesus, I will trust Thee,
Trust Thee with my soul;
Thou hast died for sinners,
Therefore, Lord, for me.

or, it may be, a verse of 'There is a green hill far away', that would carry a man's thoughts back to his childhood faith . . .

Pte Frank Pope, 10th King's Royal Rifle Corps
'History of the War'
A Trench,
A Stench,
Some scraps of French,
Some horrible German vapours;
A Shell,
A Yell
No more to tell,
Bar a paragraph in the papers!

Rev. Edward Tanner, attd 2nd Worcestershire Rgt
An incident occurred when my battalion was engaged on 'Working Parties' outside the Menin Gate at Ypres. The Boche were at the time sending over time-bombs, i.e. bombs which did not explode immediately upon impact but which were timed to go off at unexpected intervals afterwards. On this particular occasion, one of our lads, only a boy, was in a temporary latrine when one of these bombs exploded and blew both him and the latrine to pieces. Some time later I saw one of the sergeants coming towards me

carrying a sandbag. 'This is all we could find, sir, of Pte . . .' he
said. 'Never mind, Sergeant, we'll give him a Christian burial.' So
a small grave was dug, the sandbag reverently laid in it and the
committal words spoken. Afterwards I wrote to the lad's mother
and told her that her boy had been given a Christian burial, and
later received a most grateful letter in a rather large hand,
thanking me and adding, 'I'm so glad my dear boy was buried
"comfortable"!' It was pathetic.

Maj. Sidney Greenfield, 1/6th Northumberland Fusiliers
I was hanging about outside battalion HQ waiting for it to get
dark enough for me to move when a shell (whizzbang, I think)
landed just beside me and I was hit. It was just as if someone
had taken a sledgehammer and hit my spine. I was completely
paralysed from the shoulders downwards so had little pain. I
clearly remember the shudder as I hit the ground and was quite
conscious. A piece of the shell had hit my shoulder blade where
it apparently split in two, one piece coming out above the other
shoulder blade. The other piece hitting the spine thus causing
the paralysis and then passing on and lodging between the
shoulder blade and lung. I well remember the call 'stretcher-
bearers', 'stretcher-bearers', the reply 'No stretchers'. 'Find one,
it's an officer.' It could not have been long before they came
along and took me to the Medical Officer who examined me and
put on a temporary dressing and instructed them to take me
back.

This journey is one I am not likely to forget easily. The country
here near Langemarke was comparatively flat and was just a mass
of shell holes, so many that they were often joining up to one
another and all full of water almost to the brim. Winding between
them was the duckboard track down which they had to carry me.
Each time a shell came over anywhere near to us they almost
dropped me and lay flat for safety. Being paralysed, the fact of
dropping me was not causing any alarm but I was desperately

worried lest I should roll off the stretcher and drown in a shell hole as I could do nothing whatever for myself.

How long this journey took I do not know but at last we reached a light railway and my stretcher was pushed on to the base of a truck and I was left to look at the sky whilst no doubt they returned to bring back further casualties. At the entrance was a padre with a pencil and pile of field cards and when he came up with the request 'Can I write to your mother?' this brought tears and it was only with great difficulty I could give the necessary name and address.

After a brief examination I was sent to a Casualty Clearing Station. By what means I have no recollection. My next recollection was the x-ray machine and two young fellows who were operating it. Apparently the operator had been killed the previous night by a bomb on the site and these two were standing in with little or no experience of an x-ray machine. Their conversation was far from encouraging and was roughly like this: 'Now we have got to find where it is . . . is it this knob?' 'No.' 'Try that one.' 'Try turning that one.' 'No, that doesn't seem to be right.' 'Ah, There it is.' 'Where's the pencil. We must mark where it is. Now we have to find out how deep it is.' After some time they seemed to be satisfied. In my condition and knowing little about electrical machines such as x-ray I wondered whether I should be electrocuted and was more relaxed when I was taken back to bed.

Pte Christopher Massie, 76 Brigade, 25th Div., RAMC
Though the average Englishman is not by any means an outspoken patriot, the Londoner is always a great citizen. One, I remember, had been wounded for a fifth time. I watched him wrestle back to consciousness after being on 'the table'; his humorous perplexity at the drunken things he was helplessly saying in a brave battle for reason. Then, when he became lucid, he laughed at himself. 'Gor! That's the fif' time I've bin wounded. Jerry's only got to drill three more 'oles in me to make me a flute.'

Rev. Montague Bere, Army Chaplain's Department
(Temp. Chaplain 4th Class)

The recent fighting had given a lot of work to the Casualty Clearing Stations but the majority of cases were evacuated so fast that I doubt having missed much. My colleague at 20 CCS told me that he prayed with a dying man, thinking him Church of England; that the Roman Catholic padre anointed him, thinking he was Roman Catholic; and that the nonconformist came in at the end and buried him as a Wesleyan, which he was.

Pte Frank Harris, 6th King's Own Yorkshire Light Infantry

The ridge still smoked, I observed, but it smoked when we moved up and it will smoke when we have moved down. Visualise, if you can, an apparently endless ridge, an apparently impossible slope, every foot a scum-filled crater of its own, spewing forth devilish, huge volcano-like fumes, hanging in the air for miles, and you have a rough and ready picture of the view that greets our eyes. Those blokes who emerge including, I suppose, myself: are these gaunt, hollow-eyed, hollow-cheeked, haggard looking objects really human beings? Are they really flesh and blood or khaki-tattered, mud-bespattered scarecrows looking for a grave? After all, we have been gunned at and shot at for a week, all shed blood, gone without water and food, but choose what we are, we really must endeavour to get away from here and get out.

Driver Percival Glock, 281 Brigade, 56th Div., RFA

We had to consider ourselves very lucky indeed if we had four or five hours sleep at one time. Sometimes we had no 'Official' sleep for a week at a time. What I mean by official sleep is sleep that you could have without being troubled by the thoughts of being caught. If we had a minute or two to spare we used to flop down wherever we were in the mud or on the side of the road on the horse's back and fall to sleep directly and nothing on earth could wake us except someone giving you a good hard kick or punch. Of course the officers or NCOs never kicked or punched us; that would never do. They made allowances for us as no one can keep awake for ever, but all the same we got severely reprimanded as a matter of form. On one occasion we were at the ammunition dump waiting to load up, I, with the rest, flopped down beside the horses in about a foot of nice sticky mud, it was a lovely soft bed and naturally I was asleep in about half a tick. I was awakened by a blessed horse treading on my foot, I got up wondering where I was, I'd been dreaming of Blighty I think, I couldn't see anything or anybody for a minute or so as it was pitch black but I could hear everybody talking about fifteen yards away, I was told old Fritz had been dropping bombs and one had dropped there and they were trying to do something for the poor fellows who had caught pieces. That might give one an idea what our sleep was like, drop a bomb almost on you and still you sleep on.

Sapper Albert Martin, 41st Signal Coy, RE

When we reported in at the signal office Buchanan gave me a mug half full of rum but my hand was so shaky that I spilt most of it down my clothes. It was 8.30 a.m. and for forty hours we had been on the go without food or sleep . . . The cooks got us some breakfast and I almost fell asleep over it, and then lay down outside the entrance to the sap but was warned that it was not a safe place to go to sleep in as a man was killed there yesterday. So I washed and shaved as well as my shaky hand would let me and went downstairs. Sergeant Oxley lent me his bed and an overcoat and I was soon fast asleep.

Slept most of yesterday and all last night so feel pretty fit today except that I am a bundle of nerves. Any sudden noise makes me give ridiculous involuntary starts so that I drop anything I happened to be holding. My hand still shakes too much to permit letter writing without causing people to wonder what is the matter with me.

Temp. Lt Col George Archibald Stevens, Officer Commanding 2nd Royal Fusiliers

I used to visit the men and their officers daily, and I know what they suffered. Some of them had to give in and limp with swollen feet to a more or less comfortable place further back. It is a wonder that any of them were able to stand it. Wet through for six days, legs caked in mud, boots reduced to paper, nerves on edge, sick with apprehension and shock, there they remained on the alert because their officers were prepared to stick it with them, and their officers cheered them up because they knew that it all depended on them. The whole place was floating in mud and heroism.

A week's excitement and sleeplessness with continuous mud thrown in has certain results. The elation passes away, the spirit in which you despise all discomfort and danger, and you begin to realise that you are worn out. Some people will break down suddenly, most will only realise how tired they are when they are given a bed to sleep in and how dirty they are when they go to the baths for a wash.

As far as the mere rest goes, a few days is enough for that. The best means of mental recuperation would be for us all to scatter and each follow his own particular bent. Some would go fishing, and some could go to the mountains and scale precipices, and some would send for their wives and families and go to the seaside. I would probably stay here, but I would not wear uniform; I would go out with the picturesque old shepherd and stand in a long cloak like his and let the rain and wind beat upon me, and think and think. Or else I would go and visit the good-humoured little priest in the village and tell him that he should not be a Roman Catholic but a dour and honest Presbyterian. Or else I would go from one village to another and sit in the local pubs and learn the views of everybody on everything. After these high flights I should descend to the mere commonplace of war again, with reluctance no doubt, but much refreshed.

As it is, however, we remain here and are never away from one another. The contracting chamber of military discipline closes its walls on us, narrowing the circle of our interests more and more, forcing our minds to a smaller and a smaller compass, destroying all or almost all of those things we cherished before we became soldiers, till our old aims disappear, and our former delights pass out of sight. And then we have only one interest; we are units in a machine; we give ourselves up to our duty with regard to the men under us, so that we may carry out with them the wishes of the men over us.

Pte John McCauley, 2nd Border Rgt

The one thing which we all feared more than death was that we might betray our fear to each other. In moments of wildest panic and fright, our first thought was to control our real feelings from everybody else. I felt that I would far sooner die than that my comrades should know how much afraid I was in the trenches, and in open battle it was torture at times to keep our fears to ourselves, yet we all resorted to different tricks of pretence. I kept up the great sham day after day.

Gnr George Hollett, 217th Siege Batt., RGA

At last we were ready to turn in. We rolled ourselves in the blanket, lay on the damp-proof sheet on the ground and blew out the candles. I had just begun to doze off when – whee-ee – a German shell screamed overhead and burst just across the railway somewhere. It was the first I had heard and it put me in a blue flunk properly, more than I ever was in any place after. I was afraid to say anything to Hicks, in case he should say I had 'wind-up' which would have been quite true. I found afterwards that he had been just the same as I had. A few more shells came at intervals, and as they seemed to get no closer I became more reassured and finally dropped off to sleep.

Lt Edward Allfree, 111th Siege Batt., RGA

Our nightly game of bridge in the mess was sometimes disturbed by shellfire. I remember we were having a game one evening, between tea and dinner, when the shells began coming over. No one took any notice or said anything for some time, though, I am sure, each one was feeling somewhat anxious. It was most distracting, when considering whether to double 'three no trumps', to be at the same time wondering where the next one was coming to. Then you would hear the scream overhead, and down it would come with a crashing roar, and the splinters would whistle over the shed. Someone might murmur 'Seemed a bit closer, that one' and someone else would say, 'Two hearts', and over would come another one. But no one seemed to want to be the first to move. At last I decided to stick it no longer. It seemed too silly to be sitting there, playing bridge, when, at any moment, a shell might fall through the roof, and dispatch all the officers of the battery at once. So I said, 'Look here, I don't think this is good enough – they are coming too damned close – I'm going to clear.' The rest readily agreed that it was time we went. And so, to the trenches at the flank we adjourned, and there waited till Jerry saw fit to leave off. They were certainly falling very near the mess, and when we returned we found that two splinters had passed through the wooden side of the shed.

Lt Alan May, 49th Machine Gun Coy, MGC

Not far in advance of our front parapet I saw a couple of our lads who had gone completely goofy, perhaps from concussion. It was pitiful; one of them welcomed me like a long-lost friend and asked me to give him his baby. I picked up a tin hat from the ground and gave it to him. He cradled the hat as if it were a child, smiling and laughing without a care in the world despite the fact that shells were exploding all around. I have no idea what happened to the poor chap but if he stayed there very long he must have been killed.

Lt Gerald Brunskill, 1/5th Royal Sussex Rgt (Cinque Ports)

While bombs were being dropped in Poperinge a few nights ago, close to 'B' Company transport lines, one man, Private Saunter (who had previously had shell shock) got it badly again. An

RAMC sergeant, who thought he was merely windy, went over to him and said, 'Pull yourself together, my man, it's all right', whereupon he received a terrific biff on the nose, subsequently having to go to hospital! Poor Saunter then ran amok, and, being a pretty hefty chap, laid several people out before he was finally captured and sent to hospital also.

Capt. Eric Whitworth, 12th South Wales Borderers

I was sent for yesterday because one of my men was in a fit; he had had two, they said, by the time I got there. I sent for my invaluable Company Sergeant Major and he, by pressing back his thumbs, brought him round and I with great harshness ordered him to get up and walk, and, instead of allowing him to be carried on the stretcher which had been brought, I started him walking back to the Medical Officer. It was all, I believe, an effort to get out of the trenches!! And I expect the MO to return him to duty today.

L/Cpl Charles Moss, 18th Durham Light Infantry (Durham Pals)

It was nearly dark when we got out of the communication trench. Here we found a great dump where troops from other regiments who had been relieved were leaving fighting material which they had salvaged from the battlefield.

We left on this dump a Lewis gun that we had picked up in the front line on the Saturday morning after the attack. But when the gun which we carried back to the battalion was checked the next day, it was found, by the number – which we had not been able to check in the dark – that we had left our Lewis gun on the dump, and brought away with us the one we had found. I got into trouble over this mistake. The incident gave further proof to me of the callousness and inflexibility of army routine and discipline. We had survived five days and nights of exhausting experiences, but they stood for nothing in comparison to having brought the wrong gun back to the battalion.

2/Lt John Godfrey, 103 Field Coy, RE

The amount of Engineer stores used in this war is extraordinary, especially in trenches and dugouts. I carry up an average of a ton and a half a night, and more of course when there is anything on. I am glad to say the army has learnt to be more economical. We must save thousands of pounds a day by 'salvage' – collection of stuff lying about. I know one corps saved one million pounds' worth of stuff in a month in a battle area.

Signaller Charles Birnstingl, 1/9th The London Rgt (Queen Victoria Rifles)

There are notices one sees stuck on boards by the roadside: 'Every 18-pounder shell costs x and an x inch shell cots £13, pick it up now, and save yourself further taxation.' Other popular notices were those directing you to 'pick up nails'. Hundreds of horses lose their hooves through nails. 'Pick it up now and put it here' (a box by the roadside). There are also boxes for rubber from tyres, and for brass.

Rev. Roger Bulstrode, Hon. Chaplain to the Forces (2nd Class)

One of my strongest impressions of war is the waste, the appalling, wicked, inconceivable waste. Much waste is, of course, inevitable under conditions so entirely uneconomic as those of war. If every pound were wisely spent, if every bullet and shell reached its mark, if no ships were sunk and no cargoes lost, the cost of war would be enormously reduced. But these conditions are unattainable even in a model war. For instance, while we were on the Somme, the enemy made many attempts to blow up an ammunition dump. One day, some fifteen planes came over, and the last one succeeded in dropping a bomb which hit the target. That dump was 'going up' for several days afterwards with a continuous cannonade – sheer waste, and heart-rending loss. But it could not be helped, it was inevitable.

The waste I have in mind was neither inevitable nor necessary –
it seemed wanton. Sometimes, for instance, when camps were
moved, great heaps of rations were left behind – precious butter,
cheese or jam was simply scrapped. I have seen dugouts and
trenches lined with bully beef tins (unopened), and this when our
friends in England were going short of needed food. I believe that
in the early days a rule was applied that no unit might underdraw
its rations. So if a battalion went into action eight hundred strong
and came out at half its strength, the quartermaster might apply
for rations for four hundred, but eight hundred were issued!

---

*Coming out of action and going into divisional rest, perhaps twenty or
thirty miles behind the lines, was welcomed by all officers and men, but
it was not an occasion for relaxation. For the officers in particular there
was an enormous amount of administrative work to be undertaken, not
least dealing with the effects of those who had been killed or wounded,
and re-equipping those who remained.*

Capt. George McMurtie, 7th Somerset Light Infantry
All the company papers were in an awful mess. I had a nominal roll
of all the men made up, the company roll having been lost in the
attack. I sent in a list of casualties to the orderly room and then
paraded the company for indents for kit. There was not a man with
a complete kit – box respirators, ammunition, bayonets, hats,
webbing, socks – everything was missing. We made out a huge
list of kit and made an indent for them. Throughout the battalion
there was only one Lewis gun, with no magazines. All these had
been lost. I had only about thirty men, one CQMS who was
invaluable at that time and Sergeant Peaty, who was acting CSM.
There were no other officers in the company. There was an
accumulation of two weeks' mail. This had to be sorted out
and all the letters of the wounded or missing had to be signed to

that effect. This was a huge job but after a good deal of work, I at last got through them all. Parcels which arrived for men who were casualties were distributed amongst their old section.

The first morning we woke to find that the rations had not turned up and so each Company Commander had to go round and buy food for the company. I managed to get potatoes, meat, bread and butter and the company had a very good breakfast. I had to see about latrines being made, fire buckets being put outside the billet and shades to candles. Every day lists came from various Casualty Clearing Stations giving names of officers and men of the battalion who had been evacuated, and soon lists of men who had been taken prisoner also began to arrive. Meanwhile, letters started coming to me asking for information about men whom their relatives had not heard from for several weeks . . .

It was tremendous being out in this lovely country. Everything was quiet and peaceful – a nice bed to get into at night, a decent room with tables, chairs, sofa and a fire, and a horse available to ride. The work was also most interesting, reorganising and re-equipping the company, gradually training the drafts as they arrived, training new NCOs and teaching them their duties, getting to know the men really well, looking to all their comforts, putting right all their grievances, and doing everything one could for them; and by so doing getting them to realise that a Company Commander is out to look after them and not to do them down at every turn.

Lt George Foley, 7th Somerset Light Infantry
I had to take 'Company Office', which filled me with considerable alarm. At a stated hour, I would take my seat, probably a biscuit box, in my office. The sergeant major would then in stentorian tones marshal a delinquent before me. With an attempt at severity, which I always felt to be extremely feeble, I pick up the charge sheet, and read out the 'crime'. The witness then clears his throat, and rolls out a parrot-like jargon. 'Sir, on the night of

the so-and-so, I saw the accused to so-forth, etc, etc.' I then sternly
enquire of the victim if he has anything to say. Words fail him at
the last moment, and he murmurs incoherently. I pretend to
weigh his remarks judicially, and strive to appear suitably severe,
but feel a frantic and idiotic sympathy with the man. The sergeant
major coughs scathingly, as if to imply that, in his opinion, the
accused stands self-convicted. Eventually I breathe hard, a cold
sweat gathers on my brow, and I mutter 'five days' CB' [confined
to barracks] or words to that effect.

Sapper Albert Martin, 41st Signal Coy, RE

In accordance with orders, Bradley, MacDougall, Enticknap, and I
this morning proceeded by cycle to divisional headquarters for a
course in wireless. We have to go each morning this week. The
distance is only a few km but we have to be over there before 9
a.m. When we were returning this dinnertime, Enticknap and I
called in a little café and had some coffee, leaving our cycles
outside the window. My luck was out, for up came a Military
Policeman and demanded our names and numbers, etc. We could
see our cycles from where we sat, but that isn't good enough for
the army – you must have your hand on it. So now I am 'for it' for
wilful negligence of Government property.

Our new officer arrived – Lieutenant The Hon. H. M. Sylvester –
with the accent on the 'ves' if you please – and I was immediately
pulled up before him to answer the serious charge concerning the
bicycle. As it was the first case brought before him, I was dismissed
with a caution. He appears to be a very merry sort of fellow and we
both had rather a job to treat the matter seriously, but Sergeant
Twycross stood by looking very austere. He has a big realisation of
the dignity and importance of a sergeant, Royal Engineers.

Capt. George McMurtie, 7th Somerset Light Infantry

When dealing out punishment, I had to be careful. It was obvious
that if I gave too hard a sentence, the men would resent it, begin to

dislike me and things would not go smoothly as they had done up to then. On the other hand, if I was too lenient, the company would take advantage of it and discipline would immediately go. Again, I was always very careful to give any man who was brought up before me a good chance of speaking for himself to explain the circumstances. This was especially important when a man was brought by the CSM or NCO who had a dislike or was 'down' on him. If I was not careful, I should be punishing him unjustly – nothing upsets a man and for that matter the whole company more than when a man is unjustly or too severely punished. Bullying was never any good. With some men, the crime they had committed was just a little carelessness; they might be good men and very keen to keep their conduct sheet clean and so an 'admonish' would be enough. Other men with bad crime sheets would require a heavy sentence. Here again, there was a striking example in the company.

A private called Tavinor had a very full crime sheet. He had been attached to a tunnelling company for some time and rejoined the company. At first I had some trouble with him but after a bit he improved wonderfully. I was chatting to him and laughingly remarked that he had not been up for Company Office for a long time. His reply was that he was now being treated properly and that his long crime sheet was due to a Company Commander before me who took a violent dislike to him, treated him harshly and made him give up hope of ever getting out of a crime.

2/Lt Harold Jones, 12th South Wales Borderers

Xmas Day found us in the front line again. The men had read somewhere that on this day the Germans were going to signal all along their line that they had had enough. The signals were to be blue lights. It was pathetic to hear them discussing what they would do when it was all over. I did my best to prepare them for disillusionment and Jerry soon did the rest. He strafed us unmercifully most of the day and all night.

2/Lt Arthur Richardson, 116th Siege Batt., RGA

Christmas Day: Snowing hard. Helping to build the 'dining hall' for the men on the canal bank. A lovely place was made by the fitters from the doorposts of ruined houses in Ypres and waterproof canvass covering.

Men's dinner at 1 p.m. – a tophole show: consisted of roast pork, beef, Xmas pudding, apples, oranges, nuts and wine: cigarettes by the ton. Acted as waiter dishing out beer. Singsong during the afternoon.

We [the officers] had a tophole dinner at night – soup, turkey (17 lbs bought in Poperinge) Xmas pudding (mother's!) fruit, nuts, champagne, whiskey, port etc, etc: a truly splendid feast.

31 December: Night quiet. Sat up and 'saw' the new year in! We all drank to a 'Prosperous and a Happy New Year, in the hope that it may bring Peace'. How I thought of you all in dear old England, sitting up doing the same thing!

1918

The War in 1918

The enforced retirement of Russia from the war gave Germany a short window of opportunity to transfer around one million men from the Eastern to the Western Front, in order to launch a final knockout blow against the Allies. This was no secret. The Allies knew for months that such an assault was inevitable. However, such had been the losses at Ypres in the previous year's campaign that the Prime Minister, Lloyd George, was determined that his Commander-in-Chief would not have the manpower to plan, never mind prosecute, a spring offensive. In furtherance of this aim, he deliberately restricted the number of men sent to the Western Front in the first weeks of 1918. By March, German manpower had increased by around a third in four months; Allied manpower was down a quarter since the previous summer.

Anticipating an enemy attack, Haig set about a programme of reform on the Western Front, creating zones of defence, strong-points and positions of interlocking fire. As the build-up behind enemy lines continued, raids were undertaken in order to capture prisoners who might reveal the date when the offensive would begin.

The British and French did not have to wait long. The Germans planned to attack the line where British and French forces met, splitting the Allies and driving a wedge between them before pushing the British back north towards the Channel ports. On 21 March, a storm of German shells tore into the lightly held front lines, and within hours, helped by a heavy spring fog, the German infantry attacked, with storm troopers quickly enveloping the defences. Once again the forward line was bypassed and strongpoints ignored, as troops poured through gaps in the forward defences and into second, then third, line trenches almost before the defenders knew they were there. Artillery was captured or hastily pulled out of the line, weakening the ability of the guns to break up the enemy's advance. Confusion reigned.

The weight of the attack had fallen on the British Fifth Army around St Quentin, the Germans chasing and harrying the British troops as they fell back. Owing to the Fifth Army's retreat, the neighbouring Third Army was forced to pull back across the Somme, handing over all the land taken at such cost in 1916. Within days, the German army had crossed the Somme and was bearing down on the strategically important city of Amiens. Such was the pace of the advance that the German soldiers became just as exhausted as the defenders. They had also been shocked at the abundance of supplies available to the Allied troops, as abandoned canteens were overtaken by German soldiers who stopped to help themselves to the supplies. The blockade on Germany and the country's own economic mismanagement had bitten deep into the national economy. All Germany's endeavours had been utilised for the army at the neglect of the civilian population, who were suffering great privations. This in turn had affected the supply of raw materials and food to the army, creating a spiral of social and industrial decline that proved impossible to arrest, let alone reverse.

The German attack had not been decisive, so its High Command switched the thrust of the offensive north to Flanders, where an attack was made close to Armentières. The intention of this was to seize two commanding heights close to the Ypres Salient, forcing a British evacuation of the ground, and a retirement again to the Channel ports, but, as with so many initial battlefield successes, the momentum could not be maintained as the defenders fell back, thereby shortening their supply chain and con-

centrating resources while the attackers lengthened theirs. Both
sides knew the significance of the operations, Haig urging his men
to even greater efforts with a personal message on 11 April to all
British soldiers to stand firm: 'With our backs to the wall, and
believing in the justice of our cause each one of us must fight on to
the end.' The German attack petered out, still a long way short of a
very important rail junction at Hazebrouck and still twenty-five
miles from the closest Channel port.

There were further German attacks, most notably on the
Chemin des Dames, where trench warfare had begun almost four
years earlier. Yet with each attack the Germans only dissipated
what strength they had left. Allied prisoners of war could see the
ramshackle support behind the German troops, and how old, and
how young, many of those soldiers were; how ill equipped were
the rank and file. Those prisoners were in no doubt that Germany
would lose the war. The German attacks ground inexorably to a
halt in June and early July, leaving them in defence of large
salients that bulged into Allied lines. The effect of these inconclusive battles on undermining German morale should not be
underestimated, a depression made worse by the arrival and
deployment of American combat troops. Men of the American
Expeditionary Force (AEF) were pouring into France by the
boatload. Their number would reach nearly 1.4 million by
November. There was a momentary pause in July before the
Allies returned to the offensive, in what has been characterised as a
hundred days of a rolling offensive that threw the Germans back
across the battlefields and into fresh, untouched rural territory
beyond.

The first pin-pricks began in July, but it was a huge Allied
attack on 8 August which signalled the start of the counter-
offensive. This time troops swept once more over the Somme
battlefield, carried forward with overwhelming artillery and air
support. The Germans, outgunned and outnumbered, collapsed,
offering little effective resistance. Huge numbers of prisoners were

taken on a day that the German High Command would record as 'the black day of the German army in the history of the War'.

The war was lost. It was now just a question of how long German soldiers could hold out, coupled with the will of the military authorities back home to keep them there. Over the next three months, the Germans fought a tenacious rearguard action, but when the Hindenburg Line was breached in September there was no new defensive line to fall back on. Prisoners fell into Allied hands in increasing numbers, although even as late as early November few soldiers on the ground expected anything other than the war continuing into 1919, as the Germans pulled back to the homeland and defended the Rhine.

It was not to be. After failed attempts to procure a negotiated ceasefire, the Germans capitulated, agreeing to all Allied demands in order to gain an armistice and an end to the fighting. They pulled back to their pre-war frontier, at the same time relinquishing control of Alsace and Lorraine, the two disputed lands seized by the Germans from the French in the war of 1870. As the Germans retreated, they were followed closely by the Allies. On 1 December the Allies crossed the border into Germany and took control of the Rhineland, one of the jewels in Germany's industrial crown. They would remain there not just while a lasting peace was negotiated between the victorious Allies and imposed upon the Germans, but for a further ten years. On 29 June 1919, the Treaty of Versailles was reluctantly signed by the Germans, five years to the day since the Austrian heir to the throne, Archduke Franz Ferdinand, had been assassinated in Sarajevo, sparking the international crisis that had led to war.

Awards and Medals

For a conflict which lasted well over four years, there is a particular dearth of campaign medals for the Great War. Regardless of how many battles he fought in, irrespective of which continent a man served on, the greatest number of medals he could receive (other than an award for gallantry) was three, and the majority of those who served in the war received only two. The three medals were the 1914 Star or the 1914–15 Star (only one would be awarded, depending on service), the British War Medal and, lastly, the Victory Medal. The three were affectionately known as Pip, Squeak and Wilfred (after the *Daily Mirror* comic-strip characters). However, to qualify for either of the 'Stars', a man had to be serving abroad before 1 January 1916, so that a clear majority of five million men who fought received only two medals, known just as affectionately as Mutt and Jeff (also comic-strip characters).

This was very different from the Second World War, when separate campaign medals were awarded for service in such places as North Africa, Italy and Burma. In the Crimean War and the South African War, clasps rather than extra medals were given, to be worn on a medal ribbon, indicating participation in different battles or campaigns. In the Great War only one clasp was awarded and that was for those who saw action (within range of enemy guns) in the first four months of the war. There was no individual recognition or clasp for fighting at the Battle of Loos, on the Somme, or at Ypres.

Frank Richards, a regular soldier who served throughout the war, was scathing about the lack of distinction. The men who served at the bases behind the lines were entitled to exactly the same medals as those in the trenches and wore them, he felt, 'more proudly'. In earlier wars, the bar or clasp had been all-important. 'A pukka old soldier would be very ashamed to wear a war medal that did not have a bar attached. They were known as bare-arsed medals.' Richards wondered if the American Indian tradition of carrying scalps was not preferable: at least it would indicate who had done what. 'The Red Indians were vain but they were honest.'

Two medals for up to three years' overseas service was small return for such hard work and indicated neither actions fought nor time served. When nineteen-year-old Private Edgar Smallman of the 1st Welsh Guards set sail for France on the afternoon of 10 November 1918, disembarking at Boulogne that evening, he still ended up with the same medals for twenty-four-hours' active service overseas as a man who served for three years, on the Somme, Arras, at Passchendaele, Cambrai and in many other battles besides.

This lack of distinction annoyed some veterans. A few old soldiers, especially those who missed receiving the '14–15 Star by a matter of days, purchased and took to wearing the medal regardless, thus indicating two things to the casual observer: firstly, that the man was a regular, territorial or a volunteer and not a conscript. Since conscription was introduced in January 1916, no conscript received the 1914–15 Star. For 1914 Kitchener Volunteers, in particular, this was a very important distinction. They had enlisted at the beginning of the war and did not want people to think that they had been coerced into serving their country. And secondly, the 1914–15 Star carried the clear implication that the wearer might have served abroad for some considerable time, and had probably seen front line action.

There were, of course, gallantry medals which would show that active service had been seen and courage displayed above and beyond the call of duty. There were five principal distinctions: the Victoria Cross for all, regardless of rank; the Distinguished Service

Order (DSO) for officers; the Military Cross (MC) for officers and warrant officers; the Distinguished Conduct Medal (DCM); and the Military Medal (MM) for NCOs and other ranks. Fewer than 200,000 gallantry medals were awarded, roughly one in twenty-five servicemen receiving such recognition. Another 140,000 men were mentioned in dispatches, although many of these also won a gallantry medal. While large numbers of men had been recognised for bravery, clearly the vast majority had received nothing; although they might have been equally courageous, their actions went unnoticed.

Inevitably, amongst those who received no recognition there was sometimes scepticism about the 'quality' of awards. The Military Medal was instituted in March 1916 and was given as a lesser distinction than the DCM (which also came with a £20 gratuity). The MM conferred nothing else on an individual; no extra pay, and no citation published in the *London Gazette* detailing the reason for the award. For some soldiers that was good enough; for others there was a charge that Military Medals 'were sent up with the rations', to be distributed as largesse by an officer. The problem was that in spite of the MM's wide distribution (and its officer equivalent, the MC), there was no clear policy for its award. No supporting eyewitness corroboration was required, only that an individual had undertaken a specific act of gallantry, or, more vaguely, shown gallantry over a specified period. This caused a certain amount of (largely unwarranted) resentment against those serving well behind the lines. In 1917, after much front line service, Private Charles Heare was sent down with a friend to corps headquarters, many miles behind the lines.

'What a tremendous lot of DCMs, Military Medals and other honours!' he wrote. 'On making enquiries, we find these officers and men have never seen a shell burst or heard enemy rifle fire; they've only seen shells on trucks. Full rations and good pay. One man told us, "Our sergeant, who had the DCM and MM, is a cool man up the line. Shells were bursting on the right of us when we were running out a [telephone] line. Bursting about two hundred yards away and our sergeant was quite cool." I found out afterwards the nearest they have been is divisional headquarters and they call that up the line! RE Signals, Army Service Corps and Ordnance Corps are full of medals. It seems a joke. The infantry are saying that they are so far from the war, they don't know if they are in the army or the navy.'

In fact many of those who had received such honours were infantrymen badly wounded or simply worn out from front line service. They had been awarded medals for bravery in the field much earlier in the war and were now working at the base camps. It was a fact sometimes ignored by those who had taken their place in the trenches.

It was for this reason that men like Private Norman Cliff, who received an MM after a big operation, felt such awards were devalued because he believed that similar recognition had gone to NCOs behind the lines. 'I could not help being incensed myself when only a remnant of our battalion survived a particularly grim engagement into which we were flung at a moment's notice to plug a breach in a very fluid line, and the RSM, who had remained behind in charge of the stores, was decorated.'

Such sentiments were not the preserve of other ranks. Lieutenant Colonel Henry Dillon, in a letter written in October 1916, noted the disparity. The battalion had recently come out of action and the divisional general had come down to say a few kind words to the men, which had been appreciated. The battalion had suffered heavy casualties, including seventeen officers killed or wounded, roughly half the battalion's complement. Those who remained were doing two officers' jobs. Dillon was delighted that six men had been awarded Military Medals and although he had recommended several officers for awards he had yet to hear anything. 'One fellow I think is sure to get the Military Cross. He was severely wounded in the advance about 6 a.m. but carried on till 2 p.m. He then went out with four men and went over a thousand yards into the German line. Captured seven Huns, located a field gun and Hun observation post. He came and gave me his report at 5.30 and had to be carried away.' It was remarkable that it was only a Military Cross that he seemed destined for. 'It makes one a little sad,' wrote Dillon, 'to think that people at Le Havre and Rouen [base camps] get DSOs and this chap, who was a land agent only a few months ago, will probably only get the MC.'

The award of the Military Cross for this action seems richly deserved. However, Frank Richards recalled another incident in which, during a German attack, an officer had called on his own men to surrender. The order was ignored by a more experienced and more senior officer, and the men had fought on, successfully. The senior officer was awarded the DSO, and the platoon officer who had called on the men to surrender was awarded the MC, recalled Richards. 'He really deserved something different.'

'There is the most awful humbug going on over honours and [they] have precious little value now,' wrote Lieutenant Colonel George Stevens, DSO, Commanding Officer of the 2nd Royal Fusiliers. 'I have had many men, fine fellows, runners, scouts, stretcher-bearers, patrol leaders, etc, whom I have recommended for honours turned down because they "only did their duty", and yet one sees a certain class of officer wearing decorations "for a specific act of bravery in face of the enemy" who one knows never went within miles of the same enemy, and after all every staff officer, who is generally profusely decorated and helps himself to foreign orders, is "only doing his duty".'

The exception was the Victoria Cross. This was the highest distinction (only 633 were awarded throughout the entire course of the war) and was usually beyond reproach. It could not be awarded without the highest display of 'conspicuous courage' and was awarded by the Sovereign alone, after advice. Nevertheless, there could be grumbles. Private James Garrard, who was to win the DCM and MM during the war, serving with the 9th Cheshire

Regiment, felt he had been overlooked when an officer with whom he had helped take a pillbox was given the highest decoration. 'I took a couple of messages over the open to headquarters, for which I were awarded the MM, but rushing the pillbox (Potsdam Farm) and stopping the retreat I never got a mention, but Lt Colvin got the VC for that. Such is life.'

Military distinctions were designed to recognise (and encourage) bravery on the battlefield. In the majority of cases, awards were given for the right reasons, although undoubtedly there were many who received nothing but who displayed the most remarkable example to others. For the vast majority of men, who simply did their job, the army provided other distinctions to acknowledge their contribution to the effort. A brass wound stripe, worn on the left sleeve for each occasion of injury, was a clear indication of service. Blue and red chevrons stitched on to the right tunic sleeve indicated years abroad: a blue badge for every completed year from 1915, a red one for those who had served in 1914. Yet in both cases these were only worn while a man was in khaki and not (officially) once he had returned to civilian life. Then, the only indication, other than an obvious physical injury, that a man had seen action was the award of a Silver War Badge. These were given to men who, because of illness or injury, were deemed unfit for further service. However, if a man was wounded but continued his service until the end of the war, no such badge was given.

For millions of men, Mutt and Jeff were all there was from a thankful nation to commend soldiers, sailors and airmen for months and even years of service to King and Country. This paucity in number reflected the subsequent paucity of help offered to the men in terms of housing, pensions and welfare; those empty promises made on behalf of a nation by politicians who wished to build a 'land fit for heroes'.

Soldiers' Memories

Lt Edward Allfree, 111th Siege Batt., RGA

I am sitting there in this little dark dugout, in a battered-in Hun trench, out in the midst of that awful shell-strafed mud swamp, with the rain splashing down outside in a vain attempt to make the mud muddier, and the stillness occasionally disturbed by the wail of a shell, followed by that shattering roar as it buries itself, explodes, sends up a fountain of mud and smoke and splinters, making yet another crater in that already shell-pocked ground, with one candle burning while I make my day's entry in my little diary, when the field telephone at my elbow buzzes. What does it mean? Is it an SOS or a target coming through to be fired at, this time of night? I have visions of myself sliding about in the rain and mud and darkness, getting the detachments on to the guns. I take up the receiver. 'What's that? Will you kindly repeat that message one hundred times?' The telephonist repeats:– 'Order just come through, sir, from HA Group Headquarters, that Mr Allfree is to go on leave on the 12th. inst!' Joy of joys – leave at last – the night is no longer gloomy or dull. I want to go and wake someone else, and shout the news in his ear. It seems too good to be true – the idea of getting away from this beastly spot for ten whole days at home!

Sapper Albert Martin, 41st Signal Coy, RE

Up very early and packed everything up in readiness. Got away soon after 9 a.m. Tramped to the crossroads at the other end of the town and then jumped on a lorry which took me very nearly to the gates of the rest camp where I reported to the sergeant major. He examined my warrant rather critically and said he thought that I should not have presented myself there until tomorrow. After some deliberation, he said, 'All right, fall in with today's party at 12.45.' At Bray station, our passes were briefly scanned and stamped but I managed to crush through in a crowd and so on to a train where I chummed up with a motor-cyclist corporal. We left Bray at 2.30 and crawled down to Calais which we reached between eight and nine, and we marched across the town from one station to another. Here we had to wait for a couple of hours with only a small Salvation Army canteen anywhere near. It was a regular fight to get anything to eat, but we managed it, and at 11 p.m. we were crowded into trucks again and resumed our journey to Boulogne.

At daybreak we were still some distance from Boulogne but we arrived there about eight o'clock . . . Down on the quayside a notice instructed leave men to fall in at 11.30, so we just strolled about a bit and had a basin of porridge in a canteen . . . Then commenced a close and careful scrutiny of our warrants by MPs who came down the ranks and another examination as we passed on to the gangway and yet another when we stepped on to the boat. It was a terribly rough crossing; the boat was blown right round three times. I was about the only one on board who was not seasick and we did not arrive in Folkestone until a quarter past three. Trains were waiting and soon we were speeding up to London. As we looked out of the carriage windows, it required a distinct mental effort to realise that the people we saw walking about were English and spoke the same language as we did – so accustomed have we become to seeing only civilians of other nations who jabber in French or gargle in Flemish.

Driver Percival Glock, 281 Brigade, 56th Div., RFA
The first three or four days one is home after, say, eighteen months away seems more like a dream than anything else, but one soon

wakes up to the fact that you have to go back. What struck me as funny was how ignorant I was as to how the war was going on, all I knew was of one particular part and everybody else had the whole fighting line at their fingertips. I was also struck by the numbers of fellows going about all poshed up in khaki and swanking as to what they had done in France. I was speaking to one of these fellows and happened to mention St Pol, which at that time was quite twenty miles from the firing line. The fellow jumped at the sound of the word (as he probably heard it somewhere) and said, 'My word, that's a pretty hot shop now, isn't it? I was there the week before last.' I didn't call him a liar as he was about three times my size.

Capt. George McMurtie, 7th Somerset Light Infantry

We got to town about 7 p.m. There was the usual bustle at Victoria, everyone was very happy, wives were meeting husbands, sweethearts were embracing and there was a big crowd at the barrier on the lookout for friends. I took a tube to Russell Square, I had an old Burberry covered with mud and a pack and was evidently 'back from the front' and felt a great hero, with everyone staring at me.

It was great having a really good meal in a dining room with a tablecloth, serviettes, bright lights, and everything cooked and served in a civilised fashion once more. I went to bed pretty tired that night, clean sheets and all the comforts of a London hotel soon got me asleep. Having had a glorious hot bath and a good breakfast, I walked to the tube and soon got to Paddington. On the way down, I talked to a very nice lady and gentleman who asked me all about the Cambrai show and the reasons for our withdrawal. I got home to Bristol by midday and then started the best two weeks I have ever spent.

Pte Christopher Massie, 76 Brigade, 25th Div., RAMC

The sight of London drew me, as I knew it would. My first glance at the wonderful city was a greater emotional experience than sixteen months of active service. Familiar streets took me back to my unfamiliar self. I went about searching anxiously for fragments of my life.

Some people ask you: 'What is it like out there?' knowing with instinctive apprehension exactly what it is like!

But England and London! There is a light and lovely side. Those wonderful girls working the trams and buses and railway stations, delivering papers, milk and bread. To Tommy, 'on leave', London is a dazzling revue of enchanting feminine uniforms. These girls are kind to us chaps who have come back for a breather. They have a special inflection in their voices all for us. A special greeting, a quiet sympathy, for all the world as if we were invalids who require special treatment. And so we do.

Sgt Arthur Cook, 1st Somerset Light Infantry
It was heavenly to be in dear old England again, and in such peaceful surroundings it was difficult to realise that many of our men were daily laying down their lives within so short a journey from our countryside. Another pleasure was to be able to walk about with a straight back and no ducking from shells.

Pte Charles Heare, 1/2nd Monmouthshire Rgt
I have a few days in Northampton and on to Pontypool: fourteen days' leave soon go. It all seems strange to me but somehow I am not happy. I feel it is not my place. I feel somehow I belong to another world, not this civilisation. Every day seems the same here, although I have been looking forward to my leave and waited so long. Now it seems I am longing to get back. Why, I don't know.

Maj A. G. P. Hardwick, 59th Field Ambulance, RAMC
With much trepidation and misgivings I left Newquay this morning by the 9.30am train – the aforesaid fears being on account of a pair of ferrets that I was taking back to France to fight the rats. I had arranged by wire for Alan [his brother] to meet

me at Paddington if he got his leave from the gunner school at Weedon.

The ten days at home have been splendid and although I can't recall how the days were spent, at any rate I enjoyed every moment. My golf was bad, my bridge was bad, but my appetite was grand! I could not get a carriage to myself at Truro and so I had to put 'the menagerie' out in the corridor, as their smell was a bit stronger than their bite!

Alan was at Paddington all right, resplendent in a white band around his cap and a new pair of spurs, and so he was eminently fitted for the post of 1st whip and I allowed him to carry the pets. We then took a taxi to Regent's Palace and found out that a double room had been reserved for us – but, oh no! No animals were allowed in the hotel. However, by going round to another door and walking in as if we were carrying 'a present for a good boy', we managed to smuggle the beasts up to the bedroom. I had a pocket full of bread saved from lunch and so we gave them a good feed of bread and water at once and strapped them down again.

Alan was called at 5am as he had to catch a dashed early train to Euston and so he had his breakfast upstairs! I bagged all his milk and so the ferrets had a grand breakfast. They made a devil of a row during the night, scratching away at the box and squeaking so much that I quite expected to hear of a complaint from the next door neighbour.

Sgt Arthur Cook, 1st Somerset Light Infantry

The journey back to France is one I shall never forget; the sea was just about as cross as it could possibly be, our old paddle boat was tossed about like a cork, we had to lie down flat and grip each other to avoid being washed overboard by the huge waves that dashed over, drenching us to the skin; everybody was vomiting over each other and retching their hearts out, you could not tell spew from spray. We must have looked a sorry lot on landing! The next morning, Pte Hawkins was found dead in his bivouac, the poor fellow had overtaxed his heart on the boat. We were very sad at the loss of this old soldier who had survived all the perils of this war from the beginning.

Driver Percival Glock, 281 Brigade, 56th Div., RFA

Everybody in the train and boat were right fed up. Anyway, we managed to get back and went straight up the line again. If ever I felt windy, I did then, for about two days. At the least sound I would almost jump out of my skin. It was a very quiet part of the line, too, hardly saw a shell burst, but the cause of the windyness was coming from peaceful surroundings straight into the line. After two days I got settled down again in the same old style, didn't care a button.

Pte Robert Cude, 7th The Buffs (East Kent Rgt)

Entrain for Hazebrouck, arriving midday. Go to rest house for a few hours and soon get into a fight, for two Aussies arrive back from leave, and in consequence of their bragging conversations, in which they tell us that they get Blighty leave every four and a half months, they strike a bad patch. They are on a staff job somewhere. Some of the men here have been two years without leave and directly the Aussies started, they were subjected to a running fire of questions with regard to the justice of it all. Then the trouble started; either they had too much spirits or else did not realise the danger of their answers, for they did not attempt to stave it off. They were beaten unmercifully, and their nice new clothes were in rags before they had finished, and kicked out of the gates. Rather too bad, but merited just the same.

In comparison with many Empire troops, the British Tommy was neither well paid nor given much in the way of leave. For the most part, the difference was grumblingly accepted, except when it was undiplomatically rubbed in. On the whole, the British had a healthy respect for the Australian and New Zealand troops (Anzacs), not just for their

*fighting spirit but for their morale in general and their relaxed
indifference to authority.*

Pte Reginald Wilkes, 16th Royal Warwickshire Rgt (3rd Birmingham Pals)

We have been working with a company of Anzac Engineers from
New Zealand lately and a fine set they are. Most of them were gold
miners previously. This particular lot are rather elderly and in
many cases well educated. The total lack of side, swank or class
distinctions amongst them is most refreshing. It is fine to hear the
officers calling the men by their Christian names and so on. It is
very funny to see one of these colonials go up to a young English
officer and say, 'Mate, can you tell us the time please?' Their
conventions and way of speaking to officers, etc, would send some
of our old soldiers crazy. It is Tom, Dick and Harry all the way
round with them, no 'Sirring' and saluting.

2/Lt Harold Jones, 2nd South Wales Borderers

Second Lieutenant Dickinson, when on rest, was walking along a
road when he met two Aussies. As was their general rule they
failed to salute Dickinson and he had the nerve to stop them and
attempt to reprimand them. One of them drawled, 'Who are yer?'
'I am an officer,' said Dickinson. 'Oh,' said the Aussie 'Then you
are the bugger I've been looking for. Hold my coat, Bill, while I
spank him.' When Dickinson saw the man prepare for action he
made a bolt for it, but of course came back to tell us of his lucky
escape. He thought it a great joke.

Pte Charles Heare, 1/2nd Monmouthshire Rgt

One night going up through Hazebrouck I hear a crash, a shell, I
thought, but I see a Military Policeman lying on the road outside a
café. He has been thrown through a large plate-glass window and
his head is in a mess. I hear movement inside the café so I get on
my bicycle and fly. Always keep out of trouble is best.

The next day the divisional signals officer sends for me. 'What time were you in Hazebrouck last night, Heare? Your message is timed 10.30 p.m. from here and 11 p.m. at your battalion, is that right?' 'Yes, sir,' I say. 'What did you see when you came back?' 'I didn't come back that way owing to shells dropping in Hazebrouck, I went around the Steenvoorde–Cassel road, sir.' 'All right, Heare, you may go, but a Military Policeman was found dead on the road this morning, early.' I felt pleased to get away. Two days later an Australian sergeant stopped me. 'Your name is Heare, 2nd Monmouthshires?' I said, 'Yes.' 'Well,' he says, 'come and have a bottle. I want to have a talk with you.' Off we go. 'You were in Hazebrouck when the MP went through the window and you have been questioned. Isn't that right?' 'What of it?' I say. He is like an ox, six foot. I told him all I knew. 'You haven't told a soul then. Well done, Taffy. The boys were having a drink. They found a heap of bottles, full, and they were playing the piano when an MP of yours came in. "Get out!" he says. "Go to hell!" said the boys. The MP drew a revolver. "Get out, you wasters", and he came in the door. One of our fellows behind the door hit him over the head with a full bottle and we threw him through the window. So now you know all, Taffy. You promise to keep mum?' 'Yes,' I say, 'for sure. I don't want trouble.' 'Well done,' he says. 'Here's a drink from the boys who don't want trouble.' He gave me fifty francs.

————————

The dislocation many men felt on home leave often caused widespread bitterness and resentment amongst those who had so looked forward to a trip back to Britain. War fatigue had set in, and, while few doubted the righteousness of the cause, some felt anger nevertheless.

Pte Robert Cude, 7th The Buffs (East Kent Rgt)

Reading the various articles from the papers, one is taught to believe that war is such a glorious thing and that every man jack of us is anxious to kill, etc, and incidentally is delighted to be serving.

I am disgusted with England and the chaps walking about labelled 'indispensable'. I hate and loathe them as 'parasites'. It is a fact that England alone tolerates 'conscientious objectors' of all her Allies and, as such, is held up to ridicule. I have a spark of pity for them, but for any man of military age, whatever his responsibilities, to be allowed to say he is 'indispensable' I think is the greatest insult that the people of England can hurl at their own men, who are giving their all so that Jerry shall not be top dog. I cannot forget how our division, and we are one of several, had to remain in the line, month after month during 1915/16, because no other troops were available for a relief.

Cpl David Rowlands, 15th Durham Light Infantry
Perhaps you would like to know something of the spirit of the men out here now. Well, the truth is every man jack is fed up almost past bearing, and not a single one has an *ounce* of what we call patriotism left in him. No one cares a rap whether Germany has Alsace, Belgium or France *too* for that matter. All that every man desires now is to get done with it and go home. Now that's the honest truth, and any man who has been out within the last few months will tell you the same. In fact, and this is *no* exaggeration, the greatest hope of a great majority of the men is that rioting and revolt at home will force the government to pack in on *any* terms. Now you've got the *real* state of affairs 'right from the horse's mouth' as it were.

Pte Daniel Sweeney, 1st Lincolnshire Rgt
Our boys are having a terrible time in the trenches. They are up to the waist in mud and water, each side of the roads there are dead horses and men, carts, motor lorries, etc, in hundreds. Our transport have managed to get the rations up to the boys and have only lost two horses and one man up to now. The Somme was

bad enough but this is a thousand times worse. The censor, if he reads my letters, may say that I am chancing my arm for sending this news. All I can say to him is let the papers publish what the troops out here are really doing, also the torture they are going through, then perhaps the public will realise that a man out here in the fighting forces deserves better treatment than he gets. There are men now in the trenches fast dying of cold, they go sick, see the doctor, go back and try and stick it until they get relieved. I am not running our doctor down, he is a good man but he has his orders from others.

Gnr Ernest Drane, 197th Siege Batt., RGA

Saturday evening, sitting in a ditch (somewhere in France) watching Fritz shell our gun positions – not daring to move for planes overhead looking for us. We have no food or drink, cannot fire our guns and cannot shift. What should I be doing at home, probably helping to bath the children, then a quiet walk in the garden, with a cigarette. Ah well! Perhaps I shall wake up and find that this is all a dream.

Capt. George McMurtie, 7th Somerset Light Infantry

I was sitting in the company headquarters talking to two lance corporals when a shot went off just outside and a Private Gosney who was on gas sentry rushed in, shrieking and fell to the floor. He had shot himself through the leg rather badly and things looked pretty bad for him as he was already under arrest pending court martial on the charge of not having returned from leave on the proper date. We bound him up and I detailed a stretcher party to take him to the first aid post. After he had gone I had to make out a statement of evidence and sent it to battalion headquarters.

On 12 March I had to give evidence at the court martial of Private Gosney. He was brought on a stretcher in an ambulance, looking very ill. It was the first time I had seen him since the accident and I discovered that he had had his leg amputated. I thought he would certainly be found guilty [of a self-inflicted wound] because the evidence was so strong against him, although I thought it was an accident. His crime sheet was also one of the worst I have ever seen. Anyhow, having been sworn in I gave my evidence and left. Luckily for Gosney the court did not ask to see his conduct sheet, and somehow he was acquitted.

Lt Harold Jones, 2nd South Wales Borderers

After church parade one Sunday we had a very dramatic but unpleasant experience. We were ordered to 'form square' and into the middle between two military policeman marched one of our men, handcuffed. Behind came the brigade adjutant and other red tabs. The man was supposed to be in my platoon but I had never seen him, he having deserted before I took over and, although arrested, deserted again. On this occasion he had been found in a French village, in civilian clothes, and had been there a considerable time. The brigade adjutant stepped to the front and read out the findings of a Field General Court Martial – that Pte—— be shot for desertion. The man turned to his escort and said, 'In the morning, I suppose.' He was taken to a caged-in tent and sat in the open all day, exchanging greetings with all who passed. We played a game of rugby in the same field and he was an interested spectator. He was shot next morning, and although he boasted he would never go up the line he faced death bravely. The men had little sympathy for him. 'Why should we go up time after time and he continually dodge it?' was their reasoning. In any case, he had many chances to make good but never attempted to do so, and had succeeded only in getting several escorts into trouble by giving them the slip. I believe his grave bears the inscription 'accidentally killed'.

Maj. A. G. P. Hardwick, 59th Field Ambulance, RAMC
Saturday 16 March
We found that the division is still in the Cambrai sector. We went to the 'Aux Huitres' and had a gorgeous dinner of oysters and

lobster while waiting for the car. Arrived at Peronne; we decided to stay there for the night with the M.A.C. people. They were delighted with the ferrets, which they persuaded me to let loose in the mess – but they were not quite so pleased when the little beggers 'forgot themselves' in all four corners of the room! Everyone is very 'windy' here and there are terrific rumours of the Boche attacking any day. The last three days an attack has been expected every morning and the C.O. says that prisoners have stated that an attack is to be made between the 17th and the 19th. We were told that every morning we have been putting down terrific barrage at 'stand-to'. All the roads and bridges round here are mined, etc, and so altogether we seem to have returned to a delightful area. Thank goodness our division is still out of the line.

Monday 18 March
Beautiful weather. Had the ferrets out for a trial run amongst the old shell holes. The old buck is dashed good and almost immediately got first blood. He killed a decent-sized rat in a blind hole and we had to dig it out. It was only a trial run as they had had a huge breakfast but it shows they are all right.

George McMurtie, Harold Jones and Major Hardwick soon had other things to attend to, not least of which were the preparations for the German offensive. They had only nine more days to wait before the enemy threw everything he had into what turned out to be his last great offensive of the war, in a desperate bid to seal victory before American troops arrived in force. On 21 March, the 7th Somerset Light Infantry were in close reserve. Soon after the Germans attacked, they were pulled back to dig in close to the St Quentin Canal.

Pte George Fleet, 7th Queen's (Royal West Surrey Rgt)
The events of that fatal morning left us gasping at their intensity and the rapidity with which the Germans had advanced. Standing there, gazing into the early dawn with a rifle at firing point, I

expected a German at any moment to rise from the ground before me. Undoubtedly he would have bayoneted me and thus ended my existence once and for all.

I, with three others and an officer, were detailed to act as guides to the remnants of the battalion holding the front line, or rather a number of posts representing our forward front. Most had been killed or taken prisoner but the remainder had been carefully gathered together in a quarry with which we were in touch. At any moment Jerry might surround these men. On reaching the quarry, we were each given a number of men to guide back to safety, and fate decreed I should be allotted the last batch. I found my way easy at first, but suddenly all contact with the previous section was lost. We were up against a solid mass of barbed wire. Somewhere there should be an opening, but panic seized me and I forced everyone to crawl beneath the wire, the officer cursing me for an utter fool. Perhaps I was, but every minute counted and I feared for my own life as much as for theirs. I also knew we were retreating at 3.30 and that information had been received that a German barrage would be put down at 4.00. My watch recorded nearly 2.30. I had no idea how much further we had to go. I knew our lines to be near the barbed wire but was this the wire I had in mind?

Capt. George McMurtie, 7th Somerset Light Infantry
We passed frightened peasants clearing out of their homes and going back with as much of their household goods as they could carry. They had been through one German occupation and were not going to chance another. It was a pitiable sight seeing old men and women and young children hurrying along as best they could with terror in their eyes. We began to get rather anxious about how things were going . . . We passed a cooker overturned in the road and a stream of men came past us, many wounded, amongst whom were a great many gunners, some carrying gun sights. They told of an awful barrage, of swarms of Germans attacking, and of our men being shot down or surrounded.

A Company was in support of D Company which, under Captain Foley, was guarding the bridges. He had an RE officer with him, who had orders to blow up the bridges as soon as the Huns appeared. It was a fine warm day so with my runner I decided to walk up to the bridge to see Foley. I had only gone halfway when machine-gun fire broke out and came unpleasantly close to me.

Capt. George Foley, 7th Somerset Light Infantry
Machine-gun bullets were sweeping up and down the road and whistling all round us. This was a more startling development than I had expected; we hurried on as fast as we could up the road, meeting on the way, Jones, the brigade intelligence officer, who shouted to us that the Germans had reached the canal bank, various excited Royal Engineer personnel were making good their escape. I was naturally anxious to find out if the destruction of the bridges had been successful; while we were running towards the canal I noticed several heavy explosions and concluded that all was well. To my disgust I found that while the main road bridge, a heavy iron structure, was broken in half with the two ends forming a sort of V in the water, a temporary wooden erection of the Royal Engineers, fit for heavy traffic, further north, was still perfectly intact.

Pte George Fleet, 7th Queen's (Royal West Surrey Rgt)
I had but one thought, to reach our lines as quickly as possible, which I did quite safely, the only casualties being a few torn trousers and tunics. Within the next hour, orders were received to be ready to retire at any moment. A direct confrontation had again been postponed, and that soothed my troubled nerves. We turned our backs on the enemy and started to retire, an operation that lasted until late that afternoon, when we took up a position on a hill. Thankful for the rest, I sank down into the bracken. My feet were weary and my body limp. I only wanted to get away from the fighting, to leave behind the noise of shells and machine guns.

Capt. George Foley, 7th Somerset Light Infantry
We had not gone many yards when straight ahead of us we saw some men crossing a railway line in single file. I immediately took it that they marked the spot where battalion headquarters was established and was hurrying on, when my orderly, whose sight was considerably better than mine, suddenly stopped short. He took a good look at the figures ahead of us, and then announced in no uncertain voice that they were Germans. This discovery came as rather a shock. At the worst I had imagined that the enemy might have forced a crossing of the canal, but to find the position which only a few hours before had been wired to me as a battalion headquarters, actually occupied by the enemy was utterly staggering.

Capt. George McMurtie, 7th Somerset Light Infantry
The end was very near and we were captured. A German on a horse came up and led me to believe that he wanted my revolver and kit and so I gave him my revolver. He took it and fired a round into the ground. I had heard as everyone else had of the awful treatment by the Germans of their prisoners and so thought this German was trying my revolver in order to shoot me. I waited but nothing happened. I was told to take the rest of my kit off and then, being very thirsty, got my water bottle out, filled it from a stream and at last got a drink, the first one for twenty-four hours.

Capt. George Foley, 7th Somerset Light Infantry
Further concealment was useless, and we were in one of those plights when a soldier has to consult whatever conscience he may possess, and choose between a death of doubtful glory, but obvious futility, or surrender.

At twenty yards' distance the leading Hun raised his rifle and aimed it with dispassionate care at my head. It seemed to me that to be shot like a pig in a poke was in no way furthering the cause of the Allies. Consequently, and in rather less time than it takes to tell (the man had large fingers playing about his trigger), I indicated that we were willing to capitulate. Somewhat to our surprise, the Hun, evidently a gentleman, lowered his weapon, at the same time pointing out that our best course was eastward. We complied.

In a few minutes we had joined the little straggling despondent groups who were trailing back through the German lines. With all those grey figures round us, I had the sensation of being swallowed alive.

Pte George Fleet, 7th Queen's (Royal West Surrey Rgt)

Our rest proved short-lived. On the skyline could be observed little black specks moving over the hills from where we had come. Like ants they appeared, so many there were and so methodical their movements. The enemy had followed quickly on our heels. He had tracked us down, and as my eyes took in the vision of those hordes of advancing Germans, my heart sank. I knew I could never escape, that my baptism of fire and slaughter was at hand and I must prepare to face it. Nearer and nearer they came and my blood ran cold as I realised they must eventually come up against us – and that dusk was descending. Behind us a wood, a dense mass of trees and undergrowth. To retreat through this in the dark would be madness, yet no other escape offered itself. With the little time left, we attempted to dig some kind of cover.

Capt. George McMurtie, 7th Somerset Light Infantry

We soon got on the move and arrived in Ham. All the streets were full of Huns, looting the houses, nearly every man I saw was carrying a bottle of wine, some had biscuits, cigarettes, tobacco and chocolates, which they had taken from the large canteen. They all stared at us and I envied them because they had food. I was very hungry having only had a slice of bread, butter and marmalade the evening before and that morning two army biscuits which I had taken from a dead man's haversack. We passed a man pushing a trolley with a huge box of Huntley and Palmer's biscuits. I tried to get a packet from him but all I got was a snarl.

Capt. George Foley, 7th Somerset Light Infantry

As we approached the village we had to pass through a wave of the enemy just emerging. Their bayonets glistened, and they were filled evidently with the lust for blood, and the desire to kill everything in khaki within sight. Never was frightfulness more fiercely displayed, and how we got through them unstuck I cannot imagine.

Shortly after crossing the canal, we met a battalion. The officer in command, a typical German with his hideous spectacles, rode up to us and shouted something in his native tongue, which we, of course, failed entirely to understand. This rather annoyed him, and I thought we were 'for it', but he merely called up one of the cycle orderlies who were following the battalion, and detailed him as our escort. Then with the words, 'Behold, your guide, gentlemen', he saluted and rode away.

Pte George Fleet, 7th Queen's (Royal West Surrey Rgt)

How I feared to be left alone that night or sent on a journey! At long last dawn arrived, only to display a heavy mist through which nothing could be observed. We went forward – we fired — the enemy replied – we paused for the fog to lift – and then just in front of us I saw a German machine-gun post. I am sure I was trembling all over from fright, or, if you like, from sheer funk. The scrap began and as the moments flew by, it became hotter and hotter. We left our cover and took up another position. Bewilderment – anxious glances — lack of any kind of leadership, or was it we realised we were outnumbered? – a fellow running – others following. I quickly joined them. Back under cover of the wood, we paused. An officer took command of the situation and held us together for a few hours, but later, to our distress, we discovered the machine-gunners were almost out of ammunition. For a while the semblance of a fight was put up, but finally the cry 'Every man for himself!' was shouted by the officer in charge.

Nothing has ever put fear into me as that cry did. I ran through the wood not knowing in which direction I was heading, urged on by sheer fright. I and several other fellows had been running for some time when suddenly we came upon open ground. We paused to take our bearings but the bullets commenced to churn up the turf beneath our feet. Again we took to our heels. In the distance we saw a road down which vehicles of all kinds were hurrying helter-skelter. Crossing a fairly narrow and shallow stream, we gained this road and joined the motley crowd. Horse-drawn gun carriages seem to have pride of place as the drivers lashed the animals to a frenzy to escape capture. The Germans, hot on our track, were pushing forward quicker than we could retreat.

Pte Thomas Bickerton, 2nd Essex Rgt

We were bombarded with everything the Germans had got, but the quality of their shells was not very good, otherwise I wouldn't have been telling this story. We were standing to during this bombardment, and never went into a dugout or took any shelter of any kind. Our firing bay and the one next door seemed to bear charmed lives. At daybreak we could see the Germans advancing down the valley. Of course we immediately let loose with everything we had. I frantically filled magazines until my fingers would hardly move. We had a system of Very lights to send up immediately we were attacked and this would call for artillery fire on no-man's-land. We sent up our Very lights, but nothing happened. The artillery had been withdrawn and it appeared to us that we were going to be sacrificed.

Pte George Fleet, 7th Queen's (Royal West Surrey Rgt)

Sheer chaos reigned – already it was late in the afternoon – men and officers, tired and haggard, many severely wounded, hurrying away in odd groups – a sprinkling of civilians scampering along with a few personal possessions – supply wagons and guns rushing by at breakneck speed – all the paraphernalia of a great army dashing headlong to the rear – eager to escape a persistent and powerful pursuer. Where would it all end? What would happen to me in this awful turmoil? At last, under cover of darkness, we were collected and sorted out into battalions. Each given a couple of blankets and instructed to snatch a few hours' rest. In an open field adjacent to a small village, we settled down.

We woke to the dawn to the crackle of machine guns. Once more we retreated, once more the day was spent marching, marching from a victorious and triumphant enemy. But now it was a more orderly retirement. This continued for at least another couple of days. I was hungry. There had been little to eat except 'hard rations'. The agony of thirst nagged me, thirst being harder to bear than hunger. Occasionally I drank water from wayside ditches and, although discoloured, it afforded me great consolation. My feet were sore yet we could not pause. On and on we must go until at last, on the fifth day, the whole battalion and probably portions of others were lined up in a huge square in what appeared to be open country. Save for some artillery scampering across the skyline on our right, presumed to be French, and an occasional shot in the distance, everything was fairly quiet, although shrapnel could be seen bursting in the far distance. Yet there we were, lying on our stomachs in the open. Why? I asked my neighbour the reason. It meant a fight to a finish, he said. My finish, I thought.

Pte Thomas Bickerton, 2nd Essex Rgt
The Germans had broken through on our right hand and on our left, but owing to our commanding position we seemed to be able to hold them at bay. We sent back runners to battalion headquarters for instructions. The first two runners were either killed or taken prisoner; the third runner came back to tell us the Germans were cooking breakfast in our battalion headquarters kitchen. By this time we were running short of ammunition and

had started to dig up some of the ammunition which had been buried and, in consequence, was very dirty. This caused endless trouble on the Lewis gun as it had to be stripped. Our Number 1 was a first-class chap, and stuck at it until he was thoroughly exhausted and Number 2 took over. He became exhausted, too, and it is quite impossible to hold a Lewis gun forward against the rebound unless you are really feeling fit. It came to my turn and I'll admit that I couldn't stick it for long. The gun seized up and we stripped it down and put in a new barrel – we carried a spare with the spare parts. By this time we were mentally and physically exhausted and wondering what the end would be. It was obviously very near. I went into the next firing bay to see if our platoon commander was there, and he was sitting on the fire step in the corner with a revolver in his hand. I think he had shot himself rather than be taken prisoner.

Pte George Fleet, 7th Queen's (Royal West Surrey Rgt)
Secretly, I registered a determination to be out of that square if it were humanly possible. Eagerly I scanned around for places to which I could run for cover. In the course of a few hours, when shots began to whizz through the air and the atmosphere had become a trifle hot, the square collapsed, the result of movement by certain men to obtain better cover. The brigadier, seeing the break-up of his lovely square, tried to stem the tide but failed, and again we retreated towards the village of Bapouf. At the other side of the village, we were lined up across a field to meet the approaching enemy but again the scheme was abandoned. Eventually we retired from the fray and moved towards another village, some kilometres distant, where we were to stay the night. We were told not to remove any clothing and to be ready to don our equipment and move off at a moment's notice. Tired out, we flung ourselves down, hoping to obtain a few hours' sleep.

About two o'clock in the morning we were awakened and told to be ready to move off in five minutes. The Germans were expected to take the village within the next couple of hours. Our weary tramp recommenced and in spite of fatigue we were thankful to be marching away from the firing line. At dawn we halted and I recall sleeping in a dugout beside a road until late in the morning. Jerry had not made the progress anticipated and for this we were all thankful. For the rest of the day and the following night we stayed beside this road, then moved on to more comfortable billets in a small village much damaged by shellfire but which afforded a little comfort. With rest, food and drink, we became normal human beings again.

Sometimes when I attempt to relive that week, it seems ridiculously impossible. That it actually happened to me, that I experienced those events, seems incredible. Each day was an age and the horrible thought would take shape in my mind that the war was endless. I felt as one must feel on being sent to prison. My mind became a blank. The mud – when it rained – and often when it did not – the lice (how utterly wretched I felt the first time I found one on me) – the dead. Unless one has experienced these things, it is impossible to describe the conditions. If you are in no way sensitive to body filth and lice, if disgusting sights have no terror for you, if mud and rats do not revolt you, if dead bodies and the smells that frequently emanate from them do not make you retch, then probably you did not suffer unduly, unless a German bullet or shell played havoc with your anatomy. But to me all this was vile and revolting. The period I spent in France reduced me to a mere automaton.

Pte Thomas Bickerton, 2nd Essex Rgt

Two peculiar things stick in my mind: one of my comrades received a tiny piece of shrapnel through his jugular vein and he came to me and I put on a dressing; blood was spurting in a thin stream from his vein. I sent him down into the dugout. We were sending all the wounded down into the dugout – it must have been sadly overcrowded and I wondered what happened to them when the Germans got into the trench. The other incident concerned a man who had never got down from the fire step during the whole of the attack – he must have fired his rifle just at the point when he was shot through the head. His rifle rebounded, pitched across the trench, he came backwards and hung suspended by his legs over the rifle, and there he hung until someone pushed him down.

The Germans were almost up to our trench, and a corporal tied his white handkerchief to his bayonet and stuck it up over the trench. The Germans called on us to come out. By this time their barrage had lifted, but there was a fair amount of machine-gun fire from our isolated heavy machine guns. Our Number 1 had stripped the gun and taken the spare parts over the back before giving himself up, so that the Germans should not be able to use it on us. Those of us who were gunners had torn our Lewis gun badges off our jackets because we were afraid of what might happen to us. All arms had to be abandoned and we were instructed to run with our hands over our heads towards the German rear. I had not got far before I was pulled up by a German flourishing a dagger. They liked to carry these things about with them. Fortunately I had the presence of mind to whip out my pocket wallet which I thrust into his hand, and whilst he was looking at it, I ran on. Our heavy machine guns were still firing and my next encounter with a German was when one of them pulled me down into a shell hole. I wondered what was going to happen, but he was anxious that I shouldn't be shot! He indicated to me that we were both in danger from this machine gun. I quote both these instances to indicate the difference between Germans – some good, some bad.

Lt H. R. Alexander, 2nd Irish Guards

The 2nd Battalion Irish Guards were in the process of taking over the line when a German attack started. My right company actually got into the front line trench at the same time as the Germans entered it, with the result that on the right of the line there was hand-to-hand fighting, bombing, etc. I then formed a defensive right flank with my reserve company. All that night, Germans who had lost their way were brought into my HQ. One prisoner I asked what his orders were, said, 'Our company commander brought us up to the front line and said, "Do you see that star?" (pointing to a bright star in the sky). "Now march." ' He said, 'We just cut our way through any wire we came to and went on until we lost ourselves.'

Pte George Fleet, 7th Queen's (Royal West Surrey Rgt)
How frantically I dug that night, and how slow I appeared beside the others! I ached in every limb. Looking towards the skyline, we beheld figures silhouetted against the brightness that precedes the dawn. It was difficult with the light behind them to distinguish their nationality, yet they were within hailing distance. Slowly it filtered through to us that we were the front line and the figures were Jerries. They, too, were anxious to obtain cover yet seemed unaware of our presence and we were careful not to display ourselves.

The German advance had been halted near Amiens. Fifty miles had been covered in just a few days. The Germans now switched the direction of their attack north, close to Armentières. It was another critical moment in the campaign. British soldiers would once again be called upon to given their all, led frequently by officers of extraordinary calibre.

Pte Charles Heare, 1/2nd Monmouthshire Rgt
On high ground, we can see the Germans near Nieppe marching down the road with their artillery, as well as our khaki fellows marched back as prisoners. It is a strange sight. The battalion is falling back all the time and we never know where to find our colonel or adjutant. We all look like wild men now. No wash, or

shave. General Freyberg, VC, rushes into brigade headquarters and calls out most of us orderlies. He gets a Lewis machine gun and rushes up the road, saying there is a break in the line. We stop at a crossroads and I feel windy over this. 'You!' General Freyberg says to me, 'Get down to fire the gun.' After the general has left, a corporal says, 'Let me take charge of the gun, I am a machine-gunner.' 'Well,' I say, 'all I know is to pull back the cocking handle, look through the sights and press the trigger. I had a few minutes' lesson once.' I am not shifting from here, though. General Freyberg says stay. You don't know him like I do. He is the very idea of discipline and with him you stay where you are put. After a few hours, General Freyberg passes again and I am sent to look for Colonel Evans. I find him with Sergeant Witts, who says, 'Have you made a will yet, Charley?' 'Why?' I ask. 'Only four men are going to see the end of this war, Douglas Haig, the Master Baker, the Paymaster and Sergeant Witts. I have told you.'

2/Lt Harold Jones, 2nd South Wales Borderers

We had the long and nervy tramp down the duckboards and then picked up a light railway to Poperinge with a further tramp to a roadside camp which we reached about 9 a.m. Breakfast was taken and then all told they could go to bed, in tents and huts. I had been in my sleeping bag about ten minutes when the alarm sounded and we all had to turn out again. General Hunter Weston had arrived and we had to form a square as he wished to address us. He started off by saying he had very good news for us. 'Another chance for you gallant boys to distinguish yourselves (ironical cheers).' The Portuguese were supposed to be holding a piece of front near Estaires but on the first sign of Jerry animosity had bolted with the result that Jerry had broken through and was hourly widening the gap. 'You boys shall have the honour of stemming his advance and I am arranging for you to set off at once.' It was not a very diplomatic way of breaking such news to men who were already dead tired and many of the men walked away in disgust. Lots were immediately drawn to decide what officers were to go as 10 per cent of the battalion were to be left behind to form a nucleus in case it was wiped out.

Pte Charles Heare, 1/2nd Monmouthshire Rgt

The Germans are pressing. Artillery and aeroplanes are giving us socks [hell]. All are retiring fast and everyone is played out and lousy. General Freyberg loses his voice. At brigade headquarters only the divisional telephone wire is in use. Standing by, the General says, 'Quiet, take the phone and repeat what I say – 34th Division. All our men are played out. Ask for the general.' A voice answers, 'Your message is delivered. The general is having dinner. Hold out. He will talk to you after dinner.' I am hoping his dinner will choke the swine. 'Hang on at all costs' came back the order. But General Freyberg says, 'The men are all done in, they will only be taken prisoners.' Our battalion falls back again. It is a job to find them. A friend says, 'We shall be walking through one of these times and giving our message to the Kaiser.'

A boy comes down the road crying. He is mad by the look of him. He looks about seventeen. 'I've had enough of this!' he screams. I try to reason with him. 'Go sick, then you can get away, go to a doctor, he will send you down.' He is crying all the time. Off he goes.

2/Lt Harold Jones, 2nd South Wales Borderers

We reached Neuf Berquin about midday and were ordered to dismount. My company was told to make its headquarters at a farm at the entrance to the town. The farmer and his family were still there and in fact none of the inhabitants appeared to have left the town which was now under shellfire for the first time. The poor people were too scared to get away as all the roads were being shelled methodically by Jerry. Walking down the street I saw one of our gun teams come trotting along when it received a direct hit and was wiped out. To add to the confusion enemy aeroplanes were flying low and firing their machine guns at all and sundry. One woman was killed on her doorstep. The plane that did this flew over our farmyard and holding a Lewis gun on a man's shoulder and another at the trigger we gave it a magazine at point-blank range and to our joy brought it down in the adjoining field. The two occupants set it on fire before we could get to them and then kamaraded in the approved style. They put on quite the 'Conquering Hero' air and demanded an officer's escort. We had a dickens of a job to stop the men putting paid to their account but in the end had them well under way care of two Tommies. They had to pass the house where the woman was killed and the husband ran out and before he could be stopped hit one of the prisoners a terrific blow in the face.

Pte Charles Heare, 1/2nd Monmouthshire Rgt

We got our Colonel Evans. He looks worried now and needs a rest. Whenever we go to him, night or day, he is always pleasant and says 'thank you'. A real gentleman, and it is a pleasure to do anything for him. The battalions are to fall back on a ridge where a trench is to be made. All orderlies join their battalions and the 2nd Monmouthshires are the last to retire. All goes well. It is dark and I report back. 'Now,' says General Freyberg, 'we are the last to leave and if the enemy come and catch us, we must fight to the last man.' We are all in a farmhouse and there is a grunt and bump at the door. I lose two years' growth and feel cold but it is only a farm pig. What a fright!

'All outside now,' says General Freyberg. 'To the last man, before capture.' 'What do you think of it all?' I ask a Worcester orderly. 'Blast him and his last-man business. If he wants another VC, he can earn it. My arms are going up.' I keep close to him. A man shouts for help in a nearby barn; he is wounded in both legs. The General gets the man on his shoulders and says, 'Off we go.' He carries the man all the way. We all get back safe without trouble, although bullets are flying around.

2/Lt Harold Jones, 2nd South Wales Borderers

Orders arrived late in the day for the battalion to move out to meet the enemy and check his advance. Our colonel was home on leave, but the 2nd-in-Command was an equally capable soldier and would stick to the last, and he impressed upon us that was our duty. On leaving the town, we encountered hordes of our men leaving the line in disorder. They were completely out of control and we found it impossible to rally them. Our men kept stolidly on, although it was not very encouraging for them. There was no sign of any of our batteries and, quite as bad from our point of view, we did not meet a single staff officer, and were thus quite out in the blue. We passed deserted farms with the cows in their sheds waiting to be milked. Some of the men did the milkmaid touch and then released them to fend for themselves. Aeroplanes worried us when filing across fields, but by all kneeling and giving them ten rounds rapid fire, we scared them away.

When dusk arrived we found ourselves on fairly high ground and Major S—— decided to make a stand here. We put our men to digging a trench and, realising the necessity of being under cover by dawn, they worked with a will. There was no sign of Jerry and all was quiet. It was raining and, with my Company Commander, I had been lying down under my trench coat trying to get a little sleep. Finding it too cold, I got up and at the same moment a Jerry machine gun in front of us opened out and with his first burst hit me in the foot. It burned like the Old Nick and I was hopping about on one leg, chanting that I was hit. The stretcher-bearers got hold of me, took off my boot and sock and said I had got a 'Blighty'. They bandaged me up, cut my boot so that I could walk and, I am pleased to remember, with the best wishes of all sent me away to battalion HQ. My batman came with me. I found the MO in BHQ and he labelled me 'down the line' and again with best wishes and congratulations I hobbled on my way.

I left all in battalion HQ in a very cheerful mood. They were blissfully ignorant of their immediate fate. Half an hour after I left them they were all surrounded and either killed, captured or reported missing. We went into that affair 22 officers and about 500 men. Barring the padre, I was the only officer who came through and the men were under thirty. All this I learnt when I returned from hospital. I felt that I should have been with them but eased my conscience by the fact that I was a genuine casualty, and the longer I delayed getting proper treatment, the more danger there was of aggravating the wound. To be candid, it was only a bullet wound in the big toe, but extremely painful. I discovered the Casualty Clearing Station in the dark, owing to the fact that there was an ambulance car outside. Seeing no signs of life – it was a farmhouse – I walked into the kitchen and the sight that met my eyes gave me a view of the other side of war. There was an oil lamp in the middle of a big kitchen table and sitting on the benches with their heads and arms on the table, lying on the floor and sprawling in chairs, were doctors and orderlies all fast asleep and obviously dog tired. I had not the heart to disturb them, so got down on the floor myself with my batman. Some little time later, one of my neighbours became restless and finally noticed me. He at once became alive to the situation. They had been rushed up there to await casualties and I was the first. He dressed my wound, made me a cup of tea and said I would be going down on the ambulance. They had collected some refugees who would accompany me. The other doctors were now awake and one asked if by any chance I had a cigarette. By the best of luck I had three tins of fifty, and knowing I was going storewards I said they could have the lot. Such was their delight that with very little persuasion they would have labelled me a permanent 'Blighty'.

The critical stage of the German offensive had passed by the end of April. A new one in May on the Chemin des Dames was initially successful, but ran out of steam. The Germans were desperate. They

*launched smaller and increasingly ineffectual attacks that did nothing
but dissipate their strength yet further. The Allies could draw breath. It
would still require enormous effort and great loss of life to bring the war
to a close. Both sides continued to hold within their ranks experienced
troops as well as young, seemingly fearless men who would fight to the
finish. One of those was twenty-year-old Second Lieutenant Digby
Dickinson. He came from an army family: his brother, two cousins and
uncle and great uncle were all former or serving military men. Digby
might have bolted from a fight with a tough Australian but his* joie de
vivre *on the battlefield was unwavering, and he had the unbridled
devotion of the men serving under him.*

2/Lt Harold Jones, 2nd South Wales Borderers

One very funny but true yarn concerned Second Lieutenant
Dickinson. He was just a wild schoolboy and treated everything
as great sport.

He had orders to improve the wire on his front and took a party
out to work. As was to be expected he had lost his wire cutters so
his sergeant very reluctantly lent him his pair. After finishing the
job and returning to the trench the sergeant asked for the return of
his wire cutters. 'Oh damn, I've lost the bally things', and running
out to the wire he started striking matches until he brought into
play all the enemy machine guns in that area. He stuck it until his
search was successful and then accused those who upbraided him
as being 'windy'.

We were being held in readiness for the expected German
offensive and all too soon orders came to move up to the reserve
line. My company's sector had a farm on its flank and we made this
our HQ. During the day we all came back to the farm, manning
the trenches only at night. One very hot day when some of us were
dozing in the 'parlour' we were alarmed to hear a machine gun
rattling away and much shouting. Thinking the Germans had
made a very successful surprise attack we rushed out to find our
irresponsible young officer Dickinson was trying to hit the weath-

ercock on top of the barn. The shouting was due to the fact that
the trajectory of the bullets was such that they were falling on the
men's latrine in the distant corner of the field. It was very amusing
to see the men bolting for cover holding up their trousers with
both hands. When they discovered who the gunner was they had a
jolly good laugh themselves. They could see nothing wrong in
anything he did.

---

*One of the first signs of a collapse in German morale occurred on 19
July. The small town of Meteren had been fought over in 1914, when,
during a short engagement, the Germans had been pushed back and the
town taken with little damage. In 1918 it was pulverised into a
splintered heap by British artillery. The subsequent attack quickly
wrested the town from enemy hands. The significance of the victory was
far greater than the taking of Meteren, important though it was. The
predominance of Allied artillery was clear for all to see, as was the
dejection of the enemy. The attack also encapsulated much about the
advances made in Allied strategy, and how new, imaginative techniques
to improve battlefield success were being readily used. At Meteren these
included bombardments mixing smoke with gas shells to 'educate' the
enemy to expect gas whenever smoke was deployed. In a subsequent 'smoke
only' attack, the enemy would automatically wear their gas masks,
making visibility difficult and fighting awkward. The time of the
attack was unusual, set at 7.55 a.m., when the enemy would have stood
down from the parapet and placed breech covers on their machine guns.
There was one further innovation.*

Gen. H. H. Tudor, General Officer Commanding 9th Div.
Enemy aircraft which invariably came over our trenches at dawn
would spot the [assault] troops in the trenches. So we got 2,000
yards of coconut fibre matting, which was practically the same
colour as the soil on the edge of the front trench. We painted a

black line with tar about a foot wide along the centre of it and stretched it across the trench on poles along the whole of the front line, leaving only gaps for the sentries. We got the RAF to test this behind the line and the pilots reported it was practically indistinguishable from an empty trench. The troops moved in during the night and actually had breakfast under the matting.

The ingenious methods used prior to and during the attack stunned the enemy and brought rapid success.

Lt Col B. R. Kirwan, RFA

The remarkable, in fact astonishing, point about the operation was the ready way in which the Germans surrendered. We saw crowds running forward with their hands up. We had never seen anything like it before, in fact, so far as resistance goes, it represented a bound almost from one extreme to another. We felt then that the tide had very definitely turned and that the end could not be far off.

2/Lt Harold Jones, 2nd South Wales Borderers

Digby Dickinson was going 'over the top' in the morning and I was to follow him up, go through his line and finally take up position on a new line in advance. I stayed some time with him discussing our attack and getting some idea of the ground.

Next day – 18 August – was the day of our contemplated capture of Oultersteene. Zero hour was the unusual time of 11 a.m. Both sides were in the habit of dozing just then and it was hoped to spring a surprise. My position in support commanded a good view of the front line and it was a wonderful sight to see our barrage drop on the German wire right on the stroke of time. Ten minutes after zero hour I was to lead my platoon from the support trench, reinforce Dickinson's advance line and then go ahead and take up a position commanding the railway embankment. It had always been our experience that once an attack was launched the opposition concentrated their artillery fire on the support lines of the attackers and we fully expected a rough passage. We came through all right and were very jubilant when we met German prisoners making their way hurriedly back to our rear. I found Dickinson's men holding a captured German post, but they were very depressed. Dickinson had been killed. It spoilt the day for us. We had captured Oultersteene but one of our dead was Dickinson! He died in just the same happy-go-lucky way he had lived with us. As soon as our barrage lifted he saw a party of Germans in a shell hole making signs of surrender. Instead of calling to them, he jumped out towards them. Unfortunately there was a German officer there who did not wish to surrender and he fired his revolver point-blank at Dickinson. This was not treachery on the part of the German as our men said he was trying to rally his party. They all met the fate of Dickinson very promptly and when we arrived no quarter was being given. After giving my men a breather, we pushed on to our objective and set about converting shell holes into a fairly decent trench. The day had been most successful, we had done what we had been asked to do, taken a considerable number of prisoners and machine guns, and our casualties had not been heavy.

Pte George Fleet, 7th Queen's (Royal West Surrey Rgt)
With August began the final 'push', the 'push' that terminated the war. Luckily, I missed the first attack on Albert, on which front we were now stationed. Later, when the line to the right of Albert had to be straightened, I found myself involved. The early hours of the morning saw us lined up in no-man's-land, waiting for the barrage, timed for four o'clock. The guns commenced. We moved forward in small sections, reached what appeared to be an empty trench, fired several shots into it, then jumped in and out quickly. The trench appeared to be unused and as Jerry had a habit of vacating his front line at night, we could only guess whether or

not we had entered his domain, the terrain being one network of trenches.

Dawn had now broken, doing its best to illuminate an intense fog, as step by step we moved forward, peering into the mist. At last we hit upon another trench. It was empty and for all we knew it could have been the one we had just left. Apart from our small group we could see nothing, having lost contact with those either side of us. The thought of death or how to escape it concerned us all, but the continuous noise racked our nerves and there must have been many at the borderline of insanity. Soon other forms appeared and to our joy they spoke English, some of our own fellows only too glad to make contact with us.

Those engaged on our right and left had obtained their objectives but on our section Jerry had held on, rendering the position precarious for those battalions operating with us. Suddenly the colonel appeared, picking up officers and men as he passed. He made no attempt to force anyone to follow him but his action was such that all accepted his leadership and supported him. In a few moments the German machine-gunners were busy. We moved forward in short, sharp runs, dropping to the ground after each advance. The bullets whizzed through the air, bombs were thrown in each direction, shells seen to explode everywhere, men dropped beside me, many badly mutilated, others sagging to the ground dead. A short time and our objective was achieved, but this brave man, instead of seeking cover, ran up and down the open ground at the rear of the captured trench directing operations. Machine guns were creating an unearthly din, bombs were thrown heedlessly in order to cause confusion amongst the enemy. He was a tall man, an easy target for a bullet. Within a few minutes he fell to the ground, shot through the head.

Jumping into the trench, I landed upon two dead Germans, the bodies oozing as they took my weight. Instantly I moved to another fire step. Those two faces gazing at me for the rest of the day would have driven me frantic. The din, that awful din of battle, continued for hours, but with the passing of the day and the defeat of the enemy, it quietened down. The fear of a counter-attack, for which we had to prepare, caused a chill to run down my spine. It never materialised. This left us in peace, except for an occasional shell, and for an hour or so we could sleep – and forget.

So it went on from day to day. Pushing him back, attacking one day, resting the next. Oh, those nerve-racking barrages, the terrible fear as you listen to a shell coursing through the air, wondering where it will land, the never-ending machine-gun fire. Towards the last months of the war, one battalion would press on the heels of another, forcing Jerry back a further mile or two.

We pushed on across open country and to another sunken road that skirted the enemy. His position had been ascertained and we were to attack from this point. Our men commenced to climb the embankment, only to be swept back by deadly machine-gun fire. Officers were hastily summoned for consultation whilst several platoons stood crowded together in this narrow road. Standing at the head of this group, I quickly sensed the danger and moved to the rear, but with caution in order not to draw attention to myself. My instinct proved correct. A few minutes later a shell burst in almost the exact spot where I had stood, killing outright six of my fellows. Somehow I sensed the enemy had our position under his direct observation. Consternation followed and we were thrust into trenches either side of the road. The attack was abandoned. In the morning, other troops crossed our trenches to continue the good work. Either Jerry had retreated or some other strategy evolved, but the heavy firing of the previous day did not repeat itself.

2/Lt Harold Jones, 2nd South Wales Borderers

Zero hour was an hour after dawn. Just before zero hour an enemy plane flew over, spotted us and brought down heavy artillery fire. We were packed in the trench very closely and a direct hit would be costly. One shell landed on my left and knocked out a platoon. The wounded were taken to a dressing station immediately behind us and in a few minutes that also received a direct hit and burst into flames. This was not a very encouraging start to our day. Our barrage opened to time and away we went, glad to get out of that wretched trench.

The Lancashire Fusiliers formed the first wave and they had heavy losses. I came across seven of their men piled up one on top of the other, dead, in front of a house. A machine gun inside had mowed them down as they attempted to rush it. We quickly cleared the town and reached the open country. Very suddenly a dense fog came along and the gas alarm was given. Visibility was so bad that I received news from the leaders that they were taking cover where they were and passing this information back the whole attack was suspended. Out of curiosity I made my way back to the house that had caused so much trouble. In one of the rooms I discovered a hopelessly wounded German. He was crying out piteously. Going outside I spotted a German officer coming along the road with a crowd of fellow prisoners and I beckoned him into the house to comfort the poor fellow, who was obviously beyond aid. This officer could speak English and told me the Germans understood the war had ended otherwise they would have put up resistance to our attack. Doubtless he said this to discount any idea I had of a big victory that day. He was very much on his dignity and it was amusing to see him walking off alone shunning his fellow prisoners who were passing along in scores.

Lt John Godfrey, 103 Field Coy, RE
7.9.18
Well, the war is proceeding very successfully, *n'est-ce pas*? Up here we are getting on bit by bit: down below things go forward very steadily. There are great rumours going about that the Boche are really going to hop it. It is quite certain now that the German day is done, & the effect on the British Army is immense.

19.9.18

However, the war is going exceedingly well, and with any luck the show may be over next year. It rather depends on the psychology of the Hun proletariat. If they really get wind of all our successes, & realise all's up, it is quite possible they will try to take it out of the party responsible – viz. the Prussian grandees. I expect to see the whole affair go on for a bit more yet, and then crack suddenly and gloriously.

Optimism was growing in inverse proportion to the pessimism sweeping the German army. Propaganda leaflets, dropped by aircraft on enemy lines, had been a common occurrence, but significantly they were now being picked up by the side that had dropped them. The Reverend Kenelm Swallow, MC, found this English propaganda in a German billet shortly after the enemy had vacated it.

Arithmetic!

A sum for German soldiers

1. Between 15 July and 24 August 1918 more than 100,000 German soldiers were captured by the Allied troops in France. In addition to this, the German army has suffered extreme losses in wounded and killed.

2. Monthly reinforcements of 300,000 fresh American troops are arriving in France with the armies of the Entente.

Even more significantly, a German note dropped on British lines was picked up on 24 September. It was found just five days before the British attacked the last deep defensive position held by the enemy, and it called for a negotiated peace conference:

'We are of the firm conviction that all belligerents owe to mankind to examine in common whether it is not possible to put an end to this frightful struggle now, after so many years of costly but undecided fighting whose whole course points towards an understanding. The Imperial and Royal Government therefore propose to the Governments of all the belligerent states to send delegates in the near future to a place of a

neutral country . . . with a view to a confidential and not binding conference on the main principles of a treaty of peace.'

Pte William McNeil, 46th Machine Gun Coy, MGC

On 28 September 1918, we were resting between two villages that our troops had taken a day or two previously. Now Major Windeley, ex-Canadian Division, our Company Commander, Machine Gun Corps, had us paraded outside some old German dugouts near which we had our transport lines. During my three years eight months of active service with the 46th Division, I had never known an officer on the eve of an attack to talk to us as our officer did that afternoon. I remember, when he had us paraded there, how determined and grim he looked.

He told us he had only got a few minutes to spare, but he felt it his duty to have a word or two with us before we commenced what turned out to be one of the most successful feats of arms during the war.

He said, 'I want to tell you, men, that in the morning our division has the honour to be chosen to attack the enemy on the canal. We must cross that canal and I know that our GOC has great confidence in us. If we succeed, and succeed we must, it may be that our armies will be able to advance along the whole British front.'

We knew what we were about to attempt, as the 'Hindenburg Line' and the 'Canal du Nord' were considered by those in the know to be almost impregnable. We got our 'iron rations' from the quartermaster sergeant and then waited until it was time to get on with the job.

Everything was death-like still, even the star shells over the firing line seemed to be dull. The village was busy as we passed through, plenty of troops about and wagons dumping shells and rations for the artillery. The village looked ghastly as the star shells threw their shadows on the ruins. We knew what this lull meant, and occasionally someone would ask, 'What time's the artillery going to kick off?'

We were just entering the village of Jeancourt when *bang*, I was knocked stone deaf for a minute or two as a gun was fired from the hedge on the side of the road as I was just passing. It must have been a twelve-inch gun and perhaps the signal for the bombardment to start. I felt that shell skim my head and my hair seemed to be singed by the flash. 'Well, what a near one,' I thought as I recovered from that shock and struggled with my animals, who were startled and quite frantic. That shell only missed my head by inches. 'Keep low in your saddles,' shouted an artillery officer as he came dashing through a gap in the hedge and told our officer to put a spurt on through that lane.

Then everything went mad, our mules included, for at least 3,000 guns belched forth all at once, flashes everywhere, moans, shrieks, screams and sighs from our shells as they sailed away on their destination of death and maiming. Our animals backed, reared, plunged and snorted, some turned and twisted as mules will when suddenly frightened and jibbing; they led the drivers a lively dance. They were really panic-stricken for a minute or two, but our lads held them and calmed them enough to proceed.

Still the crashing and banging from our guns went on. They seemed to be everywhere, they must have been almost wheel to wheel. Eighteen-pounders, heavies and howitzers, all going together in artillery rapid fire, and then some shells came over from the enemy's lines all mixed up in that village bedlam.

Crump, bang, crump! Jerry's shells landed in the centre of the road twenty yards ahead, but we kept going forward. Blimey, I'll bet some muttered their prayers along that road. I know I did. Suddenly, down went my animals in one of the newly made shell holes. The fumes were still rising from within. 'Shell holes on the right, pass it down.' I could hear those drivers passing that message all down the column. Others were stumbling in the holes the same as I had done, and I could hear them swearing and creating.

Our artillery were now banging away more furiously. If one of our gunners dropped, another took his place, and with tunics off and shirts open at the throat, they kept pegging away, although the guns by now must have been black hot.

I thought of the poor devils who were under that awful barrage, and then I thought of that dreadful barrage they put us under on Hill 60 and Sanctuary Wood in 1915 when we could not answer back as our shells were then scarce and limited. I also thought of the pounding they gave us earlier in the year at Givenchy, Gore and La Bassée in April when they tried their big offensive. If Mr Lloyd George had heard that bombardment, I wonder whether he would have been proud or sorry, perhaps both. As we went forward with those wagons, I felt proud of the strength of Britain but damned sorry for those grey-clad Jerries on the side of that canal.

Here and there we passed a smashed wagon or two and a team of dead and dying animals, and, occasionally, some lead drivers would have to drag them to the side of the road to clear it for the transport to pass. The officers would put the dying animals out of their misery with their revolvers. We had a job to get our mules to pass them, for as soon as they saw a dead animal, their ears would shoot up and they would stop, then just as suddenly dash forward again.

Our artillery fire became more intense and rapid and we knew that soon the battle would be on in grim earnest. I could picture our infantry, the Staffords, whom our Machine Gun Company were attached to in the front line, shaking hands and wishing one another the best of luck, while waiting for the order to go over the canal and at them.

Our first guns then lifted the barrage from the enemy's front line on to their support and reserve lines, whilst our heavy guns swept the enemy's roads and back areas with shrapnel. We heard the sound of machine-gun and rifle fire and knew that our infantry were attacking. Then Jerry's artillery opened out on our infantry and all roads leading to the line, and we knew that a few more names were being added to our Roll of Honour.

The attack so far had been a great success and the casualties
fewer than had been expected. Through the mist came the German
prisoners in twos and threes, straggling along and fed up, but
glad, it seemed, to be out of that inferno with their whole skin.
We stood on that road for an hour or more, awaiting orders, and
still the German prisoners kept filing past us. Some could talk
English and offered us souvenirs, watches, cigarettes, lighters and
German coins.

At last orders came to get busy and away we went again, over
the canal bridge and into Bellenglise, where we saw hundreds of
German prisoners being collected in groups as they were brought
in, also a few howitzers and field guns and wagons that had been
taken. Now the fog was clearing we could see a thousand yards in
front of us. In one direction, we could see three or four of our tanks
crawling through a field and along the edges. They looked in the
distance like 'chats' or 'lice' crawling along the seams of a lousy
shirt!

The enemy was not going to be allowed much peace or any
chance to counter-attack, for there was already a fresh Infantry
Division moving through us to carry on the work. The 6th
Division it was and by twelve o'clock that day were hard and
fast at it with the enemy whilst our division, 46th, were having a
breather after bagging forty guns and howitzers, hundreds of
machine guns, 5,000 prisoners, the canal, and three villages, as
well as going forward four or five miles.

Sgt Walter Sweet, 1/2nd Monmouthshire Rgt
Our company were fairly comfortable in a captured German gun
site where had been left their canvas huts and other stuff. The
sergeants' mess was in a shed with a corrugated roof and after we
had had tea (at which I produced a cucumber from home, to the
delight of the others) the talk was 'How long will we be here?'
About a week or ten days was predicted, so old Sergeant Wilks
thought we ought to have a cooking range. Someone had seen a

good one in a cottage half a mile away. It was decided to get it
and six of us carried it over barbed wire, etc, and eventually got
it home. Old Wilks took on the job of erecting it and making a
smoke pipe. I turned in and slept in a corner. Next morning the
range was all in place and the chimney fitted. A fire had been
lit. Breakfast time came and old Wilks was sat in front of the
stove frying some bacon and bread – feeling very pleased with
himself, having spent most of the night working on it. Someone
came and leaned against the doorpost blocking the light. Old
Wilks turned and saw the orderly sergeant grinning at him like
a Cheshire cat.

'What! We are not moving, are we?' asked Wilks. 'Yes,' said
the orderly sergeant. 'We have to be ready to move off in one
hour's time.'

At this, old Wilks flew into a rage and said, 'Gor, strike me
ruddy well pink!' and with that bashed at the stove with the frying
pan until the handle came off, then he picked up his hammer and
finished it off, leaving it completely smashed up. We all laughed
but sympathised with him a bit after all his hard work.

Lt John Godfrey, 103 Field Coy, RE
9.10.18
Things go on well here. There is a bit of a respite at present, but
not for long, I expect. I dislike the sit-down-and-wait parts: when
one is shoving on every day for a bit, the war is much more
cheerful. Still, there is not much doubt that the Hun has all his
baggage packed up ready for an unhindered exit.

12.10.18
The war goes well. We are getting into very fine country, with
lovely grass and trees about, the only jar being the permanent
damp.

I am feeling exceedingly fit: the wet doesn't seem to make a
scrap of difference to anyone's health. You may find me swallow-

ing the whole family's rations when I come home, so look out! I have the appetite of a horse.

15.10.18
This is real good war with much advancing and pinching of stuff from the Boche. I wouldn't have missed this end of the war for worlds. It is worth all the rest.

27.10.18
We have built some bridges lately: lorry bridges as well as horse-traffic stuff. The Boche has done millions of pounds' worth of damage to the canals, and the plight of the civilians he has left behind is often pitiable. He really is a disgusting brute. An officer in my company saw a little kid of five who had had all his fingers shot off by some drunken beast of a Hun two years ago – it is almost incredible, isn't it? But all the civvies are very cheerful now, and there has been the usual cheering 'les braves Anglais' and all that business – but it doesn't last long. However, they are all pleased to have one billeted on them, which is more than can be said of some of the rapacious vultures back in the old area. Those same must have made thousands of pounds out of the ordinary Tommy.

2/Lt Harold Jones, 2nd South Wales Borderers
15 Oct. – our colonel called all his officers for a conference. Sitting on the edge of a makeshift bed he read out the day's work ahead. It was the intention to take Courtrai. Information had come in to the effect that the Germans were preparing to make a stand but that for some distance the ground was clear. B Company – my company – would form the first wave and I was to be the direction officer. I was given points on the map and compass bearings and had it impressed on me to keep well ahead so that a good line could be maintained.

Zero hour was at 9 a.m. We took up our positions, the barrage duly dropped. It was to be a creeping barrage and at the first alteration of range I was to move forward. Patrols had reported there were no Germans immediately in front of us but as soon as we showed ourselves we had proof that the patrols had not done their work properly, if they had done it at all. A terrific burst of machine-gun fire accompanied by artillery opened out on us and before I had covered 100 yards I was lying on the ground with my right leg shot off above the knee and my right shoulder badly smashed! My runner was lying on top of me shot through the stomach. Jerry was there in strength waiting for us. He got 50 per cent of my company alone, some of them men who had been right through the war. Although so very badly wounded and apparently bleeding to death, incredible as it may sound, I did not lose consciousness. As wave after wave of the attack passed I called for stretcher-bearers. Quite properly they would not stop. A few fellows tried to cheer me by telling me I had a 'Blighty' but I had great doubt as to whether I should see home again.

Notwithstanding my apparently hopeless state I was quite interested in the progress of my comrades. I can visualise now the grey strained faces that passed me and how they all avoided a second look at me and my runner who were no doubt a ghastly sight. One boy, bless him, did stop and give me a sip of his water bottle. I saw my colonel pass with his little staff of runners and he had a look of grim determination on his face doubtless engendered by the heavy casualties we had received. At long last a stretcher party came along. They put my runner on one but I would not allow them to touch me! I wriggled on to the stretcher myself. My bearers were two lusty Scotchmen. After carrying me some distance they put me down and seeing my eyes closed argued as to whether it was worthwhile taking me any further. I was too weak to join in the argument but fortunately some German prisoners came along and were commandeered to carry me and very gentle they proved to be. We reached the dressing station safely and I was soon sent on to the field hospital where the amputation of my leg was completed. Thanks to wonderful surgery my arm was saved. This day's fighting was the last in which my battalion took part and notwithstanding our heavy casualties was a great success. It was very hard luck on me to have come right through only to be knocked out at the end but I have no grouse. I realise that I had been exceptionally lucky to have lasted so long.

Pte Charles Heare, 1/2nd Monmouthshire Rgt

We get to a large town called Courtrai. The Germans have retired. The people in this town, about 40,000 of them, go mad seeing us. They have been under German rule for four years. They put flags out, and in windows have photos of the Belgian King and Queen. They all seem crazy at being free.

The division headquarters is shelled. I feel more windy now than ever. We find a good cellar but are called out to help the wounded. One man has his leg hanging on by a piece of skin. I try to help him but he yells. A doctor arrives and tells me to hold his leg as he cuts it off. 'Now throw it away,' he says. What a feeling that leg gives me, to hold it. Now all the man wants is a fag which the doctor gives him. About a dozen horses of the divisional headquarters are killed. The people of Courtrai come out, men, women, girls and boys, and cut lumps off the horses and carry them away, quite happy.

Capt. Eric Whitworth, 12th South Wales Borderers

For us it is a great war; our victorious career has gone on, capturing famous towns, crossing an important river (the Lys) and releasing the inhabitants literally in thousands. For me, incidentally, one of the most interesting features of it all is finding out what the treatment of the country has been by the Germans. It is first hand from inhabitants and only six to eight hours after the Germans have evacuated. Most speak Flemish only, but I can always find some to talk French, and I find myself talking more freely than I have ever before. The inhabitants' houses and furniture remain untouched; but all their living cows, chickens, sheep and grain have been taken without paying a penny. In many cases, at the moment inhabitants are living on vegetables. I was lunching yesterday on bully beef sandwiches during a halt and dropped a piece in the sand. Madame picked it up and asked if she might have it, and told me she had not tasted meat for many weeks. Luckily, brigade headquarters always have surplus rations and I have fed many refugee families, and I have had given me a delightful souvenir. I fed a whole family of three children and two women for two days and in return Madame gave me a Belgian franc of 1914 in which is cut the head of King Albert. For four years the Germans had objected to its being used; it has a single ring to hang it round the neck, and she was actually wearing it. It will make a historic locket for someone.

Pte Charles Heare, 1/2nd Monmouthshire Rgt

We leave Courtrai, and reach Robaix. It is Sunday. All the people are out, waving flags and cheering us like mad. The people give us anything they have. All of us have feather beds which they had to provide for German troops on rest. 'Perhaps someone has slept here,' says my mate Black, 'who had made us run like hell.'

There are signs here of the German retreat. Railway and canal bridges are blown down. When the Kaiser and Crown Prince came to Robaix Headquarters, the civilians were all turned out to line the streets. The officers would shout 'hip hip hurrah' while the French lads would say 'bastards' under their breath. The word is the same as in our language. A nice swear word.

Sgt Maj. Arthur Cook, 1st Somerset Light Infantry

1 November: The attack began at 5.15 a.m., under cover of the fiercest barrage I had ever experienced, from 2,000 cannons and hundreds of machine guns carrying out indirect fire. It was pitch dark when we started, the only light coming from bursting shells; the din was indescribable, speech was hopeless. Whistles and

signals were out of the question, we just blindly blundered on, close up to the barrage that was blasting everything in front of us and shrouding us in its cloudy fumes. The flash of the bursting shells showed up the blanched faces of the lads in action for the first time, and the barrage that was intended to terrify and break the morale of the enemy was scaring our young warriors stiff – they were half stunned by the unearthliness of it, but it was sweet music to us 'old uns'.

Dawn broke as the attack progressed and we were able to see what was going on. The earth was vomiting forth clods, bodies, trees, houses, in fact anything that came in the way of the blasted line. There were no deep dugouts, what trenches we passed were shallow and hurriedly dug by a retreating enemy . . . The smoke from the bursting shells set up a thick fog screen and caused us to lose our direction slightly. Captain Osborne observed this and got his map out. I saw the danger of this officer walking along with a Burberry on and an open map in front of him, advertising himself as an officer, an obvious target for a sniper. I shouted to him, 'Put that map away, sir, it's getting light!' He replied, 'Oh, I'll be all right, Sergeant Major', but nevertheless I was worried.

It was not long before we came in contact with the enemy, who made himself unpleasant when the barrage passed over him. It seemed inconceivable that so many had survived that line of death. One of the first to be wounded was the captain, right in the stomach, a very dangerous place to be hit. Down he went and down went the company also and opened up a withering fire on the enemy. The captain was sitting up a few yards in front of me, obviously in great pain. He took something from his pocket and swallowed it. Every moment I expected to see him collapse, riddled with bullets. I approached the captain and asked him if I could do anything for him. He said, 'No, Sergeant Major. I'm finished', and he certainly looked it, but I could not leave him there; we had fought and suffered together so long. He never knew what fear was, he was the bravest officer I ever saw, and here he was lying crushed and bleeding at my feet, so I left two men to carry him back.

Our instructions were to mop up the village. This is a dangerous and thankless task, for you are an exposed target from all angles . . . Snipers, very difficult to locate and dislodge, began to pick off the men. Shells began to fall in the village, making our task still more unpleasant; the men began to group together, probably feeling there was safety in numbers, but I soon realised that a shell amongst us would have disastrous results for the remnant of my poor old company, now about thirty strong. I warned them of the danger and ordered them to spread out, but it was too late – death was on its way. The shell burst on the hard cobbles and flew in all directions, the broken cobblestones causing as much damage as the shells. Several were killed and the remainder shared the flying pieces. I was hit in the knee; it felt as though a cart horse had kicked me. I could scarcely believe I was wounded. I had begun to feel that I was immune after dodging it for 4 years. I had been with the battalion from the beginning of the war, and now had the misfortune to be hit in what proved to be their very last action.

Sgt Walter Sweet, 1/2nd Monmouthshire Rgt
We passed through a small town with very tall houses and halted there. On the opposite side of the street was a very large building used as an Army Group HQ, and a staff officer came out and told us the news. The Germans had crossed the lines at Valenciennes and asked for an armistice. That was good news and the next few days were all rumours. If a shell pitched some distance away we ran for cover and avoided the area being shelled. At ordinary times we would have taken no notice, but now the end was near, we were taking no chances of being pipped at the last minute.

A couple of days before the 11th we moved into St Denis. The sergeants were billeted in a retired policeman's house which had been abandoned. Nice little place with tiled floors and cooking range. The place had only been evacuated a few days earlier and bedding, etc, was still in place. We got a couple of mattresses from upstairs and put them on the floor of the kitchen and were very comfortable with the stove.

One of our people, scrounging, found a nice clean pan of fresh lard and another found a dump of potatoes. I volunteered to cook the chips if someone peeled the spuds. All day, rumours were going about the company that the war would finish at eleven o'clock. At eleven o'clock that night we could hear the boys up and down the street, beating tins and cheering. 'Come on,' my pal said, 'let's go out – the war is over.' It was very cold and I was comfortable, so I told him, 'Don't be a fool, haven't you been told that the first seven years will be the worst? We have only had just over four years up to now.' Out he went and no sooner had he gone than the Germans who, no doubt, could hear the cheering, sent over a couple of salvos of shells which burst behind the houses.

Pte Charles Heare, 1/2nd Monmouthshire Rgt
People out cheering all the way. Drink free and plenty. Tomorrow some say the Armistice is to be signed, but it may be another army rumour. We find some potatoes and make tea and chips to celebrate the occasion. Off again next day, where we are told on the road that at eleven o'clock the war is over. 'What's to become of us now?' says Black. 'We have lived this life, now we shall have to start all over again.'

Sgt Maj. Arthur Cook, 1st Somerset Light Infantry
11 Nov. [England]
Hospital routine went on much the same as usual until the electrifying news came through that the Germans had asked for an armistice. I don't know whether to be pleased or otherwise over my circumstances, for I had been waiting for a nice Blighty wound for years and now I have got it and landed nicely in

England, they have gone and stopped the blinking war! What would I give to be with the battalion now!

I have always been a firm believer in prayer and after what I have been through during my war years, my faith is stronger than ever. As long as I live, I shall remember the many hundreds of pals left behind who were not as lucky as I was. One cannot help reflecting on this day and feeling thankful that the slaughter of human beings is over.

Sgt Walter Sweet, 1/2nd Monmouthshire Rgt

The morning of 11 November was very cold with a white frost. Moving off, we marched down the village to the bridge which the Royal Engineers had just completed. They had had a rough time and we saw several of their lads lying on the side of the roadway. I could not help thinking what bad luck to get it now that the end was so near.

I was in a barn in a village called Celles getting our boys settled in when the colonel walked in, wished us good day and looked at his watch. 'It is 10 a.m. Men, I am pleased to tell you that in one hour's time the war will be over and you will all be able to return to your homes again. The Armistice comes in force at 11 a.m. today.'

Well! After all the rumours, here it was straight from the horse's mouth. The colonel had told us himself! We did not cheer but just stood, stunned and bewildered. Soon after, we had to move again and about 10.50 a.m. were halted and told to fall out for a rest. Then just before 11 a.m. the order came to fall in again. I was sergeant of the leading platoon and just in front of me was the CO. With the HQ detachment and wagons, he had joined up with our company for the march. He was looking at his watch, and at the stroke of 11 a.m. he raised his hand and told us that the war was now over. We cheered and with our tin hats on and our rifles held aloft, cheered again. Next came the shock – we had to continue the march. We had thought that we would stay put wherever we happened to be, but as it was drizzling rain and there was nothing but muddy fields in sight, I was not sorry.

The old hands plodded on, with their thoughts miles away, hardly realising that the day had come at last. The noisy section of the new lads who had come up last thing started shouting that everyone should throw all their picks and shovels away, and cursed and called our officers everything they could. A corporal and myself went back along the platoon and threatened to bash anyone who threw anything away with the butts of our rifles and soon had order restored.

Some little time later we were stopped and had to get on the side of the road to let a wagon pass. This stopped in front of us and to our surprise some of the HQ lads starting unloading a drum and musical instruments. It was a band!! They formed up and played 'Colonel Bogey'. The boys took up the tune and to my delight started 'Oh Johnny, Oh Johnny, we do love you, Oh Johnny, Oh Johnny we do love you!' It was a tribute to our colonel, who was a fine gentleman, and as one noted grumbler said, 'He is a father to us all.' No one would hear a word against him at any time.

Lt John Godfrey, 103 Field Coy, RE

Next morning was 11.11.18, and the news got to every unit before eleven o'clock. We had had some warning that the Armistice might be starting any day, and when the news actually came, there was nothing much more than a 'Thank God for that'.

In the evening, the villager in whose house we were billeted took us out to the garden at the back, and began digging in a weed-grown patch. He grubbed out bottle after bottle of long-preserved wine, and we crowded into his front room, where, it being very cold outside, the stove and its long pipe were heated red-hot: we toasted everyone in turn. By then I could talk fairly adequate French. Turning out afterwards into the bitter cold very nearly bowled me over: but I crawled into bed and slept.

Anyway, the bally war is over, which is the great thing. It is a joy so great that nobody yet realises here what it means. I am certain I can't realise what peace is. To think that I shall not have to toddle up among the 'obus'es [shells] and mitrailleuses [machine guns] again and never hear another shell burst. It is simply unimaginable.

Everyone here took it very quietly. There was a little cheering when the news came round at about midday on the 11th: and that was all. As a matter of fact, I had by far my most strenuous bridge repair that day, and didn't finish until 1 a.m. the next morning: so it didn't make any difference, and hasn't yet – outwardly.

The only difference is that that feeling of oppression at the back of one's brain is slowly lifting.

For many years afterwards, the German generals peddled the idea that the German army had never been beaten in the field but that they were the victims of a 'stab in the back' by weak politicians and an ineffectual public effort. Brigadier General Rees, who had served abroad since August 1914, knew differently. He had been taken prisoner in the fighting on the Chemin des Dames in May 1918, and when the war ended he was released and found his way to Berlin, where, on 14 December, with another former POW, he witnessed the German army's homecoming.

Brig. General Hubert Rees, Officer Commanding 150th Brigade, 50th Div.

We found that crowds were beginning to line the streets and that the Prussian Guards were about to make their celebrated entry into Berlin. Having a vantage point where our uniforms would not be too conspicuous, we watched the march. Much was subsequently written about their 'victorious' entry but the right word seemed to me to be pathetic. It was merely a homecoming. Companies much under strength and composed of boys and men over-age. Officers without swords, who were turned out into the street as soon as they reached their barracks. Weapons rusty and equipment stained. Machine-gun limbers drawn by a motley collection of broken-down horses. As a military spectacle, it was lamentable. Very few Englishmen saw it, yet when we got back to England a few days later, every placard announced 'Victorious entry of Prussian Guards into Berlin'.

After spending a night just short of the Dutch frontier, we reached The Hague and reported at our embassy. There I fully expected to find everyone thoroughly cheerful at the successful conclusion of the war. To my amazement I found a most anxious group, firmly convinced that Hindenburg [the German army Chief of Staff] was collecting a great army near Hanover to renew the war. It took me the best part of two hours' hard talking to convince our ambassador that his information was all wrong. I was then sent off with letters to the War Office and to Mr Balfour [Foreign Secretary], and spent two days in London telling sundry important people that we really had won the war and that the Germans knew it.

My only explanation of what seems a curious phenomenon is that, the armies having lost contact with each other, the Allies were solely dependent on the reports of secret agents. The agents, who knew perfectly well that the war was over, saw no object in making further reports. The result was a state of intense anxiety amongst responsible people who, faced with a complete absence of any real news, were half inclined to give credence to the wildest rumours.

Aftermath

Lt George Foley, 7th Somerset Light Infantry
Within forty-eight hours of landing at Leith, I was in our beautiful home on the Quantock Hills. For me the toil and dangers of the greatest war in the world's history were over, leaving behind them many sad memories of irreparable loss, but also a heritage of wider experience, and a truer knowledge of life. Although at times the price to pay was almost intolerable, I would not at any cost have forgone them.

Pte John McCauley, 2nd Border Rgt
Before receiving my demobilisation papers, I was requested to appear before the colonel of the battalion. He asked me to remain in the army for another year, and explained that the work of collecting dead bodies and burying them in the cemeteries which were to be laid out in the vicinity of the battlefields was to be commenced, and men with some experience of that work were needed. I gently but firmly declined to remain in the army for any purpose. He made a personal plea, and spoke of the high pay that was being offered, but I was adamant.

Shortly after our return to England, small detachments of men were going back to their homes each day to attempt to pick up the threads of their life at the place where many left off to plunge into war. Our journey from Flanders Fields to Calais, then Folkestone, then Shorncliffe, and finally London, was an unforgettable experience. Cheering crowds, waving flags and band music everywhere. In London my contract duly ended. Handshakes with old comrades – fine fellows with whom I had shared experiences that will live in the memory as long as life shall last – and then out into London's streets to be swallowed up in the swirling multitude.

Such courage and nerve as I possessed were stolen from me on the blood-drenched plains of northern France. How often do I feel that loss today! Devil's Trench, and many other trenches in France and Flanders, have helped to make me a weakling. They took away many of the attributes which contributed to my manhood, sapped up my courage, shattered my nerves, and threw me back into a 'civilised' world again broken in spirit and nerve, and the coward that I am. They might as well have taken my body, too.

Pte Christopher Massie, 76 Brigade, 25th Div., RAMC

Some little time ago, whilst acting as a ward orderly, a patient who had just previously come from the operating theatre asked me to ease his right arm. I turned down the blankets, to find that his right arm had been amputated. The poor fellow's jaw dropped – as well it might – and then he said: 'They should not have done that. I shall not be able to work any more. I suppose they will give me a sum of money, and after that is gone I shall beg or starve. They ought not to have taken my arm off; I could move my fingers. If I had got better like that I could have worked. Now I shall never work again.'

There was no word or thought that his country might be grateful to him. On the other hand, it is the general attitude of soldiers to refer to the representatives of their country with great contempt and suspicion. With great bitterness this soldier added to his previous remarks: 'There was a silver ring on the middle finger of that arm you have lopped off. But it's all weighed in and sold, ain't it? Bloody nice game this is. I can't work any more.' And so the refrain went on until he left for the hospital train: 'Bloody nice thing. Can't work any more. Took off my right arm. If it had been my left – but there you are. Can't work any more.'

Far from coming home straight away, a large number of British troops remained in France undertaking battlefield clearance aided by German prisoners of war. Finding bodies and clearing munitions was an emotionally trying and often dangerous job. Other soldiers were more fortunate. They were sent to the Rhineland as an occupying force, remaining for several months until the Versailles Peace Treaty was signed in June 1919.

Pte John Dearden, 4th Duke of Wellington's Rgt

I was one of the salvaging party of the 4th Duke of Wellington's on the 10th [December] last. I was present when Captain Kirk, MC, issued orders to all ranks, giving us the precautions we were to take in the salvaging of ammunition. I had just placed a shell on the dump, and the platoon officer told me to put it down gently. I had got about five yards away when I heard an explosion. I turned around and saw three men on the ground. The shell I placed on the dump was a trench mortar shell, and I saw No.5 3096 Pte Abbot, A and No. 45225 Pte Hardy, GF carrying towards the dump what appeared to be the same sort of shell, which I had just put down.

Capt. Alfred Kirk, 4th Duke of Wellington's Rgt

I was in command of the party who were salvaging ammunition on the 10th inst. I gave out on parade the orders received from the colonel in command of the battalion, which were as follows: that ammunition of all description must be salvaged, that shells and grenades were to be collected into small dumps and that any duds that were found were not to be touched, and that the attention of the nearest officer was to be called to them. I also warned the men that if they found anything that looked at all suspicious they were to leave it until they received further orders from an officer. I was 200 yards away when an explosion occurred, and on getting to the spot I found two men killed and five injured. These men, [Abbot and Hardy] along with others, had been employed making a small dump of shells of various descriptions under the supervision of an officer.

Pte Charles Heare, 1/2nd Monmouthshire Rgt

We leave Cologne. We move. Stop. Start again, then are pushed into a siding for hours, then move off again slowly. We get out and walk beside the train to get warm. Only biscuits and bully beef to eat. I have some tea and sugar and we get hot water from the engine. After years, it seems, we call at Huy. Food is waiting for us. Off again. I don't know what day it is.

At last we get to the land we knew, the Ypres sector. How strange it seems, all smashed up. 'What was it for?' says one in the truck. 'What have we got for it, or anyone else?' I am held spellbound. I can't shake this feeling off me. 'How do you account for us living through it all?' I ask Black. 'Luck, a lot. Good hearing. A good sense of danger and mostly a free hand to move about off crossroads and the first six months at Le Bizet to get used to it and a month at Ypres in 1915 to wake us up and get us settled to it,' he says. This Ypres has a hold on me.

Down to Calais for the night. What a grand finale! We do ourselves justice and then back to the tent. In the morning, breakfast and we fall in and move off to the docks and board an American troopship, a posh affair. We land at Dover and get straight into a train. Snow everywhere. We stop at Chiseldon for a night, what a hole. After many parades, we move off to Swindon with our discharge in our pockets. We entrain for Newport, then a long wait for a train to Pontypool. At last we are on our final journey. Black says, 'How do you feel about it all, Charley?' 'Oh, all right,' says I. 'I am thinking,' says Black. 'We have had to protect one another from danger, share our sleep and food. We have seen a lot happen, seen many killed, seen thousands of dead, as many dying. We have had romping good times and horrid bad ones together but now we must part and start a new life. Well, let's hope we have lived through it all for a good purpose.'

Pontypool at last. My discharge in my pocket and my sandbag of goods on my shoulder; I'm back home.

Pte John McCauley, 2nd Border Rgt

Patriotism was rarely known and never understood in the front line. Hard, iron discipline took its place, a discipline which even meted out death if it was not rigidly observed. Whether you did your duty or neglected your duty, you faced death. It was a common saying among the fighting men that the nearer you were to death in the army, the less pay you received. If ever a man endured untold agonies for his country during the war, it was the 'bob a day' infantryman.

'They died that England might live.' Every day I hear these words ringing in my ears, like the daily dinning of the shellfire of years ago. What if they who died could come back and survey this sorry world, and see what it was fought for? I wonder what their thoughts would be? Perhaps they would say, 'We are better and happier in our world.' Who knows?

Sgt A. A. Long, RE, 3 March 1919, describing to his wife a visit to the battlefields

We have heard repeatedly of the mud of low-lying Flanders. It must be seen for one to realise fully what it is like. Even now, long after the churning of it has ceased, one has to pick one's way very carefully to avoid sinking to the tops of one's boots in the greasy stuff. It is impossible to conceive how men managed to exist in the waterlogged trenches and muddy, reeking dugouts, under fire all the while. Three bent and battered tanks were lying derelict near by and I climbed into one which had had half one side blown off. The steel is twisted all shapes, but of course it must have been subjected to shelling for a long time after being disabled. The litter of a modern battlefield is lying all about – broken rifles, bayonets, hand grenades – still dangerous stick bombs, shell cases, unexploded shells ('duds' as they are called) – those I saw being mostly German and all pointing towards Ypres – helmets, boots, equipments, etc, everywhere, these suggestive of some tragic happening to the owner. In one place a complete soldier's pack left behind told its own story. Human bones were lying about the shell holes. Protruding from the side of one shell hole, the rims of two steel German helmets were visible. One of our fellows pulled one helmet out and that had a story of its own. The crown had a long deep dent, evidently caused by a piece of shell which had penetrated the steel and must have killed the wearer instantly. What struck the onlooker most, I think, was the manner in which the ground had been cut up by the shells. The shell holes just here were literally edge to edge, and one had to make one's way along the 'rims'. Ordered trenches and pathways were completely obliterated, whilst further afield were tremen-dous holes (now filled with water, making sizeable ponds) suggestive of mine craters. And amongst all this confusion I came across one of the first signs of spring – a piece of henbit in blossom, and this made me think of you and home in our beautiful Bassett, and Lord's Wood.

We did not need to stop here long, for what we saw in a limited area was typical of the rest of the open battlefields. We returned to the car and had lunch, afterwards continuing our journey through the old lines occupied by the enemy. We soon reached the spot where the village of Zonnebeke once stood – now a heap of rubble. Thence we went on a road along part of the famous Passchendaele Ridge and leading (as the map indicated) to Becalaere. This place was distinguished by the name on a board, all other evidence of a village being completely absent! We were now well in the German area and signs of Fritz's hasty retirement began to appear everywhere. Stacks of unused shells, rifle and machine-gun ammunition were left on the roadsides, heaps of war material of all sorts laid about, while here and there stood a smashed gun, and in one case an abandoned steam road roller – this last being unable to travel fast enough!

Saddest of all were the crosses we passed, which were scattered about the fields in ones and twos and, occasionally, a small group of four or more in an out of the way corner. All signified hasty burial, some our own men, others German soldiers. On one cross was scrawled 'two unknown soldiers'! Several crosses were lying about anyhow – these, if originally marking graves, had been blown from the spot they were intended to mark. I only noticed one cemetery which had been knocked about by shells and this one had suffered badly, the headstones being scattered about the place.

. . . I cannot say I enjoyed the trip, for the sights, to me, were too fraught with tragedy. I could not look upon the devastation and chaotic condition of the countryside without thinking of all the slaughter and bitter suffering resulting from the awful events which had occurred in the area visited. And one is forced to reflect that man has indeed sunk very low, to use his superior intellect in fashioning means of dealing death and destruction all round. All this in an enlightened age – and to what purpose? Man is indeed a refined savage, and war is a hideous spectre born of the devil. If this war is the last and the world becomes the better for it – well and good, if not, God help the world!

Driver Percival Glock, 281 Brigade, 56th Div., RFA

'Death Valley', just behind Combles. This was a very appropriate name for it. Chamber of Horrors wouldn't have been a bad name. There were sights in this valley that I shall not attempt to put on paper, as it is my intention to forget all the horrors of war if possible and also for anyone who has not seen, heard or experienced such things it is not wise for them to know, or, in the words of the old saying, 'ignorance is bliss'. I would give anything if I could forget them, but I don't expect everybody to understand what I mean.

Pte George Fleet, 7th Queen's (Royal West Surrey Rgt)

Imagine for an instant moving across open country, every tree and hedge shot away and the ground pitted with shell holes, some shallow, some deep, missiles dropping around you, with no place for cover except the holes the shells themselves have made. The disgusting stench of dead bodies, horses and men, the smell from exploding bombs, your feet in mud inches thick, men dropping about you and you must go on. Your stomach may be empty, your throat parched, your body ache from sheer exhaustion and irritated by lice, and when you drop down at night, rats will play hide and seek over your body. That is war.

Pte Christopher Massie, 76 Brigade, 25th Div., RAMC

Do not neglect the graves of the heroes. Do not forget that these have died for your necessity. Died, in so many cases without romance, almost ridiculously, hung on barbed wire like scare-crows, or mixing their blood with the rain and filth of some lonely shell hole, or among strangers, to whom no sacred wish can be expressed, at a dressing station. Do not forget the long days and nights of privation and physical wretchedness which precede this end. Barbed wire is terrible, because your heart tears against it as well as your hands and garments. Apart from its hideous usefulness in catching men like flies, the endless prospect of entanglements form a sort of mesh out of which the mind cannot escape. And think of the oozing trenches with their ominous stench, always collapsing till the clay is knee-deep, and cover is hardly obtainable, and comfort not at all. Think of the wearisome and highly dangerous fatigues – the impossibility of getting one's clothes dry and one's body clean. And all the petty, tiresome circumstances of routine when there is nothing specially doing.

Sgt William Peacock, 1st South Wales Borderers

England was saved. *Yes*, that is what our soldiers have done for you. How are we going to be rewarded for our services? It is a case for the whole world to consider. Just think of the trials and hardships we had to endure to keep those foes from our shores. We are owed a debt of honour. My boys, we are proud of you, heroes all.

Pte John McCauley, 2nd Border Rgt

Last week Armistice-tide crept upon us, and slipped away into history once again. A grim, yet solemn, reminder of that awful era of world war; somehow, I like to see it come round. It gently stirs tender memories. In the two minutes' silence I see great hosts of khaki-clad figures, phantom figures, the ghosts of yesterday. The long line of soldier comrades, such noble comrades they were, march before my blurred vision. I see them in battalions, brigades, divisions, army corps, and I distinctly hear their cry: 'In honouring the dead, forget not the living. Remember us, but remember too, those who survived.'

Pte Will Bird, 42nd Bttn (Royal Highlanders)

After I returned from the war, there seemed no way in the world to get my souvenirs [including the Roman sword] back. Orders had been given that nothing was to be carried in our packs but army issues. The story ran that all packs would be searched. So I had to be content with getting no more than my diaries out of France. At Vimy Ridge was a gentleman of the engineers, Major Simpson, and he was kindness itself. When I mentioned my problem, he told me he could ship anything from France to any organisation, but not to an individual. So he made a large strong box that would hold everything, and I became at that moment the President of the Frontliners' Association of Nova Scotia. The box was shipped to me at Amherst. The contents went on display in many towns and cities on Remembrance Day, and are now in the Military Museum on Citadel Hill, Halifax.

ACKNOWLEDGEMENTS

I would like to thank the highly encouraging and supportive staff at Bloomsbury, particularly Bill Swainson, my commissioning editor, for his enthusiasm and kindness, and Emily Sweet for her excellent editorial advice and support. I am also very grateful to Nick Humphrey, Colin Midson, David Mann, Lisa Fiske, Ruth Logan, Polly Napper and Andrew Tennant for their unwavering support in helping to bring *The Soldier's War* to fruition under considerable time pressure. Additionally, I would like to express my gratitude to Richard Collins for his expert editorial comments and assiduous reading of the text, helping to iron out many small queries.

A very special mention must be made of my close friend Jeremy Banning. Without his superb research skills and his willingness to persevere under considerable time restrictions, this book would not just have been much poorer, it would not have been possible at all; I thank him for his remarkable diligence and attention to detail. I should also like to thank Peter Barton for his enthusiastic support and generosity in supplying me not only with information but also with photographs; his kindness and friendship are much appreciated. Just as invaluable was Stuart Arrowsmith, who was extremely generous in lending me irreplaceable photographs and documents from his private collection, including: the memoirs of Lt Alfred G. Richardson, 116th Siege Battery, Royal Garrison Artillery; the memoirs of Gnr George Hollett; the private photographs of Pte Frederick Main, 1/5th London Rgt; the recollections of Sgt Harold Bisgood, 2nd London Regiment, and the photographs he took while serving on the Western Front. I am equally thankful to Lawrence Brown, and to Dr and Mrs Smallcombe, for the kind loans of their privately owned images. I am also very grateful to Taff Gillingham for reading through the text and pointing out a number of small errors; his expertise is second to none. Thanks also go to Simon Jones, Vic and Diane Piuk, and Sanjeev Ahuja, John and Suzie Keating, Clair Banning, Mark Banning, and Alan and Kathleen Branch.

Especial mention should be made of my wonderful agent, Jane Turnbull, whose duty of care knows no bounds and who has always been totally and unflinchingly supportive of all I have done: thank you so much, Jane.

My deepest thanks must go to my family: to my mother, Joan van Emden, who, as always, has been absolutely remarkable in her astute editorial comments, while her keenness of eye has picked up small faux pas on my part; I am grateful as always. I am also deeply in debt to my wife, who must sometimes feel like a war widow as deadlines loom and I retreat to my study for what must seem like weeks on end; her support has been wonderful while she has been caring for our eighteen-month-old son Benjamin.

I would like to thank the following people for permission to reproduce extracts from diaries, letters or memoirs written by their Great War relatives: Nigel Armstrong-Flemming (extracts from the memoirs of Capt. Herbert Flemming); Carol Ashburner (extracts from the papers of Pte Frank Pope); Susan Ashton (quotes from the papers of Pte Robert Cude, MM); Mrs Peggy Edmonds (extracts from the memoirs of Maj. S. R. Greenfield); Ann Evans (extracts from the papers of Pte H. L. Chase, MM); Tim Hardwick (extracts from the papers of Maj. A. G. P. Hardwick, MC); Jean Harris (extracts from the memoirs of F. E. Harris); R. H. Hubbard (extracts from the memoirs of Henry Russell); Harold Jones (quotes from the memoirs of his father, Harold Jones); Sir Bayley Laurie (extracts from the papers of Capt. John Laurie); E. Lindholt (quotes taken from the papers of Lt Alan May); H. A. Long (quotes from a letter written by Sgt A. A. Long, RE); Miss D. B. Macgregor (extracts from the papers of Lt R. Macgregor); Laurence Martin (for extracts from the diary of Sapper Albert Martin); Mrs S. Martin (extracts from the letters of her uncle, Roland Mountfort); Mrs J. Nesfield (quotes taken from the papers of Gerald Brunskill); Julie Nightingale (extracts from the letters of Lt Dennis Neilson-Terry); Mrs J. Price (quotes taken from the papers of Pte Sydney Fuller); Diana Stockford (extracts from the diary of Brig. General H. C. Rees, CMG, DSO); Mavis Williams (extract from the diary of Frank Williams).

I am grateful to Tony Lund for alerting me to the diary of Sgt Bradlaugh Sanderson. Further extracts from his diary will appear in *Blood in the Summer Wine: A History of Holmfirth and District during the Great War, 1914–1919*, to be published in June 2009. Thank you also to Nik Racine for the use of the diary of Pte James Racine. The full diary can be viewed and downloaded from www.archive.org.

SOURCES AND CREDITS FOR TEXT AND PHOTOGRAPHS

Text

Imperial War Museum: By kind permission of the Department of Documents, Imperial War Museum, Lambeth Road, London, SE1 6HZ. With thanks to Roderick Suddaby, Anthony Richards and Clare Sexton from the Department of Documents.

Maj. General G. Brunskill, CB, MC – 03/6/7; H. L. Chase, MM – 06/54/1; R. Cude, MM – PP/MCR/C48; S. T. Fuller – 86/32/1; A. G. P. Hardwick, MC – 98/14/1; A. G. May – 88/46/1; Frank Pope – 06/55/1; Gnr Stanley Collins, 137th Heavy Batt. – Misc. 41 (736), RGA; Lt E. C. Allfree – 77/14/1; Rev. M. A. Bere – 66/96/1; T. A. Bickerton – 80/43/1; Lt J. T. Capron – 87/33/1; Lt Col H. M. Dillon, DSO – 82/25/1; A. E. Douglas – 98/28/1; E. J. Drane – 99/36/1; Brig. T. I. Dun, DSO, MC – P267; Capt. W. S. Ferrie – 03/19/1; M. R. Evans – P473; P. A. Glock – 99/84/1; Maj. S. R. Greenfield, MC – 05/8/1; F. E. Harris – 06/29/1; Rev. E. E. Hayward – 97/33/1 (letter from Pte V. W. Garratt); A. Higginson – 95/1/1 (anonymous account taken from this file); E. J. Higson – 01/45/1; Lt Col F. W. Johnson – 88/56/1; A. A. Long – 06/30/1; Lt R. Macgregor – 05/39/1; Brig. P. Mortimer – P253; R. D. Mountfort – Con Shelf; 2/Lt D. Neilson-Terry – 01/38/1; C. T. Newman – 03/5/1; Brig. General H. C. Rees, CMG, DSO – 77/179/1; D. L. Rowlands – 93/20/1; H. Russell – 76/119/1; R. J. Smith – PP/MCR/186; Brig. General G. A. Stevens, CMG, DSO – 06/5/2; D. J. Sweeney – 76/226/1; F. R. Williams – 05/54/1.

Every effort has been made to trace copyright holders, and the author and the Imperial War Museum would be grateful for any information which might help to trace those whose identities or addresses are not currently known.

The Liddle Archive: By kind permission of the Liddle Collection, Leeds University Library, Woodhouse Lane, Leeds, LS2 9JT (www.leeds.ac.uk). With thanks to Richard Davies.

J. R. Bellerby – GS 0117; J. McCauley – GS 1000; D. N. Lissenburg – GS 0970; C. Birnstingl – GS 0143.

Staffordshire Regiment Museum: By kind permission of the Staffordshire Regiment Museum, Whittington Barracks, Lichfield, Staffordshire, WS14 9PY (www.staffordshireregimentmuseum.com). With many thanks to Dr Erik Blakeley, Willie Turner and Jeff Elson.

Extracts from diary of 21793 Pte W. McNeil, 1/5th South Staffordshire Regiment, later 46th Bttn, MGC, 46th (North Midland) Division, 1914–18 – Acc. No. 4783.

Soldiers of Gloucestershire Museum: By kind permission of the Soldiers of Gloucestershire Museum, Custom House, Gloucester Docks, Gloucester, GL1 2HE (www.glosters.org.uk). With thanks to George Streatfield, David Read and Graham Gordon.

Personal Accounts and Papers. Great War 1914–1918 (Box I): Memories of the 8th Bttn by Pte J. E. L. Baynes.

Transcripts of letters (Box 23): Letters from J. C. Proctor, 13th Bttn, Gloucestershire Rgt, August 1914–December 1918 – Acc. No. 4762.

The letters of 2/Lt C. W. Winterbotham, 1/5th Bttn, Gloucestershire Rgt.

Durham County Record Office: Reproduced by kind permission of Durham County Record Office, County Hall, Durham, DH1 5UL.

'My Part in the Battle of the Somme' by Sergeant Charles Herbert Moss, 18th Bttn, Durham Light Infantry – Ref: D/DLI/7/478/4.

Surrey History Centre: By kind permission of Surrey History Centre, 130 Goldsworth Road, Woking, Surrey, GU21 6ND. With thanks to Julian Pooley, Mike Page and Paul Young.

Account by Pte George Fleet of his WWI service – QRWS/30/FLEE/1; Lt Col J. R. Longley diaries 1915 – ESR/25/LONG/2, 3 & 5.

Somerset Record Office: By kind permission of the Duty Archivist, Somerset Record Office, Obridge Road, Taunton, TA2 7PU (www.somerset.gov.uk/ archives) and Lt Col Mike Motum, Somerset Military Museum, Somerset County Museum, Taunton Castle, Taunton, TA1 4AA.

Arthur Henry Cook diary – DD/SLI/17/1/40; George McMurtrie diary – DD/SLI/ 17/1/65; Diary 1914–1919, 2/Lt W. R. H. Brown, MC (all quotes used are when he was a private in the 1/4th Oxford & Buckinghamshire Light Infantry) – DD/ SLI/17/1/38.

King's Own Scottish Borderers Regimental Museum: By kind permission of the King's Own Scottish Borderers Regimental Museum, The Barracks, The Parade, Berwick-upon-Tweed, TD15 1DG (www.kosb.co.uk/museum). With thanks to the Regimental Secretary and Ian Martin.

Capt. A. J. M. Shaw, 1st Bttn – KOSB T/1/13.

Royal Engineers Museum: By kind permission of the Royal Engineers Museum, Prince Arthur Road, Gillingham, Kent, ME4 4UG (www.remuseum.org.uk). With thanks to Rebecca Cheney and her staff.

Diary and letters of J. T. Godfrey.

Trustees of the Army Medical Services Museum and the Wellcome Library: Reproduced by kind permission of the Trustees of the Army Medical Services Museum, Keogh Barracks, Ash Vale, Aldershot, GU12 5RQ (www.ams-museum .org.uk). The papers are held in the Royal Army Medical Corps Muniment Collection at the Wellcome Library, 210 Euston Road, London, NW1 2BE (http://library.wellcome.ac.uk).

'War Journal of a Poultice Walloper', F. J. Aylett – RAMC/1751.

Diary of Capt. Henry Wynyard Kaye, MD, RAMC, while serving in the war with No. 8 Casualty Clearing Station from 17 October 1915 to 23 August 1916 – RAMC/739.

Royal Regiment of Fusiliers Museum (Royal Warwickshire): By kind permission of the Royal Regiment of Fusiliers (Royal Warwickshire) Museum, St John's House, Warwick, CV34 4NF (www.warwickfusiliers.co.uk). With thanks to Stephanie Bennett and David Baynham.

Lt William Vince – 2005.9 Vince; Pte Reginald Wilkes.

The Royal Green Jackets Museum: By kind permission of the Royal Green Jackets Museum, Peninsula Barracks, Romsey Road, Winchester, Hampshire, SO23 8TS (www.royalgreenjackets.co.uk). With thanks to Mrs Christine Pullen. Diary of Lt Col R. T. Fellowes, 1st Rifle Brigade – Ref: 7A-0617; diary of Maj. F. W. L. Gull, Rifle Brigade – 0347-AB7A.

The Regimental Museum of the Royal Welsh: By kind permission of the Regimental Museum of the Royal Welsh (formerly South Wales Borderers & Monmouthshire Regimental Museum), The Barracks, Watton, Brecon, Powys, LD3 7EB (www.rrw.org.uk). With many thanks to Martin Everett and Celia Green.

Pte C. P. Heare, 1/2nd Monmouthshire Rgt, unpublished diary, July 1913–March 1919 – 1997.139; war diary of C. S. M. Cornelius Love, DCM, 2nd Monmouthshire Rgt – 1999.147; Capt. QM Ernest Kirkland Laman, MBE, MC, 2nd South Wales Borderers – 2005.70; history of the Great War by Sgt W. Peacock – D94.74; Sgt W. G. R. Sweet, C Company, 2nd Monmouthshire Rgt – 1991.138; letters and articles of Capt. E. E. A. Whitworth, MC, MA, Croix de Guerre 1914–1919 – 1992.22; memoirs of 2/Lt Harold Jones, South Wales Borderers – 2001.98.

The Fusiliers Museum of Northumberland: By kind permission of the Fusiliers Museum of Northumberland, The Abbott's Tower, Alnwick Castle, Alnwick, NE66 1NG (www.northumberlandfusiliers.org.uk). With thanks to Lesley Frater and her staff.

Pte John Scollen – ALNFM: 880; diary and letter of A. O. Terry, 23rd Bttn, Northumberland Fusiliers (4th Tyneside Scottish), January 1916–July 1918 (34th Div.); reminiscences of the Great War by Alan Angus, 8th Bttn, Northumberland Fusiliers, 11th Div. 1914–1918.

Magdalene College, Cambridge: By kind permission of Dr Luckett at Magdalene College, Cambridge University. With special thanks to the sub-librarian Ms Philippa Grimstone.

The private correspondence of George Mallory, 40th Siege Batt., RGA.

The King's Own Royal Border Regiment Museum: By kind permission of the Border Regiment & King's Own Royal Border Regiment Museum, Queen Mary's Tower, The Castle, Carlisle, CA3 8UR (www.kingsownbordermuseum.btik.com). With thanks to Stuart Eastwood and Tony Goddard.

Lt C.H.M Whiteside, 7th Bttn – 11/G2/001/29A; the war letters of Leonard and Walter Ewbank, 1915–1917 – 30/C/030/61A; diary of Pte E. H. Wanless – 09/A2b/016/24A.

The Tank Museum, Bovington: By kind permission of the Tank Museum,

Bovington Camp, Bovington, Dorset, BH20 6JG (www.tankmuseum.co.uk). With thanks to Janice Tait and David Fletcher.
Gnr V. S. Archard – WW1/ARCHARDVS; Driver H. E. Emans – WW1/ EMANSHE; Gnr A. H. R. Reiffer, MM – WW1/REIFFERAHR.
Museum of Army Chaplaincy: By kind permission of the Museum of Army Chaplaincy, Amport House, Amport, Hampshire, SP11 8BG (www.army.mod.uk/ chaps). With thanks to David Blake.
'An Army Chaplain's Work in Wartime' by The Reverend E. V. Tanner, MC – a talk given at Weymouth College in the 1920s in abridged form; *A Parson in Khaki* by The Reverend R. Bulstrode, Hon. Chaplain to the Forces (2nd Class).

Photographs
Surrey History Centre: By kind permission of Surrey History Centre, 130 Goldsworth Road, Woking, Surrey, GU21 6ND.
Photo album incl. Third Battle of Ypres, showing Lt Fred Lovell, 8th East Surrey Rgt. The photographs were taken by the Australian Medical Officer, Capt. Birrie, MC – ESR/25/LOVE/1; 2nd Queen's (Royal West Surrey Regiment) photographs May 1916–October 1917 by H. B. Secretan, MC – QRWS/30/SECR/1.
The Regimental Museum of the Royal Welsh: By kind permission of the Regimental Museum of the Royal Welsh (formerly South Wales Borderers & Monmouthshire Regimental Museum), The Barracks, Watton, Brecon, Powys, LD3 7EB (www.rrw.org.uk).
1/2nd Monmouthshire Rgt at Le Bizet, 1915, photographs by Evelyn Byrde – MBA 2071, MBA 2067.
Imperial War Museum, London: By kind permission of the picture library of the Imperial War Museum, Lambeth Road, London, SE1 6HZ.
Q51128; Q60707; HU63277B; Q49750; Q49751.
Liddell Hart Centre for Military Archives, King's College, London: By kind permission of the Trustees of the Liddell Hart Centre for Military Archives, King's College, London. With thanks to Katharine Higgon.
Photo of dummy in trenches taken from Foulkes papers – 6/84.
Somerset Record Office: By kind permission of the Duty Archivist, Somerset Record Office, Obridge Road, Taunton, TA2 7PU (www.somerset.gov.uk/ar- chives) and Lt Col Mike Motum, Somerset Military Museum, Somerset County Museum, Taunton Castle, Taunton, TA1 4AA.
Photograph album of the 1st Bttn during WWI – DD/SLI/15/7/44; photograph album 1914–1919 – DD/SLI/15/7/16; photograph of R. S. M. Gamlin, 6th Bttn, in hospital, 1915 – DD/SLI/15/7/80.
Staffordshire Regiment Museum: By kind permission of the Staffordshire Regiment Museum, Whittington Barracks, Lichfield, Staffordshire, WS14 9PY (www.staffordshireregimentmuseum.com).
1/6th North Staffordshire Rgt war photographs, John Auden – 4216; 1st North Staffordshire Rgt, Flanders, 1915–1917 album – 4358; 1/6th South Staffordshire Rgt, Flanders, 1915, P. J. Slater – 5074 & 5075.

First Plate Section
Page
 1. Full page – Stuart Arrowsmith (*hereafter* SA)
 2. Top left – IWM; middle – author's collection (*hereafter* AC); bottom – IWM
 3. Top left – AC; top right – SA; middle and bottom – AC
 4. Top left – Somerset Record Office (*hereafter* SRO) ref: DD/SLI/15/7/44; top right – AC; middle – Peter Barton (*hereafter* PB); bottom – SRO ref: DD/SLI/15/7/16
 5. Top – AC; middle – AC; bottom left – Staffordshire Regiment Museum (*hereafter* SRM), ref: 5075; bottom right – AC
 6. Top left – SRO ref: DD/SLI/15/7/16; top right – SRM, ref: 4216; middle – PB; bottom – Pen & Sword (*hereafter* P&S)
 7. Top – The Regimental Museum of the Royal Welsh (*hereafter* RMRW), ref: MBA 2071; middle – AC; middle right – PB
 8. Top – IWM; bottom – Dr Smallcombe (*hereafter* DrS)
 9. Top – IWM; bottom – AC
 10. Top left – SRM, ref: 5075; middle – PB; bottom – P&S
 11. Top – PB; middle – Liddell Hart Centre for Military Archives (*hereafter* LHCMA), ref: Foulkes, 6/84; bottom – RMRW, ref: MBA 2067
 12. Top – P&S; middle – SRM, ref: 5075; bottom right – DrS
 13. Top right – SRM, ref: 5074; middle left – AC; middle right – SRM, ref: 5074; bottom – P&S
 14. Top – SRM, ref: 4216; middle – IWM; bottom left – DrS; bottom right – P&S
 15. Top – AC; bottom – SRO ref: DD/SLI/15/7/80.
 16. Full page – DrS

Second Plate Section
Page
 1. Full page – Surrey History Centre (*hereafter* SHC), ref: ESR/25/LOVE/1
 2. & 3. All photos – SA
 4. Top left – SRM, ref: 4216; top right – AC; middle & bottom – Lawrence Brown
 5. 6. & 7. All photos – AC
 8 & 9. SHC, ref: ESR/25/LOVE/1
 10. All photos – SHC, ref: ESR/25/LOVE/1
 11. 2nd photo down – AC; all other photos SHC, ref: ESR/25/LOVE/1
 12. All photos – SHC, ref: ESR/25/LOVE/1; bottom – SHC, ref: QRWS/30/SECR/1
 13. Top left – SHC, ref: ESR/25/LOVE/1; top right – SHC, ref: ESR/25/LOVE/1; middle – SRM, ref: 5075; bottom – AC
 14. Top – Lawrence Brown; middle left – AC; middle right – SRM, ref: 4358; bottom left – AC; bottom right – AC
 15. All photos – AC
 16. Full page – AC

INDEX